FORGING A CONVENTION FOR CRIMES AGAINST HUMANITY

Crimes against humanity comprised one of the three categories of crimes elaborated in the Nuremberg Charter. However, unlike genocide and war crimes, they were never set out in a comprehensive international convention. This book represents an effort to complete the Nuremberg legacy by filling this gap. It contains a complete text of a Proposed Convention on crimes against humanity in English and in French, a comprehensive history of the Proposed Convention, and fifteen original papers written by leading experts on international criminal law. The papers contain reflections on various aspects of crimes against humanity, including gender crimes, universal jurisdiction, the history of codification efforts, the responsibility to protect, ethnic cleansing, peace and justice dilemmas, amnesties and immunities, the jurisprudence of the ad hoc tribunals, the definition of the crime in customary international law, the ICC definition, the architecture of international criminal justice, modes of criminal participation, crimes against humanity and terrorism, and the interstate enforcement regime.

Leila Nadya Sadat is the Henry H. Oberschelp Professor at Washington University School of Law and Director of the Whitney R. Harris World Law Institute. She is also the holder of the Alexis de Tocqueville Distinguished Fulbright Chair at the University of Cergy-Pontoise, in Paris, France, for spring 2011. A distinguished expert in international criminal law and human rights, Sadat is the Director of the Crimes Against Humanity Initiative, a three-year project to study the problem of crimes against humanity and draft a comprehensive convention addressing their punishment and prevention. A prolific scholar, Sadat is the author of *The International Criminal Court and the Transformation of International Law: Justice for the New Millennium*.

Internationally renowned experts and Steering Committee members gathered at Washington University in St. Louis' historic Ridgley Hall for the April 2009 Meeting of the Crimes Against Humanity Initiative. Ridgley Hall was the site of the 1904 Inter-Parliamentary Union resolution that ultimately led to the convening of the 1907 Hague Peace Conference.

Photo credit: Mary Butkus/WULAW Photographic Services

Forging a Convention for Crimes Against Humanity

Edited by

LEILA NADYA SADAT

School of Law, Washington University in St. Louis

CAMBRIDGE
UNIVERSITY PRESS

32 Avenue of the Americas, New York, NY 10013-2473, USA

Cambridge University Press is part of the University of Cambridge.

It furthers the University's mission by disseminating knowledge in the pursuit of education, learning, and research at the highest international levels of excellence.

www.cambridge.org
Information on this title: www.cambridge.org/9781107676794

© Cambridge University Press 2011

This publication is in copyright. Subject to statutory exception and to the provisions of relevant collective licensing agreements, no reproduction of any part may take place without the written permission of Cambridge University Press.

First published 2011

First paperback edition 2013

A catalog record for this publication is available from the British Library.

Library of Congress Cataloging in Publication data
Forging a convention for crimes against humanity / [edited by] Leila Nadya Sadat.
p. cm.
ISBN 978-0-521-11648-0 (hardback)
1. Crimes against humanity.   I. Sadat, Leila Nadya.   II. Title.
K5301.F665   2011
345'.0235—dc22   2010035665

ISBN 978-0-521-11648-0 Hardback
ISBN 978-1-107-67679-4 Paperback

Cambridge University Press has no responsibility for the persistence or accuracy of URLs for external or third-party Internet Web sites referred to in this publication and does not guarantee that any content on such Web sites is, or will remain, accurate or appropriate.

Contents

Figures and Maps		*page* vii
Crimes Against Humanity Initiative: Steering Committee		viii
Biographies of Contributors		ix
Foreword		xvi
Richard J. Goldstone		
Preface and Acknowledgments		xix
Leila Nadya Sadat		
	Crimes Against Humanity and the Responsibility to Protect	1
	Gareth Evans, Keynote Address delivered June 11, 2009	
1.	History of Efforts to Codify Crimes Against Humanity: From the Charter of Nuremberg to the Statute of Rome	8
	Roger S. Clark	
2.	The Universal Repression of Crimes Against Humanity before National Jurisdictions: The Need for a Treaty-Based Obligation to Prosecute	28
	Payam Akhavan	
3.	Revisiting the Architecture of Crimes Against Humanity: Almost a Century in the Making, with Gaps and Ambiguities Remaining – the Need for a Specialized Convention	43
	M. Cherif Bassiouni	
4.	The Bright Red Thread: The Politics of International Criminal Law – Do We Want Peace or Justice? The West African Experience	59
	David M. Crane	
5.	Gender-Based Crimes Against Humanity	78
	Valerie Oosterveld	
6.	"Chapeau Elements" of Crimes Against Humanity in the Jurisprudence of the UN Ad Hoc Tribunals	102
	Göran Sluiter	

7. The Definition of Crimes Against Humanity and the Question
   of a "Policy" Element 142
   Guénaël Mettraux

8. Ethnic Cleansing as Euphemism, Metaphor, Criminology,
   and Law 177
   John Hagan and Todd Haugh

9. Immunities and Amnesties 202
   Diane Orentlicher

10. Modes of Participation 223
    Elies van Sliedregt

11. Terrorism and Crimes Against Humanity 262
    Michael P. Scharf and Michael A. Newton

12. Crimes Against Humanity and the International Criminal Court 279
    Kai Ambos

13. Crimes Against Humanity and the Responsibility to Protect 305
    David Scheffer

14. Re-enforcing Enforcement in a Specialized Convention
    on Crimes Against Humanity: Inter-State Cooperation, Mutual
    Legal Assistance, and the *Aut Dedere Aut Judicare* Obligation 323
    Laura M. Olson

15. Why the World Needs an International Convention on Crimes
    Against Humanity 345
    Gregory H. Stanton

Appendices
I. Proposed International Convention on the Prevention
   and Punishment of Crimes Against Humanity 359
II. Proposition de Convention Internationale sur la Prévention
    et la Répression des crimes contre l'humanité 403
III. A Comprehensive History of the Proposed International
     Convention on the Prevention and Punishment of Crimes
     Against Humanity 449
     Leila Nadya Sadat
IV. Propuesta de Convención Internacional para la
    Prevención y la Sanción de los Crímenes de Lesa Humanidad 503

Testimonials and Endorsements
1. Washington Declaration on Crimes Against Humanity 579
2. Kigali Declaration 588
3. The Fourth Chautauqua Declaration: August 31, 2010 591

Index 595

Figures and Maps

FIGURES

4.1. The West African Joint Criminal Enterprise.	page 69
8.1. Sudan-Darfur chain of command, 2003–2004.	188
8.2. Chronology of key events and monthly death estimates from survey and news counts of killings, January 2003–September 2004.	191
8.3. Combined roles of GoS and Janjaweed with ethnic protection in racial targeting of ethnic cleansing and mass atrocities in Darfur.	196
8.4. Cross-level interaction of separate and/or combined forces with settlement density on individual racial intent.	199
8.5. Cross-level interaction of collective racial intent with bombing on total victimization (standardized).	200

MAPS

8.1. Settlement cluster map of racial epithets and total victimization and sexual victimization.	193
8.2. Janjaweed militia leaders' areas of operation.	198

Crimes Against Humanity Initiative
Steering Committee

Leila Nadya Sadat, Chair
Henry H. Oberschelp Professor of Law
Director, Whitney R. Harris World Law Institute
Washington University School of Law

Professor M. Cherif Bassiouni
DePaul University College of Law;
President Emeritus, International
Human Rights Law Institute;
Distinguished Research
Professor of Law Emeritus

Justice Richard J. Goldstone
Former Chief Prosecutor, International
Criminal Tribunals for the Former
Yugoslavia and Rwanda

Professor William A. Schabas
Director, Irish Centre for Human
Rights, National University of Ireland,
Galway

Ambassador Hans Corell
Former Under-Secretary-General for
Legal Affairs and the Legal Counsel of
the United Nations

Mr. Juan E. Méndez
Visiting Professor, Washington College
of Law, American University; Former
Special Advisor to the Secretary-
General of the UN on the Prevention
of Genocide

Judge Christine Van den Wyngaert
International Criminal Court

Biographies of Contributors

CRIMES AGAINST HUMANITY STEERING COMMITTEE MEMBERS

M. Cherif Bassiouni is a Distinguished Research Professor of Law *Emeritus*, and founder and President *Emeritus* of the International Human Rights Law Institute, DePaul University College of Law. Bassiouni has previously served as Member, then Chairman, of the Security Council's Commission to investigate war crimes in the former Yugoslavia (1992–1993); Commission on Human Rights' Independent Expert on The Rights to Restitution, Compensation and Rehabilitation for Victims of Grave Violations of Human Rights and Fundamental Freedoms (1998–2000); Vice-Chairman of the General Assembly's Ad Hoc Committee on the Establishment of an International Criminal Court (1995); and Chairman of the Drafting Committee of the 1998 Diplomatic Conference on the Establishment of an International Criminal Court.

In 1999, Bassiouni was nominated for the Nobel Peace Prize for his contributions to international criminal justice and the creation of the International Criminal Court. He has received numerous medals and awards for his service to the international community.

Hans Corell served as Under-Secretary-General for Legal Affairs and Legal Counsel of the United Nations from March 1994 to March 2004. He was the Secretary-General's representative at the Rome Conference on the Establishment of an International Criminal Court.

From 1962 to 1972, Corell served in the Swedish judiciary. In 1972, he joined the Ministry of Justice where he became Director of the Division for Administrative and Constitutional Law in 1979. In 1981, he was appointed Chief Legal Officer of the Ministry. He was Ambassador and Under-Secretary for Legal and Consular Affairs in the Foreign Ministry from 1984 to 1994.

In 2004 Corell retired from public service and is now engaged *inter alia* as legal adviser, lecturer, and member of different boards and committees, including in the International Bar Association. He is Chairman of the Board of Trustees of the Raoul Wallenberg Institute of Human Rights and Humanitarian Law at Lund University, Sweden.

Richard J. Goldstone was the first Chief Prosecutor of the International Criminal Tribunals for the former Yugoslavia and Rwanda. He has also served on the Constitutional Court of South Africa and the UN Independent International Committee that investigated the Iraq Oil for Food program (the Volcker Committee). Goldstone chaired the South African Commission of Inquiry Regarding the Prevention of Public Violence and Intimidation (the Goldstone Commission) and the International Independent Inquiry on Kosovo. In 2009 he led the United Nations Fact Finding Mission on Gaza.

In January 2008, Goldstone received the World Peace through Law Award from the Whitney R. Harris Institute. In May 2009, he also received the prestigious MacArthur Award for International Justice from the John D. and Catherine T. MacArthur Foundation. Goldstone is a foreign member of the American Academy of Arts and Sciences and an honorary member of the Association of the Bar of New York City.

Juan E. Méndez is Visiting Professor at the Washington College of Law, American University. From 2004 to 2009, Méndez was the President of the International Center for Transitional Justice. He also served as the executive director of the Inter-American Institute of Human Rights in Costa Rica (1996–1999) and as a member and President of the Inter-American Commission on Human Rights of the Organization of American States (2000–2003). From 2004 to 2007, Méndez was appointed the UN Special Adviser to the Secretary-General on the Prevention of Genocide.

Additionally, Méndez worked with Human Rights Watch for fifteen years, concentrating his efforts on human rights issues in the western hemisphere. In 1994, he became General Counsel of Human Rights Watch, in which capacity he was responsible for the organization's litigation and standard-setting activities.

On October 1, 2010, the UN Human Rights Council appointed Méndez the Special Rapporteur on Torture and CID Treatment or Punishment.

Leila Nadya Sadat is the Henry H. Oberschelp Professor at Washington University School of Law and Director of the Whitney R. Harris World Law Institute. She will be the Alexis de Tocqueville Distinguished Fulbright Chair at the University of Cergy-Pontoise in Paris, France, in spring 2011.

Sadat is an internationally recognized authority and prolific scholar. She is the author of the award-winning *The International Criminal Court and the Transformation of International Law: Justice for the New Millennium*. Her most recent articles include: "A Rawlsian Approach to International Criminal Justice," "On the Shores of Lake Victoria: Africa and the International Criminal Court," "Understanding the Complexities of International Criminal Tribunal Jurisdiction," and "The Nuremberg Paradox."

Sadat was a delegate to the 1998 Rome Diplomatic Conference and the 2010 ICC Review Conference in Kampala, Uganda. She has held leadership positions in many organizations and is a member of the American Law Institute.

William A. Schabas is the Director of the Irish Centre for Human Rights and the Chair in human rights law at the National University of Ireland, Galway. He has published extensively on international human rights law, and his work has been cited by many of the world's national and international courts, including the U.S. Supreme Court, the Judicial Committee of the Privy Council, the International Court of Justice, and the European Court of Human Rights. Schabas currently holds the Vespasian V. Pella Medal for International Criminal Justice of the Association Internationale de Droit Penal.

Schabas has participated in international human rights missions on behalf of nongovernmental organizations, and from 2002 to 2004 he served on the Sierra Leone Truth and Reconciliation Commission. He was also an NGO delegate to the Rome Conference on the Establishment of an International Criminal Court in July 1998 and the Kampala Review Conference in June 2010.

Christine Van den Wyngaert is a specialist in international criminal law, criminal procedure, and comparative criminal law. In January 2009, she was elected a judge on the International Criminal Court. Van den Wyngaert has also served as a judge at the International Criminal Tribunal for the former Yugoslavia and a judge ad hoc at the International Court of Justice in the Arrest Warrant case (2000–2002).

As a professor at the University of Antwerp, a researcher, and the author of many books, Van den Wyngaert has made a considerable contribution to the development of international criminal law. She was also a rapporteur for the International Law Association on extradition and human rights and a general reporter for the Association Internationale de Droit Pénal in Budapest relating to international cooperation to combat organized crime. Van den Wyngaert has been awarded doctorates honoris causa by the University of Uppsala (2001) and the University of Brussels (2009).

OTHER CONTRIBUTORS

Payam Akhavan is a Professor of International Law at McGill University and formerly Senior Fellow at Yale Law School. He was the first Legal Advisor to the Office of the Prosecutor at the International Criminal Tribunals for the former Yugoslavia and Rwanda. Akhavan has also served as counsel before the International Court of Justice and other tribunals. He is cofounder of the Iran Human Rights Documentation Centre. His essay "Beyond Impunity: Can International Criminal Justice Prevent Future Atrocities?" was selected by the International Library of Law and Legal Theory as one of "the most significant published journal essays in contemporary legal studies."

Kai Ambos is a Professor of Criminal Law, Criminal Procedure, Comparative Law, and International Criminal Law at the University of Göttingen, Germany. He is the author and editor of numerous publications on German and international criminal law. Ambos worked as a (senior) research Fellow for international criminal law and Hispanic America at the Max-Planck Institute for Foreign and International Criminal Law. In 2003, he was appointed Chair of criminal law, criminal procedure, comparative law, and international criminal law at the Georg-August-Universität Göttingen. As of 2006, Ambos is also a judge of the district court of Göttingen.

Roger S. Clark is a Board of Governors Professor at Rutgers School of Law-Camden. He served as a member of the UN Committee on Crime Prevention and Control between 1987 and 1990. In 1995 and 1996, he represented the government of Samoa in arguing the illegality of nuclear weapons before the International Court of Justice. Since 1995, he has represented Samoa in negotiations to create the International Criminal Court and to enable it to exercise its jurisdiction over the crime of aggression. Clark has written widely on issues of human rights, decolonization, international organization, and international criminal law.

David M. Crane is a Professor of Practice at Syracuse University College of Law. From 2002 to 2005, he was the founding Chief Prosecutor of the Special Court for Sierra Leone, thus becoming the first American chief prosecutor of an international war crimes tribunal since Justice Robert Jackson and Telford Taylor in 1945. Prior to his departure from West Africa, Crane was made an honorary Paramount Chief by the Civil Society Organizations of Sierra Leone. Crane has more than three decades of public service experience in the U.S. federal government. In 2006, he founded Impunity Watch (http://www.impunitywatch.com), a law review and public service blog.

Gareth Evans is the Chancellor of Australian National University, Professorial Fellow at the University of Melbourne, and President Emeritus of the International Crisis Group, which he headed from 2000 to 2009. He was a member of the Australian Parliament for twenty-one years and a cabinet minister for thirteen years, including as Foreign Minister from 1988 to 1996. He cochaired the International Commissions on Nuclear Non-Proliferation and Disarmament (2008–2010) and on Intervention and State Sovereignty (2000–2001), which initiated the "responsibility to protect" concept. Evans has written and edited nine books, including *The Responsibility to Protect: Ending Mass Atrocity Crimes Once and for All* (Brookings Institution Press, 2008).

John Hagan is the John D. MacArthur Professor of Sociology and Law at Northwestern University and Codirector of the Center on Law & Globalization at the American Bar Foundation in Chicago. He received the Stockholm Prize in Criminology in 2009. Hagan is the editor of the *Annual Review of Law & Social Science*. He is the coauthor, with Wenona Rymond-Richmond, of *Darfur and the Crime of Genocide* (Cambridge University Press, 2009), which received the Albert J. Reiss Distinguished Publication Award and the Michael J. Hindelang Book Award.

Todd Haugh is an Instructor of Legal Writing at DePaul University College of Law. Haugh's scholarship focuses on issues related to sentencing, criminal procedure, and international criminal law. While in private practice, Haugh focused on white-collar criminal defense and commercial litigation at Winston & Strawn, LLP and Stetler & Duffy, Ltd. He also served as a law clerk to the Hon. Suzanne B. Conlon, Senior District Judge for the Northern District of Illinois. Haugh received a BA with honors in political science from Brown University and a JD, *cum laude*, from the University of Illinois College of Law.

Guénaël Mettraux appears as defense counsel before international and internationalized criminal jurisdictions. He is a guest professor in a number of universities and has published extensively in international law, including three books published by Oxford University Press. His latest book, *The Law of Command Responsibility* (Oxford University Press, 2009), won the Lieber Prize for 2009 book of the year from the Lieber Society of the American Society of International Law.

Michael A. Newton is a Professor of the Practice of Law at Vanderbilt University Law School. He is an expert on accountability and conduct of hostilities issues, having helped negotiate the Elements of Crimes for the International Criminal Court. As the Senior Advisor to the Ambassador-at-Large for War Crimes Issues, U.S. Department of State, Newton coordinated U.S. support of accountability mechanisms worldwide. Newton served as Professor of International and Operational Law at the Judge Advocate General's School and later taught at West Point. He currently serves as senior editor of the *Terrorism International Case Law Reporter* series published annually by Oxford University Press.

Laura M. Olson currently serves as a Supervisory Program Analyst in the U.S. Department of Homeland Security's Office of Civil Rights and Civil Liberties. Olson's chapter in this volume was completed prior to her government appointment, and the views expressed herein do not represent those of the U.S. Department of Homeland Security or the U.S. government. She served for ten years as Legal Advisor to the International Committee of the Red Cross (ICRC). Her writing covers matters of international humanitarian law, transitional justice, and the relationship between international humanitarian and human rights law during armed conflict.

Valerie Oosterveld is an Assistant Professor of Law at the University of Western Ontario. Previously, she served in the Legal Affairs Bureau of Canada's Department of Foreign Affairs and International Trade, where she provided legal advice on issues of genocide, crimes against humanity, and war crimes, especially with respect to the International Criminal Court, the International Criminal Tribunals for the former Yugoslavia and Rwanda, and the Special Court for Sierra Leone. Oosterveld was a member of the Canadian delegation to the International Criminal Court negotiations and subsequent Assembly of States Parties. She has published extensively on gender issues in international criminal law.

Diane Orentlicher is a Professor of International Law and Codirector of the Center for Human Rights and Humanitarian Law at Washington College of Law, American University (currently on leave). In 2009, Orentlicher was appointed to serve in the Obama administration as Deputy, Office of War Crimes Issues, Department of State. Orentlicher's contribution to this volume was completed before she became an employee of the U.S. Department of State. The views set forth in her chapter do not necessarily reflect those of the U.S. Department of State or the U.S. government.

Michael P. Scharf is the John Deaver Drinko-Baker & Hostetler Professor of Law and Director of the Frederick K. Cox International Law Center at Case Western Reserve University School of Law. Scharf cofounded and directs the Public International Law and Policy Group, which was nominated for the 2005 Nobel Peace Prize for providing pro bono legal assistance to state and nonstate entities involved in peace negotiations and war crimes prosecutions. Scharf served previously as Attorney-Adviser for UN Affairs at the U.S. Department of State and is the author of thirteen books, including three that have won national book-of-the-year honors.

David Scheffer is the Mayer Brown/Robert A. Helman Professor of Law and Director of the Center for International Human Rights at Northwestern University School of Law. He served as the U.S. Ambassador-at-Large for War Crimes Issues during the second Clinton administration and as Senior Adviser and Counsel to the U.S. Permanent Representative to the United Nations from 1993 to 1996. Scheffer led the U.S. delegation in the UN talks creating the International Criminal Court and helped negotiate the establishment of the International Criminal Tribunals for the former Yugoslavia and Rwanda, the Special Court for Sierra Leone, and the Extraordinary Chambers in Cambodia.

Göran Sluiter is a Professor of International Criminal Law, in particular the Law of International Criminal Procedure, at the University of Amsterdam and a lawyer at Böhler Advocaten, a law firm in Amsterdam specializing in international criminal law, with cases at the Khmer Rouge Tribunal and the ICC, among others. In his research, Sluiter focuses on determining general doctrines within the framework of international law of criminal procedure, which could form the basis of improved procedural law. He is member of the editorial board *of International Criminal Law Review* and of the editorial committee of the *Journal of International Criminal Justice*.

Gregory H. Stanton is the Research Professor in Genocide Studies and Prevention at the Institute for Conflict Analysis and Resolution of George Mason University and the President of Genocide Watch. He founded the Cambodian Genocide Project in 1982 and drafted the rules for the Khmer Rouge Tribunal. Stanton also founded the International Campaign to End Genocide in 1999. From 2007 to 2009 he was president of the International Association of Genocide Scholars. Stanton served in the

State Department from 1992 to 1999, where he drafted the United Nations Security Council Resolutions that created the International Criminal Tribunal for Rwanda.

Elies van Sliedregt is a Professor of Criminal Law at VU University Amsterdam. She is a member of the editorial board of the *Leiden Journal of International Law* and president of the International Criminal Law Network. In 2006, van Sliedregt was awarded the Modderman Prize, the highest scientific distinction in the field of criminal law in The Netherlands. Van Sliedregt is a member of The Young Academy of The Royal Netherlands Academy of Arts and Sciences. Her research interests lie in the field of international, European, and comparative criminal law.

Foreword

Richard J. Goldstone

It is appropriate at the outset to pay warm tribute to Whitney Harris who played a key role in establishing the initiative on a Convention for Crimes Against Humanity. Whitney was one of the leading prosecutors at Nuremberg and worked closely with U.S. Chief Prosecutor Justice Robert Jackson. It was my distinct privilege to have met Whitney in Nuremberg and hear him deliver the opening address in 1995 at a seminar to mark the fiftieth anniversary of the Nuremberg Trials against the major Nazi leaders. His voice resonated in the very courtroom where that trial was held, as the immortal words of Justice Robert Jackson took on a new and urgent meaning.

The Whitney R. Harris World Law Institute at Washington University in St. Louis functions as a center for instruction and research in international and comparative law. It is the home of the project. Those of us involved with the project rejoiced in having the support and advice of Whitney and we are sad that he passed away before the completion of the project. We console ourselves with the knowledge of how much a Convention on Crimes Against Humanity meant to him and how much satisfaction he received from it. His warmth and moving words will always be associated with it. He attended the opening conference in St. Louis, and a video-taped message watched at the final conference, shortly before his death, will always remain with us.

The idea and inspiration for the project came from Professor Leila Nadya Sadat, the Henry H. Oberschelp Professor of Law and Director of the Harris World Law Institute at Washington University in St. Louis. A recognized academic leader in the field of international law, she became aware of an important vacuum in international humanitarian law. While there is a convention dealing with genocide, and the Geneva Conventions deal with serious war crimes, there is no convention that covers crimes against humanity. The absence of the latter has negative implications for the growing international recognition of the need to withdraw impunity for war criminals. The absence of such a convention came to the fore in the case before the International Court of Justice in which Bosnia and Herzegovina brought an action against Serbia under the jurisdiction conferred on that Court by the Genocide Convention.[1] Bosnia sought a declaration that genocide had been committed in its territory during the wars of the early 1990s, and it also claimed compensation. The Court recognized the many serious violations of the laws of armed conflict

---

[1] International Convention on the Prevention and Punishment of Genocide, *adopted* Dec. 9, 1948, 78 U.N.T.S. 277.

committed by Bosnian Serb troops. It also recognized that Serbia was either responsible for some of those crimes or could, at least, have taken steps to prevent them. More particularly, the Court found that crimes against humanity had been perpetrated. However, because the jurisdiction of the Court was limited to genocide, these other crimes were not before them and they slipped off the table. Genocide was held to have been proven only in the massacre of some 8,000 Muslim men and boys in Srebrenica in July 1995. What was missing was a convention on crimes against humanity that would have given the International Court of Justice jurisdiction not only in respect of the crime of genocide, but crimes against humanity as well.

Leila Sadat decided to launch this project and applied her customary efficiency and infectious enthusiasm to it. She set up a steering committee under her leadership, and I was delighted and honored to be one of its six members together with Professor M. Cherif Bassiouni (also appointed to lead the drafting of the convention), Dr. Hans Corell, the former Legal Counsel of the United Nations; Juan E. Méndez, President Emeritus of the International Center for Transitional Justice; Professor William A. Schabas, the Director of the Human Rights Center of the National University of Ireland at Galway; and Judge Christine Van den Wyngaert, a judge of the International Criminal Court.

From its very first meeting, the members of the Steering Committee agreed that the project and the proposed convention should in no way be prejudicial to the International Criminal Court or contradictory to the provisions of the Rome Treaty. The *Proposed Convention* that has now been drafted reflects that concern and agreement. In particular, after many discussions and much consideration, the definition of "crimes against humanity" that appears in the Convention is identical to that found in the Rome Treaty. Consideration was also devoted to whether an optional protocol might be preferred rather than a convention. For a number of reasons, a convention was the route followed. One of the decisive considerations was that a convention would contain important provisions directed toward the prevention of crimes against humanity and not only their prosecution after they had been committed. Another is that non–States Parties to the Rome Treaty would be able to ratify a convention whereas an optional protocol would be open to ratification only by States Parties.

Again, on the Initiative of Leila Sadat, three outstanding conferences were held at which papers relevant to the *Proposed Convention* were convened – in St. Louis, The Hague, and Washington, D.C. Some of those papers appear in this book.

I would suggest that the need for a convention on crimes against humanity is an obvious one. Not only will it fill a vacuum in international humanitarian law, but it would enable States and international organizations to adopt appropriate measures aimed at preventing serious crimes against civilian populations. Again, it would be another positive step toward the withdrawal of impunity from war criminals. It would also encourage States to place themselves in a position to exercise their right of complementarity and investigate alleged crimes against their nationals in preference to having the International Criminal Court do so.

It remains for me to express the hope that the recognition of the need for a convention on crimes against humanity will gain political traction. States need to ratify it and speedily introduce domestic legislation to give effect to its provisions.

I warmly congratulate Leila Sadat for having initiated and brought this project to a successful conclusion.

Preface and Acknowledgments

Leila Nadya Sadat

This book represents the culmination of more than one hundred years of effort in the development of international criminal law. With extraordinary support and input from nearly 250 noted experts from around the world, a complete *Proposed International Convention on the Prevention and Punishment of Crimes Against Humanity* has finally been elaborated. It is my sincere hope that the *Proposed Convention*, along with the collected scholarly articles and drafting history set forth herein, will serve as a foundation for the consideration – and ultimate adoption by States – of a crimes against humanity convention, a still-missing and essential piece of the framework of international humanitarian and international criminal law.

During the trials of the German and Japanese leaders by the Allies following World War II, crimes against humanity emerged as an independent basis of individual criminal liability in international law. Although the so-called Martens Clause of the 1907 *Hague Convention Respecting the Laws and Customs of War on Land* referenced the "laws of humanity, and … the dictates of the public conscience" as protections available under the law of nations to human beings caught in the ravages of war, this language was too uncertain to provide a clear basis for either State responsibility or criminal liability under international law.[1] Subsequently, crimes against humanity were specifically included in the Charters of the International Military Tribunals at Nuremberg[2] and Tokyo[3] to address depredations directed against civilian populations by the State – including the State of the victims' nationality. Indeed, it was in many ways the most revolutionary of the charges upon which the accused were convicted, for its foundations in international law were so fragile.[4] Following the trials, the Nuremberg Principles embodied in the IMT Charter and Judgment were adopted by the General Assembly in 1946[5] and

---

[1] See, e.g., Leila Sadat, *The Interpretation of the Nuremberg Principles by the French Court of Cassation: From Touvier to Barbie and Back Again*, 32 COLUM. J. TRANSNAT'L. L. 289, 296–300 (1994).

[2] Charter of the International Military Tribunal – Annex to the Agreement for the Prosecution and Punishment of the Major War Criminals of the European Axis, Aug. 8, 1945, 58 Stat. 1544, 82 U.N.T.S. 280.

[3] Charter of the International Military Tribunal for the Far East, Jan. 19, 1946, *amended* Apr. 26, 1946, T.I.A.S. No. 1589, 4 BEVANS 20.

[4] The other was the crime of waging an aggressive war.

[5] *Affirmation of the Principles of International Law Recognized by the Charter of the Nuremberg Tribunal: Report of the Sixth Committee*, U.N. GAOR, 1st Sess., pt. 2, 55th plen. mtg. at 1144, U.N. Doc. A/236 (1946) (also appears as G.A. Res. 95, U.N. Doc. A/64/Add.1, at 188 (1946).

codified by the International Law Commission in 1950.[6] Thus, "crimes against humanity," whatever their uncertain legal origin, had apparently found a firm place in international law as a category of offenses condemned by international law for which individuals could be tried and punished. The codification of the crime of genocide – itself a crime against humanity – lent some truth to this assumption; however, the important achievement of the Genocide Convention's adoption and entry into force in 1951[7] was overshadowed by Cold War politics. Indeed, no trials for genocide took place until 1998, when Jean-Paul Akayesu, mayor (*bourgmestre*) of the town of Taba, was convicted by the International Criminal Tribunal for Rwanda (ICTR) for his role in the slaughter that had engulfed Rwanda in 1994.[8] Crimes against humanity percolated in the legal systems of a handful of countries that had domesticated the crime, such as France, and certain elements of their prohibition could be found in new international instruments prohibiting torture and apartheid.[9] Scholarly articles periodically appeared as well. But the promise of "never again," as many have observed before me, was repeatedly dishonored as the mass atrocities committed in the second half of the twentieth century unfolded before the eyes of the world, bloody in their carnage and the human toll they exacted, and shocking in their cruelty and barbarism.[10] There was little accountability of any kind exacted from those responsible for these crimes against humanity – *ces crimes contre l'esprit* – whether committed by government officials or military leaders, rebels, insurgents, or low-level perpetrators. The Nuremberg promise remained unfulfilled.[11]

---

[6] Documents of the second session, including the report of the Commission to the General Assembly, [1950] 2 Y.B. Int'l L. Comm'n 374, U.N. Doc. A/CN.4.SER.A/1950/Add.I.

[7] Convention on the Prevention and Punishment of the Crime of Genocide, G.A. Res. 260 (III) A, 78 U.N.T.S. 277, *entry into force* Jan. 12, 1951 (Dec. 9, 1948) [hereinafter Genocide Convention].

[8] Prosecutor v. Akayesu, Case No. ICTR-96-4-T, Judgment, ¶ 494 (Sept. 2, 1998).

[9] *See* International Convention on the Suppression and Punishment of the Crime of Apartheid, G.A. Res. 3068, U.N. Doc. A/RES/3068 (July 18, 1976); Convention against Torture and Other Cruel, Inhuman or Degrading Treatment or Punishment, U.N. Doc. A/Res/39/46 (Dec. 10, 1984); Organization of American States, Inter-American Convention to Prevent and Punish Torture, Feb. 28, 1987, O.A.S.T.S. No. 67; Council of Europe, European Convention for the Punishment of Torture and Inhuman or Degrading Treatment of Punishment, Feb. 1, 1989, E.T.S. 126.

[10] One recent study has suggested that between 1945 and 2008, between 92 million and 101 million persons were killed in 313 different conflicts, the majority of whom were civilians. In addition to those killed directly in these events, others have died as a consequence, or had their lives shattered in other ways – through the loss of property; through victimization by sexual violence; through disappearances, slavery and slavery-related practices, deportations and forced displacements, and torture. M. Cherif Bassiouni, *Assessing Conflict Outcomes: Accountability and Impunity*, *in* THE PURSUIT OF INTERNATIONAL CRIMINAL JUSTICE: A WORLD STUDY ON CONFLICTS, VICTIMIZATION, AND POST-CONFLICT JUSTICE 6 (M. Cherif Bassiouni ed., 2010).

[11] In 1989, the Cold War ended with the fall of the Berlin Wall, and this began to change. The International Criminal Court project, which had lain fallow, was restarted with the introduction of a resolution into the General Assembly by Trinidad and Tobago, leading a coalition of sixteen Caribbean nations, and work on the Draft Code of Crimes continued at the International Law

One of the most horrific examples of post–World War II crimes against humanity was the Cambodian "genocide" discussed by Gareth Evans in this volume. From 1975 to 1979, the Khmer Rouge regime killed an estimated 1.7 million–2.5 million Cambodians, out of a total population of 7 million.[12] Although now popularly referred to as a "genocide," legally that is a difficult case to make. Indeed, there has been a great deal of criticism and worry generated by the decision of the co-prosecutors of the Extraordinary Chambers for Cambodia to bring charges of genocide against several former high-ranking leaders of the Khmer Rouge regime, for fear that the charges will not be legally possible to prove.[13] For the most part, individuals were killed, tortured, starved, or worked to death by the Khmer Rouge not because of their appurtenance to a particular racial, ethnic, religious, or national group – the four categories to which the Genocide Convention applies – but because of their political or social classes, or the fact that they could be identified as intellectuals.[14] While theories have been advanced suggesting ways that the Genocide Convention applied to these atrocities,[15] and an argument can certainly be made that some groups were exterminated *qua* groups (such as Buddhist monks, whose numbers were reportedly reduced from 60,000 to 1,000),[16] most experts agree with Evans' chilling assessment that:

> [F]or all its compelling general moral authority, the Genocide Convention had absolutely no legal application to the killing fields of Cambodia, which nearly everyone still thinks of as the worst genocide of modern times. Because those doing the killing and beating and expelling were of exactly the same nationality, ethnicity, race and religion as those they were victimizing – and their motives were political, ideological and class-based ... the necessary elements of specific intent required for its application were simply not there.[17]

Once again, the international community had failed both to prevent the commission of mass atrocities and to provide the legal tools necessary to react to their

---

Commission. *See Report of the Commission to the General Assembly on the work of its forty-eighth session*, [1996] 2 Y.B. Int'l L. Comm'n 15–42, U.N. Doc. A/CN.4/SER.A/1996/Add.1; *see also* LEILA NADYA SADAT, THE INTERNATIONAL CRIMINAL COURT AND THE TRANSFORMATION OF INTERNATIONAL LAW: JUSTICE FOR THE NEW MILLENNIUM (2002).

[12] *See generally* Craig Etcheson, After the Killing Fields: Lessons from the Cambodian Genocide 118–20 (2005).

[13] Order on Request for Investigative Action on the Applicability of the Crime of Genocide at the ECCC, 002/19-09-2007-ECCC-OCIJ, Dec. 28, 2009; *see* Peter Maguire, Op-Ed., *Cambodia's Troubled Tribunal*, N.Y. TIMES, July 28, 2010, *available at* http://www.nytimes.com/2010/07/29/opinion/29iht-edmaguire.html; *see also* William A. Schabas, *Problems of International Codification – Were the Atrocities in Cambodia and Kosovo Genocide?* 35 NEW ENG. L. REV. 287 (2001).

[14] *See* SAMANTHA POWER, "A PROBLEM FROM HELL": AMERICA AND THE AGE OF GENOCIDE 87–154 (2002).

[15] Hurst Hannum, *International Law and Cambodian Genocide: The Sounds of Silence*, 11 HUM. RTS. Q. 82 (1989) (describing the mass atrocities in Cambodia as an "auto genocide").

[16] POWER, *supra* note 14, at 143.

[17] Gareth Evans, *Crimes Against Humanity and the Responsibility to Protect*, in this volume, at 3.

occurrence.[18] As war broke out in the former Yugoslavia, and the Rwandan genocide took place with the world watching in horror, the international community reached for the Nuremberg precedent only to find that it had failed to finish it. This made the task of using law as an antidote to barbarism a difficult and complex endeavor. The uncertainty in the law was evidenced by the texts of the Statutes for the International Criminal Tribunals for the former Yugoslavia (ICTY) and Rwanda (ICTR), which contained different and arguably contradictory definitions of crimes against humanity, a notion difficult to square with the idea of universal international crimes.[19] M. Cherif Bassiouni underscored this problem in an important, but little noticed, article appearing in 1994 entitled "'Crimes Against Humanity': The Need for a Specialized Convention," in which he lamented the "existence of a significant gap in the international normative proscriptive scheme, one which is regrettably met by political decision makers with shocking complacency."[20]

With the adoption of the International Criminal Court (ICC) Statute in 1998, crimes against humanity were finally defined and ensconced in an international convention. The ICC definition is similar to earlier versions but differs in important respects, such as the requirement that crimes against humanity be committed "pursuant to a State or organizational policy."[21] However, it was a convention that *by its own terms* did not purport to represent customary law, but only law defined for the purposes of the Statute itself.[22] (Whether it has *subsequently* come to represent customary international law was debated during the course of this Initiative).[23] Moreover, even if the ICC definition ultimately represents customary international law, it applies only to cases to be tried before the ICC. Although presumably ICC Party States can and will adopt the ICC definition as domestic law (and are encouraged to do so pursuant to the principle of complementarity), the ICC Statute provides no vehicle for inter-State cooperation. Putting it more simply, the adoption of the Rome Statute advanced the normative work of defining crimes against humanity considerably but did not obviate the need to fill the *lacunae* in the legal framework as regards the commission of atrocity crimes, most of which are crimes against

---

[18] The international community eventually negotiated an agreement with the Cambodian government to establish a court known as the Extraordinary Chambers in the Courts of Cambodia for the trial of a handful of former Khmer Rouge leaders in 2003. Agreements between the United Nations and The Royal Government of Cambodia Concerning the Prosecution Under Cambodian Law of Crimes Committed during the Period of Democratic Kampuchea, U.N.-Cambodia, June 6, 2003, 43 U.N.T.S. 2329.

[19] The Statute for the IMT at Tokyo and Control Council Law No. 10, *supra* notes 2 and 3, also differed slightly from the Nuremberg definition.

[20] M. Cherif Bassiouni, *"Crimes Against Humanity": The Need for a Specialized Convention*, 31 COLUM. J. TRANSNAT'L. L. 457 (1994).

[21] Rome Statute of the International Criminal Court art. 7(2)(a), July 17, 1998, U.N. Doc. A/CONF.183/9 [hereinafter ICC Statute].

[22] *See, e.g.*, ICC Statute, art. 7(1)("for the purpose of this Statute, 'crime against humanity' means ....").

[23] See Guénaël Mettraux, *The Definition of Crimes Against Humanity and the Question of a "Policy" Element*, in this volume; Kai Ambos, *Crimes Against Humanity and the International Criminal Court*, in this volume.

humanity, and not genocide, and many of which are crimes against humanity, and not war crimes. As the ad hoc tribunals begin to close down, shoring up the capacity for national legal systems to pick up cases involving crimes against humanity appears imperative if the small gains achieved during the past two decades of international criminal justice are not to be reversed. This is particularly true as regards crimes against humanity, for recent experience demonstrates that crimes against humanity have been committed and charged in all situations currently under examination before the international criminal tribunals (and the ICC) to date.

As Richard J. Goldstone notes in the *Foreword* to this volume, the case of *Bosnia v. Serbia* before the International Court of Justice[24] again evidenced the difficulty this normative gap engenders. For the debate in that case, centering upon whether the mass atrocities in Bosnia committed during the 1990s constituted genocide, missed the point. Although the Court recognized that many serious violations of the laws of armed conflict and crimes against humanity had been committed by Bosnian Serb troops, because the Court's jurisdiction was limited to genocide,[25] these other crimes were not before them, and they "slipped off the table."[26] Of the nearly 200,000 deaths, 50,000 rapes estimated to have occurred, and the 2.2 million forcibly displaced as a result of the Serb ethnic cleansing campaign,[27] genocide was held to have been proven only in the massacre of some 8,000 Muslim men and boys in Srebrenica in July 1995.[28] What was missing was a convention on crimes against humanity that would have given the International Court of Justice jurisdiction not only in respect of the crime of genocide but for crimes against humanity as well.[29]

Thus, in 2008, the Whitney R. Harris World Law Institute, under my direction, launched the Crimes Against Humanity Initiative. As the *Comprehensive History* to the *Proposed Convention* explains,[30] the Initiative had three primary objectives: (1) to study the current state of the law and sociological reality as regards the commission of crimes against humanity; (2) to combat the indifference generated by an

---

[24] Richard J. Goldstone, *Foreword*, in this volume.
[25] Genocide Convention, *supra* note 7, art. IX.
[26] Goldstone, *supra* note 24, at xviii.
[27] These numbers are estimates of the number of deaths, rapes, and forcibly displaced as a result of the armed conflict in Bosnia. AMNESTY INTERNATIONAL, THE WOMEN OF BOSNIA AND HERZEGOVINA ARE STILL WAITING 5, nn. 9, 14 & 15 (2009). Some critics claim that these numbers are overestimates and have been politicized. *See, e.g., id.*
[28] Case Concerning the Application of the Convention on the Prevention and Punishment of the Crime of Genocide (Bosn. & Herz. v. Serb. & Mont.), 2007 I.C.J. 91, ¶ 297 (Feb. 26, 2007). In its recent June 2010 judgment, the ICTY found that there is enough DNA evidence to identify at least 5,336 individuals, but evidence continues to be discovered so the numbers could be as high as 7,826. Prosecutor v. Popović, Case No. IT-05-88-T, Judgment, ¶ 664 (June 10, 2010).
[29] Article 26 of the *Proposed Convention* does this. *See* Proposed International Convention on the Prevention and Punishment of Crimes Against Humanity, in this volume. Of course, the same can be said for the actions brought to the Court by Croatia and Serbia as well. *See* Case Concerning the Application of the Convention on the Prevention and Punishment of the Crime of Genocide (Croatia v. Serbia), 2008 I.C.J. 118 (Nov. 18, 2008).
[30] Leila Nadya Sadat, *A Comprehensive History of the Proposed International Convention on the Prevention and Punishment of Crimes Against Humanity*, in this volume, App. III.

assessment that a particular crime is "only" a crime against humanity (rather than a "genocide"); and (3) to address the gap in the current law by elaborating the first-ever comprehensive specialized convention on crimes against humanity.

The Initiative has progressed in phases, each building upon the work of the last. The publication of this volume, including the papers herein and the *Proposed Convention*, represents the culmination of the first three phases of the Initiative: (I) *preparation* of the project and methodological development; (II) *private study* of the project through the commissioning of the papers in this volume, the convening of expert meetings, and collaborative discussion of draft treaty language; and (III) *public discussion* of the project with relevant constituencies and the publication of the *Proposed Convention*. Ambitious in scope and conceptual design, the project is directed by a Steering Committee of renowned experts and has drawn on the Harris Institute's connections, particularly overseas, to assemble a truly extraordinary international effort on the elaboration of a proposed convention on crimes against humanity.

During Phase II, the papers in this collection, written by leading experts, were presented and discussed at a conference held at the Washington University School of Law on April 13–14, 2009. They were then revised for publication.[31] They address the legal regulation of crimes against humanity and examine the broader social and historical context within which they occur. Each chapter was commissioned not only to examine the topic's relationship to the elaboration of a future treaty, but to serve as an important contribution to the literature on crimes against humanity in and of itself.

Each of the fifteen papers in this collection is a gem. The papers range from technical discussions of specific legal issues such as modes of responsibility (van Sliedregt), immunities and amnesties (Orentlicher), enforcement (Olson), and gender crimes (Oosterveld) to broader conceptual treatments of earlier codification efforts (Clark), the definition of the crime in the Rome Statute and customary international law (Ambos and Mettraux), and the phenomenon of ethnic cleansing (Hagan & Haugh). Several of the papers contrast the ICC and ad hoc tribunal definition of crimes against humanity and were very helpful to the discussions as the drafting effort progressed (see, e.g., Sluiter); the same can be said for the many other contributions to the volume, which addressed specific topics such as crimes against humanity and terrorism (Scharf & Newton), universal jurisdiction (Akhavan), and the Responsibility to Protect (Scheffer). David M. Crane's contribution outlining "Operation Justice" in Sierra Leone is an outstanding case study of "peace and justice" in action; likewise, M. Cherif Bassiouni's exposé on "revisiting the architecture of crimes against humanity" is a magisterial account of the crime's development during the past century.

---

[31] One paper, on *Re-enforcing Enforcement*, was commissioned subsequent to the April meeting based upon the emphasis in that meeting on inter-State cooperation as a principal need for the Convention. Laura M. Olson, *Re-enforcing Enforcement in a Specialized Convention on Crimes Against Humanity: Inter-State Cooperation, Mutual Legal Assistance, and the* Aut Dedere Aut Judicare *Obligation*, in this volume.

In discussing the scholarly work, more questions were raised than answered. What was the social harm any convention would protect? Atrocities committed by the State, or a broader concept that would include non-State actors? Would a new legal instrument prove useful in combating atrocity crimes? How would any new instrument interact with the Rome Statute for the International Criminal Court? The lengthy discussions that transpired are memorialized in the *Comprehensive History* found in Appendix III and will no doubt continue after this book has been published, but it should be emphasized that the discussion and elaboration of the Convention's provisions are deeply intertwined with the academic work accomplished at the same time.

As the initial scholarly work was undertaken, a preliminary draft text of the convention, prepared by Cherif Bassiouni, was circulated to participants of the April meeting to begin the drafting process. As the Initiative progressed, nearly 250 experts were consulted, many of whom submitted detailed comments (orally or in writing) on the various drafts of the proposed convention circulated or attended meetings convened by the Initiative either in the United States or abroad. Between formal meetings, technical advisory sessions were held during which every comment received – whether in writing or communicated verbally – was discussed as the Convention was refined. The *Proposed Convention* went through seven major revisions (and innumerable minor ones) and was approved by the members of the Steering Committee as it now appears in Appendices I (in English) and II (in French) in this volume. The *Comprehensive History* appearing in Appendix III describes the drafting process as well as the debates that surfaced during the *Proposed Convention's* elaboration in detail.

The *Proposed Convention*, we hope, will begin, not end, debate. Elaborated by experts without the constraints of government instructions (although deeply cognizant of political realities), it is, we believe, an excellent platform for discussion by States with a view toward the eventual adoption of a United Nations Convention on the Prevention and Punishment of Crimes Against Humanity. The *Proposed Convention* builds upon and complements the ICC Statute by retaining the Rome Statute definition of crimes against humanity but has added robust interstate cooperation, extradition, and mutual legal assistance provisions in Annexes 2–6. Universal jurisdiction was retained (but is not mandatory), and the Rome Statute served as a model for several additional provisions, including Articles 4–7 (Responsibility, Official Capacity, Non-Applicability of Statute of Limitations) and with respect to final clauses. Other provisions draw on international criminal law and human rights instruments more broadly, such as the recently negotiated Enforced Disappearance Convention, the Terrorist Bombing Convention, the Convention Against Torture, the United Nations Conventions on Corruption and Organized Crime, The European Transfer of Proceedings Convention, and the Inter-American Criminal Sentences Convention, to name a few.[32]

---

[32] A complete list is found in the table at the back of the *Proposed Convention* found in Appendixes I and II of this volume.

Yet although we benefited from the existence of current international criminal law instruments, the creative work of the Initiative was to meld these and our own ideas into a single, coherent international convention that establishes the principle of State Responsibility as well as individual criminal responsibility (including the possibility of responsibility for the criminal acts of legal persons) for the commission of crimes against humanity. The *Proposed Convention* innovates in many respects by attempting to bring prevention into the instrument in a much more explicit way than predecessor instruments, by including the possibility of responsibility for the criminal acts of legal persons, by excluding defenses of immunities and statutory limitations, by prohibiting reservations, and by establishing a unique institutional mechanism for supervision of the Convention. Echoing its 1907 forbear, it also contains its own Martens Clause in paragraph 13 of the Preamble. Elaborating the twenty-seven articles and six annexes of the treaty was a daunting challenge, and one that could not have been accomplished without the dedication and enthusiasm of many individuals.

First, I am deeply grateful to M. Cherif Bassiouni for his extraordinary contributions in leading the drafting effort and his service as a member of the Initiative's Steering Committee. I am equally grateful to Hans Corell, Richard J. Goldstone, Juan Méndez, William A. Schabas, and Christine Van den Wyngaert – the other members of the Steering Committee – for their leadership. Each member of the Initiative's Steering Committee brought tremendous energy and expertise to the project, guiding its methodological development and conceptual design and carefully reading, commenting on, and debating each interim draft of the *Proposed Convention* extensively. The collegial spirit with which our discussions were carried out and our work engaged helped enormously in keeping us on track, and the collective wisdom and experience of my colleagues made working on this project both delightful and inspiring. I really cannot thank them enough.

As with all such projects, many supported the effort without being on the front pages of it, so to speak. Of special note are the experts that gave generously of their time and talent, particularly Morten Bergsmo, Robert Cryer, Larry Johnson, Guénaël Mettraux, Laura M. Olson, Göran Sluiter, and Elies van Sliedregt, who attended one or more technical advisory sessions and contributed extensively to the elaboration of the Convention's text. In addition, our Senior Cash Nickerson Fellows, including Amitis (Amy) Khojasteh, Yordanka Nedyalkova (who also served as Associate Director of the Institute), B. Don Taylor III (who also served as Executive Director of the Institute), and Neill Townsend, did a marvelous job assisting with the project in so many ways – we are grateful for their enthusiasm and dedication. Our student Fellows did a terrific job as well, including Genevra Alberti, McCall Carter, Erika Detjen, Shannon Dobson, Andrew Esterday, Margaret LeBlanc, Jason Meyer, Stephanie Nickerson, Sarah Placzek, and Margaret Wichmann. We could not have managed the project without the institutional and personal support of Mark Wrighton, Chancellor of Washington University in St. Louis; Kent Syverud, Dean of the School of Law; Michael Peil, Associate Dean for International Programs;

Sherrie Malone, my faculty assistant; Linda McClain, the Institute's former Assistant Director; and Shelly Ford, the Institute's new Administrative Coordinator.

Our major conferences outside of St. Louis would not have been successful without the assistance of Carsten Stahn and the Grotius Centre at Leiden University, Wim Blockmans and The Netherlands Institute for Advanced Study, the City of The Hague, and The Brookings Institution. We are particularly grateful to Brookings for its superb support and organization of our final Phase III conference, particularly Brookings' President Strobe Talbott, Deputy Director and Senior Fellow Andrew Solomon, and Project Manager Jacqueline Geis. Robert S. Brookings endowed Washington University in St. Louis and the prestigious Washington, D.C., think tank that bears his name, and it is therefore somehow fitting that these two legacy institutions should collaborate on this important project.

We could not have undertaken this effort at all without the extraordinary support provided by Steven Cash Nickerson, Washington University alumnus, who gave generously to support the first three phases of the Initiative. Cash believed in this project from its inception, supporting it himself, and thereby helping us to raise monies elsewhere. We are grateful to the United States Institute of Peace, Humanity United, and the Brookings–Washington University Academic Venture Fund for additional, critical financial support. Finally, we thank our other institutional partners – the American Society of International Law, the International Law Association (American Branch), and the International Association of Penal Law (American Branch) – for their support of the Initiative's work as well.

At the end of the day, however, it is perhaps to Whitney R. Harris, former Nuremberg Prosecutor, to whom we are most indebted. For it was Whitney who, along with his fellow trial counsel, first prosecuted crimes against humanity at Nuremberg; Whitney who endowed the Institute bearing his name, providing it with the means to carry on his life's work; and Whitney who served as our counselor, advisor, and friend on this project, as with so many before it. I am sorry that he did not live to see it bear fruit.

One cannot embark on an endeavor such as this without being keenly aware of the currents of history. Here, in the heartland of America, calling for the elaboration of an international convention embodying international legal principles for the settlement of international problems, is not new. The Resolution responsible for the convening of the Second Hague Peace Conference – from which emanated the 1907 Hague Convention – issued from the Inter-Parliamentary Union meeting in St. Louis, Missouri, on the occasion of the 1904 World's Fair.[33] Indeed, the participants in the first meeting of the Initiative in April 2009 gathered in historic Ridgley Hall on the Washington University campus for a photograph, which was taken in the same room in which, 105 years earlier, the Inter-Parliamentary Union

---

[33] Editorial Comment, *The Second Peace Conference of the Hague*, 1 AM. J. INT'L L. 431 (1907). The hopes of that second Peace Conference, however, and the 1907 Convention it produced, were soon dashed as European leaders led their countries into the terrible war that followed.

had issued its call for peace. Nor is it unheard of for a group of experts[34] or an academic institution to spearhead an effort such as this. Witness, for example, the Harvard Research project in international law, which produced three draft conventions, published in 1935.[35] The authors of that project cautioned that the "drafts [were] completed within the limits of a rigorous time-schedule, by men already burdened with exacting duties; and these facts should be borne in mind in any appraisal of the work done."[36] We hope that our work fares somewhat better, although the men and women who contributed to it, of course, were under the same constraints of busy schedules and deadlines.

What will become of the *Proposed International Convention on the Prevention and Punishment of Crimes Against Humanity*? Phase IV of the Initiative contemplates a global awareness campaign to help make the Convention a reality. But will States embrace this "academic offering" and take up the challenge to negotiate a convention for the suppression of crimes against humanity? Or will indifference continue to be the hallmark of international policy?

As Whitney R. Harris admonished us, shortly before his death:

> The challenge to humanity is to establish and maintain the foundations of peace and justice upon the Earth for the centuries to come. We must learn to end war and protect life, to seek justice and find mercy, to help others and embrace compassion. Each person must respect every other person and honor the God who made this incredible mystery of human life a reality.[37]

I hope that this Initiative, undertaken by the Institute that bears his name, will contribute to the realization of these goals.

August 3, 2010

---

[34] The International Law Association, for example, elaborated a draft statute for an international criminal court in 1926. INTERNATIONAL LAW ASSOCIATION, REPORT OF THE THIRTY-FOURTH CONFERENCE (1927).
[35] *Codification of International Law*, 29 AM. J. INT'L L. (Supp.) (1935).
[36] *Id.* at 8.
[37] Whitney R. Harris, *This I Believe*, written and recorded for National Public Radio, June 12, 2006.

Crimes Against Humanity and the Responsibility to Protect

Keynote Address by Gareth Evans
President, International Crisis Group

I

Mobilizing an effective international response to the scourge of crimes against humanity is, for those of us in the world of policy and ideas who spend a lot of our time trying to do just that, nearly always a matter of more than just abstract, intellectual commitment. I have found that for the great majority of us that commitment has welled up from some personal experience that has touched us, individually, very deeply. For many that will be bound to be scarifying family memories of the Holocaust; for others the experience of personal loss or closely knowing survivors from Rwanda or Srebrenica or any of the other mass atrocity scenes of more recent decades; for others still, perhaps, the awful sense that they could have done more, in their past official lives, to generate the kind of international response that these situations required.

For me it was my visit to Cambodia in the late 1960s. I was a young Australian making my first trip to Europe, to take up a scholarship at Oxford. Inexhaustibly hungry for experience, like so many of my compatriots before and since, I spent six months wending my way by plane and overland through a dozen countries in Asia, and a few more in Africa and the Middle East as well. In every one of them, I spent many hours and days on student campuses and in student hangouts, and in hard-class cross-country trains and ramshackle rural buses, getting to know in the process – usually fleetingly but quite often enduringly, in friendships that have lasted to this day – scores of some of the liveliest and brightest people of their generation.

In the years that followed, I have often come across Indonesians, Singaporeans, Malaysians, Thais, Vietnamese, Indians, Pakistanis, and others whom I either met on the road on that trip or who were there at the time and had a store of common experiences to exchange. But among all the countries in Asia I visited then, there is just one, Cambodia, from which I never again, in later years, saw *any* of those students whom I had met and befriended, or anyone exactly like them – not one of those kids with whom I drank beer, ate noodles, and careened up and down the dusty road from Phnom Penh to Siem Reap in child-, chicken-, and pig-scattering share taxis.

The reason, I am sadly certain, is that every last one of them died a few years later under Pol Pot's murderous genocidal regime – either targeted for execution in the killing fields as a middle-class intellectual enemy of the State or dying, as more than a million did, from starvation and disease after forced displacement to labor in the countryside. The knowledge, and the memory, of what must have happened to those young men and women is something that haunts me to this day.

That memory certainly was a core motivation during the long and grueling years in the late 1980s and early 1990s that I worked as Australian Foreign Minister, along with my Southeast Asian, Chinese, American, and UN colleagues, to find and implement a sustainable basis for peace in Cambodia. It was a recurring motif as I watched, impotently and from a distance, the tragic events in Central Africa and the Balkans work themselves out through the mid- to late 1990s.

It was what made me accept with alacrity the offer of the Canadian government in 2000 to jointly lead a distinguished international commission charged with the task of trying to find, once and for all, a conceptual and practical answer that would unite, rather than continuing to divide, the international community in preventing and responding to mass atrocity crimes, a task that I think we in large measure accomplished by introducing and elaborating the concept of "the responsibility to protect," the core elements of which are too well known to this audience for me to need to spell them out in detail: That the primary responsibility for protecting its people from atrocity crimes is that of the sovereign State itself; other States have a responsibility to assist it to do so; but if, as a result of either incapacity or ill-will, a State is manifestly failing to give that protection, the responsibility to take appropriate action – which might in an extreme case involve the use of coercive military force – shifts to the wider international community.

It has what kept me engaged ever since – through membership of UN panels, writing a book, and constant advocacy around the world – in the even bigger task of winning and consolidating genuine international acceptance and recognition of this concept as a new global norm and, even more importantly, achieving its effective application in practice as new conscience-shocking situations continue to arise.

And it is what makes me intensely committed to the great enterprise on which this panel of experts is now engaged, on the initiative of the Harris Institute at the Washington University School of Law under the admirable leadership of Professor Leila Sadat, to draft and secure the ultimate adoption of a new Convention on Crimes Against Humanity, to fill a gap that has all too obviously become apparent in the array of legal instruments available to deal with atrocity crimes, notwithstanding the emergence of the International Criminal Court – not least the need for national courts around the world to have clear-cut jurisdiction to deal with these cases, and for there to be in place mechanisms to enable effective international cooperation in the investigation and punishment of perpetrators.

I congratulate Leila Sadat, Cherif Bassiouni, Richard Goldstone, and the other distinguished members of the Steering Committee for this project, and all those

II

The beginning of wisdom for me on this subject was the realization, very early on, that for all its compelling general moral authority, the Genocide Convention had absolutely no legal application to the killing fields of Cambodia, which nearly everyone still thinks of as the worst genocide of modern times. Because those doing the killing and beating and expelling were of exactly the same nationality, ethnicity, race, and religion as those they were victimizing – and their motives were political, ideological, and class-based rather than having anything to do with the characteristics described in the Genocide Convention – the necessary elements of specific intent required for its application were simply not there.

And for all the well-intentioned attempts that have been made many times since – most obviously in Darfur – to try to argue that the "g" word, properly understood, does have application to a much wider range of crimes against humanity, and remains the best linguistic vehicle for energizing mass support and high-level governmental support for effective action in response to newly emerging atrocity situations, the hard truth is that this approach is a lost cause. Lawyers remain lawyers, and there will always be good and compelling legal arguments why the Genocide Convention just does not reach many of the cases we morally want it to – resulting in propaganda victories again and again for those who least deserve to have them as claims or charges are reduced by commissions or courts from genocide to "only" crimes against humanity.

Rhetorically and politically it has always made more sense, following David Scheffer, to make "atrocity crimes" or "mass atrocity crimes" the dominant working concept, rather than becoming caught in the technical cul de sacs of defining the difference between genocide, crimes against humanity, and war crimes, and trying to explain where ethnic cleansing – not a clearly defined crime at all – fits into the other three.

So now it is time, when the debate does have to turn to *legal* remedies, to make "crimes against humanity" the dominant, resonating legal concept, the centrepiece of the argument in the media, and among policy makers, and not just a kind of afterthought category – what one is reduced to when genocide for one technical reason or another is ruled out, or when one has to sweep up some smaller bits and pieces.

"Crimes against humanity" is broad enough conceptually to embrace certainly genocide and ethnic cleansing (if not war crimes, which we will continue to have to refer to separately, but that does not seem a problem). It is a concept with an intellectual and international law pedigree going back a century. Linguistically, the phrase "crimes against humanity" is surely rich and powerful enough for it to carry the moral and emotional weight we want it to. Quite apart from all the good technical reasons for having a new Crimes Against Humanity Convention, the campaign to adopt it should put the concept of crimes against humanity right back on the central pedestal where it belongs.

III

I see this effort marching in lockstep with the continuing effort to entrench and operationalize the new norm of the responsibility to protect (R2P). They are wholly complementary exercises – in essence, the legal and political faces of the same coin. Persuading the UN General Assembly to endorse the responsibility to protect principle, as was achieved at the 2005 World Summit, was all about winning acceptance for the core idea that crimes against humanity and other mass atrocity crimes were everybody's business, not – as they had been for centuries, and even for the first six decades of the UN's existence – nobody's business.

Promoting the *language* of "the responsibility to protect," rather than "the right to intervene," which had so hopelessly divided the global north and south throughout the 1990s, was all about creating the conditions where – when another Cambodia, or Rwanda, or Bosnia, or Kosovo came along, as it surely would – the reflex international response would be not to retreat behind article 2(7) of the Charter and the pretense that this was somehow a matter "essentially within the domestic jurisdiction" of the State in question, but a consensus response that something had to be done, with the only argument being what and how.

For all the bumps and grinds and reverses along the way – and there have been many – I remain personally confident that the consolidation of the responsibility-to-protect norm, as the overall framing principle for international debate on this subject, and the basic guide to appropriate action, is on course.

There remain some conceptual challenges – ensuring that the scope and limits of the doctrine are universally understood, that it is seen to be not about conflict generally or human rights generally or, even more grandly and broadly, human security generally, but about a narrow subset of extreme cases, involving the commission – or likely commission – of mass atrocity crimes, with crimes against humanity at the core. Looked at this way, there are probably no more than ten or fifteen cases at any given time where it is appropriate for the political and policy debate to be conducted in responsibility to protect terms – because large-scale atrocity crimes are being committed, seem imminently about to be committed, or are on a path to being committed in the reasonably near term if appropriate remedial action is not taken, by the State itself or others assisting it. By contrast, there are likely to be 70 or 100 or more country or regional situations where at any given time it is appropriate to talk about conflict prevention or resolution strategies, responses to human rights abuses of various kinds, or reactions to other kinds of human security concerns.

There also remain conceptual challenges in explaining, in an environment where there is still considerable dissimulation going on, as well as genuine uncertainty, which particular cases are properly characterized as responsibility to protect situations and which are not: Why it is, for example, to take those cases most debated in recent times, that the coalition invasion of Iraq in 2003 and Russia's invasion of Georgia in 2008 were *not* justified in R2P terms; that the Burma-Myanmar cyclone in 2008 was not an R2P case, but could have been if the generals' behavior had been characterizable as so recklessly indifferent to human life as to amount to a crime against humanity, which in the event it was not; that Somalia and the Congo for many years, Darfur since 2003, and Sri Lanka in the 2009 military endgame have been properly characterized as R2P cases, but where the international community's response has been, for one reason or another, unhappily inadequate; and that Kenya in early 2008 is the clearest case we have had of an exploding situation being widely, and properly, characterized as an R2P one, and where the international community's response – in this case diplomatic mediation – did prove to be adequate to bring it under control.

In addition to the conceptual challenges, there certainly remain institutional ones, in ensuring for a start that well-intentioned States facing atrocity crime problems get in practice all the assistance they need – and which the 2005 UN resolution clearly encourages other States to give them – in terms of capacity building, effective policy formulation and delivery, and – if things get rough and they call for it – the necessary security support. It means also putting in place worldwide the early-warning and response capability, the diplomatic and civilian response capability, the legal response mechanisms, and – for extreme cases – the coercive military capability to ensure that the international community, if it has the will, can deliver the appropriate response to whatever new atrocity crime situation comes along demanding its engagement, again as clearly authorized by the 2005 UN resolution.

One issue that arises in this context is whether, when it comes to putting in place appropriate legal response mechanisms, it is necessary or desirable for the responsibility to protect norm itself to be given some more formal legal status, for example, as David Scheffer has suggested, by incorporating appropriate provisions in the proposed Crimes Against Humanity Convention. In its present draft form, this is focused on individual criminal responsibility, and limits State responsibility essentially to introducing the necessary legislative and other measures to make that real. Scheffer suggests that the Convention also contain State Responsibility provisions expressly prohibiting the commission of crimes against humanity by any State Party entity itself, and requiring States Parties to act, as a matter of legal obligation, in accordance with the 2005 UN resolution.

My own instinct, for what it is worth, although I would certainly be happy to see this debated further, is that while such an exercise would certainly give new weight and prominence to the responsibility to protect norm, and that anything that reinforced the obligations of States to act constructively and not destructively in relation to atrocity crimes would be hugely welcome, the risks probably outweigh the benefits. It would be nightmarishly difficult to get States to sign up to direct legal liability of the kind proposed, be a major distraction that would work against them signing up to anything else, and would in any event not make a great deal of practical difference because any enforcement action against a State itself would have to be a matter for the Security Council, and if the 2005 UN Resolution is to be taken seriously, it already has that role.

In addition to the conceptual and institutional challenges I have described, proponents of the responsibility to protect will always face a political challenge – to activate the real-world response that is actually required to avert or halt an atrocity crime catastrophe. That means having in place mechanisms and strategies to ensure both peer-group pressure, by government friends of R2P, to energize the highest levels of governmental and intergovernmental decision-making, and bottom-up grass roots action to kick the decision makers into action if they are showing signs of hesitation.

Mobilizing political will in any policy context whatsoever, national or international, requires the coming together of good information, good organization, and good arguments. As to the last, it is helpful that "national interest" is now a much broader concept than it used to be. It's not quite as easy now as it was for Chamberlain in the 1930s to talk of faraway countries with people of whom we know nothing: We do know now that States that cannot or will not stop internal atrocity crimes are the kind of States that cannot or will not stop terrorism, weapons proliferation, drug and people trafficking, the spread of health pandemics, and other global risks that every country in the world has a stake in ending.

There is still a long way to go before we can be confident that the automatic consensual reflex of which I spoke earlier will cut in at the time it should and in the way it should in every new case that arises, and longer still before we can credibly claim that the responsibility to protect principle in all its dimensions has evolved into a rule of customary international law. But the evidence is of advance rather than reverse, particularly with the large measure of consensus that seems to have emerged around the UN Secretary-General's report on the implementation of the responsibility to protect, prepared after long consultations by his special adviser Edward Luck, and, although still not debated by the UN General Assembly at the time of this writing, expected to be formally received with little or no dissent.

The importance of the report is that it does not retreat in any way on the basic principles as they were adopted in 2005, and focuses very constructively on what States need to do for themselves, what others need to do to assist them, and the kinds of prevention, reaction, and rebuilding measures that may need to be employed if a State is unreceptive to self-help or assistance, and atrocity crime alarm bells are ringing. What is intriguing is that some of the States who were last to join the consensus in 2005, and have been most resistant since in expressing support for the concept, have now very definitely changed course, with India's Foreign Minister Pranab Mukherjee, for example, saying publicly in April this year that the Government of Sri Lanka had a clear "responsibility to protect" its civilians at extreme risk in the final operations of the military against the Tamil Tigers.

IV

Maybe my confidence is a little premature, but one of the things that has most sustained me over forty years of public life, more than twenty of them working in international affairs, is a fairly unquenchable sense of optimism: a belief that even the most horrible and intractable problems are solvable; that rational solutions for which there are good, principled arguments do eventually prevail; and that good people, good governments, and good governance will eventually prevail over bad.

When it comes to international relations, and in particular the great issues of war and peace, violence, and catastrophic human rights violations with which we are concerned here, there is a well-established view that anyone who approaches things in this kind of generally optimistic frame of mind must be incorrigibly naïve, if not outright demented. Certainly in the case of genocide and atrocity crimes – either directly committed by a government against its own people or allowed to happen by a government unable or unwilling to stop it – it is hard for even the incorrigibly naïve to remain optimistic.

In this world we inhabit – full of cynicism, double standards, crude assertions of national interest, high-level realpolitik, and low-level maneuvering for political advantage – it is very easy to believe that ideas do not matter very much. But I believe as passionately now as I ever have in my long career – starting and finishing in the world of nongovernmental organizations, but with much time between in politics and government – that ideas matter enormously, for good and for ill. For all the difficulties of acceptance and application that lie ahead, there are – I have come optimistically, but firmly, to believe – not many ideas that have the potential to matter more for good, not only in theory but in practice, than that of the responsibility to protect.

In the cause of advancing that responsibility, there can be few more constructive contributions to be made than strengthening the direct normative constraints against committing crimes against humanity – sharpening the applicable law, trying to universalize its application, and ensuring its effective enforcement through worldwide cooperation. In all of this, nothing less than our common humanity is at stake, and this group can be collectively very proud of what it is doing to advance it.

1

History of Efforts to Codify Crimes Against Humanity

From the Charter of Nuremberg to the Statute of Rome

Roger S. Clark[*]

I. THE NUREMBERG CHARTER

The modern usage of the words "crimes against humanity"[1] dates from the Nuremberg Charter, article 6(c) of which reads as follows:

> CRIMES AGAINST HUMANITY: namely, murder, extermination, enslavement, deportation or other inhumane acts committed against any civilian population, before or during the war, or persecutions on political, racial or religious grounds in execution of or in connection with any crime within the jurisdiction of the Tribunal, whether or not in violation of the domestic law of the country where perpetrated.[2]

I doubt very much that the drafters of the Nuremberg Charter who gathered in London from June 26 to August 8, 1945 saw themselves as engaged in a codification exercise. In retrospect, the characterization is perhaps not inappropriate, although the term "crimes against humanity," which provided a catchy title in the Charter to go along with "crime against peace" and "war crimes," did not make an appearance in the drafting until the very last moment.[3] Until then, the talk had been of

---

[*] Board of Governors Professor, Rutgers University School of Law, Camden, New Jersey. Adviser to Samoa in the negotiations on the International Criminal Court. Any opinions expressed in this chapter should not be attributed to that Government.

[1] The author has previously discussed various aspects of this history in Roger S. Clark, *Crimes against Humanity at Nuremberg*, in THE NUREMBERG TRIAL AND INTERNATIONAL LAW 177 (George Ginsburgs & V. N. Kudriavtsev eds., 1990), and Roger S. Clark, *Crimes against Humanity and the Rome Statute of the International Criminal Court*, in INTERNATIONAL AND NATIONAL LAW IN RUSSIA AND EASTERN EUROPE: ESSAYS IN HONOR OF GEORGE GINSBURGS 139 (Roger Clark, Ferdinand Feldbrugge & Stanislaw Pomorski eds., 2001). The most comprehensive study is M. CHERIF BASSIOUNI, CRIMES AGAINST HUMANITY IN INTERNATIONAL LAW (2d rev. ed. 1999). *See also* Christopher K. Hall et al., *Article 7, Crimes against Humanity in* COMMENTARY ON THE ROME STATUTE OF THE INTERNATIONAL CRIMINAL COURT: OBSERVERS' NOTES, ARTICLE BY ARTICLE 159 (2d ed. 2008); Margaret McAuliffe deGuzman, *The Road from Rome: The Developing Law of Crimes against Humanity*, 22 HUM. RTS. Q. 335 (2000).

[2] Charter of the International Military Tribunal art. 6 (c) *in* 1 TRIAL OF THE MAJOR WAR CRIMINALS BEFORE THE INTERNATIONAL MILITARY TRIBUNAL 10, 11 (1947). In a Protocol signed on October 6, 1945, the comma before "or persecutions" in the text above replaced the semicolon that appeared there in the original text adopted in London on August 8, 1945. On the "semi-colon Protocol," see *infra* notes 14–17.

[3] Clark, *Crimes against Humanity at Nuremberg*, *supra* note 1, at 189–90. Sir Hersch Lauterpacht has been credited with providing this inspired touch. Jacob Robinson, *The International Military Tribunal and the Holocaust: Some Legal Reflections*, 7 ISR. L. REV. 1, 3 (1972).

"atrocities," "persecutions," and sometimes "deportations" (it apparently being understood that these were for the purpose of slave labor).[4]

Probably the closest example of usage hinting at what would be "codified" in London was in the declaration of May 28, 1915 by the Governments of France, Great Britain, and Russia concerning the massacres of the Armenian population in Turkey, killings to which the term "genocide" has also since been applied. The three-power declaration described these atrocities as "crimes against humanity for which all members of the Turkish Government will be held responsible together with its agents implicated in the massacres."[5] The declaration makes the novelty of the complaint clear: This is not a complaint about war crimes inflicted on an adversary; it is about what citizens of the Ottoman Empire were doing to other citizens of the Empire. That would become the gravamen of crimes against humanity at Nuremberg – crimes by Germans against fellow Germans. The 1915 usage of the term, while carefully dealing with situations to which the laws of international armed conflict do not – by their terms at least – apply, nonetheless echoes the principle of the Martens clause of the Fourth Hague Convention.[6] Specifically, to the extent certain matters are not particularly dealt with in the Convention, "the inhabitants and the belligerents shall remain under the protection of and subject to the principles of the law of nations, as established by and prevailing among civilized nations, by the laws of humanity, and the demands of the public conscience."[7] Whereas the Hague Convention applied by

---

[4] *Id.* Under the Rome Statute of the International Criminal Court, article 7(1)(d), it is clear that a deportation is, in itself, unlawful, without any further object. *Rome Statute of the International Criminal Court*, United Nations Diplomatic Conference of Plenipotentiaries on the Establishment of an International Criminal Court, July 17, 1998, U.N. Doc. A/CONF.183/9 (1998) [hereinafter *Rome Statute*].

[5] *Quoted in* Egon Schwelb, *Crimes Against Humanity*, 23 BRIT.Y.B. INT'L L. 181 (1946). Neither the Turkish Government, nor its agents were ultimately "held responsible." There were provisions (articles 226–30) in the aborted 1920 Treaty of Sèvres between the Allies and Turkey that contemplated trials both for war crimes and for internal "massacres" (the term "crimes against humanity" does not appear), but the point was not pursued in the final peace treaty done at Lausanne in 1923. *See also* COMM'N ON THE RESPONSIBILITY OF THE AUTHORS OF THE WAR AND ON ENFORCEMENT OF PENALTIES, MARCH 1919 REPORT PRESENTED TO PRELIMINARY PEACE CONFERENCE (1919) (recommending, over dissent of U.S. and Japanese members, criminal prosecution of those "guilty of offenses against the laws and customs of war or the laws of humanity").

[6] The Hague Conventions applied to war between States, not to internal conflicts or massacres. The much later provisions of common article 3 of the 1949 Geneva Conventions and Protocol II of 1977 to those Conventions provide criminal proscriptions concerning noninternational armed conflict that will often overlap with crimes against humanity (and perhaps genocide). Particular depredations can often, in the modern expanded legal universe, be characterized legally in different ways. *See generally* José Doria, *Whether Crimes against Humanity Are Backdoor War Crimes*, in THE LEGAL REGIME OF THE INTERNATIONAL CRIMINAL COURT: ESSAYS IN HONOUR OF PROFESSOR IGOR BLISHCHENKO 645 (José Doria, Hans-Peter Gasser & M. Cherif Bassiouni eds., 2009).

[7] Convention (No. IV) respecting the Laws and Customs of War on Land, with Annex of Regulations, done at the Hague pmbl., Oct. 18, 1907, 205 CONSOL. T.S. 277. Doria, *supra* note 6, at 646, attributes the origin "in the modern era" of the notion of crimes against humanity to the reference in the preamble to the Declaration of Saint Petersburg on fixing "technical limits within which the necessities of war ought to yield to the demands of humanity." *See* Declaration Renouncing the Use, in Time of War, of Explosive Projectiles Under 400 Grammes Weight, Dec. 11, 1868, 138 CONSOL. T.S. 297, *reprinted in* 1 AM. J. INT'L L. 95 (Supp.1907) (adopted at Saint Petersburg by the International Military Commission). Once again, "war" at the relevant time denoted a reference to international armed conflict. This was not a matter of what leaders did to their own subjects.

its terms only to "war" in the sense of international armed conflict, the Martens spirit certainly had some rhetorical power in the Armenian context.

In even earlier usage, "crime against humanity" had a narrower meaning, applying to the slave trade[8] and perhaps even slavery itself.[9]

I have summarized elsewhere[10] the process by which article 6(c) of the Nuremberg Charter was negotiated at the London Conference in 1945. That summary relied heavily on Justice Robert Jackson's report to the U.S. President,[11] the nearest to an "official" account of what happened. I do not intend to repeat all that material here, but a few comments about the development of the final language will help illuminate the views the participants apparently had of the nature of the crimes with which they were concerned.

The first draft of what became article 6 of the Charter, presented by the United States to its allies at the San Francisco meeting at which the United Nations Charter was finalized, listed various acts that eventually fell under the rubric of crimes against peace and war crimes. It then added:

> This declaration shall also include the right to charge and try defendants under this Agreement for violations of law other than those recited above, including but not limited to atrocities and crimes committed in violation of the domestic law of any Axis Power or satellite or any of the United Nations.[12]

What is interesting about this draft is that it contemplated trials applying what was explicitly domestic law, the domestic law both of Germany and that of those members of the Allies that had been affected by German depredations. In terms of jurisdictional theories, I take it that the Allies contemplated that, as the victorious powers following a surrender, they might exercise Germany's "active personality" power to prosecute

---

[8] See Robert Lansing, Notes on World Sovereignty, 1 AM. J. INT'L L. 13, 25 (1921) (distinguishing between piracy, "a crime against the world" and the slave trade, "a crime against humanity"). (Although it was published in 1921, a note to this article suggests that it was written in 1906.) Lansing did not apparently have a broader view of the concept; he was one of the U.S. dissenters in 1919 to the legality of the proposal to try German leadership. In an unusual case in which he was justifying the extradition of a slave trader to Cuba, without the benefit of an extradition treaty, President Abraham Lincoln reported to the Senate that "a nation is never bound to furnish asylum to dangerous criminals who are offenders against the human race." See discussion in 1 JOHN BASSETT MOORE, ON EXTRADITION AND INTERSTATE RENDITION 33–35 (1891). This must be an early example of a similar usage.

[9] See Jordan J. Paust, Threats to Accountability after Nuremberg: Crimes against Humanity, Leader Responsibility and National Fora, 12 N.Y.L. SCH. J. HUM. RTS. 545, 549 (1996) (quoting 1872 oration by George William Curtis). See also Letter from George Washington Williams to the U.S. Sec'y of State (1890), quoted in ADAM HOCHSCHILD, KING LEOPOLD'S GHOST: A STORY OF GREED, TERROR AND HEROISM IN COLONIAL AFRICA 112 (1999) (describing King Leopold's rule in the Congo as a crime against humanity). William Schabas has also discovered an even earlier, but different, usage in French, with Robespierre's reference to Louis XVI as a "criminel envers l'humanité." WILLIAM A. SCHABAS, THE ABOLITION OF THE DEATH PENALTY IN INTERNATIONAL LAW 5 (2d ed. 1997).

[10] Clark, Crimes against Humanity at Nuremberg, supra note 1, at 181–92.

[11] REPORT OF ROBERT H. JACKSON, UNITED STATES REPRESENTATIVE TO THE INTERNATIONAL CONFERENCE ON MILITARY TRIALS (1947).

[12] Id. at 24.

its nationals for what they did in Germany and elsewhere. Moreover, as delegated to by the members of the Allied group by then calling itself "the United Nations," an appropriate tribunal might exercise the power of the members over what happened on their individual territories or perhaps (a passive personality theory) to their nationals.[13] Instead of pursuing this line, article 6 ultimately adopted an approach that regarded (what later in the process came to be called) crimes against humanity as general principles of law, and thus proscribed by international law, rather than specific examples of the law of particular States. Indeed, in what was an obvious effort to cut off the argument that German law provided a justification or prescription for the crimes, the last phrase of article 6(c) asserts the illegality of the crimes in question "whether or not in violation of the domestic law of the country where perpetrated."[14]

A significant feature of the Nuremberg definition was the requirement that the crimes against humanity take place "in execution of or in connection with any crime within the jurisdiction of the Tribunal." I have argued elsewhere that this represented a jurisdictional limit on the Nuremberg Tribunal itself, rather than something inherent in the substantive concept of a crime against humanity.[15] The context of this phrase took some interesting turns. In the final version of the English text that was agreed on in London, the text defining crimes against humanity was broken by a semicolon. The first part of the definition referred to "murder, extermination, enslavement, deportation, and other inhumane acts committed against

---

[13] This concept of the delegation of national power to an international tribunal, not pursued further in the Nuremberg process, seems to be the basis of the May 30, 2007 Security Council resolution approving an Agreement between the United Nations and the Lebanese Republic on the establishment of a Special Tribunal for Lebanon. S.C. Res. 1757, U.N. Doc. S/RES/1757 (May 30, 2007). The Tribunal's jurisdiction is composed entirely of crimes defined under Lebanese law. *See also* Conference on Sec. and Cooperation in Eur. (CSCE), *Proposal for an International War Crimes Tribunal for the Former Yugoslavia*, U.N. Doc. S/25307 (Feb. 9, 1993) (Rapporteurs Corell, Türk and Thune) (applicable law "a number of provisions from the Penal Code of the Former Socialist Federative Republic of Yugoslavia"). The Nuremberg Tribunal's discussion of its own jurisdiction reflects some ambivalence about whether it is exercising jurisdiction that any of the Allies might have taken following the Surrender, or whether it is exercising collectively a form of universal jurisdiction that any of them might have exercised individually. Thus the Tribunal commented: "The making of the Charter was the exercise of the sovereign legislative power by the countries to which the German Reich unconditionally surrendered; and the undoubted right of these countries to legislate for the occupied territories has been recognized by the civilized world." Later, it added:

> The Signatory Powers created this Tribunal, defined the law it was to administer, and made regulations for the proper conduct of the Trial. In doing so, they have done together what any one of them might have done singly; for it is not to be doubted that any nation has the right thus to set up special courts to administer law.

International Military Tribunal (Nuremberg) Judgment and Sentences, 41 AM. J. INT'L L. 172 (1947) [hereinafter Nuremberg Judgment].

[14] This theme was picked up in Principle II of the International Law Commission's 1950 formulation of the Nuremberg Principles: "The fact that internal law does not impose a penalty for an act which constitutes a crime under international law does not relieve the person who committed the act from responsibility under international law." Int'l Law Comm'n, *Report of the International Law Commission on its Second Session*, U.N. GAOR, 5th Sess., Supp. No. 12, U.N. Doc. A/1316 (1950).

[15] Clark, *Crimes against Humanity at Nuremberg*, supra note 1, at 195–96.

any civilian population, before or during the war" – and ended with the semicolon. Then followed the words: "or persecutions on political, racial or religious grounds in execution of or in connection with any crime within the jurisdiction of the Tribunal ...." The logical interpretation of a paragraph so broken by the semicolon was that the legal/factual requirement of a connection to "any crime within the jurisdiction of the Tribunal"[16] applied only to the persecution variety of crimes – the murders and other depredations were subject to no such limitations. Where the semicolon came from is a puzzle – it was not to be found in the immediately preceding drafts. At all events, in a Protocol signed on October 6, 1945, the comma before "or persecutions" replaced the semicolon that appeared there in the original text adopted in London on August 8, 1945.[17] Thereafter, it was clear that "in execution of or in connection with" modified all the varieties of crimes against humanity in the Charter.[18]

II. CONTROL COUNCIL LAW NO. 10[19]

I also doubt that the drafters of Control Council Law No. 10 saw their task as codifying the concept of crimes against humanity, but they added some interesting elements to the earlier effort. For example, Law No. 10 did not, on its face at least, contain a limitation requiring a connection to other crimes within the jurisdiction of the military tribunals that were expected to be set up pursuant to it.[20] Nevertheless, these

---

[16] Most likely this required a connection to a crime against peace; that is to say, the prosecution must prove a connection to the conspiracy to wage aggressive war rather than a freestanding desire to exterminate certain groups.

[17] On the "semi-colon Protocol," see Clark, *Crimes against Humanity at Nuremberg*, *supra* note 1, at 190–92. The protocol asserts that a discrepancy had been found to exist in the French and English texts, and that these were being corrected to conform to the Russian version. Something strange was happening, but the common purpose to narrow the scope of the provision cannot be gainsaid.

[18] Hence the statement in the Tribunal's Judgment that:

> To constitute Crimes against Humanity, the acts relied on before the outbreak of war must have been in execution of, or in connection with, any crime within the jurisdiction of the Tribunal. The Tribunal is of the opinion that revolting and horrible as many of these crimes were, it has not been satisfactorily proved that they were done in execution of, or in connection with, any such crime.

Nuremberg Judgment, *supra* note 13, at 249.

[19] For the sake of completeness, mention should be made of the Charter of the International Military Tribunal for the Far East. The language therein was taken uncritically from the Nuremberg Charter. It read:

> Crimes against Humanity: Namely, murder, extermination, enslavement, deportation, and other inhumane acts committed against any civilian population, before or during the war, or persecutions on political or racial grounds in execution of or in connection with any crime within the jurisdiction of the Tribunal, whether or not in violation of the domestic law of the country where perpetrated.

Charter of the International Military Tribunal for the Far East art. 5(c), Jan. 19, 1946, T.I.A.S. No. 1589. No one was ultimately convicted of such crimes in Tokyo. *See generally* NEIL BOISTER & ROBERT CRYER, THE TOKYO INTERNATIONAL TRIBUNAL: A REAPPRAISAL (2008).

[20] Control Council Law No. 10 was issued in Berlin on December 20, 1945 by the leaders of the military occupying forces of the United States, United Kingdom, France, and the Soviet Union.

subsequent trials for the most part followed the International Military Tribunal's lead in requiring a connection to an aggressive war. There were, however, dicta indicating that a broader view of crime against humanity was possible.[21] The Law also made specific reference to "imprisonment, torture and rape" that had not been mentioned specifically in the Nuremberg Charter. Both listings were, however, somewhat openended in their reference to "other inhumane acts." Control Council Law No. 10 asserted, moreover, that its list was "including but not limited to" the listed acts.[22]

III. THE INTERNATIONAL LAW COMMISSION AND THE NUREMBERG PRINCIPLES

On December 11, 1946, the United Nations General Assembly adopted a resolution in which it "reaffirm[ed] the principles of international law recognized by the Charter of the Nuremberg Tribunal and the Judgment of the Tribunal" (without saying what those principles were); it directed the International Law Commission (then called the Committee on the Codification of International Law) to "formulate" those principles.[23] The International Law Commission (as it became known in the interim) produced its distillation of the Nuremberg Principles in 1950.[24] Principle I restated the fundamental Nuremberg tenet that "[a]ny person who commits an act which constitutes a crime under international law is responsible therefore and liable to punishment."[25] Principle VI spoke to Nuremberg's recognition of crimes against peace, war crimes, and crimes against humanity. Crimes against humanity were defined in Principle VI as "murder, extermination, enslavement, deportation and other inhuman acts done against any civilian population, or persecutions on political, racial or religious grounds, when such acts are done or such persecutions are carried on in execution of or in connection with any crime against peace or any war crime."[26] This is the essence of the Nuremberg Charter's

---

The Law defined Crimes against Humanity as "[a]trocities and offenses, including but not limited to murder, extermination, enslavement, deportation, imprisonment, torture, rape, or other inhumane acts committed against any civilian population, or persecutions on political, racial or religious grounds, whether or not in violation of the domestic laws of the country where perpetrated." Allied Control Council Law No. 10, Punishment of Persons Guilty of War Crimes, Crimes Against Peace and Against Humanity art. 2(a), Dec. 20, 1945, 3 OFFICIAL GAZETTE OF THE CONTROL COUNCIL FOR GERMANY 50–55 (1946).

[21] *See generally* TELFORD TAYLOR, FINAL REPORT TO THE SECRETARY OF THE ARMY ON THE NUERNBERG WAR CRIMES TRIALS UNDER CONTROL COUNCIL LAW NO. 10, AT 224–26 (1949). Other writers at the time were arguing against such limitations. *See* Joseph Y. Dautricourt, *Crime against Humanity: European Views on its Conception and its Future*, 40 J. CRIM. L. & CRIMINOLOGY 170 (1949).

[22] *See supra* note 20 and accompanying text. Perhaps "inhumane acts" is not entirely open-ended; at a minimum, it has to be interpreted *ejusdem generis* with the specific items on the list.

[23] *Affirmation of the Principles of International Law recognized by the Charter of the Nürnberg Tribunal*, G.A. Res. 95 (I), at 188, U.N. Doc. A/64/Add.1 (Dec. 11, 1946).

[24] *Report of the International Law Commission, supra* note 14, at 11–14.

[25] *Id.*

[26] *Id.*

language, but instead of a general reference to a crime within the jurisdiction of the Tribunal, there is a specific requirement for a nexus to crimes against peace or war crimes.

IV. THE GENOCIDE CONVENTION

The drafting of the Genocide Convention[27] is usually treated in the literature with great reverence. From the perspective of continuing further codification of crimes against humanity, which had proven to be a serviceable concept in Nuremberg, the effort devoted to genocide was, to my mind, something of a disaster.[28] It entailed taking out a significant part, but far from all, of the field covered by crimes against humanity and subjecting it to a badly drafted definition that included a specific intent that would be hard to prove. "Genocide" as defined in the 1948 Convention has obvious connections to the "persecution" part of the Nuremberg definition of crimes against humanity. Article II of the Convention provides that:

> In the present Convention, genocide means any of the following acts committed with intent to destroy, in whole or in part, a national, ethnical, racial or religious group, as such:
>
> (a) Killing members of the group;
> (b) Causing bodily or mental harm to members of the group;
> (c) Deliberately inflicting on the group conditions of life calculated to bring about its physical destruction in whole or in part;
> (d) Imposing measures intended to prevent births within the group;
> (e) Forcibly transferring children of the group to another group.[29]

The term "crime against humanity" does not find a home in the Genocide Convention. Instead, the parties confirm in article I of the Convention that "genocide, whether committed in time of peace or in time of war, is a crime under international law which they undertake to prevent and punish."[30] This includes both a strong use of the term "crime under international law" (later used to strengthen arguments for universal jurisdiction over genocide, although this is not required by the Convention itself) and a decoupling of the crime from the requirement of a connection to armed conflict – or, indeed, any other crimes. It became a clearly free-standing case of evil that the international community pledged itself to suppress.[31]

---

[27] Convention on the Prevention and Punishment of the Crime of Genocide, Dec. 9, 1948, 78 U.N.T.S. 277 [hereinafter Genocide Convention] (entered into force Jan. 12, 1951).
[28] Raphael Lemkin is credited with inventing the word "genocide." I once spent several hours reading his papers at the New York Public Library. I came away with the impression of a giant, if somewhat confused, ego so focused on immortalizing his word that he missed the bigger picture and was defeated on many drafting points.
[29] Genocide Convention, *supra* note 27, art. II.
[30] *Id.* art. I.
[31] For good measure, the literal language of the Convention itself does not require that the *génocidaire* have any connection with a State, group, or organization. *Cf. infra* note 36. The Elements of genocide

The Genocide Convention provides an important lesson for the present exercise on crimes against humanity in one other respect. It is a Convention on *prevention* as well as punishment, and in *Bosnia and Herzegovina v. Serbia and Montenegro*,[32] the International Court of Justice interpreted it as containing strong elements of State responsibility as well as individual criminal responsibility.[33]

V. THE INTERNATIONAL LAW COMMISSION'S DRAFT CODE OF CRIMES AGAINST THE PEACE AND SECURITY OF MANKIND

In addition to asking the International Law Commission to formulate the Nuremberg Principles, the General Assembly also asked the Commission to produce a Draft Code of Offenses (later "Crimes") against the Peace and Security of Mankind. This second project proceeded on the basis that the Nuremberg crimes – crimes against peace, war crimes, and crimes against humanity – were part of a broader category, the details of which would emerge through rational analysis. Suffice it to say that this five-decade effort was controversial from the start, although it was not put out of its misery until 1996 when the Commission "concluded" its work with a "Code" that contained essentially the Nuremberg crimes and genocide, along with crimes against United Nations-associated personnel.[34]

> adopted by the Assembly of States Parties of the International Criminal Court contain a (controversial) provision that the drafters of the Elements thought implicit in the Convention:
>
> > The conduct took place in the context of a manifest pattern of similar conduct directed against [the targeted] group or was conduct that could itself effect such destruction. Preparatory Comm'n for the Int'l Criminal Court, *Report of the Preparatory Commission for the International Criminal Court: Finalized draft text of the Elements of Crimes*, art. 6, U.N. Doc. PCNICC/2000/1/Add.2 (Nov. 2, 2000) [hereinafter Elements of Crimes].

[32] Application of the Convention on the Prevention and Punishment of the Crime of Genocide (Bosn. & Herz. v. Serb. & Mont.) 2007 I.C.J. 91 (Feb. 26).

[33] *See generally* Roger S. Clark, *State Obligations under the Genocide Convention in Light of the ICJ's Decision in the Case Concerning the* Application of the Convention on the Prevention and Punishment of the Crime of Genocide, 61 RUTGERS L. REV. 75 (2008). Article III of the Convention contemplates individual and State responsibility for those who commit genocide (apparently as principals), conspiracy (of the inchoate variety) to commit genocide, direct and public incitement to commit genocide, attempt to commit genocide, and complicity to commit genocide. This could provide a model for the present drafting, but there are other, perhaps more current, models such as article 25 (3) of the Rome Statute of the International Criminal Court. *See* Roger S. Clark, *Drafting a General Part to a Penal Code: Some Thoughts Inspired by the Negotiations on the Rome Statute of the International Criminal Court and by the Court's First Substantive Law Discussion in the* Lubanga Dyilo *Confirmation Proceedings*, 19 CRIM. L.F. 519, 542–50 (2008).

[34] Draft Code of Crimes against the Peace and Security of Mankind art. 18, *in Report of the International Law Commission on the work of its forty-eighth session*, U.N. GAOR, 51st Sess., Supp. No. 10, U.N. Doc. A/51/10 (1996) [hereinafter 1996 Draft Code]. The draft (art. 9) also included an obligation to extradite or prosecute, without prejudice to the jurisdiction of an international criminal court. The list of acts is now "closed" ("any of the following acts"). Compare the open-ended list, *infra* note 38 ("such as"). The flexibility is now in the last subparagraph ("other inhumane acts"). The International Law Commission, charged by the Assembly with codification and progressive development of international law, spent nearly half a century working sporadically on a Draft Code of Crimes against the Peace and Security of

The treatment of crimes against humanity was fairly straightforward in early drafts. Thus in 1950, the Commission's draft, although not using the term "crimes against humanity," clearly had the concept in mind when it included the following "acts" among those proscribed by international criminal law:

> Murder, extermination, enslavement, deportation and other inhuman acts done against a civilian population, or persecutions on political, racial or religious grounds when such acts are done or such persecutions are carried on in execution of or in connexion with any crime against peace or war crimes as defined by the Charter of the International Military Tribunal.[35]

This definition still denies crimes against humanity any freestanding status; here they must be "committed in execution of or in connexion with any crime against peace or war crimes." The Commission's 1951 formulation restructured the provision, included a reference to the relevant acts being done by the authorities of a State or by private individuals,[36] and added a reference to "cultural" as one of the proscribed grounds of persecution. The addition of "cultural" was plainly of considerable significance in view of the narrower list of forbidden bases of discrimination in the Genocide Convention.[37] "Cultural" remained in the 1951 version, which also kept the requirement of a connection to other crimes. It read:

> Inhuman acts by the authorities of a State or by private individuals against any civilian population, such as murder, or extermination, or enslavement, or deportation, or persecutions on political, racial, religious or cultural grounds, when such acts are committed in execution of or in connexion with other offences specified in this article.[38]

Mankind. Major drafts appeared in 1950, 1951, 1954, and, after a long hiatus, in 1991 and 1996. The most comprehensive collection of crimes was contained in its 1991 draft that, however, jettisoned the Nuremberg categories of crimes against peace, war crimes, and crimes against humanity. What had been crimes against humanity were covered fairly comprehensively by "genocide," "apartheid," and "systematic or mass violations of human rights." See [1991] 2(2) Y.B. Int'l L. Comm'n 1, 101–04, U.N. Doc. A/CN.4/SER.A/1991/Add.1 (Part 2). The Commission's final effort in 1996 reestablishes the categories but empties them of much of their content. See Timothy L. H. McCormack & Gerry J. Simpson, *The International Law Commission's Draft Code of Crimes against the Peace and Security of Mankind: An Appraisal of the Substantive Provisions*, 5 CRIM. L.F. 1 (1994) (discussing 1991 Draft Code); Rosemary Rayfuse, *The Draft Code of Crimes against the Peace and Security of Mankind: Eating Disorders at the International Law Commission*, 5 CRIM. L.F. 43 (1997) (discussing 1996 draft).

[35] Text of a Draft Code of Offenses against the Peace and Security of Mankind suggested as a working paper for the International Law Commission. [1950] 2 Y.B. Int'l L. Comm'n 277, Crime No. VIII (2), U.N. Doc. A/CN.4/SER.A/1950/Add.1. The Rapporteur tried to explain that this was a residual category that did not include those acts that were criminalized as genocide. Later drafters gave up trying to make any clean distinction and conceded that there would be overlap.

[36] 1996 Draft Code, *supra* note 34. The reference to "private individuals" inaugurated a decades-long debate about whether crimes against humanity required state action or some other kind of "group" connection. It became part of the debate about the appropriate "threshold" to render something an international crime. See *infra* notes 39 and 56 for the Rome Statute's solution.

[37] WILLIAM A. SCHABAS, GENOCIDE IN INTERNATIONAL LAW 179–89 (2000). "Cultural" wandered in and out of subsequent formulations of the persecution branch of crimes against humanity until it found a permanent home in the Rome Statute.

[38] Draft Code of Offences against the Peace and Security of Mankind art. 2 (9), [1951] 2 Y.B. Int'l L. Comm'n 59, U.N. Doc. A/CN.4/SER.A/1951. The words "such as" left the catalog somewhat

By 1954, the connection with other crimes had been removed, not without controversy among the members of the Commission,[39] and the definition read:

> Inhuman acts such as murder, extermination, enslavement, deportation or persecutions committed against any civilian population on social, political, racial, religious, or cultural grounds by the authorities of a State or by private individuals acting at the instigation or with the toleration of such authorities.[40]

There was, moreover, another new basis on which the persecution branch of crimes against humanity was forbidden, namely on "social" grounds.[41]

The 1991 version of the Draft Code continued to avoid the term "crimes against humanity." Now the Code referred to "systematic or mass violations of human rights." It provided:

> An individual who commits or orders the commission of any of the following violations of human rights:
> - murder
> - torture
> - establishing or maintaining over persons a status of slavery, servitude or forced labor
> - persecution on social, political, racial, religious or cultural grounds in a systematic manner or on a mass scale; or
> - deportation or forcible transfer of population
>
> shall, on conviction thereof be sentenced [to ...].[42]

The armed conflict requirement would not be reinserted. There was no requirement (as found in later drafts) that the perpetrator be acting on behalf of a State or organization. Accompanying explanatory notes recorded that the Commission had drafted this provision with current developments in human rights in mind, and that

---

open-ended. The "other offences specified" were aggression (including planning and preparation for it), war crimes, and genocide.

[39] There was a great deal of debate about whether there was something about crimes against humanity that required a functional connection to other international crimes to distinguish them from "ordinary" crimes. That year, 1954, there was an acceptance that the words "by the authorities of a State or by private individuals acting at the instigation or with the toleration of the authorities," which the Rapporteur had added to the 1951 text, provided a satisfactory basis for determining what was truly international. See [1954] 1 Y.B. Int'l L. Comm'n 131–48, U.N. Doc. A/CN.4/SER.A/1954. More recent discussions would speak of a "threshold requirement," but this term was not used in the 1950s debates. The Rome Statute of the International Criminal Court, article 7, has a threshold that requires an attack on a civilian population and some kind of State or organizational policy. See Rome Statute, supra note 4, art. 7.

[40] Draft Code of Offences against the Peace and Security of Mankind art. 2(11), [1954] 2 Y.B. Int'l L. Comm'n 151–52.

[41] "Social," insisted upon by Hersch Lauterpacht in the ILC, did not survive beyond the 1991 Draft Code nor did it find its way into the Rome Statute.

[42] Draft Code of Crimes against the Peace and Security of Mankind, Text of Draft Articles provisionally adopted by the Commission on first reading, article 21, in Report of the International Law Commission on the work of its forty-third session, 94, 103, U.N. Doc. A/CN.4/SER.A/1991/Add.1 (Part 2) (1991).

"bearing in mind that the draft Code is a criminal code and the principle of *nullem crimen sine lege*, the Commission deemed it necessary to make an exhaustive list of acts, unlike the list contained in the 1954 draft Code."[43]

In one respect, the drafters of the 1991 version felt bold enough to incorporate a development that was becoming solidified in customary law at the time. Article 6 of the draft imposed an obligation to try or extradite: "A State in whose territory an individual alleged to have committed a crime against the peace and security of mankind is present shall either extradite or try him."[44]

The ultimate 1996 version brought the term "crimes against humanity" back in from the cold and came much closer again to the Nuremberg formulation. It had a comprehensive set of acts that would have significant influence on what was contained two years later in the Rome Statute of the International Criminal Court. The 1996 Draft Code contained this:

> A crime against humanity means any of the following acts, when committed in a systematic manner or on a large scale and instigated or directed by a Government or by any organization or group:
> (a) murder;
> (b) extermination;
> (c) torture;
> (d) enslavement;
> (e) persecution on political, racial, religious or ethnic grounds;
> (f) institutionalized discrimination on racial, ethnic or religious grounds involving the violation of fundamental human rights and freedoms and resulting in seriously disadvantaging a part of the population;
> (g) arbitrary deportation or forcible transfer of population;
> (h) arbitrary imprisonment;
> (i) forced disappearance of persons;
> (j) rape, enforced prostitution and other forms of sexual abuse;
> (k) other inhumane acts which severely damage physical or mental integrity, health or human dignity, such as mutilation and severe bodily harm.[45]

One noteworthy feature of this codification was the way in which the Commission sought again to narrow the scope of "other inhumane acts," on this occasion by giving examples, although the language still arguably left "other" manifestations at large.

---

[43] Id. at 103. The notes add: "It was pointed out in the Commission that a practice of systematic disappearances of persons was also a phenomenon that deserved to be specifically mentioned in the draft Code." Id. at 104. Apparently it was not deserving enough, since it did not make the cut then, although it did make it into the 1996 version and into the Rome Statute, *supra* note 4.

[44] Id. art. 6(1). Paragraph 3 added that the obligation to try or extradite did "not prejudge the establishment and jurisdiction of an international criminal court." Id. art. 6(3).

[45] 1996 Draft Code, *supra* note 34, art. 18. The draft (*id.* art. 9) also included an obligation to extradite or prosecute, without prejudice to the jurisdiction of an international criminal court. The list of acts is now "closed" ("any of the following acts"). Compare the open-ended list, *supra* note 38 ("such as"). The flexibility is now in the last subparagraph ("other inhumane acts").

VI. THE STATUTES OF THE TRIBUNALS FOR THE FORMER YUGOSLAVIA AND RWANDA

Crimes against humanity are one of three crimes, along with genocide and war crimes, that feature in the Statutes of the two ad hoc Tribunals created by the United Nations Security Council to deal with serious violations of international humanitarian law committed in the former Yugoslavia and Rwanda. The main significance of those two drafting efforts was to demonstrate that there was still some fluidity in the understanding of what the threshold requirement is, or should be, for crimes against humanity. Thus, article 5 of the Statute of the Tribunal for the former Yugoslavia[46] confers jurisdiction over a list[47] of crimes against humanity "when committed in armed conflict, whether international or internal in character."[48] Article 3 of the Statute of the Rwanda Tribunal,[49] however, had a different threshold requirement, namely that the crimes must be "committed as part of a widespread or systematic attack against any civilian population on national, political, ethnic, racial or religious grounds."[50] There is no reference here to any requirement of a connection to armed conflict. Minus the requirement of "national, political, ethnic, racial or religious grounds," the attack requirement would find its way into the Rome Statute of the International Criminal Court.[51]

VII. THE ROME STATUTE OF THE INTERNATIONAL CRIMINAL COURT[52]

Article 7 of the Rome Statute, which contains the Statute's proscription of crimes against humanity, is a close descendant of article 6(c) of the Nuremberg Charter[53] and of articles 5 and 3, respectively, of the Statutes of the Tribunals for the former Yugoslavia[54] and Rwanda.[55] A striking feature of article 7 is its threshold requirement

---

[46] Statute of the International Criminal Tribunal for the former Yugoslavia, S.C. Res. 827, U.N. Doc. S/RES/827 (May 25, 1993) [hereinafter *ICTY Statute*].

[47] The list is terse: (a) murder; (b) extermination; (c) enslavement; (d) deportation; (e) imprisonment; (f) torture; (g) rape; (h) persecutions on political, racial and religious grounds; and (i) other inhumane acts. It will be noted that "persecutions" are not further modified by any requirement of a connection to other crimes, although the whole article requires a connection to armed conflict – though not to war crimes.

[48] *ICTY Statute*, *supra* note 46, art. 5.

[49] Statute of the International Criminal Tribunal for Rwanda, S.C. Res. 955, U.N. Doc. S/RES/955 (Nov. 8, 1994) [hereinafter *ICTR Statute*]. The Rwanda Statute contained the same list of specific acts constituting crimes as that of the ICTY, referred to in *supra* note 46.

[50] *ICTR Statute*, *supra* note 49, art. 3 (chapeau to crimes against humanity).

[51] *Rome Statute*, *supra* note 4.

[52] One additional feature of the Rome Statute that merits attention in the present codification exercise is the general part of the Statute. In particular, attention should be given to whether to incorporate something from article 25 on Individual Criminal Responsibility and the structural understandings (mental and material elements) in article 30 of the Statute. *See infra* notes 86–96.

[53] Charter of the International Military Tribunal, *supra* note 2, art. 6(c).

[54] *See supra* note 46.

[55] *See supra* note 49.

that for any of the proscribed "acts" to come within the definition of a crime against humanity, it must be "committed as part of a widespread or systematic attack directed against any civilian population, with knowledge of the attack."[56]

The requirement that there be an "attack" on a civilian population was plainly intended as a jurisdictional threshold for the International Criminal Court (ICC). Not every murder, rape, and other such acts are a matter of international concern or, of more immediate significance, come within the jurisdiction of the Court. This matter has its origin in the limitations on the kinds of offenses that could be prosecuted at Nuremberg under the rubric of crimes against humanity.[57] There, it will be recalled, the offenses of crimes against humanity had to be "committed against any civilian population" and be "in execution of or in connection with any crime within the jurisdiction of the tribunal."[58] I have argued elsewhere that this was a jurisdictional limitation on the Tribunal rather than an inherent substantive limitation in the concept of a crime against humanity.[59] The Tribunal for the former Yugoslavia has noted limits on *its* jurisdiction (the requirement of a connection to armed conflict) but added that:

> It is by now a settled rule of customary international law that crimes against humanity do not require a connection to international armed conflict. Indeed, as the Prosecutor points out, customary international law may not require a connection between crime against humanity and any conflict at all. Thus, by requiring that crimes against humanity be committed in either internal or international armed conflict, the Security Council may have defined the crime in Article 5 more narrowly than necessary under customary international law ....[60]

It might perhaps be noted at the outset that the word "armed" (as in "armed attack")[61] does not appear in the definition. Typically there will be violence, but this need not be proved as a distinct element. A great deal of attention was given at meetings of the Preparatory Committee on the Statute and in Rome to whether the attack had to be both widespread *and* systematic, or whether either one would suffice. "Widespread" has objective connotations of size, a kind of volume threshold rather than a statement about the subjective purposes of those in charge. The ordinary meaning of "systematic," on the other hand, seems more subjective and has connotations of a deliberate plan (a policy, perhaps). There was a widespread jubilation among the nongovernmental organizations (NGOs) and the like-minded States

---

[56] *Rome Statute, supra* note 4, art. 7.
[57] It is also a close relative of the limitation in the human rights area that organs such as the former Commission on Human Rights may not be able to act in individual cases but have more room where the violations are "gross." *See generally* HOWARD TOLLEY, JR., THE U.N. COMMISSION ON HUMAN RIGHTS 55–82 (1987). See also the ILC's efforts to narrow international jurisdiction, *supra* notes 36, 39.
[58] Nuremberg Charter, *supra* note 2, art. 6(c).
[59] Clark, *Crimes against Humanity at Nuremberg, supra* note 1, at 194–96.
[60] Prosecutor v. Tadić, Case No. IT-94-1-T, Decision on Defence Motion for Interlocutory Appeal on Jurisdiction, ¶ 141 (Oct. 2, 1995).
[61] For this reason, leaning on the self-defense provision of article 51 of the UN Charter, which uses the term "armed attack," does not appear useful.

in Rome that the disjunctive "or" in the final text represented a great victory. It would be easier for a prosecutor to prove than if both prongs were required. I am not altogether sure that this euphoria was warranted. The victory for the disjunctive is tempered by the definition of "attack" in paragraph 2(a):

> Attack directed against any civilian population" means a course of conduct involving the multiple commission of acts referred to in paragraph 1 against any civilian population, pursuant to or in furtherance of a State or organizational policy to commit such attack.[62]

"Multiple" must catch most cases of "widespread" unless one can imagine numerous incidents that are nevertheless not widespread (a difficult intellectual feat, to my mind). "Policy" (of a State or an organization) is pretty close to "systematic," as far as I can tell. In short, if an incident meets the definition of paragraph 2(a), that is, it involves a multiplicity of acts and has a policy behind it, the "additional" elements of widespread *and* systematic seem *both* to have been met anyway! Put it the other way around, if you like: Something close to both widespread and systematic appears to be required by the very definition of "attack."[63]

Occasionally, the Rome Statute adds new matter to the earlier instruments, or includes material that has come in and out in the various formulations, such as disappearances and apartheid. For the most part, however, when it departs from earlier definitions, it is because it spells out in more detail items that were implicit in them. In particular, paragraph 2 of article 7 offers definitions for many terms that had never been defined in earlier manifestations of crimes against humanity.[64]

The reference to gender as a proscribed ground for persecution in article 7(1)(h) is, for example, a new element when viewed against the Nuremberg

---

[62] *Rome Statute, supra* note 4, art. 7(2)(a). Note the way in which the threshold question for international liability is dealt with, in part, by requiring a state or organizational connection (such as a terrorist or otherwise dissident group). *See supra* notes 36, 39, 57.

[63] Some of the drafters of The Elements were concerned that an attack could occur by omission. This resulted in creative ambiguity. Paragraph 3 of the Introduction to the Elements of crimes against humanity reads:

> "Attack directed against a civilian population" in these context elements is understood to mean a course of conduct involving the multiple commission of acts referred to in article 7, paragraph 1 of the Statute against any civilian population, pursuant to or in furtherance of a State or organizational policy to commit such attack. The acts need not constitute a military attack. It is understood that "policy to commit such attack" requires that the State or organization actively promote or encourage such an attack against a civilian population.

Elements of Crimes, *supra* note 31, art. 7. An accompanying footnote reads:

> A policy which has a civilian population as the object of the attack would be implemented by State or organizational action. Such a policy may, in exceptional circumstances, be implemented by a deliberate failure to take action, which is consciously aimed at encouraging such attack. The existence of such a policy cannot be inferred solely from the absence of governmental or organizational action.

Id. art. 7 n.6.

[64] Article 7 was adopted by consensus in the Preparatory Commission for the Court in 2000. The Elements were approved without change, again by consensus, at the first meeting of the Court's

document.[65] It is, however, consistent with more recent developments in the international law of discrimination. Some participants in the drafting contended that "forced pregnancy" and "any other form of sexual violence of comparable gravity" represented new developments; others thought them implicit in the earlier instruments. "Rape," "sexual slavery," and "enforced prostitution" were more obviously implicit in the earlier instruments (and "rape" was sometime referred to by name), although prosecutions for them were uncommon and, when there were prosecutions, they tended to be under the rubric of war crimes rather than crimes against humanity.[66] Article 7 is, indeed, the most detailed definition to date of crimes against humanity. It represents both a "codification" and (to a small degree) a "progressive development" of international law[67] as those terms are understood in the United Nations Charter.[68] One thing that became very apparent to me during the ICC negotiations was just how difficult it is to get agreement on what represents the current customary law on any particular issue. Article 7 thus represented the limit of what a highly political process, functioning with consensus in mind, would bear. Some of us thought that we had been forced to stop short of the existing general law, whereas others thought we were on the (possibly wrong) side of developing it. It is probably possible to forge a consensus, at the least, around the proposition that the customary law definition of crimes against humanity was crystallized with the adoption of the Rome Statute on July 17, 1998.[69]

> Assembly of States Parties in 2002. They may be found at http://daccessdds.un.org/doc/UNDOC/GEN/N00/724/27/PDF/N0072427.pdf?OpenElement. Article 7(1)(h), on the other hand, contains a generic and somewhat open-ended reference to "[o]ther inhumane acts of a similar character intentionally causing great suffering, or serious injury to body or to mental or physical health." *Rome Statute*, *supra* note 4, art. 7(1)(h). Professor Oosterveld has noted that international tribunals have recognized a "wide range of criminal acts" as coming within this category. This includes sexual and physical violence on dead bodies, forced undressing of women and marching them in public, beatings, torture, humiliation, psychological abuse, confinement in inhuman conditions, and forced marriage. Valerie Oosteveld, *The Special Court for Sierra Leone's Consideration of Gender-based Violence: Contributing to Transnational Justice?*, 10 HUM. RTS. REV. 73, 89 (2009).
>
> [65] *See generally* Valerie Oosterveld, *The Definition of "Gender" in the Rome Statute of the International Criminal Court: A Step Forward or Back for International Criminal Justice?*, 18 HARV. HUM. RTS. J. 55 (2005).
>
> [66] *See generally* Kelly D. Askin, *Women and International Humanitarian Law*, *in* 1 WOMEN AND INTERNATIONAL HUMAN RIGHTS LAW 51–54 (Kelly D. Askin & Dorean M. Koenig eds., 1999) (contrasting failure to charge German leadership with such crimes and prosecution of Japanese leadership). *See also supra* note 6 on the overlap between the concepts of war crimes and crimes against humanity.
>
> [67] Either in the guise of customary law or of general principles of law. *See* Statute of the International Court of Justice art. 38 (1) (b), (c), June 26, 1945, 59 Stat. 1055, 33 U.N.T.S. 993. The most convincing explanation of the legal status of crimes against humanity in 1945–1946 was as general principles of law. *See* Clark, *Crimes against Humanity at Nuremberg*, *supra* note 1, at 193–94. Subsequent practice adds custom to the general principles. The ICC Statute now gives it a treaty basis. The issue for the present project is whether a more specific basis is needed.
>
> [68] *See* U.N. Charter art. 13 (the General Assembly to initiate studies and make recommendations for, inter alia, "encouraging the progressive development of international law and its codification.").
>
> [69] Whether the article 7 offenses represented customary law, so that it might be appropriate to prosecute them consistently with the principle of legality, caused some heart-searching when implementing legislation was being drafted. Canada, for example, domesticated into its criminal law

History of Efforts to Codify Crimes Against Humanity 23

Significant features of the prohibition of persecution[70] are the definition of the concept, including the expanded grounds contained therein and the concluding words of the subparagraph.

The "act" of persecution is defined as:

> Persecution against any identifiable group or collectivity on political, racial, national, ethnic, cultural, religious, gender as defined in paragraph 3, or other grounds that are universally recognized as impermissible under international law, in connection with any act referred to in this paragraph or any crime within the jurisdiction of the Court.[71]

"Persecution" is further defined as "the intentional and severe deprivation of fundamental rights contrary to international law by reason of the identity of the group or collectivity."[72] Persecution played a fairly significant part in the prosecution's efforts at Nuremberg, but the Tribunal did not devote much effort to illuminating its scope. The Rome Statute is generally consistent with the somewhat sketchy discussion of the concept by the Nuremberg Tribunal, which seems to have included killing political opponents and Jews and placing them in concentration camps. It also appears to have included the passage of German laws aimed at excluding Jews from economic life and from the protection of the law.[73] One suspects, however, that most of the significant cases of persecution under the Rome Statute can also be packaged under one or more of the other subparagraphs of article 7(1). Moreover, the independent scope of the persecution provision is limited by the closing words of subparagraph 1(h), which require that the persecution must be "in connection with any act referred to in this paragraph or any crime within the jurisdiction of the Court."[74] This is a completely unnecessary limitation, insisted upon by those

---

crimes against humanity where the relevant act "at the time and place of its commission constitutes a crime against humanity according to customary international law or by virtue of its being criminal according to general principles of law recognized by the community of nations." It added that, "[f]or greater certainty, crimes described in articles 6 and 7 and paragraph 2 of article 8 of the Rome Statute are, as of July 17, 1998, crimes according to customary law and may be crimes according to customary international law before that date." Crimes against Humanity and War Crimes Act, 2000 S.C., ch. 24, § 6 (Can.). On the other hand, New Zealand, having in mind both the possible presence of criminals fleeing from the former Yugoslavia and Rwanda and the desirability of certainty, bluntly claimed jurisdiction over those charged with crimes against humanity as defined in the Rome Statute effective January 1, 1991. International Crimes and International Criminal Court Act 2000, 2000 S.N.Z. No. 26, §§ 8, 10 (N.Z.).

[70] *Rome Statute, supra* note 4, art. 7(1)(h) (basic proscription); *id.* art. 7(2)(g) (definition of "persecution").

[71] *Id.* art. 7(1)(h). Paragraph 3 of article 7 "defines" the controversial term "gender" as follows, using language agreed on at earlier United Nations Conferences:

> For the purpose of this Statute, it is understood that the term "gender" refers to the two sexes, male and female within the context of society. The term "gender" does indicate any meaning different from the above.

Id. art 7(3).

[72] *Id.* art. 7(2)(g).

[73] *See generally* Clark, *Crimes against Humanity at Nuremberg, supra* note 1, at 195–97.

[74] *Rome Statute, supra* note 4, art. 7(1)(h).

who had already adequately narrowed the scope of the article with its chapeau. It is, of course, left over from the Nuremberg jurisdictional requirement that all crimes against humanity had to be "in execution of or in connection with" other crimes within the jurisdiction of the Tribunal.[75] Fears that somehow "ordinary" persecution would become criminal were quite groundless in light of the chapeau's requirement for proving an "attack." My reading of the drafting history is that the attack requirement was designed as a general threshold and an alternative to that in the Nuremberg Charter.[76] Those who insisted in reinserting something like the Nuremberg language specifically in the persecution provision were confused and thought a further limitation necessary.

"Enforced disappearance of persons" is defined to mean:

> the arrest, detention or abduction of persons by, or with the authorization, support or acquiescence of, a State or a political organization, followed by a refusal to acknowledge that deprivation of freedom or to give information on the fate or whereabouts of those persons, with the intention of removing them from the protection of the law for a prolonged period of time.[77]

While the naming of this concept and the exposition of its elements dates from the 1980s,[78] there are earlier examples that might just as easily have been given the name, such as Stalin's gulag or Hitler's "Night and Fog" Decree.[79]

---

[75] See supra notes 16-19. As a practical matter, the Nuremberg Tribunal focused on the need to show a connection to a crime against peace.

[76] The words "widespread or systematic attack against any civilian population" make their first appearance as a jurisdictional threshold in article 3 of the Statute of the International Tribunal for Rwanda. ICTR Statute, supra note 49, art. 3. The Statute of the Tribunal for the former Yugoslavia, article 5, on the other hand, has a threshold for crimes against humanity that reads: "when committed in armed conflict, whether international or internal in character, and directed against any civilian population." ICTY Statute, supra note 46, art. 5.

[77] Rome Statute, supra note 4, art. 7(2)(i). The language is based on preambular paragraph 3 of the 1992 U.N. Declaration on the Protection of All Persons from Enforced Disappearance, G.A. Res. 47/133, at 207 U.N. GAOR, 47th Sess., Supp. No. 49, U.N. Doc. A/47/49 (Dec, 18, 1992). The reference to a "political organization" does not appear in the 1992 Declaration. See also Inter-American Convention on the Forced Disappearance of Persons, June 9, 1994, reprinted in 33 I.L.M. 1529 (1994). In 2006, the crime of forced disappearance received its own specific convention, the U.N. International Convention on the Protection of All Persons from Enforced Disappearance, G.A. Res. 61/177, U.N. Doc. A/RES/61/177 (Jan. 12, 2007). Preambular paragraph 4 of the 1992 Declaration characterizes the "systematic practice" of enforced disappearance as "of the nature of a crime against humanity." Article 5 of the 2006 Convention states that "[t]he widespread or systematic practice of enforced disappearance constitutes a crime against humanity as defined in applicable international law and shall attract the consequences provided for under such applicable international law."

[78] Maureen R. Berman & Roger S. Clark, State Terrorism: Disappearances, 13 RUTGERS L.J. 531 (1982).

[79] Darryl Robinson, Defining Crimes against Humanity at the Rome Conference, 93 AM. J. INT'L L. 43, 58 n.76 (1999), reads the Nuremberg Tribunal's discussion of the Night and Fog Decree as characterizing the disappearances taking place under it as included in the Nuremberg Charter's "other inhumane acts" category of crimes against humanity. In fact, the discussion to which he refers is addressed primarily to war crimes in the occupied countries, coming within article 6(b) of the Charter. Nevertheless, given the Nuremberg Tribunal's frequent intertwining of war crimes and crimes against humanity, the example could be apt for crimes against humanity. (To the

"The crime of apartheid" is defined as "inhumane acts of a character similar to those referred to in paragraph 1, committed in the context of an institutionalized regime of systematic oppression and domination by one racial group over any other racial groups or groups and committed with the intention of maintaining that regime."[80] A few years ago, in an exercise in which many of the group involved in the current project also participated, I echoed the comment of the International Law Commission that the practice is now so deeply condemned by the world's conscience that it is inconceivable that a modern code of crimes against the peace and security of mankind would omit a specific reference to apartheid.[81] Yet the Law Commission's final version of its Code in 1996 did just that, certainly by name.[82] So too did the ICC Statute until an advanced stage of the Rome Conference.[83] It was left to the South African delegation to insist on its inclusion.[84] My hunch, however, is that the addition is more symbolic than anything else, and that the proscribed actions are already caught elsewhere in paragraph 1.[85] It is an example (not inappropriate) of the use of the law as affirmation, exclamation, or denunciation – rather than a string in the prosecutorial bow that is likely to see a lot of action.

VIII. THE ROME STATUTE'S "ELEMENTS OF CRIMES"

One final piece of codification remains to be noted. Article 9 of the Rome Statute of the International Criminal Court requires the Assembly of States Parties of the

---

extent that it differentiated between the categories, the Nuremberg Tribunal generally spoke of war crimes in occupied territory and crimes against humanity in Germany itself, often including Austria and sometimes Czechoslovakia in the latter category. Clark, *Crimes against Humanity at Nuremberg, supra* note 1, at 197–98).

[80] *Rome Statute, supra* note 4, art. 7(2)(h). This definition is derived ultimately from that in the 1973 International Convention on the Suppression and Punishment of the Crime of Apartheid, G.A. Res. 3068, at 75, U.N. GAOR, 28th Sess., Supp. No. 30, U.N. Doc. A/9030 (Nov. 30, 1973). In article I of the Convention, the parties "declare that apartheid is a crime against humanity." *Id.* art. 1.

[81] Roger S. Clark, *The Crime of Apartheid, in* I INTERNATIONAL CRIMINAL LAW 643, 662 (M. Cherif Bassiouni ed., 2d ed. 1999) (written early in 1996 before the ILC completed its final draft and referring to the 1991 draft and explanation in [1991] 2 Y.B. Int'l L. Comm'n 102 (Part 2)).

[82] The Commission's 1996 Draft Code did, however, include "institutionalized discrimination" that the Commentary to the 1996 Draft Code, *supra* note 34, at 99, describes as "the crime of apartheid under a more general denomination."

[83] The closest hint that it might be included was in footnote 17 of the Draft Statute forwarded by the Preparatory Committee to Rome. Referring to the draft language on "other inhumane acts," it noted that "[i]t was also suggested that the list of acts should include institutionalized discrimination." *See Report of the Preparatory Committee on the Establishment of an International Criminal Court, in* THE STATUTE OF THE INTERNATIONAL CRIMINAL COURT: A DOCUMENTARY HISTORY 128 (M. Cherif Bassiouni ed., 1998).

[84] Apartheid is, however, defined with sufficient breadth so that it would not only catch what happened in South Africa.

[85] The language of the Apartheid Convention was derived substantially from that of the Genocide Convention, and many of the incidences of apartheid would also be caught by that Convention and by article 6 of the Rome Statute which is almost verbatim from the Genocide Convention.

Court to adopt "Elements of Crimes" that are to "assist the Court in its interpretation of articles 6, 7 and 8." The drafting of such Elements by the Preparatory Commission for the Court provided a further opportunity to clarify some aspects of the definitions, and also to try to come to terms with the structure of crimes contained in the "general part" (Part III) of the Rome Statute.[86]

The Rome Statute represents the most comprehensive effort at drafting a general part contained in any existing global instrument. During the negotiations that led up to Rome, there was a comprehensive attempt to conceptualize both the physical (or "material") components of the treaty crimes and their associated mental elements. The effort to formulate a general concept of the material elements of the crimes contained in the Statute was abandoned at Rome,[87] but the drafters of the Elements of genocide, crimes against humanity, and war crimes were able to discern a general structure from article 30 of the Statute, which is headed "mental element." Article 30 provides that "unless otherwise provided," the "material elements"[88] of a crime need to be accompanied by "intent and knowledge."[89] For purposes of the article, a person is said to have "intent" where "(a) [i]n relation to *conduct*, that person means to engage in the conduct;" and "(b) [i]n relation to a *consequence*, that person means to cause that consequence or is aware that it will occur in the normal course of events."[90] "Knowledge," for the purpose of the article, "means awareness that a *circumstance* exists or a consequence will occur in the ordinary course of events."[91]

From article 30 can thus be inferred both a default rule that intent and knowledge are the culpability rules in the absence of clear indications to the contrary, and that the "material" (or physical) elements of the treaty crimes can be conceptualized in terms of "conduct," "consequences," and "circumstances." The drafters of the Elements, including those on crimes against humanity, structured their product

---

[86] See generally THE INTERNATIONAL CRIMINAL COURT: ELEMENTS OF CRIMES AND RULES OF PROCEDURE AND EVIDENCE (Roy Lee et al. eds., 2001); Roger S. Clark, *The Mental Element in International Criminal Law: The Rome Statute of the International Criminal Court and the Elements of Offences*, 12 CRIM. L.F. 291 (2001).

[87] See generally Roger S. Clark, *Drafting a General Part to a Penal Code: Some Thoughts Inspired by the Negotiations on the Rome Statute of the International Criminal Court and by the Court's First Substantive Law Discussion in the* Lubanga Dyilo *Confirmation Proceedings*, 19 CRIM. L.F. 519, 521–23 (2008).

[88] For most of the negotiation leading up to and at Rome, the term "physical" appeared in what became article 30. At a late stage, it was replaced with the word "material" by the Drafting Committee at Rome. Many civil law commentators use the word "objective" to describe such elements, and I am aware of no common law jurisdiction that uses the term "material" quite the way it is used in article 30 and The Elements. The Model Penal Code, for example, has a different usage for the word "material." Clark, *supra* note 86, at 527 n.25. This is a good example of the importance of trying to interpret the Rome Statute on its own terms and not bringing to it intellectual baggage that is entirely derivative from one's own legal system.

[89] *Rome Statute, supra* note 4, art. 30(1).

[90] *Id.* art. 30(2) (emphasis added).

[91] *Id.* art. 30(3) (emphasis added).

along these lines. As an example, the Elements of the crime against humanity of murder (article 7(1)(a) of the Statute) read as follows:

1. The perpetrator killed one or more persons.
2. The conduct was committed as part of a widespread or systematic attack against a civilian population.
3. The perpetrator knew that the conduct was part of or intended the conduct to be part of a widespread or systematic attack against a civilian population.[92]

Element 1 is a basic conduct element, to which the default rule of intent and knowledge applies. The Introduction to the Elements of crimes against humanity notes that the last two elements "describe the context in which the conduct must take place."[93] Element 2 is an example of a circumstance element or what the Elements describe as a "contextual circumstance"; it sets out the fundamental jurisdictional basis for raising crimes against humanity to the level of international crimes.[94] The third element gives effect to the "knowledge" requirement in the chapeau to article 7.[95]

Similar lists of elements have been made for the other kinds of crimes against humanity enshrined in article 7.[96] The Pre-Trial Chambers of the Court have been making significant use of The Elements in their first substantive decisions. As more case law emerges from the Trial and Appeals Chambers of the Court, it will no doubt indicate areas where there is room for further refinement of the Elements for crimes against humanity and perhaps even amendment of the Statute.

Codification (and re-codification), it would seem, is always a work in progress.

---

[92] Elements of Crimes, *supra* note 31, art. 7(1)(a). The introduction to the Elements of crimes against humanity notes that "[t]he acts need not constitute a military attack." *Id.*
[93] *Id.* (Introduction to crimes against humanity).
[94] Article 30 does not distinguish between "contextual" (essentially "jurisdictional" in American terms) and other circumstance elements. The Elements use the category to describe the elements that, in each instance, make genocide, war crimes, and crimes against humanity "international." *See* Clark, *supra* note 86, at 324.
[95] The default rule of article 30 would probably get the same result, but the chapeau has its own requirement of knowledge. The introduction to the Elements of crime against humanity explains:

> However, the last element should not be interpreted as requiring proof that the perpetrator had knowledge of all characteristics of the attack or the precise details of the plan or policy of the State or organization. In the case of an emerging widespread or systematic attack against a civilian population, the intent clause of the last element indicates that this mental element is satisfied if the perpetrator intended to further such an attack.

Elements of Crimes, *supra* note 31, art. 7.
[96] The Pre-Trial Chambers of the Court have been grappling with the structure of the Statute and The Elements, sometimes slipping into national modes of analysis rather than the *sui generis* one contained in the Statute. *See* Roger S. Clark, *Elements of Crimes in Early Confirmation Decisions of Pre-Trial Chambers of the International Criminal Court*, 6 N.Z.Y.B. INT'L L. (2008).

2

The Universal Repression of Crimes Against Humanity before National Jurisdictions

The Need for a Treaty-Based Obligation to Prosecute

Payam Akhavan[*]

I. INTRODUCTION

The fascination of jurists with international criminal tribunals has often eclipsed the fundamental role of national jurisdictions in eradicating impunity for crimes against humanity. The practice of the International Criminal Tribunals for the former Yugoslavia (ICTY) and Rwanda (ICTR) has demonstrated that the inordinate cost and length of proceedings impose a serious limitation on the quantity of trials. Both tribunals were supplemented by other jurisdictions, such as the war crimes chambers in Bosnia and Herzegovina and in Kosovo and national trials and traditional *gacaca* proceedings in Rwanda. The "complementarity" scheme of the Statute of the International Criminal Court (ICC Statute) has institutionalized the primary responsibility of national courts in prosecuting international crimes. Beyond the confines of the ICC, however, the scope of responsibility of domestic jurisdictions in international law is clearly incongruent with a partnership between national and international courts. In particular, there is a conspicuous normative *lacuna* in the repression of crimes against humanity based on the exercise of universal jurisdiction by national courts. The creation of such an obligation may be the single most important argument in favor of the adoption of an International Convention on Crimes Against Humanity (Convention).

The principle of "universal jurisdiction" was proposed but expressly rejected by the drafters of the ICC Statute. Instead, with the exception of referrals by the Security Council under Chapter VII of the United Nations Charter, ICC jurisdiction is limited to those instances where crimes are committed either on the territory of a State Party or by its nationals. Instruments, such as the 1948 Convention on the Prevention and Punishment of the Crime of Genocide (Genocide Convention), limit the obligation of States Parties to prosecute this category of aggravated crime against humanity only when committed on their territory. The 1968 Convention on the Non-Applicability of Statutory Limitations to War Crimes and Crimes Against Humanity (Statutory Limitations Convention) includes an obligation to extradite,

---

[*] S.J.D. (Harvard). Professor of International Law, McGill University, Montreal, Canada. Formerly Legal Advisor, Office of the Prosecutor, International Criminal Tribunal for the former Yugoslavia, The Hague, The Netherlands. The assistance of Max Reed and Samantha Jones in preparation of this article is gratefully acknowledged.

presumably, though not necessarily, as requested by the territorial State. With respect to the crime against humanity of *apartheid*, the 1973 International Convention on the Suppression and Punishment of the Crime of Apartheid (Apartheid Convention) permits, but does not require, the exercise of universal jurisdiction by States Parties. Since crimes against humanity no longer require a nexus with armed conflict, they are equivalent to massive human rights violations, and thus human rights treaties covering prohibited acts that constitute their *actus reus* (e.g., murder, torture, etc.) may provide an alternate basis in treaty law for universal repression. Beyond the *locus delicti* principle, however, the International Covenant on Civil and Political Rights (ICCPR) obligates States to provide effective remedies for extraterritorial violations only where the State Party exercises effective jurisdiction (e.g., in occupied territories). Human rights treaties, such as the Convention Against Torture (CAT), provide for extraterritorial jurisdiction based on the *aut dedere aut prosequi* or "primary universal repression" principle, but obviously only with respect to the crime of torture. Although humanitarian law treaties, such as the 1949 Geneva Conventions and Additional Protocol I of 1977, require the exercise of universal jurisdiction over "grave breaches," this applies only to war crimes committed in international armed conflicts.

This piecemeal international lawmaking process results in a manifest absurdity: If a soldier commits mass murder in an international armed conflict and is arrested in a third State, the national courts of that State are under an obligation to prosecute; but if he commits the same mass murder in an internal armed conflict, the third State is under no obligation to prosecute. Similarly, outside the context of armed conflict, if a prison official commits torture, he may be liable and prosecuted before the national courts of a third State, but not if he simply murdered the victims without first torturing them. These examples forcefully illustrate the need for a treaty that adequately addresses this significant loophole in international law.

Although clarity of treaty obligations is preferable, it is arguable that prosecution of crimes against humanity based on universal jurisdiction can still be based on customary law or general principles of international law. This would have the advantage of extending to all States and not merely to those that are States Parties to particular treaties. There is evidence supporting the view that in general international law States have a *right* to exercise universal jurisdiction. Despite the emerging "soft law," however, there is little evidence of a universal repression *obligation* under the *lex lata*.[1] Thus, until the *lex ferenda* crystallizes into customary law or is recognized as a general principle, the exercise of universal jurisdiction is essentially at the discretion of States. The practice of States with universal jurisdiction

---

[1] The Third Report of the International Law Commission (ILC) on the Obligation to Extradite or Prosecute states that although the "number of international treaties containing the obligation *aut dedere aut judicare* is growing every year ... [t]hat formulation alone cannot serve as sufficient background for the codification of a generally binding customary rule." *See* International Law Commission, *Third Report on the Obligation to Extradite or Prosecute*, ¶ 24, U.N.G.A. A/CN.4/603 (June 10, 2008) (*prepared by* Zdzislaw Galicki).

legislation demonstrates that there is little incentive in using limited resources to prosecute crimes that, however heinous, have no immediate connection with that State.[2] In Canada, for instance, almost a decade after the enactment of the Crimes Against Humanity and War Crimes Act (CAHWCA),[3] and despite an official "no haven" policy, there has been only a single prosecution. This reality further underscores the need for a Convention that creates obligations of universal repression.

II. DOES EXISTING TREATY LAW REQUIRE UNIVERSAL REPRESSION OF CRIMES AGAINST HUMANITY?

The point of departure for determining the utility of a Convention is to assess whether and to what extent existing treaty law requires States to prosecute crimes against humanity based on the universal jurisdiction principle. The most relevant instrument in this respect is the ICC Statute. Aside from the sparsely ratified Statutory Limitations Convention discussed below, it is the only treaty that prohibits crimes against humanity as such and arguably creates an implicit obligation to prosecute. The Genocide Convention, as discussed below, only covers extreme forms of persecution and thus only relates to a narrow category of crimes against humanity. The same applies to the Apartheid Convention that only covers the crime of *apartheid* that in substance is also a particular form of persecution.[4]

Crimes against humanity are within the jurisdiction of the ICC pursuant to article 7 of the Statute. The definition contained therein both codifies customary law as of 1998 but also progressively develops some important aspects of the crime. With respect to national jurisdictions, paragraph 6 of the Preamble recalls that "it is the duty of every State to exercise its criminal jurisdiction over those responsible for international crimes." This duty is not expressly contained in any of the operative provisions of the Statute. It is arguably implicit in article 17(1)(a), which provides that "the Court shall determine that a case is inadmissible where: The case is being investigated or prosecuted by a State which has jurisdiction over it, unless the State is unwilling or unable genuinely to carry out the investigation or prosecution." However, this provision only applies to situations where a State Party (or

---

[2] Although seventeen countries have initiated criminal investigations and prosecutions into international crimes committed elsewhere, only twenty-six convictions have been secured. *See* Joseph Rikhof, *Fewer Places to Hide? The Impact of Domestic War Crimes Prosecutions on International Impunity*, 20 CRIM. L.F. 1, 14 (2009).
[3] Crimes Against Humanity and War Crimes Act, R.S.C., ch. 24 (2000) (Can.).
[4] *See, e.g., Rome Statute of the International Criminal Court*, United Nations Diplomatic Conference of Plenipotentiaries on the Establishment of an International Criminal Court, July 17, 1998, U.N. Doc. A/CONF.183/9 [hereinafter *Rome Statute*] ("'Persecution' means the intentional and severe deprivation of fundamental rights contrary to international law by reason of the identity of the group or collectivity"); *id.* art. 7(2)(h) ("'The crime of apartheid' means inhumane acts of a character similar to those referred to in paragraph 1, committed in the context of an institutionalized regime of systematic oppression and domination by one racial group over any other racial group or groups and committed with the intention of maintaining that regime.").

defendant) contests the exercise of jurisdiction by the Court on the grounds that national courts are able and willing to investigate and prosecute. In other words, as the ICC Appeals Chamber held in the *Katanga Case*, although "States have a duty to exercise their criminal jurisdiction over international crimes ... under the Rome Statute, the Court does not have the power to order States to open investigations or prosecutions domestically."[5]

Notwithstanding the absence of an express duty to prosecute, it is observed by commentators that:

> The principle of complementarity also has a role to play in ensuring that national jurisdictions implement the necessary legislation to enable them to play a more active role in the prosecution of international crimes. To the extent, then, that the ICC provides an impetus to national prosecutions of genocide, crimes against humanity, and war crimes, it is to be welcomed.[6]

Nonetheless, whatever implicit duty to prosecute may arguably exist does not extend to universal jurisdiction.[7] In the Rome Conference negotiations, there was a dispute as to "whether there was an obligation to proceed on the basis of 'universal jurisdiction' or on a territorial or national basis."[8] Article 12(2) resolved this dispute by expressly restricting the Court's jurisdiction to instances where the State "on the territory of which the conduct in question occurred" or the State "of which the person accused of the crime is a national" is a party to the Statute. Thus, if a person who is not a national of a State Party commits crimes against humanity on the territory of a non-State Party, the question of whether national courts are able or willing to prosecute becomes irrelevant. In other words, beyond these two situations, mere custody of a person accused of crimes against humanity does not entail any obligations under the ICC Statute.[9]

Another important treaty is the Genocide Convention. ICTY jurisprudence states that "when persecution escalates to the extreme form of wilful and deliberate acts designed to destroy a group or part of a group, it can be held that such persecution

---

[5] Prosecutor v. Katanga, Case No. ICC-01/04-01/07-1497, Judgment on the Appeal of Mr. Germain Katanga against the Oral Decision of Trial Chamber II of 12 June 2009 on the Admissibility of the Case, ¶¶ 85–86 (Sept. 25, 2009), *available at* http://www.icc-cpi.int/iccdocs/doc/doc746819.pdf
[6] 2 THE ROME STATUTE OF THE INTERNATIONAL CRIMINAL COURT: A COMMENTARY 1906 (Antonio Cassese, Paola Gaeta & John R.W.D. Jones eds., 2002).
[7] Currently only eleven European Union and eight African Union member states have universal jurisdiction legislation for all three of the core crimes set forth in the Rome Statute. *Council Report, The AU-EU Expert Report on the Principles of Universal Jurisdiction*, at 11, 19, COM (2009) 8672/09 (April 16, 2009).
[8] *Id.* at 13.
[9] It is evident, of course, that in case of a referral by the Security Council acting under Chapter VII of the UN Charter (pursuant to article 13(b) of the ICC Statute), the jurisdiction of the Court is not restricted by either the nationality or territoriality principles. In other words, as in the case of the Darfur region of the Sudan, the Security Council may, as an enforcement measure, vest the Court with jurisdiction even where the territorial State or State of nationality is not a party to the Statute.

amounts to genocide."[10] Considering the substantial overlap with the crime against humanity of persecution, the Genocide Convention therefore only applies to a narrow category of prohibited conduct within the broader category of crimes against humanity. Nonetheless, and despite its designation as the "crime of crimes,"[11] article 6 provides only that persons charged with genocide "shall be tried by a competent tribunal of the State in the territory of which the act was committed." Thus, the obligation to prosecute is limited to the *locus delicti*, although this "does not prevent a State from exercising universal jurisdiction in a genocide case."[12]

Another relevant treaty, though of limited application, is the 1968 Convention on the Non-Applicability of Statutory Limitations. It was adopted in the context of prior resolutions condemning Portuguese colonial rule and apartheid in South Africa. It was an attempt to criminalize colonial and racist policies and was thus surrounded by considerable political controversy at the time, notwithstanding the legal content of its provisions. Article IV of the 1968 Convention obligates States Parties "to adopt, in accordance with their respective constitutional processes, any legislative or other measures necessary to ensure that statutory or other limitations shall not apply to the prosecution and punishment" of war crimes and crimes against humanity. With a view to ensuring such prosecutions, article III further provides that States Parties shall "undertake to adopt all necessary domestic measures, legislative or otherwise, with a view to making possible the extradition, in accordance with international law" of persons responsible for such crimes. Thus, the Convention only recognizes a limited obligation to extradite, presumably, though not necessarily, upon a request by the territorial State. There is, however, no express obligation to exercise universal jurisdiction over crimes against humanity. Furthermore, it is noted that because of the politicization of the 1968 Convention at its inception, there are only forty-five States Parties to the Convention.[13] Nonetheless, as discussed below with respect to customary law, certain of its provisions may reflect *opinio juris*.

The Apartheid Convention, which followed and gave effect to some of the initial aspirations of the Statutory Limitations Convention's proponents, is also worthy of consideration because it relates to yet another type of persecution. Article V of the Apartheid Convention provides in relevant part that persons charged with the crime of apartheid "may be tried by a competent tribunal of any State Party to the Convention which may acquire jurisdiction over the person of the accused." Thus, even though the Apartheid Convention permits universal jurisdiction, it does not create an obligation in this regard. In this respect, article V is substantially the same as the result obtained by application of article VI of the Genocide

---

[10] Prosecutor v. Kupreskić, Case No. IT-95-16-T, Judgment, ¶ 636 (Jan. 14, 2000).
[11] Prosecutor v. Kambanda, Case No. ICTR-97-23-S, Judgment and Sentence, ¶ 16 (Sept. 4, 1998).
[12] Case Concerning the Arrest Warrant of April 11, 2000 (*Dem. Rep. Congo v. Belg.*), 2002 I.C.J. 63 (Feb. 14) (separate opinion of Judges Higgins, Kooijmans, and Buergenthal, ¶ 27) [hereinafter *Arrest Warrant Case*, opinion of Judges Higgins, Kooijmans & Buergenthal].
[13] Convention on the Non-Applicability of Statutory Limitations, Nov. 26, 1968, 754 U.N.T.S. 73.

Convention, which does not require but also does not prohibit the exercise of universal jurisdiction.

Another possible basis for universal repression may be found in human rights treaties. The contemporary definition of crimes against humanity, at least as codified under article 7 of the ICC Statute, has definitively eliminated the requirement of a nexus with armed conflict. Thus, it is now widely recognized that "crimes against humanity are no longer linked to the laws of war but rather to human rights law."[14] ICTY jurisprudence reflects this contemporary incarnation of the Nürnberg Law. In the *Blaškić* case, for instance, the Appeals Chamber considered "charges of killing and causing serious injury" as persecutions in light of "the inherent right to life and to be free from cruel, inhuman or degrading treatment or punishment ... recognized in customary international law and ... embodied in Articles 6 and 7 of the ICCPR, and Articles 2 and 3 of the ECHR."[15] Without a link to armed conflict, the prohibition of crimes against humanity is tantamount to the criminalization of massive human rights violations. Thus, it may be argued that an obligation to prosecute isolated human rights violations that qualify as the *actus reus* of crimes against humanity subsumes the prosecution of such conduct when committed on a "widespread or systematic" scale. A duty to prosecute may be found in article 2(3) of the ICCPR providing that States Parties shall "ensure that any person whose rights or freedoms as herein recognized are violated shall have an effective remedy." For instance, with respect to the prohibition of torture, the Human Rights Committee has held that "[a]mnesties are generally incompatible with the duty of States to investigate such acts; to guarantee freedom from such acts within their jurisdiction; and to ensure that they do not occur in the future. States may not deprive individuals of the right to an effective remedy."[16] Similarly, in the case of *Bautista de Arellana v. Colombia*, the Committee held that:

> [P]urely disciplinary and administrative remedies cannot be deemed to constitute adequate and effective remedies within the meaning of article 2, paragraph 3, of the *Covenant*, in the event of particularly serious violations of human rights, notably in the event of an alleged violation of the right to life.[17]

---

[14] Kai Ambos & Steffen Wirth, *The Current Law of Crimes Against Humanity: An Analysis of UNTAET Regulation 15/2000*, 13 CRIM. L.F. 1, 24 (2002).

[15] Prosecutor v. Blaškić, Case No. IT-95-14-A, Judgment, ¶ 143 (July 29, 2004). ICCPR and ECHR refer to the International Covenant on Civil and Political Rights and the European Convention on Human Rights, respectively.

[16] Committee on Civil and Political Rights, *General Comment No. 20: Article 7 (Prohibition of Torture, or Other Cruel, Inhuman or Degrading Treatment or Punishment)*, 44th Session (March 10, 1992), *available at* http://www.unhchr.ch/tbs/doc.nsf/0/6924291970754969c12563ed004c8ae5?Opendocument.

[17] Committee on Civil and Political Rights, *General Comment No. 31, Nature of the General Legal Obligation Imposed on States Parties to the Covenant*, ¶ 19, CCPR/C/21/Rev.1/Add.13 (May 29, 2004).

There is a similar obligation in American,[18] European,[19] and African[20] regional human rights treaties as well. For instance, in *Velásquez-Rodríguez v. Honduras*, the Inter-American Court of Human Rights interpreted "effective remedy" to mean that there is a duty to "punish any violation of the rights recognized by the Convention."[21] Nonetheless, ICCPR article 2(1) limits the obligation of States Parties to respect and to ensure the human rights of "all individuals within its territory and subject to its jurisdiction." As the Committee has noted: "This means that a State Party must respect and ensure the rights laid down in the Covenant to anyone within the power or effective control of that State Party, even if not situated within the territory of the State Party."[22] Beyond extraterritorial application to persons within the effective control of a State Party, however, there is no obligation to prosecute human rights violations committed on the territory of other States.

The closest approximation of "universal jurisdiction" in human rights treaties is the *aut dedere aut prosequi* principle. This is more accurately described as the principle of "primary universal repression" because jurisdiction is exercised only if there is no extradition, presumably, though not necessarily, to the territorial State.[23] A report by Amnesty International identifies twenty-one international treaties negotiated between 1929 and 2000 that impose a duty to extradite or prosecute.[24] Of these, the only relevant ones for crimes against humanity are the CAT and possibly the International Convention for the Suppression of Terrorist Bombings. It should be noted that arguably, non-territorial States may also invoke the "extradite or prosecute" obligations of such treaties, giving it a broad scope. For instance, the Application by Belgium against Senegal before the International Court of Justice with respect to the prosecution of Hissène Habré for crimes committed in Chad has been initiated based primarily on the CAT.[25] Belgium is requesting extradition not as a territorial State, but based on a broad principle of universal jurisdiction. Nonetheless, the narrow substantive scope of these treaties limits application of "primary universal repression" to a specific list of prohibited acts that comprise the *actus reus* element of crimes against humanity. Thus, for instance, in order to benefit from

---

[18] American Convention on Human Rights, art. 2, July 18, 1978, O.A.S.T.S. No. 36, 1144 U.N.T.S. 123.
[19] European Convention for the Protection of Human Rights and Fundamental Freedoms, art. 13, November 4, 1950, 213 U.N.T.S., 222 EUR. T.S. 5.
[20] African Charter on Human and Peoples' Rights, art. 7, June 27, 1981, OAU Doc. CAB/LEG/67/3 rev. 5, 21 I.L.M. 58.
[21] Velásquez-Rodríguez v. Honduras, Inter-Am. Ct. H.R. (ser. C) No. 4, ¶ 166 (July 29, 1988).
[22] Committee on Civil and Political Rights, *General Comment No. 31*, *supra* note 17, ¶ 10.
[23] *Arrest Warrant Case*, opinion of Judges Higgins, Kooijmans & Buergenthal, *supra* note 12, ¶ 35.
[24] Amnesty International, *Universal Jurisdiction: The Duty Of States To Enact And Enforce Legislation: Chapter 14: Overcoming Obstacles To Implementing Universal Jurisdiction 2001*, AI Index IOR 53/017/2001, Aug. 31, 2001, *available at* http://www.amnesty.org/en/library/asset/IOR53/017/2001/en/dom-IOR530172001en.html.
[25] *See* Press Release, ICJ, Belgium Institutes Proceedings Against Senegal and Requests the Court to Indicate Provisional Measures (February 19, 2009), *available at* http://www.icj-cij.org/docket/files/144/15052.pdf?PHPSESSID=9f882d286e5a532c59d9cbce6eb2c90c.

the *aut dedere aut prosequi* provisions of the CAT, the *Pinochet* case had to focus on accusations of torture rather than murder or disappearances.[26]

The most robust "universal jurisdiction" obligation is that pertaining to the "grave breaches" provisions of the 1949 Geneva Conventions and Additional Protocol I of 1977. Article 49 of the First Geneva Convention, article 50 of the Second Geneva Convention, article 129 of the Third Geneva Convention, and article 146 of the Fourth Geneva Convention, all of 12 August 1949, provide, in identical terms, as follows:

> Each High Contracting Party shall be under the obligation to search for persons alleged to have committed, or to have ordered to be committed, ... grave breaches, and shall bring such persons, regardless of their nationality, before its own courts. It may also, if it prefers, and in accordance with the provisions of its own legislation, hand such persons over for trial to another High Contracting Party concerned, provided such High Contracting Party has made out a *prima facie* case.

This provision is also incorporated by reference in article 85(1) of Additional Protocol I. The jurisprudence of the International Court of Justice recognizes that:

> The stated purpose of the provision was that the offences would not be left unpunished (the extradition provisions playing their role in this objective). It may immediately be noted that this is an early form of the *aut dedere aut prosequi* to be seen in later conventions. But the obligation to prosecute is primary, making it even stronger.[27]

In other words: "No territorial or nationality linkage is envisaged, suggesting a true universality principle."[28] Nonetheless, the "grave breaches" provisions only apply to international armed conflicts. As noted by the ICTY Appeals Chamber in the *Tadić* case:

> The international armed conflict element generally attributed to the grave breaches provisions of the Geneva Conventions is merely a function of the system of universal mandatory jurisdiction that those provisions create. The international armed conflict requirement was a necessary limitation on the grave breaches system in light of the intrusion on State sovereignty that such mandatory universal jurisdiction represents. State parties to the 1949 Geneva Conventions did not want to give other States jurisdiction over serious violations of international humanitarian law committed in their internal armed conflicts – at least not the mandatory universal jurisdiction involved in the grave breaches system.[29]

---

[26] Richard Falk, *Assessing the Pinochet Legacy: Whither Universal Jurisdiction*, in UNIVERSAL JURISDICTION: NATIONAL COURTS AND THE PROSECUTION OF SERIOUS CRIMES UNDER INTERNATIONAL LAW 97, 115 (Stephen Macedo ed., 2006).
[27] *Arrest Warrant Case*, opinion of Judges Higgins, Kooijmans & Buergenthal, *supra* note 12, ¶ 30.
[28] *Id.* ¶ 31.
[29] Prosecutor v. Tadić, Case No. IT-94-1, Decision on the Defence Motion for Interlocutory Appeal on Jurisdiction, ¶ 80 (October 2, 1995).

Thus, to the extent that "grave breaches" of humanitarian law and crimes against humanity overlap, there exists a treaty basis for universal repression, but not in an internal armed conflict. In summary, whether under human rights or humanitarian law treaties, there is no comprehensive basis for ensuring the exercise of universal jurisdiction, or even of "primary universal repression," with respect to crimes against humanity.

III. DOES GENERAL INTERNATIONAL LAW REQUIRE UNIVERSAL REPRESSION OF CRIMES AGAINST HUMANITY?

Absent a treaty law basis for universal repression, it may still be argued that a Convention on Crimes Against Humanity is superfluous insofar as general international law, whether customary law or general principles, imposes such obligations. This may be derived in particular from the status of crimes against humanity as part of *jus cogens*. ICTY jurisprudence, for example, recognizes that "most norms of international humanitarian law, in particular those prohibiting war crimes, crimes against humanity and genocide, are also peremptory norms of international law or *jus cogens*, i.e., of a non-derogable and overriding character."[30] This view has also been espoused by distinguished publicists, such as Cherif Bassiouni[31] and Ian Brownlie.[32] The question is whether this exalted normative status imposes any obligations for the universal repression of crimes against humanity.

In terms of State practice, 45 countries have ratified the Convention on the Non-Applicability of Statutory Limitations for War Crimes and Crimes against Humanity, and of the 111 States Parties to the ICC, the majority have either already incorporated or begun to incorporate domestically the provisions of the ICC Statute, including the prohibition of crimes against humanity.[33] In contrast, a survey by Joseph Rikhof, Senior Counsel for the Crimes Against Humanity and War Crimes Section of the Department of Justice of Canada, concludes that "very few domestic cases have dealt with crimes against humanity."[34] To the extent that domestic legislation constitutes State practice, irrespective of whether it is actually implemented or not, the case for a customary law right is rather compelling. It is recognized that the tendency to equate *opinio juris* with State practice with respect to human rights norms blurs the distinction between customary law and general principles as different sources of international law. In this respect, it is noted that the status of crimes against humanity as part of *jus cogens* may be derived from either source. However, the international jurisprudence thus far only suggests that *jus cogens* status may create a right to

---

[30] Prosecutor v. Kupreskić, Case No. IT-95-16-T, Judgment, ¶ 5320 (January 14, 2000).
[31] M. CHERIF BASSIOUNI, CRIMES AGAINST HUMANITY IN INTERNATIONAL CRIMINAL LAW 210 (1999).
[32] IAN BROWNLIE, PRINCIPLES OF PUBLIC INTERNATIONAL LAW 515 (5th ed. 1998).
[33] *See* Overview of the Rome Statute Signatories, Ratifications and Implementing Legislation, *available at* http://www.iccwomen.org/whatwedo/projects/docs/Overview_Implementing_Legislation.pdf.
[34] Rikhof, *supra* note 2, at 46.

prosecute based on universal jurisdiction, but not a duty. By way of illustration, the ICTY *Furundzija Case* indicates that:

> one of the consequences of the *jus cogens* character bestowed by the international community upon the prohibition of torture is that every State is entitled to investigate, prosecute and punish or extradite individuals accused of torture, who are present in a territory under its jurisdiction.... This legal basis for States' universal jurisdiction over torture bears out and strengthens the legal foundation for such jurisdiction found by other courts in the inherently universal character of the crime. It has been held that international crimes being universally condemned wherever they occur, every State has the right to prosecute and punish the authors of such crimes.[35]

The jurisprudence of the International Court of Justice is even more cautious in recognizing such a right. Although the majority did not address the issue of universal jurisdiction under customary law, the Separate Joint Opinion of Judges Higgins, Kooijmans, and Buergenthal in the *Arrest Warrant of 11 April 2000 Case (Democratic Republic of Congo v. Belgium)* holds that "national legislation and case law – that is state practice – is neutral as to the exercise of universal jurisdiction."[36] Nevertheless, the Opinion concurs with *Oppenheim's International Law* that:

> While no general rule of positive international law can as yet be asserted which gives to states the right to punish foreign nationals for crimes against humanity in the same way as they are, for instance, entitled to punish acts of piracy, there are clear indications pointing to the gradual evolution of a significant principle of international law to that effect.[37]

Beyond a right to exercise universal jurisdiction, there is little evidence of an obligation to do so. However, the gradual crystallization of "soft law" in recognizing such an obligation cannot be easily dismissed. For instance, Robert Cryer concludes that: "There is almost no evidence of any State practice confirming prosecution on a universal jurisdictional basis as a customary duty rather than a right. Even the most ardent supporters of such a duty are forced to concede this point."[38] This categorical assertion disregards the emergence of such a norm through the gradual bridging of the gap between the *lex ferenda* and the *lex lata*. In this regard, the adoption and widespread ratification of a Convention on Crimes Against Humanity can have a profound impact on expediting this process of convergence.

There is significant, though not unanimous, support for the view that in customary law, the *aut dedere aut prosequi* obligations contained in treaties such as the CAT give rise to a broader obligation, especially with respect to crimes against humanity.

---

[35] Prosecutor v. Furundžija, Case No. IT-95-17/1, Judgment, ¶ 156 (Dec. 10, 1998).

[36] *Arrest Warrant Case*, opinion of Judges Higgins, Kooijmans & Buergenthal, *supra* note 12, ¶ 45.

[37] *Id.* ¶ 52.

[38] ROBERT CRYER, PROSECUTING INTERNATIONAL CRIMES: SELECTIVITY AND THE INTERNATIONAL CRIMINAL LAW REGIME 90–91 (2005).

Whereas some members of the International Law Commission are of the view that "the principle *aut dedere aut judicare* was not part of customary international law and that it certainly did not belong to *jus cogens*,"[39] others observe that:

> There is no consensus among the doctrine as it concerns this question, although a large and growing number of scholars joins the opinion supporting the concept of an international legal obligation *"aut dedere aut judicare"* as a general duty based not only on the provisions of particular international treaties, but also on generally binding customary norms, at least as it concerns certain categories of crimes.[40]

Cherif Bassiouni goes so far as maintaining that *aut dedere aut judicare* has achieved *jus cogens* status because of the "common interest which all states have in the suppression of international offenses. It is a duty owing to the international community as a whole, the *Civitas Maxima*."[41] There is a growing chorus of General Assembly resolutions that, though not legally binding, reflect the *opinio juris* of States regarding the universal repression of crimes against humanity.[42] These resolutions have operated in the context of often-controversial political issues, and the substantive norms have therefore been shaped by extralegal considerations. There is, however, a distinct evolution leading from the territorial principle to a principle of "primary universal repression" reflecting variations of an *aut dedere aut prosequi* obligation. In particular, this emerging obligation relates to international judicial cooperation in the extradition by custodial States of accused persons to the territorial State. Following political controversy over Portuguese colonial rule and apartheid in South Africa, and the consequent failure of many States to ratify the Convention on Statutory Limitations as discussed earlier in the chapter, General Assembly Resolution 2583(XXIV) of 1969 revisited the issue by calling upon all States:

> to take the necessary measures for the thorough investigation of war crimes and crimes against humanity, as defined in Article 1 of the Convention on the Non-Applicability of Statutory Limitations to War Crimes and Crimes against humanity, and for the detention, arrest, extradition, and punishment of all war criminals who have not yet been brought to trial or punished.[43]

It may be recalled that article III of that Convention contained an obligation to extradite those responsible for war crimes and crimes against humanity. The following

---

[39] International Law Commission, *Second Report on the Obligation to Extradite or Prosecute*, ¶ 26, U.N.G.A. A/CN.4/585 (June 11, 2007) (*prepared* by Zdzislaw Galicki).

[40] *Id.*

[41] M. CHERIF BASSIOUNI & EDWARD M. WISE, AUT DEDERE AUT JUDICARE: THE DUTY TO EXTRADITE OR PROSECUTE IN INTERNATIONAL LAW 24 (1995).

[42] On General Assembly resolutions and *opinio juris*, see, e.g., Legality of the Threat or Use of Nuclear Weapons Case, Advisory Opinion, 1996 I.C.J. 226, ¶ 70 (July 8).

[43] *Question of the Punishment of War Criminals and of Persons who have Committed Crimes against Humanity* (Question of Punishment), G.A. Res. 2583(XXIV), 24 U.N. GAOR Supp. (No. 30), U.N. Doc. A/RES/2583(XXIV) (December 15, 1969).

year, in 1970, General Assembly resolution 2712(XXV) once again called upon States:

> to take measures, in accordance with recognized principles of international law, to arrest such persons and extradite them to the countries where they have committed war crimes and crimes against humanity, so that they can be brought to trial and punished in accordance with the laws of those countries.[44]

Again in 1970, General Assembly Resolution 2840(XXVI) affirmed that:

> refusal by states to co-operate in the arrest, extradition, trial and punishment of persons guilty of war crimes and crimes against humanity is contrary to the purposes and principles of the Charter of the United Nations and to generally recognized norms of international law.[45]

In 1973, General Assembly Resolution 3074 stipulated that:

> Persons against whom there is evidence that they have committed war crimes and crimes against humanity shall be subject to trial and, if found guilty, to punishment, as a general rule in the countries in which they committed those crimes. In that connection, States shall co-operate on questions of extraditing such persons.[46]

More recently, in December 2005, the General Assembly adopted resolution 60/147 on the Basic Principles and Guidelines on the Right to a Remedy and Reparation for Victims of Gross Violations of International Human Rights Law and Serious Violations of International Humanitarian Law. The preamble to the resolution states that:

> International law contains the obligation to prosecute perpetrators of certain international crimes in accordance with international obligations of States and the requirements of national law or as provided for in the applicable statutes of international judicial organs.

Furthermore, principle 4 provides that:

> In cases of gross violations of international human rights law and serious violations of international humanitarian law constituting crimes under international law, States have the duty to investigate and, if there is sufficient evidence, the duty to submit to prosecution the person allegedly responsible for the violations and, if found guilty, the duty to punish her or him. Moreover, in these cases, States should,

---

[44] *Question of the Punishment of War Criminals and of Persons Who Have Committed Crimes Against Humanity*, G.A. Res. 2712(XXV), 25 U.N. GAOR Supp. (No. 28) U.N. Doc. A/RES/2712(XXV) (December 15, 1970).

[45] *Question of the Punishment of War Criminals and of Persons Who Have Committed Crimes Against Humanity*, G.A. Res. 2840 (XXVI) (1971), G.A. Res. 2840(XXVI), 26 U.N. GAOR Supp. (No. 29) at 88, U.N. Doc. A/RES/2840(XXVI) (December 18, 1971).

[46] *Principles of International Co-operation in the Detection, Arrest, Extradition and Punishment of Persons Guilty of War Crimes and Crimes against Humanity*, G.A. Res. 3074(XXVIII), 28 U.N. GAOR Supp. (No. 30) at 78–79, U.N. Doc. A/RES/3074(XXVIII) (December 3, 1973).

in accordance with international law, cooperate with one another and assist international judicial organs competent in the investigation and prosecution of these violations.[47]

The cumulative weight of these General Assembly resolutions, together with widespread ratification of relevant international criminal law and human rights treaties, and additionally the establishment of institutions such as the ICTY and ICTR, the hybrid tribunals in Sierra Leone and Cambodia, and the ICC, clearly points toward recognition of the principle that notwithstanding the primary obligation of territorial States to prosecute, those responsible for crimes against humanity should not enjoy impunity in third States. Whether this is to be achieved through exercise of "universal jurisdiction" or a variant of "primary universal repression" is less important than the underlying objective of eradicating impunity for perpetrators of the most serious international crimes. In this respect, the process of negotiating and adopting a Convention on Crimes Against Humanity may, beyond creating a definitive treaty obligation for universal repression, also exploit the often-blurred line between codification of customary law and progressive development of international law, and thereby help entrench the prevailing "soft law" as an established norm of general international law.

IV. CONCLUSION

In the post-ICC international legal order, the role of national courts has become an integral aspect of the struggle to eradicate a long-prevalent culture of impunity. The effective legal regulation of prosecuting crimes against humanity, as an elementary and versatile international crime capturing all large-scale human rights and humanitarian law violations, is crucial to the success of this enterprise. The existing patchwork of treaties and customary law creates an obligation to prosecute crimes against humanity based only on the territoriality principle. The existence of a right to exercise universal jurisdiction cannot be a substitute for an obligation to ensure repression. This significant loophole is the most compelling reason for a Convention on Crimes Against Humanity. Beyond creating such a specific conventional obligation, and notwithstanding its potential impact on the crystallization of "soft law" into customary law, such an international treaty could become, together with the ICC Statute, one of the two primary pillars of the contemporary international criminal justice system. Whereas the ICC Statute confers jurisdiction on an international court, the Convention would ensure that national courts are legally empowered to discharge their share of the burden in hastening a long-awaited era of global accountability.

The view that a right to exercise universal jurisdiction is sufficient must be considered against the failure of national courts to vigorously prosecute crimes against

---

[47] *Basic Principles and Guidelines on the Right to a Remedy and Reparation for Victims of Gross Violations of International Human Rights Law and Serious Violations of International Humanitarian Law*, G.A. Res. 60/147, U.N. Doc. A/RES/60/147 (December 16, 2005).

humanity. A case in point is Canada's experience with CAHWCA. As a State strongly committed to the ICC, Canada's domestic universal jurisdiction legislation is intended to give effect to an official "No Safe Haven" policy. As a leading immigrant nation committed to multiculturalism, this policy is particularly significant for Canada in recognizing the burden that must fall on its national judiciary as an important ingredient of its global responsibilities. Canada's "Modern War Crimes Program" was initiated in 1998 to expand investigations beyond those pertaining to Nazi crimes from the Second World War. The Program has pursued a three-pronged approach in dealing with perpetrators:

> preventing suspected war criminals from reaching Canada by refusing their immigrant, refugee or visitor applications abroad; detecting such persons who have managed to come to Canada, whether they be in the refugee determination, permanent resident or citizenship processes; and by taking the necessary steps to exclude them from the refugee determination process, prevent them from becoming Canadian Citizens, or revoking their citizenship should they be detected after acquiring that status, and ultimately removing these individuals from Canada.[48]

This approach has ensured that most of those responsible for crimes against humanity and present in Canada "are not citizens or permanent residents but have come to Canada as visitors or refugee claimants."[49] Nonetheless, there are numerous suspects that are either Canadian citizens or permanent residents, and the immigration/refugee process of exclusion or deportation, although more cost-effective, is not an absolute substitute for criminal prosecutions. In the decade since the Modern War Crimes Program was initiated, the prosecution of Désiré Munyaneza for his involvement in the 1994 Rwandan genocide is the only trial under universal jurisdiction before Canadian courts. He was charged and found guilty of seven counts of genocide, crimes against humanity, and war crimes, and described as being at the "forefront of the genocidal movement."[50] If this is the record of a State as committed as Canada to eradicating impunity, then the challenge of enlisting national courts in the cause of international criminal justice becomes starkly apparent.

In this light, the adoption of a Convention on Crimes Against Humanity is but a first step in a long and tortuous road to universal accountability. In the aftermath of the Pinochet affair before the Spanish and English courts, Henry Kissinger famously remarked that:

> human rights violations, war crimes, genocide, and torture have so disgraced the modern age and in such a variety of places that the effort to interpose legal norms to prevent or punish such outrages does credit to its advocates. The danger lies in

---

[48] See DEPARTMENT OF JUSTICE, CANADA'S CRIMES AGAINST HUMANITY AND WAR CRIMES PROGRAM, MODERN WAR CRIMES PROGRAM, (Jan. 2, 2009), *available at* http://www.justice.gc.ca/eng/pi/wc-cg/mwcp-pcgc.html.
[49] *Id.*
[50] R. v. Désiré Munyaneza, [2009] R.J.Q. 1432, ¶ 2057 (Can.).

pushing the effort to extremes that risk substituting the tyranny of judges for that of governments ....[51]

Considering the scale and gravity of mass atrocities in the contemporary world, and the cynical indifference of leaders to the demands of victims for justice, the specter of "tyranny" by judges seems rather appealing.

---

[51] Henry Kissinger, *The Pitfalls of Universal Jurisdiction*, FOREIGN AFF., July/August 2001, at 86 (2001).

3

Revisiting the Architecture of Crimes Against Humanity

Almost a Century in the Making, with Gaps and Ambiguities Remaining – the Need for a Specialized Convention

M. Cherif Bassiouni

I. INTRODUCTION

International law is essentially the product of State interests. Even in this era of globalization, it remains under the long shadow of the Westphalian paradigm founded on State sovereignty. Progress, however, has been achieved as States' interests and the values that their societies embrace have converged, demanding greater conformity by States to certain human aspirations. Spurred by economic globalization, States' international cooperation has increased substantially. In some areas, it has given rise to collective decision-making processes. Among developments in which State sovereignty has given way to collective interests and values are those that occurred in the field of human rights and International Criminal Law (ICL). Both fields have been driven by ideas that with time have acquired an incrementally higher level of value recognition from broader and diverse constituencies. Admittedly, progress in these fields has been slower and more painstaking than in the economic field. What has been achieved in the fields of human rights and ICL is the result of a process of accretion that strengthened ideas about human values throughout the history of several civilizations.

History records that such accretion is the result of an evolutionary process. It begins with the emergence of an idea that then grows in its acceptance by different constituencies, and is then followed by a stage of prescriptive articulation that eventually leads to the stage of proscriptive normative formulation. Finally, it ripens into the establishment of enforcement mechanisms. Within such a process, *largo senso*, there are multiple processes involving diverse participants, operating in different arenas, employing multiple strategies and tactics, and pursuing different value-oriented goals. Thus, the evolution of an idea from its intellectual inception to its proscriptive and enforcement stages goes through many intermediate stages and may even find itself transformed or altered from its original meaning or intended purpose. Chief among the reasons for the transformation or alteration of ideas are State interests. Equally significant, however, are the imprints of events and circumstances. The historical evolution of Crimes Against Humanity (CAH) falls within the pattern described earlier, and its ultimate shape is yet to be established, although it seems to be well on its way toward a settled meaning. Still, there are several questions that need to be answered in a cogent and clear manner. Among these questions are the following:

1. What is the social/human interest sought to be protected?
2. What is the category of persons sought to be protected?
3. What is the category of perpetrators sought to be deterred?
4. What are the policy limits of individual and group criminal responsibility?
5. What are the jurisdictional elements likely to enhance the various levels of enforcement mechanisms?
6. What are the elements of the "general part"?
7. To what extent should prohibited acts be included in the "special part"?

As described below, CAH grew out of necessity imposed by circumstances. It was not the product of deliberative legislative policy planning. It continued to evolve on a precedential basis as if it was impossible to reconsider its original architecture. The developmental process has simply been a patchwork that has never benefited from an overall reconsideration of what existed in the past.

II. THE EVOLUTION OF CRIMES AGAINST HUMANITY IN INTERNATIONAL LAW

A. *The Genesis of Crimes Against Humanity*[1]

The genesis of CAH is found in the preamble of the 1907 Hague Convention (superseding the 1899 Hague Convention), which contains the words "laws of humanity."[2] This preambular language is referred to as the Marten's Clause.[3] It was intended to mean that the Convention's contents embody that which States, at the

---

[1] *See generally*, M. CHERIF BASSIOUNI, CRIMES AGAINST HUMANITY IN INTERNATIONAL CRIMINAL LAW (2d ed. 1992). A third edition is in progress and expected to be published in 2010.

[2] Convention Respecting the Laws and Customs of War on Land pmbl., Oct. 18, 1907, 36 Stat. 2277, T.S. No. 539. 3 Martens Nouveau Recueil (ser. 3) 461, *reprinted in* 2 AM. J. INT'L L. 90 (Supp. 1908) [hereinafter 1907 Hague Convention].

[3] The Martens Clause is named after the Russian diplomat and jurist who drafted it, Fyodor Martens. A similar formula appears in each of the 1949 Geneva Conventions and in the 1977 Protocols. *See* Convention for the Amelioration of the Condition of the Wounded and Sick in Armed Forces in the Field (Geneva Convention I) art. 63(4), Aug. 12, 1949, 6 U.S.T. 3114, 75 U.N.T.S. 31; Convention for the Amelioration of the Condition of Wounded, Sick, and Shipwrecked Members of the Armed Forces at Sea (Geneva Convention II) art. 62(4), Aug. 12, 1949, 6 U.S.T. 3217, 75 U.N.T.S. 85; Convention Relative to the Treatment of Prisoners of War (Geneva Convention III) art. 142(4), Aug. 12, 1949, 6 U.S.T. 3316, 75 U.N.T.S. 135; Convention Relative to the Protection of Civilian Persons in Time of War (Geneva Convention IV) art. 158(4), Aug. 12, 1949, 6 U.S.T. 3516, 75 U.N.T.S. 287; Protocol Additional to the Geneva Conventions of 12 August 1949, and Relating to the Protection of Victims of International Armed Conflicts (Protocol I) art. 1(2), June 8, 1977, 1125 U.N.T.S. 3; Protocol Additional to the Geneva Conventions of 12 August 1949, and Relating to the Protection of Victims of Non-International Armed Conflicts (Protocol II) pmbl. June 8, 1977, 1125 U.N.T.S. 609; Paolo Benvenuti, *La Clausola Martens e la Tradizione Classica del Diritto Naturale nella Codificazione dei Conflitti Armati*, *in* SCRITTI DEGLI ALLIEVI IN MEMORIA DI GUISEPPE BARILE 173 (1995).

time, considered to be the customary law and practice of States in the course of armed conflicts. Thus the Preamble states the obvious, namely that the 1907 Hague Convention included State Parties that agreed to it at the time as constituting part of the customary law and practice of States. By implication, the Convention excludes that which had not yet risen to the level of international recognition. Presumably when such level of recognition would be reached, new norms would be added.

The Preamble states:

> It has not been found possible at present to concert regulations covering all the circumstances which arise in practice. On the other hand, the High Contracting Parties clearly do not intend that unforeseen cases should, in the absence of a written undertaking, be left to the arbitrary judgment of military commanders.
>
> Until a more complete code of the laws of war has been issued, the High Contracting Parties deem it expedient to declare that, in cases not included in the Regulations adopted by them, the inhabitants and the belligerents remain under the protection and the rule of the principles of the law of nations, *as they result from the usages established among civilized peoples, from the laws of humanity, and the dictates of the public conscience.*[4]

More specifically, the origin of the term crimes against humanity goes back to 1915 when the governments of France, Great Britain, and Russia issued a joint declaration on May 28, 1915, denouncing the Ottoman government's massacre of the Armenian population in Turkey as constituting "crimes against civilization and humanity" for which all members of the Turkish government would be held responsible together with its agents implicated in the massacres.[5] Nevertheless, the Treaty of Versailles (1919) did not include such a crime.[6] The 1919 Commission, however, recommended that the law that should be applied by the High Tribunal to be established pursuant to article 228 of the said treaty ought to include: *"the principles of the law of nations as they result from the usages established among civilized peoples, from the laws of humanity and from the dictates of public conscience."*[7] As discussed below, this did not come to pass.

The term "laws of humanity" is reminiscent of natural law terminology that had been used in various ways in connection with what became known as the "Law of Armed Conflict" (LOAC). Another term having the same importance as "laws of humanity" was developed in the twelfth century CE, namely "the Laws of God

---

[4] 1907 Hague Convention, *supra* note 2, at pmbl. (emphasis added).
[5] "Crimes against humanity" is quoted in the Armenian Memorandum presented by the Greek delegation to the 1919 Commission on Mar. 14, 1919, *as reprinted in* Egon Schwelb, *Crimes Against Humanity*, 23 BRIT. Y.B. INT'L L. 178, 181 (1946). *See generally* VAHAKIN DADRIAN, THE HISTORY OF THE ARMENIAN GENOCIDE (1995).
[6] Treaty of Peace between the Allied and Associated Powers and Germany (Treaty of Versailles), June 28, 1919, 225 Consol. T.S. 188, 2 Bevans 43.
[7] *See* CARNEGIE ENDOWMENT FOR INT'L PEACE, REPORT PRESENTED TO THE PRELIMINARY PEACE CONFERENCE BY THE COMMISSION ON THE RESPONSIBILITIES OF THE AUTHORS OF WAR AND ENFORCEMENT OF PENALTIES 24 (1919), *reprinted in* 14 AM. J. INT'L L. 95 (1920) [hereinafter 1919 Commission Report] (emphasis added).

and Nature." That term was used in the 1268 criminal prosecution of Conradin Von Hohenstaufen and Frederik of Baden for crimes committed against the civilian population of Naples in the course of that city's siege and subsequent sacking; it was used again in 1474 in the trial in Breisach of Peter Van Hagenbach, when twenty-six judges representing the different parts of the Holy Roman Empire convicted the accused of crimes against the civilian population of that city.[8] This was the world's first international criminal prosecution before an international criminal tribunal.

B. *The Meaning and Scope of Laws of Humanity*

By 1907, the term "laws of humanity" included that which was deemed part of the Christian World's ideas and values. Other civilizations, some much older, had also reached the same ideas and identified the same values without evidence of the migration of these ideas and values from one civilization to the other.

Admittedly, not all civilizations premised their values, beliefs, and practices on the same basis. For example, Sun Tzu of China in the fourth century BCE posited protections for occupied civilian populations as well as limitations on the right of Chinese combatants to kill or enslave their enemies, on the basis that this would make their occupation of conquered territories and the subjugation of foreign peoples more difficult.[9] This was a policy argument not that different from the nineteenth-century arguments supporting limitations on warfare based on the mutuality of interests of the parties engaged in a conflict. In the second century BCE, the Laws of Manu in India posited the same protections/limitations as those postulated by Sun Tzu, but on the basis of the rules of chivalry that existed in High Hinduism.[10] That too was not so different from the rules of chivalry that later developed in Europe in the Middle Ages.[11] Also, there are some indications that during the fourth century BCE,

---

[8] *See* GEORGE SCHWARZENBERGER, INTERNATIONAL LAW 462–66 (1968); BAYARD TAYLOR, A HISTORY OF GERMANY: FROM THE EARLIEST TIMES TO THE PRESENT DAY 187 (1907); WOLFGANG MENZEL, GERMANY FROM THE EARLIEST PERIOD 629 (1900); A.G. DE BARANTE, HISTOIRE DES DUCS DE BOURGOGNE DE LA MAISON DE VALOIS, 1364–1477, at 16 (1839); M. Cherif Bassiouni, *World War I: "The War to End All Wars" and the Birth of a Handicapped International Criminal Justice System*, 30 DENV. J. INT'L L. & POL'Y 244 (2002); M. Cherif Bassiouni, *International Criminal Justice in Historical Perspective*, in M. CHERIF BASSIOUNI, III INTERNATIONAL CRIMINAL LAW: INTERNATIONAL ENFORCEMENT 29 (M. Cherif Bassiouni ed., 3d ed. 2008) [hereinafter I-III BASSIOUNI ICL]; William A. Schabas, *International Sentencing: From Leipzig (1923) to Arusha (1996)*, in I BASSIOUNI ICL, *supra*, at 129.

[9] *See, e.g.*, SUN TZU, THE ART OF WAR 76 (Samuel B. Griffith trans., 1971).

[10] *See* M. CHERIF BASSIOUNI, A MANUAL ON INTERNATIONAL HUMANITARIAN LAW AND ARMS CONTROL AGREEMENTS 6 (2000) [hereinafter BASSIOUNI, MANUAL]. *See also* THE BOOK OF MANU: MANUSMURTI, discussed in detail by Nagendra Singh in *Armed Conflicts and Humanitarian Law of Ancient India*, in ETUDES ET ESSAIS SUR LE DROIT INTERNATIONAL HUMANITAIRE ET SUR LES PRINCIPES DE LA CROIX-ROUGE EN L'HONNEUR DE JEAN PICTET (Christophe Swinarski ed., 1984); and COMMENTARIES: THE LAWS OF MANU (Georg Bühler trans., 1967).

[11] *See* Leslie C. Green, *The Law of Armed Conflict and the Enforcement of International Criminal Law*, 27 ANNUAIRE CANADIEN DE DROIT INTERNATIONAL 4 (1984); Leslie C. Green, *Human Rights*

the Mayans of the American continent adopted similar limitations in their warfare practices.[12] In the seventh century CE, the Muslims developed norms that were the closest to contemporary international humanitarian law, and founded them on Islamic beliefs and values. A few centuries later, between the thirteenth and sixteenth century CE, naturalists like Gentili, Vittoria, Ayala, and Suarez[13] borrowed from the writings of the Muslim Scholar Al-Shaybani.[14] They noted in their works the chivalrous and humane practices of Muslim combatants during the Crusades, particularly those practiced by Salah-el-Din el-Ayyoubi in the sieges of Karak (1189) and Jerusalem (1192).[15] Their writings extended the Aristotelian-Augustinian-Thomistic conceptions of Natural Law to make them a source of legal/moral limitation on the methods, means, and targets of warfare.

Cumulatively, these experiences that emanated from different civilizations in different parts of the world without evidence of idea borrowing from one another (except for the Christian Naturalists, who borrowed from the Muslims) could well be considered evidence that there was something broader than the "laws of humanity," which could be called the "laws of humankind."

The use of the term "humanity" in the Preamble of the Hague Convention was probably intended to mean humankind, because it referred to the human race. The term humanity includes or at least implies certain characteristics of humankind, such as human qualities and other value-oriented characteristics. The concept of humanity was developed in Greek antiquity as an outgrowth of a certain philosophical conception. It does not, therefore, refer specifically to the biological human species, as in the case of the term "humankind." As used in the Preamble of the

---

and the Law of Armed Conflict, 10 ISR. Y.B. HUM. RTS. 9 (1980) (citing Belli (1563), Ayala (1582), Gentius (1612), Grotius (1625)). See also LESLIE C. GREEN, ESSAYS ON THE MODERN LAW OF WAR (1985). For a very useful contemporary appraisal, see THE LAW OF WAR CRIMES: NATIONAL AND INTERNATIONAL APPROACHES (Timothy L.H. McCormack & Gerry J. Simpson eds., 1997).

[12] See BASSIOUNI, MANUAL, supra note 10, at 10.

[13] Id. See also Franciscus de Victoria, De Indis et de Jure Belli, in CLASSICS OF INTERNATIONAL LAW (James B. Scott ed., 1917); Francisco Suárez, On War, in 2 CLASSICS OF INTERNATIONAL LAW (James B. Scott ed., 1944); Balthazar Ayala, Three Books on the Law of War, in 2 CLASSICS OF INTERNATIONAL LAW (John P. Bate trans., 1912); Alberico Gentili, De Jure Belli Libri Tres, in CLASSICS OF INTERNATIONAL LAW (James B. Scott ed., 1933).

[14] The cases and practices of Muslim conduct in war were taught by Al-Shaybani in the eighth century and were written in a digest by el-Shahristani. The first known publication was in Hyderabad in 1335–1336, translated by Majid Khadduri in WAR AND PEACE IN THE LAW OF ISLAM. See also Roger C. Algase, Protection of Civilian Lives in Warfare: A Comparison between Islamic Law and Modern International Law Concerning the Conduct of Hostilities, 16 REVUE DE DROIT PÉNAL MILITAIRE ET DE DROIT DE LA GUERRE 246 (1977); see also, e.g., SOBHI MAHMASSANI, THE PRINCIPLES OF INTERNATIONAL LAW IN LIGHT OF ISLAMIC DOCTRINE (1966); MAJID KHADDURI, THE ISLAMIC LAW OF NATIONS (1966); SAID RAMADAN, ISLAMIC LAW, ITS SCOPE AND EQUITY (1961); MUHAMMAD HAMIDULLAH, MUSLIM CONDUCT OF STATE (1961); Ahmed Rechid, L'Islam et le Droit de Gens, 60 RECUEIL DES COURS DE L'ACADEMIE DE DROIT INTERNATIONAL DE LA HAYE 371 (1937); NAJIB ARMANAZI, L'ISLAM ET LE DROIT INTERNATIONAL (1929).

[15] Id. See also CHRISTOPHER TYERMAN, FIGHTING FOR CHRISTENDOM (2005); JONATHAN RILEY-SMITH, THE CRUSADES: A SHORT HISTORY (1990); AMIN MAALOUF, THE CRUSADES THROUGH ARAB EYES (1989); FRANCESCO GABRIELI, ARAB HISTORIANS OF THE CRUSADES (1989).

1907 Hague Convention, the term "humanity" refers to humankind, as opposed to what humanism, as derived from the term "humanity," would imply on the basis of its Greek philosophical origins. Nevertheless, the term "humanity" stuck.

When the 1919 Commission sought to expand the applicability of the 1907 Hague Convention to civilian populations that were not nationals of another State during an ongoing international armed conflict, it used the term "crimes against the law of humanity."[16] This terminological choice was understandable in that context. What it meant, however, was to be a jurisdictional extension of the applicability of the same protections contained in the 1907 Hague Convention to persons who were not of a different nationality than those of the enemy combatant State. In other words, the diversity of nationality requirement in the application of the international law of armed conflict was to be dropped as a jurisdictional requirement. At the time, this was a major step considering that the international legal order was still largely anchored to the 1648 Westphalian concept of State sovereignty.[17] The notion that international law, no matter how laudable its purposes may be, could apply directly to States with respect to their own nationals, and without the States' specific consent, was simply, to use a modern adage, a "bridge too far." The United States and Japan objected, the former relying on the proposition that the concept in question reflected "natural law" and did not have a basis in positive international law, the latter relying on legal positivism grounds.[18]

Admittedly, there was no basis in positive international law for the recognition that "crimes against the laws of humanity" existed at the time. But then, to paraphrase the French philosopher Blaise Pascal, every practice must have its beginning in some act. This is also reflected in ancient Chinese and Egyptian popular sayings to the effect that the longest journey always starts with a first step. Indeed this concept made its way in customary international law by the recognition that a custom simply does not occur out of nowhere, but that it is the product of a certain evolution, and that evolution necessarily starts with a first act. Consequently, what the members of the 1919 Commission probably meant was that this was the beginning of a new custom, and the new custom was really nothing more than the extension of the very same norms that existed for combatants and the civilian population of an enemy State to the civilian population of the State of nationality. Thus, there was no substantive legal change, but rather an expansion of the jurisdictional scope of the crime and the inclusion of a new protected group. On its face, this is not particularly offensive to the laudable purposes of the "principles of legality," except for legal systems that adhere to a rigid positivistic concept.[19]

---

[16] 1919 Commission Report, *supra* note 7, at 20.

[17] *See generally* WILLIAM P. GUTHRIE, THE LATER THIRTY YEARS WAR: FROM THE BATTLE OF WITTSTOCK TO THE TREATY OF WESTPHALIA (2003); DEREK CROXTON & ANUSCHKA TISCHER, THE PEACE OF WESTPHALIA: A HISTORICAL DICTIONARY (2001); BEYOND WESTPHALIA?: NATIONAL SOVEREIGNTY AND INTERNATIONAL INTERVENTION (Gene M. Lyons & Michael Mastanduno eds., 1995).

[18] 1919 Commission Report, *supra* note 7, at 83.

[19] *See generally* BASSIOUNI, CRIMES AGAINST HUMANITY IN INTERNATIONAL CRIMINAL LAW, *supra* note 1, at ch. 4.

For political reasons, the victorious Allies convening at Versailles in 1919 elected not to extend the concept of international criminal responsibility for "crimes against the laws of humanity" to Turkish nationals.[20] At the beginning of the peace process, the victorious Allies were inclined to do so under the Treaty of Sèvres (1920),[21] but later in the Treaty of Lausanne (1923), the accountability of Turkish officials was dropped.[22] Instead, the Treaty of Lausanne contained an unpublished addendum that provided amnesty to Turkish nationals who may have committed crimes under international law (no matter how these would be defined).

Realpolitik prevailed over the interests of justice, as it did with respect to the nonapplicability of criminal responsibility to the German Kaiser for initiating what we would now call a war of aggression. At the time, this was artfully phrased in article 227 of the Treaty of Versailles as the "supreme offense against the sanctity of treaties." Obviously, no such international crime existed, and the Kaiser was able to benefit from asylum in The Netherlands. The same could not be said for articles 228 and 229 of the same treaty, under which the Allies were to establish tribunals for the prosecution of the Germans for violations of the 1907 Hague Convention. Instead, the Allies consigned this task to Germany, where some token prosecutions were conducted in Leipzig and concluded in 1923. These experiences are interrelated and they show, like others that have occurred over time, that the architecture of CAH has suffered from weaknesses that do not derive from any inherent reasons, not because these weaknesses cannot be rectified, but because States have an interest in preserving legal weaknesses and ambiguities as escape hatches for the vulnerability of their ruling elites to international criminal responsibility.

C. Coming of Age

After the post–World War I experience, the notion of "crimes against the laws of humanity" receded to the background of international legal scholars' attention and almost disappeared from the consciousness of political leaders. Interestingly, the concept also failed to attract the interests of philosophers, theologians, and others who should have been interested in matters involving humanity, humankind, humanism, or however else one would characterize the protection of human life

---

[20] Bassiouni, *World War I: "The War to End All Wars" and the Birth of a Handicapped International Criminal Justice System*, supra note 8. See also Jackson Maogoto, *International Justice in the Shadow of Realpolitik: Revisiting the Establishment of the Ad Hoc International Criminal Tribunals*, 5/2 FLINDERS J.L. REFORM 161 (2001). See also GARY JONATHAN BASS, STAY THE HAND OF VENGEANCE (2000).

[21] The Treaty of Peace Between the Allied Powers and Turkey (Treaty of Sèvres), Aug. 10, 1920, repinted in 15 AM. J. INT'L L. 179 (Supp. 1921). Twenty countries other than Turkey signed the Treaty. The United States, however, was not a party. For further elaboration of the Treaty of Sèvres, see David Matas, *Prosecuting Crimes Against Humanity: The Lessons of World War I*, 13 FORDHAM INT'L L.J. 86 (1989).

[22] *See* Treaty of Peace Between the Allied Powers and Turkey (Treaty of Lausanne), July 24, 1923, 28 L.N.T.S. 11, *reprinted in* 18 AM. J. INT'L L. 1 (Supp. 1924).

and human dignity from certain human depredations. The state of dormancy did not remain for long, however, because new facts unfolded in the European war theater that required responses. Thus, the facts led the law.

By 1941, scholars and diplomats meeting at St. James Palace in London under the auspices of the London International Assembly began discussing the responsibility of the Axis Powers under the law of armed conflict.[23] The concept of "crimes against the laws of humanity" started to make its way back into the consciousness of these and other scholars and experts through the same legal reasoning that had prompted the members of the 1919 Commission to consider it. The idea continued to germinate in the Allies' Moscow Declaration of 1943, but still not as "crimes against the laws of humanity." Instead, war crimes and what the Soviet Union then called aggression became the focus of international attention. It was only at the London Conference of 1945 that the United States introduced the concept of "crimes against the law of humanity" and urged to have it adopted in the IMT Charter. What the United States had opposed in 1919 it came to champion in 1945. The difference was due to the newly discovered facts, the extent of their horrors, and a constituency supporting prosecutions for such crimes. The time had come for the recognition of this category of international crimes, notwithstanding national sovereignty and legal positivism. However, that meant that no time existed for a new architecture to be developed, thus CAH would have to be similar to what had been conceived in 1919.

The term was changed to "crimes against humanity" (IMT article 6(c)) to shorten it, and it was linked to "war crimes" (article 6(b)) or "crimes against peace" (article 6(a)).[24] The linkage to these crimes was, for all practical purposes, to make "crimes against humanity" an extension of the prohibitions contained in "war crimes," but without limitation of its applicability to the civilian population of another State. This was the same conceptual basis relied on in 1919. In 1945, however, there was a greater concern about how to overcome the prohibitions against ex post facto law contained in the "principles of legality" that were recognized in all legal systems, albeit with some differences, and which were likely to be raised at trial. Thus, the definition of the new crime was, for all practical purposes, the incorporation of similarly prohibited acts under the law of armed conflict that constituted "war crimes" but applicable to a State's own civilian population or that under its control. This approach did not satisfy the more rigid objections based on the then-prevailing understanding of "principles of legality" in Europe, but it nonetheless was deemed acceptable. The new paradigm merely removed the dust of time from the old one and gave it a more modern patina.

The newly recognized international crime was based on the first act in the emerging international custom that occurred in 1919. Its recognition also evidences the fact that international law is the product of past experience and that it is driven by

---

[23] *See* THE PUNISHMENT OF WAR CRIMINALS: RECOMMENDATIONS OF THE LONDON INTERNATIONAL ASSEMBLY (REPORT OF COMMISSION I) (1944).

[24] Charter of the International Military Tribunal at Nuremberg art. 6, Aug. 8, 1945, 59 Stat. 1544, 82 U.N.T.S. 279 [hereinafter IMT Charter].

new facts and emerging needs. It is seldom the product of reflective planning for prospective needs.

D. Prosecutorial and Legislative Policies and Practices

Crimes against humanity were never applied across the board to any and all persons who may have committed such a crime. Even the initial efforts of the 1919 Commission contemplated the applicability of "crimes against the laws of humanity" only to Turkish nationals who in that case were also part of the defeated powers. This subsequently changed with the adoption of the Statutes of the International Criminal Tribunal for the former Yugoslavia (ICTY) (1993)[25] and the International Criminal Court (ICC) (1998).[26] But this crime has almost always been applied selectively.

Notwithstanding the experiences of the International Military Tribunals at Nuremberg and Tokyo, Control Council Law No. 10, the ICTY, and the International Criminal Tribunal for Rwanda (ICTR), fifty-five States since World War II have incorporated "crimes against humanity," as defined in international criminal law, into their domestic criminal laws. National post–World War II prosecutions and attempted prosecutions were sparse. They include token cases in Canada, France, and Israel. Irrespective of the success or failure of these prosecutions or attempted prosecutions, they were against individuals who were either nationals of the defeated Axis powers or who were allied thereto. Germany has an extensive post–World War II record of domestic prosecutions for war crimes and other domestic crimes from 1950 to date, which includes essentially its own citizens; however, these prosecutions did not involve CAH.[27]

To date, there is no internationally agreed-on definition of this category of international crimes. In fact, there are twelve international definitions of CAH with some significant variations among them. For example, article 4 of the ICTY Statute requires a linkage between "crimes against humanity" and a "conflict of an international or non-international character."[28] This was added to the definition of the Statute by this author, who drafted it at the request of the U.N. Secretary-General's committee preparing the ICTY's statute out of concern for the questionable binding legal effect of the 1950 International Law Commission (ILC) report that dispensed with the war-connecting link. This was not the case with respect to article 5 of the ICTR Statute, which made no such distinction and, in effect, transformed the

---

[25] M. CHERIF BASSIOUNI WITH PETER MANIKAS, THE LAW OF THE INTERNATIONAL CRIMINAL TRIBUNAL FOR THE FORMER YUGOSLAVIA (1995).
[26] See generally M. CHERIF BASSIOUNI, THE LEGISLATIVE HISTORY OF THE INTERNATIONAL CRIMINAL COURT: INTRODUCTION, ANALYSIS, AND INTEGRATED TEXT (M. Cherif Bassiouni ed., 2005) [hereinafter BASSIOUNI, LEGISLATIVE HISTORY OF THE ICC].
[27] BASSIOUNI, CRIMES AGAINST HUMANITY IN INTERNATIONAL CRIMINAL LAW, supra note 1, at 41–88, 243–81.
[28] Statute of the International Tribunal for the former Yugoslavia, art. 4, S.C. Res. 827, U.N. Doc. S/RES/827 (May 25, 1993), reprinted in 32 I.L.M. 1159 [hereinafter ICTY Statute].

nature of the crime by decoupling it from any international legal element such as affecting international peace or security or deriving from an armed conflict.[29]

E. The Present Stage

The period of stagnation during the Cold War between 1948 and 1989 evidenced the arresting effect of political considerations on the development of ICL. The efforts to codify international crimes in the Draft Code of Offences Against the Peace and Security of Mankind[30] (including CAH), which started in 1947, were frustrated until 1978 when the General Assembly mandated the International Law Commission to resume its work on the Draft Code that was tabled in 1954, pending the definition of aggression.[31] The latter, which started in 1952, was finalized in 1974.[32] But as further evidence of the politicization of the ICL, the 1974 definition of aggression was made part of a nonbinding General Assembly Resolution on which the Security Council – for which it was intended – never relied upon. To date, there is no agreed definition of aggression as an international crime, no more than there is an international convention on CAH.

As to the ILC's efforts to define Crimes Against Peace and Security of Mankind, as renamed in 1978 (from the 1954 Draft Code of Offences Against the Peace and Security of Mankind), it was completed in 1996 and submitted by the ILC to the Sixth Committee of the General Assembly.[33] The text included a definition of CAH similar to that of the ICTY's statute, save for the connecting link to a conflict. The five articles of the Draft Code of Crimes were substantially more reduced and shortened from the 1991 ILC version that contained twenty-six crimes. Nevertheless, it was not adopted by the General Assembly and remains in permanent limbo.[34]

CAH is a category of international crimes that, like aggression, is laden with political implications and thus is difficult for States to endorse. There are, indeed, so many States that, in time of peace and in time of conflict, engage in human depredations against their own and other civilians. The millions of victims of tyrannical regime repressions since the end of World War II, and the repression of internal

---

[29] Statute of the International Criminal Tribunal for Rwanda, art. 5, S.C. Res. 955, U.N. Doc. S/RES/955 (Nov. 8, 1994), *reprinted in* 33 I.L.M. 1598 (1994) [hereinafter ICTR Statute].

[30] G.A Res. 174, U.N. GAOR, 2d Sess., U.N. Doc. A/519 (Nov. 21, 1947).

[31] 1954 Draft Code of Offences Against the Peace and Security of Mankind, U.N. GAOR, 9th Sess., U.N. Doc. A/2693 (1954) [hereinafter 1954 Draft Code].

[32] *See* G.A. Res. 3314, U.N. GAOR, 29th Sess., Supp. No. 31, at 143, U.N. Doc. A/9631 (Dec. 14, 1974). *See also* M. Cherif Bassiouni & Benjamin B. Ferencz, *The Crime Against Peace and Aggression: From Its Origins to the ICC, in* I BASSIOUNI ICL, *supra* note 8, at 207; and *Symposium Issue on the International Criminal Court and the Crime of Aggression*, 41 CASE W. RES. J. INT'L L., issues 2–3 (2009).

[33] *Report of the International Law Commission on the Work of Its Forty-Eighth Session*, [1996] 2 Y.B. Int'l L. Comm'n 17, 45, U.N. Doc. A/CN.4/SER.A/1996/Add.1 (Part 2) [hereinafter 1996 Draft Code of Crimes].

[34] *See* M. Cherif Bassiouni, *International Crimes: The Ratione Materiae of ICL, in* I BASSIOUNI, ICL, *supra* note 8, at 129, 131–32.

opposition by ruling regimes, whose victims can be counted in the millions, have an interest in having clear and unambiguous CAH norms that are likely to apply to them. States, however, may not. The legal elements of CAH are defined as "widespread" or "systematic" attacks on a civilian population whose specific acts are defined, respectively, in article 5 of the ICTY Statute,[35] article 3 of the ICTR Statute,[36] and article 7 of the ICC Statute[37] (all three definitions differ in some respects), which creates too many vulnerabilities for the elites of ruling regimes. Moreover, the list of acts contained in article 7 of the ICC is by far the most extensive list of acts ever produced in any of the twelve existing international definitions for CAH. The definition of genocide, though on its face a more serious crime, is nonetheless less threatening to the elites of ruling regimes because of its "specific intent" requirement. The "general intent" required in all CAH definitions, coupled with the extensive list of enumerated acts and with the catch-all provision of similar acts, is by far more threatening to these elites and to a large segment of their subordinates and the executors of such acts than the charge of genocide. This may, in part, explain why to date, there are only 114 States Parties to the ICC out of 192 United Nations Member States. To place these numbers in perspective, the Geneva Conventions of August 12, 1949 have been ratified by 194 States.[38] The reason for this high level of ratification may be explained by the fact that the conventions do not apply to purely internal conflicts, and that common article 3 of the conventions, which applies to conflicts of a noninternational character, is not exactly the same as the "grave breaches" provision that applies to conflicts of an international character. Common article 3 is jurisdictionally limited and leaves legal wiggle room as to its prohibitions and as to the consequences of its violations. Academic writers in recent years have tried to even out these differences and to treat them as if they had no legal significance, and this perspective has been advanced by the jurisprudence of the ICTY and the ICTR. I assume that the same trend will be followed in the jurisprudence of the ICC. But the practice of States and that of non-State actors lags far behind these progressive developments.

[35] ICTY Statute, *supra* note 28, art. 5.
[36] ICTR Statute, *supra* note 29, art. 3.
[37] See, e.g., Rome Statute of the International Criminal Court, United Nations Diplomatic Conference of Plenipotentiaries on the Establishment of an International Criminal Court, July 17, 1998, art. 7(2)(g), U.N. Doc. A/CONF.183/9 [hereinafter *Rome Statute*] ("'Persecution' means the intentional and severe deprivation of fundamental rights contrary to international law by reason of the identity of the group or collectivity[.]"); art. 7(2)(h) ("'The crime of apartheid' means inhumane acts of a character similar to those referred to in paragraph 1, committed in the context of an institutionalized regime of systematic oppression and domination by one racial group over any other racial group or groups and committed with the intention of maintaining that regime.").
[38] Convention for the Amelioration of the Condition of the Wounded and Sick in Armed Forces in the Field (Geneva Convention I), Aug. 12, 1949, 6 U.S.T. 3114, 75 U.N.T.S. 31; Convention for the Amelioration of the Condition of Wounded, Sick, and Shipwrecked Members of the Armed Forces at Sea (Geneva Convention II), Aug. 12, 1949, 6 U.S.T. 3217, 75 U.N.T.S. 85; Convention Relative to the Treatment of Prisoners of War (Geneva Convention III), Aug. 12, 1949, 6 U.S.T. 3316, 75 U.N.T.S. 135; Convention Relative to the Protection of Civilian Persons in Time of War (Geneva Convention IV), Aug. 12, 1949, 6 U.S.T. 3516, 75 U.N.T.S. 287.

F. The State Policy Characterization of the Crime

"Crimes Against Humanity," as first developed in the IMT Charter and then replicated, with some changes, in the IMTFE Statute and Control Council Law No. 10, was a category of crimes linked to State policy. It was committed by the combatants, agents, and representatives of a State engaged in war, who were acting in furtherance of a State's policy directed against a certain targeted civilian population. "Crimes Against Humanity" were not deemed to be the type of crimes committed by individuals for their own personal reasons. Nor was that category of international crimes deemed to be anything less than the expression of some collective will. Moreover, it was a crime that could be committed at random by a few individuals against certain other individuals chosen at random. There is some debate as to whether this is what was meant by the use of the term "persecution" in the language of the IMT, but that is another issue, in view of the Amending Protocol of October 6, 1945 to the London Charter of August 8, 1945.[39]

The jurisprudence of the ICTY, particularly the case of *Prosecutor v. Kunarac*, has not only misapplied the law with respect to the requirement of a State policy in CAH, but has done so on the basis of a misstatement of precedential authority (in footnote 114 of that opinion).[40] In it, the Tribunal relied on precedents that held to the contrary of the proposition for which these precedents were cited. To the knowledge of this writer, there has never been a similar misrepresentation of the law in the history of international criminal law cases. The only other case involving a false misrepresentation of the facts was before the IMT, where the USSR's prosecutors accused German officers of the *Wehrmacht* of the murder of some 12,000 Polish officers at the Katyn Forest, presumably taken by the Germans as POWs. Instead, it was the USSR's Red Army that had murdered them for fear that they would oppose the Communist takeover of Poland.

The *Kunarac* case,[41] in claiming that the element of State policy never existed, sought to transform the nature of CAH by making it into a crime that non-State actors can be subject to. By removing the State policy requirement, the ICTY made

---

[39] IMT Charter, *supra* note 24.

[40] Prosecutor v. Kunarac, Kovac and Vukovic, Case No. IT-96-23 & 23/1-A, Judgment (June 12, 2002) [hereinafter *Kunarac Appeals Judgment*]. The legislative history of the ICC and the history of CAH does not support the Tribunal's position, *see* BASSIOUNI, LEGISLATIVE HISTORY OF THE ICC, *supra* note 26, at 151–52; BASSIOUNI, CRIMES AGAINST HUMANITY IN INTERNATIONAL CRIMINAL LAW, *supra* note 1, at 243–81. For a critical appraisal of this decision, see William A. Schabas, *State Policy as an Element of International Crimes*, 98 J. CRIM. L. & CRIMINOLOGY 953 (2008); for a contrasting view see generally GUÉNAËL METTRAUX, INTERNATIONAL CRIMES AND THE AD HOC TRIBUNALS 172 (2005); Guénaël Mettraux, *Crimes Against Humanity in the Jurisprudence of the International Criminal Tribunals for the Former Yugoslavia and for Rwanda*, 43 HARV. INT'L L.J. 237, 271–83 (2002) (arguing that customary international law tells us that the enumerated acts will amount to CAH if they are committed *as part of a widespread or systematic attack directed against any civilian population or any identifiable group*); and Guénaël Mettraux, *The Definition of Crimes Against Humanity and the Question of a 'Policy' Element* in this volume.

[41] *See Kunarac Appeals Judgment*, *supra* note 40, ¶ 98. *See also* Prosecutor v. Blaskić, Case No. IT-95-14-A, Judgment, ¶ 120 (July 29, 2004); Prosecutor v. Kordić et al., Case No. IT-95-14/2-A, Judgment, ¶ 98 (Dec. 17, 2004).

CAH similar to domestic crimes that became international when committed on a "widespread" or "systematic" basis. This means that human rights depredations amounting to the acts described in the Statute when committed by certain State agents for their own purposes in an internal context amount to an international crime. Thus, a "widespread" practice of police torture in a given city becomes part of CAH. Similarly, the "widespread" acts of killing by drug cartels in certain countries become CAH. The implication of such a transformation of CAH needs to be carefully assessed. Whereas such an extension of international criminal responsibility is laudable, and may one day be even attainable, it is presently, to return to an earlier characterization, a "bridge too far." Admittedly, that which was a "bridge too far" in 1919 became the bridge in 1945, and maybe this new development, as legally incorrect as it is, may also ripen one day into a new paradigm of CAH. Of this new development, Schabas wrote as follows:

> In Jelisić, the ICTY had relied on a literal reading of the definition of [genocide]. The text of the definition contains no explicit requirement of a plan or policy. Similarly, with respect to crimes against humanity, the text of the Statute contains no explicit requirement of a plan or policy. On the other hand, the Appeals Chamber noted that there had been a significant debate on the matter in the case law and the academic literature. Astonishingly, however, the discussion of this important point was confined to a footnote in the judgment of the Appeals Chamber! When the authorities cited in the reference are scrutinized, it is not at all apparent how many of them assist in the conclusion that a State plan or policy is not an element of crimes against humanity.
>
> Generally speaking, the ICTYs very summary discussion of the issue of a State plan or policy with respect to both crimes against humanity and genocide has an air of the superficial. The result reached – that a State plan or policy is not a required element – appears to be a results-oriented decision rather than a profound analysis of the history of the two crimes or of their theoretical underpinnings. The ICTY also appears to have ignored the drafting histories of the crimes as well as subsequent developments such as the work of the International Law Commission.[42]

By 1998, when the ICC Statute was adopted, the war crimes connection was removed from article 7.[43] The rationale was that the evolution of customary international law from the 1950 ILC report, which concluded that "Crimes Against Humanity" applied in times of war and peace, to the 1990s Statutes of the ICTY and the ICTR and subsequent jurisprudence had achieved the level required by customary international law. The writings of "the most distinguished publicists" and other sources of international law added that CAH has reached a level of recognition deemed to constitute part of *jus cogens* – an inderogable and peremptory norm of international law.[44] This is indeed a far-reaching development since the 1919 initial effort to articulate a new international crime called "crimes against the laws of humanity."

---

[42] Schabas, *supra* note 40, at 959–60.
[43] *Rome Statute*, *supra* note 37, art. 7.
[44] M. Cherif Bassiouni, *International Crimes: Jus Cogens and Obligatio Erga Omnes*, 59 L. & CONTEMP. PROBS. 63 (1996).

III. CONCLUSION

The historical evolution of CAH, slow and tortured as it was, has not yet settled into its final form. Its nature, scope, application, and legal elements are still somewhat unsettled. This covers a range of legal issues of which the foremost is whether the nature of the crime is about State policy or not and whether the crime essentially protects a targeted civilian population.

What is meant by "civilian population," how is it to be defined, and how large or small is the protected group are questions that bring to mind, by analogy, an incident that occurred in 1920. Shortly after President Wilson announced his Fourteen Points, which included what was interpreted as a right to self-determination – though it was not – the inhabitants of a building in St. Petersburg sent a petition to the League of Nations seeking to self-determine.[45] Today's question would be whether the inhabitants of a building, or of a neighborhood, or of a village may constitute a "civilian population."

In 1994, as Chairman of the United National Security Council Commission to investigate Violations of International Humanitarian Law in the former Yugoslavia, I joined my colleagues on the Commission to find that within the province of Prijedor, genocide was committed because the targeted Muslim population (by the Serbs) was reduced by 90 percent, from an estimated 50,000 to an estimated 5,000.[46] Was the geographic area sufficient, and was it enough to encompass a targeted group within it even though the larger membership in that targeted group exceeded its local members?

Another question is whether CAH extends to the practices of State agents not acting as part of a State policy. For example, does CAH extend to the members of a given police department in a given city or village that "systematically" torture everyone suspected of a crime? And does it apply to non-State actors, such as an organized crime group, who "systematically" torture and kill people in a given region?

Other questions pertain to the "general part," such as intent and mistake of fact, as well as questions pertaining to the "special part" concerning, for example, the extent of "other inhumane acts." Moreover, such elements as "widespread" and "systematic" are, notwithstanding the ICTY and the ICTR jurisprudence, in need of clarification.

The policy and legal implications of how elastic CAH is to become will impact the willingness of States to subject themselves to this type of international criminal responsibility. More significantly, one should ask whether the expansion of CAH to non-State actors is likely to enhance compliance and strengthen international and national enforcement. Will it enhance international prosecution?

---

[45] See Robert A. Friedlander, *Self-Determination: A Legal-Political Inquiry*, 1975 DETROIT C. L. REV. 71 (1975).

[46] See *First Interim Report of the Commission of Experts Established Pursuant to Security Council Resolution 780 (1992)*, U.N. SCOR, Annex, U.N. Doc. S/25274 (Feb. 10, 1993); *id.* at Annex V (The Prijedor Report).

Will it advance inter-State cooperation in the repression of international crimes?

This is an opportunity for the international community to ponder these and other questions, and reach the conclusion that an international convention on CAH is needed – a convention that will reinforce the ICC Statute, clarify some of its slight ambiguities, and shield it from the negative consequences of the ICTY's erroneous jurisprudence mentioned earlier. More importantly, such a convention is needed to fill the gap in national criminal legislation and to become the basis for more effective bilateral and multilateral international cooperation in the prevention, control, and repression of CAH.

These policy goals cannot be achieved by altering the nature of CAH, extending it without limits to non-State actors, removing the State policy requirement, and removing the collective nature of the protected group reflected in the term "civilian population." The best approach is to have a convention redefine CAH. In time, something can be done about the ICC's article 7. The ICC's Assembly of States Parties (ASP) can adopt a clarification statement that could be deemed interpretive and thus followed by the Court. The Statute does not, however, provide for this approach. Another approach is for the Appellate Chamber of the ICC to interpret "organizational policy" as extending the requirement of State policy to non-State actors who have the capacity for developing such organizational policy. Under both approaches, State policy would apply for State actors and organizational policy would apply for non-State actors who have some of the characteristics of State actors, whereas this would not correspond to what was understood at the Rome Diplomatic Conference, as stated by this author, namely:

> Contrary to what some advocates advance, Article 7 does not bring a new development to crimes against humanity, namely its applicability to non-State actors. If that were the case, the mafia, for example, could be charged with such crimes before the ICC, and that is clearly neither the letter nor the spirit of Article 7. The question arose after 9/11 as to whether a group such as al-Qaeda, which operates on a worldwide basis and is capable of inflicting significant harm in more than one State, falls within this category. In this author's opinion, such a group does not qualify for inclusion within the meaning of crimes against humanity as defined in Article 7, and for that matter, under any definition of that crime up to Article 6(c) of the IMT, notwithstanding the international dangers that it poses.... The text [of Article 7(2)] clearly refers to State policy, and the words "organisational policy" do not refer to the policy of an organisation, but the policy of a State. It does not refer to non-State actors.[47]

Lastly, another approach would be to have a protocol to the ICC amending article 7 to specifically include non-State actors. The likelihood of that prospect for the Review Conference scheduled in 2010 is, however, very slim. Moreover, the ICC's

---

[47] BASSIOUNI, LEGISLATIVE HISTORY OF THE ICC, *supra* note 24, at 151–52. *See also supra* note 40.

amending procedures are cumbersome and require the approval of seven-eighths of States Parties.[48]

It is nothing short of amazing that since World War II, CAH has not been codified in an international Convention. Instead, we have witnessed at least twelve definitions contained in various international instruments such as the ILC's 1996 Draft Code of Crimes Against the Peace and Security of Mankind, the ICTY's article 3, the ICTR's article 5, and the ICC's article 7. Other definitions are contained in the statutes of the mixed-model tribunals established in the last few years. These diverse definitions undermine the certainty of customary international law, and this can only be cured by an international Convention.

There are two additional reasons why such a Convention is needed. The first is that, notwithstanding the fact that 114 States are part of the ICC, the Statute does not contain provisions on inter-State cooperation in connection with any of the crimes within the ICC's jurisdiction. The Statute regulates relations between the ICC and its States Parties. It does not regulate relations between States Parties. The ICC Statute does not apply to non-States Parties, nor does it apply as between States Parties and non-States Parties. Complementarity as between the ICC's States Parties cannot exist without a treaty basis, and the same is true with respect to non-States Parties' inter-State cooperation for the enforcement of CAH with States Parties. Thus, an enormous gap exists between States Parties and between States Parties and non-States Parties, which only a treaty can fill. Such a treaty should retain the definition of the ICC's article 7 in order to build on the consensus already existing between 114 States that are ICC States Parties, but add substantial and detailed provisions on the obligations of States in carrying out the maxim *aut dedere aut judicare*.[49]

Detailed and specific provisions on inter-State cooperation in the areas of fair and effective investigations, prosecutions, and punishment of persons found guilty of CAH are indispensable. Moreover, such a Convention should contain provisions emphasizing States' obligations to prevent the occurrence or recurrence of CAH.

The normative gap that presently exists in the international legal framework must, therefore, be filled. Considering that between 1948 and 2008, based on a worldwide study conducted by forty-two experts under this author's direction and recently published,[50] there have been some 310 conflicts that generated an estimated 100 million victims, and that CAH have been committed in all these conflicts, the need for a Convention is both essential and urgent.[51]

---

[48] Rome Statute, *supra* note 37, art. 121. *See also* Roger S. Clark, *Article 121 Amendments*, in COMMENTARY OF THE ROME STATUTE OF THE INTERNATIONAL CRIMINAL COURT: OBSERVERS' NOTES, ARTICLE BY ARTICLE (Otto Triffterer ed., 2d ed. 2008).
[49] *See* M. CHERIF BASSIOUNI & EDWARD M. WISE, AUT DEDERE AUT JUDICARE: THE DUTY TO EXTRADITE OR PROSECUTE IN INTERNATIONAL LAW (1995).
[50] THE PURSUIT OF INTERNATIONAL CRIMINAL JUSTICE: A WORLD STUDY ON CONFLICTS, VICTIMIZATION, AND POST-CONFLICT JUSTICE (M. Cherif Bassiouni ed., 2010).
[51] This call was urged in M. Cherif Bassiouni, *"Crimes Against Humanity": The Need for a Specialized Convention*, 31 COLUM. J. TRANSNAT'L L. 457–94 (1994).

4

The Bright Red Thread

The Politics of International Criminal Law – Do We Want Peace or Justice? The West African Experience

David M. Crane[*]

I. INTRODUCTION

International criminal law is about politics. It is a naïve Chief Prosecutor who plans for and executes his prosecution plan (if he or she has one) without keeping in mind the bright red thread of politics that permeates the entire existence of a tribunal or court. Conceived due to a political event and a creature of political compromise, politics is in the DNA of all of the justice mechanisms that make up the modern era of international criminal justice.

Today, the climate is once again politically charged as the international community begins to adjust its thinking about how to solve diplomatically, in an acceptable manner, the indictment of the sitting President of the Sudan, Omar al-Bashir. The clarion calls by various States and organizations for peace first, maybe justice later, with a mounting pressure to defer the arrest warrant for a year, are familiar. These threats, comments, and histrionics are the very same as when I unsealed the indictment of then-President Charles Taylor of Liberia in June 2003. At the end of the day, his indictment brought a more sustainable peace for the people of Liberia, and Bashir's indictment will do the same for the people of the Sudan. It will be interesting to watch how this political process plays out.

This paper will use as a case study the development, planning, and execution of a political event that ultimately set into motion the prosecution of the various warring factions of Sierra Leone in the 1990s. The events triggered a raging debate related to peace and justice. Ultimately does the international community want peace, or does it want justice? I will first consider the general arguments related to peace and justice and then review the development of the world's first hybrid international tribunal called the Special Court for Sierra Leone. Subsequently, I will take up our case study on Operation Justice and then conclude with some lessons learned and further considerations related to the question: can one have true peace without justice?

---

[*] Professor of Practice, Syracuse University College of Law. Former founding Chief Prosecutor of the Special Court for Sierra Leone, an international war crimes tribunal for West Africa, 2002–2005. I want to thank my research assistant Sarah Marquez, Syracuse University College of Law Class of 2010, for her help with this chapter.

II. BACKGROUND: DO YOU WANT PEACE OR JUSTICE – ARE THEY COMPATIBLE?

Since the end of World War II, mass atrocities such as genocide and ethnic cleansing have increasingly been at the forefront of international law and politics. This emphasis can be traced to the trend toward "increased and deliberate targeting of civilians" during warfare, with civilians now constituting almost eighty percent of casualties.[1] However, the focus on the fight against impunity and the demand for accountability has illuminated a fundamental conflict in philosophies on how individual countries and the international community as a whole should proceed following civil wars and large-scale human rights abuses: When should the pursuit of justice give way to the need to create conditions most favorable to a peaceful resolution of a conflict?[2] More specifically, is it ever appropriate to grant amnesty to those responsible for mass atrocities as a means to secure a stable transition from conflict to peace?[3] Are the goals of peace and justice mutually exclusive?

Justice for War Criminals

The possibility that State actors could be held criminally liable for State crimes emerged following World War II, when American diplomacy suggested a legal approach to determining the fates of the surviving leaders of Nazi Germany and Japan.[4] Whereas leaders such as Stalin and Churchill favored large-scale, summary executions, a process of criminal trials prevailed.[5] The trials at Nuremberg and Tokyo "conveyed to the world the full horror of the Nazi period to a wide segment of the public."[6]

Although the Cold War made these types of international trials less feasible, Nuremberg and Tokyo set very important precedents. First, according to Nuremberg Prosecutor and U.S. Supreme Court Justice Robert Jackson, the trials documented Nazi war crimes "with such authenticity and in such detail that there can be no responsible denial of these crimes in the future."[7] Along with creating an undeniable record of the horrors of the era, Nuremberg and Tokyo contributed to the legitimization of international law.[8]

Since the end of the Cold War, there has been renewed intergovernmental interest in prosecuting those responsible for human rights abuses.[9] There are

---

[1] Rama Mani, *Balancing Peace with Justice in the Aftermath of Violent Conduct*, 48 Dev. 25 (2005).
[2] Beatriz Pavon, *Combating Impunity: Transitional Justice in the Aftermath of Mass Atrocities*, 41 U.N. Chron. 22 (2004); David Tolbert, *International Criminal Law: Past and Future*, 30 U. Pa. J. Int'l L. 1281, 1282 (2009).
[3] Pavon, *supra* note 2, at 22.
[4] Richard Falk, *Criminal Accountability in Transitional Justice*, 12 Peace Rev. 81 (2000); Lisa J. LaPlante, *Outlawing Amnesty: The Return of Criminal Justice in Transitional Justice Schemes*, 49 Va. J. Int'l L. 915, 923 (2009).
[5] Falk, *supra* note 4.
[6] *Id.*
[7] Michael P. Scharf, *From the eXile Files: An Essay on Trading Justice for Peace*, 63 Wash. & Lee L. Rev. 339, 348 (2006).
[8] David O. Friedrichs, *The Paradoxes of Transitional Justice*, 12 Peace Rev. 155 (2000).
[9] Falk, *supra* note 4.

several arguments in support of prosecutions. First, prosecutions are necessary to legitimize the legal system and discourage future human rights abuses.[10] Prosecution is vital to not only deter those responsible for the specific crimes at issue but also to send a message to the world that these types of abuses will not be tolerated.[11]

Several well-known examples are illustrative of how the failure to seek justice following human rights abuses has led to more conflict, destruction, and killing. After Charles Taylor was forced from power, and before his eventual trial, he was allowed to live in exile at a seaside villa in Nigeria.[12] From this location, he ordered the assassination of President Conte of Guinea.[13] Although the plot was unsuccessful, it shows how former leaders who are not brought to justice can continue to create chaos.[14]

Sending a message to leaders of other countries is also an important type of deterrence. In maybe one of the most notorious and well-documented statements made after genocide went largely ignored by the international community, Adolph Hitler responded to concerns about his plans of genocide by stating "who now remembers the Armenians?," a reference to the massacre of more than one million Armenians during World War I.[15] Similarly, after serving as the Prosecutor of the International Criminal Tribunal for the former Yugoslavia, Richard Goldstone stated his belief that the Serbs took note of the international community's failure to prosecute criminals such as Pol Pot, Idi Amin, Saddam Hussein, and Mohammed Aidid before pursuing their course of human rights abuses.[16]

Second, pursuing justice following human rights abuses is often seen as a moral duty to the victims of these crimes.[17] When dealing with crimes such as rape and murder, prosecutions can "give significance to the victims' suffering and serve as a partial remedy for their injuries."[18] An extension of the argument is that by acknowledging victims and their pain, prosecutions can lessen the likelihood of vigilante justice by those who feel that their suffering was never redressed.[19]

Finally, bringing war criminals to justice creates an indelible record of the crimes committed. Nuremberg Prosecutor Robert Jackson first noted the importance of this function following World War II, and the argument still holds true today. Trials help bring out the truth and extent of human rights abuses in both an official and public fashion.

---

[10] Scharf, *supra* note 7, at 349.
[11] *Id.*; Charles P. Trumbull IV, *Giving Amnesties a Second Chance*, 25 BERKELEY J. INT'L L. 283, 284 (2007).
[12] Scharf, *supra* note 7, at 348.
[13] *Id.*
[14] *Id.*
[15] Trumbull, *supra* note 11, at 305.
[16] *Id.*
[17] Scharf, *supra* note 7, at 348.
[18] *Id.*
[19] *Id.*

Does the Pursuit of Justice Inhibit Peaceful Resolutions?

Despite the arguments in favor of the prosecution of war criminals, many still believe that amnesty or exile can be appropriate in certain situations. The main argument in favor of subordinating justice to peace is that "insisting on criminal prosecutions can prolong the conflict, resulting in more deaths, destructions, and human suffering."[20] To that end, during the last quarter-century, countries including Angola, Argentina, Brazil, Cambodia, Chile, El Salvador, Guatemala, Haiti, Honduras, Ivory Coast, Nicaragua, Peru, South Africa, Togo, and Uruguay have granted amnesty for war crimes to former leaders as part of peace agreements.[21]

The rationale for promoting peace at the expense of prosecutions is that by retaining amnesty and asylum as bargaining chips, peace negotiations are far more likely to be successful.[22] Leaders who believe that a trial and a guilty verdict are inevitable following surrender have nothing to lose by continuing their reign of terror and are far less likely to participate in successful negotiations.[23] Thus, an insistence on justice in the face of resistance can endanger both peace and peacekeepers. It is also argued that traditional criminal prosecutions are often not tailored to the circumstances of particular conflicts, and that those responsible for the prosecutions fail to consider other, more effective mechanisms.[24]

Many of those advocating granting amnesty in certain circumstances disagree with the premise that prosecutions have any deterrent effect. Because many of those committing human rights crimes cannot be viewed as rational actors, it is argued that even if provided with objective information, these war criminals assume they will win the war and view the odds of facing punishment as highly unlikely.[25] In addition, there is little empirical evidence that publicized trials have deterred other human rights abuses; in fact, many of the worst atrocities in Yugoslavia occurred after the inception of the International Criminal Tribunal for the former Yugoslavia.[26]

Finally, there is disagreement over the idea that traditional prosecutions actually bring out the truth. Although proponents of this argument agree that full factual accounting is necessary to achieve peace, they argue that evidence and testimony may be excluded during the trial process as required by due process.[27] Moreover, they argue, witnesses' credibility will be attacked during testimony, undermining the defendant's responsibility and accountability.[28] Furthermore, because of limited

---

[20] *Id.* at 342.
[21] *Id.*
[22] Tolbert, *supra* note 2, at 1291.
[23] *Id.*
[24] Philip Kastner, *The ICC in Darfur – Savior or Spoiler?*, 14 ILSA J. INT'L & COMP. L. 145, 149 (2007).
[25] Kathleen Ellen MacMillan, *The Practicability of Amnesty as a Non-Prosecutory Alternative in Post-Conflict Uganda*, 6 CARDOZO PUB. L. POL'Y & ETHICS J. 199, 220 (2007).
[26] *Id.* at 219.
[27] *Id.* at 214–15.
[28] *Id.* at 215.

resources, trials will focus on the regime leaders, as well as leaving untouched the cases of victimizers who were also victims.[29]

Although many scholars cast the overarching peace-versus-justice debate in black and white, an emerging viewpoint posits that both peace and justice can be pursued following conflict. Importantly, prosecutors must first "take into account the potential of any trials to create difficulties for fragile new democratic regimes attempting to move forward in a spirit of rebuilding and reconciliation."[30] Emphasis is placed on the sequencing of events in a manner that decreases the possibility that peace and justice jeopardize each other.[31]

The pursuit of justice in the guise of criminal prosecutions is viewed as one aspect of a multifaceted approach. Other important steps should be taken to prevent the recurrence of human rights abuses, including the establishment of truth commissions that allow all victims to be heard, reparations, and the disqualification of perpetrators from government and politics.[32] An important part of any multifaceted approach is cooperation between the international community and recovering societies to determine how best to adapt these approaches to fit each country's particular needs.[33]

A New Justice Mechanism – The Special Court for Sierra Leone

1. The Request

In March 1991, the tragedy of the civil war in Sierra Leone began with an invasion from Liberia into the eastern diamond fields of that backwater of a country.[34] The invasion consisted of various units and criminal elements from across West Africa, to include the Revolutionary United Front led by Foday Sankoh, Guineans, Burkinaps, Liberians, and Special Forces from Libya.

For more than ten years, a joint criminal enterprise, led by then-President Charles Taylor, on behalf of Muammar Ghadafi, murdered, raped, maimed, and mutilated around 1.2 million human beings to further their own personal criminal gain by moving diamonds about for guns and cash.[35] These guns and cash were used in the overall geopolitical plan to turn all of West Africa into a Libyan fiefdom. Many of

---

[29] Id.
[30] Friedrichs, *supra* note 8.
[31] Yasmin Sooka, *Dealing with the Past and Transitional Justice: Building Peace Through Accountability*, 88 INT'L REV. RED CROSS 311 (2006).
[32] Pavon, *supra* note 2, at 22.
[33] Id. at 23.
[34] For an overview of the conflict, see DAVID PRATT, SIERRA LEONE: THE FORGOTTEN CRISIS, (1999), *available at* http://www.globalsecurity.org/military/library/report/1999/crisis-e.htm (Report to the Ministry of Foreign Affairs [Canada]). For a more detailed history of the ten-year civil war, see Babafemi Akinrinade, *International Humanitarian Law and the Conflict in Sierra Leone*, 15 NOTRE DAME J.L. ETHICS & PUB. POL'Y 391 (2001).
[35] Alhaji M. S. Bah, *Diamonds and Mercenaries: Exploring the Dynamics of the Sierra Leone Conflict*, 29 PEACEKEEPING & INT'L REL. 1 (2000).

the players in this horror were graduates of the terrorist training camps in Libya.[36] In this armed conflict, the combatants committed atrocities beyond description. Sierra Leone became a killing field, truly a hell on earth.

In 2000, the President of Sierra Leone, Tejan Kabbah, a retired United Nations employee, wrote the Secretary-General of the United Nations Kofi Annan, asking him for assistance in developing an accounting mechanism for the apparent war crimes and crimes against humanity perpetrated in his country.[37] The domestic court system, in large part, no longer existed and was incapable of dealing with prosecuting up to 30,000 alleged perpetrators.

2. The Response

Faced with the enormity of the tragedy, the United Nations was compelled to act, despite a great deal of initial reluctance. At the time, the world was frustrated with the cost of international criminal justice. The International Criminal Court did not exist, and the ad hoc tribunals were moving slowly forward with no end in sight, because none had a prosecution plan or an exit strategy. The cost was high, coming in at more than $250 million per year to sustain the effort in The Hague and Arusha. The total cost for the two tribunals in 2000 was more than $1.2 billion.[38] The Security Council was not going to sanction another ad hoc effort. The question at the time was: Could international criminal justice be effectively and efficiently applied in a politically acceptable time frame? Essentially, this was a political question.

In August 2000, the Security Council passed a resolution calling on the Secretary-General to study the problem and recommend an alternative mechanism to deal with what took place in Sierra Leone.[39] The result was the development of the world's first hybrid international war crimes tribunal called the Special Court for Sierra Leone.[40] In January 2002, the United Nations, on behalf of the international community, signed a treaty with the Republic of Sierra Leone creating this bold new experiment in international accountability.[41]

In April of that same year, I was appointed Chief Prosecutor; I arrived in Sierra Leone in August 2002 with a ten-phase prosecution plan. We were already in phase three when I arrived on a rainy day with my special assistant and political advisor,

---

[36] STEVEN D. ROPERT & LILIAN A. BARRIA, DESIGNING CRIMINAL TRIBUNALS: SOVEREIGNTY AND INTERNATIONAL CONCERNS IN THE PROTECTION OF HUMAN RIGHTS 31 (2006).

[37] Letter from Ahmad Tejan Kabbah, President of Sierra Leone, to Kofi Annan, U.N. Secretary-General, U.N. Doc. S/2000/786, Annex (June 12, 2000); Lome Peace Agreement between the Government of Sierra Leone and the Revolutionary United Front of Sierra Leone, July 7, 1999, *available at* http://www.undemocracy.com/S-1999-777.pdf.

[38] *See* ROPERT & BARRIA, *supra* note 36, at 29 (discussing concerns regarding the cost of international criminal justice at the time of the creation of the Special Court for Sierra Leone).

[39] S.C. Res. 1315, U.N. Doc. S/RES/1315 (Aug. 14, 2000).

[40] Statute of the Special Court for Sierra Leone, Jan. 16, 2002, 2178 U.N.T.S. 138.

[41] Agreement Between the United Nations and the Government of Sierra Leone on the Establishment of a Special Court for Sierra Leone arts. 1, 2, Jan. 16, 2002, U.N. Doc. S/2002/246/Annex.

along with my Chief of Investigations. I had three suitcases and no place to live, yet we went straight to work according to the plan.

3. The Mandate

Our mandate was to prosecute those who bore the greatest responsibility for war crimes and crimes against humanity stemming from the ten-year-long civil war in Sierra Leone.[42] As stated earlier, international tribunals are creatures of political events, and their conception is one of political compromise. The compromise for this international tribunal was "greatest responsibility."[43]

The international community got it right this time. This mandate, a political document, allowed me to accomplish my goals within a politically acceptable time frame. It was now up to my plan and the hard work of the Office of the Prosecutor working together with the Registrar and his team to achieve the efficiency and effectiveness aspects of the Security Council's directive.

4. Execution

As I have alluded to, I developed a plan that laid out our work in Sierra Leone over a period of three to four years. The phases and milestones followed a standard common law pattern. Frankly, it was not rocket science, just good old common sense, dedication, and hard work. The plan was broken down into five parts: office setup, investigation/indictment, pretrial, trial, and appeals. Currently, the Court is in the appeals phase, with the exception of the trial of former President Charles Taylor.[44] The Court is scheduled to complete all of its work in 2010–2011.

Our execution of the plan called for some unique and innovative ideas, including creating an academic consortium, establishing an outreach and legacy plan to include the town hall program, a witness management program, along with a new format for the indictments.

The academic consortium: It was designed to be an education program for law students, as well as a support mechanism for the Office of the Prosecutor. The academic consortium proved its worth by saving my office countless hours and millions of dollars in attorney time. As an education program, hundreds of law students have had the unique opportunity to be involved in a real-world international prosecution. Their work product, supervised by a professor, has been exceptional and has contributed to the advancement of international criminal law.

The Outreach and Legacy program: It must be understood that an international war crimes tribunal is for and about the victims, their families, their towns, and their

---

[42] Statute of the Special Court for Sierra Leone, *supra* note 40, art. 15.
[43] *See* The Secretary-General, *Report of the Secretary-General to the Security Council on the Establishment of a Special Court for Sierra Leone*, U.N. Doc. S/2000/915 (Oct. 4, 2000).
[44] The leadership of the Revolutionary United Front were convicted essentially as charged in early March 2009.

districts. A busy tribunal tends to lose sight of this important fact. After all, it is the people who will have to live with the results, thus it is imperative that they understand and respect the process. This can only be done by reaching out and having an ongoing dialog with them. We did this in Sierra Leone through our outreach and legacy program. The cornerstone in the Special Court's outreach program was the town hall meeting concept, originally started by me on my arrival in Sierra Leone. During my first four months in the country, I literally walked the entire countryside, listening to the people of Sierra Leone – my client – tell me about what took place there during the decade-long civil war. It allowed me, in some small way, to appreciate the pain and the suffering that took place. Additionally, it allowed them to see their prosecutor and to ask him questions. During the three years this program was in place, I spoke to thousands upon thousands of West Africans, returning many times to report to them on how their court was doing. Augmented by an Outreach Office within the Registry, the program became a huge success. The International Criminal Court has established a similar program, modeled on our work in Sierra Leone. Legacy is also a key to success for any tribunal. From the very beginning, we attempted many programs, some with great success. Our goal was to leave a dedicated cadre of lawyers, investigators, and court administrators in Sierra Leone who could begin to rebuild the devastated judiciary and to establish respect for the rule of law. The legacy program is ongoing. I left Sierra Leone in the summer of 2005, secure in the knowledge that West Africans understood that the law can be fair, that no one is above the law, and that the rule of law is more powerful than the rule of the gun.

The witness management program: Any prosecutor worth his salt will ensure that his witnesses are accounted and cared for in an appropriate way. This is no different at the international level, yet prior to our arrival in West Africa, such a program had never been attempted before. Because of the fact that all of our evidence would come from witness testimony, we needed to ensure their testimony was truthful, accurate, and that they were secure in the knowledge that they would be protected, based on the threat level assessed over time. Our intent, working with the Victims and Witness Support Unit within the Registry, was to make sure that all witnesses for the prosecution arrived safe, healthy, briefed, and with knowledge of the process they were about to undergo. For witnesses in a third-world setting, with competing cultural perspectives, this could take up to two years, particularly for child and female victims of horrors not describable in this setting. Of the 300 witnesses who testified overall, very few refused to testify. Only one witness died, and that was due to natural causes. This is a credit to our witness management team.

Charging and formatting: Early on in the prosecution plan, I wanted to change the way persons accused of international crimes are charged. My review of indictments coming out of the other tribunals showed that those indictments were too long, inaccurate, and fraught with potential legal land mines. This had to change. What we finally decided to do was to make the indictment simple and direct. As a prosecutor in the United States, I firmly believed in the principle that if you plead it, you have to prove it. Thus, we did something that had never been done before: notice pleading. The indictments are shorter, tighter, cleaner, yet give the indictees the degree of notice required for them to understand the crimes they committed, where they committed them, and when. These indictments have withstood legal challenge.

III. THE CASE STUDY: OPERATION JUSTICE

The initial success of my office's plan was not legal, but political and military, deriving from solid leadership and management principles learned from three decades of practicing law, as well as leading and managing various organizations. My legal training had little to do with developing the prosecution's strategic plan and its early execution. This part of the chapter will look at how my office developed, planned, organized, and executed Operation Justice – the takedown of all of the existing indictees found in Sierra Leone in a one-hour-long arrest operation, with the hope of minimal disruption and as few casualties as possible.

1. The Preparations

Discussions of an arrest operation began a month before I even left for Sierra Leone. I had put together an initial team of Americans to assist me in the development of my strategic plan, a plan I had made public in May 2002 at the United States Institute of Peace in Washington, DC.[45] As we considered a myriad of personnel, logistical, and operational issues, we realized early on that actually being in the country where the alleged war crimes had taken place, with the perpetrators of those crimes roaming freely about the area, would be a challenge to the success or failure of my strategic plan.[46]

It is important to note that the planning for the arrest operation was being done simultaneously with the investigation of an initial list of potential indictees to include major political figures in West Africa, all of whom were not interested in seeing the Special Court, and my office in particular, succeed.[47] Each figure in the investigation was well aware of the role they and others played in the decade-long civil war that had plagued Sierra Leone and Liberia, as well as Guinea and the Ivory Coast.

Our July 2002 meeting took place in Washington, DC. I had just retired from the federal service, and we were all technically working for the Special Court. Alan White and Bobby Bridges had just returned from a week-long advance trip to look

---

[45] The initial team was Dr. Alan White, Chief of Investigations; Frank Fountain, Chief of Prosecutions; Michael Pan, Special Assistant; Bobby Bridges, Legal Administrator; Terry Spearman, Legal Administrator. Present at the USIP briefing were representatives from key NGOs, the U.S. Government, and the United Nations.

[46] It ended up being a great help in the execution of Operation Justice itself. Being on the scene is a definite advantage for a prosecutor executing his prosecution strategy.

[47] Such potential indictees included three heads of State: Muammar Ghadaffi of Libya; Blasé Campare of Burkina Faso; and Charles Taylor of Liberia. Additionally, I considered the President of Sierra Leone, Tejan Kabbah, and his sitting Minister of Interior, Hinga Norman.

for a possible headquarters for my office and a place to live, as well as to link up with the Inspector General of the Sierra Leone National Police, Keith Biddle. Their assessment was grim. Though they had found what appeared to be a good location for the Office of the Prosecutor, called Seaview, they were overwhelmed by the sheer magnitude of the destruction of the area. There was no running water to speak of and only intermittent electricity.

Seaview was a two-acre compound with a solidly built mansion and high walls topped by razor wire. The Lebanese merchant who had built it two decades ago had planned the house to be a virtual fortress defended from any threat, with bullet-proof windows, an indirect driveway to deter any vehicle crashing both the gates and the front door, and a front door that was blast-proof, strong enough to withstand fire from a rocket-propelled grenade. The challenge, however, was that it was largely gutted after having been the scene of a battle between members of the Armed Forces Revolutionary Council and ECOMOG troops in the late 1990s. Though a group of Canadian peacekeepers had been housed there prior to our arrival, the Seaview compound needed work before it could house our office and apartments.

Despite the drawbacks, Seaview was the best place to defend and to carry out our initial work securely – a major priority of mine throughout our setup phase.[48] This aside, we reviewed potential indictees and agreed to send Frank Fountain to meet with a key insider witness in Burkina Faso to discuss his possible support to the investigations and to assess his credibility.[49] Frank would leave at the beginning of August and meet us in Freetown two weeks later.

Additionally, we agreed that when the time came in March of the following year to arrest our indictees, we would have to do it in a sweeping operation, taking all of them down at once.[50] This would take the support of many nations and organizations to successfully complete. The planning began with various milestones and the identification of key players to assist my office in the arrest operation we called "Operation Justice." At this point, the operation was classified "highly sensitive," with limited persons given access to the plan.[51]

The operation would involve several local, regional, and international players, all of which had to be approached for their initial support. This would begin in late July in London, followed by discussions in Freetown with the American Ambassador, the

---

[48] My biggest fear throughout my time in Sierra Leone was that one of my people would be kidnapped and used as a bargaining chip to get me to drop charges against an indictee. That potential threat remained throughout my time in Sierra Leone.

[49] Doug Farah of the *Washington Post* had asked for assistance in protecting this witness from an imminent assassination attempt by President Charles Taylor in July 2002. We would eventually have to send a plane with our investigators in early December 2002 to save that witness from a death squad that had been launched according to a confidential source in Taylor's government to take out the witness and his family. We beat the death squad by an hour.

[50] Because the main actors were still living and working in Sierra Leone with tremendous political clout or influence, and to limit the potential disruption of the Special Court and the sitting government, it was essential for a simultaneous takedown.

[51] We mirrored the protection of our documents similar to the U.S. classification system: Confidential/Secret = Operationally Sensitive; Top Secret = Operationally Highly Sensitive.

British High Commissioner, the UN peacekeeping force, and the Inspector General of the Sierra Leone National Police.

My initial trip to London began on July 27, 2002, lasting several days. Our intent was to meet key persons in the Foreign Commonwealth Office and the Defence Ministry at Whitehall. The focus was to outline my strategic plan and to develop a level of trust and confidence in that plan before I left for Freetown. I also flew to The Hague to outline my strategy to the Dutch government. My initial impression was that the British government was impressed but skeptical. The Dutch were polite yet held their cards close to their chest.

We flew to Freetown on August 6, 2002 and were hosted by Keith and Suzanne Biddle.[52] We stayed in their home for more than two weeks while we prepared Seaview for occupation. It was an onerous task, yet by the third week, Seaview was ready for operations. Frank Fountain arrived from Burkina Faso after his meetings with the insider witness. His assessment was favorable and he felt that the witness could be trusted. The witness gave us some initial material that we began to review, along with some leads to key witnesses who all turned out to be important. It was this witness, among others, who would help us crack the inner circle of Charles Taylor, Blasé Compare, and Muammar Ghadafi, and who also helped us understand the extent of the West African Joint Criminal Enterprise.

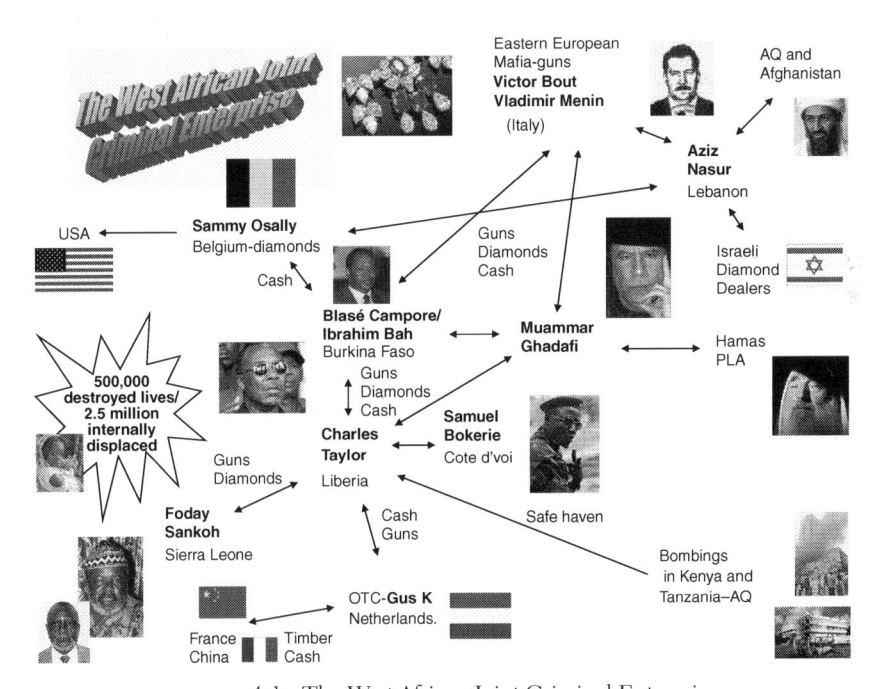

FIGURE 4.1. The West African Joint Criminal Enterprise

---

[52] The Biddles were a wonderful couple who had lived in Freetown for years. Keith Biddle was a retired senior inspector of police in Britain and had been seconded to help the President of Sierra Leone rebuild the Sierra Leone National Police. Without Keith Biddle, we would have been severely hampered in the initial setup of our investigative plans. He left Sierra Leone in May 2003.

During this time frame, I met with Alan Jones, the British High Commissioner, and asked if he would be willing to host monthly meetings of what I called the Security Group, made up of those individuals who would be the most interested in the progress of the investigation, the players, and their eventual arrest. Each of the members of the Security Group would all play a key role in Operation Justice.

I also began to establish a relationship with the American Ambassador, Pete Chavez, the UN Secretary-General's Special Representative (SRSG) Alieu Adenige, and his deputy, Alan Doss.[53] I also reached out to the Chief of Staff of the peacekeeping force, Brigadier James Ellery. Another key player would be the Commander of the British training team, Brigadier Adrian Freer, along with Keith Biddle, the Inspector General of the Sierra Leone National Police. The Security Group was a roundtable to discuss the practical, political, and diplomatic aspects of my work in developing my prosecution case against those who bore the greatest responsibility for the tragedy in Sierra Leone.

Alan Jones agreed to host these secret meetings starting in September. At that initial meeting, I outlined for them the progress of our initial setup, our phased-in personnel plan, along with a general discussion of those I was investigating without revealing any names. Frankly, it was understood by all of these gentlemen who the "local favorites" were. Importantly, I told them that as we got closer to the launch of Operation Justice, I would give them appropriate warnings and specific briefings on their needed support. They knew that Operation Justice would be a simultaneous arrest operation of all of the indictees at the same time, because arresting the key players one at a time would be political suicide and would place the entire region in jeopardy.

September of 2002 was a busy month. My plan called for the Office of the Prosecutor to be at full operational capacity by November 1, with two task forces working on the investigation of the leadership of the Civil Defense Force and the Revolutionary United Front/Armed Force Revolutionary Council, respectively. In the latter task force, we also had a group developing a plan to investigate and arrest the sitting President of Liberia, Charles Taylor, the most powerful warlord in Africa at the time and very much a threat to our work.[54] That month, I also met with the Security Group to review our setup and inform them about the information operation we had developed against the possible indictees.

---

[53] I developed close professional relationships with most of the members of the Security Group. Only the American Ambassador at the time, Pete Chavez, was a reluctant player and largely unhelpful throughout his tenure there. I never understood why. I also did not trust the Secretary-General's Special Representative in Sierra Leone, Alieu Adenigi, who was blatantly trying to undercut the work of the Special Court and tried to secret two of our potential indictees out of Sierra Leone on "agricultural scholarships" to Nigeria a month before Operation Justice was to be launched. I was told of this by a very senior deputy. I sent a note that simply stated that if he did what he was contemplating, I would have him arrested for obstruction of justice. This was passed on to senior officials at the United Nations. The two indictees, Issa Sesay and Morris Kallon, never left Sierra Leone. Adenigi was never told about Operation Justice because of his attitude and this scam.

[54] Also during this time frame, my very capable Deputy Desmond DeSilva had been put in charge of our appellate team and was well into drafting the responses to ten potential pretrial motions

The information operation was to divert the attention of the citizens of Sierra Leone and the indictees away from the planning of Operation Justice, already initially set for March 2003. The plan called for me to openly discuss our general work – the depth and scope of the investigation – with the local and regional press on a regular basis. Comments like "the investigation is complex" and "my office won't be ready to go to trial for at least a year" were regular sound bites that were printed and broadcast until just a few days before the execution of Operation Justice. None of my comments were untrue and were delivered with as much detail as possible to ensure plausibility. We wanted the indictees to be looking the other way when we came in to arrest them. At the end of the day, the information operation worked like a charm.

In the fall of 2002, I began to meet separately with the members of the Security Group to review their possible support for Operation Justice. It was during this time frame that the SRSG was cut out of the process for unreliability and possible sabotage. He never knew we were meeting. The Chief of Staff of the peacekeeping force, Brigadier Ellery, met with me secretly and promised support of his Pakistani Special Operations quick reaction force during the arrest operation. All this was kept from the SRSG up to the day of the operation. His deputy, Alan Doss, was part of the Security Group as well. They agreed to provide backup helicopters to transport the indictees to a temporary detention facility on Bonthe Island.[55]

The Inspector General of the Sierra Leone National Police Keith Biddle quietly informed the President of Sierra Leone Tejan Kabbah that he was part of a discussion group working with the Office of the Prosecutor on our investigation, as he was required to do under the Statute for the Special Court for Sierra Leone.[56] President Kabbah very adroitly gave him permission, telling Biddle that he would stay completely out of the investigation and that he was to represent him in the process. Biddle began to train a select team of trusted police for the operation about a month prior to the event.[57] A week from the takedown, various indictees were placed under surveillance by the investigations section of my office's and Biddle's teams.[58]

The cornerstone of Operation Justice was the support of the British High Commissioner Alan Jones. He was able to open doors to the Blair government,

---

related to jurisdiction that we predicted would be filed by the various defense teams. We kicked in the new academic consortium that was of great assistance to the Deputy Prosecutor. Of the various motions filed by the defense teams in the fall of 2003, Desmond's appellate team won them all.

[55] The detention facility was an old abandoned jail facility on Bonthe Island, 165 kilometers southwest of Freetown. We used the ruse of a legacy project by the Special Court to help rebuild the jail for the police. The Sierra Leone National Police were technically under the Ministry of Interior run by a future indictee, Hinga Norman, head of the Civil Defense Force during the civil war.

[56] Rule 8, Rules of Procedure and Evidence, Special Court for Sierra Leone (as amended at Sixth Plenary, May 14, 2005).

[57] Biddle never told them what they were organized and trained for until the moment of the various arrests.

[58] We had the best of the detectives and other police seconded to us throughout my tenure in Sierra Leone. During those early days, the bulk of our investigations unit was Sierra Leonean National Police. Not once did we doubt their loyalty and not once did they let us down.

which turned out to be critical. I made a few trips to London, the most important being my secret meeting in early January 2003 with the Ministry of Defence and the Foreign Commonwealth Office, during which the British agreed to provide direct military support to the operation. This was due to our patient building of trust and confidence in our ability to plan and execute Operation Justice. The United Kingdom put itself out on a huge political limb when it agreed to provide us with this necessary support.

The agreement essentially provided that I would alert them in a sequence of weeks prior to the arrest operation, now set for the second week in March. Only the British and Keith Biddle knew the exact date. The Americans and the UN peacekeepers would be alerted a week from the date. A week prior to the operation, the Ministry of Defense would send the Spear Point battalion of Ghurkas from the Parachute Regiment for annual training in Sierra Leone, a regular event there. The training exercise would be to land and secure Sierra Leone's one and only commercial airport. This would allow a possible evacuation point for persons needing to leave should violence break out during the execution of Operation Justice. It would also be a base for follow-on British troops should the situation dictate such a measure.

Also, Britain agreed to the movement of the British Navy's West African Squadron to Sierra Leone a few days before the operation. The squadron was to sortie just over the horizon. On the day of execution, the HMS *Iron Duke*, a British frigate, would arrive just off the coast of Sierra Leone and would sail up and down the coast, visible to everyone as a show of force by Great Britain.

After I flew back to Freetown from my meetings in London, I began to finalize the drafting of the indictments for my signature and presentment to a duty judge for approval. This process had to happen before we could launch Operation Justice. I signed eight indictments in a moving signing ceremony in my office on March 3, 2003. Indictment number one was President Charles Taylor, number two was Samuel "the mosquito" Bockarie, and number three was Foday Sankoh. The others were essentially the leadership of all of the warring factions that had destroyed Sierra Leone in the 1990s. My acting Chief of Prosecutions Brenda Hollis took the indictments and flew the next day to London where the duty judge reviewed all of the indictment packets and signed them in the late evening of Friday, March 7.

When informed of this by Hollis, I gave the green light for Operation Justice to take place on Monday, March 10, 2003. That week, I met with the Security Group and told them the arrests were imminent and to begin to finalize their plans. Brigadier Ellery put the quick reaction force on alert, the Americans laid on three contract helicopters to transport the indictees to Bonthe Island, the Spear Point Battalion, now in country at the airport in Sierra Leone, was alerted, and the British West African squadron was moved into place.

I gave a press conference at the Sierra Leone press club in downtown Freetown highlighting the complexity of the case and that trial of any of the indictees would be months away. This came out in the press at the end of the week. I also gave a speech at the UN peacekeeping headquarters on Saturday, March 7, also highlighting that our investigations could take years.

As stated earlier, surveillance was placed on all of the indictees; the teams reported back to Alan White, Chief of Investigations, and Keith Biddle on the whereabouts of their various targets. The landing zones for the helicopters were discretely cleared and monitored, and final preparations at the temporary detention facility were made. All was in place; it was now time to execute Operation Justice, set for the early morning of Monday, March 10.

2. The Execution

March is a time of good weather in Sierra Leone, usually clear, with the winds blowing down from the Sahara keeping the air drier and the breezes cool. It was just such a day when I finally met with the arrests teams assembled in the basement at Seaview. My Chief of Investigations, Alan White, was in charge of Operation Justice assisted by his able deputy, Gilbert Morisette, from Canada. I recall how solemn everyone was at the time. We had no idea whether this would be a day of triumph or disaster. I was concerned that we would miss someone who would promptly disappear into the bush and perhaps start the civil war all over again. It was an historic and seminal moment, indeed.

I left the basement and went to a meeting with my political advisor, Mike Pan, to arrange for a press conference at 4:00 PM at UN headquarters in Freetown. Its purpose was to tell the world about Operation Justice and who was indicted and arrested. We reviewed my statement to the world's press. Present was my new Chief of Prosecutions, Luc Cote, who had arrived a few days earlier and could only watch in wonder the execution of a plan started several months earlier. Pan left to arrange for the press conference, the topic of which was left generic because the United Nations was not aware of the operation in general. Recall that only Brigadier Ellery and the Deputy SRSG knew of the operation. During this morning meeting, it was agreed that I would only tell the SRSG when I was assured the operation was completed. We then waited. It was a long morning, indeed.

Due to final adjustments, the takedown was moved to noon. The HMS *Iron Duke* was alerted and began to steam toward Freetown. The arrest teams moved into position, the helicopters flew to the rally points, and the detention facility was standing by to receive any and all of the indictees. Precisely at noon, March 10, six of the eight indictees were arrested throughout the Freetown area.[59] The current Minister of the

---

[59] I sealed the indictment against President Charles Taylor, who was in Liberia. Samuel Bockarie was in the Ivory Coast, fomenting rebellion there on behalf of Taylor. Johnny Paul Koroma, former head of the Armed Forces Revolutionary Council, was missing after he fled Sierra Leone in an unsuccessful attempt to topple the government in January 2003. He was never seen again, although it has now been discovered that Koroma had been murdered and his body cut up and scattered in the jungle. Bockarie, along with his entire family, was murdered by Taylor in Liberia. Taylor sent Bockarie to me in a box on my birthday – May 29, 2003.

Interior, Hinga Norman, was arrested at his desk; others were seized on streets, in prison, or lured to a police station where they were handed over to the arrest team. As each indictee was arrested, he was handcuffed and moved quickly by a police vehicle to the helicopter landing zones, from which he was whisked off to Bonthe Island for processing. James Johnson from my office, head of the task force who was to try the leadership of the Civil Defense Force, was put in charge of ensuring that each indictee was read his rights, given a copy of his indictment, and handed over properly to the Registry and the detention facility under Robert Parnell, the Special Court's Chief of Security.

Operation Justice lasted fifty-five minutes. I was called by Alan White around 1:00 PM that all of the targets had been seized and were flying in three helicopters toward Bonthe Island. I then called the SRSG, Alieu Adenige, who was sitting in a barber's chair getting a haircut, and told him about Operation Justice. He was stunned. He began to shout, and I hung up. There was nothing he could do. During this time frame, the HMS *Iron Duke* cruised slowly back and forth off Lumley Beach at general quarters. It was an impressive sight.

Not a shot was fired, no one was injured or killed, and the region was quiet, although the "talking drum" was already sounding throughout the area.[60] Word was quickly out that the Minister of the Interior had been arrested at his desk by the Special Court. I left for UN headquarters around 3:30 PM and could see people in the streets talking excitedly. At 4:00 PM, I was introduced by the UNAMSIL press secretary where I read my prepared remarks. I was not going to take any questions. I told the world and the people of Sierra Leone of the indictment and arrest of most of those who had murdered, raped, maimed, and mutilated over 500,000 Sierra Leoneans. Not announced was the indictment of President Taylor next door in Liberia. That indictment was sealed.

When I left UN headquarters around 4:15 PM, the word had gotten out officially, and people were dancing in the streets. They celebrated well into the evening hours. As I had declared in my statement to the press, "tomorrow the people of Sierra Leone would awake to a new dawn." I would like to think that they did.

IV. LESSONS

Most of the key lessons learned from the creation and development of the world's first hybrid tribunal were politically based. Its ultimate success, particularly in its first year, was as much political as legal. Most of my work for three years was political and diplomatic in focus. Once my prosecution plan was in place, my Chief of Prosecutions would monitor and lead the two trial teams in prosecuting the leadership of the three warring factions in three joint criminal trials. I traveled throughout

---

[60] An impressive means of communication, information is passed by word of mouth at an astonishing rate. I was always impressed and used this to my advantage throughout my tenure, including the information operation.

the world talking to politicians and diplomats, seeking to gain political momentum. Part of this was seeking their assistance in the handover of now publicly indicted President of Liberia Charles Taylor to the Court. The political process of building a political base for that handover would consume my entire last year as Chief Prosecutor. His handover would happen several months after I left in a political decision by the United States and Nigeria, with the backing of the United Nations and Great Britain. All this is another story, but it illustrates just how bright that red thread of politics can be in a successful prosecution strategy. So what have we learned from all this?

Political Lessons Learned in General
The mandate of a tribunal has to be realistic. We were able to do our work efficiently and effectively because we had a workable mandate that matched the expectations of the international community. "Greatest responsibility" was the key phrase within the mandate that permitted the tribunal in Sierra Leone to succeed. The numbers of individuals that we now considered to indict went from 30,000 to around twenty. We could get the job done in a politically acceptable time frame.

Another lesson learned is that a tribunal is most effective when it is located in the region of the conflict. To the extent possible, regional tribunals need to be located right where the crimes occurred. It allows for the victims to see justice done and renews or restores faith in the rule of law. The downside to such a placement is security, as recent events in Iraq illustrate.

Again, outreach is essential to assist in the understanding of the importance of the rule of law and international justice. This helps build a local political base that can sustain support for a justice mechanism. A tribunal can only complete its work if the citizens of the region appreciate and understand why the international community is there seeking justice and accounting for the various international crimes allegedly committed. At the end of the day, it will be the people living in the area who will have to live with the results.

A tribunal also must be finished with its work in five years, if possible. Without the political support of the citizens, the various States, the region, or the international community in general, a tribunal will not completely succeed in seeking justice for the victims of the atrocities that have taken place. The longer the tribunal remains, the greater the chances that the vital support of the populace and their political leaders will begin to fade. This had already happened in Rwanda and, to some extent, in the Balkans.

A further lesson learned is that a truth commission is essential to building a sustainable peace, which also bolsters the political environment in the country. We were able to show that both a truth commission and a war crimes tribunal could work side by side in helping restore peace to a country and to a region. In my mind, you must have both truth and justice to ensure that a sustainable peace develops. One without the other makes the peace somewhat illusory. Simply put, truth plus justice equals a sustainable peace.

Hiring local nationals is also a key to success practically and politically. We hired professionals from the region at the start of our work and were very proud of the dedication and the bravery of our African colleagues. More importantly, the people of Sierra Leone saw their barristers in court representing them before the tribunal. There was not one time where I doubted the abilities of our West African trial counsel and investigators. The experience and training gained by them dovetailed very nicely into our legacy program, as they will remain to continue the fight to return the rule of law to the region.

Consideration of regional cultures establishes confidence in the rule of law. The people have to understand that the justice we are seeking is the justice that will aid them in restoring their societies to a proper balance. Cultural perspectives must be respected and factored into the prosecutorial strategy and plan. This also assists the investigators and witness managers in preparing West African witnesses to testify before an international tribunal in a way that they understand.

The Political Challenges

Indifference: My biggest political challenge was the indifference of the international community toward the work of the tribunal. This war-crimes-weary world, particularly as related to Africa, simply feels incapable of dealing with the atrocities. The ruin of more than one million lives still did not stir the hearts of the Western world.

Political resolve: Additionally, a further challenge was sustaining the will to see even, arguably, a successful tribunal through to a just conclusion. For example, halfway through the life of the Special Court, we simply ran out of donations and had to scramble to seek a subvention grant from the United Nations to see us through our third year.

Mandate enforcement: A tribunal can only be successful if those properly indicted under statutory guidelines and the law are turned over to it for a fair trial. This is certainly true in the case of the Special Court. Prior to his eventual handover to the Court in March 2006, Charles Taylor was in a type of political limbo in Calabar, Nigeria, after I unsealed the seventeen-count indictment against him in June 2003. At the time, it was the appropriate thing to do to get him out of Liberia so the peace process could move forward in Accra, Ghana. Today, Charles Taylor sits in a jail cell in The Hague, being prosecuted for what he did to Sierra Leone.[61]

V. CONCLUSION

A study of the creation of a tribunal or court will show that it is truly a political creature. I hope that this chapter causes the reader to appreciate the depth and scope of this point by my detailed discussion of the planning and execution of Operation Justice by my office. The success or failure of future prosecutions hinges on a full

---

[61] The Prosecution, led by Brenda Hollis, rested its case against Taylor at the end of the first week of March 2009.

understanding of politics and diplomacy to ensure justice at the end of the day. Ignore the role of politics, and there certainly is the possibility of failure, frustrating victims, and stunting the development of modern international criminal law.

In my mind, a successful Chief Prosecutor must be selected as much for his political and diplomatic skills as for his legal acumen. The law is not enough in this day and age to carry through the complex prosecution of those who commit war crimes, crimes against humanity, and genocide without such a person and those skills.

Legal success, the rendering of justice, is based on a myriad of factors, much of which is politically driven. One can see in the case study presented that the diplomacy and military planning of many parties working closely with a Chief Prosecutor experienced in all aspects of law, politics, and diplomacy formed the practical basis by which the legal rules of procedure and evidence could begin the process of justice. Without the success of Operation Justice, the legal process would not have happened in the timely manner that it did in Sierra Leone.

5

Gender-Based Crimes Against Humanity

Valerie Oosterveld

Gender-based crimes against humanity are prevalent in situations of insecurity, such as armed conflict.[1] Several gender-based crimes against humanity have been recognized in the statutes of international criminal tribunals, such as the Rome Statute of the International Criminal Court (ICC)[2] and in the case law of these tribunals. This recognition has largely focused on crimes against humanity of sexual violence, especially rape and sexual slavery. Less developed is the recognition of the crime against humanity of gender-based persecution and other crimes that are gendered but may not contain sexual aspects. This chapter begins by examining what is meant by the term "gender" when referring to gender-based crimes against humanity. Next, the chapter explores the ways in which gender-based crimes have been reflected in current international criminal law. This section first describes legal developments related to sexual violence crimes: rape, sexual slavery, enforced prostitution, forced pregnancy, enforced sterilization, and other forms of sexual violence. Then, current international law on other gender-based crimes against humanity is considered, such as the Rome Statute's definition of gender-based persecution and the Special Court for Sierra Leone's definition of forced marriage. This paper then discusses other prohibited acts with gendered aspects, such as enslavement and torture. It concludes with recommendations for gender-based prohibited acts that should be reflected in any future crimes against humanity codification. It also raises questions that will need to be considered by drafters of a treaty codifying crimes against humanity.

I. WHAT IS MEANT BY "GENDER"?

The term "gender" is often used within the United Nations as a synonym for "women."[3] Similarly, references to gender within international criminal law usually focus on prosecutions by the International Criminal Tribunals for the former

---

[1] This has been recognized by the Security Council: *Women and peace and security*, U.N. S.C. Res. 1888, U.N. SCOR, 6195th Mtg., pmbl. ¶ 3, U.N. Doc. S/RES/1888 (Sept. 30, 2009).
[2] *Rome Statute of the International Criminal Court*, United Nations Diplomatic Conference of Plenipotentiaries on the Establishment of an International Criminal Court, July 17, 1998, U.N. Doc. A/CONF.183/9 (1998) [hereinafter *Rome Statute*].
[3] Hilary Charlesworth, *Not Waving but Drowning: Gender Mainstreaming and Human Rights in the United Nations*, 18 Harv. Hum. Rts. J. 1, 14 (2005).

Yugoslavia and Rwanda (ICTY and ICTR, respectively), the Special Court for Sierra Leone (SCSL), and the ICC of sexual violence crimes committed against women.[4] This recognition of sexual violence committed against women within the context of international crimes is groundbreaking and important but only represents part of an understanding of gender. Gender should be understood as something much wider in both scope and meaning than "women" or "sexual violence committed against women." This is because gender is not the same as sex. Feminist theorists have critiqued the international criminal tribunals for collapsing gender into sex, for seeming to understand gender solely as sex, and therefore to understand a gendered analysis of international crimes simply as an analysis of sexual crimes.[5]

Although there is no single accepted definition of gender within feminist legal theory, gender is usually understood as a socially constructed concept of "maleness" and "femaleness" that can vary across cultures and over time. For example, the United Nations Office of the Special Adviser on Gender Issues ("OSAGI") defines the term "gender" as referring to:

> the social attributes and opportunities associated with being male and female and the relationships between women and men and girls and boys, as well as the relations between women and those between men. These attributes, opportunities and relationships are socially constructed and are learned through socialization processes. They are context/time-specific and changeable. Gender determines what is expected, allowed and valued in a women [sic] or a man in a given context. In most societies there are differences and inequalities between women and men in responsibilities assigned, activities undertaken, access to and control over resources, as well as decision-making opportunities. Gender is part of the broader socio-cultural context. Other important criteria for socio-cultural analysis include class, race, poverty level, ethnic group and age.[6]

Similar approaches can be found elsewhere within the United Nations. Some UN bodies emphasize a distinction between the terms "gender" and "sex," such

---

[4] The ICTY, ICTR, and SCSL have entered convictions for the crime against humanity and the war crime of rape, and all three tribunals have adopted definitions or elements for this prohibited act. *See, e.g.*, Prosecutor v. Akayesu, Case No. ICTR-96-4-T, Judgment, ¶ 688 (Sept. 2, 1998); Prosecutor v. Furundžija, Case No. IT-95-17/I-T, Judgment, ¶ 185 (Dec. 10, 1998); Prosecutor v. Brima et al., Case No. SCSL-04-16-T, Judgment, ¶ 693 (June 20, 2007) [hereinafter *Brima Trial Judgment*]. These tribunals, as well as the ICC, have also examined sexual slavery, sexual torture and other forms of sexual violence. On sexual slavery, see *id.* ¶ 708; and Prosecutor v. Katanga and Ngudjolo Chui, ICC-01/04-01/07, Decision on the Confirmation of Charges, ¶ 343 (Sept. 30, 2008). On enslavement of a sexual nature, see Prosecutor v. Kunarac et al., Case No. IT-96-23-T and IT-96-23/I-T, Judgment, ¶¶ 539, 542 (Feb. 22, 2001) [hereinafter *Kunarac Trial Judgment*]. On sexual torture, see, e.g., *Furundžija, supra*, ¶¶ 163–64. On other forms of sexual violence, such as forced nudity, see *Akayesu, supra*, ¶ 697.

[5] Karen Engle, *Feminism and its (Dis)Contents: Criminalizing Wartime Rape in Bosnia and Herzegovina*, 99 Am. J. Int'l L. 778, 815 (2005); Katherine M. Franke, *Gendered Subjects of Transitional Justice*, 15 Colum. J. Gender & L. 813, 822–23 (2006).

[6] U.N. Office of the Special Adviser on Gender Issues and Advancement of Women, *Gender Mainstreaming, Concepts and Definitions*, available at http://www.un.org/womenwatch/osagi/conceptsandefinitions.htm (last visited Apr. 17, 2010) [hereinafter OSAGI].

as this definition of gender used by the Special Rapporteur on Violence Against Women: "the socially constructed roles of women ascribed to them on the basis of their sex."[7] Most others, including more recent definitions, do not contrast gender with sex, focusing instead – as in the OSAGI definition above – on the social construction of male/female distinctions.[8]

The concept of gender includes several significant aspects. First, gender is an understanding rooted in a specific time. How gender is constructed is not static or innate.[9] A social construction of gender may, at any given time, seem unchanging or representing tradition,[10] but can also "change quite rapidly in response to policy and changing socioeconomic conditions."[11] Second, the construction of gender is strongly influenced by culture. Cultural assumptions affect the roles men and women are expected to play, the value placed on these roles, and how these roles intersect.[12] It is important to note that these assumptions can vary within a culture over time and at the same time. For example, the strength of these assumptions may differ from rural to urban cultural settings. "Historically, different cultures construct gender in different ways so that women's [or men's] roles, the value that their society places on those roles, and the relationship with men's [or women's] roles may vary considerably over time and from one setting to another."[13] Finally, it is crucial to understand that the concept of gender is multidimensional and intersectional – that is, it intersects with other variables, such as age, class, race, ethnicity, poverty level, sexual orientation, political, and economic context.[14]

---

[7] World Conference Against Racism, Racial Discrimination, Xenophobia, and Related Intolerance, Geneva, Switz., July 30-Aug. 10, 2001, *Review of Reports, Studies and Other Documentation for the Preparatory Commission and the World Conference*, ¶ 10, U.N. Doc. A/CONF.198/PC.3/5 (July 27, 2001) [hereinafter *Review of Reports*]. Another, more detailed approach distinguishing the terms "gender" and "sex" can be found in the U.N. High Comm'r for Refugees, *Guidelines on International Protection: Gender-Related Persecution within the Context of Article 1A(2) of the 1951 Convention and/or Its 1967 Protocol Relating to the Status of Refugees*, at 1, U.N. Doc. HCR/GIP/02/01 (May 7, 2002) [hereinafter UNHCR Guidelines].

[8] For a review of definitions used within the World Health Organization, United Nations Environment Program, United Nations Development Program, International Labour Organization, and elsewhere, see Valerie Oosterveld, *The Definition of "Gender" in the Rome Statute of the International Criminal Court: A Step Forward or Back for International Criminal Justice?*, 18 HARV. HUM. RTS. J. 55, 66–69 (2005).

[9] *See, e.g.,* UNHCR Guidelines, *supra* note 7, ¶ 3. For other examples, see Oosterveld, *supra* note 8, at 70.

[10] U.N. Div. for the Advancement of Women, *The Role of Men and Boys in Achieving Gender Equality*, at 14 n.4, U.N. Doc. EGM/MEN-BOYS-GE/2003/Report (Jan. 12, 2004) [hereinafter UNDAW].

[11] WORLD BANK, ENGENDERING DEVELOPMENT THROUGH GENDER EQUALITY IN RIGHTS, RESOURCES AND VOICE, A WORLD BANK POLICY RESEARCH REPORT 2, at 24 (2001) [hereinafter WORLD BANK].

[12] Oosterveld, *supra* note 8, at 69.

[13] U.N. Econ. & Soc. Council, Comm'n on Human Rights, *Report of the Expert Group Meeting on the Development of Guidelines for the Integration of Gender Perspectives into United Nations Human Rights Activities and Programmes*, ¶ 13, U.N. Doc. E/CN.4/1996/105 (Nov. 20, 1995).

[14] UNDAW, *supra* note 10, at 14 n.4; *Review of Reports*, *supra* note 7, ¶ 10; OSAGI, *supra* note 6; WORLD BANK, *supra* note 11, at 24.

As a result of these differing variables, international tribunals prosecuting crimes years after a conflict or event must take measures to understand the construction of gender (by society, by the perpetrators) as it was understood by the relevant culture(s) at the time and in the place of the events in question. It will also be important to analyze the key intersectionalities at play in any given crime. For example, it is important to explain how age plus gender may have influenced the choice of young girls as forced "wives" for combatants in a past conflict, such as that in Sierra Leone or in an ongoing conflict such as that in the Democratic Republic of the Congo. In turn, this information can inform evaluations of *mens rea*, harm to victims, and penalties.

Gender is a multilayered concept deserving of an equally complex understanding. This raises the question of whether the term should be defined within a treaty directed at codifying crimes against humanity. There is a strong argument to be made against defining the term within such a treaty. Depending on how the treaty is structured, the term is likely to first appear in a provision setting out the crime against humanity of persecution.[15] The Rome Statute lists the prohibited act of persecution in article 7(1)(h) as:

> persecution against any identifiable group or collectivity on political, racial, national, ethnic, cultural, religious, gender as defined in paragraph 3, or other grounds that are universally recognized as impermissible under international law, in connection with any act referred to in this paragraph [setting out the prohibited acts] or any crime within the jurisdiction of the Court.[16]

The only term in the Rome Statute's list of persecutory grounds that is defined is gender. This is despite the fact that other grounds may not be clearly defined within international criminal law – for example, "cultural" may also be open to variations of interpretation. Therefore, one could conclude that the term "gender" should similarly be left to judicial (or other) interpretation and determination. This is the approach of the UN General Assembly, Security Council, and Economic and Social Council in State-negotiated resolutions using the term "gender."[17] This was also the approach adopted with respect to the outcome documents of a number of

---

[15] This is the case in the *Proposed International Convention on the Prevention and Punishment of Crimes Against Humanity*, in this volume, App. I, art. 3(1)(h) [hereinafter *Proposed Convention*].

[16] *Rome Statute*, *supra* note 2, art. 7(1)(h).

[17] The term "gender" is regularly used without definition in General Assembly and Security Council resolutions and statements. *See, e.g.*, Statement by the President of the Security Council, *Protection of civilians in armed conflict*, U.N. Doc. S/PRST/2009/1, at 4 (Jan. 14, 2009); *Women and peace and security*, S.C. Res. 1820, U.N. SCOR, 5916th Mtg., ¶ 11, U.N. Doc. S/RES/1820 (June 19, 2008); *Women and peace and security*, S.C. Res. 1325, U.N. SCOR, 4213th Mtg., ¶¶ 5, 7, 8, 10, 15–17, U.N. Doc. S/RES/1325 (Oct. 31, 2000); *Follow-up to the Fourth World Conference on Women and full implementation of the Beijing Declaration and Platform for Action and the outcome of the twenty-third special session of the General Assembly*, G.A. Res. 63/159, U.N. GAOR, 63rd Sess., ¶¶ 3, 7, 12–22, 24–30, U.N. Doc. A/RES/63/159 (Feb. 4, 2009); U.N. Econ. and Soc. Council, *Strengthening of the Coordination of Emergency Humanitarian Assistance of the United Nations*, U.N. Doc. E/2004/L.35 (July 23, 2004).

UN World Conferences.[18] Even where there has been contention among States as to the use of the term "gender" within UN documents, the solution has largely been to leave the term undefined.[19]

On the other hand, one of the arguments made during the Rome Statute negotiations by those States wishing to include a definition of the term "gender" was that the term is unclear and the principle of legality requires a definition. The Rome Statute defines "gender" in the crimes against humanity article as follows:[20] "For the purposes of this Statute, it is understood that the term "gender" refers to the two sexes, male and female, within the context of society. The term 'gender' does not indicate any meaning different from the above."[21] This definition refers to maleness and femaleness within the context of society, and thus arguably captures the understanding of gender as a socially constructed category. However, one can legitimately question whether this definition – agreed to only after difficult and contentious diplomatic negotiations, and containing opaque and circular language – adds much to satisfy the principle of legality.[22] It is not an ideal precedent.

The *Proposed International Convention on the Prevention and Punishment of Crimes Against Humanity* proposes the inclusion of a definition of the term "gender" that replicates the definition found in the Rome Statute.[23] In this author's view,

---

[18] See, e.g., World Conference on Human Rights, June 14–25, 1993, *Vienna Declaration and Programme of Action*, ¶¶ 18, 38, 42, U.N. Doc. A/CONF.157/23 (July 12, 1993) [hereinafter *Vienna Declaration*]; World Summit for Social Development, Copenhagen, Den., Mar. 6–12, 1995, *Copenhagen Declaration on Social Development and Programme of Action*, ¶¶ 7, 16, 20, 22, 27–30, 36, 45, 47, 53, 56, 70, 73, 74, 77, 83, 91, U.N. Doc. A/CONF.166/9 (Apr. 19, 1995).

[19] For example, there was diplomatic disagreement on the use of the term "gender" during the negotiations for the Beijing Declaration and Platform for Action, but the solution was that the President of the Conference would make a statement indicating that the word "gender" as used in the outcome document was to be interpreted and understood "in [its] ordinary, generally accepted usage" and that "there was no indication that any new meaning or connotation of the term, different from accepted prior usage, was intended in the Platform for Action." Fourth World Conference on Women, Beijing, P.R.C., Sept. 4–15, 2001, *Report of the Fourth World Conference on Women*, Addendum, Annex IV, U.N. Doc. A/CONF.177/20/Rev.1 (Jan. 1, 1996) [hereinafter *Beijing Declaration*]. This approach was followed the next year in the 1996 Habitat World Conference, U.N. Conference on Human Settlements, Istanbul, Turk., June 3–14, 1996, *Report of the United Nations Conference on Human Settlements*, Annex I, ¶ 46, U.N. Doc. A/CONF.165/14 (Aug. 7, 1996), which includes a footnote stating: "The statement on the commonly understood meaning of the term "gender," presented at the Fourth World Conference on Women by the President of the Conference, is reproduced in Annex V to the present report." One exception to this trend was the 2001 *Durban Declaration and Programme of Action*, World Conference Against Racism, Racial Discrimination, Xenophobia and Related Intolerance, Durban, S. Afr., Aug. 31-Sept. 8, 2001, at 5, 75 n.1, U.N. Doc. A/CONF.189/12 (Jan. 1, 2002), in which the Rome Statute definition of "gender" (discussed *infra*) was included.

[20] This definition is replicated in United Nations Transitional Administration in East Timor Regulation No. 2000/15, section 5.1. U.N. Transitional Admin. In East Timor, Regulation on the Establishment of Panels with Exclusive Jurisdiction over Serious criminal Offenses, § 5.1 UNTAET/REG/2000/15 (June 6, 2000) [hereinafter UNTAET Reg. 2000/15]. The UNTAET regulations replicated the Rome Statute's crimes and definitions almost verbatim.

[21] *Rome Statute*, *supra* note 2, art. 7(3).

[22] For an explanation of the negotiating history, see Oosterveld, *supra* note 8, at 58–66.

[23] *Proposed Convention*, in this volume, App. I, arts. 3(1)(h) and 3(3).

if an explanation of the term "gender" is to be included in a crimes against humanity convention (or, similarly, in a domestic statute codifying this crime),[24] it would be prudent to aim for a clearer definition that more obviously satisfies the principle of legality. The definition should state that gender is the social construction of maleness and femaleness. In addition, the definition should indicate that this social construction can vary within and across cultures, over time, and may be influenced by its intersection with other factors, such as age. Given the trend within the United Nations system (and elsewhere) toward defining gender without reference to biology, it is not necessary to refer to sex.

In sum, there are compelling arguments against the inclusion of a definition of "gender" in a treaty codifying crimes against humanity. However, if States wish to include a definition in order to be sure to satisfy the principle of legality, then a definition indicating that gender is the social construction of maleness and femaleness and can vary within and across cultures, over time, and may be influenced by its intersection with other factors (such as age) is to be preferred.

II. GENDER-BASED CRIMES AGAINST HUMANITY RECOGNIZED WITHIN INTERNATIONAL CRIMINAL LAW

A. Prohibited Acts of Sexual Violence

This section details different kinds of sexual violence that have been recognized as prohibited acts within crimes against humanity: rape, sexual slavery, enforced prostitution, forced pregnancy, enforced sterilization, and other forms of sexual violence. Given the historical silence concerning the criminality of acts of sexual violence, the relatively recent explicit recognition of these acts as crimes against humanity is a welcome step forward within international criminal law. With the exception of forced pregnancy, all of the acts of sexual violence can be committed against women, men, girls, or boys.

1. Rape

Rape is listed as a crime against humanity in the Statutes of the International Criminal Tribunals for the former Yugoslavia and Rwanda[25] and the Special Court

---

[24] There may be States that wish to adopt a domestic statute specifically on crimes against humanity that have already adopted the definition of crimes found in the Rome Statute of the International Criminal Court, including the gender definition. In this case, "gender" could be left undefined in the crimes against humanity statute, or the Rome Statute definition could be adopted. Although opaque, the Rome Statute definition does refer to the core content of gender and should provide guidance to a court to determine whether the crime against humanity of gender-based persecution has taken place.

[25] Statute of the International Criminal Tribunal for the former Yugoslavia Annex art. 5(g), S.C. Res. 827, U.N. Doc. S/RES/827 (May 25, 1993) [hereinafter ICTY Statute]; Statute of the International Criminal Tribunal for Rwanda Annex art. 3(g), S.C. Res. 955, U.N. Doc. S/RES/955 (Nov. 8, 1994) [hereinafter ICTR Statute].

for Sierra Leone,[26] the Rome Statute of the ICC,[27] the UNTAET Regulations,[28] the Law on the Establishment of the Extraordinary Chambers in the Courts of Cambodia,[29] and in Control Council Law No. 10.[30] There should be no question that rape must be included as a prohibited act within a treaty codifying crimes against humanity. Where there is likely to be discussion, however, is on the definition of rape that might be included in any affiliated list of elements of crimes. There is no single definition in use among the international and internationalized tribunals today. Rather, there are a number of definitions, some more often relied upon than others. These definitions have stirred debate among international commentators, especially (but not only) around whether nonconsent is or is not properly part of the elements of rape.

The first definition of rape was articulated by an ICTR Trial Chamber in the 1998 *Akayesu* judgment and subsequently relied on or referred to in other ICTR and ICTY judgments.[31] The *Akayesu* approach defines rape broadly and conceptually as a "physical invasion of a sexual nature, committed on a person under circumstances which are coercive."[32] Shortly after, an ICTY Trial Chamber in the *Furundžija* judgment defined rape in a more descriptive manner (perhaps out of concern for satisfying the principle of legality) as:

(i) the sexual penetration, however slight:
   (a) of the vagina or anus of the victim by the penis of the perpetrator or any other object used by the perpetrator; or
   (b) of the mouth of the victim by the penis of the perpetrator;
(ii) by coercion or force or threat of force against the victim or a third person.[33]

A third approach was introduced in 2001 by an ICTY Trial Chamber in the *Kunarac et al.* judgment. This definition adopts the description of body parts of

---

[26] Statute of the Special Court for Sierra Leone art. 2(g), Jan. 16, 2002, 2178 U.N.T.S. 138 [hereinafter SCSL Statute].

[27] *Rome Statute*, *supra* note 2, art. 7(1)(g).

[28] UNTAET Reg. 2000/15, *supra* note 20, § 5.1(g).

[29] Law on the Establishment of the Extraordinary Chambers in the Courts of Cambodia for the Prosecution of Crimes Committed During the Period of Democratic Kampuchea, Oct. 27, 2004, NS/RKM/1004/006, *available at* http://www.eccc.gov.kh/english/cabinet/law/4/KR_Law_as_amended_27_Oct_2004_Eng.pdf.

[30] Allied Control Council Law No. 10, Punishment of Persons Guilty of War Crimes, Crimes Against Peace and Against Humanity art. 2(a), Dec. 20, 1945, 3 OFFICIAL GAZETTE OF THE CONTROL COUNCIL FOR GERMANY 50–55 (1946).

[31] Prosecutor v. Delalic et al., Case No. IT-96-21-T, Judgment, ¶ 478 (Nov. 16, 1998); Prosecutor v. Musema, Case No. ICTR-96-13-T, Judgment and Sentence, ¶¶ 220, 226 (Jan. 27, 2000); Prosecutor v. Niyitegeka, Case No. ICTR-96-14, Judgment and Sentence, ¶ 456 (May 16, 2003).

[32] *Akayesu*, *supra* note 4, ¶ 598.

[33] *Furundžija*, *supra* note 4, ¶ 185. Schabas notes that this more positivistic approach was likely taken due to concerns about possibly breaching the *nullem crimen sine lege* principle. WILLIAM A. SCHABAS, THE UN INTERNATIONAL CRIMINAL TRIBUNALS: THE FORMER YUGOSLAVIA, RWANDA AND SIERRA LEONE 209 (2006).

the second approach but changes the coercion/threat of force element to one of nonconsent:

> the *actus reus* of the crime of rape in international law is constituted by: the sexual penetration, however slight:
>
> (a) of the vagina or anus of the victim by the penis of the perpetrator or any other object used by the perpetrator; or
> (b) of the mouth of the victim by the penis of the perpetrator; where such sexual penetration occurs without the consent of the victim. Consent for this purpose must be consent given voluntarily, as a result of the victim's free will, assessed in the context of the surrounding circumstances. The *mens rea* is the intention to effect this sexual penetration, and the knowledge that it occurs without the consent of the victim.[34]

Within the ICTY and the ICTR, the *Kunarac et al.* approach appears to be used more often than the first two approaches.[35] A similar nonconsent-based approach has been adopted by the Special Court for Sierra Leone.[36]

A fourth approach is articulated in the ICC's elements of crimes but represents a mix of the first two approaches because these were the only definitions rendered by the ICTY and the ICTR at the time the ICC's elements were being drafted. However, the ICC's approach includes a broader definition than that found in the second approach and essentially avoids the nonconsent element included in the third approach.[37]

These varying approaches, especially the differences regarding whether or not a nonconsent element is appropriate in international criminal law, have been critiqued by

---

[34] *Kunarac Trial Judgment*, *supra* note 4, ¶ 460. This definition was confirmed on appeal. Prosecutor v. Kunarac et al., Case No. IT-96-23/I-A, Judgment, ¶ 128 (June 12, 2002) [hereinafter *Kunarac Appeals Judgment*].

[35] *See, e.g.*, Prosecutor v. Kvočka et al., Case No. IT-98-30/1-T, Judgment, ¶¶ 177–79 (Nov. 2, 2001); Prosecutor v. Semanza, Case No. ICTR-97-20-T, Judgment and Sentence, ¶¶ 344–46 (May 15, 2003); Prosecutor v. Kajelijeli, Case No. ICTR-98-44A-T, Judgment and Sentence, ¶ 915 (Dec. 1, 2003); Prosecutor v. Kamuhanda, ICTR-99-54A-T, Judgment, ¶¶ 709–10 (Dec. 22, 2004). The appeals judgment in *Gacumbitsi* explains that nonconsent is an element, but it is not necessary, as a legal matter, for the Prosecution to introduce evidence concerning the words or conduct of the victim or the victim's relationship to the perpetrator. Nor need it introduce evidence of force. Rather, the Trial Chamber is free to infer nonconsent from the background circumstances, such as an ongoing genocide campaign or the detention of the victim. Prosecutor v. Gacumbitsi, Case No. ICTR-2001-64-A, Judgment, ¶ 155 (July 7, 2006).

[36] *Brima Trial Judgment*, *supra* note 4, ¶¶ 693–94.

[37] ANNE-MARIE L.M. DE BROUWER, SUPRANATIONAL CRIMINAL PROSECUTION OF SEXUAL VIOLENCE: THE ICC AND THE PRACTICE OF THE ICTY AND THE ICTR 131–35 (2005). The relevant ICC elements are:

> 1. The perpetrator invaded the body of a person by conduct resulting in penetration, however slight, of any part of the body of the victim or of the perpetrator with a sexual organ, or of the anal or genital opening of the victim with any object or any other part of the body.
> 2. The invasion was committed by force, or by threat of force or coercion, such as that caused by fear of violence, duress, detention, psychological oppression or abuse of power, against such person or another person, or by taking advantage of a coercive environment, or the invasion was committed against a person incapable of giving genuine consent.

a number of commentators.[38] For example, Schomburg and Peterson, as well as de Brouwer and McDougall, argue that sexual violence qualifying as genocide, crimes against humanity, or war crimes occurs under inherently coercive circumstances that negate any possibility of genuine consent.[39] Schomburg and Peterson note that a "widespread or systematic attack against a civilian population generates highly coercive circumstances," so "[a]ny sexual act that is so related to the overall context will therefore occur under coercive circumstances that rule out the possibility of genuine consent."[40] They conclude that, at most, the issue of consent should be treated as an affirmative defense that may be raised in exceptional cases.[41] On the other hand, Engle posits that presumed coercion "essentially makes consensual sexual relationships legally impossible, in some set of circumstances," including those found in the *Kunarac* case.[42] In Halley's view, assumptions regarding consent during conflict could lead to convictions of men who could prove consent.[43] Campbell argues that such debates concerning consent fail to address "the more problematic issue of the nature of the harm itself, namely, whether the harm is the coercive or the sexual aspect of the assault."[44]

To conclude, it should be uncontroversial to include rape as a crime against humanity. Intensive discussion will likely occur, however, around the drafting of any affiliated elements of the crime. Specifically, there will need to be consideration of whether or not it is appropriate to include nonconsent as an element of the crime that a prosecutor would need to prove beyond a reasonable doubt, or whether consent should be treated as a defense.

Preparatory Comm'n for the Int'l Criminal Court, *Report of the Preparatory Commission for the International Criminal Court: Addendum, Part II, Finalized Draft Text of the Elements of Crimes*, art. 7(1)(g)-1, U.N. Doc. PCNICC/2000/1/Add.2 (Nov. 2, 2000) [hereinafter ICC Elements of Crimes] (footnotes omitted). Rule 70 of the ICC's Rules of Procedure and Evidence addresses the parameters of consent raised as a defense. Preparatory Comm'n for the Int'l Criminal Court, *Report of the Preparatory Commission for the International Criminal Court, Finalized draft text of the Rules of Procedure and Evidence*, rule 70, U.N. Doc. PCNICC/2000/1/Add.1 (Nov. 2, 2000) [hereinafter ICC Rules].

[38] See, e.g., Engle, *supra* note 5; Kristen Boon, *Rape and Forced Pregnancy Under the ICC Statute: Human Dignity, Autonomy, and Consent*, 32 COLUM. HUM. RTS. L. REV. 625 (2001); Kirsten Campbell, *The Gender of Transitional Justice: Law, Sexual Violence and the International Criminal Tribunal for the Former Yugoslavia*, 1 INT'L J. TRANSITIONAL JUST. 411 (2007); Janet Halley et al., *From the International to the Local in Feminist Legal Responses to Rape, Prostitution/Sex Work, and Sex Trafficking: Four Studies in Contemporary Governance Feminism*, 29 HARV. J.L. & GENDER 335 (2006); Catharine A. MacKinnon, Essay, *Defining Rape Internationally: A Comment on Akayesu*, 44 COLUM. J. TRANSN'L L. 940 (2006).

[39] Wolfgang Schomburg & Ines Peterson, *Genuine Consent to Sexual Violence Under International Criminal Law*, 101 AM. J. INT'L L. 121, 124 (2007); DE BROUWER, *supra* note 37, at 120–24; U.N. Econ. & Soc. Council, Sub-Comm'n on Prevention of Discrimination and Prot. of Minorities, *Contemporary Forms of Slavery: Systematic rape, sexual slavery and slavery-like practice during armed conflict*, ¶ 25, U.N. Doc. E/CN.4/Sub.2/1998/13 (June 22, 1998) (prepared by Gay J. McDougall).

[40] Schomburg & Peterson, *supra* note 39, at 130.

[41] *Id.* at 139.

[42] Engle, *supra* note 5, at 804.

[43] Halley et al., *supra* note 38, at 381.

[44] Campbell, *supra* note 38, at 418.

2. Sexual Slavery

Sexual slavery was explicitly recognized as a prohibited crime against humanity for the first time in the Rome Statute and since then in the UNTAET Regulations and the Statute of the Special Court for Sierra Leone.[45] Sexual slavery was included in the Rome Statute as a crime against humanity and a war crime without much debate. There was some discussion about the difference between sexual slavery and enforced prostitution, and whether sexual slavery should be identified as a separate crime from enslavement.[46] In the end, States were persuaded that sexual slavery is a prevalent contemporary crime warranting express recognition, that the prohibition on sexual slavery was sufficiently established in existing law, that listing the crime would increase the gender sensitivity of the Rome Statute, and that sexual slavery is conceptually distinct from certain other forms of enslavement or slavery-like practices.[47] It would likely be entirely uncontroversial to include sexual slavery in any treaty codifying crimes against humanity.[48] Indeed, three accused were recently convicted of this crime against humanity by the Special Court for Sierra Leone.[49]

Following lengthy negotiations on the slavery aspect,[50] the relevant elements of crimes for sexual slavery are listed in the ICC's Elements of Crimes document as:

1. The perpetrator exercised any or all of the powers attaching to the right of ownership over one or more persons, such as by purchasing, selling, lending or bartering such a person or persons, or by imposing on them a similar deprivation of liberty. [fn 18]
2. The perpetrator caused such person or persons to engage in one or more acts of a sexual nature.[51]

Footnote 18 to subsection 1 mentioned earlier states:

It is understood that such deprivation of liberty may, in some circumstances, include exacting forced labour or otherwise reducing a person to a servile status as defined in the Supplementary Convention on the Abolition of Slavery, the Slave Trade, and Institutions and Practices Similar to Slavery of 1956. It is also understood that the conduct described in this element includes trafficking in persons, in particular women and children.[52]

---

[45] *Rome Statute*, *supra* note 2, art. 7(1)(g); UNTAET Reg. 2000/15, *supra* note 20, § 5.1; SCSL Statute, *supra* note 26, art. 2(g).
[46] Valerie Oosterveld, *Sexual Slavery and the International Criminal Court: Advancing International Law*, 25 MICH. J. INT'L L. 605, 616–25 (2004).
[47] *Id.* at 625.
[48] For the history of the inclusion of sexual slavery in the Rome Statute, see *id.* at 611–15.
[49] Prosecutor v. Sesay, Kallon and Gbao, Case No. SCSL-04-15-T, Judgment, 678, 682, 685 (Mar. 2, 2009).
[50] *See* description in Oosterveld, *supra* note 46, at 627–41.
[51] ICC Elements of Crimes, *supra* note 37, art. 7(1)(g)-2. When listing the elements of crimes, this chapter does not replicate the overarching elements required for all crimes against humanity.
[52] *Id.* art. 7(1)(g)-2 n.18.

In addition, the title listed in the Elements of Crimes document – "crimes against humanity of sexual slavery" – has the following footnote appended to it: "Given the complex nature of this crime, it is recognized that its commission could involve more than one perpetrator as part of a common criminal purpose."[53]

Some commentators have critiqued these elements. For example, Argibay feels that the Elements document "adopts an unreasonably narrow definition of enslavement which it then extends to sexual slavery," namely an emphasis on commercial exchange or similar deprivation of liberty.[54] This was also the view expressed in the nongovernmental Women's International War Crimes Tribunal "Comfort Women" Judgment.[55] The Special Rapporteur on systematic rape, sexual slavery, and slavery-like practices during armed conflict, citing the "purchasing, selling, lending or bartering" language, argued that "it is unnecessary and inappropriate to require any element of commercial transaction for the crime of sexual slavery."[56] These concerns seem not to have materialized, at least with respect to the ICC. In the Decision on Confirmation of Charges in *Katanga and Ngudolo Chui*, the Pre-Trial Chamber noted that the illustrative list is not exhaustive and found reasonable grounds to believe that sexual slavery may have been committed in circumstances that did not involve a commercial transaction.[57]

Recently, the Special Court for Sierra Leone's Trial Judgment in *Sesay et al.* adopted the ICC's elements of crimes for sexual slavery (minus the footnotes), adding a third element: "The Accused intended to exercise the act of sexual slavery or acted in the reasonable knowledge that this was likely to occur."[58] The Trial Chamber also adopted the following indicia of enslavement identified by the ICTY in *Kunarac et al.*: "control of someone's movement, control of physical environment, psychological control, measures taken to prevent or deter escape, force, threat of force or coercion, duration, assertion of exclusivity, subjection to cruel treatment and abuse, control of sexuality and forced labour."[59]

It is clear that sexual slavery should be included in any listing of prohibited acts in a treaty on crimes against humanity. The only point for further discussion would be how best to define the elements of slavery: follow the elements provided in the ICC's Elements document and used by the Special Court for Sierra Leone, or adopt elements which more clearly do not require any commercial element.

---

[53] *Id.* art. 7(1)(g)-2 n.17.
[54] Carmen M. Argibay, *Sexual Slavery and the "Comfort Women" of World War II*, 21 BERKELEY J. INT'L L. 375, 388 (2003).
[55] Prosecutors and Peoples of the Asia-Pacific Region v. Hirohito Emperor Showa, Case No. PT-2000–1-T, Judgment, ¶¶ 630–32 (Dec. 4, 2001) (Women's International War Crimes Tribunal for the Trial of Japan's Military Sexual Slavery).
[56] U.N. Comm'n on Human Rights, Sub-Comm'n on the Promotion and Prot. of Human Rights, *Contemporary Forms of Slavery, Systematic rape, sexual slavery and slavery-like practices during armed conflict: Update to the final report submitted by Ms. Gay J. McDougall, Special Rapporteur*, ¶¶ 8, 29, 50, U.N. Doc. E/CN.4/Sub.2/2000/21 (June 6, 2000).
[57] *Katanga and Ngudolo Chui*, *supra* note 4, ¶¶ 343, 347–54.
[58] *Sesay, Kallon and Gbao*, *supra* note 49, ¶ 158.
[59] *Id.* ¶ 160 (citing *Kunarac Trial Judgment*, *supra* note 4, ¶ 543).

3. Enforced Prostitution

The term "enforced prostitution" was listed for the first time as a crime against humanity in the Rome Statute.[60] The term, however, had been used in international humanitarian law and conventions against slavery for quite some time.[61] Prior to the adoption of the Rome Statute, enforced prostitution had also been referred to as a crime against humanity.[62] After the adoption of the Rome Statute, the UNTAET Regulations and the Statute of the Special Court for Sierra Leone listed enforced prostitution as a crime against humanity.[63]

The inclusion of enforced prostitution as a crime against humanity in the Rome Statute was uncontroversial, although there was some corridor discussion about whether enforced prostitution was an outdated term that should be replaced by a reference to sexual slavery.[64] In the end, States decided to include reference to both enforced prostitution and sexual slavery to differentiate between the two and to capture cases that may not satisfy the definition of slavery.

The negotiations on the elements of the crime of enforced prostitution provided States with the chance to illustrate how enforced prostitution is different from sexual slavery. These negotiations prompted debate focused around two interlinked issues: first, how a person might be forced to undertake sexual acts, short of enslavement; and, second, whether a benefit (monetary or otherwise) was required to be exchanged for the sexual acts, what might constitute a benefit, and to whom any benefit must accrue.[65] A majority of States agreed that the common understanding of prostitution encompasses the idea that the perpetrator or another person expects or obtains monetary or other advantage in exchange for or in connection with the sexual acts.[66] However, they also agreed that "advantage" should be understood in

---

[60] *Rome Statute*, *supra* note 2, art. 7(1)(g); UNTAET Reg. 2000/15, *supra* note 20, § 5.1(g); SCSL Statute, *supra* note 26, art. 2(g).

[61] For example, the 1919 Commission on the Responsibility of the Authors of the War and on Enforcement of Penalties (created by the Paris Peace Conference) listed "abduction of girls and women for the purpose of enforced prostitution" in its list of World War I war crimes. YOUGINDRA KHUSHALANI, DIGNITY AND HONOUR OF WOMEN AS BASIC AND FUNDAMENTAL HUMAN RIGHTS 11–12 (1982). The Fourth Geneva Convention indicates that women shall be especially protected against any attack on their honor, in particular against enforced prostitution. Geneva Convention of 1949 Relative to the Protection of Civilian Persons in Time of War art. 27, Aug. 12, 1949, 75 U.N.T.S. 287, 306. For a summary of other references, see Oosterveld, *supra* note 46, at 616–18.

[62] The Secretary-General, *Report of the Secretary-General Pursuant to Paragraph 2 of Security Council Resolution 808 (1993)*, at 13, ¶ 48, U.N. Doc. S/25704 (May 3, 1993); Int'l Law Comm'n, *Draft Code of Crimes Against the Peace and Security of Mankind*, art. 18(j), *in Report of the International Law Commission on the Work of its Forty-Eighth Session*, U.N. GAOR, 51st Sess., Supp. No. 10, U.N. Doc A/51/10 (1996).

[63] SCSL Statute, *supra* note 26, art. 2(g); UNTAET Reg. 2000/15, *supra* note 20, § 5.1(g).

[64] For more detail, see Oosterveld, *supra* note 46, at 618–22.

[65] *Id.* at 643–46.

[66] Eve La Haye, *Article 8(2)(b)(xxii)-Rape, Sexual Slavery, Enforced Prostitution, Forced Pregnancy, Enforced Sterilization, and Sexual Violence*, *in* THE INTERNATIONAL CRIMINAL COURT: ELEMENTS OF CRIMES AND RULES OF PROCEDURE AND EVIDENCE 184, 193 (Roy S. Lee et al. eds., 2001).

a complex sense: It could be advantage of sexual access to the perpetrator or a person linked to the perpetrator, material advantage (such as the exchange of goods or services for sex) benefiting the perpetrator or another person, or psychological advantage of the perpetrator or another person over the victim or a person linked to the victim.[67] Some States expressed the view that the person expecting an advantage could be the victim, hoping not to be tortured or killed.[68]

The relevant elements adopted, therefore, were:

1. The perpetrator caused one or more persons to engage in one or more acts of a sexual nature by force, or by threat of force or coercion, such as that caused by fear of violence, duress, detention, psychological oppression or abuse of power, against such person or persons or another person, or by taking advantage of a coercive environment or such person's or persons' incapacity to give genuine consent.
2. The perpetrator or another person obtained or expected to obtain pecuniary or other advantage in exchange for or in connection with the acts of a sexual nature.[69]

These elements distinguished enforced prostitution from sexual slavery. Enforced prostitution involves a person obtaining or expecting to obtain pecuniary or other advantage in exchange for sexual acts, whereas sexual slavery does not require a showing of advantage (as the test focuses upon the exercise of powers attaching to the right of ownership).[70] This approach seems to provide some welcome clarity to the prohibited act of enforced prostitution.

4. Forced Pregnancy

The crime against humanity of forced pregnancy was first codified within the Rome Statute.[71] The term "forced pregnancy" had been used previously in United Nations documents, such as the 1993 *Vienna Declaration and Programme of Action* and the 1995 *Beijing Declaration and Platform for Action*.[72] Subsequent to the adoption of the Rome Statute, both the UNTAET Regulations and the Statute of the Sierra Leone Special Court included forced pregnancy as a crime against humanity.[73] The crime against humanity (or war crime) of forced pregnancy has not been charged or prosecuted at any of these tribunals.

---

[67] Oosterveld, *supra* note 46, at 645.
[68] La Haye, *supra* note 66, at 193.
[69] ICC Elements of Crimes, *supra* note 37, art. 7(1)(g)-3.
[70] Oosterveld, *supra* note 46, at 646.
[71] *Rome Statute*, *supra* note 2, art. 7(1)(g). It is also listed as a war crime in articles 8(2)(b)(xxii) and 8(2)(e)(vi).
[72] *Vienna Declaration*, *supra* note 18, ¶¶ 18, 38; *Beijing Declaration*, *supra* note 19, ¶¶ 114, 132, 135.
[73] SCSL Statute, *supra* note 26, art. 2(g); UNTAET Reg. 2000/15, *supra* note 20, § 5.1(g).

The diplomatic negotiations surrounding the inclusion of this act in the Rome Statute were difficult. Forced pregnancy was proposed for inclusion into the draft Statute in order to capture the type of acts reported to have occurred during the conflict in Bosnia and Herzegovina, in which Bosnian women were raped, made pregnant, and held captive until abortion was not a likely option.[74] The rapists' intent seemed to be – apart from harming the victims physically and psychologically – to force these women to bear children considered by the rapists to be Serb.[75] In addition, the proposing and supporting States wished to capture other types of circumstances that might occur in the future in which women are forcibly made and kept pregnant (in a context satisfying the crimes against humanity or war crimes chapeau).[76] In response, the Holy See, Ireland, and other States expressed concern that the crime of forced pregnancy might impose on States the obligation to provide abortion services to women made forcibly pregnant.[77] A compromise was eventually reached to define forced pregnancy to mean "the unlawful confinement of a woman forcibly made pregnant, with the intent of affecting the ethnic composition of any population or carrying out other grave violations of international law. This definition shall not in any way be interpreted as affecting national laws relating to pregnancy."[78]

Some questions arise from the definition of forced pregnancy enunciated in the Rome Statute and the corresponding elements of crime: Is there a minimum temporal requirement for the "confinement"?[79] Must the confinement and forced impregnation be committed by the same person?[80] What is the effect of the phrase "This definition shall not in any way be interpreted as affecting national laws relating to pregnancy" on an ICC prosecution? Depending on whether a definition similar to that of the Rome Statute was adopted within a crimes against humanity convention, these questions might be relevant.

---

[74] Cate Steains, *Gender Issues*, in THE INTERNATIONAL CRIMINAL COURT: THE MAKING OF THE ROME STATUTE, ISSUES, NEGOTIATIONS, RESULTS 357, 366 (Roy S. Lee ed., 1999).

[75] *Id.*

[76] *Id.* An example of another context is when women are forcibly made and kept pregnant for the purposes of medical experimentation. Darryl Robinson, *Defining "Crimes Against Humanity" at the Rome Conference*, 93 AM. J. INT'L. L. 43, 53 n.63 (1999).

[77] Steains, *supra* note 74, at 366–67.

[78] *Rome Statute*, *supra* note 2, art. 7(2)(f). The relevant element of crime adopted for this prohibited act is: "The perpetrator confined one or more women forcibly made pregnant, with the intent of affecting the ethnic composition of any population or carrying out other grave violations of international law." ICC Elements of Crimes, *supra* note 37, art. 7(1)(g)-4.

[79] Some commentators argue that confinement should be interpreted broadly to include any deprivations of liberty no matter the length. *See, e.g.*, DE BROUWER, *supra* note 37, at 146. Boon suggests that a broad interpretation is appropriate. Boon, *supra* note 38, at 662.

[80] Draft elements had indicated that the accused confined one or more women, "[s]uch woman or women had been forcibly made pregnant," and "[t]he accused intended to keep the women or women pregnant," thus clarifying that the perpetrator need not be the one who forcibly made the woman or women pregnant. *Discussion paper proposed by the Coordinator: Article, paragraph 2 (b) (xxii)*, PCNICC/1999/L.5/WGEC/RT.6 (1999). However, this formulation was opposed by some delegations and the decision was taken to revert to a close reproduction of the Rome Statute definition. La Haye, *supra* note 66, at 194–95. Boon suggests that, even so, it is reasonably clear

5. Enforced Sterilization

The crime against humanity of enforced sterilization was first codified by the Rome Statute, and then again in UNTAET Regulation 2000/15.[81] Its inclusion in the Rome Statute was first inspired by the kinds of acts described in the post–World War II *Medical Case* and other cases stemming from medical experimentation or mass sterilization in concentration camps,[82] and second, from reports of violent sexual acts taking place during conflicts that resulted in severe reproductive damage (including sterilization).[83]

In the Rome Statute, this prohibited act is listed among sexual violence crimes. This is because enforced sterilization can occur through sexually violent means. For example, Askin notes that sterilization may occur as a result of sexual mutilation or damage (such as castration, use of a weapon or object to rape, or through violent/multiple rapes), sexually transmitted disease, or forced or botched abortions.[84] Many World War II "comfort women" lost their reproductive capacity as a result of their sexual slavery.[85] In this respect, this act is properly placed within the list of sexually violent acts.

However, enforced sterilization may also occur as a result of medical procedures affecting reproductive capacity that are not necessarily the result of sexual violence. The *Medical Case* described how drugs, X-rays, and surgery were used to test ways in which to conduct rapid, widespread sterilization.[86] Some of these methods may not be considered "sexual" in a manner similar to rape, sexual slavery, enforced prostitution, and forced pregnancy. Thus, it may be useful to consider whether this prohibited act should remain on the list of prohibited acts of sexual violence or be listed separately.

The ICC's elements of crime for enforced sterilization are listed as:

1. The perpetrator deprived one or more persons of biological reproductive capacity.[19]
2. The conduct was neither justified by the medical or hospital treatment of the person or persons concerned nor carried out with their genuine consent.[20]

Footnote 19: The deprivation is not intended to include birth-control measures which have a non-permanent effect in practice.

---

that the perpetrator need not be the one who forcibly made the woman or women pregnant. Boon, *supra* note 38, at 660.

[81] *Rome Statute*, *supra* note 2, art. 7(1)(g); UNTAET Reg. 2000/15, *supra* note 20, § 5.1(g). This act is not included in the Statute of the Special Court for Sierra Leone. See SCSL Statute, *supra* note 26.

[82] United States v. Karl Brandt, 2 Trial of War Criminals Before the Nuremberg Military Tribunal Under Control Council Law No. 10 (1950) (also referred to as the Medical Case). See examples provided in Kelly D. Askin, *The Jurisprudence of International War Crimes Tribunals: Securing Gender Justice for Some Survivors*, in LISTENING TO THE SILENCES: WOMEN AND WAR 125, 146 (Helen Durham & Tracey Gurd eds., 2005).

[83] As detailed in, for example, HUMAN RIGHTS WATCH, SHATTERED LIVES: SEXUAL VIOLENCE DURING THE RWANDAN GENOCIDE AND ITS AFTERMATH (1996).

[84] Askin, *supra* note 82, at 145–46.

[85] *Id.*

[86] For a summary, see Harvard Law School Library Nuremberg Trials Project, *available at* http://nuremberg.law.harvard.edu/php/docs_swi.php?DI=1&text=medical.

Footnote 20: It is understood that "genuine consent" does not include consent obtained through deception.[87]

The second element seems to imply that the prohibited act of enforced sterilization is likely to occur in a medical setting. Given that enforced sterilization can also occur outside of such a setting (for example, through rape), any elements of crime adopted for a crimes against humanity treaty should allow for a broad understanding of where and how sterilization results.

6. Other Forms of Sexual Violence

Within the Rome Statute, the crimes against humanity listing of sexual violence crimes ends with a basket clause, classifying as a prohibited act along with the acts listed above, "any other form of sexual violence of comparable gravity."[88] The comparable gravity wording was inserted to satisfy those States concerned that, absent this phrase, the basket clause might not meet the principle of legality due to its perceived vagueness. Whereas the UNTAET Regulations replicate the comparable gravity wording, the Statute of the Special Court for Sierra Leone's basket clause is simply "any other form of sexual violence."[89]

The open-ended reference to "any other form of sexual violence" was included in the Rome Statute to capture other kinds of sexual violence that are not explicitly named in the list of sexual violence crimes, but are also of concern to the international community. The ICC's elements of crime for this basket clause are:

1. The perpetrator committed an act of a sexual nature against one or more persons or caused such person or persons to engage in an act of a sexual nature by force, or by threat of force or coercion, such as that caused by fear of violence, duress, detention, psychological oppression or abuse of power, against such person or persons or another person, or by taking advantage of a coercive environment or such person or persons' incapacity to give genuine consent.
2. Such conduct was of a gravity comparable to the other offences in article 7, paragraph 1(g) of the Statute.
3. The perpetrator was aware of the factual circumstances that established the gravity of the conduct.[90]

The examples of force or coercion are taken from those referred to in the elements for rape and enforced prostitution. These elements were influenced by the definition of sexual violence adopted by the ICTR in *Akayesu*: "any act of a sexual nature which is committed on a person under circumstances which are coercive. Sexual violence is not limited to physical invasion of the human body and may include acts which do not involve penetration or even physical contact."[91] Examples

---

[87] ICC Elements of Crimes, *supra* note 37, art. 7(1)(g)-5.
[88] *Rome Statute, supra* note 2, art. 7(1)(g).
[89] UNTAET Reg. 2000/15, *supra* note 20, § 5.1(g); SCSL Statute, *supra* note 26, art. 2(g).
[90] ICC Elements of Crimes, *supra* note 37, art. 7(1)(g)-6.
[91] *Akayesu, supra* note 4, ¶ 688.

of sexual violence identified by the ICTY and ICTR include forced nudity or forced undressing,[92] sexual mutilation, forced marriage, and forced abortion.[93] (Note that forced marriage is not solely a sexual violence crime and is therefore discussed as a gender-based crime in more detail below.)

The inclusion of a residual basket clause within the Rome Statute to ensure inclusion of other sexual violence crimes was relatively uncontroversial. There was some concern expressed by nongovernmental organizations that the phrasing "of comparable gravity" would be interpreted by the ICC as meaning that the sexual violence would have to look like rape. However, the negotiations on the elements of crimes clarified that the sexual violence conduct must be of a gravity comparable to any of the other offenses in article 7(1)(g), and not only rape.[94] This is consistent with the ICTY and ICTR's understanding of sexual violence as including a wide range of acts, from those that invade sexual organs to humiliating acts that do not involve physical contact. This has been the approach of the Special Court for Sierra Leone to date.[95]

One would expect that States would wish to include a basket clause referring to other forms of sexual violence within a crimes against humanity treaty in order to capture sexual violence crimes that have not been already named above, such as sexual mutilation, forced impregnation not accompanied by forcible confinement, and forced sexual intercourse or other sexual acts with family members. The question that would likely require some discussion is whether to include a reference to comparable gravity, as was done in the Rome Statute, or to exclude such a reference, as was done in the Statute of the Special Court for Sierra Leone.

B. Other Gender-Based Acts

This section explores three gender-based acts: gender-based persecution, forced marriage, and forced abortion/miscarriage. Just as it is important to recognize that gender is a far wider concept than of sex, it is crucial to understand that gender-based acts comprise much more than sexual violence, even though sexual violence may be an aspect of a gender-based act.

1. Gender-Based Persecution

Even though persecution has long been recognized as a crime against humanity, the Rome Statute was the first international criminal justice instrument to include gender

---

[92] *Id.* ¶ 697.
[93] These last three examples are provided in *Kvočka, supra* note 35, ¶ 180 n.343.
[94] Darryl Robinson, *Article 7(1)(g)-Crime Against Humanity of Rape, Sexual Slavery, Enforced Prostitution, Forced Pregnancy, Enforced Sterilization, or Any Other Form of Sexual Violence of Comparable Gravity, in* THE INTERNATIONAL CRIMINAL COURT: ELEMENTS OF CRIMES AND RULES OF PROCEDURE AND EVIDENCE 93, 93 (Roy S. Lee et al. eds., 2001).
[95] Prosecutor v. Brima et al., Case No. SCSL-04-16-T, Decisions on Defence Motion for Judgment of Acquittal Pursuant to Rule 98, ¶ 111 (Mar. 31, 2006).

as a ground for persecution.⁹⁶ The inclusion of gender within the list of persecutory grounds in the Rome Statute followed on the recognition of gender-related forms of persecution within international refugee law since 1985.⁹⁷ The Rome Statute includes gender among a number of grounds, namely political, racial, national, ethnic, cultural, religious, or other grounds that are universally recognized as impermissible under international law.⁹⁸ Persecution is defined in the Rome Statute as "the intentional and severe deprivation of fundamental rights contrary to international law by reason of the identity of the group or collectivity."⁹⁹ The UNTAET Regulations similarly include gender as a ground for persecution and define it in the same way.¹⁰⁰

The ICC has not yet charged individuals with gender-based persecution, but the ICTY and ICTR have identified certain gender-specific acts as amounting to persecution. For example, in *Nahimana*, the ICTR Trial Chamber indicated that the social construction of Tutsi women as "seductive agents of the enemy" by the media in Rwanda "made the sexual attack and killing of Tutsi women a foreseeable consequence of the role attributed to them."¹⁰¹ The ICTY has also indicated that acts of sexual violence such as rape can be persecutory acts.¹⁰²

The Rome Statute definition of persecution was subject to negotiation because some States expressed concern that the inclusion of persecution as a prohibited act within the crimes against humanity provision could turn a criminal court into a human rights court.¹⁰³ Thus, a definition was drafted to indicate that persecution has a specific threshold requiring an "intentional and severe deprivation of fundamental rights contrary to international law" and a connection with other crimes within the jurisdiction of the Court.

---

⁹⁶ For more detail, see Valerie Oosterveld, *Gender, Persecution, and the International Criminal Court: Refugee Law's Relevance to the Crime Against Humanity of Gender-Based Persecution*, 17 DUKE J. COMP. & INT'L L. 49 (2006).

⁹⁷ In 1985, the United Nations High Commissioner for Refugees Executive Committee issued a conclusion that

> [r]ecognized that States, in the exercise of their sovereignty, were free to adopt the interpretation that women asylum-seekers who face harsh or inhuman treatment due to their having transgressed the social mores of the society in which they lived may be considered as a "particular social group" within the meaning of article 1 A, paragraph 2, of the 1951 United Nations Convention relating to the Status of Refugees.

U.N. High Comm'r for Refugees, *Report of the Executive Committee on the Programme of the United Nations High Commissioner for Refugees on the Work of its Thirty-Sixth Session, Addendum to the Report of the United Nations High Commissioner for Refugees*, ¶ 115(4)(k), U.N. Doc. A/40/12/Add.1 (Jan. 10, 1986).

⁹⁸ *Rome Statute, supra* note 2, art. 7(1)(h) ("Persecution against any identifiable group or collectivity on political, racial, national, ethnic, cultural, religious, gender as defined in paragraph 3, or other grounds that are universally recognized as impermissible under international law, in connection with any act referred to in this paragraph or any crime within the jurisdiction of the Court.").

⁹⁹ *Id*. art. 7(2)(g).

¹⁰⁰ UNTAET Reg. 2000/15, *supra* note 20, §§ 5.1(h), 5.2(f).

¹⁰¹ Prosecutor v. Nahimana et al., Case. No. ICTR-99-52-T, Judgment and Sentence, ¶ 1079 (Dec. 3, 2003).

¹⁰² Prosecutor v. Brđanin, Case No. IT-99-36-T, Judgment, ¶ 1008 (Sept. 1, 2004).

¹⁰³ Robinson, *supra* note 78, at 53.

Early in the negotiations on defining persecution, the term "gender" was added to the list of potential prohibited grounds. At the time, it was placed in square brackets as part of the debate over whether to include an illustrative or exhaustive list of prohibited grounds of persecution, rather than for any definitional concern.[104] Later, however, some States did raise concern about the meaning of the term as a persecutory ground.[105] These States appeared to be concerned that inclusion of the term "gender" within the crime against humanity of persecution could create a persecutory ground based on sexual orientation,[106] or could lead to the classification of certain laws and practices that affect women in their countries as crimes against humanity.[107] After lengthy and contentious negotiations, a definition of "gender" was adopted.[108] The definition did not, as some claim, exclude sexual orientation from being considered within the context of gender or exclude the socially constructed context that is key to an understanding of gender.[109] Rather, it left the issue of sexual orientation and the case-specific understanding of the "context of society" to be judicially determined.

In line with the Rome Statute, any treaty codifying crimes against humanity should include gender as a persecutory ground. If the ICC negotiations are a guide – and they may not be, given the ever-growing use of the term "gender" (without definition) within the United Nations Security Council and General Assembly – there may be calls by some States for the term "gender" to be defined. For the reasons articulated in the first section of this chapter, these calls should be deferred. However, if they cannot, a clearer definition, indicating that gender is the social construction of maleness and femaleness and can vary within and across cultures,

---

[104] Preparatory Comm'n on the Establishment of an Int'l Criminal Court, *Decisions Taken by the Preparatory Committee at Its Session Held from 11 to 21 February 1997*, Annex 1, at 4, 5 n.7, U.N. Doc. A/AC.249/1997/L.5 (Mar. 12, 1997).

[105] For example, Azerbaijan, Bahrain, and Kuwait. United Nations Diplomatic Conference of Plenipoteniaries on the Establishment of an International Criminal Court, Rome, Italy, June 15-July 17, 1998, *25th meeting of the Committee of the Whole*, ¶ 61, U.N. Doc. A/CONF.183/C.1/SR.25 (July 8, 1998) [hereinafter Summary Record of the 25th Meeting] (comments of the representative of Azerbaijan); United Nations Diplomatic Conference of Plenipoteniaries on the Establishment of an International Criminal Court, Rome, Italy, June 15-July 17, 1998, *27th meeting of the Committee of the Whole*, ¶ 22, U.N. Doc. A/CONF.183/C.1/SR.27 (July 8, 1998) (comments of the representative from Bahrain); United Nations Diplomatic Conference of Plenipoteniaries on the Establishment of an International Criminal Court, Rome, Italy, June 15-July 17, 1998, *28th meeting of the Committee of the Whole*, ¶ 13, U.N. Doc. A/CONF.183/C.1/SR.28 (July 8,1998) (comments of the representative from Kuwait).

[106] Under international refugee law, gender-based claims of persecution on the basis of sexual orientation have been recognized. It was the view of many States that the interpretation of "gender" to include persecution on the basis of sexual orientation was not only desirable, but also necessary to prosecute the kind of homophobic persecution that had occurred in World War II.

[107] For example, the delegate from Azerbaijan asked if a gender-based persecution provision could "imply that a conviction by a national court for homosexual acts might be regarded as persecution and thus fall within the jurisdiction of the Court as a crime against humanity." Summary Record of the 25th Meeting, *supra* note 105, ¶ 61. See also Oosterveld, *supra* note 8, at 63, 65–66.

[108] Oosterveld, *supra* note 96, at 57–59.

[109] *See* Oosterveld, *supra* note 8, at 76–80 (discussing assumptions to this effect and the actual history of the negotiations).

over time, and may be influenced by its intersection with other factors (such as age), is to be preferred over a carbon copy of the Rome Statute's definition.

2. Forced Marriage

The Prosecutor of the Special Court for Sierra Leone charged a number of the accused with the crime against humanity of inhumane acts using evidence of forced marriage. Forced marriage occurred in Sierra Leone when girls and women were abducted (often in circumstances of extreme violence) and then forcibly assigned to male combatants to serve as "wives."[110] These "wives" were expected to submit to sex with their "husbands" on demand, as well as to cook, wash clothes, and carry possessions for them.[111] These "wives" were also expected to remain loyal to, and protect the property of, their "husbands."[112] Many of these wives were subjected to physical, emotional, and sexual violence, and some contracted sexually transmitted diseases during their time spent as a "wife."[113] Many became pregnant and were forced to bear, care for, and rear the children, often under very difficult circumstances.[114] Girls and women who served as "wives," and their children, have been negatively stigmatized in Sierra Leonean society and suffer long-lasting harm as a result.[115]

The analysis of forced marriage by a Trial Chamber of the Special Court can serve as a cautionary tale regarding the importance of understanding the difference between gender-based and sexual crimes. This Trial Chamber dismissed the charge related to forced marriage for redundancy, finding that evidence adduced on forced marriage was "completely subsumed" by that of the crime against humanity of sexual slavery.[116] This is despite the nonsexual nature of some of the evidence, for example, evidence related to forced household labor and portering. This mischaracterization was corrected by the Appeals Chamber, which held that forced marriage is different from sexual slavery, and can be defined as:

> a situation in which the perpetrator through his words or conduct, or those of someone for whose actions he is responsible, compels a person by force, threat of force, or coercion to serve as a conjugal partner resulting in severe suffering, or physical, mental or psychological injury to the victim.[117]

The Appeals Chamber's definition of forced marriage raises some questions that will need to be addressed if forced marriage is included as a prohibited act within a crimes against humanity treaty. What does "conjugal" association mean? Is the

---

[110] Prosecutor v. Brima et al., Case No. SCSL-04-16-A, Judgment, ¶ 190 (Feb. 22, 2008) [hereinafter *Brima Appeals Judgment*].
[111] *Brima Trial Judgment*, *supra* note 4, ¶ 711.
[112] *Id.* ¶¶ 31–32 (separate opinion of Judge Doherty).
[113] *Id.* ¶ 15 (separate opinion of Judge Sebutinde).
[114] *Brima Appeals Judgment*, *supra* note 110, ¶ 190.
[115] *Brima Trial Judgment*, *supra* note 4, ¶ 48, 51 (separate opinion of Judge Doherty); *Brima Appeals Judgment*, *supra* note 110, ¶ 199.
[116] *Brima Trial Judgment*, *supra* note 4, ¶¶ 713–14.
[117] *Brima Appeals Judgment*, *supra* note 110, ¶ 196.

definition gender-neutral?[118] Does the definition reinforce patriarchal notions of marriage and, if so, is this worrisome?[119]

The Special Court's Prosecutor charged the act of forced marriage under the crime against humanity of other inhumane acts because the Special Court's Statute did not specifically list "forced marriage" as a prohibited act. The Special Court's Appeals Chamber determined that forced marriage satisfies the elements of "other inhumane acts."[120] It stated that it is "firmly of the view that acts of forced marriage were of similar gravity to several enumerated crimes against humanity including enslavement, imprisonment, torture, rape, sexual slavery and sexual violence."[121] Given the recent jurisprudential development of this act, including a definition, forced marriage need not always be considered within the category of "other inhumane acts"; it could certainly be listed as a separate prohibited act within a crimes against humanity treaty. Jain agrees, arguing that:

> [t]he defining element of forced marriage is the imposition of a marital relationship without the consent of the party to the marriage. The lack of consent is what distinguishes a forced marriage from a valid marriage and emphasizes what is at the heart of forced marriage, the severe violation of individual autonomy and right to self-determination.[122]

Alternatively, the prohibited act of forced marriage could be listed in combination with other gender-based acts that are not mainly or exclusively sexual in nature, such as enforced sterilization and forced abortion.[123]

3. Forced Abortion or Forced Miscarriage

The ICC's *Lubanga* case has heard evidence related to forced abortion (though this act has not been charged as such). On March 18, 2009, a former militia soldier testified that abducted girls who became pregnant in the camps of Lubanga's militia were pressured to have abortions or they were chased away.[124] Although forced abortion (or forced miscarriage) is not listed in any international criminal justice statute

---

[118] In the Extraordinary Chambers of the Courts of Cambodia, Co-Lawyers for the Civil Parties have filed an application requesting that Co-Prosecutors investigate forced marriage during the Khmer Rouge period. Kaig Guek Eav ("Duch"), Case No. 001/18–07–2007-ECCC/TC, Civil Parties' Co-Lawyers' Request for Supplementary Preliminary Investigations (Feb. 9, 2009) (on file with the author).

[119] Valerie Oosterveld, *The Special Court for Sierra Leone's Consideration of Gender-based Violence: Contributing to Transitional Justice?*, 10 Hum. Rts. Rev. 73, 85 (2009); Valerie Oosterveld, *The Special Court for Sierra Leone, Child Soldiers and Forced Marriage: Providing Clarity or Confusion?*, 45 Can. Y.B. Int'l L. 131, 158 (2009).

[120] *Brima Appeals Judgment*, supra note 110, ¶¶ 197–203.

[121] *Id.* ¶ 200.

[122] Neha Jain, *Forced Marriage as a Crime against Humanity: Problems of Definition and Prosecution*, 6 J. Int'l Crim. Just. 1013, 1031 (2008).

[123] Although not discussed in this chapter, forced maternity/forced childrearing (as a result of, for example, forced marriage or rape) could also qualify as a separate gender-based act and be added into this list.

[124] Meribeth Dean, *Pregnant Girls Forced to Abort*, Mar. 18, 2009, *available at* www.LubangaTrial.org/2009/03/18/pregnant-girls-forced-to-abort/ (official ICC transcript not available at the time of writing).

as a crime against humanity, this crime should be considered for inclusion because of its resemblance to the harm done in forced sterilization, which is an explicitly recognized prohibited act under the umbrella of crimes against humanity.

Like forced sterilization, forced abortion (or forced miscarriage) may or may not involve a physical invasion of an individual's (in this case, always a female's) sexual organs and therefore may more properly be listed as a gender-based act. An example of forced abortion involving nonphysical invasion is given in the *Lubanga* evidence, in which girls took traditional medicine to induce miscarriages.[125] The International Military Tribunal at Nuremberg recorded evidence of forced abortion likely involving physical operations.[126] Askin convincingly notes that if a woman (or girl) is subjected to violence, including sexual violence, which results in a miscarriage, that act could be prosecuted as forced abortion (or forced miscarriage) if the pregnancy was known or obvious and the miscarriage is a foreseeable outcome of the violence.[127]

The specific elements of forced abortion (or forced miscarriage) might include: 1) the perpetrator caused the termination of pregnancy of a woman by force, threat of force or coercion, such as that caused by fear of violence, duress, detention, psychological oppression, or abuse of power, against such person or persons or another person, or by taking advantage of a coercive environment or such person's or persons' incapacity to give genuine consent – wording from the elements of sexual violence; or 2) the conduct was neither justified by the medical or hospital treatment of the persons or persons concerned nor carried out with their genuine consent – wording from the elements of enforced sterilization. As with enforced sterilization, the latter wording may not clearly capture forced abortion (or forced miscarriage) resulting from, for example, individuals jumping on the abdomen of a pregnant woman.[128]

C. Other Prohibited Acts With Gendered Aspects

Gender-based acts have been prosecuted by the ICTY, the ICTR, and the Special Court for Sierra Leone as the crimes against humanity of torture, enslavement, and other inhumane acts. For example, in *Akayesu*, the ICTR's Trial Chamber convicted

---

[125] *Id.*

[126] For example, Askin refers to IMT transcripts stating that, in the Nazi concentration camps, "[t]he Jewish women, when they arrived in the first months of pregnancy, were subjected to abortion," and that official Nazi policy required that non-German women were to be obliged to have their fetuses "removed by operation in a hospital." Askin, *supra* note 82, at 150.

[127] *Id.* at 151.

[128] Askin has proposed two approaches, defining forced abortion as "treatment, whether medically induced or otherwise, which results in a woman losing her pregnancy against her will and in violation of international norms," Askin, *supra* note 82, at 150, and, in an earlier book, elements including:

1) That the accused committed or ordered to be committed certain acts against a certain named or described person;
2) That such person was known to be pregnant at the time the act(s) were committed;
3) That the accused committed or order[ed] to be committed the acts with the intent to cause the person to lose the pregnancy;
4) That the acts were wrongfully committed against the will, without the consent, or by coercion of the woman; and
5) That a loss of pregnancy resulted from the act.

the accused of inhumane acts on evidence of forced nudity.[129] In *Niyitigeka*, the accused was convicted by the ICTR of the inhumane acts of castration of Kabanda and sexual mutilation of a dead Tutsi woman.[130] In *Tadić*, sexual mutilation of a male prisoner was categorized as an inhumane act.[131] Enslavement and torture were proven through the use of sexual violence evidence in the ICTY's *Kunarac et al.* case.[132]

It is important to maintain the ability to prosecute gender-based acts under the umbrella of other prohibited acts not listed earlier, such as extermination, enslavement, torture, or inhumane acts. First, the commission of the other prohibited acts may take place in a gendered manner. As an example, the prohibited act of extermination may take place by targeting two parts of a civilian population in different ways: men for summary execution by gunfire and women for sexual mutilation until death. In this case, it is crucial to consider these acts together to prove the prohibited act of extermination. Second, a particular act may be proven using, among various kinds of evidence, gender-based acts. The Special Court for Sierra Leone Appeals Chamber has confirmed the approach of the ICTY and ICTR that evidence of sexual violence may be used to prove the crime against humanity of other inhumane acts.[133] Finally, although it is generally best to charge the acts that most precisely describe the evidence,[134] there may be times when, "due to the sensitivities of the survivors or other legitimate reasons," a prosecutor may wish to consider gender-based acts under the heading of another prohibited act.[135]

III. PROPOSALS FOR A CRIMES AGAINST HUMANITY TREATY

To be relevant to the nature of current and future armed conflicts, a treaty codifying crimes against humanity should reflect a range of gender-based prohibited acts. These should include acts of sexual violence: rape, sexual slavery, enforced prostitution, and forced pregnancy, as well as a basket clause capturing other forms of sexual violence. A crimes against humanity treaty should also list acts that may or may not contain sexual aspects but that are gender-based, such as gender-based persecution, forced marriage, enforced sterilization, and forced abortion/miscarriage.

KELLY DAWN ASKIN, WAR CRIMES AGAINST WOMEN: PROSECUTION IN INTERNATIONAL WAR CRIMES TRIBUNALS 399–400 (1997).

[129] *Akayesu*, *supra* note 4, ¶ 697.
[130] *Niyitegeka*, *supra* note 31, ¶¶ 462–463.
[131] Prosecutor v. Tadić, Case No. IT-94-1-T, Judgment, ¶ 729 (May 7, 1997).
[132] *Kunarac Trial Judgment*, *supra* note 4, ¶ 883; *Kunarac Appeals Judgment*, *supra* note 34, ¶¶ 149–150.
[133] *Brima Appeals Judgment*, *supra* note 110, ¶ 186.
[134] *See* DE BROUWER, *supra* note 37, at 166.
[135] Askin, *supra* note 82, at 151.

Some of the acts proposed for inclusion carry with them questions that may need to be addressed, either when discussing their inclusion or when considering elements of crimes:

- Rape: Which of the four definitions of rape currently in use by international tribunals, if any, should be followed? Is it appropriate to include nonconsent as an element of the crime that a prosecutor would need to prove beyond a reasonable doubt, or should consent be treated as a defense?
- Sexual slavery: How best to define the elements of slavery: follow the elements provided in the ICC's Elements document and used by the Special Court for Sierra Leone, or adopt elements that more clearly do not require any commercial element?
- Forced pregnancy: Is there a minimum temporal requirement for the "confinement"? Must the confinement and forced impregnation be committed by the same person? If included, what is the effect of the phrase "This definition shall not in any way be interpreted as affecting national laws relating to pregnancy" on a prosecution?
- Enforced sterilization: Should this prohibited act be listed among the sexual violence crimes or separately listed with gender-based crimes? Should the ICC's elements be replicated (referring to a medical setting) or should a broader approach be explicitly taken?
- Other forms of sexual violence: Should a reference to comparable gravity be included, as was done in the Rome Statute, or excluded, as was done in the Statute of the Special Court for Sierra Leone?
- Gender-based persecution: Must the term "gender" be defined?
- Forced marriage: What does "conjugal" association mean? Is the definition applicable to both female and male victims? Does the definition reinforce patriarchal notions of marriage and, if so, is this worrisome?
- Forced abortion/miscarriage: How should this act be defined? Is one term (abortion or miscarriage) preferable to the other?
- Other prohibited acts: Are the other prohibited acts listed in the draft treaty worded in such a way as not to exclude the use of gendered evidence to prove those acts?
- Finally, the question should be considered as to whether the term "gender" requires definition. Can it be left undefined?

6

"Chapeau Elements" of Crimes Against Humanity in the Jurisprudence of the UN Ad Hoc Tribunals

Göran Sluiter

I. INTRODUCTION

Crimes against humanity is the common element in the law and practice of the International Criminal Tribunal for the former Yugoslavia (ICTY) and the International Criminal Tribunal for Rwanda (ICTR). It is the glue that ties these institutions together in terms of their subject matter jurisdiction. Looking at the judgments of the ICTY, one notices the difficulty in securing convictions for genocide, but crimes against humanity figure prominently in both indictments and convictions, with the exception of a few cases only dealing with war crimes.[1] At the ICTR, genocide is the focus in practically all cases, but each genocide accusation is backed up by crimes against humanity accusations, especially extermination, murder, and persecution; thus the ICTR confirms the (historically) close relationship between both sets of crimes.[2] But the ICTR rarely convicts for war crimes, for the reasons that the prosecution does not tend to include it in the indictment and that in (early) case law, ICTR Trial Chambers found no nexus between genocidal acts and the armed conflict.[3] As far as the Special Court for Sierra Leone (SCSL) is concerned, it has no jurisdiction over genocide, but only over war crimes, crimes against

---

[1] In the following cases, the indictments concentrated on war crimes only: Prosecutor v. Delalić, Mucić, Delić and Landžo, Case No. IT-96-21-T, Judgment (Nov. 16, 1998); Prosecutor v. Furundžija, Case No. IT-95-17/1-T, Judgment (Dec. 10, 1998); Prosecutor v. Aleksovski, Case No. IT-95-14/1-T, Judgment (June 25, 1999); Prosecutor v. Strugar, Case No. IT-02-42-T, Judgment (Jan.31, 2005); Prosecutor v. Hadzihasanović and Kubura, Case No. IT-01-47-T, Judgment (Mar. 15, 2006); Prosecutor v. Orić, Case No. IT-03-68-T, Judgment (June 30, 2006); Prosecutor v. Boškoski and Tarčulovski, Case No. IT-04-82-T, Judgment (July 10, 2008).
[2] See WILLIAM A. SCHABAS, THE UN INTERNATIONAL CRIMINAL TRIBUNALS – THE FORMER YUGOSLAVIA, RWANDA AND SIERRA LEONE 185 (2006).
[3] The existence of a nexus between the conduct of the accused and the armed conflict in Rwanda in 1994 was not established by the ICTR Trial Chambers in: Prosecutor v. Musema, Case No. ICTR-96-13, Judgment and Sentence, ¶¶ 973–74 (Jan. 27, 2000); Prosecutor v. Ntakirutimana, Cases No. ICTR-96-10 & ICTR-96-17, Judgment and Sentence, ¶ 861 (Feb. 21, 2003); Prosecutor v. Rutaganda, Case No. ICTR-96-3, Judgment and Sentence, ¶¶ 442–43 (Dec. 6 1999); Prosecutor v. Akayesu, Case No. ICTR-96-4, Judgment, ¶ 640 (Sept. 2, 1998); Prosecutor v. Kamuhanda, Case No. ICTR-99-54, Judgment and Sentence, ¶ 739 (Jan. 22, 2004); in a way also in Prosecutor v. Kayishema and Ruzindana, Cases No. ICTR-95-1 and ICTR-96-10, Judgment, ¶ 617 (May 21, 1999). Especially in more recent case law, the ICTR Trial Chambers seemed more inclined to establish a nexus between the armed conflict and certain "acts of genocide." Prosecutor v. Ntagerura et al., Case No. ICTR-96-10-A, Judgment and Sentence, ¶ 793 (Feb. 25, 2004); Prosecutor v.

humanity, and a limited set of crimes under Sierra Leonean law.[4] All judgments of that court deal with allegations of both war crimes and crimes against humanity.[5]

Thus, the UN ad hoc tribunals truly are crimes against humanity courts and undeniably have in their practice contributed significantly to the definition and understanding of the crime. For the drafting of a crimes against humanity convention, their work is of great significance. Although the quantity of case law dealing with crimes against humanity is certainly impressive, this contribution is concerned with its quality and will, as a result, critically assess choices made and approaches adopted by the UN ad hoc tribunals. The focus is on tracing back the origin of the ad hoc tribunals' case law and providing insight as to the jurisprudential choices made. This serves the ultimate purpose of answering the question whether the foundations of the ICTY and ICTR case law on crimes against humanity are as strong as we may be tempted to believe. The answer to this question is especially relevant if one seeks to critically address and compare alternative definitions and approaches to crimes against humanity, like in the International Criminal Court (ICC) Statute. When differences exist and/or when aspects of the ad hoc tribunals' case law leave something to be desired, the question imposes itself to what extent the law and jurisprudence of the UN ad hoc tribunals should be regarded as authoritative guidance when drafting a convention on crimes against humanity. On the basis of the analysis in this chapter, which is not complete but at least exemplary as to how the UN ad hoc tribunals have dealt with crimes against humanity, I intend to answer this question.

I will confine my discussion to the chapeau elements in crimes against humanity. It would clearly exceed the scope of this work to include an analysis of punishable acts; furthermore, others deal with two very important punishable acts elsewhere in this volume.[6]

Before moving to an analysis of the chapeau elements in the case law of the UN ad hoc tribunals, two preliminary paragraphs are in order. First, I will sketch the legal framework as it developed since the first definition of crimes against humanity in the International Military Tribunal (IMT) Charter; only definitions of crimes against humanity that have in fact been applied by international criminal tribunals are taken into account. Second, I will discuss briefly the discovery of rules of international law and use of interpretative methods at the ad hoc tribunals because this is of significant importance for understanding and evaluating their jurisprudence.

Semanza, Case No. ICTR-97-20, Judgment and Sentence, ¶ 518 (May 15, 2003); Prosecutor v. Bagosora, Case No. IT-98-41-T, Judgment and Sentence, ¶¶ 2231–36 (Dec. 18, 2008).

[4] Statute of the Special Court for Sierra Leone, U.N. Doc S/2002/246, Appendix II, Jan. 16, 2002, 2178 U.N.T.S. 138, arts. 2–5.

[5] Prosecutor v. Fofana and Kondewa, Case No. SCSL-04-14-T, Judgment (Aug. 2, 2007); Prosecutor v. Sesay, Kallon and Gbao, Case No. SCSL-04-15-T, Judgment (Mar. 2, 2009); Prosecutor v. Brima, Kamara and Kanu, Case No. SCSL-04-16-T, Judgment (June 20, 2007).

[6] *See* Valerie Oosterveld, *Gender-based Crimes Against Humanity*, in this volume; Michael P. Scharf and Michael A. Newton, *Terrorism and Crimes Against Humanity*, in this volume.

It will be noticed that the discussion in this chapter concentrates to a large degree on the ICTY. This tribunal was the first to be confronted with the interpretation of the law on crimes against humanity. Leaving aside a few decisions in the framework of Rule 61,[7] the first relevant and authoritative rulings on crimes against humanity can be encountered in the *Tadić* jurisdiction appeal judgment from October 2, 1995,[8] and then in the *Tadić* trial judgment from May 7, 1997.[9] The ICTR followed with the *Akayesu* trial judgment on September 2, 1998.[10] The prevailing importance of ICTY case law, when compared to the ICTR, also was occasioned by the fact that crimes against humanity, as a serious basis – or even the most serious basis – for conviction, were in initial case law regularly challenged on appeal, the first judgment dating to July 15, 1999 (*Tadić*).[11] This was not the case at the ICTR, however, where genocide was the primary and major concern for individuals convicted by a Trial Chamber, and generally speaking, the focus on appeal was on factual rather than legal issues. As a result, the first appellate judgment at the ICTR dealing with legal aspects of crimes against humanity was in the *Gacumbitsi* case, as late as July 7, 2006.[12]

As for the SCSL, it issued judgments long after the first jurisprudence of the ICTY and the ICTR on crimes against humanity had settled many important issues.[13] Furthermore, in respect of substantive international criminal law, including crimes against humanity, these judgments contribute very little to the development of the law, except for confirming the approaches adopted and choices made in the jurisprudence of the ICTY and the ICTR.

II. THE LEGAL FRAMEWORK FOR EVALUATING ICTY AND ICTR CASE LAW

A proper analysis of the ad hoc tribunals' case law regarding crimes against humanity must be preceded by a short excursion into the statutory definitions of crimes against

---

[7] Prosecutor v. Nikolić, Case No. IT-94-2-R61, Review of the Indictment Pursuant to Rule 61 of the Rules of Procedure and Evidence (Oct. 20, 1995); Prosecutor v. Martić, Case No. IT-95-11-R61, Review of the Indictment pursuant to Rule 61 of the Rules of Procedure and Evidence (Mar. 8, 1996); Prosecutor v. Rajić, Case No. IT-95-12-R61, Review of the Indictment pursuant to Rule 61 of the Rules of Procedure and Evidence (Sept. 13, 1996); Prosecutor v. Mrkšić et al., Case No. IT-95-13-R61, Review of the Indictment Pursuant to Rule 61 of the Rules of Procedure and Evidence (Apr. 3, 1996); Prosecutor v. Karadžić and Mladić, Case Nos. IT-95-5-R61 and IT-95-18-R61, Review of the Indictments Pursuant to Rule 61 of the Rules of Procedure and Evidence (July 11, 1996).
[8] Prosecutor v. Tadić, Case No. IT-94-1-AR72, Decision on the Defence Motion for Interlocutory Appeal on Jurisdiction (Oct. 2, 1995).
[9] Prosecutor v. Tadić, Case No. IT-94-1-T, Judgment (May 7, 1997).
[10] *Akayesu, supra* note 3, ¶ 640.
[11] Prosecutor v. Tadić, Case No. IT-94-1-A, Judgment (July 15, 1999).
[12] Prosecutor v. Gacumbitsi, Case No. ICTR-2001-64-A, Judgment (July 7, 2006).
[13] Trial Judgments in the three big cases, RUF, AFRC, and CDF, date from June and August 2007 and March 2009; *see supra* note 5.

humanity. In chronological order, the authoritative definitions of crimes against humanity, as used in practice by *international* criminal tribunals and, on that basis, having found codification in some domestic legislation are set out below.

I have left out the definitions contained in so-called hybrid or internationalized criminal courts statutes, like those for East Timor's Special Panels for Serious Crimes (SPSC) and Cambodia's Extraordinary Chambers (ECCC). Although these definitions are undeniably interesting additions to the law on crimes against humanity and contain some interesting variations, their authority and impact on future developments – including the drafting of a convention on crimes against humanity – is likely to be limited. This is also due to the fact that at present, there is yet no case law on crimes against humanity from the ECCC. Whereas the Special Panels in East Timor have generated case law in respect of an interesting definition of crimes against humanity,[14] the quality of that case law leaves very much to be desired to be of real influence on the development of the law on crimes against humanity.[15]

Article 6(c) of the IMT Charter sets out the first definition of crimes against humanity used by an international tribunal:

> CRIMES AGAINST HUMANITY: namely, murder, extermination, enslavement, deportation, and other inhumane acts committed against any civilian population, before or during the war; or persecutions on political, racial or religious grounds in execution of or in connection with any crime within the jurisdiction of the Tribunal, whether or not in violation of the domestic law of the country where perpetrated.

The origin, interpretation, and application of this definition have been discussed in detail elsewhere.[16] Compared to contemporary definitions, two matters draw our immediate attention. First, the "chapeau elements" were not yet singled out and put as a threshold for applicability of the various punishable acts at the beginning of the provision on crimes against humanity. Second, although the semicolon between "war" and "or" may create some confusion, it was beyond doubt that crimes against humanity were not considered as a stand-alone category of crimes, but depended upon the commission of another crime within the IMT's jurisdiction.[17]

---

[14] For a detailed analysis of crimes against humanity in the applicable law of the East Timorese Special Panels, see Kai Ambos & Steffen Wirth, *The Current Law of Crimes against Humanity: An Analysis of UNTAET Regulation 15/2000*, 13 CRIM. L.F. 1 (2002).

[15] For example, in the SPSC Prosecutor v. Florencio Tacaqui, Case No. 20/2001, Judgment (Dili District Court, Dec. 9, 2004), the law on crimes against humanity was dealt with in a perfunctory manner, without taking into account existing and highly relevant case law on the matter. See my critical commentary in 16 ANDRÉ KLIP & GÖRAN SLUITER, ANNOTATED LEADING CASES OF INTERNATIONAL CRIMINAL TRIBUNALS 702–03 (2009).

[16] Among many others, see Egon Schwelb, *Crimes against Humanity*, in GUÉNAËL METTRAUX, PERSPECTIVES ON THE NUREMBERG TRIAL 120–66 (2008), and Mohamed E. Badar, *From the Nuremberg Charter to the Rome Statute: Defining the Elements of Crimes against Humanity*, SAN DIEGO INT'L L.J. 73 (2004).

[17] See M. CHERIF BASSIOUNI, CRIMES AGAINST HUMANITY IN INTERNATIONAL LAW 27–31 (1999).

The definition in article 5(c) of the Charter of the International Military Tribunal for the Far East (IMTFE), although heavily inspired by the IMT definition, reveals two deviations from its predecessor. First, the semicolon was replaced by a comma, confirming the required nexus between crimes against humanity and another crime within the IMTFE's jurisdiction. Second, the IMTFE Charter left out religious persecutions, probably due to the fact that the drafters were of the view that these crimes had not been committed on a large scale by the Japanese.[18]

The ICTY was the first international court to apply crimes against humanity since the IMT. The definition of the crime can be found in article 5 of its Statute. A particular need was felt to stay close to the IMT's definition, especially since the ICTY was not to be an exercise in lawmaking.[19] The standard by the UN Secretary-General was that the definition should, especially in the absence of a treaty, be beyond any doubt part of customary international law, as a result of which certain proposals for a definition had to be rejected.[20] This could, for example, explain the requirement that for the ICTY to exercise jurisdiction, crimes against humanity must be committed in an armed conflict. This requirement was later dismissed in the case law of the ICTY as merely being jurisdictional and no longer part of the present-day definition of crimes against humanity;[21] it was dropped from the ICTR's definition, but the Statute of the latter included the (jurisdictional) requirement that the attack on the civilian population had to be committed on national, political, ethnic, racial, or religious grounds.

As will be later examined, the ICTY definition was considerably confused by parts of the Report of the Secretary-General accompanying the ICTY Statute. This Report, in its function as an explanatory memorandum, appeared to offer an alternative, or parallel, definition of crimes against humanity – using the words "crimes against humanity refer to" – which, unfortunately, differed on significant points from the statutory definition.[22] Notably, the elements of "widespread and systematic attack" and the required presence of discriminatory grounds are part of this parallel definition but do not appear in the ICTY Statute. The vital question on the table for the ICTY judges was whether these additional elements in the definition of crimes against humanity set out in the Report of the Secretary-General had to be read into the statutory definition or, instead, could be largely ignored. As will be demonstrated

---

[18] Badar, *supra* note 16, at 82.
[19] The Secretary-General, *Report of the Secretary-General pursuant to Paragraph 2 of Security Council Resolution 808 (1993)*, ¶ 34, U.N. Doc. S/25704 (1993) ("In the view of the Secretary-General, the application of the principle nullum crimen sine lege requires that the international tribunal should apply rules of international humanitarian law which are beyond any doubt part of customary law so that the problem of adherence of some but not all States to specific conventions does not arise. This would appear to be particularly important in the context of an international tribunal prosecuting persons responsible for serious violations of international humanitarian law.").
[20] *See* Virginia Morris & Michael P. Scharf, An Insider's Guide to the International Criminal Tribunal for the Former Yugoslavia 77 (1995).
[21] *See infra* notes 48-49 and accompanying text.
[22] *Report of the Secretary-General*, *supra* note 19, ¶ 48.

further in this chapter, the ICTY judges had a hard time coming to grips with this question, especially since they were far from consistent in their appreciation of the UN Secretary-General's "parallel definition."

The drafting of the ICTR Statute was not the work of the UN Secretary-General. The UN Security Council, having already the benefit of the ICTY Statute and the accompanying Report from the Secretary-General, adopted the Statute directly as an annex to UN Security Council Resolution 955 (1994). Remarkably, the definition in article 3 of the ICTR Statute of crimes against humanity differs in a number of important respects from the ICTY definition. First, a nexus to the armed conflict is no longer required under the ICTR Statute; second, the ICTR definition contains the nexus "part of a widespread or systematic attack," which is not part of the ICTY definition; third, another new element in the ICTR definition is the requirement of discriminatory grounds in relation to all punishable acts; fourth, something which seems of minor importance, but may nevertheless significantly affect the interpretation of crimes against humanity, is that under article 3 of the ICTR Statute, the attack needs to be "against any civilian population," instead of "directed against any civilian population."

These differences are puzzling in light of the fact that both definitions emanate from the same source – the UN Security Council – and were adopted in a quite short period of time.[23] The deviations may in significant part be explained by the definition proposed by the Commission of Experts set up under Security Council Resolution 935 (1994), which underlined the human rights origin of crimes against humanity and added the requirement of discriminatory grounds.[24] In addition, the "parallel definition" in the Report of the UN Secretary-General accompanying the ICTY Statute must also have been influential.

The codification of crimes against humanity in article 7 of the Rome Statute in 1998 built on previous codifications, but at the same time also marked a rupture compared to the still very much IMT-inspired crimes against humanity codification at the ICTY and ICTR. First of all, contrary to the ICTY and ICTR, the codification of crimes in the ICC Statute, involving the entire international community and not having any retroactive application, was more open to lawmaking, especially in relation to crimes that had never been codified in a treaty before.[25] Second, the ICC

---

[23] Yoram Dinstein, *Crimes against Humanity after Tadić*, 13 LEIDEN J. INT'L L. 386 (2000).

[24] *See Preliminary report of the Independent Commission of Experts established in accordance with Security Council resolution 935 (1994)*, ¶ 18, U.N. Doc. S/1994/1125 (Oct. 4, 1994) ("The Commission of Experts on Rwanda considers that 'crimes against humanity' are gross violations of fundamental rules of humanitarian and human rights law committed by persons demonstrably linked to a party to the conflict, as part of an official policy based on discrimination against an identifiable group of persons, irrespective of war and the nationality of the victim, and includes acts such as the following...."). For a discussion, see LARISSA J. VAN DEN HERIK, THE CONTRIBUTION OF THE RWANDA TRIBUNAL TO THE DEVELOPMENT OF INTERNATIONAL LAW 158–59 (2005).

[25] Antonio Cassese, for example, identified areas where the definition is narrower and areas where the definition is broader than customary international law. *See* Antonio Cassese, *Crimes against Humanity*, in THE ROME STATUTE OF THE INTERNATIONAL CRIMINAL COURT: A COMMENTARY 375–77 (Antonio Cassese et al. eds., 2002).

Statute did away with "chapeau elements" in the definition, which were generally regarded as connected very strongly to particular jurisdictional contexts and not part of the customary international law definition of crimes against humanity ("armed conflict" nexus in the IMT, IMTFE, and ICTY Statutes, and the requirement of discriminatory grounds in the ICTR Statute). Third, the ICC definition paid more attention to *mens rea* elements in the definition ("with knowledge of the attack"). Fourth, the ICC definition expanded the crime's *actus reus*; this concerned both new punishable acts including enforced disappearance and apartheid, as well as expanding the scope of already punishable acts, namely deportation, imprisonment, and rape. Fifth, the ICC Statute, in combination with the Elements of Crimes, offered a detailed definition of the constituent elements of crimes against humanity, unparalleled by any previous codification.

Contrary to what appears from the previous points, the ICC codification has not only expanded the scope of application of the crime; it introduced a policy requirement in relation to the attack on the civilian population, which was never part of previous definitions and had been rejected explicitly in ICTY case law.[26]

The codification of crimes against humanity in the SCSL Statute in 2002 represents the most recent international definition in an *international* instrument.[27] After the ICTY definition, the legal team of the UN Secretary-General was given another opportunity to lay down the law. Interestingly, no two of the three definitions applicable to the UN ad hoc tribunals have been the same in a period of eight years. It demonstrates how much the crime has evolved in a relatively short period of time, but also, possibly, that a number of uncertainties still surround the crime. In drafting the SCSL Statute, the Secretary-General had the benefit of the ICC codification but only followed it to a certain extent. The "jurisdictional constraints" in the ICTY and ICTR Statutes, respectively the armed conflict-nexus and the required presence of discriminatory grounds, were abandoned, and rape was supplemented by acts of sexual violence, just like in the ICC Statute. But other changes in the law set out in article 7 of the ICC Statute, other expansions in punishable acts and the insertion of the requirement of a policy element, were not followed. All in all, the Secretary-General retained in the SCSL Statute the flexibility in the crimes against humanity definition, with certain expansion.

It is difficult to evaluate the impact of the ICTY's and, to a lesser degree, the ICTR's law and practice on subsequent codification, especially the ICC Statute.

---

[26] The issue of the policy element is the object of a separate paper in this volume; *see* Guénaël Mettraux, *The Definition of Crimes Against Humanity and the Question of a Policy Element*, in this volume.

[27] The definition in the law applicable to East Timor's SPSC dates from 2000. U.N. Transitional Admin. in East Timor (UNTAET), On the Establishment of Panels with Exclusive Jurisdiction over Serious Criminal Offenses, UNTAET/REG/2000/15 (June 6, 2000). The definition applied by the ECCC is more recent (2004) but is formally part of domestic legislation. Law on the Establishment of the Extraordinary Chambers in the Courts of Cambodia for the Prosecution of Crimes Committed During the Period of Democratic Kampuchea, Oct. 27, 2004, NS/RKM/1004/006.

Generally speaking, the ICC was meant to be more controlled by States Parties and not to allow for the degree of judicial discretion and lawmaking as is the case with the ICTY and ICTR. This has resulted in more detailed codification of every aspect of the applicable law. The content of this codification may have benefited from the ICTY's and ICTR's initial case law, but not a great deal. In the summer of 1998, only the *Tadić* October 1995 jurisdiction decision[28] and the judgment of May 7, 1997 in the same case[29] were available to the negotiating parties in Rome; there was not yet any ICTR case law dealing substantively with crimes against humanity as the *Akayesu* trial judgment was handed down in September 1998.[30] Clearly, there was much more available in terms of guidance from the ICTY and ICTR when the Elements of Crimes were drafted in 2002.

But even if a significant amount of case law, including authoritative findings by the Appeals Chamber, would have been available well before the summer of 1998, it remains to be seen to what degree this would have influenced the negotiations. Multilateral diplomatic conferences have their own dynamics. It seems, for these reasons, that the importance of the ICTY and ICTR case law for the ICC lies rather in the interpretation and practical application of elements in the definition of crimes against humanity in the ICTY and ICC Statutes, which are the same.

III. DISCOVERING AND INTERPRETING THE LAW ON CRIMES AGAINST HUMANITY

It has been said that the ad hoc tribunals have had an immense influence on the law of crimes against humanity, turning a set of abstract concepts into a fully-fledged, well-defined body of law.[31] Underlying this assessment is an active role for the judiciary, because there is, failing detailed codification, no other way to turn abstract concepts into a well-defined body of law. The quality and also legitimacy of developments in the law on crimes against humanity by the ad hoc tribunals ultimately depends on the quality of the methodology applied in discovering and interpreting the law.

The manner in which the ad hoc tribunals approach the interpretation of their legislative framework is not without criticism.[32] It is contended that there is a lack of a consistent and well-reasoned methodology in discovering and interpreting the law. It is true that the reader of ICTY and ICTR decisions and judgments is often puzzled where certain interpretations come from, what interpretative approach is

---

[28] Prosecutor v. Tadić, Case No. IT-94-1-AR72, Decision on the Defence Motion for Interlocutory Appeal on Jurisdiction (Oct. 2, 1995).
[29] *Tadić Trial Judgment, supra* note 9.
[30] *Akayesu, supra* note 3.
[31] GUÉNAËL METTRAUX, INTERNATIONAL CRIMES AND THE AD HOC TRIBUNALS 147 (2005).
[32] *See, e.g.*, ALEXANDER ZAHAR & GÖRAN SLUITER, INTERNATIONAL CRIMINAL LAW: A CRITICAL INTRODUCTION 79–108 (2008).

applied, and how interpretations relate to sources of law outside the Statutes and Rules of Procedure and Evidence.

The starting point in the discovery and interpretation of substantive international criminal law by the ICTY is the already quoted statement from the UN Secretary-General that the international tribunal should apply rules of international humanitarian law that are beyond any doubt part of customary law.[33]

The Secretary-General offers a prominent place to the principle of legality, or *nullum crimen*.[34] This certainly applies to crimes against humanity for which there is no conventional source.[35] Arguably, one should assume that the definition of crimes in the ICTY Statute is consistent with customary international law, at least that there is no expansion of individual criminal responsibility violating the *nullum crimen* rule.

The ICTY Appeals Chamber had the following to say on the relationship between the definitions of crimes in the Statute and customary international law:

> [I]t is open to the Security Council – subject to respect for peremptory norms of international law (*jus cogens*) – to adopt definitions of crimes in the Statute which deviate from customary international law. Nevertheless, as a general principle, provisions of the Statute defining the crimes within the jurisdiction of the Tribunal should always be interpreted as reflecting customary international law, unless an intention to depart from customary international law is expressed in the terms of the Statute, or from other authoritative sources.[36]

This statement is problematic in at least two ways. First, it cannot be said that the Security Council can adopt every definition of crimes against humanity inconsistent with the state of customary international law in the early 1990s; the principle of legality must be respected, as it is embodied, for example, in article 15 of the ICCPR. Limiting criminal responsibility on the basis of so-called jurisdictional requirements is unproblematic, but expanding criminal responsibility when compared to the customary international law definition is unacceptable.[37] Second, there is something utterly confusing and enigmatic in the proposition that the ICTY definition reflects customary international law, unless it does not. This truism illustrates the elusive role customary international law plays in the ICTY case law. Matters would have been much simpler and more understandable if the ICTY Appeals Chamber had

---

[33] *Report of the UN Secretary-General*, supra note 19, ¶ 34.

[34] For a detailed study on the scope of the *nullum crimen* rule in international criminal law, see MACHTELD BOOT, NULLUM CRIMEN SINE LEGE AND THE SUBJECT MATTER JURISDICTION OF THE INTERNATIONAL CRIMINAL COURT (2002).

[35] It is therefore not necessary to pay attention to the question to what degree treaty law can be a basis for criminal liability; see on this matter ZAHAR & SLUITER, supra note 32, at 88–92.

[36] *Tadić Appeals Judgment*, supra note 11, ¶ 296 (footnotes omitted).

[37] In this respect, it is telling that the Appeals Chamber, in footnote 356, only refers to the example of a jurisdictional limitation on the definition of crimes against humanity: "For instance, the express requirement in Article 5 of a nexus with an armed conflict creates a narrower sphere of operation than that provided for crimes against humanity under customary international law." *Id.* ¶ 296 n. 356.

presented the *true* definition of crimes against humanity, namely as it stood under customary international law in the early 1990s, and then thoroughly explored its relationship to the statutory definition. In light of the principle of legality, the result would then be, I assume, that the customary international law definition would "correct" the statutory definition when the former would be more favorable to the accused; it would be ignored if the statutory definition contains inconsistent elements expanding the scope of criminal responsibility.

It is not only the use of customary law as a "tool of convenience" that has plagued the case law of the ad hoc tribunals; it is also the quality of methods of discovering customary international law that leaves something to be desired.[38] With so many gaps or uncertainties in the applicable law, one may be tempted to adopt a more pragmatic view toward identifying rules of customary law. However, the criticism from international lawyers is that, among other things, the ad hoc tribunals tend to directly translate their policy objectives into customary international law.[39] Thus, at times, one has the impression that the identification of rules of customary international law in the case law of the ICTY and ICTR represents a choice as to what is right and/or logical, instead of having a solid basis in State practice and *opinio juris*. This also concerns crimes against humanity. One could even say that in the absence of a treaty and in the absence of significant State practice, a very convincing customary international law basis is debatable. The matter is best exemplified by labeling certain elements of the crime in the ICTY and ICTR Statutes as "jurisdictional requirements" and thereby indicating that these elements (nexus with armed conflict and discriminatory intent) are not part of the crime's customary international law definition. But this is quite a statement in respect of a crime that, by definition, has developed out of the exercise of jurisdiction, namely by the IMTs. Although it may be true, a convincing analysis of State practice and *opinio juris* still has to be conducted. As it has been expressed by one author, many Chambers of the ad hoc tribunals have been too ready to brand norms as customary, without giving any reason or citing any authority for that conclusion.[40]

It is not difficult to point out some of the weaknesses in the customary international law foundations of crimes against humanity. It all starts with the acknowledgment that a *new* category of crimes was created at the IMTs, emphasizing that there was certainly not any rule of customary international law prior to that time.[41] Second,

---

[38] For a discussion of the application of customary international law by the ICTY, see Lorenzo Gradoni, L'attestation de droit international pénal coutumier dans la jurisprudence du Tribunal pour l'ex-Yougoslavie. <<Régularités>> et <<règles>>, in LES SOURCES DU DROIT INTERNATIONAL PÉNAL 25, 25–74 (Mireille Delmas-Marty, Emanuella Fronza & Elisabeth Lambert-Abdelgawad eds., 2004).

[39] André Nollkaemper, The Legitimacy of International Law in the Case Law of the International Criminal Tribunal for the former Yugoslavia, in AMBIGUITY IN THE RULE OF LAW, THE INTERFACE BETWEEN NATIONAL AND INTERNATIONAL LEGAL SYSTEMS 19 (T.A.J.A. Vandamme & Jan-Herman Reestman eds., 2001).

[40] METTRAUX, *supra* note 31, at 15.

[41] *Tadić Appeals Judgment*, *supra* note 11, ¶ 618.

the mandate of the ILC in 1950 merely consisted of formulating Nuremberg principles and not passing any judgment as to their legal status. It is therefore difficult to regard this codification as evidence of customary international law. Third, there is very limited State practice in the prosecution of crimes against humanity; in most States, crimes against humanity have not been penalized.

Bearing in mind the problems in discerning rules of customary international law, especially in respect of crimes against humanity, it is worth recalling that the UN Secretary-General in his report instructed the ICTY to only use sources that are "beyond any doubt" part of customary international law. Certainly, such a "doubt" can be said to exist in relation to certain jurisprudential choices made by the ad hoc tribunals.

Generally speaking, there are two modalities of discovery of customary international law at the ICTY and ICTR, both of which are perfunctory. First, there are the sweeping statements, in the sense of "there can be no doubt that …," which *ab initio* preempt any serious inquiry into the customary international law foundations. A good example in respect of crimes against humanity can be found in the *Tadić* trial judgment: "Since the Nürnberg Charter, the customary status of the prohibition against crimes against humanity and the attribution of individual criminal responsibility for their commission have not been seriously questioned."[42]

Second, there are instances where Chambers have embarked upon an inquiry of State practice and *opinio juris* and, on that basis, discovered a rule of customary international law; one may wonder, however, whether that inquiry in terms of both its quantity and quality satisfies the conditions attached to State practice and *opinio juris*. Put simply, too little or unimportant State practice and corresponding *opinio juris* were examined, or the distinctive elements of State practice and *opinio juris* were conflated.

This should not make us lose sight of the fact that the primary methods of interpretation focus on a provision's content and its object and purpose in a given context; hence, customary international law only seems to become relevant as a source of law when there is a legality problem, in the sense that the use of interpretative techniques should not result in retroactive expansion of a crime's definition (the contrary is allowed). Yet, it seems that the ad hoc tribunals are keen on foregoing the primary methods of interpretation – as set out in articles 31–33 of the Vienna Convention on the Law of Treaties (VCLT), possibly supplemented by generally accepted interpretative methods in relation to domestic criminal law provisions – for an interpretation in the context of customary international law. Regarding article 5 of the ICTY Statute, the *Tadić* Appeals Chamber said: "in case of doubt and whenever the contrary is not apparent from the text of a statutory or treaty provision, such a provision must be interpreted in light of, and in conformity with, customary international law."[43]

---

[42] *Id.* ¶ 623.
[43] *Id.* ¶ 287.

This is confusing because, first of all, customary international law is, first and foremost, a source of law and not an interpretative tool; this confusion between methods of interpretation and discovery of the law is not uncommon at the ad hoc tribunals. Furthermore, we do not know now whether customary international law allows for "re-interpretation" of the text, even if this would be inconsistent with the methods of interpretation set out in articles 31–33 of the VCLT. The confusion is exacerbated when the *Tadić* Appeals Chamber, in the same judgment, repeating findings of the International Court of Justice, puts the interpretative method of article 31 of the VCLT at the center: "The first duty of a tribunal which is called upon to interpret and apply the provisions of a treaty is to endeavour to give effect to them in their natural and ordinary meaning in the context in which they occur."[44]

The reader has difficulty in understanding whether customary international law, as a source of law capable of, in certain circumstances, trumping the statutory definition, or textual interpretation should prevail in approaching the definition of crimes against humanity; it seems a choice must be made.

However, as will follow from the analysis further in this chapter, no consistent choice was made, and the chambers quite easily shifted from a "textual interpretation" to a "customary international law interpretation," with the emphasis, however, being on the latter in respect of crimes against humanity. This is very confusing. For example, when the textual interpretation becomes the prevailing approach in respect to a certain element – the absence of discriminatory intent in the written definition of article 5 of the ICTY Statute – one cannot help but think how consistent use of this interpretative method could affect the analysis of other elements. The problem is, however, that any consistent use of interpretative methodology cannot be found for the very simple reason, in this author's view, that it would result in applicable law close to the text but quite far from the outcome desired by chambers.

A few observations must be made in relation to the generally expansive view on international criminal law that seems to be adopted by ICTY and ICTR judges, because this may seem to underlie the inconsistent and confusing approach toward discovering and interpreting the law. The following was said by the *Milutinović* Trial Chamber: "In order to give full effect to the object and purpose of customary international law prohibiting crimes against humanity, it is necessary to adopt a broad definition of the key terms that extends as much protection as possible."[45]

A puzzling statement, which hardly conforms to the position and role of the adjudicator; furthermore, the reverse of this statement, namely that the *nullum crimen* rule cautions against any "broad definition," seems far more appropriate to me. But in its candor, the *Milutinović* Trial Chamber revealed what is known to many who have been closely following the jurisprudence of the ad hoc tribunals from the beginning: There is an enormous, almost unstoppable desire to develop and expand

---

[44] *Id.* ¶ 282.
[45] Prosecutor v. Milutinović et al., Case No. IT-05-87-T, Judgment, ¶ 147 (Feb. 26, 2009).

the law, and a solid approach to discovering and interpreting the law seems to have been made subordinate to that desire.

Bearing in mind the apparent weaknesses of the *ad hoc* tribunals as to their methods in discovering and interpreting the law, I now proceed with the discussion of the chapeau (both material and jurisdictional) elements of crimes against humanity, as interpreted and developed in the case law of the *ad hoc* tribunals.

IV. THE CHAPEAU ELEMENTS OF CRIMES AGAINST HUMANITY

A. *"When Committed in Armed Conflict"*

Article 5 of the ICTY Statute only attributes jurisdiction over crimes against humanity "when committed in armed conflict, whether international or internal in character." None of the subsequent definitions used by the ICTR, the ICC, and the SCSL contains this requirement. Hence, it seems for the contemporary definition of crimes against humanity to be of very limited value.

In his Report on the ICTY Statute, the UN Secretary-General said the following: "Crimes against humanity are aimed at any civilian population and are prohibited regardless of whether they are committed in an armed conflict, international or internal in character."[46] This is very different language than the text of article 5. It was already mentioned that the role of the Report of the Secretary-General in interpreting crimes against humanity has not been clear. In my view, it should be regarded as an important "parallel definition" of crimes against humanity, implying that limitations in the definition in the Statute that are not part of the report are in principle of a "jurisdictional" nature.[47] The case law of the ICTY also made it very clear from the beginning that this was a jurisdictional limitation, inherited from the Nuremberg definition, which could by no means be regarded as a contextual element in the contemporary definition of crimes against humanity.

In the October 1995 jurisdiction decision in *Tadić*, the Appeals Chamber dismissed the argument raised by the defense that, following "Nuremberg law," a nexus requirement between a crime against humanity and a war crime – the ICTY lacking jurisdiction over aggression – should still be read into the definition.[48] Furthermore,

---

[46] *Report of the Secretary-General, supra* note 19, ¶ 47.
[47] Conversely, the judges are much less keen on accepting limitations set out in the report when these are not part of the statutory definition. See *Tadić Appeals Judgment, supra* note 11, ¶ 295 ("It should be noted that the Secretary-General's Report has not the same legal standing as the Statute. In particular, it does not have the same binding authority. The Report as a whole was 'approved' by the Security Council (see the first operative paragraph of Security Council resolution 827 (1993)), while the Statute was 'adopted' (see operative paragraph 2). By 'approving' the Report, the Security Council clearly intended to endorse its purpose as an explanatory document to the proposed Statute. Of course, if there appears to be a manifest contradiction between the Statute and the Report, it is beyond doubt that the Statute must prevail. In other cases, the Secretary-General's Report ought to be taken to provide an authoritative interpretation of the Statute.").
[48] *Tadić Decision on the Defence Motion for Interlocutory Appeal on Jurisdiction, supra* note 8, ¶ 140.

the Appeals Chamber firmly stated – without substantive research into the matter, however – that "[i]t is by now a settled rule of customary international law that crimes against humanity do not require a connection to international armed conflict." The judgment continues: "[t]hus, by requiring that crimes against humanity be committed in either internal or international armed conflict, the Security Council may have defined the crime in Article 5 more narrowly than necessary under customary international law."[49] The Appeals Chamber repeated this in the *Tadić* Appeals Judgment of July 1999.[50] The Appeals Chamber concluded its discussion by repeating its findings that an armed conflict existed in the former Yugoslavia, but it did not offer any guidance as to how to approach the (jurisdictional) nexus between a crime against humanity and this armed conflict.

In its judgment of May 1997 in *Tadić*, the ICTY Trial Chamber used statements from UN Security Council members to interpret "when committed in armed conflict" to mean "during a period of armed conflict";[51] this interpretation was preceded by the finding that the Statute was more restrictive than customary international law on this point.

The Trial Chamber's interpretation can be criticized for not keeping with the ordinary meaning of the provision: "in armed conflict" is something else than "during a period of armed conflict." It illustrates that methods of interpretation are used by the ICTY arbitrarily and selectively. A textual interpretation is passed over, whereas below we will see that in relation to another perceived element of the crime, the requirement of discriminatory intent, the Appeals Chamber focused very much on this method of interpretation.

Another problematic aspect is that the *Tadić* Trial Chamber *seemed* to eliminate a substantive nexus requirement for crimes against humanity by merely requiring a temporal and geographical connection to an armed conflict. However, it reintroduced it via the back door, by requiring that "the act and the conflict must be related to or, to reverse this proposition, the act must not be unrelated to the armed conflict."[52] By inserting this requirement, the question arises as to what the substantial difference is between the crimes against humanity and the war crimes nexus. It was not elaborated on by the Trial Chamber.

But the Trial Chamber's judgment was reversed by the Appeals Chamber. The latter said:

> A nexus between the accused's acts and the armed conflict is *not* required, as instead suggested by the Judgement. The armed conflict requirement is satisfied by proof that *there was* an armed conflict; that is all that the Statute requires, and in so doing, it requires more than does customary international law.[53]

---

[49] *Id.* ¶ 141.
[50] *Tadić Appeals Judgment*, *supra* note 11, ¶ 249.
[51] *Tadić Trial Judgment*, *supra* note 9, ¶ 631.
[52] *Id.* ¶ 634.
[53] *Tadić Appeals Judgment*, *supra* note 11, ¶ 251 (confirmed in Prosecutor v. Kunarac, Kovač and Vuković, Case No. IT-96-23 & IT-96-23/1-A, Judgment, ¶ 83 (June 12, 2002)).

This is not convincing. *In* armed conflict conveys an ordinary meaning that goes beyond requiring that there merely *was* an armed conflict.

However, the Appeals Chamber's dictum was uncritically followed by Trial Chambers, in the sense that all that is required now is the existence of an armed conflict at the time and place relevant to the indictment, but no material nexus between the acts of the accused and the armed conflict.[54] Most recently, the Trial Chamber in *Milutinović* said that the armed conflict requirement for article 5 requires two parts: (a) there was an armed conflict; and (b) the offenses charged in the indictment are objectively linked, both geographically and temporally, with the armed conflict.[55]

As to what this geographical and temporal linkage entails, the law of armed conflict may be of guidance. Although analogy with humanitarian law in the interpretation of "committed in armed conflict" was dismissed, the *Kunarac* Trial Chamber saw no problem in the following statement: "Once the existence of an armed conflict has been established, international humanitarian law, including the law on crimes against humanity, continues to apply beyond the cessation of hostilities."[56] This would mean that the ICTY has jurisdiction over crimes against humanity committed beyond the cessation of hostilities and covering the entire territory controlled by warring factions, even when the theater of combat is far away.

It seems that this requirement is not difficult to meet, except maybe for the period between the conclusion of the Dayton Peace Agreements in 1995 and the outbreak of the Kosovo armed conflict in March 1999.[57] But this has never proven problematic in jurisprudence where the existence of an armed conflict has been relatively easily accepted.

It may seem that the previously mentioned and related case law is quite obsolete for contemporary thinking on crimes against humanity and the drafting of a Convention. However, from the perspective of interpretative methodology, it is instructive that the ICTY has done its very best to ignore as much as possible the nexus requirement. It has expressed dissatisfaction at several occasions, by emphasizing that this is just a "purely jurisdictional requirement."[58] Whereas this may be true, *lex dura, sed lex*, and it must be properly interpreted. It seems to me that the approach by the *Tadić* Trial Chamber, trying to insert at least some substance into the nexus requirement, was an honest and better attempt at proper statutory interpretation than the selective picking by other chambers from the law of armed conflict, namely only those aspects aimed at expanding the ICTY's jurisdiction over crimes against humanity.

---

[54] *See* Prosecutor v. Kunarac, Kovač and Vuković, Case Nos. IT-96-23-T and IT-96-23/1-T, Judgment, ¶ 413 (Feb. 22, 2001); Prosecutor v. Kupreškić and others, Case No. IT-95-16-T, Judgment, ¶ 546 (Jan. 14, 2000); Prosecutor v. Vasiljević, Case No. IT-98-32-T, Judgment, ¶ 38 (Nov. 29, 2002); Prosecutor v. Limaj et al., Case No. IT-03-66-T, Judgment, ¶ 180 (Nov. 30, 2005).
[55] *Milutinović et al.* Trial Judgment., *supra* note 45, ¶ 140.
[56] *Kunarac, Kovač and Vuković Trial Judgment*, *supra* note 54, ¶ 414.
[57] *See* SCHABAS, *supra* note 2, at 189.
[58] *Kunarac, Kovač and Vuković Trial Judgment*, *supra* note 54, ¶ 83.

B. "Directed against Any Civilian Population"

The element that a crime against humanity must be committed against "any civilian population" has been a core element of the definition since the crime's codification in the Nuremberg Statute. The notion of a civilian population as a protected category confirms the nature of crimes against humanity as a collective crime, together with the requirement of widespread and/or systematic attack.[59] The reference to "*any* civilian population" is the innovative part of crimes against humanity compared to war crimes and also its very *raison d'être* in the IMT Statute, because it permitted prosecution against acts committed against a State's own population, such as the German Jews, who were not covered by the law of armed conflict, certainly not an international armed conflict.[60]

As a contextual element, "directed against any civilian population" must be carefully distinguished from the acts and conduct of an individual; the latter must be part of an attack directed against any civilian population, but there is no requirement that the individual victim is a civilian. It also seems that in its case law the ICTY – and subsequently the ICTR – at times confused this element with defining a class of victims.[61] The use of the word "directed" raises the question whether there should be a purpose-based or objective, result-based interpretation of civilian population. Indeed, that an attack is "*directed*" against a "civilian population" may be a vital element in how to define civilian population in both qualitative and quantitative terms. If the object and purpose of an attack are to be decisive, and the attack was at least capable of targeting a civilian population, the actual composition of the civilian population, including the presence of noncivilian elements, should not be of overriding importance. Providing an answer to this question is somewhat overshadowed by definitional inconsistency. "Directed against" is part of the ICTY and the ICC definition, but does not appear in the IMT, the ICTR, and the SCSL counterparts.

This may explain why, in their case law, the ICTY and the ICTR have not managed to fully clarify the issue. The *Tadić* Trial Chamber, confronted with the difficult task of being the first having to resolve all these issues, limited itself to two aspects: "what must the character of the targeted population be and how is it to be determined whether an individual victim qualifies as a civilian such that acts taken against the person constitute crimes against humanity."[62] It thus focused on "civilian population" and did not deal with "directed."

The *Tadić* Trial Chamber, in requiring an individual victim to be a civilian, introduced an element not required by the definition, and subsequent case law has rightly ruled that a noncivilian also can be a victim of crimes against humanity, as long as

---

[59] See *Tadić Trial Judgment, supra* note 9, ¶ 644 ("[T]he population element is intended to imply crimes of a collective nature and thus exclude single or isolated acts ....").
[60] See METTRAUX, *supra* note 31, at 165.
[61] See ZAHAR & SLUITER, *supra* note 32, at 207.
[62] *Tadić Trial Judgment, supra* note 9, ¶ 636.

the act was part of an attack directed against a civilian population.[63] Furthermore, the Chamber seemed to contradict itself later in the judgment by ruling that acts committed against noncivilian individuals among a predominantly civilian population also may qualify as crimes against humanity.[64]

More important, however, is the *Tadić* Chamber's interpretative approach to "civilian population." The Chamber uses the laws of war as a source of guidance. It started off by opining that "the targeted population must be of a predominantly civilian nature; the presence of certain non-civilians in their midst does not change the character of the population."[65] It then moved on to explore the definition of civilian. It openly struggled with relevant sources, humanitarian law provisions, and domestic case law, especially the French *Barbie* case where no strict distinction between civilians and noncivilians was maintained, and concluded: "Despite the limitations inherent in the use of these various sources, from Common Article 3 to the Barbie case, a wide definition of civilian population, as supported by these sources, is justified."[66] The Chamber did not inform us, however, what this wide definition in fact amounts to.

The *Kunarac* appeals judgment takes a different, purpose-based approach by concentrating on "directed against." As a result, it paid less attention to defining "civilian population," confining itself to the requirement that the civilian population subjected to the attack must be the primary rather than an incidental target of the attack.[67] What matters, in the approach of the Appeals Chamber, is "to determine whether the attack may be said to have been so directed," that is, against the civilian population as the primary target.[68] To determine whether this is the case, a Trial Chamber needs to consider a nonexhaustive list of factors:

- the means and method used in the course of the attack;
- the status and number of the victims;
- the discriminatory nature of the attack and the nature of crimes committed in its course;
- the resistance to the assailants at the time;
- the extent to which the attacking force may be said to have complied or attempted to comply with the precautionary requirements of the laws of war.[69]

It is interesting to see to what degree the *Kunarac* test has been followed by Trial Chambers in subsequent case law. There is still a discernible tendency to require that the civilian population be composed predominantly of civilians, as proposed by the

---

[63] See, e.g., *Kupreškić and others Trial Judgment*, supra note 54, ¶ 568.
[64] *Tadić Trial Judgment*, supra note 9, ¶ 658.
[65] Id. ¶ 638.
[66] Id. ¶ 643.
[67] *Kunarac, Kovač and Vuković Trial Judgment*, supra note 54, ¶ 91.
[68] Id.
[69] Id. (confirmed in Prosecutor v. Blaškić, Case No. IT-95-14-A, Judgment, ¶ 105 (July 29, 2004)).

Tadić Trial Chamber, but not, in my view, an absolute requirement in *Kunarac*. The confusion has not ended, given the most recent ICTY judgment in *Milutinović*, of February 26, 2009. Here the Trial Chamber sought to combine the *Tadić* approach and the *Kunarac* approach: First, as in *Tadić*, it analyzed "civilian population," resorting to the laws of war to define civilian and then using the "predominantly civilian" standard, without giving a numerical threshold but indicating that a case-by-case approach was necessary.[70] Next, it used *Kunarac* to interpret "directed against."[71] The Trial Chamber, in all likelihood in an endeavor to be comprehensive, did not address the question whether both approaches are not, to a certain degree, mutually exclusive, or whether the element "directed against any civilian population" can in fact be separated into two distinct analyses and determinations without distorting its proper interpretation. Interestingly, the combination of the *Tadić* and *Kunarac* approaches sets out a high threshold for crimes against humanity, in direct contrast with the *Milutinović* Trial Chamber's own interpretative approach.

It was a good effort by the *Kunarac* Appeals Chamber to turn a still rather abstract element into a more workable definition. The Chamber was right, in my view, to concentrate on "directed against." Indeed, the factors it lists, applying largely a methodology of deduction, enable chambers to conclude whether or not an attack was *directed* against a civilian population. Whereas in *Kunarac*, the purpose-based approach clearly prevails over the result-based approach, the latter is not fully negated; in other words, an attack that may be intended to target only civilians, or predominantly civilians, but in fact only makes noncivilian victims, or predominantly noncivilian victims, is unlikely to qualify as a crime against humanity. This objective element in the *Kunarac* test is covered by the status of the victims, implying that an attack *directed* against a civilian population must at least result in a significant number of civilian victims, but this is clearly something else than requiring that a population is predominantly of a civilian composition. Interestingly, it seems not to have been fully grasped by the ICTY's Trial Chambers, as demonstrated above by the *Milutinović* judgment.

One may wonder, however, to what extent a purpose-based approach, as set out in *Kunarac*, can survive in the long run. In the ICC definition of "attack directed against civilian population," the word "directed" seems no longer to have any independent significance. What seems to matter in article 7(2)(a) of the ICC Statute is the actual commission of acts against a civilian population and not whether these "acts" were directed against that population. We must also acknowledge that the purpose-based approach of the *Kunarac* Appeals Chamber does not find support in the definitions in the ICTR and the SCSL Statutes, where the word "directed" has been omitted.

The *Kunarac* dictum arguably should also have put an end to some of the confusion as to the class of victims. Crimes against humanity contain no requirements as to the status and/or position of *individual* victims. However, in *Martić*, the Trial

---

[70] *Milutinović et al.*, *supra* note 45, ¶¶ 147–48.
[71] *Id.* ¶ 149.

Chamber maintained the position that the class of victims should consist of civilians and that, following the laws of war, persons *hors de combat* can thus not be victims of crimes against humanity.[72] Repeating the *Kunarac* findings, the Trial Chamber was, on this point, overruled by the Appeals Chamber, which held that "[t]here is nothing in the text of article 5 of the Statute, or previous authorities of the Appeals Chamber that requires that individual victims of crimes against humanity be civilians."[73]

The importance of the word "directed" is also apparent in relation to the question how to define "population" in quantitative terms. The *Kunarac* Appeals Chamber, confirmed by the *Blaškić* Appeals Chamber,[74] said the following:

> the use of the word "population" does not mean that the entire population of the geographical entity in which the attack is taking place must have been subjected to that attack. It is sufficient to show that enough individuals were targeted in the course of the attack, or that they were targeted in such a way as to satisfy the Chamber that the attack was in fact directed against a civilian "population", rather than against a limited and randomly selected number of individuals.[75]

The interpretation of the word "directed" is here of crucial importance as well.

C. "Widespread or Systematic Attack"

At the heart of the definition of crimes against humanity as a collective crime is that individual punishable acts must be part of a widespread or systematic attack. However, just by looking at the definitions cited above, one immediately notices that this contextual element is not part of the IMT and the ICTY statutory definition. Yet, the UN Secretary-General in his report to the ICTY Statute included it in his "parallel definition."[76]

Again, the ICTY was put in the awkward position of having to deviate from the written definition and thereby required to abandon the primary means of interpretation of international instruments, namely the ordinary meaning of terms. Furthermore, the ICTY must have felt uncomfortable by having to pick the "good" parts of the "parallel definition" of the UN Secretary-General's report, namely the requirement of widespread and systematic attack, while at the same time leaving the "bad" parts – the requirement of discriminatory intent for every crime against humanity – for what they were.[77]

At least the ICTY Trial Chamber in *Tadić* was consistent in its deference to the Secretary-General's definition, in that it accepted both the "widespread or systematic attack" and the discriminatory intent as requirements that had to be read in article 5 for the ICTY to exercise jurisdiction. It could arguably do so because these

---

[72] Prosecutor v. Martić, Case No. IT-95-11-T, Judgment, ¶ 56 (June 12, 2007).
[73] Prosecutor v. Martić, Case No. IT-95-11-A, Judgment, ¶ 307 (Oct. 8, 2008).
[74] *Blaškić Appeals Judgment*, *supra* note 69, ¶ 105.
[75] *Kunarac, Kovač and Vuković Trial Judgment*, *supra* note 54, ¶ 90.
[76] *Report of the Secretary-General*, *supra* note 19, ¶ 47.
[77] On the matter of discriminatory intent, see *infra* Section IV.D.1.

were both limitations to individual criminal responsibility for crimes against humanity, which, being limitations, were consistent with the *nullum crimen* rule. In respect of the discriminatory intent, however, this was done rather reluctantly.

Regarding the requirement of a widespread or systematic attack, it is unclear what its legal status was in the eyes of the *Tadić* Trial Chamber; it simply said, "it is now well established that the requirement that the acts be directed against a civilian 'population' can be fulfilled if the acts occur on either a widespread basis or in a systematic manner. Either one of these is sufficient to exclude isolated or random acts."[78]

This seems an elegant way not to draw attention to the defective definition of crimes against humanity in the ICTY Statute, by tying it to another element in that definition. But clearly, even though it must be acknowledged that "population" and "widespread or systematic attack" have in common the notion of crimes against humanity as a form of mass crime – system criminality – they are also distinct and autonomous elements in the definition. Rather, the matter lends itself to determining whether it is an element of the crime under customary international law in the early 1990s, instead of seeking to connect it to other and distinctive elements.

The *Tadić* Appeals Chamber was not directly called on to rule on this element of crimes against humanity, but it did support an approach of "inference," namely that from "directed against any civilian population," it follows that the acts of the accused must compromise part of a pattern of "widespread and systematic crimes."[79]

The *Blaškić* Trial Chamber followed this approach, stating that "widespread or systematic attack" was "implied," not only in "civilian population," but also in some of the punishable acts; it was said that extermination, enslavement, and persecutions do not refer to single events.[80] It referred to the inclusion of this element in the definition set out in the ICTR and the ICC Statutes, concluding that "there can be no doubt that inhumane acts constituting a crime against humanity must be part of a widespread or systematic attack against civilians."[81] However, the ultimate and, in my view, decisive determination that this element was part of customary international law in the early 1990s has not been made.

In subsequent case law, the foundation of this element, which is not part of the definition in the ICTY Statute, has never been seriously challenged. Trial chambers tend to confine themselves to answering the question whether this element has been satisfied,[82] and on appeal the issue was never addressed, probably because it inserts a threshold favorable to the accused. It is interesting, however, that the insertion of this element in the statutory definition is based on "inference" and "implication" rather than a determination as to this element's status as customary international law. It begs the question: If it is contended that this element can very well be

---

[78] *Tadić Trial Judgment, supra* note 9, ¶ 646.
[79] *Tadić Appeals Judgment, supra* note 11, ¶ 248.
[80] Prosecutor v. Blaškić, Case No. IT-95-14-T, Judgment, ¶ 202 (Mar. 3, 2000).
[81] *Id.*
[82] See most recently *Milutinović et al., supra* note 45, ¶¶ 150–51.

read into other elements in the definition, why has it been inserted in all posterior codifications?

The analysis further in the chapter concentrates on "attack." The requirement of this attack having to be widespread or systematic is very closely related to the issue of a policy requirement. As this matter is the object of a separate work, I will only offer some brief observations.

1. "Attack"

In respect to the definition of attack, one must be cautious with isolating it from other elements. What must be borne in mind is that in the ICTR, the ICC, and the SCSL definitions – and thus possibly also for the ICTY – "attack" is doubly qualified because it is preceded by "widespread or systematic" and followed by "directed against any civilian population." But by laying too much emphasis on these qualifiers, there is a significant risk that "attack" itself is not autonomously defined, as seems to be the case with article 7(2)(a) of the ICC Statute. That particular provision pretends to define "attack directed against a civilian population," but does not help us as to what "attack" means in qualitative terms; rather, this particular provision seemingly is concerned with defining "widespread or systematic."

Regarding the definition of "attack," there was an opportunity for the ICTR to take the lead in the development of the law. The *Tadić* Trial Chamber, still looking for a way to "insert" widespread or systematic attack in the statutory definition, concentrated on "widespread or systematic" commission of the punishable *acts* and did not elevate *attack* to an independent element.[83] From the perspective of the Trial Chamber, this was understandable, given that it was approaching crimes against humanity on the basis of a substantive nexus of punishable acts to the armed conflict and also decided that a policy must exist to commit these crimes. Hence, when the punishable acts must have a substantive relation to armed conflict and must also be part of a policy, it indeed seems too much to also demand that punishable acts are part of an *attack*, thereby requiring a chamber to determine that no less than three nexi have to be satisfied.[84]

Thus, the *Akayesu* Trial Chamber was the first to be called on to propose a convincing approach to this element of the crime, which was clearly articulated in the ICTR Statute. Unfortunately, it was not very helpful in defining "attack." Indeed, without any proper reasoning, the Chamber said:

> The concept of attack may be defined as a unlawful act of the kind enumerated in Article 3(a) to (i) of the Statute, like murder, extermination, enslavement etc. An attack may also be non violent in nature, like imposing a system of apartheid, which

---

[83] *Tadić Trial Judgment*, supra note 9, ¶¶ 644–49.
[84] Interestingly, the Trial Chamber did quote from one of the Rule 61 decisions (The Prosecutor v. Mile Mrkšič and others (*Vukovar Hospital* case), Review of the Indictment Pursuant to Rule 61 of the Rules of Procedure and Evidence, Case No. IT-95-13-R61, T.Ch.I, 3 Apr. 1996, ¶ 30),

is declared a crime against humanity in Article 1 of the Apartheid Convention of 1973, or exerting pressure on the population to act in a particular manner, may come under the purview of an attack, if orchestrated on a massive scale or in a systematic manner.[85]

The Trial Chamber's weakness in statutory interpretation was underscored when it held, in the next paragraph, that the *act* instead of the *attack* must be directed against the civilian population, in spite of different language in the definition in the Statute.[86]

The absence of any reasoning relating to the definition of attack and the absence of proper interpretative methodology are striking. Apparently, the Trial Chamber wished to move away from any analogy with the term "attack" in the laws of war. One also notices the conflation with punishable acts and "systematic or widespread," in the sense that any of the punishable acts committed in a widespread or systematic manner would qualify as an "attack" in the meaning of the definition. This, again, raises the question of what the autonomous meaning of attack is. The Trial Chamber is confusing the reader when it opens up the definition of attack to "exerting pressure on the population to act in a particular manner." We do not know where this interpretation comes from. Moreover, the reference to the Apartheid Convention begs answers to a broad range of questions that cannot be addressed here.[87] Again we witness that there is not even an attempt at discerning rules of customary international law applicable in 1994.

With the *Tadić* Trial Chamber on the wrong foot – substantive nexus with armed conflict and policy requirement – and the *Akayesu* Trial Chamber seemingly incapable of providing the term "attack" with a properly reasoned definition, urgent resolution of the matter – preferably at the appellate level – was required. Admittedly, this was not an easy task, for at least three reasons. First, the term "attack" has an ordinary meaning, involving acts of violence, which may not correspond with a broader protective function underlying crimes against humanity. Second, related to that, to justify such broader interpretation, analogy with the laws of war has to be prevented. For example, under article 49(1) of the First Additional Protocol to the Geneva Conventions, "attacks" are defined as "acts of violence against the adversary, whether in offense or in defense." However, analogy with humanitarian law had been resorted to in the interpretation of other elements in the definition of crimes against humanity, for example, "civilian population." This raises the difficult question when analogy with the laws of war is appropriate in defining the scope of

---

where there was the explicit requirement that the punishable acts must be part of a widespread or systematic attack. *Tadić Trial Judgment, supra* note 9, ¶ 649.

[85] *Akayesu, supra* note 3, ¶ 581.
[86] *Id.* ¶ 582.
[87] For example, what is the status of apartheid as a crime against humanity, and if it is an independent punishable act, is there not a problem in respect of "double counting" regarding both the contextual element of an attack and the definition of the punishable act? Furthermore, is a system of apartheid ultimately not by definition of a violent nature?

crimes against humanity. Third, given the absence of the word "attack" in both the IMT and the ICTY definitions, it would be difficult to find a solid basis in customary international law for "attack" as an autonomous element of the crime.

The Appeals Chamber in *Tadić* devoted its energy essentially to reversing the Trial Chamber's substantive link to armed conflict, saying that "a nexus with the accused's acts is required, however, *only* for the attack on 'any civilian population'."[88] Whereas it may have been correct to opine that the Trial Chamber in *Tadić* had exceeded the requirements of customary international law,[89] it substituted this with "attack" – and the corresponding nexus – without exploring the customary law foundations for that particular element or addressing any of the definitional questions referred to earlier. Ultimately, the scope and content of "attack" in the crimes against humanity definition has its foundation in the rejection of a different (jurisdictional) element, namely "committed in armed conflict."

The confusion in respect of "attack" was not resolved in the *Blaškić* trial judgment, where this element was not addressed at all.[90] The *Kunarac* Trial Chamber, however, listed it as the first element: "(i) there must be an attack."[91] This judgment sets out, for the first time, the five subelements for the crimes against humanity chapeau. It has, with slight variations in content and order, been followed ever since, up to and including the *Milutinović* judgment of February 26, 2009.[92]

The definition provided by the *Kunarac* Trial Chamber leaves something to be desired. There was no inquiry into customary international law, nor was it made clear what interpretative methodology was applied. The Trial Chamber was on safe grounds by indicating that the attack must comprise a course of conduct and not just one particular act; it based this conclusion on "directed against any civilian population," but it may, of course, also be covered by "widespread or systematic."[93] But what is an "attack"? We witness an awkward approach. Without any preparatory work, a definition is immediately provided: "an 'attack' can be described as a course of conduct involving the commission of acts of violence."[94] "Acts of violence" seem indeed discernable and workable notions, consistent also, in my view, with the ordinary meaning of the word "attack." But then we witness the continuing struggle of appropriate analogy with the laws of war, leading to the following puzzling dictum:

> The term "attack" in the context of a crime against humanity carries a slightly different meaning than in the laws of war. In the context of a crime against humanity, "attack" is not limited to the conduct of hostilities. It may also encompass situations of mistreatment of persons taking no active part in hostilities, such as someone in detention. However, both terms are based on a similar assumption, namely that

---

[88] *Tadić Appeals Judgment, supra* note 11, ¶ 251.
[89] *Id.*
[90] *Blaškić Trial Judgment, supra* note 80.
[91] *Kunarac, Kovač and Vuković Trial Judgment, supra* note 54, ¶ 410.
[92] *Milutinović et al., supra* note 45, ¶ 260.
[93] *Kunarac, Kovač and Vuković Trial Judgment, supra* note 54, ¶ 415.
[94] *Id.*

war should be a matter between armed forces or armed groups and that the civilian population cannot be a legitimate target.[95]

Thus, after attack was defined as "acts of violence," "situations of mistreatment" are introduced as part of the definition. But should this then be violent mistreatment or does it also allow for nonviolent mistreatment? Furthermore, it is not explained what is to be understood by a "slightly different meaning" compared to the laws of war, on what basis this is justified, and how this affects the already provided definition of "attack." As was already mentioned, in article 49(1) of Additional Protocol I, an attack is defined as acts of violence against the adversary. One can see that "against the adversary" is ill-suited to apply by analogy – this is already inevitable on the basis of the definition "directed against the civilian population." But leaving that out, one has a definition – acts of violence – which is useful and consistent with the word's ordinary meaning and finds a very solid basis in international law. It is not substantiated how "mistreatment" can be added to that definition, or nonviolent measures or exerting pressure on the population as provided for in the *Akayesu* trial judgment.[96]

The definition of attack, as an autonomous element in crimes against humanity, has still not been clarified in ICTY and ICTR case law. The discussion tends to focus on the distinction between armed conflict and attack, and on the determination whether an attack was directed against a civilian population.[97] For example, in *Milutinović* the Trial Chamber stated:

> The concept of an "attack" is not identical to that of an "armed conflict", seeing as an attack can precede, outlast, or continue during an armed conflict, but need not be a part of it. "Attack in the context of a crime against humanity can be defined as a course of conduct involving the commission of acts of violence. It is not limited to the use of armed force; it encompasses any mistreatment of the civilian population." In addition, there is no requirement that an attack directed against a civilian population be related to the armed conflict.[98]

Thus, the *intrinsic* definition of attack remains unclear, especially the question of intensity, namely whether nonviolent measures can constitute an attack and if so, on what basis, and what minimum requirements regarding intensity of mistreatment should be applied.

One explanation for a definition of attack beyond its ordinary meaning of "violent acts" is an interpretation of the element in light of the punishable acts and the crime's (current) applicability in times of peace as well. Clearly, not all punishable acts are or need to be accompanied by acts of violence. When committed on a widespread or systematic basis in a nonviolent context, an interpretation of attack requiring acts of violence means that such crimes should go unpunished as crimes against humanity; this may not be consistent with the contemporary view that crimes against

---

[95] *Id.* ¶ 416 (footnotes omitted).
[96] *Akayesu*, *supra* note 3, ¶ 581.
[97] *See* overview and analysis by METTRAUX, *supra* note 31, at 156–61.
[98] *Milutinović et al.*, *supra* note 45, ¶ 144 (footnotes omitted).

humanity may be committed in times of peace. If, as an alternative, mistreatment can also be of a significantly less serious nature than any of the nonviolent punishable acts, such as exerting pressure on the population – whatever that may mean – as proposed in the *Akayesu* trial judgment,[99] then this risks no longer corresponding to the definition of attack in its ordinary meaning.

2. "Widespread or Systematic"

The scale of the attack is in part determined by its target – the civilian population – but even more so by the requirement that it must be widespread or systematic. The *Tadić* Trial Chamber said that this requirement serves the purpose of a threshold excluding isolated or random acts from the notion of crimes against humanity.[100] Indeed, the nature of crimes against humanity as a form of mass or system criminality is predicated upon a broader, systematic or widespread attack against a civilian population. The ICTY and ICTR chambers ultimately managed to develop relatively sound interpretations of widespread or systematic, but not without considerable difficulty in their early case law.

The *Tadić* Trial Chamber was preoccupied with dismissing the defense's views that the attack should be widespread *and* systematic – based on such language in the UN Secretary-General's report and in the French text of the ICTR Statute. It therefore did not really focus on the substantive meaning of the terms "widespread" and "systematic"; this was also made difficult, as was already mentioned, by the Trial Chamber's insecurity as to what "widespread/systematic" referred to – the attack or the punishable acts.

Akayesu, however, did offer a definition, but it was very general and no reasoning was provided for its origin:

> The concept of widespread may be defined as massive, frequent, large scale action, carried out collectively with considerable seriousness and directed against a multiplicity of victims. The concept of systematic may be defined as thoroughly organized and following a regular pattern on the basis of a common policy involving substantial public or private resources. There is no requirement that this policy must be adopted formally as the policy of a state. There must however be some kind of preconceived plan or policy.[101]

Here manifests itself the notion of "policy" as an element of crimes against humanity, already adopted as a requirement by the *Tadić* Trial Chamber.[102] Given the current contrast between the law of the ICC (definition of attack in article 7(2)(a) of the ICC Statute) and the ICTY and ICTR case law, which has clearly abandoned the

---

[99] *Akayesu*, *supra* note 3, ¶ 581.
[100] *Tadić Trial Judgment*, *supra* note 9, ¶ 648.
[101] *Akayesu*, *supra* note 3, ¶ 580 (footnotes omitted).
[102] At the ICTR, *Akayesu* was followed in *Kayishema and Ruzindana*, *supra* note 3, ¶ 123; *Musema*, *supra* note 3, ¶ 204; Prosecutor v. Bagilishema, Case No. ICTR-95-1A-T, Judgment, ¶ 78 (June 7, 2001). The *Semanza* Trial Chamber was the first where, following *Kunarac* Appeals Chamber,

policy element,¹⁰³ the latter is one of the big unresolved questions regarding crimes against humanity. Guénaël Mettraux has written an extensive paper on this topic, and I will refrain from dealing with this question here.

The *Kunarac* Trial Chamber set out two fundamental parameters in interpreting "widespread or systematic," both of which are supported by a logical interpretation of the entire definition of crimes against humanity, but which may not be properly appreciated when separating elements in their analysis.

First, the Trial Chamber ruled that "widespread or systematic" is a relative notion, dependent upon the population targeted.¹⁰⁴ Second, we were reminded that only the attack and not the individual acts of the accused must be "widespread or systematic"; a single act could therefore be regarded as a crime against humanity if it takes place in the relevant context.¹⁰⁵

The Appeals Chamber in *Kunarac* was aware of the increasingly important role attributed to policy in the interpretation of "systematic" in *Blaškić*, which was endorsed in *Kordić and Čerkez* (the latter judgment was not yet available to the *Kunarac* Trial Chamber).¹⁰⁶ The Appeals Chamber must have felt it was time to stop the case law of Trial Chambers developing in the wrong direction.

The *Blaškić* Trial Chamber came up with the idea that "systematic" referred to the following four elements:

- the existence of a political objective, a plan pursuant to which the attack is perpetrated or an ideology, in the broad sense of the word, that is, to destroy, persecute or weaken a community;
- the perpetration of a criminal act on a very large scale against a group of civilians or the repeated and continuous commission of inhumane acts linked to one another;
- the preparation and use of significant public or private resources, whether military or other;
- the implication of high-level political and/or military authorities in the definition and establishment of the methodical plan.¹⁰⁷

It is not only the increasing importance of the policy element, but also the creation of "sub-elements" that are generally unfounded and unsubstantiated, such as

---

the policy requirement was no longer considered a separate legal element of the crime. *Semanza*, *supra* note 3, ¶ 329.

¹⁰³ *Kunarac, Kovač and Vuković Appeals Judgment*, *supra* note 53, ¶ 283.
¹⁰⁴ *Kunarac, Kovač and Vuković Trial Judgment*, *supra* note 54, ¶ 430. Having determined that and allowing for a system where elements mutually influence one another, the question arises whether there is a minimum independent core of "widespread or systematic." Especially when "attack against a civilian population" may be interpreted as including relatively small areas or sections of population, the question arises if an attack just against a small section of a population can still be regarded objectively as widespread or systematic.
¹⁰⁵ *Id.* ¶ 431.
¹⁰⁶ *Prosecutor v. Kordić and Čerkez*, Case No. IT-95-14/2-T, Judgment, ¶ 201 (Feb. 26, 2001).
¹⁰⁷ *Blaškić Trial Judgment*, *supra* note 80, ¶ 203 (footnotes omitted).

the use of resources and the implication of high level authorities, which must have filled the *Kunarac* Appeals Chamber with concern.

The *Kunarac* Appeals Chamber's findings can still be considered as the basis for subsequent case law and lie at the heart of the currently prevailing interpretation of the requirement "widespread or systematic," including the rejection of a policy requirement, and are worth quoting in full:

> 94. As stated by the Trial Chamber, the phrase "widespread" refers to the large-scale nature of the attack and the number of victims, while the phrase "systematic" refers to "the organised nature of the acts of violence and the improbability of their random occurrence". The Trial Chamber correctly noted that "patterns of crimes – that is the non-accidental repetition of similar criminal conduct on a regular basis – are a common expression of such systematic occurrence".
>
> 95. As stated by the Trial Chamber, the assessment of what constitutes a "widespread" or "systematic" attack is essentially a relative exercise in that it depends upon the civilian population which, allegedly, was being attacked. A Trial Chamber must therefore "first identify the population which is the object of the attack and, in light of the means, methods, resources and result of the attack upon the population, ascertain whether the attack was indeed widespread or systematic". The consequences of the attack upon the targeted population, the number of victims, the nature of the acts, the possible participation of officials or authorities or any identifiable patterns of crimes, could be taken into account to determine whether the attack satisfies either or both requirements of a "widespread" or "systematic" attack vis-à-vis this civilian population.
>
> 96. As correctly stated by the Trial Chamber, "only the attack, not the individual acts of the accused, must be widespread or systematic". In addition, the acts of the accused need only be a part of this attack and, all other conditions being met, a single or relatively limited number of acts on his or her part would qualify as a crime against humanity, unless those acts may be said to be isolated or random.
>
> 97. The Trial Chamber thus correctly found that the attack must be either "widespread" or "systematic", that is, that the requirement is disjunctive rather than cumulative....
>
> 98. Contrary to the Appellants' submissions, neither the attack nor the acts of the accused needs to be supported by any form of "policy" or "plan." There was nothing in the Statute or in customary international law at the time of the alleged acts which required proof of the existence of a plan or policy to commit these crimes. As indicated above, proof that the attack was directed against a civilian population and that it was widespread or systematic, are legal elements of the crime. But to prove these elements, it is not necessary to show that they were the result of the existence of a policy or plan. It may be useful in establishing that the attack was directed against a civilian population and that it was widespread or systematic (especially the latter) to show that there was in fact a policy or plan, but it may be possible to prove

these things by reference to other matters. Thus, the existence of a policy or plan may be evidentially relevant, but it is not a legal element of the crime.[108]

This seems a solid interpretation, and it is undeniably to be preferred over the approaches in *Blaškić* and *Akayesu*. However, there is an intriguing element in the Appeals Chamber's reasoning, which reveals the weakness of the foundations of the jurisprudence on crimes against humanity. It is said that nothing in the Statute or in customary international law supports the "policy requirement." But an important analysis should have preceded that finding. The requirement of "widespread or systematic attack" is, like the policy requirement, *not* part of the Statute, meaning that its insertion in the definition can only have a basis in customary international law. Until this day, none of the ICTY chambers has conducted the analysis whether this element is in fact part of customary international law and what that source of law tells us about its interpretation. Only when that analysis would have been convincingly made could it have been claimed that the "policy element" has no place in the definition.

Be this as it may, in the practice of the ad hoc tribunals, the *Kunarac* findings on "widespread or systematic" remain relevant and authoritative. As a result, the requirement of "systematic or widespread" no longer causes any significant difficulty, neither is it the subject of any controversy within the law and practice of these Tribunals.

D. Mens Rea *Aspects: Discriminatory Intent and Knowledge of the Attack*

The chapeau elements of crimes against humanity have raised two distinct *mens rea* aspects in the ad hoc tribunals. First, there was the issue of whether, like genocide, a specific discriminatory intent was required for crimes against humanity. Second, it needed to be determined if, and to what degree, the accused must have knowledge of the contextual elements.

1. Discriminatory Intent (or Discriminatory Attack?)

By discriminatory intent, or motive, it is to be understood that to constitute a crime against humanity, each of the punishable acts must be committed on discriminatory grounds, namely on national, political, ethnic, racial, or religious grounds. This requirement seems to be consistent with the general notion of crimes against humanity as a "discriminatory crime," attacking individuals because of membership to a group – based on its proximity to genocide and having its origin in the Holocaust. However, as an element of the crime's definition, in the Statutes of the IMTs and the ICTY, it can only be found for the punishable act of persecution. In respect of the ICTY, the "requirement" of discriminatory intent was set out in the "parallel definition" in paragraph 48 of the Report of the Secretary-General.[109] It was also an element of the

---

[108] *Kunarac, Kovač and Vuković Appeals Judgment, supra* note 53, ¶¶ 94–98 (footnotes omitted) (findings confirmed in *Blaškić Appeals Judgment, supra* note 69, ¶¶ 100–02).

[109] *See supra* note 19.

ICTR's statutory definition. The two more recent codifications, the ICC and the SCSL Statutes, do not contain the discriminatory intent requirement. It thus seems that for contemporary law and practice, the ad hoc tribunals' approach to this matter is of limited significance. However, it is nevertheless instructive to explore the ad hoc tribunals' jurisprudence because it may shed light on the question of whether rejection of this requirement in recent codifications has a firm basis in customary international law.

The *Tadić* Trial Chamber was in a difficult position. It did not have the benefit, like the Appeals Chamber in 1999, of other codifications (ICC) or more developed and advanced discussions on the matter. The Trial Chamber's approach was still defendable. A decisive factor was the fact that discriminatory intent was in the Secretary-General's "parallel definition" and in the ICTR Statute. Therefore, it can be argued that the Secretary-General considered discriminatory intent to be part of the definition.[110] This approach is also consistent with the ICTY's position toward other elements of crimes against humanity that were not set out in the statutory definition – "widespread or systematic attack" – but were nevertheless applied, in part, on the basis of the language in the Report of the Secretary-General. True, the Tribunal did not conduct an analysis of customary international law on the matter, but this was, unfortunately, not unusual. An analysis of customary international law has not been conducted in respect to other chapeau elements as well, most notably "widespread or systematic," and where it has been done, it has not always been convincing. Furthermore, both the language of the Report and the more recent ICTR codification caused the Trial Chamber to adopt the view that the definition was effectively part of the Statute. This view now finds support in the literature which indicates that it was indeed the Secretary-General's firm view that discriminatory intent was part of the crimes against humanity chapeau elements.[111] Given this context, the Trial Chamber cannot be heavily reproached for not exploring customary international law. It can, however, be criticized on two other points.

First, it did not interpret the matter of discriminatory intent in light of the entire definition of crimes against humanity. This is especially true as regards the crime of persecution, which also requires discriminatory intent for that particular punishable act. One way of doing this is no longer requiring discriminatory intent as a *mens rea* aspect, but tying it to the attack. This was the solution adopted in ICTR case law, as will be further explored below. It was also the approach of the Trial Chamber in *Tadić* in its application of the law to the facts, which focused on the attack and not on the *mens rea* of Mr. Tadić.[112] Second, after having determined that a discriminatory intent is a requirement for each crime against humanity, the Trial Chamber made no attempt at analyzing what is to be understood by this requirement. It simply concluded that "the attack on the civilian population was conducted against only the non-Serb portion of the population because they were non-Serbs," and left it at that.[113]

---

[110] *Tadić Trial Judgment, supra* note 9, ¶ 652.
[111] Larry Johnson, *Ten Years Later: Reflections on the Drafting*, 2 J. INT'L CRIM. JUST. 372 (2004).
[112] *Tadić Trial Judgment, supra* note 9, ¶ 652.
[113] *Id.*

The *Tadić* Appeals Chamber, possibly inspired by the definition adopted in the Rome Statute,[114] reversed the trial judgment and concluded that a discriminatory element is not required for all acts punishable as crimes against humanity.[115] Predictably, it relied heavily on the clear language of the Statute: "the wording of Article 5 is so clear and unambiguous as to render it unnecessary to resort to secondary sources of interpretation such as the Secretary-General's Report. Hence, the literal interpretation of Article 5 of the Statute ... must necessarily prevail."[116] This is quite remarkable and highly selective, because the "literal interpretation" method has not been resorted to in respect to other elements in the definition.

In addition to the "literal/textual interpretation" technique, the Appeals Chamber resorted to logical interpretation of the provision as a whole, using the presence of discriminatory intent in persecution as a punishable act:

> This specification [presence of discriminatory intent in persecution] would be illogical and superfluous. It is an elementary rule of interpretation that one should not construe a provision or part of a provision as if it were superfluous and hence pointless: the presumption is warranted that law-makers enact or agree upon rules that are well thought out and meaningful in all their elements.[117]

Again, this interpretative method is now resorted to, but often is not used at all. As to the presumption that rules are "well thought out and meaningful in all their elements," this begs the question how one should then consider the definition in the ICTR Statute.

The Appeals Chamber also emphasized in this regard the importance of conformity with customary international law of any definitional element:

> The same conclusion is reached if Article 5 is construed in light of the principle whereby, in case of doubt and whenever the contrary is not apparent from the text of a statutory or treaty provision, such a provision must be interpreted in light of, and in conformity with, customary international law. In the case of the Statute, it must be presumed that the Security Council, where it did not explicitly or implicitly depart from general rules of international law, intended to remain within the confines of such rules....
>
> A careful perusal of the relevant practice shows that a discriminatory intent is not required by customary international law for all crimes against humanity.[118]

The zeal with which customary law and methods of interpretation are used in this instance to reject a certain interpretation represents a selective and arbitrary use of interpretative methods, which risks undermining the entire foundation of the law of crimes against humanity. Moreover, the Appeals Chamber's reversal is not based on

---

[114] *Tadić Appeals Judgment, supra* note 11, ¶ 291.
[115] *Id.* ¶ 305.
[116] *Id.* ¶ 295.
[117] *Id.* ¶ 284.
[118] *Id.* ¶¶ 287–88.

a proper reading of the Trial Chamber's judgment and ignores a possible alternative interpretation of "discriminatory grounds."

The Report of the Secretary-General[119] and article 3 of the ICTR Statute quote this part of the definition: "committed as part of a widespread or systematic attack against any civilian population on national, political, ethnic, racial or religious grounds." From a textual interpretation, it cannot be inferred whether the discriminatory grounds regard "committed" or "attack." The French text of article 3 of the ICTR Statute arguably allows for both interpretations. Of course, there is a huge difference between the two possible interpretations.

As was already mentioned, the ICTY did not separate the two possible interpretations. The *Tadić* Trial Chamber began by focusing on discriminatory *intent*, but concluded that the *attack* had in fact been discriminatory.[120] The Appeals Chamber should have noticed this discrepancy and paid attention to both possible interpretations, especially since tying discriminatory grounds to the attack would have weakened its argument of "logical interpretation." It is not difficult or illogical to combine the requirement that the attack must be based on discriminatory grounds with the specific *mens rea* of discriminatory motive for the punishable acts of persecution. Furthermore, it would have required an additional focus to its examination of customary international law.

The case law of the ICTR suggests that the connection between the attack and the discriminatory grounds is therefore not a strange idea. In early trial judgments such as *Akayesu*,[121] *Kayishema and Ruzindana*,[122] and *Musema*,[123] the discriminatory grounds were exclusively related to "committed" and thus were regarded as an element of *mens rea* covering all punishable acts. But a new view on the matter was advanced in the *Bagilishema* trial judgment, saying that the discriminatory grounds "should, as a matter of construction, be read as a characterization of the nature of the 'attack' rather than of the *mens rea* of the perpetrator."[124] The reasoning came in a footnote:

> Had the drafters of the Statute sought to characterise the individual actor's intent as discriminatory, they would have inserted the relevant phrase immediately after the word "committed", or they would have used punctuation to set aside the intervening description of the attack. In addition, they would have taken care to modify Article 3(h) to redress the resulting repetition of qualifiers. As noted by the Appeals Chamber in *Tadić* (correcting the Trial Chamber's adoption in that case of a supposedly implicit requirement of discriminatory intent for all crimes against humanity under Article 5 of the ICTY Statute), "a logical construction of Article 5 also leads to the conclusion that, generally speaking, this requirement is not laid down for

---

[119] See *supra* note 19.
[120] *Tadić* Trial Judgment, *supra* note 9, ¶¶ 650–52.
[121] *Akayesu*, *supra* note 3, ¶¶ 583–84.
[122] *Kayishema and Ruzindana*, *supra* note 3, ¶ 130.
[123] *Musema*, *supra* note 3, ¶ 208.
[124] *Bagilishema*, *supra* note 102, ¶ 81.

all crimes against humanity. Indeed, if it were otherwise, why should Article 5(h) specify that "persecutions" fall under the Tribunal's jurisdiction if carried out 'on political, racial and religious grounds'. This specification would be illogical and superfluous. It is an elementary rule of interpretation that one should not construe a provision or part of a provision as if it were superfluous and hence pointless: the presumption is warranted that law-makers enact or agree upon rules that are well thought out and meaningful in all their elements."[125]

All later judgments at the ICTR have followed this interpretation.[126] Although the *Bagilishema* Trial Chamber used the *Tadić* Appeals Chamber's own "logical interpretation" approach, it directly challenged the Appeals Chamber in its conclusion that a logical interpretation would remove the requirement of discriminatory intent from the definition. It demonstrates that a logical construction of article 3 of the ICTR Statute, or article 5 of the ICTY Statute, is quite possible with the inclusion of discriminatory grounds. Yet, the *Tadić* appeals judgment has not been seriously questioned in ICTY case law.

This is not to suggest that I advocate the presence of discriminatory grounds in respect to the attack. I see the negative sides to it, like a definition of attack being qualified in three respects: "widespread or systematic," "directed against any civilian population," and launched on discriminatory grounds. This could be quite burdensome even if in the ICTR it was generally easily proven. But the matter has never been properly explored in the case law of the ICTY.

2. Knowledge of Contextual Elements

Both the substantive nexus between the punishable act and the attack as well as the required corresponding *mens rea*, knowledge of the attack, connect the chapeau elements to the concrete conduct of individuals.

It seems reasonable that individual criminal responsibility depends on the accused's knowledge that his acts are part of a broader attack. This may be regarded as imperative in light of the fact that a single, isolated act can qualify as crimes against humanity as well. So if the allegations against the accused are that he has engaged in mass or system criminality, which is represented by crimes against humanity, knowledge of the broader context seems inevitable. There is a significant difference with the contextual element of armed conflict for war crimes. For war crimes, the punishable act need not be *part* of the armed conflict. Conversely, for crimes against humanity, the punishable acts must be *part* of the attack. It is therefore not unreasonable to regard the existence of an armed conflict as a simple and objective

---

[125] *Id.* ¶ 81 n.79 (footnotes omitted).
[126] *See, e.g., Semanza, supra* note 3, ¶ 331; Prosecutor v. Kajelijeli, Case No. 98–44A-T, Judgment and Sentence, ¶ 877 (Dec. 1, 2003); Prosecutor v. Gacumbitsi, Case No. ICTR-2001-64-T, Judgment, ¶ 301 (June 17, 2004); Prosecutor v. Muhimana, Case No. ICTR-95-1B-T, Judgment and Sentence, ¶ 9 (Apr. 28, 2005); Prosecutor v. Seromba, Case No. ICTR-2001-66-I, Judgment, ¶ 359 (Dec. 13, 2006); *Bagosora et al., supra* note 3, ¶ 2166.

contextual element bringing in the applicability of the laws of war. However, even in that context the argument has been made, and there is case law,[127] that the individual must have knowledge of the existence of an armed conflict.[128]

Having said this, knowledge of the attack cannot be found as an element of crimes against humanity in the Statutes of the IMTs, the ICTY, and the ICTR. It is part of the ICC codification but, surprisingly, is left out of the SCSL Statute. If we were to resort to a textual interpretation, knowledge of the attack cannot be regarded as a *mens rea* element of the crime. Since this element is favorable to the accused, we would need, from a *nullum crimen* perspective, evidence of the existence of a rule of customary international law in the early 1990s to supplement the statutory definition.

The codification in the ICC Statute does not solve all questions. The scope of knowledge – just the attack or also that the attack targeted the civilian population and was widespread or systematic – and the relationship of this mental element to the general provision on *mens rea* (article 30) still need to be sorted out in ICC case law. The ICTY and ICTR jurisprudence may assist on the first question, but not on the second.

With the battle in *Tadić* concentrating on discriminatory intent, there was not much attention to other aspects of *mens rea*. The Trial Chamber did not mention knowledge of the attack at all, either as the result of an oversight or perhaps because the Trial Chamber considered that if discriminatory intent was proven, knowledge of the broader attack was no longer necessary. An additional complication was that the Trial Chamber confused discriminatory intent with a discriminatory attack. If it is the attack that has to be discriminatory – instead of the acts – then it seems obvious that for individual accountability, knowledge thereof is required.

The *Tadić* Appeals Chamber did not address the "knowledge" issue in its opinion on the question of discriminating intent. Rather, it evoked it during the discussions on the nexus with armed conflict and in rejecting the requirement that crimes against humanity cannot be committed for purely personal motives.[129] The Appeals Chamber used the interpretative technique of "inference" (clearly if it would have resorted to a literal interpretation, the "knowledge" requirement could never have been sustained):

> The Appeals Chamber agrees that it may be inferred from the words "directed against any civilian population" in Article 5 of the Statute that the acts of the accused must comprise part of a pattern of widespread or systematic crimes directed against a civilian population and that the accused must have *known* that his acts fit into such a pattern.[130]

---

[127] Prosecutor v. Naletilić and Martinović, Case No. IT-98-34-A, Judgment, ¶ 116 (May 3, 2006); *Boškoski and Tarčulovski, supra* note 1, ¶ 295.
[128] *See* Kai Ambos, Internationales Strafrecht 239 (2008).
[129] *Tadić Appeals Judgment, supra* note 11, ¶ 248.
[130] *Id.* (footnotes omitted).

There is thus a double inferential leap. I can follow the Appeals Chamber as far as the first one is concerned, namely that there must be a nexus between the attack and the punishable acts. However, knowledge of this nexus does not automatically follow from the definition of the crime in the Statute. We thus do not know where this second inference comes from,[131] especially whether it is motivated by customary international law. Finally, it is important to note that, according to the Appeals Chamber, the accused must have knowledge of certain subelements, namely "attack" (or here: pattern), which was "widespread or systematic," and which was "directed against a civilian population."

In ICTR case law preceding the *Tadić* appeals judgment, the knowledge requirement – if mentioned at all (it is not in the *Akayesu* trial judgment) – seemed inspired very much by the ICC definition. Thus, in *Kayishema and Ruzindana*, the Trial Chamber said there must be knowledge of the attack.[132] But it clearly viewed "attack" in the broad sense, including all qualifiers:

> The Trial Chamber agrees with the Defence. Part of what transforms an individual's act(s) into a crime against humanity is the inclusion of the act within a greater dimension of criminal conduct; therefore an accused should be aware of this greater dimension in order to be culpable thereof. Accordingly, actual or constructive knowledge of the broader context of the attack, meaning that the accused must know that his act(s) is part of a widespread or systematic attack on a civilian population and pursuant to some kind of policy or plan, is necessary to satisfy the requisite *mens rea* element of the accused. This requirement further compliments the exclusion from crimes against humanity of isolated acts carried out for purely personal reasons.[133]

The requirement of double knowledge – namely concerning the existence of an attack, in its qualified sense, and the nexus between attack and punishable act – has been consistently applied in ICTY and ICTR case law and has not undergone significant developments. However, the degree of knowledge – actual or other – has been taken on by the *Blaškić* Trial Chamber in a lengthy discussion:

> ii. Knowing participation in the context
>
> 251. The accused need not have sought all the elements of the context in which his acts were perpetrated; it suffices that, through the functions he willingly accepted, he knowingly took the risk of participating in the implementation of that context.
>
> 252. This is what emerges from the spirit of the Statute, from the case-law of both this Tribunal and the ICTR and from the Judgment of the French *Cour de Cassation* rejecting Maurice Papon's appeal against the Judgment of the Indictments Chamber of the Bordeaux Appeals Court (hereinafter the "*Papon* case").

---

[131] See Milutinović et al., supra note 45, ¶ 154 ("[N]o authority was cited for the proposition that the accused must know that the conduct charged fits into the pattern of crimes …").
[132] *Kayishema and Ruzindana*, supra note 3, ¶ 133.
[133] *Id.* ¶ 134.

253. As concerns the spirit of the Statute, the Trial Chamber is of the view that an accused who, in his capacity as a commander, participates in the commission of a mass crime must question the malevolent intentions of those defining the ideology, policy or plan in whose name the crime is perpetrated.

254. Moreover, the nexus with the institutional or *de facto* regime, on the basis of which the perpetrator acted, and the knowledge of this link, as required by the case-law of the Tribunal and the ICTR and restated above, in no manner require proof that the agent had the intent to support the regime or the full and absolute intent to act as its intermediary so long as proof of the existence of direct or indirect malicious intent or recklessness is provided. Indeed, the Trial Chambers of this Tribunal and the ICTR as well as the Appeals Chamber required only that the accused "knew" of the criminal policy or plan, which in itself does not necessarily require intent on his part or direct malicious intent ("… the agent *seeks* to commit the sanctioned act which is either his *objective* or at least the method of achieving his objective"). There may also be indirect malicious intent (the agent did not deliberately seek the outcome but knew that it would be the result) or recklessness, ("the outcome is foreseen by the perpetrator as only a probable or possible consequence"). In other words, knowledge also includes the conduct "of a person taking a deliberate risk in the hope that the risk does not cause injury".

255. The person who has "knowledge" of the plan, policy or organisation as part of which the crimes take place is not only the one who fully supports it but also the one who, through the political or military functions which he willingly performed and which resulted in his periodic collaboration with the authors of the plan, policy or organisation and in his participation in its execution, implicitly accepted the context in which his functions, collaboration and participation must most probably have fit.[134]

This analysis is complicated by the fact that the *Blaškić* Trial Chamber still required a policy element, which led to the discussion to what degree the perpetrator must be aware of this policy or participate in it. As to the issues regarding the scope of the accused's knowledge (how much should an accused know about the attack) and the degree of knowledge, the *Kunarac* Appeals Chamber set the standard still applicable today:

> Concerning the required *mens rea* for crimes against humanity, the Trial Chamber correctly held that the accused must have had the intent to commit the underlying offence or offences with which he is charged, and that he must have known "that there is an attack on the civilian population and that his acts comprise part of that attack, or at least [that he took] the risk that his acts were part of the attack." This requirement, as pointed out by the Trial Chamber, does not entail knowledge of the details of the attack....
>
> For criminal liability pursuant to Article 5 of the Statute, "the motives of the accused for taking part in the attack are irrelevant and a crime against humanity may be

---

[134] *Blaškić Trial Judgment, supra* note 80, ¶¶ 251–55 (footnotes omitted).

committed for purely personal reasons." Furthermore, the accused need not share the purpose or goal behind the attack. It is also irrelevant whether the accused intended his acts to be directed against the targeted population or merely against his victim. It is the attack, not the acts of the accused, which must be directed against the target population and the accused need only know that his acts are part thereof. At most, evidence that he committed the acts for purely personal reasons could be indicative of a rebuttable assumption that he was not aware that his acts were part of that attack.

104. The Appellants' contention that a perpetrator committing crimes against humanity needs to know about a plan or policy to commit such acts and that he needs to know of the details of the attack is not well founded. Accordingly, the Appeals Chamber rejects this part of the common grounds of appeal.[135]

Compared to the knowledge of the armed conflict required for war crimes, the knowledge requirements for crimes against humanity are more demanding. For war crimes, it is not required that the accused knew of the nexus between his acts and the armed conflict, whereas knowledge that acts are part of the attack is required for crimes against humanity. It seems that there is a slightly different approach to the nexus requirement between the two sets of crimes. In respect to war crimes, the *mens rea* of the accused may be relevant to establish the nexus and is probably for that reason not a separate *mens rea* element.[136] But for crimes against humanity, the case law initially dealt with the objective and subjective *nexus* elements in a combined test, but later on the *mens rea* element, "knowledge that acts were part of the attack," seemed to have gained the status of an independent element.

E. Nexus between Punishable Acts and the Attack

The definition of all core crimes suffers from the same difficulty, namely that the "chapeau" or "contextual" elements must be adequately connected to individual punishable acts. It is this connection that truly makes certain conduct particularly blameworthy. This chapter has already explored the issue of a nexus between the attack and individual punishable acts from a *mens rea* perspective (knowledge of the attack). But what is required in terms of *actus reus*?

There is nothing concrete to assist us in the Statutes of the IMTs and the ICTY. All other subsequent statutory definitions – the ICTR's, the ICC's, and the SCSL's – require that a punishable act be "part" of the attack. On the basis of textual interpretation, two things can be concluded. First, to determine whether a punishable act is "part" of a widespread or systematic attack against a civilian population, we must

---

[135] *Kunarac, Kovač and Vuković Appeals Judgment, supra* note 53, ¶¶ 102–04 (footnotes omitted).
[136] The *Kunarac* appeals judgment sets out a four-pronged test to determine whether a nexus can be established, and two of the prongs consider the accused's *mens rea*: The existence of an armed conflict must, at a minimum, have played a substantial part in the perpetrator's ability to commit it, *his decision to commit it*, the manner in which it was committed or *the purpose for which it was committed*. *Id.* ¶ 58.

have a good understanding of what "attack" exactly means and be able to provide sufficient details of that attack as to scope, duration, intensity, and so on. Second, the question arises whether "part of" should be, in nexus terms, regarded as a high standard. As was already explored, the "jurisdictional" nexus required for crimes against humanity at the ICTY, in respect of armed conflict, has in practice been reduced to "during armed conflict." In respect to war crimes, the nexus requirement has given rise to case law where flexible notions, such as "under the pretext or under the guise of armed conflict," suffice to satisfy the nexus requirement. Arguably, the war crimes nexus may be said to have a lower threshold, because crimes have to be committed *in* armed conflict and not as *part* of it.

In respect to war crimes, it has always been extremely important to determine precisely when and where the armed conflict took place, because only acts committed in the course of such a conflict and immediately following the cessation of hostilities can qualify as war crimes. The problem with the notion of "widespread or systematic attack against any civilian population" is that similar precision is far more difficult because the attack tends to be the result of a series of (violent) acts launched against a civilian population that may just gradually evolve into a *widespread or systematic* attack. But making that determination is inevitable, in my view, to be able to answer the question of whether an act was part of the attack; it also implies that acts that may have been vital to reaching the threshold of a widespread or systematic attack cannot qualify as crimes against humanity because they were not yet part of it.[137]

Looking at the case law of the ad hoc tribunals, there is a striking discrepancy in approach to the war crimes nexus and the crimes against humanity nexus. Whereas they have endeavored to indicate with precision the beginning, duration, scope, and territorial reach of armed conflicts, the same cannot be said for "attacks" in the analyses of crimes against humanity. Clearly, this is a complex task, because (a) there may be a great number of different attacks, whereas armed conflict tends to require the one determination as to the start of hostilities between organized groups; and (b), as previously mentioned, it is extremely difficult to determine at which moment in time an attack becomes widespread or systematic, especially if there is, in my view, still no proper understanding as to what attack exactly means. Nevertheless, more precision in making the determination of "part of the attack" than is currently the case is in order.

The ad hoc tribunals do not seem to have struggled a great deal with this lack of precision in their case law. The *Tadić* Trial Chamber understandably did not give this particular nexus much attention because it operated on the basis of a substantive nexus to the armed conflict. The *Akayesu*, *Kayishema/Ruzindana*, and *Musema*

---

[137] For a contrary view, see *Kunarac, Kovač and Vuković Appeals Judgment*, *supra* note 53, ¶ 100, on this point, which says that a crime committed before the main attack against the civilian population or away from it could still, if sufficiently connected, be part of that attack. But if "main attack" is to be understood as the vital "widespread or systematic attack," I do not see how any crime committed *before* such a widespread or systematic attack materialized could ever be part of it.

Trial Chambers, although specifically called on to explore this matter as part of the statutory definition, paid no attention to it, too occupied as they were with interpreting "widespread or systematic."[138]

The *Tadić* appeals judgment ruled that "the crimes must be committed *in the context of* widespread or systematic crimes directed against a civilian population ...."[139] Only the *Kunarac* Trial Chamber systematically addressed this requirement, holding:

> There must exist a nexus between the acts of the accused and the attack, which consists of:
>
> (i) the commission of an act which, by its nature or consequences, is objectively part of the attack; ...
>
> It is sufficient to show that the act took place in the context of an accumulation of acts of violence which, individually, may vary greatly in nature and gravity...
>
> Finally, the Trial Chamber notes that, although the attack must be part of the armed conflict, it can also outlast it.[140]

The *Kunarac* Appeals Chamber confirmed this test,[141] which has since been consistently employed with some slight elaborations and variations.[142]

V. CONCLUSION

It is not possible to draw predominantly positive conclusions in respect to the ICTY and ICTR jurisprudence on the chapeau elements of crimes against humanity. An examination of the treatment and development of these elements throughout their jurisprudence evokes a number of critical remarks. However, in defense of the ad hoc tribunals, the presence of a number of "mitigating circumstances" must first be acknowledged. The most important of them is undeniably the absence of a firm, stable, and convincing legislative framework. The tribunals were confronted with different and conflicting definitions: one in the ICTY Statute, one "parallel" definition in the Report of the Secretary-General to the ICTY Statute, one in the ICTR Statute, one in the ICC Statute, and one in the SCSL Statute. If the international community did not display a firm understanding of the content of this crime, how can judges be expected to do so? It simply was a legislative nightmare, requiring enormous creativity on the part of the judges. Furthermore, it proved very difficult to repair or supplement the confusing legislative context with a solid interpretative methodology and convincing sources of international law. Failing the existence of any treaty on the matter, the content of crimes against humanity very much depended on customary international law, of which there was, and is, quite little.

---

[138] *Akayesu, supra* note 3; *Kayishema and Ruzindana, supra* note 3; *Musema, supra* note 3.
[139] *Tadić Appeals Judgment, supra* note 11, ¶ 255 (emphasis added).
[140] *Kunarac, Kovač and Vuković Trial Judgment, supra* note 54, ¶¶ 418–20 (footnotes omitted).
[141] *Kunarac, Kovač and Vuković Appeals Judgment, supra* note 53, ¶ 99.
[142] *See* METTRAUX, *supra* note 31, at 161–63.

Mention must be also made of the role of the ICTY/ICTR Appeals Chamber in the development of the law. The latter has an important role to play but is highly dependent on the appellate points made by the parties, and not all legal issues and questions of interpretation were presented to it. What is more, the Appeals Chamber in initial decisions, like the *Tadić* case, was confronted with so many issues that it was indeed difficult to address all of them thoroughly, and certain errors and oversights inevitably ensued from this.

Whereas there are thus certainly mitigating circumstances, this is no reason to refrain from criticism. As with many aspects of the law of the ad hoc tribunals, the important decisions and choices were made in the early case law. Even if they fundamentally disagreed with these choices, subsequent Trial Chambers could not significantly deviate from these initial findings without risking the invalidation of earlier judgments. Hence, one should not be overly impressed with references to a great number of judgments in support of particular findings and conclusions. There is a lot of uncritical repetition going on, and what matters is the origin and quality of the initial solution proposed.

Going back to the "roots," the following critical observations have to be made, which affect the ICTY and ICTR legacy on crimes against humanity and also our thinking on the appropriate definition in a Convention.

First, in assessing the legacy of the ad hoc tribunals, we must distinguish between the ICTY and the ICTR. The former has clearly taken the lead in developing the law. The ICTR's initial jurisprudence, with some exceptions, like the *Bagilishema* judgment, provided for little to no reasoning in the interpretation of crimes against humanity, or did so in a perfunctory manner.

Second, no clear and convincing interpretative methodology was established and applied from the beginning. As a result, methods of interpretation were used in an arbitrary and selective manner, and at times the methods in interpreting and discovering the law have been confused.

Third, the role of customary international law in relation to the statutory definitions has remained obscure. One can doubt whether the instruction of the Secretary-General that only rules which are without doubt part of customary international law can be applied has been followed consciously and consistently by the ad hoc tribunals. The importance attributed to the *nullum crimen* rule by the Secretary-General seems not to have inspired a cautious approach toward establishing rules of customary international law. Rather, as was mentioned earlier, development and expansion lie at the heart of the Tribunals' approach toward the law.

Fourth, when the ad hoc tribunals have tried to identify rules of customary international law, the result is not always convincing. At times, both the quantity and quality of their examination of State practice and *opinio juris* leaves much to be desired.

It follows from this study of the interpretation and application of the chapeau elements in crimes against humanity by the ad hoc tribunals that there is every reason to be critical. Undeniably, their case law has "developed" the law on crimes against humanity considerably, but one can doubt what the quality of its foundation is. It is therefore difficult to say whether the law of the ICTY and ICTR on crimes against humanity is stronger or better than a definition agreed on by the international community in the Rome Statute. In my view, the very simplistic contention that the ICC Statute embodies a political compromise, and that the law of the ad hoc tribunals truly represents the current status of customary international law on crimes against humanity, is without merit.

For a Convention on Crimes against Humanity, this also means that from a perspective of the quality of the law, there are no convincing reasons to prefer the law of the ICTY and ICTR over the law of the ICC. Even if the ICC law lacks a basis in customary international law, it represents a definition supported by a significant majority of States. Some of the interpretations adopted by the ad hoc tribunals, however, suffer from a twofold flaw. First, they are improperly presented as the only possible interpretation or as representing customary international law. Second, these interpretations come from just a handful of judges, namely those that were active in the early case law. In terms of legitimacy in the development of international law, widespread participation of States is more convincing.

7

The Definition of Crimes Against Humanity and the Question of a "Policy" Element

Guénaël Mettraux

I. INTRODUCTION

It has been debated for some time in the literature whether or not the definition of crimes against humanity includes an element of "policy."[1] With a view to answering this inquiry, the general question about the existence of that requirement may be subdivided into four separate queries:

(i) What does the requirement of "policy" mean to its proponents?
(ii) What is at stake in this debate?
(iii) What are the *pros* and *cons* supporting each side of the debate?
(iv) What is the position of international law on this issue?

Each of these subquestions will be addressed in turn.

II. WHAT IS THE REQUIREMENT OF "POLICY" SUPPOSED TO MEAN?

The first difficulty that one encounters when discussing this issue pertains to the meaning of "policy." To the extent that an element of "policy" is put forth as a constitutive requirement of crimes against humanity, one would expect a clear understanding of what that expression is intended to refer to. However, there is little indication in the literature – and even less in existing practice – as to what that requirement exactly means. Nor is it entirely clear whether its supporters all agree on what the concept should encompass. Unless the definitional contours of that expression are sufficiently clear, there is a genuine risk that it will not be understood by all in the same manner. In this context, as in others, "a difference in the mere form of words does in several cases make a difference in law."[2] Also, if such an element is said to form part of the definition of crimes against humanity, ambiguity as to its real

---

[1] For the sake of transparency, the present author should disclose the fact that, in earlier publications, he has taken the view that no element of "policy" forms part of the definition under customary international law. He maintains that view to this day. *See generally* Guénaël Mettraux, *Crimes against Humanity in the Jurisprudence of the International Criminal Tribunals for the Former Yugoslavia and for Rwanda*, 43 Harv. Int'l L.J. 237, 271–83 (2002); Guénaël Mettraux, International Crimes and the ad hoc Tribunals 172 (2005) [hereinafter Mettraux, International Crimes].

[2] Dean v. Dean [1891] 3 Ch. 150, 155 (U.K.).

meaning could have serious – primarily evidentiary – consequences for the parties to a criminal trial (in particular, the accused) and for the judges alike. In criminal law, lack of clarity and ambiguities are to be avoided since they may create great unfairness, not just to the defendant, but also to the prosecuting authorities. Without a clear indication as to what this expression implies, neither the prosecution nor the defense is in a position to effectively meet their case. Definitional ambiguity feeds evidentiary uncertainty. Part of the difficulty with the "policy" requirement lies in the linguistic haziness underlying that expression. During the drafting of the Nuremberg Charter, the representative of the United Kingdom, Sir David Maxwell Fyfe, expressed reservations about the use of the word "policy" in relation to the crime of aggression. He explained: "Our difficulty is that 'policy' is rather a loose word in English and is inclined to be used by people when they want to get out of expressing a concrete meaning."[3]

The expression seems to carry with it the idea that some sort of plan or agreed scheme was devised by authorities to commit crimes. The description given by the supporters of that requirement is in many respects similar in nature to the Anglo-Saxon concept of "conspiracy," an agreement to commit crimes, although in such a case the agreement relates not to specific criminal offenses, but provides for an environment of criminal permissiveness and impunity. For the purpose of defining crimes against humanity, this "policy" element appears to be intended to create a legal linkage between otherwise disparate crimes committed in the context of an attack against a civilian population. From an evidentiary point of view, it would require prosecuting authorities to establish, not only the commission of widespread or systematic crimes against members of a civilian population as part of an "attack," but also that these crimes were the material consequence and the expression of an existing agreed-on agenda to commit crimes with a view to attain a particular goal or end. For the purpose of the present article, the concept of "policy" may therefore be understood to refer to the following idea: An agreement, plan, or practice pursued by or on behalf of a government, authorities, or bodies, official or nonofficial, for the purpose or with a view to commit, aid, or support criminal activities.

III. THE STAKES

Why does it matter that such an element should or should not form part of the definition of crimes against humanity?

---

[3] International Conference on Military Trials, London 1945, *Minutes of Conference Session of 19 July 1945, concerning the definitions of crimes within the jurisdiction of the IMT*, reprinted in REPORT OF ROBERT H. JACKSON, UNITED STATES REPRESENTATIVE TO THE INTERNATIONAL CONFERENCE ON MILITARY TRIALS, LONDON 1945, at 301 (1949), *cited in* David Hunt, *The International Criminal Court – High Hopes, "Creative Ambiguity" and an Unfortunate Mistrust in International Judges*, 2 J. INT'L CRIM. JUST. 56, 65 (2004).

A. Judicial Significance

Judges seized of a case in which crimes against humanity form part of the charges need to know what this concept entails and what elements form part of its definition. Without a sufficient degree of legal certainty, they are simply unable to fulfill their mandate in relation to such a criminal offense. Furthermore, in the context of criminal trials, criminal judges will need more than a general sense of what that definition and its element might be.[4] They need to be able to identify, based on the definition of that crime, the evidence that would be relevant to their findings of fact. If the element of "policy" does not form part of the law applicable in their jurisdiction, no such inquiry needs to be made.

Judges also need clarity as regards the elements of that offense to determine whether they have jurisdiction over the crime in question, whether the case is adequately pleaded, whether the defense can validly raise "defenses" in relation to any element of that offense, whether the court is entitled to prevent parties from asking questions not relevant to the definition of that offense, and, at the end of the trial, whether the prosecution has met its burden in relation to each and every element of the offense.

B. Evidential and Prosecutorial Significance

Judges are not the only trial participants who need clarity as regards the definition of this criminal offense. Prosecuting authorities need clear guidance as regards (i) the information and material that they need to look for and collect as part of their investigation; and (ii) the evidence that they need to produce at trial to meet their burden of proof in relation to this category of crime.

As will be discussed further in this chapter, the adoption of a "policy" element would have the effect of making it more difficult for the prosecution to meet its case in relation to alleged crimes against humanity than would be the case without one. Not only would the prosecution have to establish an additional fact (i.e., the existence of a "policy" to commit crimes), but it would have to identify and obtain evidence relevant to prove that fact. Unless that phrase ends up being interpreted as no more than a loose coincidence of converging evidence, suggesting that there was more to the crimes than the coincidence of unrelated events, the prosecution might have difficulties uncovering evidence of a plan or agreement to commit crimes and even greater difficulties to associate any particular defendant with such a plan. This, in itself, is no sufficient basis to object to the inclusion of this element, but it is a factor of relevance to decide whether it should or should not be included.

---

[4] See, e.g., Prosecutor v. Hadžihasanović et al., Case No. IT-01-47-AR72, Decision on Interlocutory Appeal Challenging Jurisdiction in Relation to Command Responsibility, ¶ 34 (July 16, 2003).

The adoption of a "policy" element would also be significant for the defense in cases where crimes against humanity form part of the charges. If that element is adopted, the defense could contest its existence in a particular case and challenge the existence of any connection or relationship between the conduct of the accused and the policy behind the underlying offenses.

C. Political and Historical Significance

The finding that a "policy" somehow accompanied the crimes that form the background of charges could be, historically and politically, important for the nation concerned with those crimes. To the extent that such a "policy" existed in a particular context where crimes were committed, a judicial finding to the effect that it did exist might also contribute to ensuring that the court's findings are in tune with the reality of the facts on the ground and thus contribute to the accurate historical retelling of those events.

A finding to that effect could also have implications as regards the responsibility of States whose organs or agents have been involved in the planning or execution of such a policy.

IV. THE DOCTRINAL *PROS* AND *CONS*

Each side in the academic debate has accused the other of having a political or prosecutorial agenda behind its position. To some extent, both sides are correct to make that suggestion. The debate over the requirement – or not – of "policy" and the answer given to the question of whether or not such a requirement forms part of the definition of crimes against humanity under customary international law is to a large extent tainted by the views of writers as to the role and function of that category of crimes. With it has come a certain degree of selectivity in citing the authorities relevant to each side of the argument and little critical effort to evaluate their positions.

Despite the appearance sometimes created by decisions and judgments of international criminal tribunals, various aspects of the definition of crimes against humanity have hardly hardened into customary law.[5] This explains that the debate over the definition of that crime is also a debate over its soul, over what it *should* be, as much as over what it is. The debate over the "policy" element is as much a debate over whether it does or does not form part of the definition of crimes against humanity, as it is a debate over whether it should or should not be part of it. Those who support the inclusion of such an element wish to give this crime an added dimension, a more global and greater political significance, whereas the other camp generally wants to keep it focused, penal, and more prosecution-friendly.

The focus of this chapter will be primarily directed at the question of whether or not existing practice and precedents support the inclusion of such an element in

---

[5] See, e.g., METTRAUX, INTERNATIONAL CRIMES, *supra* note 1, at 13 *et seq.*

the definition of crimes against humanity. Whereas the precedents, authorities, and state practice available on this issue will be reviewed in the next part of this chapter, the present section will briefly consider and assess the arguments in support and against the inclusion of a "policy" element in the definition of crimes against humanity.

A. *The Pros – Why a "Policy" Requirement Should Form Part of the Definition of Crimes Against Humanity*

The arguments in support of the requirement of "policy" generally fall into one of the following categories:

1. The Inclusion of a "Policy" Element Better Reflects the Historical Reality That Crimes Against Humanity Have Generally Been Committed in the Context and as Part of a State-Based or State-Organized Criminal Campaign or Policy

This argument is probably the strongest in support of the position that a requirement of "policy" should form part of the definition of crimes against humanity. It is also, for the most part, correct as a matter of historical or factual experience.[6]

In response, it could be said that such a factual coincidence says little about the need for – let alone the existence as a matter of law of – this element of the definition of crime against humanity. If it were to be established statistically, for instance, that in most cases of murders, the perpetrator is acting in pursuance of a morally repulsive goal, this would not justify that "morally repulsive goals" should become a required element of the crime of murder and that acts committed for any other reason would therefore be disqualified as murders. A criminal offense cannot be (re)defined in light of the factual situations it is called upon to sanction. It is the definition of the offense that determines the contours of the factual matrix that is relevant to the charges, not the other way around. Finally, it cannot be excluded that mass atrocities could occur without any policy sustaining them – unless one defines "policy" in such a way as would require a tribunal to stretch the meaning of that concept so far as to render it all but meaningless.

2. Without Such an Element, the Currency of Crimes Against Humanity Would Be Devaluated

It is part of the argument in support of a "policy" element that, unless this requirement is recognized as forming part of the definition of crimes against humanity, the

---

[6] For a historical and sociological discussion of State-organized massacres, see YVES TERNON, L'ÉTAT CRIMINEL: LES GÉNOCIDES AU XXEME SIÈCLE (1995), and BRENDA UEKERT, RIVERS OF BLOOD: A COMPARATIVE STUDY OF GOVERNMENT MASSACRES (1995).

stigma that attaches to that category of crimes would be undermined or devaluated. An element of planning, if it can be linked to the perpetrator, would render his conduct more serious because it would imply an element of premeditation (or criminal organization) on his part, which would aggravate his conduct. Again, this consideration is meritorious.

It could be argued, however, that the "currency" argument may be countered by pointing to the fact that the gravity of the offense is already fully sustained by the existing chapeau elements of crimes against humanity ("a widespread or systematic attack against a civilian population.")[7] It could further be said that, as with any other international crime, the definition of crimes against humanity has to strike a balance between depth (of gravity) and breadth (of application): The more specific and serious the definition of the offense – as with genocide – the narrower the scope of its application and the narrower its reach. It could finally be pointed out that at Nuremberg, perhaps the gravest of crimes were characterized as crimes against humanity whether or not there was any suggestion of an element of "policy" forming part of their definition.[8]

3. The Definition of a Crime May Not Be Decided by Evidentiary Considerations, in Particular the Ease with Which the Prosecution Might Be Able to Prove the Charges

It is sometimes suggested by the supporters of the "policy" requirement that its exclusion could not be based on the argument that including it would render prosecution of crimes against humanity simpler and conviction more certain. Although the argument is not per se invalid, it could easily be responded that neither could this element of "policy" be added to the definition of crimes against humanity with a view to prevent the definition of that crime from getting too broad. In this sense, the argument – in its positive or negative formulation – is self-justifying and without much weight. It is true, however, that the inclusion of such a requirement would impact the scope of potential prosecutions for crimes against humanity and the "ease" with which this crime could be successfully prosecuted.[9] In other words, the inclusion of such a requirement – if it is given a meaningful evidentiary content – would make it more difficult for the prosecuting authorities to meet their case.

4. Without Such an Element, Isolated or Domestic Crimes Could Qualify as Crimes Against Humanity

It has been argued by a number of authors that unless such an element is included, the definition of crimes against humanity could come to cover crimes such as

---

[7] For a definition of that phrase, see METTRAUX, INTERNATIONAL CRIMES, *supra* note 1, at 155–72.
[8] See *infra* § V(B).
[9] See *infra* § IV(A).7.

organized crime or serial killings, which should not come within the framework of an international offense. This argument has merit.

There is indeed a risk that the concept of crime against humanity could be applied to all sorts of conduct that, at first sight, would seem not to *fit* with the traditional understanding of what this notion is intended to criminalize. This, however, appears to be the consequence not of the existence (or not) of a requirement of "policy," but of the general lack of clarity and specificity of the definition of crimes against humanity. In that sense, adding an element of "policy" would not necessarily exclude those scenarios from the theoretical scope of that offense. In other words, the inclusion of a "policy" requirement does not seem to provide any answer to the stated fear.

It should be noted, furthermore, that those who have advanced this argument do not appear to have located a single, real-life example that would support their argument. Instead, it would seem that the existing elements of the definition and prosecutorial discretion have generally protected the concept of crimes against humanity from such definitional *débordement*.

5. The Perpetrators of Crimes Against Humanity Are Always Policy Makers or Individuals with a Policy or Organizational Role, Which Sets Them Apart from Mere Executioners

It is also sometimes suggested that the perpetrators of crimes against humanity are always or mostly high-ranking officials or policy makers, in the general sense, and that the definition of the crime should reflect that reality. The record of existing trials for crimes against humanity does not support such a contention. In addition, it mistakes prosecutorial strategy and jurisdictional considerations (as regards the sort of defendants that international justice should be interested in) on the one hand and elements of the criminal offense on the other. In fact, the record of war crimes trials since World War II indicates that a vast number of relatively lowly individuals have been prosecuted and convicted for crimes against humanity. It is now accepted under customary international law that not just high-ranking leaders and officers may be convicted for crimes against humanity, but also executioners or foot-soldiers.[10]

---

[10] Low-level defendants such as Akayesu (at the ICTR), Kunarac, Kovač, and Vuković (at the ICTY) are only examples of a much broader pattern. In the *Todorović and Radić* Judgment, the Appellate Panel of the State Court of Bosnia and Herzegovina noted that "the criminal culpability of lower-level, direct perpetrators for crimes against humanity, is founded upon their knowing participation in a widespread or systematic attack against a civilian population through the commission of an underlying crime. The conviction of such persons for crimes against humanity neither attributes responsibility for the attack itself nor constitutes collective responsibility for all crimes committed as part of the attack." Prosecutor v. Todorović and Radić, Appeal Judgment, X-KRZ-07/382, ¶ 104 (Feb. 17, 2009) (Ct. of Bosnia and Herzegovina, Appellate Division) [hereinafter *Todorović and Radić Appeal Judgment*].

The above argument might result, in part, from the confusion that exists between those elements that form part of the definition of international crimes and those requirements that are constitutive elements of a given form of criminal liability. As early as 1950, Jean Graven had pointed out the confusion surrounding the element of "policy" and made it clear that, in his view, the existence of a policy or plan did not constitute an element of crimes against humanity. Rather, it might be relevant to certain particular forms of participation in such crimes:

> En revanche, s'il est naturel et juste de punir 'entente' active et agissant en vue du crime, il est erroné de subordonner l'existence et la punition du crime lui-même à la préexistence d'une entente ou d'un 'complot', comme on a voulu le faire souvent à la suite du statut et du jugement de Nuremberg. C'est là, juridiquement, une confusion que rien ne justifie et dont il faut désormais absolument se garder.[11]

Thus, if and where the defendant has taken part in the planning or policy-making exercise that led to or accompanied the commission of mass atrocities, the prosecution would be armed with the necessary tools to prosecute this person and take into consideration any "policy" role that he might have had in that process – not through the definition of crimes against humanity, but by selecting the relevant form of liability to prosecute him. The doctrines of "conspiracy," "incitement/instigation," and "joint criminal enterprise" already capture this sort of criminal involvement in the commission of crimes against humanity.

B. The Cons – Why a Requirement of "Policy" Should Not Form Part of the Definition of Crimes Against Humanity

The arguments against the addition of a "policy" requirement – in addition to the general argument that no such requirement exists under customary international law, which will be considered further in this chapter – generally fall into one of the following categories:

1. The Concept of "Policy" Is Too Loose and Uncertain to Apply in a Criminal Context

One of the main reasons advanced against the inclusion of this concept in the definition of crimes against humanity is that the concept of "policy" is unclear and not capable of any precise legal definition. Rather than being conducive to a better understanding of the concept of crimes against humanity, it is suggested that the use of such an expression would further undermine the quest for a clear and

---

[11] Jean Graven, *Les Crimes contre l'Humanité*, RECUEIL DES COURS, 1950-I, 433, 560. Graven also pointed out the mistaken interpretation of the last paragraph of article 6 of the Nuremberg Charter, which some courts (and authors) have wrongly interpreted as a general requirement that there be a plan or a policy accompanying a crime against humanity. *Id.* at 560 n.4.

workable definition of crimes against humanity. As already noted earlier, this argument certainly has some merit, but it could not in itself serve to exclude such an element from the definition of crimes against humanity as a sufficiently precise definition could be found for it. It is an unfortunate reality of international criminal law that the definition of many of its concepts and prohibitions have been loaded with terms and expressions that end up meaning nothing or little, like "weasel words" that promise to mean something but end up having no or very little evidential significance.

2. The Inclusion of This Concept Risks Creating an Opportunistic and Political Use of This Category of Crimes

More serious, in this author's view, is the suggestion that unless the concept of "policy" is defined with sufficient clarity, it risks being used to shield and protect from prosecution nationals or officials from those States that a court or tribunal does not wish, or does not feel capable of prosecuting. The way in which the Prosecutor of the International Criminal Court has dealt with allegations of crimes as part of his "Iraq investigation" is telling in that respect. In the part of the Prosecutor's response to communications received in relation to this matter, the ICC Prosecutor had this to say:

> Very few factual allegations were submitted concerning genocide or crimes against humanity. The Office collected information and examined the allegations. The available information provided no reasonable indicia that Coalition forces had the "intent to destroy, in whole or in part, a national, ethnical, racial or religious group as such," as required in the definition of genocide (Article 6). Similarly, the available information provided no reasonable indicia of the required elements for a crime against humanity, i.e. a widespread or systematic attack directed against any civilian population (Article 7).[12]

The Prosecutor did not specify further what part of that phrase was evidentiarily insufficient, nor did he specify whether the requirement of "policy" contained in article 7 of the Statute played any part in his considerations. However, the negative potential of that requirement may be observed from another part of the Prosecutor's response, which deals with allegations of war crimes. Article 8(1) of the ICC Statute provides that "the Court shall have jurisdiction in respect of war crimes *in particular when committed as part of a plan or policy* or as part of a large-scale commission of such crimes."[13] In his Response, the Prosecutor of the ICC stated: "This threshold

---

[12] Letter from Luis Moreno-Ocampo, Chief Prosecutor of the International Criminal Court (Feb. 9, 2006), *available at* http://www.icc-cpi.int/Menus/ICC/Structure+of+the+Court/Office+of+the+Prosecutor/Comm+and+Ref/Iraq/.

[13] Rome Statute of the International Criminal Court art. 8(1), July 17, 1998, U.N. Doc. A/CONF.183/9 (emphasis added) [hereinafter *ICC Statute*].

is not an element of the crime, and the words 'in particular' suggest that this is not a strict requirement. It does, however, provide Statute guidance that the Court is intended to focus on situations meeting these requirements."[14]

As a former ICTY Judge has noted, there is a real risk that "[b]ehind an apparently doctrinal issue, it is possible to perceive the concern of some States which are keen to prevent investigations into criminal conduct which, although clearly criminal, had not been orchestrated or supported by them."[15] The signs are not encouraging, and the inclusion of concepts such as a "policy" requirement, unless adequately defined and duly policed in their application, could have the unfortunate effect of creating de facto immunities for the citizens and officials of politically potent States. Commenting on article 7 of the ICC Statute, former ICTY Judge David Hunt had this to say:

> Less obvious, and possibly more insidious, are the limitations which were implanted within the very definitions of crimes which limit the scope of the Court's inquiry. One good example is the reference in the definition of crimes against humanity to a requirement that such crimes must have been committed as a result of or in connection with some sort of "policy." Such a requirement was repeatedly mentioned by States as a necessary shield against the prosecutions of crimes which were not actively supported or orchestrated by a State or a similar entity. Many States were afraid that, in the absence of such a limitation, isolated criminal conduct and other "unfortunate" accidents during military operations could be prosecuted under that article. As pointed out by one author, "the introduction of this element of 'policy' [in the definition of crimes against humanity] was a highly political affair." As noted above, no such requirement of policy exists in current international criminal law. The text of Article 7 of the ICC Statute (Crimes against Humanity) is in fact a compromise between the two camps which fought over the breadth of its definition. The requirement in Article 7(2)(a) that an "attack against any civilian population" involves an element of "policy" made a compromise possible between those who wanted to prosecute all crimes against humanity and those who wanted to limit the Court's jurisdiction to crimes organized by a State or similar entity.[16]

To guard against any such risk, and should an element of "policy" be adopted, it should be

(i) defined precisely and carefully; and
(ii) in such a way as to ensure transparent, fair, and nondiscriminatory application of the definition of crimes against humanity.

If it is to serve the purposes that its supporters wish to attribute to that concept, the concept of "policy" will have to be fleshed out into something evidentially significant. This, in turn, might mean that acquittals might result because of the prosecution's

---

[14] Ocampo, *supra* note 12.
[15] Hunt, *supra* note 3, at 65.
[16] *Id.* at 65 (footnotes omitted).

inability to garner sufficient evidence of the existence of such an element. This is not in itself an argument against the inclusion of a "policy" requirement, but it is one that its supporters should be willing and ready to both acknowledge and defend.

There is a real risk that where such a vague concept forms part of the definition of an international crime (or of a form of liability) and that difficulty arises in proving it, it is effectively diluted by stealth, emptied of any evidentiary content. This phenomenon renders the requirement practically meaningless while maintaining the appearance of its relevance. The requirements of a *nexus* with an armed conflict for war crimes, for instance, or that of an agreement to commit crimes in the definition of "joint criminal enterprise" has *generally* been interpreted in such a way that it has been emptied of the better part of any content.[17]

3. This Requirement Mixes Factual Considerations with Legal or Definitional Requirements

It is correct, as noted earlier, that crimes against humanity are often, and perhaps always, accompanied by some sort of policy or plan to commit them. This, however, seems to be no argument in support of its inclusion as an element of their legal definition. These are factual considerations that the court may take into consideration, but which need not – and, in this author's view, do not – form part of the definition of the crime. No criminal offense can claim to capture each and every factual aspect of the context that characterizes a particular type of criminal conduct. Instead, criminal law provides for those elements that, if met, would bring that conduct into the realm of the law. In response, it could be said that, to the extent possible, the definition of a crime should match as closely as possible the factual patterns that it seeks to criminalize.

4. This Requirement Creates a Gap in the Protection Afforded by International Criminal Law

It is also sometimes argued that if an element of "policy" were added to the definition of crimes against humanity, a gap would open up in the protection afforded by international criminal law. Although making international law "watertight and inescapable"[18] might be an overly ambitious and not necessarily desirable objective, it is a fact that the addition of a "policy" element would have the effect of excluding

---

[17] For an encouraging exception to that broad proposition, see the Judgment of a Dutch court in The Hague, which took the view that the prosecution had failed to establish a sufficient "nexus" between the conduct of the accused – who was charged with war crimes for crimes committed in Rwanda during the genocide – and the armed conflict which the prosecution said existed at the time. Mpambara, Rechtbank's-Gravenhage [Rb.] [District Court of The Hague, Netherlands] 23 Maart 2009, LJN BI2444 (Neth.).

[18] Prosecutor v. Tadić, Case No. IT-94-1-AR72, Decision on the Defence Motion for Interlocutory Appeal on Jurisdiction, ¶ 91 (Oct. 2, 1995) (in relation to the interpretation of common article 3 of the Geneva Conventions).

from the scope of crimes against humanity a large number of crimes that could not be linked – or not sufficiently linked – to any sort of criminal policy.

In itself, such a consequence might not justify opting for a broader definition rather than for the narrower version of it. It is, however, a factor worth evaluating and weighing in this context. The crimes that might fall afoul of the "policy" requirement will not necessarily qualify as war crimes (as, for instance, where there is no armed conflict) nor as genocide (if no genocidal *mens rea* existed or where it cannot be proved). Impunity might result. Also, and indirectly, such a requirement could have the intended or unintended effect of narrowing the jurisdictional reach of international courts and tribunals. Both the ICC and national jurisdictions that have adopted the "policy" definition of crimes against humanity could refuse to exercise their jurisdiction on that basis, thus leaving potentially very serious crimes unpunished (unless they fall under any of the other categories of crimes).

This could also interfere with the jurisdictional trigger mechanism – "unable or unwilling" – of the ICC: If the ICC Prosecutor is permitted to rely on this factor (i.e., the absence of evidence of a "policy" underlying the crimes) to set aside or renounce investigations and decline to prosecute, so could local prosecutors. If local prosecuting authorities were to take the view that there is no evidence of a "policy" to commit such crimes, the prosecutors could not use such a finding to claim that the authorities are unwilling or unable to prosecute. The impunity gap might open further.

5. The Requirement Is Redundant and Unnecessary

A commentator has noted that it would appear that "the requirement of policy is simply another means of expressing the requirement that crimes against humanity be something more than random or isolated inhumane acts. In other words, the requirement of policy is the equivalent of [the] requirement of widespread or systematic scale."[19] This position seems to be correct. If the phrase "widespread or systematic attack against a civilian population" is given its due meaning, it seems that all or most of the concerns expressed by the supporters of the requirement of "policy" dissipate or become quite insignificant.

The concept of "attack" that forms part of the definition of crimes against humanity carries with it the sense of a course of conduct involving the commission of acts of violence.[20] In that sense, it is such as to exclude from the realm of this category of crimes unrelated or insufficiently related criminal occurrences. Many of the factors

---

[19] See Payam Akhavan, Defining the Ultimate Crime: Genocide and Crimes Against Humanity in International Law 59 (on file with the author).

[20] Prosecutor v. Kunarac et al., Case No. IT-96-23-T & IT-96-23/1-T, Judgment, ¶ 415 (Feb. 22, 2001) [hereinafter *Kunarac Trial Judgment*]; Prosecutor v. Vasiljević, Case No. IT-98-32-T, Judgment, ¶ 29 (Nov. 29, 2002) and references cited therein. The acts which form part of the attack need not, strictly speaking, be crimes in the sense that they need not amount to any of the offenses listed in the Statute; only those acts prosecuted as crimes against humanity have to meet the

that are evidentially relevant to establishing the existence of such an attack will, in many ways, cover the same evidential ground as would be relevant to a requirement of "policy."[21] In addition, the requirement that the attack must be directed at a civilian "population" amplifies further the element of scale that is implicit in the requirement of "attack" and has the effect of excluding from the definition of that offense isolated or random criminal occurrences.[22] So do the qualifiers of "widespread" or "systematic," which already form part of the definition of crimes against humanity.[23]

In that sense, the existing definition of crimes against humanity is perfectly capable of excluding from its realm the sort of theoretical scenarios (biker gangs, serial killers, etc.) that are put forth in support of the "policy" element.[24] If any "risk" remains as to the type of situations in relation to which the concept could possibly apply to,

---

requirement of this offense. *Id.* The Trial Chamber in *Kayishema and Ruzindana* described the *attack* as "the event in which the enumerated crimes must form part." Prosecutor v. Kayishema and Ruzindana, Case No. ICTR-95-1-T, Judgment, ¶ 122 (May 21, 1999) [hereinafter *Kayishema and Ruzindana Trial Judgment*]. The Trial Chamber in *Akayesu* gave a slightly different definition of the "attack": "The concept of 'attack' may be defined as an unlawful act of the kind enumerated in Article 3(a) to (i) of the Statute, like murder, extermination, enslavement, etc." Prosecutor v. Akayesu, Case No. ICTR-96-4-T, Judgment, ¶ 581 (Sept. 2, 1998) [hereinafter *Akayesu Trial Judgment*]; *see also* Prosecutor v. Kajelijeli, Case No. ICTR-98-44A-T, Judgment and Sentence, ¶ 867 (Dec. 1, 2003); Prosecutor v. Musema, Case No. ICTR-96-13-T, Judgment and Sentence, ¶ 205 (Jan. 27, 2000); Prosecutor v. Rutaganda, Case No. ICTR-96-3-T, Judgment and Sentence, ¶ 70 (Dec. 6, 1999). The *Akayesu* Trial Chamber further held (without providing any authority for its assertion) that an "attack" may be non-violent in character – like imposing a system of apartheid. *Akayesu Trial Judgment*, ¶ 581. The author does not agree with the view that the establishment and maintenance of such a system of apartheid can be regarded as "non-violent" or that, for that matter, any "attack" within the meaning of crimes against humanity could be non-violent in the broad sense of the word. *See also* ICC Statute, *supra* note 13, art. 7, ¶ 2.

[21] In the *Dragan Nikolić* case, for example, the Trial Chamber identified six factors relevant in determining post facto whether an "attack" against the civilian population had taken place: (i) whether there has been an authoritarian takeover of the region where the crimes have been committed; (ii) whether a new authoritarian power structure has been established; (iii) whether discriminatory measures, such as restrictions on bank accounts held by one group of citizens, or *laissez-passer* requirements have been imposed; (iv) whether summary arrests, detention, torture, and other crimes have been committed; (v) whether massive transfers of civilians to camps have taken place; (vii) whether the enemy population has been removed from the area. *See* Prosecutor v. Dragan Nikolić, Case No. IT-94-2-R61, Review of Indictment Pursuant to Rule 61 of the Rules of Procedure and Evidence, ¶ 27 (Oct. 20, 1995) [hereinafter *Nickolić Rule 61 Decision*].

[22] *See* METTRAUX, INTERNATIONAL CRIMES, *supra* note 1, at 163 *et seq*, and authorities cited therein. *See* in particular Prosecutor v. Tadić, Case No. IT-94-1-T, Opinion & Judgment, ¶ 648 (May 7, 1997) [hereinafter *Tadić Trial Judgment*] and *Kunarac Trial Judgment*, *supra* note 20, ¶ 422.

[23] *See* METTRAUX, INTERNATIONAL CRIMES, *supra* note 1, at 170 *et seq*.

[24] Although the concept of crime against humanity might not be best suited for that purpose, it could be, factually and evidentiarily, that it might be made to apply to certain categories of terror-related activities. Crimes committed as part of a widespread campaign of terrorist attacks targeting a particular civilian population could, for instance, qualify as crimes against humanity, all conditions being met. A cautious approach is warranted in such context, however, as an expansive application of the concept of crime against humanity in situations not well suited for it could have the effect of disfiguring it as a distinct category of criminal offense.

and as with many other such concepts, the diligent use of prosecutorial discretion should be regarded as capable of dealing with any such residual concerns.

In response, supporters of the requirement may say that the inclusion of a "policy" requirement would further highlight aspects of these crimes that form part of other elements of the definition but which would all be "centralized" into that concept. They might also add that rather than relying upon the prosecutor's discretion to eliminate theoretically possible situations where crimes against humanity could apply, this element would do so automatically without the need for the prosecution to exercise any discretion in that regard.

6. The Adoption of This Requirement Marks a Return to the Idea of Collective Responsibility

The creation of the ad hoc tribunals in the early 1990s and the establishment of other courts and tribunals in more recent years were thought to mark the coming of age of *individual* criminal responsibility and the end or near-end of the idea of collective liability that was increasingly seen as dangerous and outdated. The victory appears to have been short-lived and in any case far from complete.[25]

It could be argued that the inclusion of an element of "policy" in the definition of crimes against humanity marks a return to the idea of collective responsibility from which international criminal law has sought to escape. Although individuals would be the sole "recipients" of a criminal conviction for crimes against humanity, the presence of an element of "policy" might spread the stain of collective liability over an entire community or group that might not be given the benefit of a trial in which to contest the charges. The risk of this happening would be all the greater if, as precedents suggest, the ambit and scope of that "policy" is defined most broadly and without specifying those individuals who are said to have adopted or supported it.

As will be discussed further below, it seems much wiser to deal with any collective element that might have accompanied the commission of crimes against humanity not as part of the definition of the offense, but in the context of the relevant forms of liability that are being used to prosecute a particular defendant. This maintains the scope of that offense and permits the prosecution and the court to narrow the scope of the collective aspect of these crimes to those individuals (or groups of individuals) that have acted in concert to bring about the commission of these crimes. Such a course also has the benefit of avoiding the unnecessary duplication of evidence between crimes and forms of liability as would result from the inclusion of an element of "policy" in the definition of crimes against humanity.

---

[25] Concepts like "joint criminal enterprise," which have been spreading through the case law of these Tribunals, have reinjected a great deal of "collectiveness" into the body of international criminal law.

7. The Requirement of "Policy" Could Create Serious Jurisdictional Impediments

Insisting on a "policy" element may have awkward jurisdictional consequences. In a case where, for instance, the alleged "policy" that accompanied the crimes is that of a State or its organs, a defendant State in a civil law claim could raise the "act of State" doctrine to object to the justiciability of the matter. In criminal cases, State officials involved in enforcing such a policy could likewise seek to rely on their functional immunities to shield themselves from the reach of a domestic jurisdiction that wishes to prosecute them for their involvement in a policy of the State that local prosecutors regard as criminal in character. Even though the validity of such "defenses" might be subject to much academic debate, they might be enough to cause a prosecutor or a judge to refrain from proceeding.

The inclusion of a policy could also have regrettable consequences in jurisdictions like the United States where, in civil cases, doctrines such as the "political question" doctrine could have the effect of condemning to almost certain failure a civil action that relates to allegations of crimes against humanity. An insistence on the policy element could indeed have the effect of reducing or excluding the claimants' chance to obtain reparation in a case where the policy is said to have been officially sanctioned by State authorities. As was noted in a case related to crimes committed in Abu Ghraib, "the more plaintiffs assert official complicity in the acts of which they complain, the closer they sail to the jurisdictional limitation of the political question doctrine."[26] Insisting on the inclusion of a "policy" element could thus have the effect of immunizing crimes against humanity from successful civil claims in certain jurisdictions.

V. DEFINITION OF CRIMES AGAINST HUMANITY UNDER INTERNATIONAL LAW

Each side in the debate on the issue of "policy" cites as authority cases and instruments that are said to be supportive of their position, while often ignoring those authorities that would contradict their position. Below is a review of those cases and instruments that would appear to be relevant to any discussion of the state of international law on that point.

A. General Overview

Before looking into the relevant material, it must be acknowledged that there are contradictory statements as regard the state of the law on that point and some of the material under review could be open to contradictory interpretations. The

---

[26] Saleh v. Titan Corp., 436 F. Supp. 2d 55, 58 (D.D.C. 2006) (order granting in part and denying in part motion for summary judgment).

general rule of interpretation pursuant to which criminal law should be interpreted restrictively might not be of great assistance here because it could be read in two contradictory ways: First, it could be said that a requirement of "policy" could not be read into the law where it is not expressly or explicitly provided for. Second, in the alternative, it could be read in such a way as to demand that the interpretation most favorable to the accused – one that would include a requirement of "policy" – should be adopted. It is submitted, however, that when existing precedents and instruments are looked at as a whole, there is an overwhelming case in support of the view that the definition of crimes against humanity does not include a requirement of "policy" and a rather meager one supporting the opposite view.

B. The Trial of the Major Nazi War Criminals at Nuremberg

Although the term "crimes against humanity" or "laws of humanity" had been previously used, the first genuine attempt at defining crimes against humanity took place after World War II.[27] The result of this effort was embodied in article 6(c) of the Nuremberg Charter. The definition of crimes against humanity contained in the Nuremberg Charter is generally considered to be the authoritative definition under customary international law,[28] and it contains no explicit reference to a plan or a policy. It reads as follows:

> Crimes against Humanity: namely, murder, extermination, enslavement, deportation, and other inhumane acts committed against any civilian population, before or during the war, or persecutions on political, racial or religious grounds in execution of or in connection with any crime within the jurisdiction of the Tribunal, whether or not in violation of the domestic law of the country where perpetrated.[29]

Despite the absence of any reference in the Tribunal's Charter to an element of "policy," it has been argued in the literature that the policy element may be inferred

---

[27] The terminological origin of the expression "crimes against humanity" may be found as far back as the Paris Peace Conference of 1919, where reference was made to the "laws" and "dictates of humanity." See REPORT PRESENTED TO THE PRELIMINARY PEACE CONFERENCE BY THE COMMISSION ON THE RESPONSIBILITY OF THE AUTHORS OF THE WAR AND ENFORCEMENT OF PENALTIES, reprinted in 14 AM. J. INT'L L. 95, 113 (1920). However, the first indictment and classification of a crime as a crime against humanity took place in Nuremberg. See also Leo Gross, The Punishment of War Criminals: The Nuremberg Trial, 1955 NETH. INT'L L. REV. 1. See also Elisabeth Zoller, La Définition des Crimes contre l'Humanité, 3 JOURNAL DU DROIT INTERNATIONAL 549, 551 (1993).

[28] See TRIAL OF THE MAJOR WAR CRIMINALS BEFORE THE INTERNATIONAL MILITARY TRIBUNAL, NUREMBERG, 14 NOVEMBER 1945 – 1 OCTOBER 1946, at 254, 461 (1947–1949) [hereinafter IMT Judgment]: "The Charter ... is the expression of international law existing at the time of its creation." See also The Secretary-General, Report of the Secretary-General Pursuant to Paragraph 2 of Security Council Resolution 808, ¶ 35, U.N. Doc. S/25704 (May 3, 1993) (provides that the Nuremberg Charter is part of customary international law).

[29] Charter of the International Military Tribunal art. 6(c), Aug. 8, 1945, 59 Stat. 1544, 82 U.N.T.S. 279 [hereinafter Nuremberg Charter].

from the reference in the Tribunal's Charter to the phrase "political, racial or religious grounds," which has been said to apply not just to the crime of persecution, but to all crimes against humanity.[30] On closer inspection, however, the phrase does not appear to support such an interpretation. First, it is remarkable that, if that interpretation of the phrase was adopted, the requirement of policy would apply not just to crimes against humanity, but to all three categories of crimes that were within the jurisdiction of the Tribunal, including war crimes. Until the adoption of the ICC Statute,[31] however, no international instrument had suggested that to constitute a war crime, a violation of the laws or customs of war had to be committed in pursuance of some policy or plan. Instead, such a requirement has been said and shown not to form part of customary international law.[32] Furthermore, it is clear from the record of the negotiations that led to the adoption of the Nuremberg Charter that there was not one type of crimes against humanity that required an element of "racial, political or religious" discrimination, but two categories, with only one of them requiring such an element. In its *History*, the United Nations War Crimes Commission took notice of the conclusion of its Legal Committee, according to which "[t]here are two types of crimes against humanity, those of the 'murder type' (murder, extermination, enslavement, deportation and the like), and those of the 'persecution type' committed on racial, political or religious grounds."[33] The Commission also laid down for the first time what would become the requirement of a "widespread or systematic attack," which distinguishes between purely domestic crimes and crimes against humanity.[34] This definition did not include an element of "policy" as a necessary requirement.[35] In fact, it is now accepted that the requirement of a discriminatory "political, racial or religious grounds" pertains exclusively to the crime of persecution, not any of the other underlying offenses that can qualify as crimes against humanity.[36]

---

[30] William Schabas, *State Policy as an Element of International Crimes*, 98 J. CRIM. L. & CRIMINOLOGY 953, 954 (2008).

[31] ICC Statute, *supra* note 13.

[32] *See, e.g.*, Prosecutor v. Kunarac et al., IT-96-23 & IT-96-23/1-A, Judgment, ¶¶ 98–101 (June 12, 2002); *Tadić Trial Judgment, supra* note 22, ¶ 573; Prosecutor v. Mucić et al., Case No. IT-96-21-T, Judgment, ¶¶ 194–95 (Nov. 16, 1998).

[33] HISTORY OF THE UNITED NATIONS WAR CRIMES COMMISSION AND THE DEVELOPMENT OF THE LAWS OF WAR 178, 194.

[34] *See id.* at 179 ("Isolated offences did not fall within the notion of crimes against humanity. As a rule systematic mass action, particularly if it was authoritative, was necessary to transform a common crime, punishable only under municipal law, into a crime against humanity, which thus became also the concern of international law. Only crimes which either by their magnitude and savagery or by their large number or by the fact that a similar pattern was applied at different times and places, endangered the international community or shocked the conscience of mankind, warranted intervention by States other than that on whose territory the crimes had been committed, or whose subjects had become their victims.").

[35] *Id.*

[36] *See generally* Prosecutor v. Akayesu, Case No. ICTR-96-4-A, Judgment, ¶¶ 464–69 (June 1, 2001); Prosecutor v. Bagilishema, Case No. ICTR-95-1A-T, Judgment, ¶ 81 (June 7, 2001); *Kajelijeli Trial Judgment, supra* note 20, ¶ 877 (concerning the formulation of the ICTR Statute on that point).

It has also been suggested that an element of "policy" could be read into the preambular paragraph of article 6 of the Nuremberg Charter, which provides that offenders must have been "acting in the interests of the European Axis countries," thereby suggesting, it is argued, that the Charter referred to men "acting in the interest of a State."[37] The historical records of the drafting of the Nuremberg Charter would appear to contradict such a suggestion. The real function of the phrase "acting in the interests of the European Axis countries" was to make it clear that, although the law applied by the Tribunal was supposed to be universal in scope, the reference to persons "acting in the interest of a State" was to make it clear that the *jurisdiction* of the Tribunal was limited to the Nazi leaders and that did not concern any of the Allied leaders or commanders. At some stage during the negotiation of the Charter, Justice Jackson, the U.S. representative at the International Conference on Military Trials, took the view that the expression "carried out by the European Axis Powers":

> should come out of the definition because, as I said yesterday, if it is a crime for Germany to do this, it would be a crime for the United States to do it. I don't think we can define crimes to be such because of the particular parties who committed the acts, but for the purpose of meeting General Nikitchenko's suggestion that we are only supposed to deal with the Axis powers, we could in the opening paragraph state that this Tribunal has jurisdiction only over those who carried out these crimes on behalf of the Axis powers so that we could keep the idea of a limitation, but not in the definition.[38]

In fact, it is quite clear from the findings of the Nuremberg Tribunal that although a policy of extermination and crimes was engineered by the Nazi leadership, that policy was an evidentiary or factual consideration, not an element of any of the crimes that were within its jurisdiction, and certainly not crimes against humanity:

> With regard to crimes against humanity, there is no doubt whatever that political opponents were murdered in Germany before the war, and that many of them were kept in concentration camps in circumstances of great horror and cruelty. The *policy of terror* was certainly carried out on a vast scale, and in many cases was organised and systematic. The *policy of persecution, repression and murder of civilians* in Germany before the war of 1939, who were likely to be hostile to the Government, was most ruthlessly carried out. The persecution of Jews during the same period is established beyond all doubt. To constitute crimes against humanity, the acts relied on before the outbreak of war must have been in execution of, or in connection with, any crime within the jurisdiction of the Tribunal. The Tribunal is of the opinion that revolting and horrible as many of these crimes were, it has not been satisfactorily proved that they were done in execution of, or in connection with, any such crime. The Tribunal therefore cannot make a

---

[37] See Schabas, *supra* note 30, at 954, 961.
[38] International Conference on Military Trials, London 1945, *Minutes of Conference Session of 24 July 1945, reprinted in* JACKSON, *supra* note 3, at 361.

general declaration that the acts before 1939 were crimes against humanity within the meaning of the Charter, but from the beginning of the war in 1939 war crimes were committed on a vast scale, which were also crimes against humanity; and insofar as the inhumane acts charged in the Indictment, and committed after the beginning of the war, did not constitute war crimes, they were all committed in execution of, or in connection with, the aggressive war, and therefore constituted crimes against humanity.[39]

The expression "policy of terror" is, as is obvious from the following sentence of the judgment, a descriptive device akin to that of "policy of persecution, repression and murder of civilians" used in the next sentence. This expression was used by the IMT to exclude isolated crimes from the realm of crimes against humanity and capture in a few words the criminal context in which the acts of the accused took place. Today, this descriptive function is served by the concept of "attack."[40]

In addition to this general statement, the Judgment of the International Military Tribunal relating to the major war criminals dealt with the individual responsibility of several accused for crimes against humanity.[41] Nowhere in the Judgment did the Nuremberg Tribunal require a nexus between the acts of the accused on the one hand and some form of policy or plan on the other. Partly because of the requirement contained in the Nuremberg Charter that crimes against humanity be committed in execution of or in connection with any crime within the jurisdiction of the Tribunal (war crimes or crimes against peace), the court never clearly distinguished between crimes against humanity and those other crimes.[42] However, two of the accused, Streicher and von Schirach, were convicted for crimes against humanity *only*. In neither case did the Tribunal require a policy element or suggest that the crimes of the accused had to be connected to a Nazi policy, although they most certainly were in practice.[43]

---

[39] IMT Judgment, *supra* note 28, at 254.

[40] See *supra* notes 20–23 and accompanying text.

[41] In Nuremberg, sixteen of the twenty-four defendants were convicted for crimes against humanity under Count 4 of the indictment. PERSPECTIVES ON THE NUREMBERG TRIAL 749–50 (Guénaël Mettraux ed., 2008).

[42] As already pointed out, the Nuremberg Tribunal very much regarded crimes against humanity as a subsidiary crime. See, e.g., HERSCH LAUTERPACHT, INTERNATIONAL LAW AND HUMAN RIGHTS 35–36 (1950). Even more strikingly, in Tokyo, there was no explicit charge for crimes against humanity and, logically, no conviction. See also Bing Bing Jia, *The Differing Concepts of War Crimes and Crimes Against Humanity in International Criminal Law*, in THE REALITY OF INTERNATIONAL LAW – ESSAYS IN HONOUR OF IAN BROWNLIE 243 (Guy S. Goodwin-Gill & Stefan Talmon eds., 1999).

[43] For the accused Streicher, see IMT Judgment, *supra* note 28, at 304. ("*Streicher's* incitement to murder and extermination at the time when Jews in the East were being killed under the most horrible conditions clearly constitutes persecution on political and racial grounds in connection with war crimes as defined by the Charter, and constitutes a crime against humanity."). It should be noted *en passant* that his crimes committed before 1939 were excluded not because they were not somehow related to the Nazi policy (since most of them were, as is acknowledged by the IMT), but simply because they were not committed "in execution of, or in connection with any crime within the jurisdiction of the Tribunal." Concerning the accused von Schirach, see *id.* at 318–19 ("*Von Schirach* is not charged with the commission of war crimes in Vienna, only with the commission

At most, the requirement that there needed to be a plan or policy reflected the view of the American prosecution team rather than the way in which the Tribunal handled the definition of crimes against humanity. In his letter to the President of the United States, Chief Prosecutor Justice Jackson presented the prosecution case as that against the "Nazi master plan, [that] grand, concerted pattern to incite and commit the aggressions and barbarities which have shocked the world."[44] However, this view was expressly rejected by the Tribunal, which did not accept the Prosecution's submission that the "conspiracy" charge extended not just to the crime of aggressive war, but also to crimes against humanity and war crimes.[45]

On December 11, 1946, the United Nations General Assembly adopted Resolution 95(I) that affirmed the principles of international law recognized by the Charter of the Nuremberg Tribunal and Judgment of the Tribunal.[46] In 1950, the Principles of International Law Recognized in the Charter of the Nuremberg Tribunal and in the Judgement of the Tribunal were adopted. Principle VI(c), which contains a definition of crimes against humanity, again makes no mention of a policy element.[47]

In similar fashion, neither the Charter of the Tokyo Tribunal nor the Judgment of the Nuremberg Tribunal contained any indication that an element of "policy" formed part of the definition of crimes against humanity. It may thus be concluded that neither at Nuremberg nor at Tokyo an element of "policy" was regarded as forming part of the definition of crimes against humanity.

of crimes against humanity. As has already been seen, Austria was occupied pursuant to a common plan of aggression. Its occupation is, therefore, a crime within the jurisdiction of the Tribunal, as the term is used in Article 6(c) of the Charter. As a result, 'murder, extermination, enslavement, deportation and other inhumane acts' and persecutions on political, racial or religious grounds' in connection with this occupation constitute a crime against humanity under that Article.").

[44] See REPORT TO THE PRESIDENT ON ATROCITIES AND WAR CRIMES BY MR. JUSTICE JACKSON, 6 JUNE 1945, *in* JACKSON, *supra* note 3, at 42, 48. Jackson considered that linking the acts that were to be prosecuted to a common plan or policy – to wage aggressive war – was the sole legitimate reason for a State inference in another State's internal affairs:

[W]e do not consider that acts of a government towards its own citizens warrant our interference. We have some regrettable circumstances at times in our country in which minorities are unfairly treated. We think it is justifiable that we interfere or attempt to bring retribution to individuals or to states only because the concentration camps and the deportations were in pursuance of a common plan or enterprise of making an unjust or illegal war in which we became involved. We see no other basis on which we are justified in reaching the atrocities which were committed inside Germany, under German law, or even in violation of German law, by authorities of the German state. Without substantially [sic] this definition, we would not think we had any part in the prosecution of those things ....

Minutes of Conference Session of 23 July 1945, *in id.* at 333. Justice Jackson was wary of limiting the jurisdictional reach of the Tribunal to the acts of the Axis powers without being perceived as applying different standards to both sides of the conflict. *Id.* at 336. The plan or policy requirement provided a subtle way out of this dilemma.

[45] IMT Judgment, *supra* note 28, at 44. *See also* HISTORY OF THE UNITED NATIONS WAR CRIMES COMMISSION, *supra* note 33, at 196.
[46] *Reprinted in* PERSPECTIVES ON THE NUREMBERG TRIAL, *supra* note 41, at 748 (2008).
[47] Principles of International Law Recognized in the Charter of the Nuremberg Tribunal and in the Judgment of the Tribunal, adopted by the International Law Commission and presented to the General Assembly, U.N. GAOR, 5th Sess., Supp. No. 12, U.N. Doc. A/1316 (1950), *reprinted in* [1950] 2 Y.B. Int'l L. Comm'n 376, *available at* http://www.icrc.org/ihl.nsf/FULL/390.

C. Other World War II Cases

Article II(1)(c) of Control Council Law No. 10, which defined crimes against humanity for the purpose of providing a common legal basis for the national prosecutions of war criminals other than the major defendants dealt with by the International Military Tribunal, did not contain any reference to a plan or policy either. Several decisions from the Supreme Court in the British Zone did, however, refer to the need for a connection with the Nazi politico-criminal project.[48] But in doing so, the court did nothing but highlight the context in which the acts of the accused occurred, in the same manner that the Trial Chambers of the ad hoc tribunals are required to establish that the acts of the accused were part of a "widespread or systematic attack upon the civilian population."

Thus, the definition of crimes against humanity adopted in all major post–World War II cases (e.g., the *Flick*, the *Ministries*, the *Einsatzgruppen* cases, and, arguably, the *Justice* case) made no mention of a legal requirement of "policy" or plan. The decision rendered by a Dutch Special Criminal Court *In re Ahlbrecht* (No. 2) on September 22, 1948 is a fair summary of the jurisprudence under Control Council Law No. 10 on that point: It states that crimes against humanity must be construed in the limited sense of this term in the definition given by the United Nations War Crimes Commission, which the Nuremberg Tribunal adopted.[49] It continues:

> Isolated offences did not fall within the notion of crimes against humanity. As a rule systematic mass action, particularly if it was authoritative, was necessary to transform common crimes, punishable only under municipal law, into crimes against humanity which thus became also the concern of international law. Only crimes which, either by their magnitude and savagery, or by their large number or by the fact that a similar pattern was applied at different times and places, endangered the international community or shocked the conscience of mankind warranted intervention by States other than those on whose territory the crimes had been committed or whose subjects had become their victims.[50]

Again, the focus of the definition is on the scale or systematicity of the crimes and their distinctiveness, for that very reason, from isolated acts. As a consequence, the court concluded that neither the isolated shooting of a prisoner nor the ill-treatment of individual prisoners was of such a character as to come within this definition. The judgment contains no reference to any kind of plan or policy.

The proponents of the "policy" requirement generally refer to a group of cases that, they say, support the view that such a requirement exists under international

---

[48] See, e.g., Obersten Gerichtshofes für die britische Zone [OGHbrZ] [Supreme Court of the British Zone] 1949, 1 Entscheidungen des obersten Gerichtshofes für die britische Zone in Strafsachen 19; Obersten Gerichtshofes für die britische Zone [OGHbrZ] [Supreme Court of the British Zone] 1949, 2 Entscheidungen des obersten Gerichtshofes für die britische Zone in Strafsachen 231.
[49] *In re* Ahlbrecht (No. 2), 16 I.L.R. 396 (Special Crim. Ct., Arnhem, 1948; Special Ct. of Cassation, II 1949) (Neth.).
[50] *Id.*

Crimes Against Humanity and the Question of a "Policy" Element

law. They have frequently referred to the decision of the United States Military Tribunal in In re Altstötter and others, in which it is stated that:

> Crimes against humanity as defined in C.C. Law 10 must be strictly construed to exclude isolated cases of atrocities or persecutions whether committed by private individuals or by a governmental authority. As we construe it, that section provides for the punishment of crimes committed against German nationals only where there is proof of conscious participation in *systematic governmentally organised or approved procedures*, amounting to atrocities and offences of that kind specified in the act and committed against populations or amounting to persecutions on political, racial or religious grounds.[51]

This statement should, however, be read in its proper context:

(i) First, the court erroneously circumscribed the scope of crimes against humanity to crimes committed by Germans against German nationals only, thus making it particularly important to find a way to distinguish between crimes against humanity and purely domestic crimes;

(ii) Second, and in light of the previous comment, it should be noted that this finding was only meant to exclude from the scope of crimes against humanity "isolated crime by a private German individual [or] the isolated crime perpetrated by the German Reich through its officers against a private individual."[52] This is in keeping with today's requirement that the attack be directed against a civilian population, rather than against any one or several of its individual members, so as to exclude isolated acts from the scope of crimes against humanity;

(iii) Finally, the court only referred to a *State or governmental policy*, not to the Nazi policy.[53] This decision seems, for that reason only, to be of dubious assistance to those who suggest that there needs to be a policy but that it need not be a policy of the State, but possibly that of other entities.

It is interesting to note that this decision was considered by the High Court of Australia in the *Polyukhovich* case.[54] Justice Brennan, referring to the passage in question, stated that in the opinion of this tribunal, *In re Altstötter* had *not* been accepted as an authoritative statement of customary international law.[55] He continued:

> [Control Council] Law No 10 and the tribunals which administered it were not international in the sense that the Nuremberg Charter and the International

---

[51] *In re* Altstötter and others, 14 I.L.R. 278, (U.S. Military Tribunal, Nuremberg, Germany, 1947) ("The Justice Trial") (emphasis added).
[52] *Id.* at 284.
[53] In the course of its judgment, the court also referred to other instances in which States had intervened to prevent the ill treatment by another State of its own subjects. *Id.* at 981–2.
[54] Polyukhovich v. The Commonwealth of Australia and Another (1991) 172 C.L.R. 501 (High Ct. of Australia).
[55] *Id.* at 141.

Military Tribunal were international. As Dr. Schwelb observes: 'the difference between the Charter and Law No 10 probably reflects the difference both in the constitutional nature of the two documents and in the standing of the tribunals called upon to administer the law. As we have attempted to show, the International Military Tribunal is, in addition to being an occupation court for Germany, also – to a certain extent – an international judicial organ administering international law, and therefore its jurisdiction in domestic matters of Germany is cautiously circumscribed. The Allied and German courts, applying Law No 10, are local courts, administering primarily local (municipal) law, which, of course, *includes provisions emanating from the occupation authorities*.'[56]

Another often-cited case in support of the requirement of "policy" is the judgment of the Dutch Supreme Court in the *Menten* case. In *Menten*, the Dutch Supreme Court held that article 6(c) of the Nuremberg Charter required that a crime against humanity be committed in connection with some plan or policy.[57] The interpretation of article 6(c) of the Nuremberg Charter in *Menten* is a very dubious one. The court stated that the policy element underlying crimes against humanity is embedded in this definition, although the judgment conceded that such a requirement was "not expressed in so many words" in the Nuremberg Charter.[58] In fact, it is expressed in no words at all. The court made no secret of that fact later, when it clearly stated that it was giving a definition of crimes against humanity in its "restrictive sense."[59] It is also noteworthy that the Supreme Court offered no precedent for its peculiar interpretation of article 6(c) of the Nuremberg Charter.

Two other cases relied on are from France: *Papon* and *Touvier*. The French courts have applied a distinctively French and highly political definition of crimes against humanity. The definition developed by the French courts in successive trials were intentionally both inclusive (with respect to its victims, in particular by including members of the French "Resistance" into the civilian population) and exclusive (with respect to the persons responsible for those acts – only those who acted as agents of the Nazi State could be responsible, as opposed to those who acted for the pro-Nazi but French Vichy regime). The opportunistic definition of this crime adopted by French courts has been criticized elsewhere.[60] It has been accurately described as "moral evasion"[61] on the part of a State that was not ready to accept its share of the responsibility for crimes committed against some of its citizens, in particular its Jewish community.[62]

---

[56] *Id.*
[57] Public Prosecutor v. Menten, 75 I.L.R. 331 (Sup. Ct. 1981) (Neth.).
[58] *Id.* ¶¶ 362–3.
[59] *Id.*
[60] See, e.g., Leila Sadat Wexler, *The Interpretation of the Nuremberg Principles by the French Court de Cassation: From Touvier to Barbie and Back Again*, 32 COLUM. J. TRANSNAT'L L. 289 (1994).
[61] MARK OSIEL, MASS ATROCITY, COLLECTIVE MEMORY AND THE LAW 14, 157 (1997).
[62] It has taken the French judiciary more than sixty years to shed its exonerating attitude toward the actions of the French authorities (of which the requirement of a "policy" partook) and acknowledge the active part that the French authorities played in the extermination of French Jews. See the February 16, 2009 Decision of the Conseil d'Etat, Avis – Assemblée du contentieux sur le rapport

It is also useful to underline that the legal justification for the inclusion of a general requirement of such a sort was legally mistaken. According to the French Court of Cassation, the policy element was already contained in article 6 of the Nuremberg Charter, in that its last paragraph said that "[l]eaders, organizers, instigators and accomplices *participating in the formulation or execution of a common plan or conspiracy* to commit any of the foregoing crimes are responsible for all acts performed by any person in execution of such plan."[63] From the text of the Charter and from the judgment of the IMT, it is clear, however, that the participation in a plan did not constitute a general requirement or definitional element of crimes against humanity but was instead a form of criminal participation. Besides, the paragraph just mentioned applied equally to the other crimes within the Tribunal's jurisdiction: war crimes and crimes against peace. In addition, the whole body of jurisprudence of the IMT on the law of conspiracy contradicts the French courts' interpretation of article 6. The incorrectness of the French interpretation was made even clearer with the adoption of Control Council Law 10. Article II of that law, which defines crimes against humanity, contains no reference to any plan or policy, and what used to be the final paragraph of article 6 of the Nuremberg Charter is to be found in article II(2), which relates to the various forms of participation, making it clear that participation in a criminal plan is *one of many forms* of criminal participation that can apply to war crimes, crimes against peace, *as well as* crimes against humanity. This erroneous interpretation was already criticized as early as 1950 by Graven, who noted the following:

> La confusion et la généralisation de cette condition sont dues sans doute à l'alinéa final de l'article 6 du Statut de Nuremberg, disposant que 'les chefs, les organisateurs, les instigateurs et les complices qui participèrent à l'élaboration ou à l'exécution d'un plan commun ou complot destiné à commettre l'un des susdits crimes – crimes contre l'humanité compris – sont responsables des actes de toute personne ayant exécuté un tel plan ou complot.' Cela ne veut toutefois pas dire que l'instigateur ou l'exécutant d'un crime contre la paix ne soit punissable que si le crime résulte d'un tel complot.[64]

---

de la section du contentieux Séance du 6 février 2009 Lecture du 16 février 2009 No. 315499, *available at* http://www.conseil-etat.fr/cde/node.php?articleid=1340. The re-introduction of a requirement of policy would run the risk of allowing for the same type of official denial of responsibility on the part of state authorities.

[63] Nuremberg Charter, *supra* note 29, art. 6 (emphasis added).

[64] Graven, *supra* note 11, at 433, 560 n.4. *See, e.g.*, CrimC (Jer) 40/61 Attorney-General v. Adolph Eichmann [1961] IsrDC 45(3); Mugesera v. Minister of Citizenship and Immigration, [2001] IMM-5946-98 (Fed. Ct. Can.,Trial Division); *In re* Trajkovic, District Court of Gjilan, P Nr. 68/2000 (Kosovo, Federal Republic of Yugoslavia) (Mar. 6, 2001); Moreno v. Canada (Minister of Employment and Immigration), [1994] 1 F.C. 298; and Sivakumar v. Canada (Minister of Employment and Immigration), [1994] 1 F.C. 433.

Finally, the supporters of the "policy" requirement generally refer to the Canadian Supreme Court's judgment in *Finta*,⁶⁵ which stated:

> Where a crime against humanity is alleged, the trial judge's findings would have to include such issues as whether the impugned conduct was the practical execution of state policy and whether the conduct targeted a civilian population or other identifiable group of persons. The technical nature of these inquiries, unrelated as they are to matters of culpability, do not form part of the special capacity of the jury. This leads me to conclude that it is not unfair or contrary to our philosophy of trial by jury to entrust these issues to the trial judge rather than the jury.⁶⁶

Later in its Judgment, the Court added the following:

> What distinguishes a crime against humanity from any other criminal offence under the Canadian *Criminal Code* is that the cruel and terrible actions which are essential elements of the offence were undertaken in pursuance of a policy of discrimination or persecution of an identifiable group or race.⁶⁷

It is interesting to note that the criminal code applied by the Court in this case did *not* include any requirement of "policy." It is also important to note that the Court cited *no* precedents for the above findings. The Judgment suggests that it relied exclusively on the views of the expert called to testify on this point – Professor M. Cherif Bassiouni. In his academic writings, Professor Bassiouni has been a powerful supporter of this requirement, and his views certainly deserved to be given considerable weight.⁶⁸

D. *United Nations War Crimes Tribunals*

The Statutes of the ad hoc Tribunals for the former Yugoslavia and Rwanda, which were adopted by the Security Council of the United Nations, do not mention any requirement of "policy" in relation to the definition of crimes against humanity. Nor do the Reports of the Secretary-General, which accompanied these statutory instruments and are often regarded as authoritative when it comes to interpreting these instruments.⁶⁹ Nor does the Statute of the Special Court for Sierra Leone contain any requirement of "policy" in its definition of crimes against humanity. This, in

---

⁶⁵ R. v. Finta [1994] 1 S.C.R. 701 (La Forest, J., dissenting) (Can.).
⁶⁶ *Id.* at 85.
⁶⁷ *Id.* at 131.
⁶⁸ *Id.* at 141 ("Although the [*Criminal*] *Code* does not stipulate that crimes against humanity must contain an element of state action or policy of persecution/discrimination, the expert witness, M. Cherif Bassiouni, testified that at the time the offenses were alleged to have been committed, "state action or policy" was a pre-requisite legal element of crimes against humanity. Thus, in my view, the trial judge properly instructed the jury that they had to be satisfied that Finta knew or was aware of the particular factual circumstance which rendered the acts he was alleged to have committed crimes against humanity.").
⁶⁹ *See Report of the Secretary-General Pursuant to Paragraph 2 of Security Council Resolution 808*, *supra* note 28, in respect of the ICTY, and *Report of the Secretary-General Pursuant to Paragraph 5 of Security Council Resolution 955* (1994), U.N. Doc. S/1995/134 (Feb. 13, 1995), in respect of the ICTR.

itself, is further indication of the nonexistence of such a requirement under international law. Further support for this view may be found in the jurisprudence of these Tribunals, which has been said to reflect customary international law.

In one of the early cases dealing with this issue, the ICTY Trial Chamber in *Kunarac* noted that there had been some differences of approach between the jurisprudence of the ICTY[70] and ICTR,[71] that of other courts, and the history of the

---

[70] In *Nikolić*, the Trial Chamber held that to amount to a crime against humanity, the acts must be "organised and systematic." *Nikolić Rule 61 Decision, supra* note 21, ¶ 26. That meant, according to the Trial Chamber, that the underlying offense "need not be related to a policy established at State level [but that] they cannot be the work of isolated individuals alone." *Id.* In *Tadič*, the Trial Chamber held that the definition of crimes against humanity put the emphasis not on the individual victim but rather on the collective, *Tadič Trial Judgment, supra* note 22, ¶ 644, which implied in particular that there be some form of a governmental, organizational or group policy to commit these acts. The Trial Chamber added that such a policy need not be formalized and can be deduced from the way in which the acts occurred. *Id.* ¶ 653. Notably, it said that if the acts occurred on a widespread or systematic basis that would demonstrate a policy to commit those acts. Furthermore, the *Tadič* Trial Chamber held that this policy did not need to be a policy of the State, but that it could be the policy of "entities exercising de facto control over a particular territory." *Id.* ¶ 654. In *Kupreškić*, the Trial Chamber held that "there is some doubt as to whether it is strictly a requirement, as such, for crimes against humanity." Prosecutor v. Kupreškić et al., Case No. IT-95-16-T, Judgment, ¶ 551 (Jan. 14, 2000) [hereinafter *Kupreškić Trial Judgment*]. In any case, the Trial Chamber continued, "it appears that such a policy need not be explicitly formulated, nor need it be the policy of a State." *Id.* It went on to suggest that the crimes against humanity must, as a minimum, have been tolerated by a State, Government or entity. *Id.* ¶ 552. In *Blaškić*, the Trial Chamber stated that the systematic element of the attack required some form of plan or political objective. Prosecutor v. Blaškić, Case No. IT-95-14-T, Judgment, ¶¶ 203–04 (Mar. 3, 2000). However, it made it clear that this plan did not need to be organized at the State level. *Id.* ¶ 205. In addition, the Trial Chamber held that the criminal against humanity needed to know about this criminal plan or policy but did not need to intend it. *Id.* ¶ 254. Both the *Kunarac* and *Kordić* Chambers raised doubts as to the existence of a policy requirement under customary international law: the *Kunarac* Trial Chamber said that "there has been some difference of approach in the jurisprudence of the ICTY and ICTR, and in that of other courts, as well as in the history of the drafting of international instruments, as to whether a policy element is required under existing customary law." *Kunarac Trial Judgment, supra* note 20, ¶ 432. The Chamber added that it was open to question whether the sources often cited by Chambers of the ICTY and ICTR supported the existence of such a requirement. *Id.* ¶ 432 n.1109. The *Kordić* Trial Chamber held that the existence of the policy requirement was not uncontroversial. It added that it was not appropriate to adopt a "strict" view in relation to the plan or policy requirement. It concluded that "the existence of a plan or policy should better be regarded as indicative of the systematic character of offences charged as crime against humanity" rather than as an independent, additional element of the definition of this crime. Prosecutor v. Kordić and Čerkez, Case No. IT-95-14/2-T, Judgment, ¶¶ 181–82 (Feb. 26, 2001) [hereinafter *Kordić and Čerkez Trial Judgment*].

[71] In *Akayesu*, the Trial Chamber stated that the concept of systematicity may be defined as thoroughly organized and following a regular pattern *on the basis of a common policy involving substantial public or private resources. Akayesu Trial Judgment, supra* note 20, ¶ 580. According to the Trial Chamber, there must be some kind of preconceived plan or policy, but this policy need not be adopted formally as the policy of the State. *Id.* In *Kayishema and Ruzindana*, the court said that for an act of mass victimization to be a crime against humanity, it must include a policy element. *Kayishema and Ruzindana Trial Judgment, supra* note 20, ¶ 124. According to the Trial Chamber, either of the requirements of widespread or systematic are enough to exclude acts not committed as part of a broader policy or plan against a "civilian population" inevitably demands some kind of plan and, the discriminatory element of the attack specific to the ICTR Statute is, by its very

drafting of international instruments[72] as to whether, under existing customary law, a crime against humanity needs to be supported by some form of *policy* or *plan*.[73] In a footnote, the *Kunarac* Trial Chamber stated that it was open to question whether the original sources often cited by Chambers of the ICTY and ICTR in support of their argument for the existence of such a requirement in fact supported its existence.[74] The Trial Chamber did not rule upon the issue because it found that even if such a requirement existed, it had been fulfilled in the instant case.[75] Therefore, suggestions that have been made in the literature[76] that the *Kunarac* Chamber had taken this position "*en opportunité*" because it could not establish the existence of a "policy" in this particular case are without merit.

The Trial Chambers in *Kupreškić*[77] and subsequently in *Kordić and Čerkez* also raised some doubts that a plan or policy constituted an element of the definition of crimes against humanity under customary international law. The *Kordić* Trial Chamber held that this element "should better be regarded as indicative of the systematic character of offences charged as crimes against humanity."[78]

Later cases took the clear position that no such requirement existed under customary international law. Therefore, according to the United Nations Tribunals, there is no requirement under customary international law (nor under the Statutes of the Tribunals) that the acts in question be committed as a result or as part of a plan or policy to commit them.[79] Thus, for instance, in the *Kunarac* Appeal, the ICTY said the following:

> Contrary to the Appellants' submissions, neither the attack nor the acts of the accused needs to be supported by any form of "policy" or "plan." There was nothing in the Statute or in customary international law at the time of the alleged acts

---

nature, only possible as a consequence of a policy. *Id.* The Trial Chamber concluded that "to have jurisdiction over either accused, the Chamber must be satisfied that their actions were instigated or directed by a Government or by any organization or group." *Id.* ¶ 126.

[72] Whereas the ICC Statute introduces a requirement that the attack take place "pursuant to or in furtherance of a State or organizational policy to commit such attack," none of the earlier relevant international conventions which dealt with crimes against humanity contained such a requirement. *See* Convention on the Non-Applicability of Statutory Limitations to War Crimes and Crimes against Humanity, Nov. 26, 1968, 754 U.N.T.S. 73; International Convention on the Suppression and Punishment of the Crime of Apartheid, Nov. 30, 1973, 1015 U.N.T.S. 243; Convention on the Prevention and Punishment of the Crime of Genocide, Dec. 9, 1948, 102 Stat. 3045, 78 U.N.T.S. 277.

[73] *Kunarac Trial Judgment*, *supra* note 20, ¶ 432.

[74] *Id.* ¶ 432 n.1109.

[75] *Id.* ¶ 579.

[76] *See, e.g.*, Schabas, *supra* note 30, at 960.

[77] *See, e.g., Kupreškić Trial Judgment*, *supra* note 70, ¶ 551.

[78] *Kordić and Čerkez Trial Judgment*, *supra* note 70, ¶¶ 181–82.

[79] *See, e.g., Kunarac Appeal Judgment*, *supra* note 32, ¶ 98 and references cited therein; Prosecutor v. Vasiljević, Case No. IT-98-32-T Judgment, ¶ 36 (Nov. 29, 2002) [hereinafter *Vasiljević Trial Judgment*]; Prosecutor v. Naletilić and Martinović, Case No. IT-98-34-T, Judgment, ¶ 234 (Mar. 31, 2003); Prosecutor v. Blaškić, Case No. IT-95-14-A, Judgment, ¶¶ 100, 120, 126 (July 29, 2004); Prosecutor v. Krnojelac, Case No. IT-97-25-T, Judgment, ¶ 58 (Mar. 15, 2002); Prosecutor v.

which required proof of the existence of a plan or policy to commit these crimes. As indicated above, proof that the attack was directed against a civilian population and that it was widespread or systematic, are legal elements of the crime. But to prove these elements, it is not necessary to show that they were the result of the existence of a policy or plan. It may be useful in establishing that the attack was directed against a civilian population and that it was widespread or systematic (especially the latter) to show that there was in fact a policy or plan, but it may be possible to prove these things by reference to other matters. Thus, the existence of a policy or plan may be evidentially relevant, but it is not a legal element of the crime.[80]

The same finding was later reiterated many times by the ad hoc tribunals.[81] In the *Vasiljević* case, for instance, a Trial Chamber of the ICTY made the following finding:

> The Appeals Chamber has stated that neither the attack nor the acts of the accused need to be supported by any form of "policy" or "plan." There is nothing under customary international law which requires the imposition of an additional requirement that the acts be connected to a policy or plan.[82]

According to the ad hoc tribunals, the existence of a policy or plan as might form the background of crimes against humanity may, therefore, be evidentiarily relevant (for instance, to establishing the existence of a "systematic" attack on the civilian population), but it is not a legal element of crimes against humanity.

The position of the Special Court for Sierra Leone is similar. As noted earlier, the definition of crimes against humanity in its Statute does not contain any element of policy or plan.[83] Nor has the case law of that court supported the view that such an element exists under international law, and its judgments in fact support the opposite conclusion. In *Brima*, for instance, a Trial Chamber made it clear "[t]hat the crimes were supported by a policy or plan to carry them out is not a legal ingredient of crimes against humanity."[84] In two cases, *Fofana* and *Sesay*, the Special Court again reiterated that a requirement of "policy" did not form part of the definition of crimes against humanity under international law:

> The existence of a policy or plan, or that the crimes were supported by a policy or plan to carry them out, may be evidentially relevant to establish the widespread or systematic nature of the attack and that it was directed against a civilian population, but it is not a separate legal requirement of crimes against humanity.[85]

Semanza, Case No. ICTR-97-20-T, Judgment and Sentence, ¶ 329 (May 15, 2003); *Kajelijeli Trial Judgment*, *supra* note 20, ¶ 872.

[80] *Kunarac Appeal Judgment*, *supra* note 32, ¶ 98.
[81] *See, e.g., Kordić and Čerkez Trial Judgment*, *supra* note 70, ¶¶ 181–82.
[82] *Vasiljević Trial Judgment*, *supra* note 79, ¶ 36 (footnote omitted).
[83] See Statute of the Special Court for Sierra Leone art. 2, Jan. 16, 2002, 2178 U.N.T.S. 138, *available at* http://www.sc-sl.org/LinkClick.aspx?fileticket=uClnd1MJeEw%3d&tabid=176.
[84] Prosecutor v. Brima et al., Case No. SCSL-04-16-T, Judgment, ¶ 215 (June 20, 2007).
[85] Prosecutor v. Fofana and Kondewa, Case No. SCSL-04-14-T, Judgment, ¶ 113 (Aug. 2, 2007); Prosecutor v. Sesay et al., Case No. SCSL-04-15-T, Judgment, ¶ 79 (Mar. 2, 2009).

E. Legislative Instruments, Treaties, and Draft Conventions

Several countries adopted legislation or developed definitions in their national case law regarding the definition of crimes against humanity applicable in those legal systems. At least one of them – France – introduced an express requirement that the acts be related to a policy of the State,[86] but most others did not.[87] In any case, national definitions of a criminal offense may only be considered, for the purpose of defining an international offense, to the extent that they represent the general principles of law common to the major national legal systems of the world.[88] Indeed, international law cannot accept whatever definition of an international crime municipal law may contain. As stated by Justice Brennan in the *Polyukhovich* case, "[w]hat is left to municipal law is the adoption of international law as the governing law of what is an international crime."[89] Referring specifically to the issue of jurisdiction, he continued:

> If a country introduces legislation describing some offence under its own criminal law as constituting for example, piracy, and includes within that term offences which do not strictly fall within the international law definition, then that law can only be invoked to establish jurisdiction against nationals or residents of the country in question …. Equally, if a country uses in its national criminal law a definition that only partly meets the conditions of international law, especially if the offence in question has been defined in a treaty, the courts of that country would only be entitled to try those whose actions fall within its own definition.[90]

Justice Brennan concluded: "International law distinguishes between crimes as defined by it and crimes as defined by municipal law and it makes a corresponding distinction between jurisdiction to try crimes as defined by international law and jurisdiction to try crimes as defined by municipal law."[91] This statement is true with respect to jurisdiction, but also with respect to the very elements of the definition of international crimes. It is also in line with the cautious attitude of the UN Secretary-General concerning the UN Tribunals' reliance on domestic law concepts

---

[86] See Article 212–1 of the French *Penal Code* which reads as follows:

> La déportation, la réduction en esclavage ou la pratique massive et systématique d'exécutions sommaires, d'enlèvements de personnes suivis de leur disparition, de la torture ou d'actes inhumains, inspirées par des motifs politiques, philosophiques, raciaux ou religieux et *organisées en exécution d'un plan concerté* à l'encontre d'un groupe de population civile sont punies de la réclusion criminelle à perpétuité.

C. Pén. art. 212–1 (Fr.) (emphasis added).

[87] See, e.g., Canada Criminal Code, R.S.C., ch. C-46, s. 7 (3.71), (3.76) (1985); Nazi and Nazi Collaborators (Punishment) Law, 5710–1950, 4 LSI 154, s. 1(b) (1949–50) (Isr.).

[88] See, e.g., Prosecutor v. Furundžija, Case No. IT-95-17/1-T, Judgment, ¶ 177 (Dec. 10, 1998) [hereinafter *Furundžija Judgment*]. See also Kunarac Trial Judgment, supra note 20, ¶ 439.

[89] Ivan Timofeyevich Polyukhovich v. The Commonwealth of Australia and Anor (1991) 172 C.L.R. 501 (High Ct. Austl.).

[90] *Id.* at 566.

[91] *Id.* at 567.

or principles to define the jurisdiction *ratione materiae* of the Tribunals.[92] In practice, the definitions of offenses provided for in national jurisdictions can only assist the court in finding out what the definition of the offense is under international law.[93]

International conventions – prior to the adoption of the ICC Statute – are unanimous in respect of the policy element: There is simply no such requirement on record. The 1968 *Convention on the Non-Applicability of Statutory Limitations to War Crimes and Crimes Against Humanity*,[94] for example, contains no reference to a policy element in respect of crimes against humanity. Nor does the Apartheid Convention[95] or the Genocide Convention.[96]

Although not binding in any way, the Draft Codes of the ILC may provide indications of the state of the law on a particular issue. The 1954 Draft Code of Offences against the Peace and Security of Mankind prepared by the International Law Commission and its successors show a contradictory pattern as to the need, content, and role of a policy element in respect to crimes against humanity. In its first version, article 2(11) of the Draft provided that crimes against humanity had to be committed "by the authorities of a State or by private individuals *acting at the instigation or with the toleration of such authorities.*"[97] The Commentary to this article stated that the nexus with another crime had been removed but in order not to characterize any inhumane act committed by a private individual as an international crime, "it was found necessary to provide that such an act constitutes an international crime only if committed by the private individual at the instigation or with the toleration of the authorities of a State."[98]

By 1991, however, that requirement had disappeared.[99] The Commentary merely suggested that the "systematic" character of the attack may consist of a "constant

---

[92] The Secretary-General, *Report of the Secretary-General Pursuant to Paragraph 5 of Security Council Resolution 955 (1994), on the establishment of the International Tribunal for Rwanda*, ¶ 36, U.N. Doc.S/1995/134 (Feb. 13, 1995).

[93] Reliance upon the national definition of an offense is acceptable to the extent only that this definition corresponds or represents the common denominator of the major national legislation on the subject and that this definition accords with the particular international character of the environment in which it is being imported. See *Furundžija Judgment*, supra note 88, ¶¶ 177–78, and *Kunarac Trial Judgment*, supra note 20, ¶¶ 437–40, in respect of the definition of "rape."

[94] Convention on the Non-Applicability of Statutory Limitations to War Crimes and Crimes Against Humanity, Nov. 26, 1968, 754 U.N.T.S. 73.

[95] See International Convention on the Suppression and Punishment of the Crime of Apartheid, Nov. 30, 1973, 1015 U.N.T.S. 243.

[96] See Convention on the Prevention and Punishment of the Crime of Genocide, Dec. 9, 1948, 102 Stat. 3045, 78 U.N.T.S. 277.

[97] See *Report of the International Law Commission to the General Assembly*, [1954] 2 Y.B. Int'l L. Comm'n 149, U.N. Doc. A/CN.4/SER.A/1954.

[98] *Id.* at 150.

[99] Article 21 of the renamed Draft Code of Crimes against the Peace and Security of Mankind reads as follows:

> Systematic or mass violations of human rights. An individual who commits or orders the commission of any of the following violations of human rights:
> - murder
> - torture

practice *or* ... a methodical plan to carry out such violations," the plan being in the alternative.[100] In its 1994 Draft Statute for an International Criminal Court, the ILC referred, in respect of the definition of crimes against humanity, to both the definition contained in article 5 of the Statute of the ICTY and article 21 of the 1991 Draft Code of Crimes against the Peace and Security of Mankind. The Commission stated in its Commentary to article 20 that the concept of "crimes against humanity" encompasses "inhumane acts of a very serious character involving widespread or systematic violations aimed at the civilian population in whole or in part."[101] It added that the particular forms of unlawful acts were less crucial to the definition than the factors of scale and deliberate policy, as well as the acts being aimed at the civilian population.[102] Reference to a "policy" was thus a reiteration of the existing requirement of scale and systematicity. In other words, such an element added nothing to the definition of the crime. According to the ILC, the specificity of the crime is captured by the expression "directed against any civilian population" used in article 5 of the ICTY's Statute. The 1995 updated Draft Code of Crimes against the Peace and Security of Mankind did not contain any policy requirement or reference thereto.[103] Eventually, in the 1996 Draft, the chapeau of, by then, article 18 required that the

> – establishing or maintaining over persons a status of slavery, servitude or forced labour
> – persecution on social, political, racial, religious or cultural grounds in a systematic manner or on a mass scale; or
> – deportation or forcible transfer of population shall, on conviction thereof, be sentenced [to...].
>
> *Id.* art. 21.

[100] Int'l Law Comm'n, *Report of the International Law Commission on the Work of its Forty-Third Session*, Supp. No. 10, at 265–66, U.N. Doc. A/46/10 (Apr. 21-July 19, 1991).

[101] Int'l Law Comm'n, *Report of the International Law Commission on the Work of its Forty-Sixth Session*, Supp. No. 10, at 75–76, U.N. Doc. A/49/10 (May 2-July 22, 1994).

[102] *Id.*

[103] Article 21 of the 1995 Draft reads:

> Article 21 (Systematic or mass violations of human rights) An individual who commits or orders the commission of any of the following violations of human rights:
> – murder
> – torture
> – establishing or maintaining over persons a status of slavery, servitude or forced labour
> – persecution on social, political, racial, religious or cultural grounds in a systematic manner or mass scale; or
> – deportation or forcible transfer of population shall, on conviction thereof, be sentenced [to...].

Int'l Law Comm'n, *Report of the International Law Commission on the Work of its Forty-Seventh Session*, U.N. GAOR, 47th Sess., Supp. No. 10, at 47, 49, U.N. Doc. A/50/10 (May 2-July 21, 1995).

Some members of the ILC had insisted that a crime against humanity needs the support or the acquiescence of the State while other members favoured encompassing the conduct of individuals even if they had no link with the State. *Id.* In addition, in order to ensure that the Code would only apply to acts of exceptional seriousness, three criteria were *considered* – but not formally adopted – to distinguish systematic or mass violations of human rights/crimes against humanity from simple human rights violations; first, seriousness, massive nature and violation of the international legal order were proposed as helpful criteria to operate that distinction. Two other criteria were also suggested as relevant, namely the commission of a very serious act by a person who enjoyed

acts be "instigated or directed by a Government or by any organization or group."[104] The Drafting Committee of the ILC *added* this last element, in the words of its Chairman, Calero Rodrigues, in order "to prevent serial murders committed by an individual, such as those which had recently occurred in the United Kingdom of Great Britain and Northern Ireland and Australia and which were acts committed on a large scale, from being considered crimes against humanity."[105]

In 1998, the Statute of the International Criminal Court was adopted. Article 7 of the Statute, entitled "Crimes against humanity," reads as follows in its relevant parts:

> (1) For the purpose of this Statute, "crimes against humanity" means any of the following acts when committed as part of a widespread or systematic attack directed against any civilian population, with knowledge of the attack; ... (2) For the purpose of paragraph 1: (a) "Attack directed against any civilian population" means a course of conduct involving the multiple commission of acts referred to in paragraph 1 against any civilian population, *pursuant to or in furtherance of a State or organizational policy to commit such attack.*[106]

The Statute of the ICC, therefore, introduces a supplementary element of "policy" that has generally been shunned by other international courts and tribunals. The ad hoc tribunals have in fact been criticized for ignoring or disregarding the Statute of the ICC on that point.[107] There seemed, however, to be good reasons to do so. Although some questions might be raised about this, the law applicable to crimes before the ad hoc tribunals is said to reflect customary international law. It would be hard by contrast to suggest that the Statute of the ICC is a reflection of customary international law as existed in 1998. The ICTY has thus noted that:

> Depending on the matter at issue, the Rome Statute may be taken to restate, reflect or clarify customary rules or crystallise them, whereas in some areas it creates new law or modifies existing law. At any event, the Rome Statute by and large may be taken as constituting an authoritative expression of the legal views of a great number of States.[108]

---

the protection or authorization of a State and the institutionalisation of human rights violations with the support of the State. As already stated, none of these criteria was adopted at the time. *Id* at 50.

[104] Int'l Law Comm'n, *Report of the International Law Commission on the Work of its Forty-Eighth Session*, Supp. No. 10, at 93, U.N. Doc.A/51/10 (May 6-July 26, 1996).

[105] The Commentary to the Draft Code went slightly further; it states:

> The second condition requires that the act was 'instigated or directed by a Government or by any organization or group.' The necessary instigation or direction may come from the government or from an organization or a group. This alternative is intended to exclude the situation in which an individual commits an inhumane act while acting on his own initiative pursuant to his own criminal plan in the absence of any encouragement or direction from either a Government or a group or organization.

[106] *ICC Statute, supra* note 13, art. 7 (emphasis added).
[107] Schabas, *supra* note 32, at 955.
[108] *Furundžija Judgment, supra* note 88, ¶ 227.

This statement was later qualified by the Tribunal when it was made clear that "the ICC Statute does not necessarily represent the present status of international customary law," nor do its provisions "*necessarily* indicate what the state of the relevant law was at the time relevant" to the charges before the ICTY or ICTR.[109]

Thus, even if it were, the law that is relevant to the ad hoc tribunals refers to a time that precedes the adoption of the ICC Statute so that any subsequent developments would not have been relevant to their determination. Furthermore, it is clear from the records of the negotiations in Rome that article 7 is in no way a reflection of existing law, but a political compromise over contradictory views as to how broad or narrow the definition of that offense should be.[110]

In this sense, the definition of crimes against humanity in the Rome Statute is not the crystallization of existing law, but a political construction necessary to achieve compromise. This in turn is important for assessing the relevance, if any, of the ICC Statute to other courts and tribunals that are applying existing customary international law. This fact was duly noted by the ICTY Trial Chamber in paragraph 227 of the *Furundžija* case cited earlier.[111]

F. Subsequent Developments

Although it is difficult to quantify the effect and *precedential* value, if any, of the ICC Statute as far as this issue is concerned, there are some indications to be collected from subsequent international instruments and jurisprudence. First, as far as concerns the State Court of Bosnia and Herzegovina, a hybrid tribunal, it has been made clear in its case law that the definition of crimes against humanity does not include any requirement of "policy." In the most recent jurisprudence arising from the State Court, the Appellate Panel summarized the law of the chapeau of crimes against humanity in the following terms:

> The Appellate Panel recalls that the chapeau elements of crimes against humanity describe both 1) the objective context in which the accused acted – the existence of

---

[109] *Kunarac Trial Judgment, supra* note 20, ¶ 495 n.1210. The footnote continues: "The Trial Chamber also notes the definition of torture contained in Art 7(e) of the International Criminal Court Statute." *Id. See also ICC Statute, supra* note 13, arts. 7(1)(f) (crimes against humanity), 8(2)(a)(ii)-1 "Although the ICC Statute does not necessarily represent the present status of international customary law, it is a useful instrument in confirming the content of customary international law. These provisions obviously do not *necessarily* indicate what the state of the relevant law was at the time relevant to this case. However, they do provide some evidence of state *opinio juris* as to the relevant customary international law at the time at which the recommendations were adopted."

[110] The text of article 7 that was eventually adopted is essentially a compromise between two camps that fought over the breadth of the definition of crimes against humanity. Some States argued that the requirements of "widespread" and "systematic" should be conjunctive whereas others suggested that the two adjectives should come in the alternative. States in the first category were worried that a disjunctive approach would lead to overinclusiveness of the concept of crime against humanity. The recognition that the concept of an "attack against any civilian population" implied an element of policy made a compromise possible. *See* Robinson, *supra* note 16; Mettraux, *Crimes against Humanity, supra* note 1, at 279; Hunt, *supra* note 3, at 65.

[111] *See supra* note 103.

a widespread or systematic attack – and 2) the subjective nexus between that objective context and the mental state of the accused – the accused's knowledge of the widespread or systematic attack and that his acts are part of that attack.[112]

The Appellate Panel added that the criminal culpability of lower-level, direct perpetrators for crimes against humanity – which could be isolated events if linked to the widespread and systematic attack[113] – is based on their knowing participation in a widespread or systematic attack against a civilian population through the commission of one or more crimes.[114] There was no suggestion that an element of "policy" formed part of the definition of that crime. And in the *Rašević* case, a Trial Panel from the same Court made an explicit finding to the effect that an element of "policy" does not form part of the customary international law for crimes against humanity: "Under customary international law at the relevant time, the existence of a plan or policy to attack a civilian population or commit the acts that constitute such an attack need not be proven as an element of the charge of crimes against humanity."[115]

Also of interest is The Law on the Establishment of the Extraordinary Chambers in the Courts of Cambodia for the Prosecution of Crimes Committed during the Period of Democratic Kampuchea, as promulgated on October 27, 2004.[116] Article 5 of that Law, which gives the Extraordinary Chambers jurisdiction over crimes against humanity, does not contain any requirement of policy or plan.

These expressions of the law are consistent with the ad hoc tribunals' identification of customary international law and do not contain any suggestion of a requirement of "policy" or plan.

VI. CONCLUSION

The overwhelming jurisprudence and legal instruments reviewed in this chapter make it clear that international law does not seem to mandate the imposition of an additional requirement of "policy" that would require a showing that the conduct of the accused was somehow connected to a policy or plan.[117] Instead, it appears that the existence of a policy or plan is regarded as one of the factors a tribunal may take into account as a matter of evidence to conclude that an attack was directed on a civilian population rather than against one or several individual members of this population,

---

[112] *Todorović and Radić Appeal Judgment*, supra note 10, ¶ 103.
[113] *Id.* ¶ 108 (citing with approval the findings of the ICTY Appeals Chamber in *Blăskić*).
[114] *Id.* ¶ 104.
[115] Prosecutor v. Rašević and Todović, Trial Judgment, X-KR/06/275, 39 (Feb. 28, 2008) (Ct. of Bosnia and Herzegovina, Trial Division).
[116] Law on the Establishment of the Extraordinary Chambers in the Courts of Cambodia for the Prosecution of Crimes Committed During the Period of Democratic Kampuchea, Oct. 27, 2004, NS/RKM/1004/006, *available at* http://www.eccc.gov.kh/english/cabinet/law/4/KR_Law_as_amended_27_Oct_2004_Eng.pdf.
[117] *Kordić and Čerkez Trial Judgment*, supra note 71, ¶ 182.

and that this attack was indeed systematic.[118] Nor, on policy grounds, does the inclusion of such a requirement appear to be desirable. Existing requirements, if interpreted correctly, appear to be capable of maintaining the integrity of that offense while preserving the breadth of its necessary scope of application.

It might be the case, however, that the drafters of a would-be crimes against humanity convention may wish to adopt a definition of the offense that is close or identical to the one adopted in the Rome Statute, so as to prevent the multiplication of legal regimes among State Parties to the ICC. Although such a course might make it easier for States to sign up to such a convention, it would not resolve the problem of different regimes and definitions of the same offense being used in various contexts.

Furthermore, if the view was taken that an element of "policy" should form part of the definition of crimes against humanity for the purpose of such a convention, the following should be expected of the drafters:

(i) A clear and precise definition of what the concept of "policy" is supposed to encompass would have to be agreed on.
(ii) The evidentiary significance of this new requirement would have to be clearly outlined.
(iii) Safeguards should be built in against the politicization and selective use of this requirement.
(iv) Should such a requirement be adopted, it would also have to be established what effect this would have on the requisite *mens rea* for crimes against humanity: does it have to be established that the accused knew of such a "policy?" Is it enough that he was reckless as to its existence? How much information about this "policy" does he need to possess to be said to have had the requisite *mens rea*?[119]

---

[118] *Id.* It is worth pointing out that even if the *Tadić*, *Kupreškić*, and *Kayishema* Trial Chambers interpreted the element of systematicity as requiring a policy or a plan, they concurred in saying that widespread and systematic remain disjunctive requirements thus implying that proof of a policy or plan is a necessary element of crimes against humanity only when opting to establish that the attack was systematic.

[119] In this regard, the case law of the ICTY may provide some guidance. The Appeals Chamber of the ICTY has stated that, for the Prosecution to succeed in establishing the criminal responsibility of an accused in relation to any international crime within its jurisdiction, it would have to establish that each and all elements of the definition of the offense in relation to which the accused is charged must be shown to have formed part of the accused's *mens rea*, including elements of the *chapeau*. *See generally* Prosecutor v. Naletilić and Martinović, Case No. IT-98-34-A, Judgment, ¶¶ 113–14 (May 3, 2006); *see also* Prosecutor v. Kordić and Čerkez, Case No. IT-95-14/2-A, Judgment, ¶ 311 (Dec. 17, 2004).

8

Ethnic Cleansing as Euphemism, Metaphor, Criminology, and Law

John Hagan and Todd Haugh

I. INTRODUCTION

Euphemistic uses of the concept of ethnic cleansing are often traced to "the burning tradition" in the Balkans and the "final solution" in Nazi Germany. In this chapter, we review the origins of these euphemisms and consider how they form a backdrop for understanding the further metaphorical influence of the imagery of ethnic cleansing. Cherif Bassiouni and an international commission of experts revealed the incriminating influence of ethnic cleansing as an activating metaphor, and in this way turned the understanding of the term on its head.[1] The result was to spur an international response to the massive and ongoing atrocities in the former Yugoslavia. We examine the further evolution of a social scientific understanding of ethnic cleansing as a topic of criminological study – a topic that is now evolving alongside the law of ethnic cleansing and genocide in the current epicenter of mass atrocity: Darfur.

This discussion requires that we enumerate the meaning and elements of ethnic cleansing. In doing so, we adopt a distinction between "atrocity crime" and "atrocity law" as advanced by David Scheffer.[2] Accordingly, we distinguish the "criminology of mass atrocity" from "the law of atrocity." The criminology of mass atrocity involves the social scientific study of the precursors of ethnic cleansing, although it may also involve studying factors influencing whether and when these crimes will be legally prosecuted. Our use of Scheffer's distinction is less to advance the prosecution of ethnic cleansing than to increase the possibility for "real time" criminological documentation and analysis of acts of ethnic cleansing. These acts, which often extend to genocide, demand policy interventions.

Our point is that the social scientific methods of criminological documentation and analysis of acts of ethnic cleansing are important in identifying what Scheffer calls the "precursors of genocide."[3] We argue that such documentation and analysis

---

[1] The Secretary-General, *Final Report of the Commission of Experts Established Pursuant to Security Council Resolution 780 to Investigate Violations of International Humanitarian Law in the Former Yugoslavia (1992)*, ¶¶ 129–50, U.N. Doc. S/1994/674 (May 27, 1994) [hereinafter *Final Report*].
[2] David J. Scheffer, *The Future of Atrocity Law*, 25 SUFFOLK TRANSNAT'L L. REV. 389, 398 (2002).
[3] David J. Scheffer, *Genocide and Atrocity Crimes*, 1 GENOCIDE STUD. & PREVENTION 229, 229 (2006). Such precursors might include, for example, the forced migration and large-scale displacement of civilians from their homes and properties.

is a necessary first step to timely intervention. Our argument is focused as much or more on the prevention of ethnic cleansing and genocide as on its prosecution and punishment. Our conclusion is ultimately a call for a criminology of ethnic cleansing that will make the prospect of prosecuting mass atrocities less paralytic and more timely. We illustrate our argument by drawing on the events in the former Yugoslavia and Darfur.

II. ETHNIC CLEANSING AS EUPHEMISM

The history of mass atrocity is awash with euphemistic rationalizations. For example, authoritative accounts of the "burning tradition" in the Balkans, which include euphemistic references to ethnic cleansing, appear in the findings of an international observer mission sent by the American Carnegie Endowment to report on the Balkan Wars of 1912 and 1913.[4] Further reports of "cleansing" in the Balkans date back to at least the early 1800s.

In his history of the Serbs, Tim Judah writes that "Vuk Karadžić makes use of the word 'cleansed' in describing what happened to the Turks of Belgrade … in 1806."[5] He also observes that:

> [t]here was no question of this being an act of undesirable discrimination; it was simply accepted as normal for the time and place. How widespread was the massacre of the Muslims during the insurrection is unclear, yet there was no doubt that such a practice was deemed a laudable aim worth singing about.[6]

The Carnegie Endowment similarly reported that "[t]he burning of villages and the exodus of the defeated population is a normal and traditional incident of … all these peoples. What they have suffered themselves, they inflict in turn upon others."[7] The euphemistic use of the term "cleansing" was thus joined with the idea that the atrocities involved were not only acceptable but desirable. References to the burning tradition and cleansing of the population treated acts such as killing one's neighbor and burning his village as expected means to the valued end of national liberation. These practices were rationalized again throughout the 1990s in the former Yugoslavia as necessary steps toward achieving a "Greater Serbia."

The "final solution" was a euphemism for the Holocaust in Nazi Germany. This extensive linguistic subterfuge also included references to cleansing. In the preface to *Documents of the Persecution of the Dutch Jewry, 1940–1945*, it was remarked that "these men spoke not of … 'gassing' but of 'sonderbehandlung' (special treatment)."[8]

---

[4] CARNEGIE ENDOWMENT FOR INT'L PEACE, REPORT OF THE INTERNATIONAL COMMISSION TO INQUIRE INTO THE CAUSES AND CONDUCT OF BALKAN WARS 73 (1914).
[5] TIM JUDAH, THE SERBS: HISTORY, MYTH AND THE DESTRUCTION OF YUGOSLAVIA 75 (1997).
[6] Id.
[7] CARNEGIE ENDOWMENT FOR INT'L PEACE, *supra* note 4, at 73.
[8] Jacob Presser, *Preface* to DOCUMENTS OF THE PERSECUTION OF THE DUTCH JEWRY 1940–1945, at 10 (1969).

The official German memorandum outlining the final solution indicated that "this discussion had been called for the purpose of clarifying fundamental questions."[9] The memorandum went on to describe "the aim of all this being that of clearing the German Lebensraum of Jews in a legal manner,"[10] and that "in the course of the practical execution of the final settlement of the problem, Europe will be cleaned up from the west to the east."[11]

The challenge was to expose this euphemistic use of language for what it was – a label for organized acts of violent death and displacement – and turn it into a source of evidence for the elimination of violence as accepted practice.

III. ETHNIC CLEANSING AS METAPHOR

The metaphorical meaning of ethnic cleansing was captured by Mao Zedong's observation that insurgents among a civilian population are like fish swimming in water that must be drained to eliminate the fish.[12] As recently as the Darfur conflict, one Sudanese ministerial official, Ahmad Harun, made a strikingly similar statement.[13] According to the ICC Prosecutor who indicted Harun for war crimes and crimes against humanity, Harun stated that "rebels infiltrate the villages" and that the villages "are like water to fish."[14] The ICC Prosecutor noted that "[t]his proposition – that the potential rebel habitats or communities were as dangerous as the rebels – tellingly differed little from his [Harun's] statements that 'all the Fur,' or 3/4 of the population of Darfur, should be regarded as the target of the counter-insurgency campaign."[15] This exemplifies the sweeping metaphorical logic of the concept of ethnic cleansing.

Cherif Bassiouni seized the opportunity to change the term 'ethnic cleansing' from a rationalizing euphemism into an incriminating metaphor when he prepared the final report on violations of international humanitarian law in the former Yugoslavia.[16] The most incriminating part of Bassiouni's report for the International

---

[9] Protocol of the Conference held in Berlin on January 20, 1942, where measures were discussed for "Endlosung der Judenfrage," the Liquidation of the Jews (1942) *in* DOCUMENTS OF THE PERSECUTION OF THE DUTCH JEWRY 1940–1945, at 29 (1969).

[10] *Id.*

[11] *Id.* at 30.

[12] MAO ZEDONG, ON GUERRILLA WARFARE 92–93 (Samuel B. Griffith, II trans., Univ. of Ill. Press 2000) (1937).

[13] Harun was charged with fifty-one counts of crimes against humanity and war crimes by the International Criminal Court. A warrant for his arrest was issued on April 27, 2007. *See* OFFICE OF THE PROSECUTOR, INTERNATIONAL CRIMINAL COURT, THE SITUATION IN DARFUR, FACT SHEET (Feb. 27, 2007); Prosecutor v. Harun, Case No. ICC-02/05-01/07, Warrant for Arrest of Ahmad Harun (Apr. 27, 2007).

[14] Situation in Darfur, The Sudan, Case No. ICC-02/05-56, Prosecutor's Application Under Article 58(7), ¶ 147 (Feb. 27, 2007).

[15] *Id.* ¶ 148.

[16] *Final Report*, *supra* note 1, ¶¶ 129–50; *The Policy of Ethnic Cleansing*, Annex IV, U.N. Doc. S/1994/674/Add.2 (Dec. 28, 1994).

Commission of Experts established by the United Nations' Security Council was based on 131 single-spaced pages of documentation and analysis regarding the events in Prijedor (the "Prijedor report").[17] The Prijedor report was prepared by Hanne Sophie Greve and Morten Bergsmo, who joined extensive background materials with nearly 400 interviews of victims and witnesses to the events in Prijedor.[18] Names were often redacted from the report for purposes of confidentiality, but full statements were separately collected into four large volumes. These volumes were later transferred to the International Criminal Tribunal for the former Yugoslavia (ICTY) and used to guide investigations and prosecutions.

The Prijedor report argued that the facts on the ground met the elements of the crime of genocide.[19] Since Greve and Bergsmo believed the events were genocide, and since the term 'ethnic cleansing' was only then beginning to enter public discourse, they did not use this term in the report. However, when Bassiouni prepared the final report of the Commission, he included a series of introductory paragraphs that explained how, in the context of the former Yugoslavia, the term 'ethnic cleansing' was widely understood to refer to the use of force and intimidation to render an area ethnically homogeneous by removing persons of other groups.[20]

Bassiouni further explained that the policy of ethnic cleansing was linked to political doctrines involving "Greater Serbia" and claims that date as far back as the 1389 battle in Kosovo.[21] His explanation thus began to turn the rationalizing euphemism of ethnic cleansing, which was widely known and endorsed among Serbian military and political leaders, into an incriminating metaphor that social scientists could recognize as a collective framing device.[22] In this context, ethnic cleansing was a way of framing an arc-like geography of aggression that began by linking Serbia proper with Serb-inhabited areas of Croatia and Bosnia, leading to the semicircular sweep of Kosovo, sometimes called Operation Horseshoe.[23] Although the Prijedor report could not fully tell this still unfolding story, Bassiouni emphasized in the Final Report of the Commission that the pattern documented in Prijedor closely matched similar information received in other regions, including Banja-Luka, Brčko, Zvornik, and Foca.[24]

---

[17] *Final Report, Prijedor Report*, Annex V, U.N. Soc. S/1994/672/Add.2 (Dec. 28, 1994) [hereinafter *Prijedor Report*].

[18] *Id.* ¶¶ 1, 37–40.

[19] *Final Report, supra* note 1, ¶ 182; *Prijedor Report, supra* note 17, ¶ 35.

[20] *Final Report, supra* note 1, ¶¶ 129–50.

[21] *Id.* ¶ 131. Bassiouni noted that Serbian contemporary reality was particularly affected by a vivid recollection of history, even events taking place as far back as the 1300s.

[22] Robert D. Bedford & David A. Snow, *Framing Process and Social Movements: An Overview and Assessment*, 26 ANN. REV. SOC. 611 (2000). A framing device is a cognitive structure, usually consisting of a word or phrase that connects events, people, and groups into a meaningful narrative that communicates an understanding of an aspect of the social world to others.

[23] MICHAEL IGNATIEFF, VIRTUAL WAR: KOSOVO AND BEYOND 122 (2000). Operation Horseshoe was developed in autumn 1998 and authorized by Milošević in early 1999. Part of the Serbian "master plan," it called for a sweep of Kosovo by army and paramilitary groups that drove most of the population into Albania and Macedonia by late March.

[24] *Final Report, supra* note 1, ¶ 140.

Neither the Prijedor Report nor the Commission Report was presented as social science evidence. Indeed, the Report's goal was to provide a legalistic presentation of the facts. Yet crucial social facts were included, setting a social science foundation for the claim that the atrocity crime of ethnic cleansing had been committed. For example, the Prijedor report analyzed Serbian-reported census counts, establishing that between 1991 and 1993, the Muslim population in the region decreased from 49,454 to 6,124, whereas the Serbian population increased from 47,745 to 53,637.[25]

When the Prijedor team completed its report detailing the ethnic cleansing of the region, its members had no doubt about its legal meaning: "It is unquestionable that the events in Opština Prijedor since 30 April 1992 qualify as crimes against humanity. Furthermore, it is likely to be confirmed in court under due process of law that these events constitute genocide."[26] Yet it was the metaphorical framing of the events in Prijedor as ethnic cleansing that persuasively summarized what happened there.

The ethnic cleansing that occurred in Prijedor was not consistently denied by Serbian authorities. The concept of cleansing was a well-known part of Serbian culture, and its consequences were confirmed by the official Serbian census statistics. A chilling confirmation that the concept of ethnic cleansing had fully circulated through Serbian leadership circles was provided by the journalist John Burns, who reported an interview with a Serbian commander Borislav Herak. In the interview, Herak confirmed that "Serbian commanders called the Serbian operation ... 'ciscenje prostora,' or the cleansing of the region, and had told the Serbian fighters to leave nobody alive."[27]

Bassiouni succeeded in transforming the previously euphemistic use of the concept of ethnic cleansing, and its role in rationalizing death and displacement, into a powerful metaphor that locally framed genocidal crimes in Prijedor and more widely in Bosnia and Croatia.

IV. THE MEANINGS OF ETHNIC CLEANSING

Ethnic cleansing is generally understood as the systematic removal of a group or groups from an area by killing, expulsion, and/or imprisonment. A crucial concern is that the cleansing of ethnic groups is policy-driven. As Andrew Bell-Fialkoff explains, "ethnic cleansing can be understood as the expulsion of an 'undesirable' population from a given territory due to religious or ethnic discrimination, political, strategic or ideological considerations, or a combination of these."[28]

Although the UN General Assembly has identified ethnic cleansing as a violation of international humanitarian law and explicitly declared that "the abhorrent

---

[25] Id. ¶ 153.
[26] Id. ¶ 182; Prijedor Report, supra note 17, ¶ 35.
[27] John F. Burns, A Killer's Tale – Special Report: A Serbian Fighter's Path of Brutality, N.Y. TIMES, Nov. 27, 1992, at A1.
[28] Andrew Bell-Fialkoff, A Brief History of Ethnic Cleansing, FOREIGN AFF., Summer 1993, at 110.

policy of 'ethnic cleansing' ... is a form of genocide,"[29] the concept is better understood as overlapping with and extending beyond genocide. For example, in the trial of Milomir Stakić on charges of genocide in Prijedor, the ICTY Trial Chamber observed that despite obvious similarities between genocidal and ethnic cleansing policies, a "clear distinction must be drawn between physical destruction and mere dissolution of a group. The expulsion of a group or part of a group does not in itself suffice for genocide."[30]

To be genocide, ethnic cleansing must be intentional and fall within one of the categories of acts of group or partial group destruction explicitly prohibited by the Genocide Convention. The genocidal activity most likely to occur in situations of ethnic cleansing is the "deliberate[] inflicti[on] on the group conditions of life calculated to bring about its physical destruction in whole or in part."[31] Of course, the imprecise reference to whole or partial destruction is an issue for consideration. The precise and intended targeting of a group for ethnic cleansing may also be unclear. As a result, some ethnic cleansing more easily fits within the meaning of crimes against humanity, as a "widespread or systematic attack directed against any civilian population."[32]

Dražen Petrović further categorizes types of conduct recognized as component parts of ethnic cleansing. These categories include: (1) administrative measures, such as removal from employment and elected positions, and interference with mobility and access to essential goods and services; (2) other nonviolent measures, such as threatening media attention and harassment and related forms of intimidation; (3) terrorizing measures, such as deportation, detention, discrimination, and displacement, which are usually illegal, threatening, and harmful; and (4) military measures, such as attacking and laying siege to a locality, and detaining, deporting, and executing leaders and citizens.[33] However, Petrović emphasizes that all of these measures and more can also be treated as isolated violations of human rights and humanitarian law while overlooking or underemphasizing their systematic and collective structure, which is a distinctive characteristic of ethnic cleansing.[34]

To capture the systematic and collective aspect of ethnic cleansing, which he regards as central, Petrović urges particular attention be paid to the goals of cleansing acts. He also draws attention to the motivating policies of the involved parties,

---

[29] *The Situation in Bosnia and Herzegovina*, G.A. Res. 47/121, pmbl., U.N. Doc. A/RES/47/121 (Dec. 18, 1992).

[30] Prosecutor v. Stakić, Case No. IT-97-24-T, Judgment, ¶ 519 (July 31, 2003).

[31] *Convention on the Prevention and Punishment of the Crime of Genocide*, art. 2, Dec. 9, 1948, 102 Stat. 3045, 78 U.N.T.S. 277 [hereinafter *Genocide Convention*]; *Rome Statute of the International Criminal Court*, Conference of Plenipotentiaries on the Establishment of an International Criminal Court, art. 6, July 17, 1998, U.N. Doc. A/CONF.183/9 [hereinafter *Rome Statute*].

[32] *Rome Statute*, *supra* note 31, art. 7.

[33] Dražen Petrović, *Ethnic Cleansing – An Attempt at Methodology*, 5 Eur. J. Int'l L. 342, 345–48 (1994).

[34] *Id.* at 348.

both in the form of organized attacks and counterattacks. Petrović's understanding is that:

> [E]thnic cleansing is a well-defined policy of a particular group of persons to systematically eliminate another group from a given territory on the basis of religious, ethnic or national origin. Such a policy involves violence and is very often connected to military operations. It is to be achieved by all possible means, from discrimination to extermination, and entails violations of human rights and international humanitarian law.[35]

Petrović is clearly correct that the "systematic elimination" aspect of ethnic cleansing is central to its overlap with genocide, but also involves a potential extension beyond the meaning of genocide. We argue that establishing whether "systematic elimination" is present involves using a mixture of social scientific criminological and legal evidence, with the criminological evidence often playing a leading role.

Petrović identifies several forms of evidence of systematic elimination that depend on intent.[36] The degree of intent present bears on the overlapping meanings of ethnic cleansing and genocide.[37] Petrović acknowledges the rarity of finding explicit written materials and public statements of official intentions.[38] This kind of material is especially difficult to uncover in "real time," since it is often hidden from public view.

In a vivid illustration of the complex problems involved in obtaining and introducing explicit evidence of specific intent, the ICTY Trial Chamber ultimately could not accept into evidence a recorded audio intercept of General Radislav Krstić issuing a command in Srebrenica to "kill them all."[39] The rejection of this evidence occurred even though the intercept was repeatedly heard in court and subjected to extensive expert testimony.[40] This experience highlights important issues of what will be deemed "sufficient evidence" of genocidal intent. We maintain that social science documentation and criminological analysis, in addition to legal evidence, can occupy a crucial space between what we have followed Scheffer in calling the criminology of mass atrocity, as distinct from mass atrocity law.

Petrović identifies two probative indicators of genocidal intent that he regards as constituting "sufficient evidence." The first is the participation of government authorities in atrocities or their omission to prevent or punish the perpetration

---

[35] Id. at 351.
[36] Id. at 357–58.
[37] Petrović, *supra* note 33, at 357–58.
[38] Id. at 357.
[39] JOHN HAGAN, JUSTICE IN THE BALKANS: PROSECUTING WAR CRIMES IN THE HAGUE TRIBUNAL 169–73 (William O'Bar & John M. Conley eds., 2003).
[40] Id. The audio intercept was ultimately rejected based on foundation grounds. Although the recording was played in court, its poor quality led to battle of experts whether Krstić was one of the speakers. In addition, the court found it problematic that the prosecution did not introduce the recording until its rebuttal case, even though it was available prior to Krstić's cross-examination.

of these crimes.[41] The second is the identification of civilian groups rather than military forces as targets of war.[42]

Petrović also identifies more specific evidence of circumstances indicating ethnic cleansing and genocide:

> These elements could be: a profile of the population killed (sex, age, social position, specific categories, level of education, etc.), characteristics of individual crimes committed (brutality, cruelty, humiliation, etc.), the systematic nature of certain crimes (rape, destruction of property and objects necessary for survival of population, destruction of places of worship, prevention of delivery of humanitarian aid, etc.).[43]

Courts will ultimately decide which kinds and combinations of the above evidence revealed in the criminology of mass atrocity are crucial to the atrocity law of genocide and ethnic cleansing.

First, however, evidence of the above elements necessary for assessing intent must be documented and analyzed. Building on Scheffer's distinction, the range of possibilities involved in this determination opens up important space and motivation for criminological documentation and analysis of atrocity crimes – that is, a criminology of mass atrocities that can form the foundation for atrocity law determinations. We elaborate and illustrate this point next by reviewing the analyses of episodes of ethnic cleansing in Kosovo and Darfur.

V. THE KOSOVO PHASE OF THE MILOŠEVIĆ TRIAL

The early phase of the trial of Slobodan Milošević at the ICTY provides a vivid example of how the combined use of social scientific criminological documentation and analysis and more conventional eyewitness evidence may identify the necessary intent to establish the "precursors of genocide."[44] Even earlier availability of such evidence, in the manner we follow Scheffer in advocating, might arguably have more successfully forestalled the mass atrocities that took place in Kosovo.

The first phase of the Milošević trial included the testimony of Patrick Ball, a young sociologist and statistician. Ball presented results from a statistical study that, at one point, involved him retrieving data on displaced refugees through a barrage of gunfire at a Kosovo border crossing.[45] His testimony was introduced to refute Milošević's defense that NATO bombings and attacks by the Kosovo Liberation Army (KLA) were actually to blame for the exodus of refugees from Kosovo.

Ball was able to identify 4,400 persons killed in Kosovo.[46] He then used population sampling methods to estimate that the death toll in Kosovo was more than

---

[41] Petrović, *supra* note 33, at 357.
[42] *Id.* at 358.
[43] *Id.*
[44] Scheffer, *supra* note 3, at 229.
[45] Prosecutor v. Milošević, Case No. IT-02-54-T, Trial Transcript, 2146 (Mar. 13, 2002).
[46] *Id.* at 2165.

10,000.[47] Ball presented evidence that the geographic and temporal distribution of the dead across Kosovo corresponded closely to refugee movements. He concluded that the deaths and the refugee movements were the result of a common cause.[48]

The Miloščvić defense claimed the deaths and refugee movements were the joint products of NATO bombing and KLA terrorism. Yet Ball was able to show that surges in refugee flows followed Serbian military activity; that NATO bombing and KLA activity followed, rather than preceded, Serbian military activity; and that NATO and KLA actions followed increases in refugee movements. Ball testified that "the findings of this study are consistent with the hypothesis that action by Yugoslav forces was the cause of the killings and refugee flow."[49] Milošević characteristically responded during cross-examination that "statistics ... can prove anything ... and this is done to serve the purposes of the American politics aimed at enslavement."[50] He then turned, in a somewhat less *ad hominem* fashion, to the specifics of Ball's analysis.

Milošević questioned how Ball's analysis could transform the 4,211 dead into "the invented figure of 10,356" and then distribute them across time and place.[51] When Ball identified the statistical procedures involved, Milošević responded, "[s]o you distributed the assumed dead into assumed time points by applying some kind of statistical methods. How can that be a serious way of doing it? Tell me."[52] Ball explained that he and his colleagues used accepted methods to compensate for the missing data, and included cautionary warnings wherever noteworthy doubts emerged.[53]

Milošević accused Ball of simplifying war with statistics.[54] Milošević asserted that if the Tribunal took seriously Ball's hypothesis that Yugoslav forces provoked the exodus from Kosovo, then there must be some still unproven official plan.[55] This was a demand for very specific and explicit evidence of intent. As we note earlier, this type of evidence is seldom uncovered. The refusal of officials in Belgrade to allow access to Yugoslav military archives made the identification of such evidence of specific intent very unlikely. Milošević persisted: "So I'm asking you: if the Yugoslav authorities planned and carried out a centrally organized campaign, where is the plan? What is it called and who made it?"[56]

When Ball stuck to his hypothesis-driven analysis of the patterns revealed in the data on death, displacement, NATO bombing, and KLA attacks, Milošević pressed his contention that there was no credible documentary evidence of an official government plan. He followed with the observation that "you are aware of the statement

---

[47] Id. at 2166.
[48] Id. at 2204.
[49] Id.
[50] Id. at 2216.
[51] Prosecutor v. Milošević, Case No. IT-02-54-T, Trial Transcript, 2226 (Mar. 14, 2002).
[52] Id. at 2252.
[53] Id. at 2252–53.
[54] Id. at 2268.
[55] Id.
[56] Id. at 2285.

of one of the NATO Defense Ministers, the German Minister, Rudolph Scharping, who said that there was a plan, the Horseshoe Operation, and this claim was later refuted ... Are you aware of that?"[57] The Presiding Judge, Richard May, said that Operation Horseshoe was neither within Ball's expertise, nor part of his testimony.[58] Ball had established a prima facie case based on statistical patterns suggesting the deadly role of the Yugoslav forces, but it was also clear that Milošević had raised the issue of specific intent in a challenging way.

The Prosecution followed Ball's presentation of the statistical evidence with a form of eyewitness evidence. The evidence was introduced through the testimony of Paddy Ashdown, a former member of the British Parliament who played several diplomatic and administrative roles in the Balkan conflict.[59] Ashdown's involvement exemplifies Scheffer's discussion of the "precursors of genocide."

Ashdown visited the Balkans in June 1998 in an effort to observe what was then unfolding in "real time" in Kosovo.[60] Although he was denied entry to Kosovo itself, Ashdown, positioned on the Albanian side of the border, used binoculars to witness gunfire and the torching of Kosovar villages.[61] This was an indication of "the burning tradition" of ethnic cleansing in the Balkans. After reporting his observations to British Prime Minister Tony Blair, Ashdown returned to western Kosovo in September 1998.[62] Ashdown witnessed firsthand the burning and bombardment of whole villages – scenes that were captured on video.[63]

Ashdown traveled to Belgrade to meet with Milošević in person. Ashdown described during the trial what he said to the Serbian leader. He told Milošević that:

> [W]hat I had witnessed could only be described as the actions of the main battle units of the Yugoslav army in an action which could only be described as indiscriminate, punitive, designed to drive innocent civilians out of their properties, could not be explained by any targeting military operation, that this was ... not only illegal under international law, damaging to the representation of the Serbs and his nation, but also deeply counter-productive.[64]

Ashdown further reported warning Milošević that "the international community will act if you do not stop."[65]

When Milošević initiated his cross-examination of Ashdown in court, Ashdown took the opportunity to again remind Milošević of what was said.

> I said to you, in specific terms, that if you went on acting in this fashion, you would make it inevitable that the international community would have to act, and in the

---

[57] *Id.* at 2285.
[58] *Milošević*, supra note 51, at 2285.
[59] *Id.* at 2332.
[60] *Id.* at 2336.
[61] *Id.* at 2341–44.
[62] *Milošević*, supra note 51, at 2346–47.
[63] *Id.* at 2354–55; Prosecutor v. Milošević, Case No. IT-02-54-T, Trial Transcript, 2358 (Mar. 15, 2002).
[64] *Milošević*, supra note 63, at 2379.
[65] *Id.* at 2384.

end they did have to act. And I warned you that if you took those steps and went on doing this, you would end up in this Court, and here you are.[66]

Ashdown was later asked a question from one of the judges about his sense of what knowledge Milošević had of the atrocities occurring in Kosovo. Ashdown stated:

> I must presume that he [Milošević] knew about it, but I wanted to make explicitly clear that from the moment I had informed him and had drawn his attention to the provisions of international law, the Geneva Convention, from that moment onwards, he could not then deny knowledge of these facts if they were to continue.[67]

Similar testimony was offered by William Walker, the U.S. Ambassador and head of the Kosovo Verification Mission, and by Klaus Naumann, the German NATO military commander.

Patrick Ball's statistical analysis and Paddy Ashdown's eyewitness testimony constitute evidence of Scheffer's "precursors of genocide." Ball's analysis and Ashdown's testimony, as they unfolded during the trial, also illustrate what Scheffer calls atrocity law. Scheffer's further point is that by opening up a recognized and accepted space between the finding of evidence of atrocity crime and the unfolding of atrocity law, we can encourage the "real time" collection of evidence of the precursors of genocide in an even more proactive manner than this ICTY example provides. For example, if Ball's social scientific criminological analysis had been completed even earlier, in time for presentation not only to Milošević during Ashdown's Belgrade confrontation, but also at a court hearing of the evidence, it is possible that the atrocities in Kosovo might have been more effectively forestalled. This could conceivably have taken place in "real time," as the events were happening, and in advance of the retrospective unfolding of the earlier described atrocity law at the ICTY trial.

VI. PRECURSORS OF GENOCIDE AND THE ETHNIC CLEANSING OF DARFUR

Ethnic cleansing, if not genocide, is still ongoing in Darfur.[68] This presents a timely opportunity to see how a social scientific criminological approach to mass atrocity can set a persuasive foundation for intervention and legal prosecution. We present our own research on Darfur, which builds on earlier work of the U.S. State Department.

We conceive the genocide charge in Darfur to be as follows: The government of Sudan knowingly mobilized and collectivized a racially constructed division

---

[66] Id. at 2395.
[67] Id. at 2497.
[68] Prosecutor v. Harun, Case No. ICC-02/05-01/07, Warrant for Arrest of Ahmad Harun (Apr. 27, 2007) (charging fifty-one counts of crimes against humanity and war crimes, including what could be characterized as the systematic murder of the civilian Fur population in Kadoom villages).

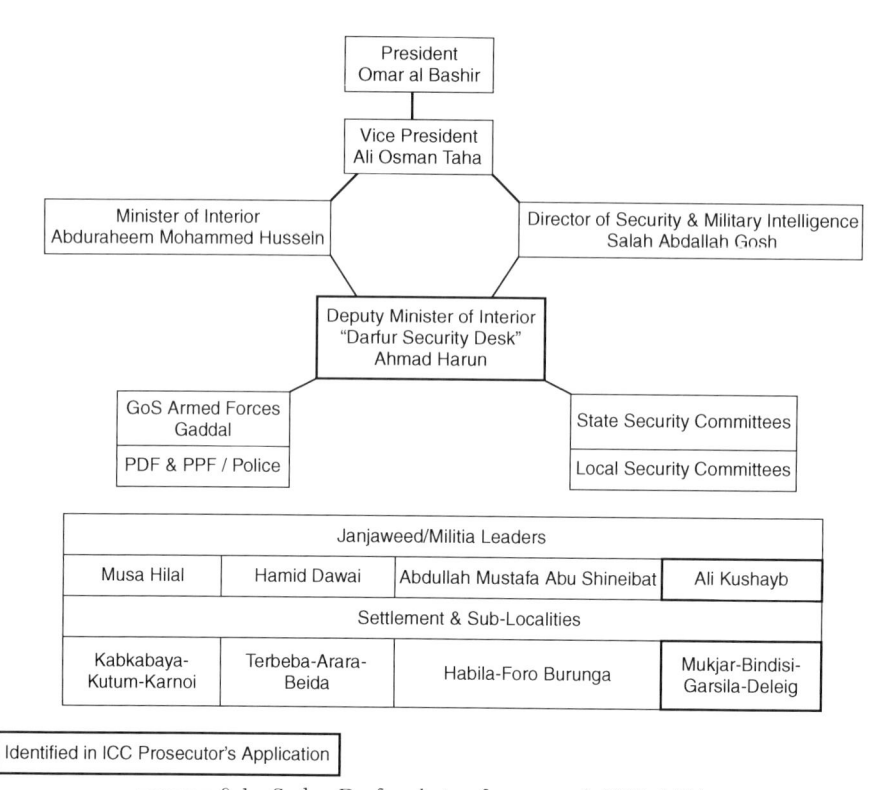

```
                          President
                         Omar al Bashir
                              │
                        Vice President
                        Ali Osman Taha
       ┌──────────────────────┴──────────────────────┐
  Minister of Interior                    Director of Security & Military Intelligence
  Abduraheem Mohammed Hussein                       Salah Abdallah Gosh
       └──────────────────────┬──────────────────────┘
                      Deputy Minister of Interior
                         "Darfur Security Desk"
                             Ahmad Harun
       ┌──────────────────────┴──────────────────────┐
  GoS Armed Forces                           State Security Committees
       Gaddal
  PDF & PPF / Police                         Local Security Committees
```

Janjaweed/Militia Leaders			
Musa Hilal	Hamid Dawai	Abdullah Mustafa Abu Shineibat	Ali Kushayb
Settlement & Sub-Localities			
Kabkabaya-Kutum-Karnoi	Terbeba-Arara-Beida	Habila-Foro Burunga	Mukjar-Bindisi-Garsila-Deleig

Identified in ICC Prosecutor's Application

FIGURE 8.1. Sudan-Darfur chain of command, 2003–2004.

between the Arab and black African groups in Darfur to intentionally bring about the death, destruction, and displacement of those black African groups. Although documentary evidence is thus far scarce, we will infer from the statistical evidence below that there was authorization from the highest levels of the Sudanese government, as indicated in Figure 8.1, for coordinated, racially targeted attacks on African farms and villages by Government of Sudan (GoS) military forces and Arab Janjaweed militias. As one refugee in the survey described below reported, "they come together, they fight together, and they leave together."[69]

The ICC Prosecutor has identified President Omar Al-Bashir, former Deputy Minister of Interior Ahmad Harun, and the militia leader Ali Kushayb as joint participants in the mass atrocities in Darfur.[70] In addition to these individuals, Figure 8.1 identifies three other militia leaders who participated in mass atrocities in connection with Deputy Minister Harun. This "chain of command" comes from the

---

[69] JOHN HAGAN & WENONA RYMOND-RICHMOND, DARFUR AND THE CRIME OF GENOCIDE 116 (2009) (quoting *Sudan: Peace But at What Price?: Hearing Before the S. Comm. On Foreign Relations*, 108th Cong. 52–62 (2004) (statement of Julie Flint, Darfur field researcher, Human Rights Watch).
[70] *Id.* at 105, 114–15.

documentation and analysis of a U.S. State Department survey of refugees in Chad, which we discuss below.

In June 2004, a U.S. official placed the Sudan government on notice that its coordinated attacks on villages in Darfur were being observed and recorded with satellite and aerial imagery.[71] Although these attacks were at a minimum signs of ethnic cleansing, as well as "precursors of genocide," the official cautioned "that the images are not hard evidence until they are corroborated by testimony of witnesses on the ground."[72] Therefore, during the following July and August, the U.S. State Department, at the direction of Secretary of State Colin Powell, conducted the Atrocities Documentation Survey (ADS). The ADS was a survey of 1,136 refugees who witnessed and experienced attacks in Darfur, but were now living in Chad.[73]

An eight-page summary of the ADS survey, which included a table of descriptive statistics and maps, formed the background for Secretary of State Powell's testimony on September 9, 2004 to the U.S. Senate Foreign Relations Committee, stating that genocide was occurring in Darfur.[74] This summary report, however, was only the first step in the development of a criminology of the mass atrocities that were still underway. We report next how we have used the ADS survey to document and analyze the mass atrocities of ethnic cleansing in Darfur. The point is to illustrate how a criminological analysis of these mass atrocities can set the foundation for the development of the atrocity law of Darfur in future prosecutions.

The ADS data uniquely and extensively documented victimization during the attacks on black African settlements in Darfur. We know of only one other systematic study of precamp violence in Darfur,[75] and none that includes sexual violence. As part of the ADS survey, refugees were asked, since the beginning of the conflict approximately eighteen months earlier: (1) when, how, and why they had left Darfur; and (2) if, when, how, and by whom they, their family, or their fellow villagers were harmed.[76]

The survey mixed the closed-ended format of health and crime victimization surveys with the semistructured format of legal witness statements.[77] With the State Department's geospatial technology, cartographers, translators, and interviewers' notations, we were able to locate 90 percent of the settlements from which the

---

[71] News Release, Monica Amarelo, American Association for Advancement of Science, Using Science to Gauge Sudan's Humanitarian Nightmare, (Oct. 26, 2004), *available at* http://www.aaas.org/news/releases/2004/1026sudan.shtml.
[72] Id.
[73] Id.
[74] BUREAU OF DEMOCRACY, HUMAN RIGHTS, AND LABOR & BUREAU OF INTELLIGENCE AND RESEARCH, U.S. DEP'T OF STATE, DOCUMENTING ATROCITIES IN DARFUR (2004), *available at* http://2001-2009.state.gov/g/drl/rls/36028.htm.
[75] Evelyn Deportere et al., *Violence and Mortality in West Darfur, Sudan (2003–2004): Epidemiological Evidence from Four Surveys*, 364 LANCET 1315–20 (2004).
[76] BUREAU OF DEMOCRACY, HUMAN RIGHTS, AND LABOR & BUREAU OF INTELLIGENCE AND RESEARCH, *supra* note 74.
[77] Cyrena Respini-Irwin, *Geointelligence Informs Darfur Policy*, GEOINTELLIGENCE, Sept./Oct. 2005, at 18, 19–22; *see also* HAGAN & RYMOND-RICHMOND, *supra* note 69, at 170.

refugees fled.[78] In total, 932 of the 1,136 refugees were identified as coming from 22 settlements, each with 15 or more respondents.[79] We cross-checked and supplemented the ADS data by rereading and recoding the extensive narratives recorded in the interviews.[80]

The ADS refugee sample provides a descriptive picture of the results of ethnic cleansing in Darfur. About 40 percent of the ADS respondents are male and they are on average thirty-seven years old.[81] Female refugees probably outnumber males because in Darfur, males are more likely to be killed, whereas females are more likely to be raped and survive, at least physically. Slightly more than half of the Africans in the sample are self-identified as Zaghawa, approximately a quarter are Masalit, and about 5 percent each are Fur and Jebal.[82] The largest concentrations of the Zaghawa fled from North Darfur, whereas most of the Masalit and Fur fled from West Darfur, with the Jebal previously concentrated in one town, Seleya, in West Darfur.[83] The documentation of the victimized groups is crucial to establishing the protected status of the victims of the mass atrocities.

Each attack narrative was read and coded to designate the attacking group as Janjaweed, Sudanese, or combined Sudanese and Janjaweed forces. About two thirds of the attacks were joint Sudanese and Janjaweed operations; nearly a fifth of the attacks involved Sudanese forces acting alone (usually in bombing attacks); and about one-tenth involved the Janjaweed alone.[84] The remaining 10 percent of cases could not be categorized but are used as a comparison group in some of our analyses.[85] The documentation of when the attacks included Sudanese military forces is crucial to establishing the role of Sudanese government policy in the mass atrocities.

During the second two-week period of the ADS interviews, a question was added asking if there were rebels actually staying in the respondent's town or village.[86] Less than 2 percent of the respondents in the sample reported a rebel presence.[87] These reports were disproportionately located in several northern settlements, such as Karnoi, near Tine, and Girgira, with the reporting of rebel presence still low, but ranging from 6 to 13 percent.[88] The documentation of rebel involvement in the settlements that were attacked is crucial to refuting the Sudanese government's defense that it was acting in proportionate self-defense against an organized insurgency.

---

[78] Id. at 22–24.
[79] Id. at 20.
[80] HAGAN & RYMOND-RICHMOND, supra note 69, at 93.
[81] Id. at 173.
[82] Id.
[83] Id.
[84] HAGAN & RYMOND-RICHMOND, supra note 69, at 173.
[85] Id.
[86] Id.
[87] Id.
[88] HAGAN & RYMOND-RICHMOND, supra note 69, at 173.

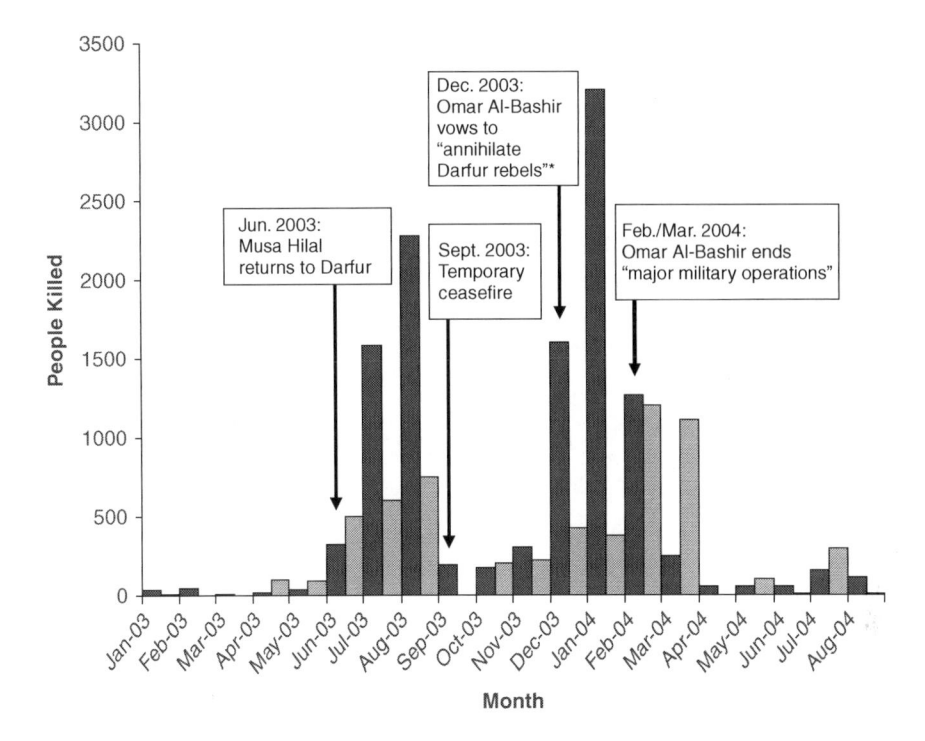

Ethnic Cleansing 191

```
3500

3000          Dec. 2003:
              Omar Al-Bashir
              vows to
2500          "annihilate
              Darfur rebels"*

       Jun. 2003:                    Feb./Mar. 2004:
2000   Musa Hilal    Sept. 2003:     Omar Al-Bashir ends
       returns to   Temporary        "major military operations"
       Darfur       ceasefire
1500

1000

500

  0
```

FIGURE 8.2. Chronology of key events and monthly death estimates from survey and news counts of killings, January 2003–September 2004.

There were two waves of attacks in Darfur, and these predictably corresponded with the peak periods of ethnic cleansing involving violent and health-related death and displacement. About a quarter of the sample fled during the first three months of first wave attacks, about half fled during the four months of the second wave of attacks, with the remaining quarter fleeing during the other thirteen months.[89] The second wave of attacks was obviously the most costly in terms of the physical destruction of the group conditions of social life for Africans in Darfur. It was during the second wave of attacks, in December 2003, that Sudanese President Omar Al-Bashir vowed to "annihilate Darfur rebels."[90] Figure 8.2 shows monthly death counts from January 2003 to September 2004, encompassing the two waves of attacks as well as the months before and after. The two sources are the ADS interviews and a separate survey based on news and NGO reports of deaths in attacks on 101 villages.[91]

[89] Id.
[90] Id. at 139–40.
[91] Id. at 139.

The death toll in Darfur for this eighteen-month period is estimated at between 200,000 and 400,000.[92]

The ADS interviews are highly detailed in recording the shouting of racial epithets – our measure of racial intent – during the attacks. The epithets are important, in part, because they provide evidence of an explicit targeting that focused the attacks in a way that went beyond the multiple ethnic tribal identities indigenous to Darfur (i.e., the Zaghawa, Fur, and Masalit). The effect of these epithets was to identify an explicit binary racial division. As we see next, although both ethnic and racial groups are protected under the Genocide Conventions, ethnic attributions are more easily dismissed as subjectively and internally adopted by the groups themselves.

The UN International Commission of Inquiry approached this distinction involving subjective and objective identity as an important issue of atrocity law. This is an example of how Scheffer argues that the exclusively legal framing of such issues can inhibit parties from acting on their responsibility to protect victimized groups.[93] The UN Commission concluded that victims of violence in Darfur were not *objectively distinct* from their attackers and recognizable as *protected ethnic or racial groups* under the Genocide Convention:

> The various tribes that have been the object of attacks and killings (chiefly the Fur, Masalit and Zaghawa tribes) do not appear to make up ethnic groups distinct from the ethnic group to which persons or militias that attack them belong. They speak the same language (Arabic) and embrace the same religion (Muslim). In addition, also due to the high measure of intermarriage, they can hardly be distinguished in their outward physical appearance from the members of tribes that allegedly attacked them.[94]

The UN Commission failed to acknowledge that racial distinctions are often socially constructed and forcefully imposed with little regard to physical difference. Racial epithets are important for both criminological and legal analysis because they capture the motivation and intent of attackers. The frequently quoted *Akayesu* decision in Rwanda[95] and the *Jelisić* decision in Bosnia[96] both emphasize the importance of spoken language in genocide. Social science evidence regarding the influence of racial epithets is shown below to have an important bearing on the criminology and law of mass atrocity in Darfur.

We examined the narrative accounts of the attacks on a case-by-case basis to find reports of victims and refugees hearing racial epithets. We recorded the content of the epithets, detailing as exactly as possible the wording of the epithets, and each individual was assigned a code indicating whether or not they heard racial epithets.

---

[92] John Hagan & Alberto Palloni, *Death in Darfur*, SCIENCE, Sept. 15, 2006, at 1578–79.
[93] Scheffer, *supra* note 3, at 248.
[94] U.N. International Commission of Inquiry, *Report of the International Commission on Darfur to the United Nations Secretary-General*, ¶ 508, U.N. Doc. S/2005/60 (Feb. 1, 2005).
[95] Prosecutor v. Akayesu, Case No. ICTR-96-4-T, Judgment, ¶¶ 698–734 (Sept. 2, 1998).
[96] Prosecutor v. Goran Jelisić, Case No. IT-95-10-T, Judgment, ¶¶ 73–77 (Dec. 14, 1999).

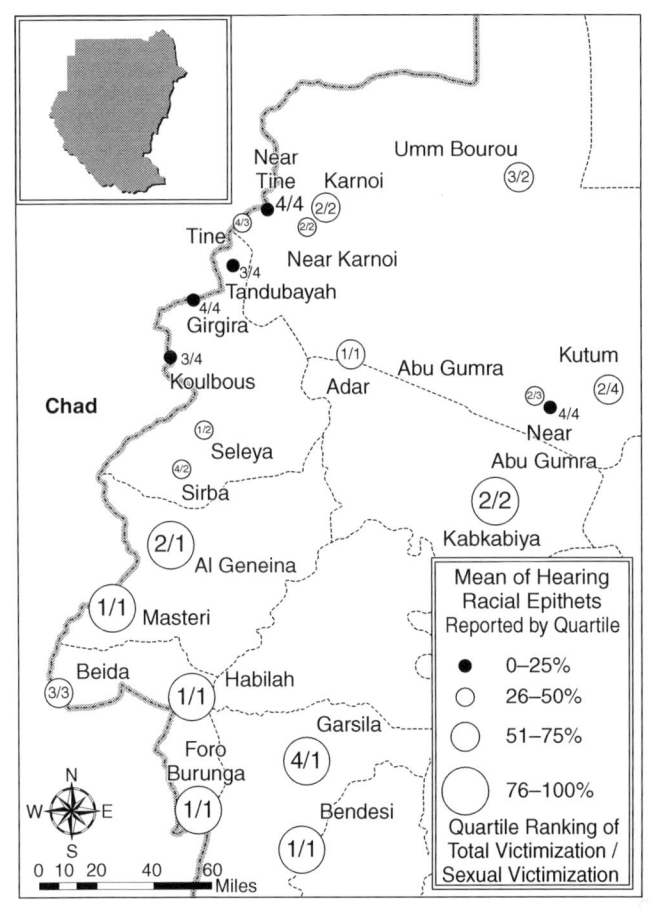

MAP 8.1. Settlement cluster map of racial epithets and total victimization and sexual victimization.

Respondents reported hearing racial epithets, as indicated on the accompanying Map 8.1, in all the settlements, with about a quarter to half of the respondents hearing them across the twenty-two settlements.[97] Overall, about one-third of the respondents heard racial epithets during the attacks.[98] These epithets were explicit, often invoking images of racial slavery, and they constitute concrete, first-person evidence of racial intent.

We argue that the racial epithets combine elements of motivation and intent, and that they were raised to compelling collective levels in the settings where they were most frequently heard. The racial component of the epithets is the motivational element. The intent element includes the targeted references to killing, raping, assaulting, looting, and destroying group life.

---

[97] HAGAN & RYMOND-RICHMOND, *supra* note 69, 172–73.
[98] *Id.*

Refugees often reported hearing the incoming forces shouting racial slurs, such as "this is the last day for blacks," "[w]e will destroy the black skinned people," "kill all the slaves," "kill all the blacks," "you are black, you deserve to be tortured like this," and "we will kill any slaves we find and cut off their heads."[99] These words and phrases shouted by the perpetrators provide insight into and evidence of the attackers' motivation and intentions during the raids on Darfurian villagers. We shorten the reference to "collective racial intent" below, but it is noteworthy that both motivation and intent are involved in the reported racial epithets.

In addition to situating the refugees in terms of prior rebel activity in their settlements and the hearing of racial epithets during the attacks, it is also important to consider the density of the population settlements in which they lived. The more densely settled areas of Darfur are also the most fertile in providing the necessary conditions for group life that are importantly highlighted in the Genocide Convention.[100] We developed a measure for density consisting of the number of settlements in an area recorded in the UN Humanitarian Information Profiles (the numerator), and the square kilometers in the area (the denominator).

Settlement density is more than a measure of the population at risk of victimization. It is also a measure of criminal opportunities and incentives, including desirable property consisting of possessions, livestock, and the settled land itself. The settlements that score highest on this settlement density measure are in the southwestern area of West Darfur, including Bendesi, Foro Burunga, Habiliah, and Masteri. Settlement of a land area effectively constitutes ownership in Darfur, and in a time of desertification and recurrent famine, access to settled land is often a crucial resource for sustaining group life. We hypothesized that the victimization characteristic of ethnic cleansing is most likely in the densely settled areas of Darfur, where opportunities and incentives for attacks and strains on resources are greatest.

This hypothesis is consistent with the Malthusian view of population growth previously applied to the Rwandan genocide by Jared Diamond.[101] According to Diamond, "population and environmental problems created by non-sustainable resource use … ultimately get solved in one way or another: if not by pleasant means of our own choice, then by unpleasant and unchosen means, such as the ones that Malthus initially envisioned."[102] Yet Diamond is not an environmental determinist, even though he argues that "population pressure was one of the important factors behind the Rwandan genocide."[103] He further allows an important role for ethnic hatred, observing that:

> I'm accustomed to thinking of population pressure, human environmental impacts, and drought as ultimate causes, which make people chronically desperate

---

[99] Id. at 172.
[100] Rome Statute, supra note 31, art. 6.
[101] JARED DIAMOND, COLLAPSE: HOW SOCIETIES CHOOSE TO FAIL OR SUCCEED 311–28 (2005).
[102] Id. at 313.
[103] Id. at 327.

and are like the gunpowder inside the powder keg. One also needs a proximate cause: a match to light the keg. In most areas of Rwanda, that match was ethnic hatred whipped up by politicians cynically concerned with keeping themselves in power.[104]

This last reference to the role of politicians controlling the State and molding what we call "collective racial intent" fits well with Flint and de Waal's description of a Sudanese security cabal in Khartoum that unleashed the Janjaweed militias on black African groups in Darfur as an explicitly planned policy.[105]

The final pieces of our descriptive portrait of the ADS sample involve its description of genocidal victimization. The classical understanding of genocide emphasizes the intentional *taking of lives* that characterizes the destruction of a group. We have noted that a more contemporary approach to genocide also focuses on the deliberate infliction of *physical conditions of life* on a group calculated to bring about its destruction. Obviously both are important and both are included in Article II of the original Genocide Convention definition.[106]

Our measurement approach involved using a report section from each survey that recorded incidents of victimization. Respondents reported attacks on themselves, their families, and their settlements, which involved bombing, killing, rape, abduction, assault, property destruction, and theft.[107] Each respondent therefore reported for him or herself together with his or her settlement.

We created a total victimization severity score based on the common law seriousness of the incidents reported for attacks on the settlements. We aggregated reports of specific incidents experienced or witnessed by each respondent in the settlement.[108] We assigned the following values to the incidents: five to reported killings; four to sexual violence or abductions; three to assaults; two to property destruction or theft; and one to displacement.[109]

To illustrate the coding of the incidents in the severity scale, consider the example of a thirty-five-year-old Masalit woman with a total severity score of fifty-two.[110] The attack reported by this woman occurred in a village near Masteri. Sudanese government troops and Arab Janjaweed militia attacked her village on September 1, 2003. Her report included twenty incidents during the attack that occurred that day. Her report includes herself, her family, and others in the village. During the attack, she was beaten (severity score of 3) and raped (4). Her father was severely beaten (3) trying to protect her, and he was subsequently abducted (4). Some women from her village were abducted (4) and held for two hours. They were beaten (3) and raped

---

[104] *Id.* at 326.
[105] JULIE FLINT & ALEX DE WAAL, DARFUR: A SHORT HISTORY OF A LONG WAR 101 (2005).
[106] *Genocide Convention, supra* note 31, art. 2.
[107] HAGAN & RYMOND-RICHMOND, *supra* note 69, at 175.
[108] *Id.* at 176.
[109] *Id.*
[110] *See also* John Hagan & Wenona Rymond-Richmond, *The Collective Dynamics of Genocidal Victimization in Darfur*, 73 AM. SOC. REV. 875, 885 (2008).

before being released. Another group of women (ages ranging from 16 to 20) were raped (4), and she personally witnessed one of the rapes and heard about the rapes from other victims. Additional villagers, including her brother, were beaten (3), shot (3), and stabbed (3). She witnessed dead bodies (5), all male, some of whom had their throats cut, and others that were shot in the head. Her village was completely destroyed (2), except for three huts that were on the far edge of the village. Theft occurred (2), including that of livestock, food, and water pots. She reports there was no rebel activity in or around her village. The only defense the villagers had was a few spears, which were no match for the attackers' guns, knives, aircraft, and pickup trucks with mounted guns. She entered Chad in February 2004, becoming one of the two to three million Darfurians displaced (1) from the mass atrocities.

To the extent that ethnic cleansing and genocide victimization encompass a group "in whole" – as, for example, a "scorched earth" policy would imply – there might be little within- or between-settlement variation in the numbers of deaths or severity of victimization of the kind whose quantitative measurement we have just described. All would be victimized. On the other hand, to the extent that this group victimization is "in part," there should be variance in both within- and between-settlement outcomes. For the criminological and legal reasons we have indicated, we were particularly interested in determining the role that racial intent played in explaining variation in Sudanese state organized victimization, along with the Janjaweed militias, of the African groups and settlements.

Our interest was thus in the settlements as much as the individuals who are the victims of the Darfur conflict as represented in the ADS sample. The hypothetical process examined in our analysis is expressed in Figure 8.3. We analyze the combined roles of GoS forces with Janjaweed militias in racially targeted mass atrocities, as well as in the selective protection of nearby Arab villagers. Selective protection as

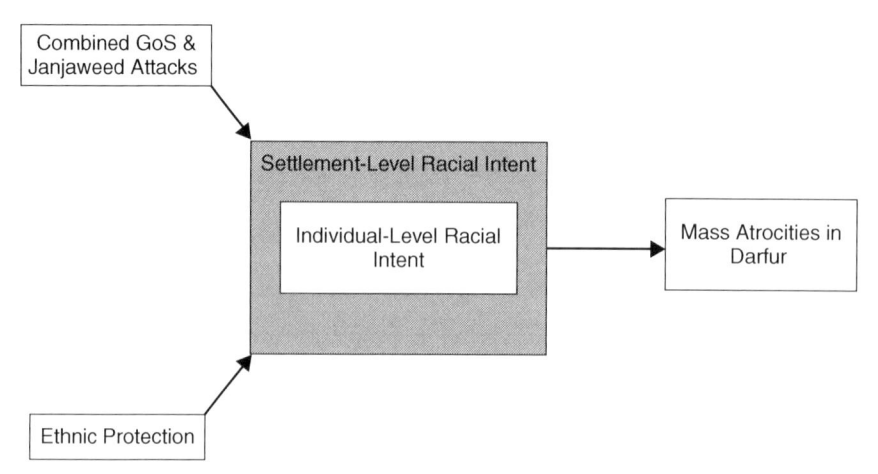

FIGURE 8.3. Combined roles of GoS and Janjaweed with ethnic protection in racial targeting of ethnic cleansing and mass atrocities in Darfur.

well as predation can be an instrumental way of separating "us" from "them" in an organizational dynamic of ethnic cleansing that results in mass atrocities.

We summarize the most important aspects of this analysis in two maps. We begin with the distribution of the racial epithets heard during attacks by the ADS respondents. First, we consider how racial epithets were distributed in terms of the characteristics of the *individuals* who heard them – that is, we answer the question: *Who* heard these epithets most often? Second, we consider how the reporting of these epithets varies across the *settlements* – that is, we answer the question: *Where* were these epithets heard most often?

At the individual level, men reported hearing racial epithets more often than women.[111] This is probably because women are less likely than men to know the Arabic words of the shouted epithets. Respondents also indicated they heard racial epithets less often in settlements with rebels.[112] This finding is strongly suggestive that the scorched-earth tactics of the attacks focused on civilians rather than on suspected rebels. Three of the four African groups – the Fur, Masalit, and Jebal – more often reported hearing racial epithets than did the Zaghawa.[113] This is likely because the Zaghawa were more often victims of bombing and air attacks than other groups – there is more opportunity to hear the epithets during ground attacks.[114] Epithets were reported less often during the first wave of attacks than at other times,[115] which suggests that the racialization of the attacks increased over the duration of the conflict.

Map 8.1 portrays the variation in reported racial epithets across the settlements. It indicates variation in the proportion of respondents reporting epithets with circles of increasing sizes (calibrated in quartiles) in the settlements. About half of the respondents in the top quartile heard racial epithets during the attacks. Thus, 45 percent of the respondents heard racial epithets in Kabkabiyah, where the militia leader Musa Hilal began his early attacks, and between 43 percent and 50 percent of respondents heard these epithets in settlements in southwestern Darfur – in Al Geneina, Masteri, Habilah, Garsila, Foro Burunga, and Benesi – the sites of attacks reported in the media as led by three other Janjaweed militia leaders.[116] The latter sites are in the more fertile and densely settled areas of Darfur.[117]

Map 8.2 outlines the locations where news media and human rights groups reported attacks occurred that were led by four militia leaders – Musa Hilal, Hamid Dawai, Ali Kushayb, and Abdullah Shineibat. The approximate areas of their operations indicated in these independent reports are designated with triangular-shaped markings on Map 8.2. These are also the areas with high reports of racial epithets and attacks in Map 8.1.

[111] HAGAN & RYMOND-RICHMOND, *supra* note 69, at 178.
[112] *Id.*
[113] *Id.*
[114] *Id.*
[115] HAGAN & RYMOND-RICHMOND, *supra* note 69, at 178.
[116] *Id.*
[117] *Id.*

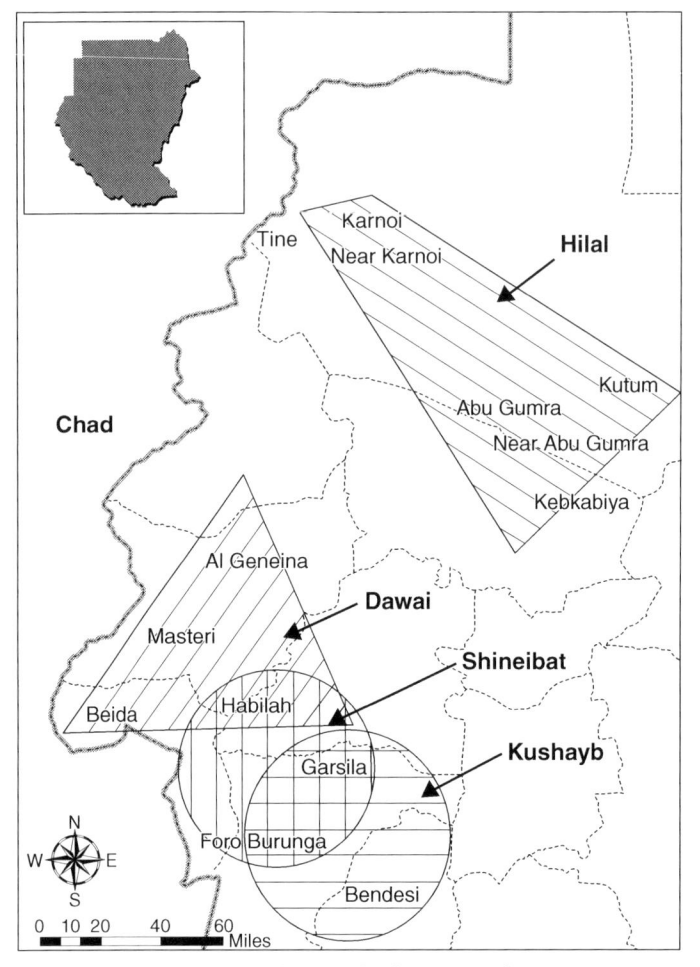

MAP 8.2. Janjaweed militia leaders' areas of operation.

Our analysis further revealed that the racial epithets we have emphasized as indicating racial intent were heard most often when the Sudanese government forces were joined with the Janjaweed in attacks and in areas of high settlement density. This finding, which reflects the effects of State military organization and policy as well as the opportunities and incentives of land-based resources that often motivate ethnic cleansing, is summarized with a bar graph in Figure 8.4. It indicates the following: When Sudanese and Janjaweed forces attack together, increased population density notably increases the hearing of racial epithets. When the Sudanese and Janjaweed forces attack separately, increased population density slightly diminishes the hearing of these epithets. Recall that the Sudanese and Janjaweed forces operate together in about two-thirds of the attacks.[118] The effect of this *combination* of forces

[118] *Id.* at 179.

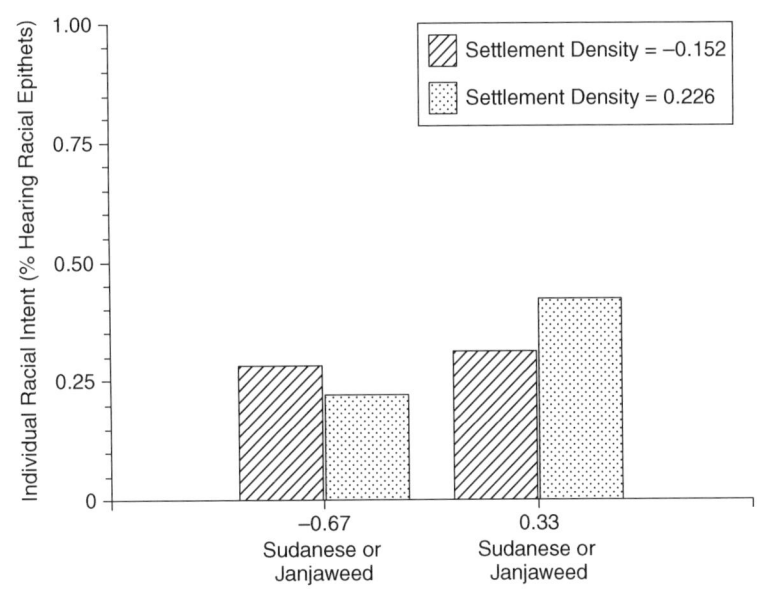

FIGURE 8.4. Cross-level interaction of separate and/or combined forces with settlement density on individual racial intent.

in the right side of Figure 8.4 – in areas representing higher population densities – is to approximately *double* the hearing of racial epithets from about 20 percent to more than 40 percent. This is compelling evidence of the organized policy role of the Sudanese State in intensifying the expression of racial intent by joining its military forces with the Janjaweed in attacks on densely settled areas of Darfur.

We next observe the impact of what we have called collective racial intent in two ways. Map 8.1 provided the first reflection of our finding of a significant effect of collective racial intent. The map showed that racial epithets were heard more often in the Kabkabiyah area, where the militia leader Musa Hilal launched his attacks, and in the southwestern settlements in West Darfur, where three other leaders had been active. Inside the circles on Map 8.1, which reflect these elevated reports of racial epithets, we also present the quartile ranks of the severity of total victimization, as operationalized earlier, as well as sexual victimization that we measured separately as the number of sexual assaults reported as occurring during the attacks.[119]

There is a clear tendency in Map 8.1 for the quartile ranking of victimization scores across settlements to coincide with the quartile ranking of reported racial epithets. Thus, top quartile victimization scores are found in five of the six settlements that also feature elevated racial epithets in the southwestern part of West Darfur. This part of West Darfur is more fertile and densely settled. The statistical models we present elsewhere show that these are also the areas where victimization is most

---

[119] *See also* John Hagan, Wenona Rymond-Richmond & Alberto Palloni, *Racial Targeting of Sexual Violence in Darfur*, 99 Am. J. Pub. Health 1386 (2009).

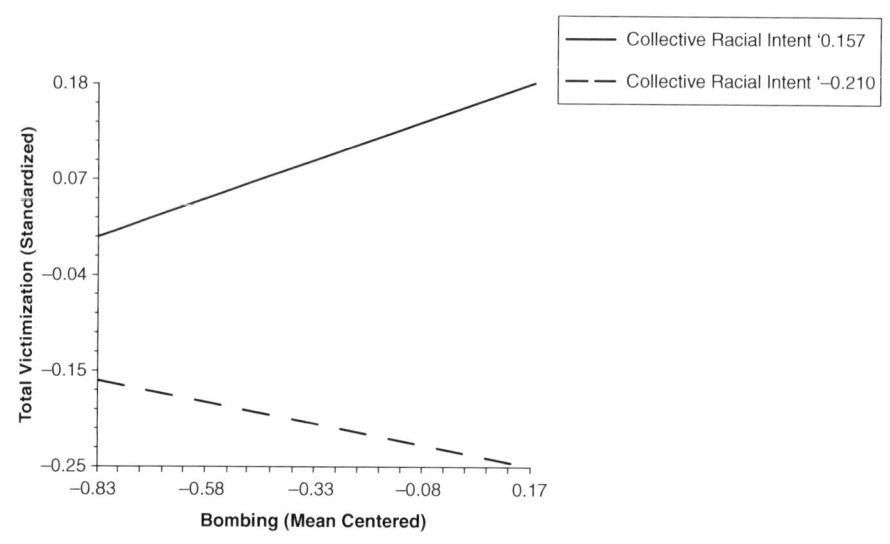

FIGURE 8.5. Cross-level interaction of collective racial intent with bombing on total victimization (standardized).

severe, and that this pattern is further mediated by the pervasiveness of the racial epithets and their collective effect in increasing victimization.[120] This part of the analysis supports Diamond's metaphor, introduced earlier, that his expectation that collective racial intent is the transformative racial spark that ignites the powder keg of settlement density.[121]

There is also a pattern in Map 8.1 of higher-level victimization scores and racial epithet reports extending from Kabkabiyah, through Adar, and northward to Kornei. This pattern of scores reflects the northern line of attacks that Musa Hilal threatened in remarks reported in the market town of Kabkabiyh, as described in ADS survey interviews.[122] It seems likely that if the levels of settlement density were as high in North Darfur as they are in the affected areas of West Darfur, the pattern observed in this part of the map would be even more striking.

An important final finding about collective racial intent and bombing is summarized in Figure 8.5. This figure indicates that at lower levels of collective racial intent, the effect of increased bombing is associated with decreasing levels of victimization, whereas at higher levels of collective racial intent, the effect of increased bombing is to elevate total victimization.[123] The basic thesis underlying our analysis is that the Sudanese government enlisted the Janjaweed militias and channeled their hostility toward black African groups as a means of more effectively gaining control over the Darfur region – out of fear that this region was escaping government control. Given

---

[120] HAGAN & RYMOND-RICHMOND, *supra* note 69, at 177–82.
[121] DIAMOND, *supra* note 101, at 326.
[122] HAGAN & RYMOND-RICHMOND, *supra* note 69, at 181.
[123] *Id.*

that the bombing by GoS planes is entirely under Sudanese State control, the combined use of the Janjaweed militias and government bombing is particularly striking evidence of the use of State power to divide and victimize subordinate groups. Figure 8.5 supplements the earlier findings in showing how, especially in densely settled areas, the concentration of bombing and collective racial hostility against African groups, such as the Fur and Masalit, produces elevated levels of victimization. The Sudanese government directed the bombing and enlisted the Janjaweed in racially animated attacks that intensified victimization. This is evidence that a joined, collective intent was enacted and accomplished.

VII. CONCLUSIONS

We propose the acceptance of a definition of ethnic cleansing, such as Petrović's, which emphasizes the enactment of an explicit policy of elimination or removal by one group against another that is defined in religious, ethnic, national, or racial terms and is organized in relation to an identified geographic area by military or sociopolitical means ranging from discrimination to extermination. Scientific research, legal scholarship, and judicial decision making can all play a role in further identifying the more exact boundaries of ethnic cleansing. More specifically, we argue that establishing the occurrence of ethnic cleansing may characteristically involve a mixture of social scientific criminological and legal evidence, with the criminological evidence playing a leading role. The challenge is to fully delineate the boundaries of ethnic cleansing in relation to genocide. Scheffer's distinction between atrocity crime and atrocity law creates a space in which this kind of documentation and analysis may occur. We have considered how this kind of documentation and analysis was undertaken in Kosovo and Darfur. These are only examples. Unfortunately, there is no shortage of other settings in which this work may be furthered.

9

Immunities and Amnesties

Diane Orentlicher*

I. INTRODUCTION

This chapter addresses two broad issues relevant to the *Proposed International Convention on the Prevention and Punishment of Crimes Against Humanity*. Section II considers how questions of official and personal immunities may arise in respect of efforts to establish responsibility for crimes against humanity. Section III addresses issues relating to amnesties for such crimes. Each section begins by reviewing relevant principles of international law that would apply unless the *Proposed Convention* established a different rule, with a view toward ensuring that any new convention on crimes against humanity (1) does not undermine progressive developments in international law; and (2) clarifies applicable rules where necessary or useful.

In brief, this chapter concludes:

- The proposed convention on crimes against humanity should explicitly provide that the official position of the accused may not absolve him or her of criminal responsibility for crimes against humanity.
- In addition, separate provisions should make clear that State officials may not successfully invoke substantive immunities to avoid civil or administrative sanctions in respect of crimes against humanity committed in their own States.
- Recent developments in law and practice suggest that States are unlikely to agree to text that commits States Parties not to invoke immunities *ratione personae* in the context of inter-State criminal proceedings.
- Turning to amnesties, recent experience with another human rights treaty suggests that States are unlikely to agree on language prohibiting amnesties for crimes against humanity, even though such language would find strong support in developing principles of international law. The wisest course in a treaty whose aim is to assure criminal accountability for crimes against humanity is to avoid explicit references to the subject of amnesties.

---

* I am grateful to Peter Chapman and Lyndsay Gorton for excellent research assistance. This chapter was written before the author's employment with the U.S. Department of State. The views expressed herein do not necessarily reflect those of the U.S. Government or Department of State.

II. IMMUNITIES

A. *Preliminary Observations*

Much of the core body of international law concerning the immunities of State officials developed in the context of inter-State relationships, addressing the circumstances in which officials of one State could be subjected to the jurisdiction of other States' courts. With the advent of international tribunals in the postwar period, questions concerning the scope of immunities that could successfully be pleaded before such courts also became a subject of international regulation. As this section makes clear, State practice in respect of international courts has had a profound impact on the law of immunities more generally. Even so, the distinction between the immunities that may be asserted before foreign courts on the one hand and international or hybrid courts on the other hand has continuing relevance – a point this chapter addresses in Section II.C.

Another crucial distinction has a significant bearing on the issues addressed in this paper – that between State officials' immunity *ratione materiae* on the one hand and their immunity *ratione personae* on the other hand.[1] Whereas immunity *ratione materiae* operates to shield the official conduct of State officials from the scrutiny of foreign (and potentially international and/or hybrid) courts,[2] immunity *ratione personae*, which attaches to the status of certain incumbent officials, operates as a procedural bar to the exercise of jurisdiction over them by the courts of another State and, potentially, by an international or hybrid court.[3] Although immunity *ratione materiae* operates alongside immunity *ratione personae*, the former generally becomes relevant – or at any rate its relevance becomes apparent – when a potential defendant's official status comes to an end, and he or she is therefore no longer entitled to claim the broader protections associated with immunity *ratione personae*.[4]

---

[1] The distinctions used here are not uniformly followed. *See* Int'l Law Comm'n, *Preliminary Report on Immunity of State Officials from Foreign Criminal Jurisdiction*, ¶¶ 78–83, U.N. Doc. A/CN.4/601 (May 29, 2008) (*prepared by* Roman Anatolevich Kolodkin, Special Rapporteur) [hereinafter *Kolodkin, Preliminary Report*]. In cases interpreting relevant principles of international law, moreover, courts have not always clearly distinguished between these two types of immunity, at times conflating or confusing the two.

[2] *See* IAN BROWNLIE, PRINCIPLES OF PUBLIC INTERNATIONAL LAW 330 (4th ed. 1990).

[3] Because this type of immunity attaches to the person of certain incumbent officials, it is often called a "personal immunity." Effectively immunizing acts performed in the exercise of official functions, this type of immunity is also sometimes described as a functional immunity.

[4] *See* Colin Warbrick & Dominic McGoldrick, *Current Developments: Public International Law; The Future of Former Head of State Immunity After Ex Parte Pinochet*, 48 INT'L & COMP. L.Q. 937, 940 (1999) ("The existence of immunity *ratione materiae* is not immediately apparent given that the personal immunity of [the] head of state has the effect of rendering any discussion of the official or non-official nature of [his] acts redundant.").

B. Immunity Ratione Materiae

1. Overview of International Law Concerning Immunity *Ratione Materiae* for International Crimes

As indicated earlier, when they are applicable, immunities *ratione materiae* serve to shield from the scrutiny of foreign courts the "acts performed by State officials acting in an official capacity, i.e., performed in fulfillment of functions of the State,"[5] even after they leave office and thus are no longer entitled to the broader immunities accorded certain incumbent officials from the exercise of foreign States' jurisdiction.[6] Although some experts see this type of immunity as essentially a procedural bar to prosecution, others emphasize that it operates in effect as a "substantive defense" and thus refer to it as a form of substantive immunity.[7]

In the view of the International Law Commission, various courts, and legal scholars, a key rationale behind this form of immunity is that actions against individuals representing a foreign State "in respect of their official acts are essentially proceedings against the State they represent,"[8] which enjoys broad, but no longer virtually absolute, immunity from the jurisdiction of foreign States. Thus "when they act in an official capacity, [individuals representing a] State do not engage their own responsibility, but that of the State; consequently their acts enjoy the immunities of the State."[9]

Postwar prosecutions by the Allied Powers played a leading role in qualifying the previously broad substantive immunities conferred by international law on government officials, including Heads of State and Government.[10] Article 7 of the Charter of the International Military Tribunal (IMT) at Nuremberg provided:

> The official position of defendants, whether as Heads of State or responsible officials in Government Departments, shall not be considered as freeing them from responsibility or mitigating punishment.[11]

---

[5] Kolodkin, *Preliminary Report*, *supra* note 1, ¶ 80.

[6] *See id.* ¶ 88.

[7] ANTONIO CASSESE, INTERNATIONAL CRIMINAL LAW 266 (2003). While describing this type of immunity as a substantive defense, Cassese also uses the phrase "functional" immunities to describe this category. *See id.* at 264–65.

[8] Int'l Law Comm'n, *Jurisdictional Immunities of States and their Property Report of the International Law Commission on the Work of its Forty-Third Session*, U.N. Doc. A/46/10 (July 19, 1991), *reprinted in* [1991] 2 Y.B. Int'l L. Comm'n Part II, at 18, U.N. Doc. A/CN.4/SER.A/1991/Add.1 (Part 2), *quoted in* Kolodkin, Preliminary Report, *supra* note 1, ¶ 88; *see also* CASSESE, *supra* note 7, at 264–66.

[9] Certain Questions of Mutual Legal Assistance in Criminal Matters (Djib. v. Fr.), Public Sitting of Jan. 25, 2008, Statement of Allain Pellet, Counsel for France, at 50, *available at* http://www.icj-cij.org/docket/files/136/14413.pdf, *quoted in* Kolodkin, Preliminary report *supra* note 1, at 42 n.173; *see also* CASSESE, *supra* note 7, at 264–66.

[10] Nuremberg and its progeny do not appear to have made parallel inroads into the immunity enjoyed by States themselves. *See* Al-Adsani v. United Kingdom, App. No. 35763/97, 34 Eur. Ct. H.R. 11, ¶¶ 61–66 (2001).

[11] The Charter of the International Military Tribunal art. 7, Aug. 8, 1945, 59 Stat. 1544, 82 U.N.T.S. 279. Although Adolf Hitler committed suicide before he could be prosecuted, one of the defendants

In its final judgment, the IMT famously articulated the principle underlying this provision, explaining:

> The principle of international law, which under certain circumstances, protects the representatives of a State, cannot be applied to acts which are condemned as criminal by international law. The authors of these acts cannot shelter themselves behind their official position in order to be freed from punishment in appropriate proceedings.... [T]he very essence of the Charter is that individuals have international duties which transcend the national obligations of obedience imposed by the individual State. He who violates the laws of war cannot obtain immunity while acting in pursuance of the authority of the State if the State in authorizing action moves outside its competence under international law.[12]

A provision similar to article 7 of the Nuremberg Charter was included in Allied Control Council Law No. 10,[13] pursuant to which the Allied Powers prosecuted German war criminals in the Allies' respective zones of occupation in Germany, and a somewhat modified version of the Nuremberg text – omitting explicit reference to Heads of State – was included in the Charter of the International Military Tribunal for the Far East.[14]

Building on the postwar precedents, the statutes of contemporary international and several hybrid tribunals have included similar provisions.[15] For example, the Statutes of the ad hoc international criminal tribunals established by the United Nations Security Council in 1993 (for the former Yugoslavia) and 1994 (for Rwanda), respectively, provide:

> The official position of any accused person, whether as Head of State or Government or as a responsible Government official, shall not relieve such person of criminal responsibility nor mitigate punishment.[16]

---

prosecuted before the IMT, Admiral Karl Doenitz, briefly served as Head of State of Germany. Doenitz succeeded Hitler as Head of State on May 1, 1945, serving in this position until Germany's surrender on May 8, 1945. Doenitz was no longer Head of State at the time of his indictment.

[12] NAZI CONSPIRACY AND AGGRESSION, OPINION AND JUDGMENT 53 (1946).

[13] Allied Control Council Law No. 10, Berlin Dec. 20, 1945, *reprinted in* 3 OFFICIAL GAZETTE OF THE CONTROL COUNCIL FOR GERMANY 50–55 (1946). Article 4(a) of this law provided: "The official position of any person, whether as Head of State or as a responsible official in a Government Department, does not free him from responsibility for a crime or entitle him to mitigation of punishment."

[14] Charter of the International Military Tribunal for the Far East, Jan. 19, 1946, T.I.A.S. No. 1589, 4 Bevans 20. Article 6 of the Tokyo Charter provides in pertinent part that "the official position, at any time, of an accused" would not by itself "free such accused from responsibility for any crime with which he is charged." This provision did not make explicit reference to Heads of State because the United States, which promulgated the Tokyo Charter, had already determined not to prosecute Japanese Emperor Hirohito.

[15] The Statute of the most recently established hybrid court, the Special Tribunal for Lebanon, does not include such a provision. *See* S.C. Res. 1757, U.N. Doc. S/RES/1757 (May 30, 2007), *available at* http://www.un.org/Docs/sc/unsc_resolutions07.htm (follow "S/RES/1757 [2007]" hyperlink).

[16] Statute of the International Criminal Tribunal for the former Yugoslavia Annex art. 7(2), S.C. Res. 827, U.N. Doc. S/RES/827 (May 25, 1993) [hereinafter *ICTY Statute*] (original text); Statute of the International Criminal Tribunal for Rwanda Annex art. 6(2), S.C. Res. 955, U.N. Doc. S/RES/955 (Nov. 8, 1994) [hereinafter *ICTR Statute*] (original text). The first defendant convicted

Article 6(2) of the statute of the Special Court for Sierra Leone (SCSL), a hybrid court established through a treaty between the United Nations and Sierra Leone,[17] provides: "The official position of any accused persons, whether as Head of State or Government or as a responsible Government official, shall not relieve such a person of criminal responsibility nor mitigate punishment." Article 29 of a law establishing another hybrid court, the Extraordinary Chambers in the Courts of Cambodia (ECCC), provides in pertinent part: "The position or rank of any Suspect shall not relieve such person of criminal responsibility or mitigate punishment."[18]

Like the international criminal tribunals that preceded it, the International Criminal Court (ICC), whose statute entered into force on July 1, 2002, may exercise its jurisdiction over Heads of State or Government (and indeed the ICC has issued an arrest warrant against the incumbent President of Sudan),[19] as well as over other members of government. The first paragraph of article 27 of the Rome Statute of the International Criminal Court (Rome Statute),[20] adopted in 1998, provides:

> This Statute shall apply equally to all persons without any distinction based on official capacity. In particular, official capacity as a Head of State or Government, a member of a Government or parliament, an elected representative or a government official shall in no case exempt a person from criminal responsibility under

---

by the International Criminal Tribunal for Rwanda (ICTR), Jean Kambanda, held the post of Prime Minister of the Interim Government of Rwanda from April 8 to July 17, 1994 – a period encompassed in his indictment for genocide and crimes against humanity. *See* Prosecutor v. Kambanda, Case No. ICTR-97-23-DP, Indictment (Oct. 16, 1997). Slobodan Milošević, who faced trial before the International Criminal Tribunal for the former Yugoslavia (ICTY) but died before his trial ended, was indicted while he was the incumbent president of the Federal Republic of Yugoslavia (FRY). Milošević, who served as president of the FRY from July 1997 until October 2000, was first indicted by the ICTY on May 22, 1999; the initial indictment was subsequently amended. Like Jean Kambanda, Milošević was charged in relation to conduct that occurred while he served as leader of his country. *See* Prosecutor v. Milošević et al., Case No. IT-99-37, Initial Indictment (Kosovo), ¶ 43 (May 22, 1999); Prosecutor v. Milošević et al., Case No. IT-99-37-I, First Amended Indictment (Kosovo), ¶ 4 (June 29, 2001); Prosecutor v. Milošević et al., Case No. IT-99-37-PT, Second Amended Indictment (Kosovo), ¶ 4 (Oct. 16, 2001). Milošević was also indicted in connection with conduct that occurred before he became president of the FRY but while he was president of the Republic of Serbia. *See* Prosecutor v. Milošević et al., Case No. IT-01-50-I, Initial Indictment (Croatia) (Sept. 27, 2001); Prosecutor v. Milošević et al., Case No. IT-02-54-T, First Amended Indictment (Croatia) (Oct. 23, 2002); Prosecutor v. Milošević et al., Case No. IT-01-51-I, 22, Initial Indictment (Bosnia and Herzegovina) (Nov. 22, 2001).

[17] Although established by treaty, the UN Security Council directed the UN Secretary-General to negotiate such a treaty. *See* S.C. Res. 1315, ¶ 1, U.N. Doc. S/RES/1315 (Aug. 14, 2000). In this respect, its mandate ultimately derives from a Security Council resolution.

[18] Law on the Establishment of Extraordinary Chambers in the Courts of Cambodia for the Prosecution of Crimes Committed during the Period of Democratic Kampuchea, NS/RKM/1004/06 (Oct. 27, 2004), *available at* http://www.eccc.gov.kh/english/cabinet/law/4/KR_Law_as_amended_27_Oct_2004_Eng.pdf.

[19] Prosecutor v. al Bashir, Case No. ICC-02/05-01/09, Warrant of Arrest for Omar Hassan Ahmad al Bashir (Mar. 4, 2009).

[20] *Rome Statute of the International Criminal Court*, United Nations Diplomatic Conference of Plenipotentiaries on the Establishment of an International Criminal Court, July 17, 1998, U.N. Doc. A/CONF.183/9 [hereinafter *Rome Statute*].

this Statute, nor shall it, in and of itself, constitute a ground for reduction of sentence.[21]

The fact that the statutes of various international and hybrid courts specially provide that official immunities otherwise applicable do not exempt defendants from criminal responsibility does not by itself answer the question whether these provisions reflect the law that would apply in the absence of such provisions. Indeed, the explicit recognition of nonimmunity in tribunal statutes could suggest that State representatives involved in drafting these texts believed it necessary to derogate from rules of substantive immunity that would otherwise apply.

Yet the principles reflected in the provisions cited earlier have, in fact, received broader affirmation. Following the postwar prosecutions, the principle recognized in article 7 of the Nuremberg Charter and affirmed in the IMT's judgment was reaffirmed in several general international legal texts. In 1946, the UN General Assembly adopted a resolution "affirm[ing] the principles of international law recognized in the Charter of the Nürnberg Tribunal and the judgment of the Tribunal" and directing the Committee on the codification of international law to formulate those principles.[22] Pursuant to the latter mandate, in 1950 the International Law Commission (ILC) adopted *Principles of International Law Recognized in the Charter of the Nürnberg Tribunal and in the Judgment of the Tribunal*.[23] Principle III (Nuremberg Principle III) affirmed:

> The fact that a person who committed an act which constitutes a crime under international law acted as Head of State or responsible Government official does not relieve him from responsibility under international law.

Various courts have concluded that Nuremberg Principle III is established in customary international law. For example, after quoting the ILC's formulation of Nuremberg Principle III in a decision rejecting a challenge to the jurisdiction of

---

[21] Describing the negotiating history of this provision, William Schabas has written: "The issue was uncontested during negotiations and there were no problems reaching agreement on an acceptable text." WILLIAM A. SCHABAS, AN INTRODUCTION TO THE INTERNATIONAL CRIMINAL COURT 231 (3d ed., 2007) (footnote omitted).

[22] *Affirmation of the Principles of International Law Recognized by the Charter of the Nürnberg Tribunal*, GA Res. 95(I), U.N. Doc. A/64/Add.1 (Dec. 11, 1946). A British judge captured the legal significance of the General Assembly's resolution this way:

> Although there may be legitimate doubts as to the legality of the Charter of the Nuremberg Tribunal, in my judgment those doubts were stilled by the Affirmation of the Principles of International Law recognised by the Charter of Nuremberg Tribunal [sic] adopted by the United Nations General Assembly on 11 December 1946.... At least from that date onwards the concept of personal liability for a crime in international law must have been part of international law.

Regina v. Bartle et al. ex parte Pinochet, [1999] 2 W.L.R. 827 (Eng.) [hereinafter *Pinochet III*] (opinion of Lord Browne-Wilkinson), *reprinted in* 38 I.L.M. 581, 589 (1999). Subsequent references to *Pinochet III* follow the pagination in Volume 38 of INTERNATIONAL LEGAL MATERIALS.

[23] Principles of International Law Recognized in the Charter of the Nürnberg Tribunal and in the Judgment of the Tribunal, Principle III (Aug. 2, 1950), *reprinted in* [1950] 2 Y.B. Int'l L. Comm'n 374, U.N. Doc. A/CN.4/SER.A/1950/Add.1.

the SCSL mounted by Charles Taylor, who had been indicted while still president of Liberia, the SCSL Appeals Chamber observed:

> As long ago as 12 December 1950 when the General Assembly accepted this formulation of the principle of international law by the International Law Commission, that principle became firmly established.[24]

Rejecting a challenge to the jurisdiction of the International Criminal Tribunal for the former Yugoslavia (ICTY) based on the official status of former Yugoslav President Slobodan Milošević, an ICTY Trial Chamber observed that the rule set forth in article 7(2) of its Statute[25] "at this time reflects a rule of customary international law."[26] In an earlier case, an ICTY Trial Chamber observed: "article 7(2) of the [ICTY] Statute and article 6(2) of the Statute of the International Criminal Tribunal for Rwanda … are indisputably declaratory of customary international law."[27]

By its nature, the principle embodied in Nuremberg Principle III makes no distinction among a foreign State's officials.[28] Regardless of their rank, a foreign State's officials should not be able successfully to claim immunity *ratione materiae* in respect of crimes against humanity.

2. The *Proposed Convention* on Crimes Against Humanity: Immunity *Ratione Materiae*

Affirmations of Nuremberg Principle III summarized in the preceding subsection might suggest that it is unnecessary to include a nonimmunity provision in the

---

[24] Prosecutor v. Taylor, Case No. SCSL-2003-01-I, Decision on Immunity from Jurisdiction, ¶ 47 (May 31, 2004) [hereinafter *Taylor Appeals Chamber Decision*].

[25] *See supra* text accompanying note 17.

[26] Prosecutor v. Milošević, Case No. IT-99-37-PT, Decision on Preliminary Motions, ¶ 28 (Nov. 8, 2001); *see also id.* ¶ 31 ("Article 7(2) of the [ICTY] Statute and article 6(2) of the Statute of the International Criminal Tribunal for Rwanda … are indisputably declaratory of customary international law.").

[27] Prosecutor v. Furundžija, Case No. IT-95-17/1-T, Judgment, ¶ 140 (Dec. 10, 1998); *see also* Prosecutor v. Blaškić, Case No. IT-95-14-AR108*bis*, Judgment on the Request of the Republic of Croatia for Review of the Decision of Trial Chamber II of 18 July 1997, ¶ 41 (Oct. 29, 1997) ("Under [the norms of international criminal law prohibiting war crimes, crimes against humanity and genocide], those responsible for such crimes cannot invoke immunity from national or international jurisdiction even if they perpetrated such crimes while acting in their official capacity."); CrimC (Jer) 40/61 Attorney Gen. of Israel v. Eichmann, [1961] IsrDC 45(3), *reprinted in* 36 I.L.R. 277, 311 (asserting that the Nuremberg principles "have become part of the law of nations and must be regarded as having been rooted in it also in the past"). *See also* OTTO TRIFFTERER, COMMENTARY ON THE ROME STATUTE OF THE INTERNATIONAL CRIMINAL COURT 786 (2d ed. 2008) (Article 27(1) of the Rome Statute "recognizes a generally accepted principle of international criminal law"); CASSESE, *supra* note 7, at 267–69. *Cf.* Institute de Droit International, *Immunities from Jurisdiction and Execution of Heads of State and of Government in International Law*, art. 13(2) (Aug. 26, 2001) (affirming that a former Head of State does not enjoy immunity from prosecution in a foreign State for acts constituting a crime under international law).

[28] Conversely, according to the ILC's Special Rapporteur Roman Anatolevich Kolodkin, when immunities *ratione materiae* apply, they are available "regardless of the level of [State officials']

proposed international convention on crimes against humanity because customary international law already clearly establishes the principle. But for reasons explained below, the better course would be to include such a provision. For reasons also explained later, the same textual provision could and should govern all criminal proceedings instituted pursuant to States Parties' obligations under the proposed convention, whether in the territorial State, in the State of the alleged perpetrator's nationality, or in the courts of another State Party exercising extraterritorial jurisdiction. In addition, separate provisions should make clear that State officials may not successfully invoke substantive immunities to avoid civil or administrative sanctions in respect of crimes against humanity committed in their own State.

Criminal prosecutions. Several criminal cases instituted in the past decade have highlighted the importance of clarity concerning the (non)availability of immunities *ratione materiae* in the context of criminal prosecutions, which occupy a central place in the *Proposed Convention's* enforcement provisions, and an explicit nonimmunity provision is the surest way to achieve this.[29] Spain's effort to prosecute former Chilean president Augusto Pinochet illustrates the point. As is well known, a Spanish magistrate sought General Pinochet's extradition from the United Kingdom, where the former Chilean leader was traveling, in October 1998. Ultimately, the United Kingdom's highest court concluded that Pinochet did not enjoy immunity *ratione materiae* from extradition for torture-related charges. Yet the wide range of opinions by the United Kingdom's Law Lords addressing Pinochet's immunity made clear that the outcome was hardly inevitable.

---

post." Kolodkin, *Preliminary report, supra* note 1, ¶ 80. *See also id.* ¶ 81 ("[A]ll State officials enjoy immunity *ratione materiae*.").

[29] The discussion that follows illustrates the point through the instructive example of the *Pinochet* case. But this is not the only case that points up the value of including an unambiguous nonimmunity provision in the text of the proposed convention on crimes against humanity.

In the *Arrest Warrant Case*, the majority opinion of the International Court of Justice (ICJ), after ruling that the immunity *ratione personae* enjoyed by an incumbent foreign minister shields him from the jurisdiction of foreign courts even with respect to a charge of crimes against humanity, observed that such a person would no longer enjoy immunity from foreign courts' jurisdiction once he or she ceased to hold the office of foreign minister "in respect of acts committed during that period of office in a private capacity." Case Concerning the Arrest Warrant of April 11, 2000 (Dem. Rep. Congo v. Belg.), 2002 I.C.J. 3, ¶ 61 (Feb. 14) [hereinafter *Arrest Warrant Case*]. In contrast to the potentially confusing phrase "private capacity," a separate opinion by three ICJ judges asserted – with notably greater clarity – that immunity *ratione materiae* applies only for "official acts" and that "serious international crimes cannot be regarded as official acts." *Id.*, Joint Separate Opinion of Judges Higgins, Kooijmans & Buergenthal, ¶ 85.

Turning to another example from a national jurisdiction: In November 2007, the Paris District Prosecutor dismissed a case that had been instituted by private complainants against former U.S. Secretary of Defense Donald Rumsfeld alleging, *inter alia*, torture. In response to a letter contesting that decision and citing the ICJ's judgment in the *Arrest Warrant Case*, the Public Prosecutor explained that the torture charges against Rumsfeld "cannot be dissociated from his functions" and thus sought to distinguish the situation from that underlying *Pinochet* case. It explained that in the latter case, the defendant "was accused of acts (kidnapping, sequestration, assassinations) that did not fall under the exercise of his functions as President but were marginal to them." Letter from Public Prosecutor of the Paris Court of Appeal to Mr. Patrick Baudouin (Feb. 27, 2008), *available at* http://ccrjustice.org/files/Rumsfeld_FrenchCase_%20Prosecutors%20Decision_02_08.pdf. Yet as

In a decision that was later vacated,[30] a five-judge appellate committee ruled by a bare majority of three-to-two that Pinochet did not enjoy immunity *ratione materiae* in respect of conduct outlawed by international law (two of the Law Lords reached the opposite conclusion – that Pinochet was entitled to immunity in respect of all of the charges for which his extradition was sought).[31] Whereas a majority of Law Lords in the vacated decision believed that Pinochet could not successfully claim immunity for *any* international crime, a majority of Law Lords on an expanded appellate panel later reached a narrower conclusion: Pinochet was not entitled to immunity *ratione materiae* in respect of certain torture-related charges.[32] Although their reasoning varied somewhat, the 1984 Convention against Torture and Other Cruel, Inhuman or Degrading Treatment or Punishment (Torture Convention)[33] played a key role in the reasoning of several Law Lords.

For example, Lord Browne-Wilkinson reasoned that this convention would be nonsensical if former Heads of State could claim immunity *ratione materiae* on torture-related charges. As he noted, the 1984 convention defines torture in a way that requires official action. It struck Lord Browne-Wilkinson as inconceivable that the same convention would exempt from criminal prosecution the official "most responsible" for torture.[34]

For present purposes, it is important to note that Lord Browne-Wilkinson's analysis turned in significant part on the Torture Convention[35] (as did the analysis of several other Law Lords, at least in part) *and* that he had to deduce nonimmunity *ratione materiae* from the text of the convention because it did not address the issue directly. Yet this was not the only possible view: Lord Goff, for example, insisted that such immunity

---

noted in the text that follows, the case against General Pinochet ultimately turned on the torture allegations against him.

[30] This decision was vacated on the ground that the appellate committee had been improperly constituted. See Diane F. Orentlicher, *Whose Justice? Reconciling Universal Jurisdiction with Democratic Principles*, 92 GEO. L.J. 1057, 1076 (2004) [hereinafter *Whose Justice?*].

[31] See *id.* at 1083 (describing *R v. Bow St. Metro. Stipendiary Magistrate, ex parte Pinochet Ugarte* (No. 1), [2000] 1 A.C. 61 (H.L.) (U.K.), *reprinted in* 37 I.L.M. 1302 (1998) [hereinafter *Pinochet I*]).

[32] One of the Law Lords on the expanded panel believed that General Pinochet was entitled to virtually absolute immunity from extradition to Spain on all of the charges presented. At the other extreme, another Law Lord doubted whether customary law provided for immunity *ratione materiae* from criminal process in general, much less for international crimes. For the other Law Lords, the Convention against Torture was crucially important. See *Whose Justice?*, *supra* note 30, at 1083–84 (summarizing the separate opinions in *Pinochet III*).

[33] Convention against Torture and Other Cruel, Inhuman or Degrading Treatment or Punishment, Dec. 10, 1984, 1465 U.N.T.S. 85. All three countries had become parties to this convention as of September 29, 1988. See *Whose Justice?*, *supra* note 30, at 1078 n.121.

[34] *Pinochet III*, *supra* note 22, at 594.

[35] Some passages of Lord Browne-Wilkinson's opinion seemed to suggest that his reasoning was broader – that he believed that there could be no claim of immunity *ratione materiae* for a crime that violates a *jus cogens* prohibition. See *id.* at 593–94 (opinion of Lord Browne-Wilkinson). Yet he went on to observe: "I have doubts whether, before the coming into force of the Torture Convention, the existence of the international crime of torture as jus cogens was enough to justify the conclusion that the organization of state torture could not rank for immunity purposes as performance of an official function." *Id.* at 594.

could not be inferred from the Torture Convention.[36] The range of approaches taken by the Law Lords to the question of Pinochet's immunity points up a risk that can readily be avoided through explicit text in the proposed convention on crimes against humanity: Unless the proposed convention clearly provides for nonimmunity *ratione materiae*, States Parties could reach different conclusions about its availability.[37]

In contrast to the textual silence of the Torture Convention concerning immunities of State officials, the Convention on the Prevention and Punishment of the Crime of Genocide (Genocide Convention),[38] the first postwar instrument aimed at transforming Nuremberg's lessons in individual responsibility into treaty law, explicitly provides that persons who have committed genocide "shall be punished, whether they are constitutionally responsible rulers, public officials or private individuals."[39] Similarly explicit language in the context of a treaty providing for extraterritorial jurisdiction over crimes against humanity would avoid the ambiguities in the Torture Convention that were highlighted in the *Pinochet* proceedings.

C. Immunity Ratione Personae

Whereas there should be no doubt that government officials' immunity *ratione materiae* does not extend to crimes against humanity,[40] the question of whether the proposed convention should seek to remove immunities *ratione personae* that would otherwise be recognized is more complex.[41] If the proposed convention were silent on this point, the most natural implication would be that the immunities *ratione personae* that otherwise

---

[36] See *id.* at 602–04 (opinion of Lord Goff).

[37] This is not to suggest that identical questions would arise in respect of crimes against humanity, with respect to which the principle of nonimmunity *ratione materiae* has been established for a longer period than with respect to the crime of torture when committed outside the context of crimes against humanity, genocide, or war crimes.

[38] Convention on the Prevention and Punishment of the Crime of Genocide, Dec. 9, 1948, 102 Stat. 3045, 78 U.N.T.S. 277.

[39] *Id.* art. IV. This convention contemplates prosecution either before courts in the territory of the State in which genocide occurred – a situation that in most circumstances would not entail violation of a foreign State's sovereign rights – or before "such international penal tribunal as may have jurisdiction with respect to those Contracting Parties which shall have accepted its jurisdiction." *Id.* art. VI. As noted below, a Belgian court concluded that because article IV of the Genocide Convention does not explicitly provide for extraterritorial jurisdiction, it does not alter the immunity *ratione personae* to which certain officials are entitled in respect of *foreign* States' courts. See *infra* note 42.

[40] While there should be no doubt, some writers and decisions have occasionally implied, perhaps unintentionally, that Nuremberg Principle III clearly applies only before international courts. As noted in this section, the distinction between international and domestic courts has greater pertinence for immunities *ratione personae*. Even so, the fact that there may be some doubt concerning the application of Nuremberg Principle III to domestic proceedings reinforces the value of including a provision that corresponds to article 7 of the Nuremberg Charter, article 7(2) of the ICTY Statute, article 6(2) of the ICTR Statute, and article 27(1) of the Rome Statute, with appropriate adaptations.

[41] This issue would not arise in respect of prosecutions by the territorial State of its own officials, but instead would arise when a foreign State or an international or hybrid court sought to institute prosecutions of a State official for crimes against humanity.

apply to a person suspected of committing crimes against humanity would shield him or her from the jurisdiction of other States' courts, and potentially also that of an international or hybrid court, until he or she ceased to hold the relevant office.

Recent State practice supports this view. For example, in a 2003 ruling concerning the asserted immunity of an incumbent Israeli prime minister, the Belgian Court of Cassation held that since the 1949 Geneva Conventions and the 1977 Protocols on the laws of war "contain no provisions that would pose an obstacle to the jurisdictional immunity the defendant can invoke before the Belgian courts," he was immune from its criminal process even in respect of grave breaches of the Geneva Conventions,[42] with respect to which States Parties are obligated to ensure prosecution. Moreover, even though the Genocide Convention *does* include a nonimmunity provision,[43] the same court concluded that, because that convention explicitly provides for prosecution only before an international court or in the courts of the territorial State, its nonimmunity provision does not override immunities otherwise available under customary law before a *foreign* State's courts.[44]

An explicit provision in the proposed convention on crimes against humanity derogating from immunities *ratione personae* as between States Parties could produce a different result.[45] But as elaborated below, proposed text to this effect could prove too much for potential adherents. Given States' reluctance to allow senior leaders in particular to face prosecution before foreign courts, proposed language providing for nonimmunity could well be opposed by a majority of States. Moreover, even if such a provision were included in the text, a large number of reservations would likely be entered. I will come back to this question after reviewing relevant developments in international law and State practice.

1. Overview of International Law Concerning Immunity *Ratione Personae* for International Crimes

Two principal rationales have been put forth in support of immunities *ratione personae*. First, and of particular importance historically, they reflect the respect that

---

[42] Cour de cassation, H.S.A. v. S.A., No. P.02.1139.F (Feb. 12, 2003) (Belg.).
[43] See *supra* notes 38–39.
[44] *Id.* A Spanish judge might have applied similar reasoning when he indicted forty current or former Rwandan military officers on counts of genocide and other human rights violations but did not indict the incumbent president of Rwanda despite evidence of his criminal responsibility. The Spanish judge believed that the Rwandan leader was entitled to Head of State immunity. *See* Al Goodman, *Spanish Judge Indicts 40 Rwandan Military Officers for Genocide*, CNN.COM/EUROPE, Feb. 6, 2008, http://edition.cnn.com/2008/WORLD/europe/02/06/spain.indictments.rwanda/index.html.
[45] In the *Gaddafi* case, the French Court of Cassation suggested that only a legally binding undertaking of this sort would overcome the immunity *ratione personae* otherwise applicable to incumbent Heads of State: "International custom precludes Heads of State in office from being the subject of proceedings before the criminal courts of a foreign State, in the absence of specific provisions to the contrary binding on the parties concerned." Cour de cassation, Chambre criminelle [Cass. crim.] Paris, Mar. 13, 2001, Bull. Crim., No. 64 (Fr.), *reprinted in* 125 I.L.R. 508, 509 (2004).

sovereign equals owe each other. This notion is captured in the Latin maxim *par in parem non habet imperium*, pursuant to which one sovereign State may not exercise its jurisdiction over another.[46] The second rationale is functional: Immunities *ratione personae* are necessary to enable certain officials to perform their duties without interference.[47]

While the immunities *ratione personae* of certain officials, notably diplomats, are well-established under customary international law, they are also addressed in various treaties.[48] That said, no international treaty deals with these immunities in a comprehensive fashion, nor is there general consensus on even such basic questions as which foreign officials – beyond serving Heads of State or Government, Foreign Ministers, and diplomats[49] – are covered by such immunities.[50]

Several relatively recent decisions provide some sense of the state of international law on this question, while highlighting the ambiguities that surround it. In *Arrest Warrant of 11 April 2000 (Democratic Republic of the Congo v. Belgium)*, the ICJ observed that "in international law, it is firmly established that, as also diplomatic and consular agents, certain holders of high-ranking office in a State such as the Head of State, Head of Government and Minister for Foreign Affairs, enjoy immunities from jurisdiction in other States, both civil and criminal."[51] Following this decision, British courts have accorded immunity *ratione personae* to an incumbent

---

[46] This rationale has had special resonance in respect of Heads of State, who historically were seen to embody a State's sovereignty. *See Pinochet III, supra* note 22, at 592 (opinion of Lord Browne-Wilkinson) ("State immunity probably grew from the historical immunity of the person of the monarch."); Tachiona v. Mugabe, 169 F. Supp. 2d 259, 264 (S.D.N.Y. 2001), *aff'd in part, rev'd in part*, 386 F.3d 205 (2d Cir. 2004) (in an older time, "the State was the monarch and the monarch was the State"); *see also* Sir Arthur Watts, *The Legal Position in International Law of Heads of States, Heads of Governments and Foreign Ministers*, 247 RECUEIL DES COURS 35 (1994); Jerrold L. Mallory, Note, *Resolving the Confusion over Head of State Immunity: The Defined Rights of Kings*, 86 COLUM. L. REV. 169, 170 (1986). A similar rationale historically supported the immunity *ratione personae* accorded diplomats, who were seen as "emanations of the king." Mark A. Summers, *Diplomatic Immunity* Ratione Personae: *Did the International Court of Justice Create a New Customary Law Rule in Congo v. Belgium?*, 16 MICH. ST. J. INT'L L. 459, 462 (2007). *Compare Pinochet III, supra* note 22, at 592 (opinion of Lord Browne-Wilkinson) ("The diplomatic representative of the foreign state in the forum state is also afforded the same immunity [as a foreign head of state] in recognition of the dignity of the state which he represents.").

[47] *See* Summers, *supra* note 46, at 462.

[48] *See, e.g.,* Vienna Convention on Diplomatic Relations art. 29, Apr. 18, 1961, 22 U.S.T. 3227, 500 U.N.T.S. 95; Convention on the Privileges and Immunities of the United Nations, Feb. 13, 1946, 21 U.S.T. 1418, 1 U.N.T.S. 15; Convention on Special Missions, Dec. 8, 1969, 1400 U.N.T.S. 231.

[49] According to the ILC's Special Rapporteur on the immunity of State officials from foreign criminal jurisdiction, "Heads of State, Heads of Governments and ministers for foreign affairs constitute, in a manner of speaking, the basic threesome of State officials who enjoy personal immunity." Kolodkin, Preliminary Report, *supra* note 1, ¶ 111. *But see* Philippe Sands, *International Law Transformed? From Pinochet to Congo…?*, 16 LEIDEN J. INT'L L. 37, 48 (2003) (asserting, in relation to the ICJ's judgment in the *Arrest Warrant Case*: "There are questions … about the Court's treatment of foreign ministers in the same breath as heads of state … given the absence of state practice supporting that approach ….").

[50] *See* Kolodkin, Preliminary Report, *supra* note 1, ¶¶ 30, 109.

[51] *Arrest Warrant Case, supra* note 29, ¶ 51.

Minister of Defense[52] and an incumbent Minister for Commerce and International Trade.[53] But whereas national courts have thus extended immunities *ratione peronae* beyond those mentioned in the *Arrest Warrant* case, the ICJ itself has indicated that their reach is not unlimited. In a 2008 decision, the Court noted "that there are no grounds in international law upon which it could be said that [the *procureur de la République* and the Head of National Security of Djibouti] were entitled to personal immunities...."[54]

In part because the scope of immunities *ratione personae* under international law is not readily ascertained, delegates to the Rome Conference on the International Criminal Court ultimately decided that they would not attempt to specify those immunities.[55] Instead, article 98(1) of the Rome Statute incorporates by reference applicable principles of international law without trying to define them more specifically, providing that the ICC cannot:

> proceed for a request for surrender ... which would require the requested State to act inconsistently with *its obligations under international law with respect to the State or diplomatic immunity of a person* ... of a third State, unless the Court can first obtain the cooperation of that third State for the waiver of immunity.[56]

If it remains unsettled precisely which officials are covered by immunities *ratione personae* (or when),[57] the ICJ's 2002 judgment in the *Arrest Warrant* case clearly addressed a separate issue: Whether, if otherwise applicable, they apply in respect of a foreign State's effort to prosecute crimes against humanity. Until this ruling, some scholars and jurists had thought that Nuremberg Principle III addressed immunities *ratione personae* as well as immunities *ratione materiae*[58] (and indeed some still maintain that the ICJ got the law wrong on this point). But the ICJ ruled otherwise in its judgment in the *Arrest Warrant* case,[59] holding that Belgium violated the immunity *ratione personae* of the incumbent foreign minister of the Democratic Republic of the Congo by issuing an international arrest warrant even though the underlying charges involved crimes against humanity.

---

[52] Re General Shaul Mofaz, Bow St. Dist. Ct., Judgment (Feb. 12, 2004) (U.K.), 53 INT'L & COMP. L.Q. 771 (2004), *available at* http://journals.cambridge.org/production/action/cjoGetFulltext?fulltextid=1523460.

[53] Re Bo Xilai (Bow St. Mag. Ct. Nov. 8, 2005) (U.K.), *reprinted in* 128 I.L.R. 713.

[54] Certain Questions of Mutual Assistance in Criminal Matters (Djib. v. Fr.), 2008 I.C.J. 136, ¶ 194 (June 4).

[55] See TRIFFTERER, *supra* note 27, at 1602–03.

[56] See also Rome Statute, *supra* note 20, art. 27(2) (emphasis added).

[57] There is not even a general consensus about such basic issues as whether immunity *ratione personae* operates when the official concerned is traveling abroad on a private visit. *See, e.g.*, Micaela Frulli, *The ICJ Judgement on the Belgium v. Congo Case (14 February 2002): A Cautious Stand on Immunity from Prosecution for International Crimes*, 3 GERMAN L.J., ¶ 3 (2002), *available at* http://www.germanlawjournal.com/print.php?id=138.

[58] See Int'l Law Comm'n, *Final Draft Articles and Commentary (1996), Draft Code of Crimes against the Peace and Security of Mankind*, commentary to Article 7, U.N. Doc. A/CN.4/L.532 (July 8, 1996).

[59] *Arrest Warrant* case, *supra* note 29.

In dicta, the Court suggested various circumstances in which officials whom international law clothes with immunity *ratione personae* could nonetheless be prosecuted for crimes against humanity. Addressing the immunities enjoyed by foreign ministers, the Court observed that these officials "enjoy no criminal immunity under international law in their own countries, and may thus be tried by those countries' courts in accordance with the relevant rules of domestic law."[60] Of course, States may waive the immunities their representatives would otherwise enjoy.[61] Third, the Court recognized – albeit in ambiguous terms[62] – that immunities *ratione personae* no longer operate once the official ceases to hold the position of foreign minister.[63]

Finally, the Court noted that even incumbent foreign ministers "may be subject to criminal proceedings before certain international criminal courts, where they have jurisdiction," citing the ICTY, the ICTR, and the ICC as examples.[64] It did not explain the reasoning behind this dictum, however, except perhaps by way of noting that article 27(2) of the Rome Statute of the ICC specifically addresses this matter (see below), nor did it otherwise offer a test for determining which international courts fall within the legally significant category of "certain international courts."[65]

Particularly in light of the ICJ's decision in the *Arrest Warrant* case, the proposed convention on crimes against humanity would doubtless be interpreted as maintaining the immunities *ratione personae* conferred by customary and treaty law unless it included a provision establishing a different rule. This conclusion is reinforced by the Rome Statute of the International Criminal Court: The drafters of that treaty did not believe that a provision explicitly recognizing the nonapplicability of official immunities along the lines of Nuremberg Principle III would automatically resolve the question whether immunities *ratione personae* apply vis-à-vis incumbent officials. Instead, immediately following the previously mentioned provision

---

[60] *Id.* ¶ 61.
[61] *Id.*
[62] *Id.*
[63] *Id.*
[64] *Id.*
[65] One possibility is that the legal basis for the distinction between national and international courts is addressed somewhat differently for each relevant international tribunal. In respect of the ad hoc tribunals, nonimmunity might flow from the authority of the UN Security Council, which established those tribunals and adopted their statutes in the exercise of its Chapter VII authority. In the case of the ICC, nonimmunity of State officials might derive from the consent of States Parties to the Rome Statute as well as from the authority of the Security Council in cases resulting from a Security Council referral. In contrast to both of these instances, the postwar tribunals' authority might derive from the fact that they were convened by Occupying Powers in effect exercising sovereign authority in Germany and Japan, respectively. In this context, the immunity accorded *foreign* States' officials would not be relevant.

Another possibility is that genuinely international courts cannot, by definition, commit the affront to sovereign equality that one State's assertion of jurisdiction over another State's senior officials would entail. This rationale figured prominently in a 2004 decision by the Special Court for Sierra Leone. Confronted with a challenge to its exercise of jurisdiction over Charles Taylor, who was still president of Liberia when indicted by the SCSL Prosecutor, the Appeals Chamber

concerning immunities *ratione materiae* (article 27(1)), the Rome Statute separately provides in article 27(2):

> Immunities or special procedural rules which may attach to the official capacity of a person, whether under national or international law, shall not bar the Court from exercising its jurisdiction over such a person.

By virtue of this provision, States Parties to the Rome Statute in effect agree to abrogate the immunities *ratione personae* as well as immunities *ratione materiae* that their officials would otherwise enjoy if they are subject to the jurisdiction of the ICC.[66]

2. Proposed Convention on Crimes against Humanity

It seems doubtful that States are prepared to accept a treaty provision that abrogates the personal immunities that their officials would otherwise enjoy under customary international law. The current legal scope of immunities *ratione personae* is so uncertain that the International Law Commission is currently studying the matter.[67] The ILC study reflects in significant part States' general apprehension,

---

reasoned that the SCSL itself qualified as an international court for purposes of the distinction drawn by the ICJ in the *Arrest Warrant Case* and concluded that Taylor did not enjoy immunity *ratione personae* or *materiae*. *See Taylor Appeals Chamber Decision, supra* note 24, ¶¶ 34–54. The Appeals Chamber offered the following rationale for the distinction drawn in the *Arrest Warrant Case*:

> A reason for the distinction ... between national courts and international courts ... would appear [to be] due to ... the principle that one sovereign state does not adjudicate on the conduct of another state; the principle of state immunity derives from the equality of sovereign states and therefore has no relevance to international criminal tribunals which are not organs of a state but derive their mandate from the international community.

Id. ¶ 51. While this explanation is pertinent to the historically important rationale for Head of State immunity – the view that a State's leader is the embodiment of its sovereignty – a second reason noted by the SCSL Appeals Chamber is more relevant to the functional justification for immunities *ratione personae*: "states have regarded the collective judgment of the international community to provide a vital safeguard against the potential destabilizing effect of unilateral judgment in this area." *Id.* (quoting *amicus curiae* brief submitted by Diane Orentlicher).

Some believe that under customary law, officials may not assert immunity before international courts. Sometimes this position is asserted in a context that emphasizes immunity *ratione materiae*. *See, e.g.*, INT'L CTR. FOR TRANSITIONAL JUSTICE, HANDBOOK ON THE SPECIAL TRIBUNAL FOR LEBANON 11 (2008) (observing that, although the Statute of the Special Tribunal for Lebanon does not include a provision affirming the relevance of Nuremberg Principle III, "[a]n emerging norm under customary international law envisages that immunity for heads of states can be lifted before international courts for certain core international crimes such as genocide, war crimes, and crimes against humanity"). In other contexts, however, the view encompasses immunity *ratione personae*. *See, e.g., Pinochet III, supra* note 22, at 660 (opinion of Lord Phillips) ("The principle of state immunity provides no bar to the exercise of criminal jurisdiction by an international tribunal, but the instruments creating such tribunals have tended, nonetheless, to make it plain that no exception from responsibility or immunity from process is to be enjoyed by a head of state or other state official.").

[66] *See* TRIFFTERER, *supra* note 27, at 791. By virtue of article 98(1) of the Rome Statute, however, States Parties cannot do the same for non-Party States, and perhaps not even in respect of third-party States that have also adhered to the Rome Statute.

[67] *See* Kolodkin, Preliminary Report, *supra* note 1, ¶¶ 1–2.

in the wake of the *Pinochet* and other high-profile attempts to exercise universal jurisdiction against incumbent and former officials, about any further erosion of official immunities. In this setting, States are unlikely to agree to a further diminution of immunities now accorded their officials under international law. States would, of course, be bound to respect any applicable provisions set forth in an international/hybrid court's statute in situations involving transfers to such a court.

D. *Immunity under Domestic Law*

The immunities *ratione personae* accorded by international law to certain State officials, which rest in part on the principle that "one State shall not be subject to the jurisdiction of another State,"[68] are not applicable before their own courts.[69] Yet national law, including constitutional law, frequently accords immunities to a State's own officials.[70] For reasons implicit in the previous sections' analysis, language in the proposed convention corresponding to Nuremberg Principle III would require States Parties to ensure that State officials are not absolved from prosecution under national law. Such a commitment would be essential to the effectiveness of the *Proposed Convention*.

III. AMNESTIES

A. *Preliminary Observations*

There is some authority for the proposition that amnesties for crimes against humanity are inconsistent with customary law,[71] but this claim is hardly uncontested. It is widely agreed, however, that international treaties that require States Parties to prosecute a defined offense, such as genocide or torture, would be breached by an amnesty exempting perpetrators of these offenses from criminal prosecution. Similarly, as elaborated further, treaties that explicitly require States Parties to provide a remedy for violations of rights enumerated therein have been interpreted implicitly to proscribe amnesties that prevent victims from accessing an effective remedy.

---

[68] *Al-Adsani v. United Kingdom*, supra note 10, ¶ 54.
[69] *See Arrest Warrant Case*, supra note 29, ¶ 61 ("Accordingly, the immunities enjoyed under international law by an incumbent or former Minister for Foreign Affairs do not represent a bar to criminal prosecution in certain circumstances. First, such persons enjoy no criminal immunity under international law in their own countries, and may thus be tried by those countries' courts in accordance with the relevant rules of domestic law.").
[70] *See* BRUCE BROOMHALL, INTERNATIONAL JUSTICE AND THE INTERNATIONAL CRIMINAL COURT 139 n.43 (2003).
[71] *See* Prosecutor v. Kallon, Case No. SCSL-2004-15-AR72(E), and Kamara, Case No. SCSL-2004-16-AR72(E), Decision on Challenge to Jurisdiction: Lomé Accord Amnesty, ¶ 82 (Mar. 13, 2004), *available at* http://www.transcrim.org/07%20SCSL%20-%202004%20-%20Kallon%20

In this setting, if the proposed convention on crimes against humanity were silent on the question of amnesties, there is a strong chance that it would be interpreted implicitly to prohibit amnesties for crimes against humanity in the event that a State Party adopted such an amnesty and the amnesty were challenged before an international court – unless, as I elaborate below, the drafting history made this interpretation implausible. The principal practical issue, then, is whether the drafters should include an explicit prohibition on amnesties. For reasons noted below, this course would be unwise.

B. Overview of International Law Concerning Amnesties for Crimes Against Humanity

If the proposed convention included a provision explicitly prohibiting States Parties from adopting an amnesty law in respect of crimes against humanity, it would be the first multilateral human rights treaty to do so.[72] Even so, various treaties that require States Parties to criminalize and prosecute certain international offenses have been interpreted to be incompatible with amnesties that prevent prosecution of those crimes.

As noted earlier, there is wide agreement among international jurists that treaties that explicitly require States Parties to penalize certain offenses and to pursue criminal prosecutions when those crimes occur would be breached by an amnesty preventing such prosecutions.[73] Examples of such treaties include the Torture

---

Kamara [hereinafter *Kallon and Kamara Decision*] (a norm to the effect that "a government cannot grant amnesty for serious violations of crimes under international law ... is developing under international law"); Zimbabwe Human Rights NGO Forum v. Zimbabwe, Comm. 245/2002, ¶ 201 (2006), *reprinted in* TWENTY-FIRST ANNUAL ACTIVITY REPORT OF THE AFRICAN COMMISSION ON HUMAN AND PEOPLES' RIGHTS, Annex III, EX.CL/322(X), *available at* http://www.achpr.org/english/activity_reports/21%20Activity%20Report.pdf [hereinafter *Zimbabwe Human Rights NGO Forum*] ("There has been consistent international jurisprudence suggesting that the prohibition of amnesties leading to impunity for serious human rights has become a rule of customary international law"); *see also* U.N. Gen. Assembly, *Report of the Special Rapporteur on the Question of Torture and Other Cruel, Inhuman or Degrading Treatment or Punishment*, ¶ 33, U.N. Doc. A/56/156 (July 3, 2001) (*prepared by* Nigel Rodley, Special Rapporteur of the Commission on Human Rights) ("[C]onsistent international jurisprudence suggest[s] that the prohibition of amnesties leading to impunity for serious human rights has become a rule of customary international law.").

In a recent decision responding to the defendant's motion to compel evidence in support of his claim that he had been promised immunity from prosecution before the ICTY if he stepped down from public office, an ICTY Trial Chamber said that it "considers it well established that any immunity agreement in respect of an accused indicted for genocide, war crimes and/or crimes against humanity before an international tribunal would be invalid under international law." Prosecutor v. Radovan Karadžić, Case No. IT-95-5/18-PT, Decision on Accused's Second Motion for Inspection and Disclosure: Immunity Issue, ¶ 25 (Dec. 17, 2008). The Chamber did not provide any citations to supporting authority or indicate whether (or if so, why) it attached legal significance to the fact that the suspect was "indicted ... before an international tribunal."

[72] For this purpose, I do not include treaties between the United Nations and a particular State establishing a hybrid court.

[73] *See, e.g., Kallon and Kamara Decision, supra* note 71, ¶ 73; CASSESE, *supra* note 7, at 314.

Convention,[74] the Genocide Convention,[75] and the Geneva Conventions of 1949[76] and Additional Protocol No. 1.

Moreover, several treaty bodies have found that amnesties pertaining to gross violations of human rights, such as torture, extrajudicial executions, and enforced disappearance, are incompatible with States Parties' obligations under the relevant treaty even though it does not explicitly require prosecution. For example the Human Rights Committee has found that States Parties to the International Covenant on Civil and Political Rights "may not relieve perpetrators from personal responsibility, as has occurred with certain amnesties," for "violations recognized as criminal under either domestic or international law, such as torture and similar cruel, inhuman and degrading treatment ..., summary and arbitrary killing ... and enforced disappearance."[77]

The most extensive treatment of this issue has occurred within the Inter-American human rights system. The Inter-American Commission and Court of Human Rights have repeatedly found amnesties preventing prosecution of gross violations of the rights protected by the American Convention on Human Rights to violate that convention – again, despite the fact that it does not explicitly impose an obligation to prosecute certain offenses.[78] In recent cases, the Inter-American Court has placed special emphasis on the duty to combat impunity for crimes against humanity.[79]

While the amnesty jurisprudence of the African Commission on Human and Peoples' Rights is significantly less developed, the Commission has found a 2000 Zimbabwean amnesty to be incompatible with the African Charter on Human and Peoples' Rights.[80] Although the European Court of Human Rights has not yet ruled on the compatibility of an amnesty with the European Convention for the Protection of Human Rights and Fundamental Freedoms, it has repeatedly found

---

[74] See ANDREAS O'SHEA, AMNESTY FOR CRIME IN INTERNATIONAL LAW AND PRACTICE 186 (2002) (asserting that the provisions of the Convention against Torture requiring States Parties to extradite or prosecute suspected torturers are "inconsistent with amnesty from criminal prosecution"); ASS'N FOR THE PREVENTION OF TORTURE & THE CTR. FOR JUSTICE & INT'L LAW, TORTURE IN INTERNATIONAL LAW: A GUIDE TO JURISPRUDENCE 19 (2008) (citing the Committee against Torture's repeated affirmation of the principle that States Parties to the Convention against Torture must "ensure that amnesty laws exclude torture from their reach").

[75] See O'SHEA, supra note 74, at 185 ("The granting of amnesty to an individual for an act of genocide or other related act under article III [of the Genocide Convention] would be a clear violation of a state's international obligations in terms of the Convention.").

[76] See CASSESE, supra note 7, at 314.

[77] U.N. Comm'n on Human Rights, General Comment No. 31 [80]: Nature of the General Legal Obligation Imposed on States Parties to the Covenant, ¶ 18, U.N. Doc. CCPR/C/21/Rev.1/Add.13 (May 26, 2004). This General Comment notes that when "committed as part of a widespread or systematic attack on a civilization population, these violations of the Covenant are crimes against humanity." Id.

[78] See, e.g., Chumbipuma Aguirre et al. v. Peru (Barrios Altos Case), Inter-Am. Ct. H.R. (ser. C) No. 75, ¶¶ 39–41 (Mar. 14, 2001).

[79] See Almonacid-Arellano et al. v. Chile, Inter-Am Ct. H.R. (ser. C) No. 154, ¶ 114 (Sept. 26, 2006); Goiburú et al. v. Paraguay, Inter-Am. Ct. H.R. (ser. C) No. 153, ¶ 128 (Sept. 22, 2006), available at http://www.corteidh.or.cr/docs/casos/articulos/seriec_153_ing.doc.

[80] Zimbabwe Human Rights NGO Forum, supra note 71, ¶¶ 211–12.

that when certain violations occur, States Parties must conduct a thorough and effective investigation capable of leading to the identification and punishment of those responsible.[81]

C. Proposed Convention on Crimes Against Humanity: Amnesties

In light of the trends summarized in Section III.B, it may seem to follow that the proposed convention on crimes against humanity should include a provision explicitly ruling out amnesties for these crimes. Yet relatively recent experience during the preparatory work for adoption of an international treaty on enforced disappearances suggests that States are not prepared to accept such explicit language.

The treaty on enforced disappearance was preceded by a 1992 UN Declaration on the Protection of All Persons from Enforced Disappearance.[82] Article 18(1) of that declaration provides: "Persons who have or are alleged to have committed [the offense of enforced disappearance] shall not benefit from any special amnesty law or similar measures that might have the effect of exempting them from any criminal proceedings or sanction." The first draft of the International Convention on the Protection of All Persons from Forced Disappearance, prepared by a working group of the UN Sub-Commission on Prevention of Discrimination and Protection of Minorities on the Administration of Justice in 1998, included a similar provision:

> The perpetrators or suspected perpetrators of and other participants in the offense of forced disappearance … shall not benefit from any amnesty measure or similar measures prior to their trial and, where applicable, conviction that would have the effect of exempting them from any criminal action or penalty.[83]

As the drafting process progressed, however, it was impossible to secure agreement about the issue of amnesties,[84] and the International Convention for the Protection of All Persons from Enforced Disappearance,[85] the text of which was adopted in 2006 and which is not yet in force, does not include a provision corresponding to

---

[81] See, e.g., Musayeva et al. v. Russia, App. No. 74239/01, Eur. Ct. H.R., ¶¶ 85–86, 116 (2007).
[82] Declaration on the Protection of All Persons from Enforced Disappearances, G.A. Res. 47/133, U.N. Doc. A/RES/47/133 (Dec. 18, 1992).
[83] U.N. Comm. on Human Rights, Sub-Comm. on the Prot. & Promotion of Human Rights, Report of the Sessional Working Group on the Administration of Justice, U.N. Doc. E/CN.4/Sub.2/1998/19, Annex, draft art. 17(1) (Aug. 19, 1998).
[84] See, e.g., U.N. Comm. on Human Rights, Report of the Intersessional Open-Ended Working Group to Elaborate a Draft Legally Binding Normative Instrument for the Protection of All Persons from Enforced Disappearance, ¶¶ 73–80, U.N. Doc. E/CN.4/2004/59 (Feb. 23, 2004). According to this report, "[s]ome delegations considered that the existence of amnesties could not be ignored, [and] that they were sometimes necessary elements of processes of national reconciliation …." Id. ¶ 76.
[85] International Convention for the Protection of All Persons from Enforced Disappearance, Dec. 20, 2006, U.N. Doc. A/RES/61/177 (opened for signature Feb. 6, 2007, but not yet in force).

article 18(1) of the 1992 declaration.[86] Summarizing the negotiations, two authors explain:

> No consensus could be found on such a delicate issue. Some delegations, notwithstanding the generally recognized need for a development of international law in view of granting broader protection to human rights, pointed out that introducing a clause expressly prohibiting any amnesty in a legally binding instrument would have been an unprecedented step and too serious a limitation to the domestic jurisdiction of States, hindering processes of national reconciliation. Other States were ready to send a clear message to international society about this serious undertaking in the fight against impunity. Given the circumstances, the Intersessional Working Group preferred not to mention the issue of amnesties, pardons or similar measures and limited itself to appealing to the good faith of governments.[87]

This experience does not mean that States would inevitably take the same approach in respect of crimes against humanity. Indeed, during a 2003 drafting session for the treaty on disappearances, "[s]everal participants said that they were not opposed to amnesty in cases of enforced disappearance which did not constitute crimes against humanity"[88] – implying that even those opposed to a general "no amnesty" clause believed that such a clause would be appropriate when it came to crimes against humanity.

Still, many States would doubtless oppose including a "no amnesty" provision in the proposed convention on crimes against humanity. In recent years, there has been robust debate about whether evolving international principles opposing

---

[86] International human rights advocates were concerned that omission of a "no amnesty" provision from the final text would set back legal developments in combating impunity that had taken place outside the drafting process. Thus while the Convention on Enforced Disappearance was being drafted, a leading human rights organization called upon States to reintroduce a "no amnesty" provision, reasoning:

> The FIDH strongly supports reintroducing a measure to ban the amnesty on enforced disappearances. *The lack of such a measure could be interpreted as a negative precedent in the construction of a customary rule, currently in preparation.* The group's refusal to prohibit the amnesty of such a serious violation as enforced disappearances would considerably weaken the scope of the instrument by enabling states to paralyse all their penal obligations and by opening up the possibility of impunity for the perpetrators of the disappearances.

Int'l Fed'n of Human Rights, *Summary of Comments by F.I.D.H. on the Draft Text 21st June 2004*, Oct. 4, 2004, *available at* http://www.fidh.org/spip.php?article2053 (emphasis added).

[87] TULLIO SCOVAZZI & GABRIELLA CITRONI, THE STRUGGLE AGAINST ENFORCED DISAPPEARANCE AND THE 2007 UNITED NATIONS CONVENTION 328–29 (2007); *see also* OLIVIER DE FROUVILLE, LA CONVENTION DES NATIONS UNIES POUR LA PROTECTION DE TOUTES LES PERSONNES CONTRE LES DISPARITIONS FORCEES: LE ENJEUX JURIDIQUES D'UNE NEGOCIATION EXEMPLAIRE 46 n.175, *available at* http://www.icaed.org/fileadmin/user_upload/df6odfdf.pdf (In French, unofficially translated via Google) (due to the difficulties in negotiating the amnesty provisions, "several states and most of the NGOs felt that the only solution was to request that this issue not [be] included in the future instrument").

[88] U.N. Comm. on Human Rights, *Report of the Intersessional Open-Ended Working Group to Elaborate a Draft Legally Binding Normative Instrument for the Protection of All Persons from Enforced Disappearance*, ¶ 52, U.N. Doc. E/CN.4/2003/71 (Feb. 12, 2003).

amnesty for serious crimes under international law may be too inflexible. In particular, many have urged that amnesties can play an important role in ending violent conflict or in clearing the way for traditional processes of reconciliation to operate effectively in the aftermath of mass atrocity.[89]

With vigorous debate on these issues still very much under way, they are unlikely to be resolved during negotiations for a convention on crimes against humanity. In all likelihood, States and human rights organizations that support a "no amnesty" provision would, in the face of proposals that dilute the strength of such a provision, conclude that it is best to exclude such language altogether.

Indeed, the likelihood of securing consensus on such a provision may be so remote that it is best not even to propose language to this effect – the approach taken in the current *Proposed Convention* on crimes against humanity. This would allow future interpretations of the *Proposed Convention* to benefit from evolving experience and international practice without undermining principles that are gaining strength through their repudiation by negotiating States.

---

[89] This same issue has been vigorously debated in the context of the ICC's indictments of key protagonists in ongoing armed conflicts. In this setting, the focus of debate has been whether the UN Security Council should exercise its power, pursuant to article 16 of the Rome Statute, to defer an investigation/prosecution undertaken by the ICC Prosecutor.

10

Modes of Participation

Elies van Sliedregt

I. INTRODUCTION

Violations of international humanitarian law entail what Röling called "system criminality."[1] Indeed, international crimes such as crimes against humanity often occur on a mass scale or in the context of systemic violence. System criminality generally concerns a plurality of offenders, particularly in carrying out the crimes. It further presupposes an *auctor intellectualis*, or an "intellectual perpetrator," pulling the strings. This can be one person, but also a group of people gathered together in a political or military structure. Any international prosecutor will acknowledge that linking those two levels – the intellectual perpetrator at leadership level and the plurality of offenders at execution level – is a difficult task. This chapter will discuss both traditional forms of liability (commission, instigation, and aiding and abetting/complicity) and crime-specific modes of liability. The latter have been conceptualized to punish "intellectual perpetrators" by way of inchoate modes of liability (conspiracy, incitement) or by linking the intellectual and execution levels (indirect perpetration, participation in a criminal enterprise, and superior responsibility).

The problem of linking crimes of foot soldiers to the masterminds is not new. In setting up the International Military Tribunal (IMT) at Nuremberg, U.S. Army Colonel Bernays devised a liability theory based on the concepts of conspiracy and membership in a criminal organization that would enable the conviction of not only the perpetrators of crimes but also their superiors and the thousands of lower-ranking Nazi culprits who had been passive observers. The theory was never fully implemented in practice. The concept of conspiracy was controversial, as was the concept of a crime of (irrefutable) membership in a criminal organization. The latter concepts were downgraded in the case law of occupation tribunals and military courts to more familiar national concepts of participating in an "association de malfaiteurs," "acting with a common purpose," and complicity liability.[2] Bernays' theory serves to illustrate the peculiarity of system criminality and the challenges it poses to principles of criminal law, above all the principle of personal culpability.

---

[1] Bernard Victor Aloysius Röling, *Aspects of the Criminal Responsibility for Violations of the Laws of War, in* THE NEW HUMANITARIAN LAW OF ARMED CONFLICT 203 (Antonio Cassese ed., 1979).

[2] ELIES VAN SLIEDREGT, THE CRIMINAL RESPONSIBILITY OF INDIVIDUALS FOR VIOLATIONS OF INTERNATIONAL HUMANITARIAN LAW 16–31 (2003).

A. Individual Criminal Responsibility

One of the fundamental principles underlying modern criminal law is the principle of individual autonomy. In the words of Ashworth, "each individual should be treated as responsible for his or her own behaviour."[3] This principle is based on the assumption that individuals have the capacity and free will to make their own choices.[4] From this follows the principle of personal responsibility. As Anthony Kenny has submitted, "it is unjust to hold individuals criminally responsible for their acts and omissions unless those acts and omissions are themselves voluntary acts and omissions."[5]

The principle that a person can only be held responsible to the degree and extent of his or her own personal fault applies equally to international criminal law. Whether it is abided by, however, is another matter. Broad liability concepts have been developed in the case law of international tribunals that threaten to exceed the limits of individual culpability. It should be noted that this is not unique to international criminal law. To meet the demands of a changed society where collective actors interact like individuals and crime is highly organized and carried out on a large scale, individual responsibility has expanded in domestic criminal law as well.[6] This should not reassure international lawmakers. On the contrary, it serves to demonstrate that in dealing with system criminality, the danger of developing liability concepts that might stray into a type of collective responsibility looms largely.

B. Domestic Prosecutions

The proliferation of international criminal tribunals and courts in the last decades of the twentieth century has influenced national criminal justice systems. National governments adopted legislation to provide the legal basis for cooperating with these institutions. They also initiated prosecutions for international crimes, albeit somewhat hesitantly. With the adoption of the Statute for an International Criminal Court (ICC Statute) in 1998 and its coming into force in 2002, the tide has turned in favor of national prosecution of international crimes.

The *Proposed International Convention on the Prevention and Punishment of Crimes Against Humanity* (*Proposed Convention*) stipulates that States have a duty to exercise criminal jurisdiction over those who allegedly commit crimes against humanity (article 10) and to cooperate fully with other States to ensure the capacity of each State to fulfill its obligations to prevent and punish crimes against humanity (preamble, cl.8).

---

[3] ANDREW ASHWORTH, PRINCIPLES OF CRIMINAL LAW 27 (3d ed. 1999).
[4] This approach is contrasted by the determinist claim that all human action is compelled and determined by causes that an individual cannot control. For a more elaborate discussion, *see* ANTHONY KENNY, FREEWILL AND RESPONSIBILITY 22–44 (1978).
[5] *Id.* at 34.
[6] VAN SLIEDREGT, *supra* note 2, at 345–46.

The question of domestic prosecutions raises the issue of the interplay between national and international norms relating to criminal responsibility. In adjudicating international crimes, domestic courts may be expected to apply international standards derived from international case or statutory law and to represent the interests of the international community – especially when exercising universal jurisdiction. The complementarity principle underlying the ICC Statute and considerations concerning legal equality will prompt an "internationalist approach" – that is, the application of international standards.[7] Especially with regard to concepts that have an international pedigree, for example, definitions of crimes and a liability concept such as superior/command responsibility, it makes sense to apply international standards,[8] even if that means disregarding (conflicting) national standards.[9]

However, an internationalist approach is not always the most appropriate approach. Under certain circumstances, it can even be undesirable. As one commentator has noted, "it is by no means self-evident that time-honoured general parts of criminal law should yield to their international equivalents, as this would probably cause unwarranted differences in the administration of criminal justice within one legal system."[10] This view is particularly compelling when international criminal law fails to offer clear guidance or is not fully crystallized.[11]

Adopting a "national approach" means that we accept a certain degree of divergence in adjudicating international crimes at the domestic level. Indeed, the shift from international to national adjudication is likely to enhance the divergence of international criminal law (ICL). Such divergence will only be increased and complicated by the fact that there is divergence at the international level as well – the law of the ad hoc tribunals and the ICC deviates with regard to certain liability concepts, most prominently with regard to superior responsibility and joint criminal enterprise (JCE).

The drafters of the *Proposed Convention* should be aware of the interplay between national and international norms of liability and aim for a liability provision that

---

[7] See *Rome Statute of the International Criminal Court*, United Nations Diplomatic Conference of Plenipotentiaries on the Establishment of an International Criminal Court, July 17, 1998, art. 17, U.N. Doc. A/CONF.183/9 [hereinafter *Rome Statute*]. By not adhering to ICC standards or modes of liability, a State Party may be regarded as "unable" to prosecute or effectively punish.

[8] See Harmen van der Wilt, *Equal Standards? On the Dialectics between National Jurisdictions and the International Criminal Court*, 8 INT'L CRIM. L. REV. 229 (2008); Elies van Sliedregt, *Complicity to Commit Genocide*, in THE UN GENOCIDE CONVENTION: A COMMENTARY (Paola Gaeta ed., 2009).

[9] As did The Hague District Court in the *Van Anraat* case with regard to the *mens rea* of complicity in genocide. Van Anraat, Arrondissementsrechtsbank [Rb.] [District Court, The Hague], 23 December 2005, LJN AU8685 § 7 (Neth.); *see also* Mugesera v. Canada, [2005] 2 S.C.R. 9, 2005 SCC 39 (Can.). One might legitimately question the precedence that was given to international standards in both cases. See Harmen van der Wilt, *Genocide v. War Crimes in the Van Anraat Appeal*, 6 J. INT'L CRIM. JUST. 557 (2008).

[10] *See* van der Wilt, *supra* note 8, at 254.

[11] *See* Public Prosecutor v. Van Anraat, Gerechtshof [Hof] [Court of Appeal, The Hague], 9 May 2007, LJN BA4676 § 7 (Neth.).

encapsulates concepts that are familiar to most national criminal justice systems and word it in neutral and loose terms. This will facilitate implementation at the national level and could limit (further) divergence. Indeed, compared to most national criminal justice systems, ICL is an undertheorized and even inconsistent body of law[12] – not necessarily an obvious choice for a national legislator or judge when the alternative is national criminal law.

C. Modalities of Liability

Conventions that are most comparable to the *Proposed Convention* – the Genocide Convention and the Convention Against Torture (CAT) – provide for liability provisions that reflect municipal criminal law concepts. The Torture Convention provides for commission, attempt, complicity, and participation in torture in article 4. Article III of the Genocide Convention lists as modes of liability commission, attempt, complicity, conspiracy, and direct and public incitement. "Commission," "complicity," and "attempt" can be termed traditional forms of liability in that they are the most common ways of committing crimes; they would make up the vast majority of cases in any domestic criminal justice system. "Conspiracy" and "incitement" are more crime-specific because they address the organized nature of international crimes and focus on the intellectual rather than the direct/physical perpetrator characteristics of what I termed earlier as system criminality.

Both modalities, "traditional" and "crime specific," feature in domestic law. This explains why many States Parties to the Genocide Convention and the CAT felt no need to specifically enact legislation with regard to the liability provisions in these treaties. It was felt that domestic criminal law already provided for such liability, whether in the unwritten common law or the general part in a (written) criminal code. The UK position with regard to article III(e) of the Genocide Convention is illustrative in this respect. The Parliamentary Secretary, when introducing the treaty to Parliament, observed that:

> [c]omplicity in genocide has not been included in Clause 2(1) because we take the view that the sub-heading in Article III (of the Genocide Convention) is subsumed in the act of genocide itself in exactly the same way as, under our domestic criminal law, aiding and abetting is a situation in which a person so charged could be charged as a principal in relation to the offence itself.[13]

There is yet another category of crime-specific modes of liability that has come to the fore since the establishment of international courts and tribunals. It concerns liability modes that have been specifically conceptualized at the international level

---

[12] As pointed out by a group of critical scholars, see Darryl Robinson, *The Identity Crisis of International Criminal Law*, 21 LEIDEN J. INT'L L. 925 (2008); GÖRAN SLUITER & ALEXANDER ZAHAR, INTERNATIONAL CRIMINAL LAW: A CRITICAL INTRODUCTION (2006).

[13] 777 PARL. DEB., H.C. (5th ser.) (1969) 480–509 (U.K.), *cited in* WILLIAM A. SCHABAS, GENOCIDE IN INTERNATIONAL LAW: THE CRIMES OF CRIMES 287 (2000).

and that have been applied to international crimes. The latter can be referred to as "atrocity-crime-specific," differing from the aforementioned crime-specific modalities. Superior responsibility is a genuine international mode of liability. Another concept that could be mentioned in this context is JCE. It differs from superior responsibility, however, in that it originates from national law (common purpose liability in English law), yet it has moved away from those origins as it has been applied and further developed in international case law. JCE is "international" to the extent that it is specifically attuned to international crimes; at least it is conceptualized on the basis of facts that relate to the commission of genocide, crimes against humanity, and war crimes, and because it merges elements derived from different national criminal justice systems.

Against this backdrop, it could be argued that States can no longer afford to rely on their respective general parts of criminal law, as did the United Kingdom with regard to the concept of "complicity" in the Genocide Convention. Certain liability concepts are so specific to international crimes that they require separate implementation at the national level. Still, the "atrocity-crime-specific" argument should not be exaggerated. Most national legal systems provide for liability concepts that capture systemic criminality. Only a limited class of liability modes qualify as "atrocity-crime-specific" in that they have no equivalent in national law because they are specifically attuned to international crimes.

In the following section, liability modes will be discerned in traditional modes of liability and (atrocity) crime-specific types of liability. Traditional modes of liability are regarded as dealing with individual forms of criminality, whereas (atrocity) crime-specific liability is specifically attuned to system criminality. Superior responsibility will be discussed in a separate section because it is a specific form of liability that warrants a more elaborate analysis.

D. Approach

It is opportune to take as a starting point international liability concepts when conducting research into responsibility for crimes against humanity. After all, most of the relevant case law is produced by international tribunals and courts. However, it is submitted that these concepts should be viewed in the light of national criminal law. This is appropriate against the background of the previously mentioned shift to domestic prosecutions. Moreover, most international modes of liability are modeled on national law. Thus, modes of participation in the CAH convention should reflect concepts of liability that can be found at the national level. It is, therefore, important to uncover the national origins of international liability concepts and to see which possible analogous concepts exist in domestic law (vertical comparison).

Any exercise of comparative criminal law made for the purpose of conceptualizing modes of liability should abide by the principle of legality (*nullum crimen sine lege*). This means that national liability concepts and theories should constitute general principles of criminal law while standards/elements derived from international statutory and case law should reflect rules of customary international law.

II. TRADITIONAL MODES OF LIABILITY[14]

A. *Commission*

The term "commission" is equivocal in that it may be used in a narrow and broad sense. In a narrow sense, it refers to direct and indirect perpetration of a crime, that is, physical and intellectual perpetration. In a broad sense, it includes both physical and intellectual perpetration and participation in a crime. Article 25(2) of the ICC Statute stipulates: "a person who commits a crimes within the jurisdiction of the Court shall be individually responsible and liable for punishment." Here, "commits" is used in a broad sense, extending to perpetration and participation. In paragraph (3)(a) of article 25, "commits" is used in the narrow sense: "commits such a crime, whether as an individual, jointly with another or through another person."

Rather than adopting the terminology of direct and indirect perpetration, the ad hoc tribunals use the verb "commit." "Committing" at the ad hoc tribunals covers direct perpetration and participation as in the common purpose doctrine, leaving aiding and abetting outside it. Indirect perpetration (perpetration through/by way of another person) is not recognized as such. In *Tadić*, the Appeals Chamber held:

> This provision (article 7(1)) covers first and foremost the physical perpetration of a crime by the offender himself, or the culpable omission of an act that was mandated by a rule of criminal law. However, the commission of one of the crimes envisaged in Articles 2, 3, 4 or 5 of the Statute might also occur through participation in the realisation of a common design or purpose.[15]

Article 4 of the *Proposed Convention* adopts almost verbatim the language of article 25 in the Rome Statute, and it seems safe to assume that the word "commits" in article 4(1) and 4(2)(a) of the *Proposed Convention* has the same meaning as "commits" in article 25(2) in 25(3)(a) of the Rome Statute.

1. Omission Liability

Most national legal systems accept that "omissive behaviour" is implied in provisions penalizing positive criminal conduct, provided verbs suggesting action are part of the crime's definition.[16] This type of omission, which is referred to as "commission

---

[14] This chapter draws from the author's book, van SLIEDREGT, THE CRIMINAL RESPONSIBILITY, *supra* note 2.
[15] Prosecutor v. Tadić, Case No. IT-94-1-A, Judgment, ¶ 188 (July 15, 1999) [hereinafter *Tadić Appeals Judgment*].
[16] JEAN PRADEL, DROIT PÉNAL COMPARÉ 235–36 (1995); HANS-HEINRICH JESCHECK & THOMAS WEIGEND, LEHRBUCH DES STRAFRECHTS, ALLGEMEINER TEIL 612–13 (5th ed. 1996).

by omission," in German terminology *"unechte Unterlassungsdelikete"*[17] or in Anglo-American terms "indirect" omissions,[18] should be distinguished from "genuine" or "direct" omissions. In the latter case, the definition of the crime constitutes criminal inaction, for example, the failure of a subpoenaed person to appear as a witness or the failure of a commander to prevent offenses committed by his subordinate. Genuine crimes of omission are usually conduct crimes, whereas crimes that qualify as commission by omission are often result crimes.

Commission by omission is a construction of doctrine and has its basis in jurisprudence. This explains why French courts and commentators reject the concept. Endorsing a very strict legality principle, French courts maintain that, in principle, there is no liability for commission by omission.[19] We must understand the French position against the historical importance of individual freedom and the concomitant strict legality principle. This explains the relatively late acceptance of a general offense of omission, such as the failure to assist a person in peril, comprised in article 223–6(2) of the Code Pénal of 1994.[20]

The failed attempt of the ICC drafters to draw up a general provision on omission should not be interpreted as rejecting omission liability altogether. In other words, silence on the part of the legislators should not be taken as to exclude omission liability from article 25 of the ICC Statute. A strict interpretation of the legality principle cannot be an obstacle to extending criminal responsibility as laid down in article 25 to include criminal omission. Article 22 of the ICC Statute does not relate to modes of criminal responsibility but to crimes. As Boot observes:

> The Statutory provision in Article 22, containing *nullum crimen sine lege*, does not concern Article 25 containing provisions on individual criminal responsibility. Article 25 only comes into play after it has been established that the "conduct in question constitutes, at the time it takes place, a crime within the jurisdiction of the Court."[21]

---

[17] JESCHECK & WEIGEND, *supra* note 16, at 605–12.
[18] A classic example of "commission by omission" in national law is the case of the parent who neglects to feed his or her child. Not feeding the child causes it to die, which amounts to murder. *See, e.g.*, R. v. Emery, (1993) 14 Crim. App. (S) 394 (U.K.), *in* ASHWORTH, *supra* note 3, at 115.
[19] PRADEL, *supra* note 16, at 236.
[20] "Sera puni des mêmes peines quiconque s'abstient volontairement de porter à une personne en péril l'assistance que, sans risque pour lui ou pour les tiers, il pouvait lui prêter soit par son action personnelle, soit en provoquant un secours." C. PÉN. ART. 223–6(2) (1994) (Fr.) (Translation: "Any person who wilfully abstains from rendering assistance to a person in peril when he or she could have rendered that assistance without risk to himself, herself, or others, either by acting personally or by calling for aid, is liable to the same penalties." 31 THE AMERICAN SERIES OF FOREIGN PENAL CODES: FRANCE (Edward A. Tomlinson ed., 1999)). *See* Kai Ambos, *Superior Responsibility*, *in* THE ROME STATUTE OF THE INTERNATIONAL CRIMINAL COURT: A COMMENTARY 850 (Antonio Cassese et al. eds., 2002).
[21] MACHTELD BOOT, GENOCIDE, CRIMES AGAINST HUMANITY, WAR CRIMES: NULLUM CRIMEN SINE LEGE AND THE SUBJECT MATTER JURISDICTION OF THE INTERNATIONAL CRIMINAL COURT 395, § 369 (2002).

It is not clear whether "commission" in the *Proposed Convention* explicitly allows for the material element to be "committed" by omission. In earlier drafts, this was made explicit. Bearing in mind the almost verbatim adoption of articles 25 and 28 of the Rome Statute in articles 4 and 5 the *Proposed Convention*, one could legitimately adopt the same approach to omission liability as in the Rome Statute: It is part of "commission liability." Moreover, bearing in mind the purpose of this treaty and the interplay with national criminal law, it is undesirable to adopt a narrow approach and only understand "commission" as to imply active conduct.

2. Perpetration

The distinction between perpetration and participation, or principal liability and secondary/accomplice liability, is recognized in most criminal law systems. The terminology that is used to refer to these forms of liability is confusing because it does not refer to similar forms of liability. Depending on which liability model one relies upon, principal liability may refer, and be limited, to physical perpetration, as in Anglo-American complicity law. Yet, it may also extend to "intellectual perpetration," such as joint perpetration and perpetration through or by means of another person. The latter are modes of liability that qualify as separate and principal modes of liability in certain civil law systems.[22] "Principal" in the latter sense has a connotation of serious moral blameworthiness. This is different in Anglo-American complicity law, where the principal/secondary distinction is a mere technical distinction. In English law, those who jointly perpetrate or instigate crimes may be referred to as "secondary parties" (those who aid, abet, counsel, or procure) and qualify as participants in a crime. Secondary parties/participants are not less culpable than principals/perpetrators. On the contrary, those who abet (instigate) crimes can be more culpable than the principal who physically commits the crime. In the sentencing stage, secondary parties/accomplices/participants receive the sentence that appropriately reflects their role.

Thus, when using concepts such as indirect and joint perpetration, we refer to secondary liability and participation in terms of Anglo-American complicity law. Not recognizing this ambiguity complicates debates and may lead to confusion, as it did at the International Criminal Tribunal for the former Yugoslavia (ICTY) with regard to JCE (is it participation or a form of perpetration/"commission"?).[23]

In the following, the term "direct perpetration" will be relied on to refer to physically committing the crime. "Indirect perpetration" will be used to refer to nonphysical/intellectual forms of perpetration, such as perpetration through or by means of another person (e.g., innocent agency, functional perpetration and

---

[22] VAN SLIEDREGT, *supra* note 2, at 61–64.
[23] *See* Elies van Sliedregt, *Joint Criminal Enterprise as a Pathway to Convicting Individuals for Genocide*, 5 J. INT'L CRIM. JUST. 184, § 3B (2007).

Organisationsherrschaft). Both direct and indirect perpetration will be regarded as forms of principal liability, like joint liability or co-perpetration. To keep a strict distinction between "perpetration" and "principal liability" on the one hand and participation on the other hand, the term "participation" will be used below to refer to what is generally considered "secondary" or accomplice liability (e.g., aiding/abetting and instigation).

3. Joint Perpetration

Joint or co-perpetration is recognized as a separate ground of liability in most civil law systems. Joint perpetration, such as the German "*Mittäterschaft*," the Belgian "coaction," or the Dutch "*medeplegen*" are distinguished from complicity as mere facilitation.[24] Co-perpetration connotes full cooperation in the crime. In those systems that recognize two types of accomplices – co-perpetrators and facilitators – it has proven difficult to distinguish between the two. Yet doing so is vital, because facilitators, who have a subsidiary status as helpers, are punished less severely than co-perpetrators.

The structure of Anglo-American complicity law, with a perpetrator who most immediately or directly *causes* the *actus reus* and an accomplice whose responsibility derives from that of the principal, has its limits.[25] It cannot capture the factual situation of two or more participants each making a direct contribution to an element of the *actus reus*. The same can be said about the situation when only one participant causes the *actus reus* while both participants share the *mens rea*. The doctrine of common purpose or JCE compensates for this "deficiency" in the Anglo-American complicity doctrine by not requiring an exact identification of the causal contributions that led to the offense(s), but rather leaving them under the cover of "joint enterprise" or "common purpose."[26] Common purpose is based on the principles of accomplice liability where the responsibility of the one is (partly) derived from the causal contribution of the other, and where joint "principals" are each liable for their joint acts and are punished for the principal crime.

French law, like Anglo-American law, has struggled to accommodate the notion of co-perpetrator or "*coauteur*" because of the derivative nature of its complicity theory, based on the notion of "*emprunt de pénalité*."[27] Under the 1810 Code, the accomplice was punished *as a* principal, whereas under article 121–7, the accomplice

---

[24] Mittäterschaft, StGB art. 25(2) (German Penal Code); Penal Code art. 66 (Belgian Penal Code); Sr art. 47(1) (Dutch Penal Code).

[25] For a discussion on the relationship between causation and complicity, see K.J.M. Smith, A Modern Treatise on the Law of Criminal Complicity 69 (1991); Sanford H. Kadish, *Complicity, Cause and Blame: A Study in the Interpretation of Doctrine*, 73 Cal. L. Rev. 323 (1985); H.L.A. Hart & Tony Honoré, Causation in the Law (1959).

[26] J.C. Smith & Brian Hogan, Criminal Law 209–34 (8th ed. 1996).

[27] Frédéric Desportes & Francis Le Gunehec, Le Nouveau Droit Pénal 494, § 566 (7th ed. 2000).

is now punished *as if he were* the principal. "*Coauteurs*" are distinguished from accomplices in that they are liable in their own right. The difference between "*coauteurs*" and accomplices is that the "*coauteur*" is *considered to have* performed the acts that constitute the offense, whereas the accomplice has performed ancillary acts with a view to assisting the offense.[28] In essence, the "*coauteur*" is a secondary party, just like any other accomplice.

The derivative nature of complicity liability in the ICTY and the International Criminal Tribunal for Rwanda (ICTR) case law has been an obstacle to recognizing the concept of joint perpetration in the case law of these institutions. By now, JCE I features as such,[29] yet as will appear below when discussing JCE more fully, there has been much debate and misunderstandings over whether co-perpetration is the same as participation in a JCE. The *Tadić* Appeals Chamber brought the concept under the heading "committing" and distinguished it from aiding and abetting a crime, which, it held, is generally couched in terms of "participating" in an offense[30] and which was found to "[u]nderstate the degree of criminal responsibility."[31] On the other hand, it referred to common purpose/JCE as "a form of accomplice liability."[32] To complicate matters even further, the Appeals Chamber used the terms "perpetrator" and "co-perpetrator" to refer to a *participant* in a JCE.[33] It thus seemed that co-perpetration as a civil law concept was cloaked in terms of Anglo-American accomplice liability. Although some Trial Chambers did not accept the term "co-perpetrator," it is by now settled in the law of the ad hoc tribunals that there is a distinction between facilitators, those aiding and abetting, and those more fully engaged in the commission of the crime as joint or co-perpetrators.[34]

Article 25(3)(a) of the ICC Statute provides for perpetration "jointly with another." The Statute thus recognizes joint perpetration as an autonomous head of participation. Joint or co-perpetration connotes two or more perpetrators who each contribute to the commission of the crime. Their cooperation must be close because their contributions are mutually attributable, holding each co-perpetrator

---

[28] JOHN BELL ET AL., PRINCIPLES OF FRENCH LAW 238 (1998).

[29] *See* Kai Ambos, *in* COMMENTARY ON THE ROME STATUTE OF THE INTERNATIONAL CRIMINAL COURT 748, margin nos. 8–9 (O. Triffterer ed., 2d ed. 2008); Kai Ambos, *Amicus Curiae Brief in the Matter of Co-Prosecutor's Appeal of the Closing Order Against Kaing Guek Eav "Duch" Dated 8 August 2008*, 20 CRIM. L.F. 353, 353–54 (2009) [hereinafter Ambos Amicus Brief].

[30] In this it relied on the text of article 2(3)(c) of the International Convention for the Suppression of Terrorist Bombings. *See Tadić Appeals Judgment, supra* note 15, ¶ 221.

[31] *Id.* ¶ 192.

[32] *Id.* ¶ 220.

[33] *Id.* ¶ 192.

[34] The *Krnojelac* Trial Chamber (headed by the Australian Judge Hunt) held that it did "[n]ot accept the validity of the distinction ... between a co-perpetrator and an accomplice" but it adopted the expression co-perpetrator "for convenience" when referring to a participant in a JCE. Prosecutor v. Krnojelac, Case No. IT-97-25-T, Judgment, ¶ 77 (Mar. 25, 2002) [hereinafter *Krnojelac Judgment*]. The *Krnojelac* Trial Chamber made a point in stating that it considered a co-perpetrator to be an *accomplice* and not a principal offender. *Id.* ¶ 75.

responsible for the whole crime. Joint perpetration in the context of article 25 of the ICC Statute equates (indirect) perpetration. Its position in subparagraph 3(a), alongside perpetration by means (indirect perpetration) and direct perpetration, warrants this conclusion.

In the *Lubanga* Confirmation Decision, co-perpetration was modeled on the German-inspired theory of "control over the crime" or the hegemony-over-the-act doctrine developed by Claus Roxin (*Organisationsherrschaft*).[35] The three forms of perpetration listed in article 25(3)(a) are brought under the common denominator of the perpetrator who "controls the commission of the crime." In interpreting the concept of "control" in joint or co-perpetration, the Pre-Trial Chamber (PTC) in *Lubanga* specified "control" as having "along with others, control over the offense by reason of the essential tasks assigned to them."[36] Moreover, it connotes a "division of the essential tasks for the purpose of committing a crime between two or more persons in a concerted manner."[37] A person can only be a co-perpetrator when he/she "could frustrate the commission of the crime by not carrying out his or her task."[38] The PTC further held that a co-perpetrator does not necessarily have to perform his/her acts at the "execution stage" of the crime.[39] The subjective requirements for co-perpetration are threefold: (i) a common plan, (ii) awareness of the offense to be committed and voluntarily acceptance of it, and (iii) awareness of an essential role in the common plan.[40] The common plan need not be "criminal," and the PTC adopted a broad interpretation of intent by assuming a volitional element when the offender is merely "aware of the risk that the objective elements of the crime result from his or her actions or omissions and accepts such an outcome by reconciling himself or herself with it or consenting to it."[41] Weigend has persuasively criticized this approach for not giving clear and objective criteria (what might be a substantial risk to one person may be a low risk to another) and for violating the wording of article 30(2) of the ICC Statute.[42]

The theory of "control over the crime" was adopted by the *Stakić* Trial Chamber in the context of JCE but not endorsed on appeal. This author questions the theory's acclaimed "general acceptance" (see PTC and *Stakić* Trial Chamber judgment) and thus its customary law status.[43]

---

[35] CLAUS ROXIN, TÄTERSCHAFT UND TATHERRSCHAFT (7th ed. 2000).
[36] Prosecutor v. Thomas Lubanga Dyilo, Case No. ICC-01/01-01/06, Decision on the Conformation of Charges, ¶ 332 (Jan. 29, 2007).
[37] *Id.* ¶ 342.
[38] *Id.*
[39] *Id.* ¶ 348.
[40] *Id.* ¶ 350(ii).
[41] *Id.* ¶ 352.
[42] Thomas Weigend, *Intent, Mistake of Law, and Co-perpetration in the* Lubanga *Decision on Conformation of Charges*, 6 J. INT'L CRIM. JUST. 471 (2008).
[43] It is applied in Germany and "exported" to Argentina and some other Spanish-speaking countries. Even within Germany it is controversial. *See* Weigend, *supra* note 42, at 471–87.

4. Proposed Convention

The *Proposed Convention* draws on article 25 of the ICC Statute and provides for joint perpetration in article 4(2)(a). It thus recognizes this form of responsibility as a separate head of liability and in that sense departs from the rigid common law division between principals and accomplices. Still, we must not exaggerate the difference between common law and civil law. The Anglo-American theory of acting with a common purpose may be seen as providing for a type of liability that can be equated to civil law joint perpetration. ICTY and ICTR case law on JCE 1 does exactly that.

B. Instigation[44]

The *Proposed Convention* stipulates in article 4(2)(b) that a person shall be liable for punishment if that person "orders, solicits or induces the commission of such a crime." These three forms of instigation are taken from article 25(3)(b) of the ICC Statute.

Black's Law Dictionary defines solicitation in rather neutral terms as "asking, enticing, urgent request." Soliciting, in the context of article 25 of the ICC Statute – and it is assumed also in the context of the *Proposed Convention* – is a mode of criminal participation and not an inchoate crime as it is in some common law legal systems. Ordering, soliciting, and inducing in article 25(3)(b) of the ICC Statute relate to one another as *specimen* to *generalis*. Inducing seems to be an umbrella term for soliciting and ordering and is defined in Black's Law Dictionary as: "to bring on or about, to affect, cause, to influence an act or course of conduct, lead by persuasion or reasoning, incite by motives, prevail on."[45] "Inducing" in article 25(3)(b) of the ICC Statute seems to constitute the lowest grade of instigation and is broad enough to cover any type of influence causing another person to commit a crime.

Whereas soliciting and inducing do not feature as participation modes in the Statutes of the ad hoc tribunals, "ordering" does appear as a form of participation in crime in article 2(3)(b) of the ILC Draft, and articles 6(1) and 7(1) of the ICTR and ICTY Statutes, respectively. "Ordering" can be a specific type of "soliciting." It requires a superior-subordinate relationship, de facto or de jure, and an underlying (subordinate) crime. Though the word "superior" does not feature in articles 6(1) and 7(1) of the ICTR and ICTY Statutes, nor in article 25(3)(b) of the ICC Statute, ordering should be interpreted as implying issuance of a command by a person "who

---

[44] Although the *Proposed Convention* does not speak of "instigation" but uses the term "soliciting," it appears appropriate to use "instigation" as a general term that covers various ways to prompt a person to commit a crime. *See also* Albin Eser, *Individual Criminal Responsibility*, in THE ROME STATUTE OF THE INTERNATIONAL CRIMINAL COURT: A COMMENTARY 795 (Antonio Cassese et al. eds., 2002).

[45] HENRY CAMPBELL BLACK ET AL., BLACK'S LAW DICTIONARY: DEFINITIONS OF THE TERMS AND PHRASES OF AMERICAN AND ENGLISH JURISPRUDENCE, ANCIENT AND MODERN 775 (6th ed. 1990).

is in a position of an authority and uses his authority to compel another individual to commit a crime."[46] A person who orders is not a secondary party or accomplice, but rather a perpetrator by means. It has, therefore, been suggested that "ordering" can be subsumed under "committing" in article 25(3)(a).[47] As article 25(3)(a) of the ICC Statute does not require an *innocent* agent like in national law, ordering can be construed as perpetration by means. As noted by the International Law Commission (ILC) Draft Commentary, "the superior who orders the commission of the crime is in some respects more culpable than the subordinate who merely carries out the order and thereby commits a crime that he would not have committed on his own initiative."[48]

The leading case in relation to "ordering" at the ICTY is the *Blaškić* case. In *Blaškić*, the Trial Chamber ruled that "ordering" implies a superior-subordinate relationship between the person giving the order and the person executing it.[49] A *dolus eventualis* standard was considered sufficient for "ordering crimes." The criminal liability of the person who gave the order was said to extend even to those crimes that had not been ordered but had merely been accepted as likely consequences. It has been argued by the German scholar Claus Roxin that when a statement cannot *objectively* be seen to provoke a certain event or act, it should not be considered an act of criminal participation by "*Anstiftung*" (instigation).[50] In light of this statement, the Trial Chamber's interpretation of "ordering crimes" in article 7(1) of the ICTY Statute can be regarded as broad. In light of the facts, however, the result does not appear to be wholly unacceptable. By ordering an attack on villages to prevent a counterattack in an atmosphere of ethnic tension, one increases the chance of a massacre. If a person accepts such a chance, imputing to the superior the consequences does not appear too far-fetched. In this case, it seemed acceptable that, though the commander did not order the crimes, he could be held responsible for having knowingly *accepted the risk* that his order would result in the commission of crimes.

1. *Proposed Convention*

What has been said about ordering, soliciting, or inducing in the context of the ICC Statute equally applies to the *Proposed Convention* because it relies on the exact same wording. The same can be said about some of the ambiguities that surround these forms of liability. For instance, how should we interpret "solicitation"? Is it a mode of liability or an inchoate crime? Is "planning" a separate mode of liability in the *Proposed Convention* as it is in the Statutes of the ICTY and the ICTR?

---

[46] See *ILC Commentary to 1996 ILC Draft Code*, art. 2, § 8.
[47] Ambos, *supra* note 29, at 491, margin no. 38.
[48] *ILC Commentary supra* note 46.
[49] Prosecutor v. Blaškić, Case No. IT-95-14-T, Judgment, ¶ 281 (Mar. 3, 2000) [hereinafter *Blaškić Judgment*].
[50] Hans-Heinrich Jescheck & Wolfgang Russ, Strafgesetzbuch: Leipziger Kommentar § 26 StGB (11th ed. 1993).

Could it be subsumed under "soliciting"? And lastly, how does "ordering" comport with "indirect perpetration," or perpetration through another person? These are questions to which there is no obvious answer at this stage. Yet, for purposes of implementation at the national level, this is not necessarily a problem. The fact that instigation as a mode of liability comes in various forms and shapes in the *Proposed Convention* will make it easier to find an equivalent at the national level and thus accommodate implementation.

C. Aiding and Abetting/Facilitation

The Tribunals for Rwanda and the former Yugoslavia provide for "aiding and abetting" as a mode of criminal participation in articles 6(1) and 7(1) of their respective Statutes. In case law, the concept has been further developed. Aiding means "giving assistance to someone," and abetting involves "facilitating the commission of a crime by being sympathetic thereto."[51] In interpreting complicity liability in international law, the Trial Chamber in *Tadić* relied on case law produced by the post-Nuremberg war crimes trials. The subsequent Nuremberg proceedings provide us with a patchwork of decisions and, on some points, an inconsistent body of law.[52] Each tribunal or court relied on concepts familiar to it, deriving from its own criminal law system. On the whole, however, the complicity concept was applied along Anglo-American lines. By "picking and choosing" from these precedents, the Trial Chamber in *Tadić* developed its own theory of complicity liability.

The *Krnojelac* judgment,[53] providing a short review of case law on aiding and abetting, lists the following elements:

(i) It must be demonstrated that the aider and abettor carried out an act which consisted of practical assistance, encouragement, or moral support to a principal offender.

(ii) The act of assistance need not have directly caused the act of the principal offender but it must have had a substantial effect on the commission of the crime by the principal offender.

---

[51] Prosecutor v. Akayesu, Case No. ICTR-96-4-T, Judgment, ¶ 484 (Sept. 2, 1998) [hereinafter *Akayesu Judgment*].

[52] As to participation and presence at the scene of the crime, this inconsistency was recognized by the Trial Chamber: "Although the court in that case [Trial of Franz Schonfeld and Nine Others, U.N. War Crimes Comm'n, XI LAW REPORTS OF TRIALS OF WAR CRIMINALS 69–70 (1949)] neither accepted nor rejected the Judge-Advocate's statement [that to incur liability the principal in the second degree must participate in the act], other cases [Trial of Adam Golkel and Thirteen Others, U.N. War Crimes Comm'n, V LAW REPORTS OF TRIALS OF WAR CRIMINALS 53 (1948); Trial of Max Wielen and Seventeen Others, U.N. War Crimes Comm'n, XI LAW REPORTS OF TRIALS OF WAR CRIMINALS 43–44, 46 (1949)] show that direct contribution does not necessarily require the participation in the physical commission of the illegal act." Prosecutor v. Tadić, Case No. IT-94-1-T, Opinion and Judgment, ¶ 679 (May 7, 1997) [hereinafter *Tadić Trial Judgment*].

[53] *Krnojelac Judgment, supra* note 34, ¶¶ 88–90.

(iii) Presence alone at the scene of a crime is not conclusive of aiding and abetting unless it is demonstrated to have had a significant or legitimising or encouraging effect on the principal offender.
(iv) The *mens rea* requires that the aider and abettor knew (in the sense that he or she was aware) that his or her own acts assisted in the commission of the specific crime in question by the principal offender.
(v) The aider and abettor must be aware of the essential elements of the crime committed by the principal offender, including the principal offender's *mens rea*.
(vi) However, the aider and abettor need not share the *mens rea* of the principal offender.[54]

Two observations can be made. First, the *mens rea* for aiding and abetting in ICTY case law is a "reduced" *mens rea* standard. The aider and abettor need not share the *mens rea* of the principal offender. It suffices that he was aware of the principal offender's *mens rea* (see (v) above). Moreover, *mens rea* needs to relate to the act of assistance. The aider and abettor needs to know, or be aware, that their act assists in the commission of the crime (see (iv) above). A "double intent" is thus required.

The second point relates to causation. While the *Tadić* Trial Chamber was of the view that the contribution needs to be "direct and substantial," that is, a straightforward *sine qua non* or "but if" approach,[55] the Trial Chamber in *Furundžija* held that a "substantial" contribution would suffice in expressing the causal link between assistance and principal crime.[56] In the context of aiding and abetting, the requirement of "directly" was found to be misleading, "[a]s it may imply that assistance needs to be tangible, or to have a causal effect on the crime." These findings may explain why the word "direct" was not used in the ICC Statute's provision on aiding and abetting.

Unlike the Statutes of the ICTY and ICTR, which seem to consider "counselling" and "procuring" subsumed under aiding and abetting, the ICC Statute deals with aiding and abetting as a facilitation-type of complicity that has a distinct status from the other modes of liability in article 25(3). The *mens rea* standard is higher than that established in the case law of the ad hoc tribunals. Aiding and abetting "for the purpose of facilitating" is a higher threshold than mere knowledge that the accomplice aids the commission of the offense.

The knowledge standard, as adopted in ICTY and ICTR case law, goes back to Nuremberg. One could persuasively argue that it is the proper standard for

---

[54] *See* RODNEY DIXON ET AL., ARCHBOLD INTERNATIONAL CRIMINAL COURTS: PRACTICE, PROCEDURE AND EVIDENCE §§ 10–15 (2003).
[55] *Tadić Trial Judgment, supra* note 52, ¶¶ 678–80.
[56] Prosecutor v. Furundžija, Case No. IT-95-17/1-T, Judgment, ¶ 232 (Dec. 10, 1998) [hereinafter *Furundžija Judgment*] (endorsed in Prosecutor v. Aleksovski, Case No. IT-95-14/1-A, Judgment, 163 (Mar. 24, 2000) [hereinafter *Aleksovski Appeals Judgment*]).

"facilitation liability" in international criminal law. This is exactly what a group of international law scholars argued when criticizing the ruling of the U.S. Court of Appeals for the Second Circuit in *Presbyterian Church of Sudan v. Talisman Energy, Inc.* Talisman Energy, Inc. was charged with aiding and abetting human rights abuses and international crimes in Sudan for providing logistical support (airfields, roads) to the military in Sudan who committed crimes against civilians.[57] The Court relied on the strict ICC standard in finding in favor of the company and holding that "plaintiffs have not established Talisman's purposeful complicity in human rights abuses."[58] As *amici curiae* before the U.S. Supreme Court, the scholars contended that under customary international law, aiding and abetting liability requires that an accused *knowingly* provide substantial assistance to the perpetrator or tortfeasor.[59] They further held that, if the ICC standard in article 25(3)(c) is to be understood as a purpose test for aiding and abetting international crimes, it does not comply with customary international law.[60]

The ICC purpose test is stricter than some of the national concepts of aiding and abetting discussed later in this chapter. Against the background of the *Talisman* amicus brief and what was said earlier on domestic implementation of the *Proposed Convention* (Section I.B.), it is somewhat surprising that the *Proposed Convention* repeats verbatim this strict *mens rea* standard in article 4(2)(c).

In common law, accessories are those who "aid, abet, counsel or procure" the commission of an offense. "Aiding and abetting" has often been taken to connote presence, whereas "counselling and procuring" traditionally refers to helping beforehand.[61] However, the view prevails that these four words should be given their ordinary meaning.[62] "Aiding" means "to give help, assistance or

---

[57] The company was taken to court under the Alien Tort Claims Act (ATCA). The Court ruled in favor of the company. Presbyterian Church of Sudan v. Talisman Energy, Inc., 582 F.3d 244, 244 (2d Cir. 2009). Another example is *Bauman v. DaimlerChrysler A.G.*, No. C-04–00194 RMW, 2007 WL 486389 (N.D. Cal. Feb. 12, 2007), where twenty-three Argentinean residents claimed that they (or their family members) were kidnapped, detained, and tortured by Argentinean state security forces acting at the direction of their former employer, Mercedes Benz Argentina. The case was dismissed for lack of personal jurisdiction. This decision was affirmed in an appeal. See http://www.morelaw.com/verdicts/case.asp?d=41133&n=07–15386&s=CA (last visited May 22, 2010).

[58] *Presbyterian Church of Sudan*, 582 F.3d at 244.

[59] Brief of Amici Curiae International Law Scholars William Aceves et al. in Support of Petitioners, Presbyterian Church of Sudan v. Talisman Energy, Inc., No. 09–1262 (Apr. 30, 2010), available at http://law.harvard.edu/programs/hrp/Talisman%20Amicus%20Final%20Filed%204.30.10.pdf [hereinafter Amicus Brief].

[60] In an overview of case law from Nuremberg to the ICTY, the ICTR, and the SCSL, the *amici* persuasively make clear that aiding and abetting under international law does not require proof of purposeful assistance. See Amicus Brief, *supra* note 59, at 5–12.

[61] SMITH, *supra* note 26, at 130. The common law on felonies equated aiders and abettors with principals in the second degree and counselors and procurers with accessories before the fact. See also ARCHBOLD CRIMINAL PLEADING, EVIDENCE AND PRACTICE § 18–9 (P.J. Richardson et al. eds., 2000).

[62] Attorney Gen.'s Reference (No. 1 of 1975), [1975] 2 All E.R. 684, 686 ("We approach section 8 of the Act of 1861 on the basis that the words should be given their ordinary meaning, if possible. We approach the section on the basis also that if the four words are employed here 'aid, abet, counsel

support."[63] "Abetting" denotes "to incite, instigate or encourage."[64] The ordinary meaning of "counselling" is to "advise" or "solicit,"[65] whereas "procuring" means "to produce by endeavour."[66] In Anglo-American law, complicity thus has its own distinctive *actus reus*: aiding, abetting, counseling, or procuring.[67] As to the *mens rea*, it was held in DPP for Northern Ireland v. Maxwell[68] that it is not necessary that the aider and abettor know the precise crime that was intended and which in the event was committed. It suffices that he knew the principal elements of the crime. The requirement is that the accomplice must have had the commission of the principal crime "within his contemplation." "Reckless knowledge" is sufficient to constitute *mens rea*, that is, the defendant had *knowledge of a risk* that a certain crime would be committed. This is a broad test, especially when bearing in mind that the defendant in DPP for Northern Ireland v. Maxwell was *persuaded to* drive the principal offenders to the scene of the crime.

Some civil law systems recognize two categories of aiders and abettors: facilitation-type complicity and full cooperative complicity.[69] The former generates a lower maximum sentence than the latter. As to its *mens rea*, a double intent is required and *dolus eventualis* can suffice as the requisite mental standard of instigation.[70] Causality plays an important role in that the contribution must have facilitated or contributed to the principal offense, but as in ICTY case law, a *sine qua non* link is not required. Aiding and abetting, as a form of accomplice liability, has an accessorial nature, that is, culpability and/or punishability is based on the principal crime. This is not only expressed through the requirement of double intent, but also in sentencing. In Dutch law, for instance, the aider and abettor (*"medeplichtige"*) can only be sentenced for the acts he intentionally facilitated or contributed to.[71]

---

or procure,' the probability is that there is a difference between each of the four words and the other three, because, if there were no such difference, then Parliament would be wasting time in using four words where two or three would do.").

[63] SMITH, *supra* note 26, at 129. "Aiding and abetting" can also include acts before the perpetration of the offense. *See* RICHARDSON, *supra* note 61, §§ 18–9, 18–10.
[64] SMITH, *supra* note 26, at 129.
[65] RICHARDSON, *supra* note 61, § 18–20. According to Smith "abet" seems indistinguishable from "counsel": "Perhaps there is no difference except that at common law 'abet' connoted incitement at the time of the offence and 'counsel' incitement at an earlier time." SMITH, *supra* note 26, at 130.
[66] Procuring requires a causal connection between what the (alleged) procurer did and the commission of the offense. RICHARDSON, *supra* note 61, § 18–22.
[67] J. Gardner, *Aid, Abet, Counsel, Procure: An English View of Complicity*, in EINZELVERANTWORTUNG UND MITVERANTWORTUNG IM STRAFRECHT. INDIVIDUAL, PARTICIPATORY AND COLLECTIVE RESPONSIBILITY IN CRIMINAL LAW 229, S. 71 (Albin Eser et al. eds., 1998); *see also* SMITH, *supra* note 25, at 20–135.
[68] [1978] 3 All E.R. 1140, (1978) 1 W.L.R. 1350 (Eng.).
[69] VAN SLIEDREGT, *supra* note 2, at 92.
[70] JESCHECK & WEIGEND, *supra* note 16, at 691–96.
[71] SR art. 49(4) (Dutch Penal Code) ("Only those actions that were intentionally facilitated or promoted by the accessory and the consequences of such actions are to be taken into consideration in sentencing.") (Translation: 30 THE AMERICAN SERIES OF FOREIGN PENAL CODES, THE NETHERLANDS (1997)).

As Holá and colleagues have discovered in their research on sentencing at the ICTY and ICTR, aiding and abetting is considered less culpable as a mode of liability than other forms of participatory liability.[72] One could argue that aiding and abetting as a mode of liability is moving away from its common law roots and developing into a "facilitation type" of liability.

1. Complicity by Omission

In the *Furundžija* Judgment, the ICTY Trial Chamber ruled that "intangible assistance" could qualify as aiding and abetting. Intangible assistance can exist through moral support and encouragement. In deliberating on the nature of Furundžija's participation in the crime, the Trial Chamber found that actual physical presence at the scene of the crime is not required.[73] It concluded a survey on customary international law relating to criminal participation with the following ruling: "[t]hat the *actus reus* of aiding and abetting in international criminal law requires practical assistance, encouragement, or moral support which has a substantial effect on the perpetration of the crime."[74]

It can be understood from post–Second World War jurisprudence that presence and authority can constitute a form of assistance. An approving spectator who is held in such esteem by the perpetrators that his presence encourages them to commit or continue to commit crime may be guilty of complicity (by omission) in a crime against humanity.[75] Mere presence as part of a crowd does not suffice – it needs to be coupled with a certain status before such presence can qualify as "aiding and abetting the commission of a crime." Thus, attending as a spectator in civilian dress a parade in which two political opponents are publicly humiliated falls short of silent approval as encouragement.[76] Moreover, the failure to act must have a significant effect on the commission of the crimes to qualify as aiding and abetting by omission.[77] In the *Akayesu* case, the ICTR argued along similar lines when it determined that the defendant, a *bourgomestre*, aided and abetted by merely being present at the scene of the crime. His inaction coupled with his status had an encouraging effect on the actual perpetrators.[78]

---

[72] *See* Barbora Holá et al., *Is ICTY Sentencing Predictable? An Empirical Analysis of ICTY Sentencing Practice*, 22 LEIDEN J. INT'L L. 79 (2009).
[73] *Tadić Trial Judgment, supra* note 52, ¶ 691.
[74] *Furundžija Judgment, supra* note 56, ¶ 235.
[75] *Id.* ¶ 207.
[76] As was decided in the "Pig-cart parade case" by the German Supreme Court in the British Occupied Zone, cited in the *Furundžija Judgment, supra* note 56, ¶ 208. The Trial Chamber concluded that the accused "[w]as found not guilty. He may have lacked *mens rea*. But in any event, his insignificant status brought the effect of his 'silent approval' below the threshold necessary for the *actus reus*." *Id.*
[77] *Blaškić Judgment, supra* note 49, ¶ 284; Prosecutor v. Delalić et al., Case No. IT-96-21-T, Judgment, ¶ 842 (Nov. 16, 1998) [hereinafter *Čelebići Trial Judgment*]; *Tadić Trial Judgment, supra* note 52, ¶ 686.
[78] *Akayesu Judgment, supra* note 51, ¶ 705.

Aiding and abetting, or complicity by omission, is supported in customary international law and endorsed in the jurisprudence of the ad hoc tribunals. It is therefore argued that "intangible support" can equally qualify as aiding and abetting under article 25(3)(c) of the ICC Statute and article 4(2)(c) of the *Proposed Convention*. As was argued in Section II.A.1, it is this author's view that omission liability can be included in article 25(3) of the ICC Statute and, therefore, in the *Proposed Convention*.

2. Proposed Convention

Having regard to what was said about aiding and abetting in the context of ICTY and ICTR case law, national legislation, and the ICC Statute, it seems that aiding and abetting in article 4(2)(c) refers to a "facilitation" type of liability that would attract a lesser sentence than co-perpetration. The text of the *Proposed Convention* does not make clear whether nontangible assistance or complicity by omission can be brought under "aiding and abetting." Still, there is no reason why it should not be part of it when domestic systems allow for such a form of complicity.

III. CRIME-SPECIFIC MODES OF LIABILITIES

A. Indirect Perpetration

"Perpetration through another person" is recognized as a separate mode of liability for the first time in international criminal law in article 25(3)(a) of the ICC Statute. Since it extends to perpetration through both innocent and culpable agents, it is likely to cover a wide range of situations. Its Anglo-American counterpart that comes closest is the doctrine of innocent agency.[79] The act of the innocent agent is as much the act of the indirect perpetrator as if the latter were present and did commit the act himself. The *actus reus* may be brought about by the act of someone who is not a participant in the crime at all (that is, who has no *mens rea*, or who has some defense, such as infancy or insanity). Such a person is usually described as an "innocent agent."[80] If the agent is not "innocent," he is considered a principal and the perpetrator by means of a secondary party, in which case ordinary accomplice liability applies.

Civil law systems are more accommodating and provide for indirect perpetration or "perpetration by means" in their domestic law. In French law, the "*auteur médiat*" is not codified but is recognized in case law as the responsible perpetrator when the actual perpetrator is used as an instrument. German law refers to perpetration by means as "*mittelbaren Täterschaft*."[81] Dutch law provides for a statutory type of "perpetration by means" for those who cause an innocent person to commit a criminal

---

[79] Kadish, *supra* note 25, at 369–72; HART & HONORÉ, *supra* note 25, at 323–24.
[80] SMITH, *supra* note 26, at 128.
[81] GEORGE P. FLETCHER, RETHINKING CRIMINAL LAW 639–40 (1978); *see also* H. Burgstaller, *in* CRIMINAL RESPONSIBILITY OF LEGAL AND COLLECTIVE ENTITIES 19–20 (Albin Eser et al. eds., 1999).

offense.[82] In both German and Dutch law, concepts have been developed to escape the rigid condition of innocence of the agent in the concept of perpetration by means, which have affected the development and use of the latter concept. In this context, we can refer to the earlier mentioned German theory of "*Organisationsherrschaft,*" or the doctrine of "hegemony-over-the-act."[83] The indirect perpetrator dominates through and within an organization the acts of the subordinates, who, as direct perpetrators, carry out the crimes conceived and ordered by the indirect perpetrators who can be referred to as commanders. The subordinates are criminally responsible together with the commanders who are in control and use the former as replaceable or fungible mediators of the act. In Ambos's words:

> [T]he direct perpetrator loses transcendence as he plays a secondary role in the execution of the act. He who dominates the system dominates the anonymous will of all the men who constitute it.[84]

The domination of the indirect perpetrator over the direct perpetrator is total, in that even if the latter refused to comply, another would automatically replace him and the commission of the acts would take place anyhow.

In Dutch law, the development of the concept of "functional perpetration" has rendered the statutory provision of "perpetration by means" virtually superfluous. According to the concept of functional perpetration, persons may be held liable for an offense they did not physically commit if they can be said to have acted through another person, irrespective of whether that other person is criminally responsible himself or herself. An offense is considered to have been functionally perpetrated when the following requirements have been met: (i) the doctrine can be applied to the offense, (ii) the violated norm was addressed to the accused, and (iii) the physical acts of another person can be imputed to him.[85] A person is held liable as the functional perpetrator of an offense because of his or her failure to prevent another person's act if they had control over those acts and accepted, or usually accepted, such acts. Intent is inferred from the acceptance of the act(s). This is taken to indicate that the functional perpetrator consciously and voluntarily refrained from intervening while having the duty to do so.[86]

The Statutes of the ad hoc tribunals do not provide for indirect perpetration. Yet in recent ICTY case law, JCE liability has been developed in such a way that it reflects traits of "*Organisationsherrschaft.*"[87] In its Judgment of April 3, 2007, the

---

[82] Sr art. 47(1) (Dutch Penal Code); *see* Alexandra van Woensel, In de Daderstand Verheven (1993) (with summary in English, *id.* at 179–82).
[83] Roxin, *supra* note 35, at 242–52, 653–54; Fletcher, *supra* note 81, at 655–56 (1978).
[84] Kai Ambos, *Individual Criminal Responsibility*, *in* I Substantive and Procedural Aspects of International Criminal Law 19 (Gabrielle Kirk McDonald & Olivia Swaak-Goldman, eds., 2000).
[85] IJzerdraad, Hoge Raad der Nederlanden [HR] [Supreme Court of the Netherlands], 23 Februari 1954, NJ 378 (Neth.).
[86] *See* van Woensel, *supra* note 82, at 96.
[87] Roxin, *supra* note 35, at 242–52, 653–54.

Appeals Chamber in *Brđanin* found that there is support in post–World War II case law[88] and in ICTY jurisprudence[89] that the principal perpetrator need not be a member of the JCE. Instead, the appellate judges found that "[w]hat matters is ... not whether the person who carried out the *actus reus* of a particular crime is a member of the JCE but whether the crime in question forms part of the common purpose."[90] To hold a member of the JCE responsible for crimes perpetrated by a nonmember, it is sufficient to show that at least one member of the JCE can be linked to a nonmember. When the latter is used by the former to carry out the common criminal purpose, the other co-perpetrators of the JCE can be held equally liable for the crimes.[91] This type of JCE liability provides for the liability of senior figures (indirect perpetrators) for crimes committed by an anonymous executive machinery (direct perpetrators) who are used as a tool to carry out the crimes planned and instigated by those leaders. The extended form of JCE, or "third category" JCE, may also trigger liability when it concerns crimes committed by nonmembers as long as it can be shown that the member who uses nonmembers as tools to carry out the *actus reus* had the requisite intent – in other words, that in the circumstances of the case, (i) it was foreseeable that such a crime might be perpetrated by one or more of the principal persons, and that (ii) he willingly took that risk.[92]

The appellate ruling in *Brđanin*, which reconceptualizes the original "mob violence type of JCE" into an "interlinked JCE," can be regarded as a breakthrough in the law on JCE.[93] This judgment enables the prosecutor at the ICTY (and the ICTR) to apply JCE entirely at leadership level, as long as it can be shown that one of the participants is linked to the physical perpetrator who is used as a tool to carry out the crime(s). The *Brđanin* ruling effectively loosens the link between the JCE participants and the principal perpetrator(s). Such "delinking" is expressed through the acceptance of nonmembership of the actual/physical perpetrator. It is also reflected in the Appeals Chamber finding with regard to the *mens rea* of "first category" JCE. The Appeals Chamber held that determining the link between the JCE member and the nonmember does not require proof of a shared agreement. Instead, "this essential requirement may be inferred from various circumstances."[94] When a JCE member uses a nonmember to carry out the crimes and the latter "[k]nows of the existence of the JCE – without it being established that he or she shares the *mens rea* necessary to become a member of the JCE," such knowledge

---

[88] Prosecutor v. Brđanin, Case No IT-99-36-A, Judgment, ¶ 404 (Apr. 3, 2007 [hereinafter *Brđanin Appeals Judgment*].

[89] *Id.* ¶¶ 408–09 (referring to Prosecutor v. Stakić, Case No. IT-97-24-A, Judgment, ¶ 98 (Mar. 22, 2006) and Prosecutor v. Krstić, Case No. IT-98-33-A, Appeals Chamber Judgment (Apr. 19, 2004).

[90] *Brđanin Appeals Judgment*, *supra* note 88, ¶ 410.

[91] *Id.* ¶ 413.

[92] *Id.* ¶ 411.

[93] On reconceptualizing legal concepts and the principle of legality, see ALBERT R. JONSEN & STEPHEN TOULMIN, THE ABUSE OF CASUISTRY: A HISTORY OF MORAL REASONING (1988).

[94] *Brđanin Appeals Judgment*, *supra* note 88, ¶ 410.

"may be a factor to be taken into account when determining whether the crime forms part of the common criminal purpose."[95] In other words, the *mens rea* requirement for participants and nonparticipants may deviate. First-category JCE liability ("sharing the *mens rea*") does not apply to a nonmember of a JCE. Thus, the principal perpetrator, when committing crimes within a detention center set up as part of a policy to ethnically cleanse a certain area, need not necessarily share the *mens rea* of the senior leaders who devised and implemented the policy of ethnic cleansing.

The *Brđanin* appellate ruling, rather than endorsing the Prosecutor's initial strategy of charging members at leadership and execution levels with a large-scale JCE, all furthering the same common criminal purpose, accepted liability for those participating in *separate* but *linked* JCEs. The leadership JCE and the execution JCE may pursue different criminal objectives but come together in the agreement between representatives of each JCE. Although the Appeals Chamber accepted that JCE liability may attach to those participating in large-scale criminal enterprises, the "interlinked JCE" seems to be the preferred theory in cases such as *Brđanin* with policy makers on the one hand and executors or "foot soldiers" on the other hand.

Two observations can be made with regard to interlinked JCE. First of all, in substantiating the existence of interlinked JCE in modern law, the Appeals Chamber relied on only two cases, the *Justice* case and the *RuSHA* case. This, to this author's opinion, is not sufficient. Indeed, it appears that the judges were themselves aware of the thin legal basis supporting the doctrine of interlinked JCE as evidenced by their statement that these cases have been "interpreted as a valid source of the *contours of* joint criminal enterprise liability in customary international law."[96]

A second observation concerns the loosening of the link between participants in the JCE at leadership level and perpetrators at execution level. This delinking may increase the possibility of guilt by association. In other words, the interlinked JCE concept with principal perpetrators who do not share the common objective of those participating at policy level may increase the risk of violating the principle of *personal* culpability. The Appeals Chamber in *Brđanin* was aware of this risk and emphasized that "JCE is not an open-ended concept that permits conviction based on guilt by association."[97] It also pointed to the elements to be proven before a conviction under the JCE doctrine can be entered, emphasizing that JCE liability, even in its interlinked form, must stay within the limits of criminal law principles. Still, certain questions remain unanswered. Does interlinked JCE mean that the participants in a JCE can be held liable for crimes for which they had no *mens rea*, not even through the "natural and foreseeable consequences" variant? In other words, can all the participants in a JCE be held responsible for deaths and killings in a detention camp where guards have been used as a tool by only one of the JCE participants and with whom they – the other JCE participants – do not share the *mens*

---

[95] *Id.*
[96] *Id.* ¶ 415 (emphasis added).
[97] *Id.* ¶ 428.

rea, or whose acts have not been accepted by them as natural and foreseeable consequences of their plan? In other words, can the *mens rea* of the member participant who uses the nonmember participant replace the *mens rea* of all the participants? If so, interlinked JCE would be a form of vicarious liability.

In *Katanga and Ngudjolo* before the ICC Pre-Trial Chamber (PTC) I, the concept of "*Organisationsherrschaft*" was applied as a means by which intellectual perpetrators, by controlling an organizational apparatus, may be held liable for crimes committed by the apparatus. The suspects were indicted for crimes committed by subordinates during and in the aftermath of an attack on civilians. The PTC required control over an organizational apparatus, based on hierarchical relations between superiors and subordinates. It required the organization to be composed of (interchangeable) "sufficient subordinates" and that "the chief, or the leader, exercises authority and control over the apparatus."[98] Under this theory of liability, the leader is a perpetrator behind the perpetrator who "mobilises the authority and power within the organisation to secure compliance with his orders."[99] Execution of the crime is secured by almost automatic compliance with orders in a "mechanized" manner, and the resulting crimes can be mutually attributed to both of the suspects.

The question arises whether this German doctrine fits the facts of the *Katanga* case. "*Organisationsherrschaft*" assumes the existence of a rigidly formal bureaucracy comparable to an authoritarian Prussian army. Does this really reflect present-day conflict in Africa? When reading the PTC Confirmation Decision in *Katanga and Ngudjolo*, one gets the feeling that this theory has been devised in the abstract, at the drawing table, rather than applied to the facts and scrutinized for its present-day viability. Moreover, the PTC ruling that indirect perpetration in its *Organisationsherrschaft* form is part of modern legal doctrine is not convincing.[100] The notion of "control over an organized apparatus of power"[101] is not widely applied and recognized in national jurisdictions; it features in German and Argentine case law, and even in those countries it is not generally accepted and applied.[102] The liability theory was specifically premised on the experience of State crime in Nazi Germany.

1. *Proposed Convention*

ICTY case law on JCE, especially as it evolved since the *Tadić* ruling, demonstrates that international criminal law needs some form of indirect perpetration. It serves to link the intellectual perpetrator to the executioner. This author, therefore,

---

[98] Prosecutor v. Katanga and Ngudjolo Chui, ICC-01/04-01/07, Decision on the confirmation of the charges, ¶¶ 512–13 (Sept. 30, 2008).
[99] *Id.* ¶ 513.
[100] *Id.* ¶ 510.
[101] *Id.*
[102] *See* Thomas Rotsch, *Neues zur Organisationsherrschaft*, 25 NEUES ZEITSCHRIFT FÜR STRAFRECHT 13 (2005); Gerhard Werle, *Individual Criminal Responsibility in Article 25 ICC Statute*, 5 J. INT'L CRIM. JUST. 953 (2007).

welcomes the fact that article 4(2)(a) of the *Proposed Convention* reproduces article 25(3)(a) of the ICC Statute providing for liability for acting "through another person." Indirect perpetration in the context of the *Proposed Convention* should not be viewed as solely referring to *Organisationsherrschaft*/control over the crime. The latter model of liability is not generally accepted, even though one Pre-Trial Chamber of the ICC seems to suggest it is. Indirect perpetration in the context of the CAH Convention should be seen to encapsulate other liability theories as well, for example, innocent agency in Anglo-American law and "functional perpetration" in Dutch law.

B. Participating in a Criminal Enterprise[103]

Prosecutors and judges at the military commissions and tribunals set up after World War II relied on a "group crime concept," in addition to the theory of accomplice liability, in prosecuting and convicting Nazi supporters who had been involved in mob violence against the Allied military and resistance forces. They based criminal liability on the concept of "acting with a common design" derived from English criminal law. Common design liability, as interpreted in these proceedings, required proof of knowledge on the part of the defendant (*mens rea*) that in some way his/her conduct contributed to the crime (*actus reus*).[104] The latter element was very vague, only limited by the condition that the cooperation in the war machine had a "real bearing" on the crime.[105] Liability under the common-design theory required a lower degree of participation than accomplice liability, which calls for a substantial effect on the crime committed by the principal offender. Moreover, the distinction between perpetrator and accomplice is irrelevant as all defendants are regarded as participants in the crime. The "common design" concept was relied on to convict concentration camp personnel[106] and those involved in mob violence.[107]

---

[103] This paragraph is based on the author's paper: Elies van Sliedregt, *Joint Criminal Enterprise as a Pathway to Convicting Individuals for Genocide*, 5 J. INT'L CRIM. JUST. 184 (2007).

[104] See Trial of Werner Rohde and Eight Others, U.N. War Crimes Comm'n, V LAW REPORTS OF TRIALS OF WAR CRIMINALS 54, 56 (1948) (British Military Court, Wuppertal, Germany 1946); Trial of Bruno Tesch and Two Others, U.N. War Crimes Comm'n, I LAW REPORTS OF TRIALS OF WAR CRIMINALS 93, 101 (1947) (British Military Court, Hamburg, Germany 1946) (*Zyklon B* case).

[105] Trial of Max Wielen and Seventeen Others, U.N. War Crimes Comm'n, XI LAW REPORTS OF TRIALS OF WAR CRIMINALS 33, 46 (1949) (British Military Court, Hamburg, Germany 1947) (*Stalag Luft III* case).

[106] Trial of Martin Gottfried Weiss and Thirty-Nine Others, U.N. War Crimes Comm'n, XI LAW REPORTS OF TRIALS OF WAR CRIMINALS 5–17 (1949) (General Military Government Court of the United States Zone, Dachau, Germany 1945) (*Dachau Concentration Camp* case).

[107] Trial of Otto Sandrock and Three Others, U.N. War Crimes Comm'n, I LAW REPORTS OF TRIALS OF WAR CRIMINALS 35, 40 (1947) (British Military Court, Almelo, Holland 1945); Trial of Erich Heyer and Six Others (The *Essen Lynching* case) *cited in* Tadić *Appeals Judgment*, *supra* note 15, ¶¶ 204–09; Trial of Kurt Goebell et al. (*The Borkum Island* cases) *cited in* Tadić *Appeals Judgment*, *supra* note 15, ¶¶ 210–13.

History seems to have repeated itself. At the ICTY, a group liability concept was devised to prosecute and convict those involved in collective crime/mob violence situations. In *Tadić*, JCE was applied in order to ascribe to Tadić the killing of five men in the village of Jaskici. Tadić had not physically committed these crimes, but the Appeals Chamber, applying the concept of common purpose/JCE, ruled that Tadić was responsible for the five deaths because members of his group committed them and because the deaths were considered "natural and foreseeable consequences" of the common purpose to ethnically cleanse the Prijidor region, to which Tadić had agreed.[108] Since the ICTY Statute does not provide for the concept of JCE, the Appeals Chamber based its findings on customary international law and subsumed it under "committing" in article 7(1) and justified this by pointing to the object and purpose of the Statute and the inherent characteristics of crimes committed in warlike situations.[109]

According to the Appeals Chamber, relevant case law shows that the notion of common purpose or JCE encompasses three distinct categories.[110] Tadić was held responsible under the Third Category, also referred to as JCE III or extended JCE. This category concerns cases where "one of the perpetrators commits an act which, while outside the common design, was nevertheless a natural and foreseeable consequence of the effecting of that common purpose."[111] The post–World War II case law, such as the *Essen Lynching* and *Borkum Island* cases that were cited in support of this category as reflecting customary international law, mainly deal with small-scale, mob violence situations.[112]

Since the *Tadić* ruling, the concept of JCE has been applied in many cases, initially only at the ICTY, and later at the ICTR as well. From a prosecutorial point of view, JCE has appeal because it captures an array of criminal conduct of those who knowingly participate in the criminal endeavor.[113] Tadić could not have been

---

[108] *Tadić Appeals Judgment, supra* note 15, ¶¶ 232–33.
[109] For the doctrine of common purpose at the ICTY and the principle of legality, see Boot, *supra* note 21, at 288–302.
[110] (i) *The first category* relates to cases where all codefendants possessing the same intent pursue a common criminal design, for instance, the killing of a certain person.(ii) *The second category* concerns the so-called "concentration camp" cases, where the requisite *actus reus* comprises the active participation in the enforcement of a system of repression, as it could be inferred from the position of authority and the specific functions held by each accused. The *mens rea* element comprised: (i) knowledge of the nature of the system and (ii) the intent to further the common concerted design to ill-treat inmates. Intent may *also* be inferred from the accused position within the camp. (iii) *The third category* concerns cases "where one of the perpetrators commits an act which, while outside the common design, was nevertheless a natural and foreseeable consequence of the effecting of that common purpose." *Tadić Appeals Judgment, supra* note 15, ¶¶ 196–204.
[111] *Id.*
[112] *Id.* ¶ 219. Sassòli and Olsen doubt the correctness of this statement as the Italian cases, unlike the *Essen Lynching* and *Borkum Island* cases, represent the application of national rather than international law. *See* Marco Sassòli & Laura M. Olson, *The Judgment of the ICTY Appeals Chamber on the Merits in the Tadić Case: New Horizons for International Humanitarian and Criminal Law?*, 82 Int'l Rev. Red Cross 733, 751–52 (2000).
[113] *See* Allison Marston Danner & Jenny S. Martinez, *Guilty Associations: Joint Criminal Enterprise, Command Responsibility, and the Development of International Criminal Law*, 93 Cal. L. Rev. 75, 102–20 (2005).

convicted for the five deaths at Jaskíci on the basis of accomplice liability provided for in article 7(1) as "aiding and abetting in a crime." The prosecution would have had to prove that Tadić had carried out acts specifically directed to assisting, encouraging, or lending moral support to the killings, and that the support had a substantial effect on the underlying crime.[114] JCE thus fills a gap by supplying a group crime concept – a basis for convicting those engaged in the "mob violence type" of system criminality.

JCE has further been used to prosecute senior political and military figures for crimes committed by others but falling within the object of a certain (criminal) policy formulated by them, for instance the plan to create a "greater Serbia" and ethnically cleanse certain areas by setting up detention camps. The extended form of JCE can be relied on to hold leaders responsible for crimes that go *beyond* the plan: detention-related crimes (rape and killing) that can be considered natural and foreseeable consequences of the common criminal policy of which the accused were aware as being the "possible outcome."[115]

The difficulty with JCE at the leadership level is the link with the physical perpetrator. Political leaders are physically remote from the battlefield, which makes it difficult to link them to those who actually commit the crimes. The interlinked JCE liability theory, developed by the ICTY Chamber in *Brđanin* (see Section III.A.) provides a solution for the linkage problem in cases of senior or military figures.

1. JCE and Aiding and Abetting

The Appeals Chamber in *Tadić* ruled that the aider and abettor carries out acts that are specifically directed to assist, encourage, or lend moral support to the perpetration of a certain specific crime. By contrast, in the case of JCE, it is sufficient for the co-perpetrator to somehow contribute to furthering the common plan or purpose. This lower standard of participation, the objective element, is offset by the fact that liability under the JCE theory requires a criminal plan or common design.[116] With aiding and abetting, the principal may not even know of the contribution of the aider and abettor.[117]

The "common purpose/plan element" is JCE's distinctive feature, making it a more serious contribution to a crime than aiding and abetting *and* capable of compensating for the lack of physical/tangible involvement in the actual commission of the crime. In the tribunals' case law, there have been attempts to interpret the "plan element" beyond its original understanding (an agreement between the actual/"physical"

---

[114] *Tadić Appeals Judgment, supra* note 15, ¶ 192.
[115] Prosecutor v. Milosević, Case No. IT-01-51-I, Initial Indictment (Bosnia and Herzegovina), ¶ 6 (Nov. 22, 2001).
[116] *See also* Katrina Gustafson, *The Requirement of an "Express Agreement" for Joint Criminal Enterprise Liability: A Critique of Brđanin*, 5 J. INT'L CRIM. JUST. 134 (2007).
[117] *Tadić Appeals Judgment, supra* note 15, ¶ 229.

perpetrator and the "nonphysical" perpetrator) by applying JCE entirely at leadership level, merely requiring the common plan to be concluded by those far removed from the actual scene of the crimes, which amounts to developing JCE into a surrogate conspiracy concept. The underlying rationale of the Trial Chamber's "explicit agreement requirement" in *Brđanin* was to dismiss such an understanding of JCE. The common purpose links the physical perpetrator to the nonphysical perpetrator and provides the basis for attributing individual criminal responsibility. It requires participants in a JCE to either share the intent in pursuing the common purpose or to foresee the crime as a natural consequence of the common purpose.[118] Satisfying these "subjective elements" would require an identification of the members of the JCE. However, this has proved problematic in practice. Inferring intent by way of circumstantial evidence has been the solution.

Haan rightfully points out that there is an inconsistency between JCE in theory and JCE in practice.[119] Not much is required to satisfy JCE's subjective elements of a common plan and *mens rea*. Moreover, recent attempts to limit JCE's expansive scope by imposing additional conditions for participation[120] result in overemphasizing the objective element. In this way, the objective-subjective balance of JCE has been reversed. The threshold for *actus reus* has been increased, while the *mens rea* threshold remains very low.[121] Against that background, the "express agreement requirement" proposed by the Trial Chamber in *Brđanin* could have been a useful additional requirement for proving participation in a JCE.[122] It limits the scope of JCE while restoring the proper subjective-objective balance, bringing JCE closer to its original meaning.

2. Nature of JCE Liability

Any attempt to identify the nature of JCE liability would first require determining what JCE is *not*. JCE is not an inchoate type of liability like conspiracy. Moreover, participating in a JCE is a route to the commission of a crime.[123] It is not a crime in itself as was suggested by the Trial Chamber in *Kvočka* and corrected in appeal.[124]

The confusion regarding the nature of JCE liability evolves around the question whether JCE liability constitutes a form of *perpetration* or *participation*. Resolving

---

[118] *Id.* ¶ 204.
[119] Verena Haan, *The Development of the Concept of Joint Criminal Enterprise at the International Criminal Tribunal for the Former Yugoslavia*, 5 INT'L CRIM. L. REV. 167, 194–95 (2005).
[120] For instance, by requiring the accused to make a substantial contribution to the JCE. Prosecutor v. Kvočka, Case No. IT-98-30/1-A, Judgment, ¶ 278 (Feb. 28, 2005) [hereinafter *Kvočka Appeals Judgment*].
[121] Haan, *supra* note 119, at 195.
[122] For another view, see Gustafson, *supra* note 116.
[123] Prosecutor v. Milutinovic et al., Case No. IT-99-37-AR72, Decision on Dragoljub Ojdanic's Motion Challenging Jurisdiction – Joint Criminal Enterprise, ¶ 20 (May 21, 2003).
[124] *Kvočka Appeals Judgment*, *supra* note 120, ¶ 91.

this confusion is particularly relevant when one attempts to answer the question whether JCE can be a basis for genocide convictions. Unlike participants, perpetrators are required to have genocidal intent themselves.

The different views that exist on the nature of JCE liability may be explained by misleading terminology. The term 'co-perpetrator' suggests that a participant in a JCE is a *principal* rather than a *participant*, who *commits* rather than *participates* in a crime. Illustrative on this point is the ruling in the *Krnojelac* case where the Trial Chamber held that participating in a JCE could not be brought under "commission" within the meaning of article 7(1) of the ICTY Statute because that notion was reserved for the principal physical perpetrator of the crime.[125] Against that background, the neutral terminology used in article 25(3)(d) of the ICC Statute, and thus article 4(2)(d) of the *Proposed Convention*, referring to "contributes to" (the commission of such a crime by a group of persons acting with a common purpose) should be welcomed.

Another reason for the perpetration-participation confusion is possibly the divergent positions in national law. In Anglo-American law, JCE liability is a form of criminal *participation*. The French legal system adopts a similar approach.[126] In German law, however, the "*Mittäter*" is considered a perpetrator.[127] In Dutch law, a "*medepleger*" qualifies as a participant.[128]

The Appeals Chamber in *Tadić* seems to have adopted the Anglo-American approach, which is hardly surprising bearing in mind JCE's origin. It held that "[t]he *commission* of one of the crimes envisaged in Articles 2, 3, 4 or 5 of the Statute might also occur through *participation* in the realisation of a common design or purpose."[129] As a result, JCE should be regarded as a form of criminal participation – a more neutral term than accomplice liability – to which principles of derivative liability apply. This is also in line with JCE's customary law status. The post–World War II concepts of "being concerned in" or "participating in a common design" generated a body of case law on which JCE liability was modeled. Past and present international case law indicates that JCE is based on Anglo-American principles and has been applied as such.

Considering JCE as a form of criminal participation would not ignore the concept's civil law origins. Firstly, the latter do not exclude branding co-perpetration as participation and secondly, JCE's civil law origins are respected in accepting that JCE, as joint perpetration, is a more serious degree of liability than aiding and abetting.

---

[125] Prosecutor v. Krnojelac, Case No. IT-97-25-T, Judgment, ¶¶ 78–87 (Mar. 15, 2002).
[126] C. PÉN. art. 121-6 (Fr.). *Complicité, Art. 121-6 et 121-7, Introduction, A et B*, JURIS-CLASSEUR PÉNAL 1–16 (Henri Angevin & Albert Chavanne eds., 1998).
[127] § 25(2) StGB. Jescheck & Weigend, *supra* note 16, at 645–46.
[128] SR art. 47(1)-(1) (Dutch Penal Code). NOYON-LANGEMEIJER-REMMELINK, WETBOEK VAN STRAFRECHT (CODE OF CRIMINAL LAW – A COMMENTARY) suppl. 121, at 324a-326a, art. 47, Dutch Penal Code, § 1a.
[129] *Tadić Appeals Judgment*, *supra* note 15, ¶ 188 (emphasis added).

The above account concludes that:

(i) JCE liability has developed into a *sui generis* concept with elements derived from both civil law and Anglo-American law.
(ii) It most closely resembles the Anglo-American doctrine of common purpose and, as affirmed in past and present international case law, has been applied as such. As a result, it should be regarded as a form of criminal participation to which principles of derivative liability apply.
(iii) JCE creates a perpetrator status for those closely involved in the commission of an international crime, which constitutes a higher degree of culpability than aiding and abetting. In that sense it takes after civil law co-perpetration.
(iv) JCE's central element and distinctive feature is the requirement of a common plan and/or purpose. JCE liability requires a lower degree of participation than aiding and abetting, which is offset by proof of a shared intent or plan/common purpose.
(v) The "common plan" element, being the central element of JCE liability, should be strictly construed to prevent it from becoming elusive.

The common purpose/JCE doctrine introduces a "foreseeable risk" test and brings within the scope of complicity the acts committed by a principal who goes off on a frolic of his own. This is why the concept was relied on in the *Tadić* case with regard to the Jaskíci murders. This type of "collateral" or extended liability is based in English law on the rule that when A and B share the common purpose of committing an offense, B is also liable for a crime that he did not intend, assist, or encourage A to commit, if he knew that A might do the act while committing the "agreed crime."[130] The criminal liability lies in participating with foresight.[131] This test is similar to the reckless knowledge test of complicity liability in English law[132] and is not very different from the mental standard for aiding and abetting at the ICTY, where one can be held liable for aiding and abetting a crime of which one is aware that it "will probably be committed."[133]

The wording of 25(3)(d) of the Rome Statute, adopted verbatim in draft article 4(2)(d) of the *Proposed Convention*, reflects the English "common purpose" doctrine

---

[130] SMITH, *supra* note 25, at 209; SMITH, *supra* note 26, at 148 (referring to the decision of the Privy Council in Chan Wing-Sing v. R. (1985) 80 Crim. App. 117 (U.K.): "[The principle] turns on contemplation .... It meets the case of a crime foreseen as a possible incident of the common unlawful enterprise. The criminal culpability lies in participating in the venture with that foresight.").

[131] ANDREW ASHWORTH, PRINCIPLES OF CRIMINAL LAW 434 (4th ed. 2003).

[132] In *DPP for Northern Ireland v. Maxwell*, [1978] 3 All E.R. 1140 (Eng.), a reckless knowledge test was introduced for complicity. As to the mental element of the accomplice, it suffices that he "[k]nows that one or more of a group of offences is virtually certain to be committed, which means that in relation to the one(s) actually committed there was knowledge only of a risk that it would be actually committed – and that amounts to recklessness." ASHWORTH, *supra* note 131, at 442.

[133] *Furundžija Judgment*, *supra* note 56, ¶ 246.

and seems to be the equivalent of the mob violence type of JCE at the ad hoc tribunals. The wording is taken from the International Convention for the Suppression of Terrorist Bombings.[134] The *mens rea* of common purpose liability in article 25(3)(d) of the ICC Statute constitutes "acting with a *common purpose*" (emphasis added). Like the previously discussed participation modes of instigation and aiding and abetting, common purpose liability requires a twofold mental standard: one relating to the contribution and one relating to the subsequent crime. As to the first, article 25(3)(d) stipulates that such contribution shall be "intentional." Intentional includes knowledge and volition. As to the second, alternatives (i) and (ii) provide two different mental standards relating to the underlying crime. "Third category" JCE does not easily "fit" the ICC common purpose concept. First of all, alternative (ii) requires knowledge of the intention of the group. With regard to "third category" JCE, the accused does not *know* of the intention of the group member who committed the additional crime. Moreover, and more importantly, the strict wording of article 30 of the ICC Statute on the mental element seems to exclude *dolus eventualis* as a valid degree of *mens rea*.

There is no equivalent of article 30 in the *Proposed Convention*. One could therefore argue that "third category" JCE can be brought under common purpose liability concept in article 4(2)(d). Cognizant of the interplay between national and international criminal law in supporting the need for a CAH treaty, one could argue that domestic law requires a proposed convention to leave room for JCE liability, including its "third category." After all, JCE has a national law pedigree. Aside from the common design theory in English criminal law, which is the closest to JCE as interpreted in *Tadić*, we can refer in this context to American law and the Pinkerton doctrine as developed by United States federal courts. According to the U.S. Supreme Court in *Pinkerton v. Unites States*,[135] each member of a conspiracy can be liable for substantive offenses carried out by co-conspirators in furtherance of the conspiracy, even when there is no evidence of their direct participation in, or knowledge of, such offenses. Liability extends to offenses that are "reasonably foreseen as a necessary or natural consequence of the unlawful agreement."[136] This reasoning is similar to the foresight test in common purpose cases, though the *Pinkerton* test puts more emphasis on the agreement.

French law penalizes "participation in a group formed or an understanding reached for the perpetration of one of the felonies specified in Articles 211–1, 212–1, and 212–2 [genocide, crimes against humanity, and war crimes], when evidenced by one or more overt acts."[137] Moreover, the French concept of "*association de*

---

[134] International Convention for the Suppression of Terrorist Bombings, Annex art. 2(3)(c), Jan. 12, 1998, G.A. Res. 164, U.N. GAOR 52d Sess., U.N. Doc. A/RES/52/164 (1998).
[135] 328 U.S. 640 (1946).
[136] *Id.*
[137] C. PÉN. ART. 212-3(1) (1994) (Fr.) (Translation: 31 THE AMERICAN SERIES OF FOREIGN PENAL CODES, FRANCE (1999)).

malfaiteurs" can also be referred to as a type of common purpose concept.[138] Dutch law provides for an analogous concept in article 140 of the Dutch Penal Code. This provision penalizes the "participation in an organization that has as its object the commission of serious offenses."[139] A participant in a criminal organization needs to be part of the organization and needs to participate or support acts that lead or directly relate to the realization of the common purpose. The participant's intent does not have to extend to all the elements of the underlying crimes. It suffices that he knew the aim and intention of the organization.[140]

3. Proposed Convention

JCE liability was initially developed and applied in international case law as compensating for the deficiencies of Anglo-American inspired complicity law. In that sense, it fulfils the same function as common purpose liability in national law. It introduces a group responsibility concept that offers a way out of complicated causality problems in mob violence situations. The way it has developed in more recent years, however, applying it as a liability theory to offenders at leadership levels, makes it a surrogate-conspiracy concept.[141] In ICTY case law, JCE has gained the function of a catch-all concept that was developed to compensate for a narrowly defined superior responsibility concept and the absence of a general conspiracy concept.

Does JCE III qualify as a crime-specific concept that should be part of the liability provision in the CAH Convention? Is there a need for such a concept alongside joint and indirect perpetration? An analysis of case law goes to show that there is a need for a concept that criminalizes participation in a group that pursues a common criminal purpose. Such participation may not necessarily imply a direct contribution to the commission of the underlying crime. Agreeing to pursue a common criminal design can suffice, and assisting in pursuing such a design can be sufficient for criminal liability. Common purpose liability or JCE requires a lower degree of participation in a crime than aiding and abetting/complicity in a crime. As the *Tadić* case and certain post–World War II case law illustrate, mob violence situations call for a liability theory like JCE and common purpose liability. Unlike conspiracy, common purpose liability requires proof of a link to the underlying offense/actual perpetrator.

---

[138] Regulated in Articles 450–1 to 450–4 of the Code Pénal. C. PÉN. ARTS. 450–1–450–4 (1994) (Fr.).

[139] Translation: 30 THE AMERICAN SERIES OF FOREIGN PENAL CODES, THE NETHERLANDS (1997).

[140] See Hoge Raad der Nederlanden [HR] [Supreme Court of the Netherlands], 18 November 1997, NJ 1998, 225.

[141] See Ambos Amicus Brief, *supra* note 29; George P. Fletcher & Jens David Ohlin, *Reclaiming Fundamental Principles of Criminal Law in the Darfur Case*, 3 J. INT'L CRIM. JUST. 539, 548 (2005); Steven Powles, *Joint Criminal Enterprise: Criminal Liability by Prosecutorial Ingenuity and Judicial Creativity?*, 2 J. INT'L CRIM. JUST. 606, 613 (2004); Danner & Martinez, *supra* note 113,

Against this background, it should be welcomed that the ICC Statute and therefore the *Proposed Convention* provide for common purpose liability. Article 4(2)(d) of the *Proposed Convention* may have a wider scope than article 25(3)(d) of the ICC Statute in that it can subsume "third category" JCE. Having said that, it is doubtful whether the JCE concept that has been developed in recent years in ICTY case law (interlinked JCE) and has been termed a surrogate-conspiracy concept should be regarded part of article 4(2)(d). The critique it has attracted for straying into collective liability – thus violating the principle of personal culpability – *and* the fact that ascribing liability to the intellectual perpetrator can be done through the concept of indirect perpetration, which is also provided for in article 4(2)(a), makes the inclusion of interlinked JCE in the *Proposed Convention* undesirable and unnecessary.

C. *Inchoate Liability: Conspiracy and Incitement*

Should conspiracy be included as a crime with regard to CAH? This is a controversial issue. On the one hand, one could argue that it would be a useful concept in capturing intellectual perpetratorship. It does away with the "linking problem" and thus prevents the development of concepts like interlinked JCE III. On the other hand, it is a controversial concept, especially in countries that have a civil law tradition (this could be nuanced, however, with recent terrorism legislation that has made the concept more widely acceptable). As a result, it was controversial in Nuremberg and controversial in drafting the ICC Statute. Moreover, the fact that indirect perpetration is encapsulated in the *Proposed Convention*, providing for (a choate type of) intellectual perpetratorship, makes the inclusion of a conspiracy concept less necessary.

Incitement to commit a crime is more acceptable as an inchoate offense than conspiracy. Its inclusion seems useful and desirable.

IV. SUPERIOR RESPONSIBILITY

Prior to World War II, superior responsibility[142] was an articulation of military practice.[143] This accounts for the term "command responsibility." A position of command generally imposed military-disciplinary responsibility;[144] only in a few cases did it entail *criminal* responsibility.[145] International adjudication in the twentieth century, in particular after World War II, has developed superior responsibility into a concept of criminal responsibility. It was World War II and its aftermath that generated the

---

at 118–19; Mark Osiel, *The Banality of Good: Aligning Incentives Against Mass Atrocities*, 105 COLUM. L. REV. 1751, 1785 (2005); van Sliedregt, *supra* note 103, at 200.

[142] Command responsibility and superior responsibility are used here as interchangeable concepts.

[143] For a historical overview, see William H. Parks, *Command Responsibility for War Crimes*, 62 MIL. L. REV. 1, 1–20 (1973); L.C. Green, *Command Responsibility in International Humanitarian Law*, 5 TRANSNAT'L L. & CONTEMP. PROBS. 319, 320–27 (1995); ILIAS BANTEKAS, PRINCIPLES OF DIRECT AND SUPERIOR RESPONSIBILITY IN INTERNATIONAL HUMANITARIAN LAW 67–70 (2002).

[144] Some trace it back to what they refer to as "the oldest military treatise in the world," written in 500 B.C. by Sun Tzu. SUN TZU, THE ART OF WAR 125 (Samuel B. Griffith trans., 1963).

[145] For an early exception, see Parks who refers to the trial of Peter Hagenbach in 1474, who was brought to trial by the Archduke of Austria for murder, rape, perjury, and other crimes. Hagenbach was tried by an international tribunal composed of judges from the allied States of the Holy Roman

leading cases on superior responsibility.[146] In these cases, the first contours of a modern concept of superior responsibility were established. Superior responsibility is premised on three constitutive elements: (i) a *functional* aspect: a superior's position entails a duty to act; (ii) a *cognitive* element: a superior must have known or should have known of crimes committed by subordinates; and (iii) an *operational* element: a superior must have failed to act.[147] These three elements have been encapsulated in article 86 of Additional Protocol I (AP I) to the 1949 Geneva Conventions, and affirmed by the case law of the ad hoc tribunals for the former Yugoslavia and Rwanda.[148] The leading case is *Prosecutor v. Dedalić et al.*, also referred to as the Čelebići case.[149] Article 28 of the ICC Statute – the most recent provision on superior responsibility, which differs from the provisions in the ICTY and ICTR Statutes in that it effectively contains two separate concepts for superior responsibility, one for military and one for nonmilitary superiors – equally reflects the three elements of superior responsibility.

A. The Scope of Superior Responsibility

The doctrine of superior responsibility punishes *in*activity.[150] Thus, with superior responsibility, a military or nonmilitary superior is held responsible for a failure to act.

> Empire. He was convicted of crimes which he, as a knight, should have prevented as he had had the duty to do so. Parks, *supra* note 143, at 4–5.

[146] See Yamashita v. Styer, 327 U.S. 1 (1946); S. v. Von Leeb *reprinted in* 2 LAW OF WAR: A DOCUMENTARY HISTORY 1421–70 (Leon Friedman ed., 1972) (*High Command* case); United States v. von List *reprinted in* 2 LAW OF WAR: A DOCUMENTARY HISTORY 1303–43 (Leon Friedmand ed., 1972) (*Hostages* case).

[147] See VAN SLIEDREGT, *supra* note 2, at 119–35.

[148] The provision reads:

> The fact that any of the acts referred to in articles 2 to 5 of the present Statute was committed by a subordinate does not relieve his superior of criminal responsibility if he knew or had reason to know that the subordinate was about to commit such acts or had done so and the superior failed to take the necessary and reasonable measures to prevent such acts or to punish the perpetrators thereof.

> Additional Protocol Relating to the Protection of Victim's of International Armed Conflicts art. 86, June 8, 1977, 1125 U.N.T.S. 3.

> The three elements were elaborated upon in the Čelebići Trial Judgment at the ICTY and confirmed in appeal: (i) the existence of a superior-subordinate relationship (functional aspect); (ii) the superior knew or had reason to know that the criminal act was about to be or had been committed (cognitive aspect); and (iii) the superior failed to take the necessary and reasonable measures to prevent the criminal act or to punish the perpetrator thereof (operational aspect). *Čelebići Trial Judgment, supra* note 77, ¶ 346; Prosecutor v. Delalić et al., Case No. IT-96-21-A, Judgment, ¶¶ 189–98, 225–26, 238–39, 256, 263 (Feb. 20, 2001) [hereinafter *Čelebići Appeals Judgment*].

[149] For comments on *Čelebići*, see Ilias Bantekas, *The Contemporary Law of Superior Responsibility*, 93 AM. J. INT'L L. 573 (1999); Matthew Lippman, *The Evolution and Scope of Command Responsibility*, 13 LEIDEN J. INT'L L. 139 (2000); Harmen van der Wilt, *Commentary on the Čelebići Judgement*, in III ANNOTATED LEADING CASES OF INTERNATIONAL CRIMINAL TRIBUNALS: INTERNATIONAL CRIMINAL TRIBUNAL FOR THE FORMER YUGOSLAVIA 1997–1999, 669–83 (André Klip & Göran Sluiter, eds., 2001).

[150] Thus, an *act* such as ordering crimes does not generate superior responsibility. An act of ordering can be prosecuted under a separate mode of liability, namely "ordering" or "instigation" (art. 6(1)/7(1) ICTR/ICTY Statutes) or "ordering, soliciting or inducing" (art. 25(3)(b) ICC Statute).

This failure can consist of two scenarios: (i) one knew, or had reason to know, that crimes were about to be committed and failed to prevent such crimes; or (ii) one did not know of crimes being committed, but once informed, failed to punish and/or report such crimes to the proper authorities. In other words, there is a pre-crime and a post-crime scenario of superior responsibility. As it appears from the decision by the ICTY Appeals Chamber in the *Hadžihasanović and Kubura* case, the post-crime scenario only generates superior responsibility when it can be established that there was a superior-subordinate relationship governed by effective control *at the time of the offense*.[151] Thus, commander Kubura, who had taken up the position of commander on April 1, 1992, was not criminally liable for crimes committed by his subordinates in January 1992 because he had no effective control over his subordinates at the time – that is, he could not have prevented the crimes. Kubura could not be held liable for past crimes even though he did not punish subordinates once he learned of them. At this point we should refer to article 28 of the ICC Statute that stipulates that "subordinate crimes" are *a result of* the superior's failure to exercise control properly. This clause in the ICC Statute rules out superior responsibility for past crimes and thus affirms the *Hadžihasanović and Kubura* interlocutory decision, at least on this particular point.

"Effective control" is a key element in the doctrine of superior responsibility. Only when a superior exercises effective control can the de facto or de jure commander/superior be held liable for crimes committed by the subordinate. "Control" is defined in the NATO glossary as:

> authority exercised by a commander over part of the activities of subordinate organisations, or other organisations not normally under his command, which encompasses the responsibility for implementing orders or directives. All or part of this authority may be transferred or delegated.[152]

Having control means having *effective* authority over subordinates.[153] This accords with the ICTY understanding of the concept of control as shaping the relationships of both direct and indirect subordination that can generate superior responsibility. Control "requires the possession of material abilities to prevent subordinate offences or to punish subordinate offenders." It governs relationships beyond rank and formal authority. Control is particularly relevant in the following three situations. Firstly, with regard to those who hold occupation or executive command. Secondly, control is instrumental in assessing a commander's responsibility for units or organizations not normally under his command.[154] Thirdly, control is the key concept in establishing the scope of de facto superior responsibility of nonmilitary superiors. This already

---

[151] Prosecutor v. Hadžihasanović and Kubura, Case No. IT-01-47-AR72, Decision on Joint Challenge to Jurisdiction (July 16, 2003).
[152] NATO STANDARDIZATION AGENCY, NATO GLOSSARY OF TERM AND ORGANISATIONS AAP-6(U) (1995).
[153] *Čelebići Trial Judgment, supra* note 77, ¶ 378 (endorsed in *Čelebići Appeals Judgment, supra* note 148, ¶¶ 256, 265–66).
[154] The ICTY confirmed this in the *Blaškić* case. *Blaškić Judgment, supra* note 49, ¶¶ 445, 451, 464.

appeared in the *Pohl* case, against defendant Mummenthey, a business manager of industries employing concentration camp labor. In *Čelebići*, the Trial Chamber ruled that, in order for the principle of superior responsibility to be applicable to nonmilitary superiors, an element of control is vital: "[t]he doctrine of superior responsibility extends to civilian superiors only to the extent that they exercise a degree of control over their subordinates which is similar to that of military commanders."[155]

"Knowledge" (of subordinate crimes) is another important ingredient of superior responsibility. The standard of knowledge varies in both national and international criminal law. "Actual knowledge," which corresponds to intention, is at one end of the spectrum, whereas "should have known," which essentially constitutes negligence, is at the other end of the spectrum.[156] The knowledge standard for superior responsibility has been the subject of extensive legal debate at the ICTY and ICTR, particularly at the ICTY. Post–World War II case law and ICRC documents have been consulted to interpret the "knew or had reason to know" standard of articles 6(3) and 7(3) of the ICTR and ICTY Statutes, giving rise to different interpretations. At the ICTY, this resulted in a divergence between two Trial Chambers: the Trial Chamber in *Čelebići*[157] and the Trial Chamber in *Blaškić*.[158] The disagreement evolved around the inclusion or exclusion of the clause "should have known" into the knowledge standard of article 7(3) of the ICTY Statute. Eventually the "dispute" was settled by the *Čelebići* Appeals Chamber that endorsed the Trial Chamber ruling by holding that "should have known," which essentially introduces a negligence standard and, in the words of the Appeals Chamber, a "general duty to know," does not reflect customary international law at the time of the offenses and, as such, is not part of the ICTY legal framework.[159] "Had reason to know" requires proof that there was "information … available to him which would provide notice of crimes committed by his subordinates."[160] The "should have known" standard, however, is codified in article 28(i)(a) of the ICC Statute as the cognitive standard for military superiors.

B. A Multilayered Concept

Superior responsibility in international law is a multilayered concept. It comprises two "liability models": (i) superior responsibility as a separate crime, and (ii) superior

---

[155] *Čelebići Trial Judgment, supra* note 77, ¶ 378.
[156] In *United States v. Medina*, 43 C.M.R. 243 (1971) *reprinted in* 2 THE LAW OF WAR. A DOCUMENTARY HISTORY 1729–38 (Leon Friedman ed., 1972), a Vietnam-related case, an American court accepted "actual knowledge" as the only appropriate standard for superior responsibility. However, the so-called Kahan commission that looked into the massacres in the refugee camps of Sabra and Shatila in Lebanon accepted a much lower "should have known" standard. REPORT OF THE COMMISSION OF INQUIRY INTO THE EVENTS AT THE REFUGEE CAMPS IN BEIRUT, Feb. 7, 1983, 22 I.L.M. 473 (1983).
[157] *Čelebići Trial Judgment, supra* note 77, ¶ 392.
[158] *Blaškić Judgment, supra* note 49, ¶¶ 322–28.
[159] *Čelebići Appeals Judgment, supra* note 148, ¶¶ 226–27.
[160] *Čelebići Trial Judgment, supra* note 77, ¶ 393.

responsibility as a form of participation/mode of liability. In the latter form, at least at the ICTY, superior responsibility requires a close link between superiors and subordinates through "control" and "knowledge."[161] Moreover, in temporal terms, superior responsibility criminalizes two types of *actus reus* pre-crime and *actus reus* post-crime. Lastly, it varies as to *mens rea*; the cognitive aspect ranges from "should have known" to "actual knowledge," where the latter corresponds to *dolus*, intention, and the former equals *culpa*, negligence.

It is instructive to look at national provisions on superior responsibility to understand the layered structure of superior responsibility. The German Code of Crimes against International Law[162] contains three provisions relating to superior criminal responsibility. A superior who intentionally omits to prevent the commission of crimes deserves the same punishment as the subordinate (article 1 § 4(1)) and can be qualified as an accomplice, whereas the failure to properly supervise the subordinate (article 1 § 13) and/or report crimes (article 1 § 14) are separate crimes of omission and as such punished more leniently. The Dutch International Crimes Act[163] provides for a "splitting solution" as well. Section 9(1) criminalizes a superior who "(a) intentionally permits the commission of such an offence by a subordinate; or (b) intentionally fails to take measures, in so far as these are necessary and can be expected of him, if one of his subordinates has committed or intends to commit such an offence." The cognitive aspect of these provisions requires actual knowledge for 1(a) and constructive knowledge ("must have known") for 1(b) – intention and recklessness, respectively. Section 9(2), on the other hand, provides for superior responsibility as a separate offense, a negligent dereliction of duty, which carries a lower sentence than the underlying (subordinate) offense:

> Anyone who culpably neglects to take measures, in so far as these are necessary and can be expected of him, where he has reasonable grounds for suspecting that a subordinate has committed or intends to commit such an offence, shall be liable to no more than two-thirds of the maximum of the principal sentences prescribed for the offences referred to in § 2.

Other national legislators have opted for one particular interpretation of superior responsibility. The UK International Criminal Court Act 2001 regards superior responsibility as a mode of liability. Section 65 of this Act incorporates almost verbatim article 28 of the ICC Statute to which it adds in paragraph 4: "A person responsible under this section for an offence is regarded as aiding, abetting, counselling

---

[161] *See* Elies van Sliedregt, *Article 28 of the ICC Statute: Mode of Liability and/or Separate Offense?*, 20 NEW CRIM. L. REV. 420, 425–27 (2009).

[162] Gesetz zur Einführung des Völkerstrafgesetzbuches, June 26, 2002, RGBl. II at 2254, *available at* http://www.iuscrim.mpg.de/forsch/online_pu.html (in all UN languages).

[163] Act of 9 June 2003, Stb. 2003, 270 (Neth.). For an English translation, see http://www.iccnow.org/resourcestools/ratimptoolkit/nationalregionaltools/legislationdebates/NL.IntCrAct.doc. For a more elaborate analysis of the ICA, see Hans Bevers et al., *The Dutch International Crimes Act, in* NATIONAL LEGISLATION INCORPORATING INTERNATIONAL CRIMES 179–97 (Matthias Neuner ed., 2003).

or procuring the commission of the offence."[164] The Canadian legislature, on the other hand, interpreted superior responsibility as a distinct offense rather than a way of committing one of the three core crimes.[165] This approach was partly prompted by constitutional difficulties.[166]

C. Remodeling Superior Responsibility

It is submitted that superior responsibility should be recognized in its various layers; thus various concepts of superior responsibility should be discerned. So far, none of the international provisions codifying superior responsibility have done that. This new Convention presents such an opportunity.

Especially when "should have known" features as the knowledge standard, superior responsibility would benefit from conceptualization as a separate offense. As a negligent mode of liability for intentional crimes, it has been referred to as "a stunning contradiction between the negligent conduct of the superior and the underlying intent crimes committed by the subordinates."[167] Consider Schabas's statement with regard to superior responsibility and the crime of genocide:

> Indeed, even the ICC will probably be required, in practice, to treat command responsibility as a separate and distinct offence. In the case of genocide, for example, it is generally recognized that the mental element of the crime is one of specific intent. It is logically impossible to convict a person who is merely negligent of a crime of specific intent. Accordingly, the Court, if Article 28 of the Statute is to have any practical effect, will be required to convict commanders of a crime other than genocide, and one that can only be negligent supervision of subordinates who commit genocide.[168]

---

[164] http://www.legislation.hmso.gov.uk/acts/acts2001/20010017.htm.

[165] *See* Crimes Against Humanity and War Crimes Act, 2000 S.C., ch. 24, § 5 (Can.) (the full title of the act is: "An Act respecting genocide, crimes against humanity and war crimes and to implement the Rome Statute of the International Criminal Court, and to make consequential amendments to other Acts."). The Act received Royal Assent on June 29, 2000. Canada's Response to the Questionnaire on the Follow-up to the 27th International Conference of the Red Cross and Red Crescent, http://www.international.gc.ca/humanitarian-humanitaire/conference_27.aspx?lang=eng.

[166] This approach was partly prompted by constitutional difficulties. As William Schabas writes:

> In effect, Canadian constitutional jurisprudence considers it contrary to principles of fundamental justice to stigmatise a person with a conviction for a serious crime like murder or rape where the mental element is one of negligence. A military commander may be convicted under the Rome Statute if he or she 'should have known' that subordinates were committing genocide. Canada's courts would be almost sure to consider genocide as a crime of terrible social stigma, and could be expected to resist any attempt to convict a commander who was merely negligent for the crime or its cognates, although such a commander would certainly be subject to prosecution for lesser crimes.

William A. Schabas, *Canadian Implementing Legislation for the Rome Statute*, 3 Y.B. INT'L HUMANITARIAN L. 342 (2000).

[167] Ambos, *supra* note 20, at 852.

[168] Schabas, *supra* note 166, at 342; *see also* Mirjan Damaška, *The Shadow Side of Command Responsibility*, 49 AM. J. INT'L L. 455 (2001).

The above discussion demonstrates how inappropriate a "should have known" standard would have been in the context of articles 6(3) and 7(3) of the ICTR and ICTY Statutes. The awkward formulation of the superior responsibility concept in the Statutes of the ICTY and the ICTR (as an extension of subordinate liability) rules out negligent liability for specific intent crimes, such as genocide and crimes against humanity.

The current concept of superior responsibility, as codified in the Statutes of the ICTY, the ICTR, and the ICC, does not do justice to superior responsibility by distinguishing the various layers/concepts that make up the concept. The distinction that *is* codified, however, is that between military and nonmilitary superiors in article 28 of the ICC Statute. For the first time in international law, a superior's status (military or nonmilitary) is linked to a certain knowledge standard: "should have known" for military superiors and "consciously disregarding information" for nonmilitary superiors. Such a distinction is unnecessary. By acknowledging the existence of various cognitive standards, we have already discerned the latter aspect as a separate layer within superior responsibility and with it an indication as to how to view superior responsibility: as a mode of liability with an actual knowledge/intent requirement or as a separate offense with a "should have known" negligence standard. Moreover, as I have discussed elsewhere, there is no principal reason for coupling these standards to a particular type of superior.[169] On the contrary, an analysis of customary and conventional international law demonstrates that the three previously discussed constitutive elements of superior responsibility give sufficient room to vary according to the type of superior.

Rather than a distinction between military and nonmilitary superiors, I would favor a "conceptual distinction" between superior responsibility as an intentional mode of liability and superior responsibility as a separate crime of negligence. Like the German and Dutch provisions on superior responsibility, I would propose a "splitting solution," distinguishing the pre-crime and post-crime scenarios while recognizing the conceptual distinction. This means providing for three concepts of superior responsibility: (i) intentionally permitting the commission of crimes by subordinates, (ii) intentionally failing to report crimes, and (iii) negligently failing to supervise subordinates.

1. *Proposed Convention*

Article 5 of the *Proposed Convention* on the responsibility of commanders and other superiors is an exact copy of article 28 of the ICC Statute. Although there may be good reason for aligning command/superior responsibility in the *Proposed Convention* to command/superior liability in the ICC Statute, this author sees it as a missed opportunity. Article 28 of the ICC Statute does not specify the three concepts of liability that make up the theory of command responsibility. Instead, it adopts the distinction made in Article 28 between military and nonmilitary superiors. This, for

---

[169] *See* VAN SLIEDREGT, *supra* note 2, at 191–92.

reasons set out above, is in essence a superfluous distinction and does nothing to identify the conceptual layers of superior responsibility.

V. CONCLUDING OBSERVATIONS

As this commentary made clear from the very outset, it is up to national legislatures to implement and model the concept of individual responsibility for crimes against humanity. Indeed, it is undesirable that the general part of criminal law would be regulated in a Convention that is primarily aimed at obliging States to establish jurisdiction over crimes against humanity and to cooperate with other States in prosecuting these crimes. Reproducing verbatim the liability provisions (articles 25 and 28) of the Rome Statute may be welcomed for reasons of uniformity or for strategic reasons, but it is not this author's preferred position. Instead, a proposed convention should be modeled after conventions like the Torture Convention, the Genocide Convention, and the Geneva Conventions. Unlike the ICC Statute and the Statutes of the ICTY and the ICTR, provisions on modes of liability in these conventions have an *expressive* function; they express the will to widen the category of possible offenders. Modes of liability in the Statutes of the ICTY, the ICTR, and the ICC have an additional function, which is to provide for the substantive law of an international court; they thus have an *empowering/jurisdictional* function.

Furthermore, it is unnecessary to regulate criminal responsibility in an international treaty. Traditional forms of liability, such as perpetration and aiding and abetting, are already the part of most national criminal law systems. Certain crime-specific concepts, such as joint criminal enterprise/common purpose liability and indirect perpetration, are familiar to domestic criminal law. In fact, these liability theories have been conceptualized at the national level. The fight against organized and white-collar crime has generated liability theories that have been at the basis of international liability theories, such as JCE. Superior responsibility, on the other hand, is a concept that has a true international pedigree. As a theory of liability, it is unique to international law, although analogous concepts exist at the national level (parental responsibility, criminal responsibility of employers).

This chapter may serve as guidance for those who are responsible for implementing a future CAH Convention, be it diplomats, lawmakers, or judges. From the analysis of criminal responsibility in international law, particularly of ICTY and ICTR case law, it appears that a number of "crime-specific" modes of liability can be distinguished, and that the *Proposed Convention* very appropriately provides for them. The analysis also goes to show that most crime-specific modalities have underpinnings in national criminal law. The above may be relied on to mirror national concepts to international equivalents – to understand how they differ and/or overlap. Superior responsibility – an international liability theory – has been analyzed and discussed in its various components. The reflections on its multilayered structure may serve to inspire implementation at the national level.

11

Terrorism and Crimes Against Humanity

Michael P. Scharf and Michael A. Newton

I. INTRODUCTION

International law currently embodies universal and strongly articulated support for the positivist premise that "any acts of terrorism are criminal and unjustifiable, regardless of their motivation, whenever and by whomsoever committed and are to be unequivocally condemned."[1] The UN General Assembly reaffirms that "no terrorist act can be justified in any circumstances,"[2] and regional instruments adhere to the same legal premise.[3] The security, stability, economic vitality, sovereignty, political independence, and citizen safety of all States are accordingly protected against terrorist acts, irrespective of how democratic or human rights abiding the government in question is. The notion that States must use their domestic processes to cooperate together in the investigation and punishment of terrorist acts therefore reflects the truism that acts of terrorism violate the essential precepts of civilization.

As a matter of qualitative jurisprudence, terrorist offenses are on substantive par with the grave breaches provisions of the 1949 Geneva Conventions, the 1948 Genocide Convention, and the provisions of the Torture Convention; the same *aut dedere aut punire* obligation that applies to grave breaches, genocide, and torture also applies to terrorism.[4] If a terrorist is found on the territory of a State Party,

---

[1] *Declaration on the Issue of Combating Terrorism*, S.C. Res. 1456, U.N. Doc. S/RES/1456 (Jan. 20, 2003). The United Nations Global Counterterrorism Strategy reiterates the "strong condemnation" of the international community and states that "terrorism in all its forms and manifestations, committed by whomever, wherever and for whatever purposes."

[2] *Measures to Eliminate International Terrorism*, U.N. Doc. A/C.6/62/L.14, U.N. GAOR, 62d Sess., Agenda Item 108 (Nov. 19, 2007).

[3] Council Framework Decision 2002/475/JHA of 13 June 2002 on combating terrorism, pmbl. (1)-(2), 2002 O.J. (L 164) 3 (EU); Convention of the Organisation of the Islamic Conference on Combating International Terrorism pmbl., July 1999, Res. No. 59/26-P Annex; OAU Ministerial Communiqué on Terrorism, Central Organ/MEC/MIN/Ex-Ord(V) (Nov. 11, 2001), *available at* www.dfa.gov.za/docs/terroau.htm; Declaration of Lima to Prevent, Combat, and Eliminate Terrorism pmbl., OAS Doc. No. OEA/Ser.K/XXXIII.1/CEITE/doc.28/96 rev.1 (Apr. 26, 1996), *available at* www.oas.org/jurdico/english/docu6.htm.

[4] Michael Scharf, *Aut dedere aut judicare*, *in* THE MAX PLANCK ENCYCLOPEDIA OF PUBLIC INTERNATIONAL LAW (2008), *available at* www.mpepil.com (reviewing the framework of modern conventions containing the *aut dedere aut punire* obligation and quoting Hugo Grotius' 1625 formulation that "[t]he state … ought to do one of two things…. It should either punish the guilty person as he deserves, or it should entrust him to the discretion of the party making the appeal.

that State has an affirmative duty arising from the modern multilateral framework either to extradite the terrorist suspect to another State that itself has the motivation and personal jurisdiction to adjudicate the offender, or in the alternative it must "without exception whatsoever and whether or not that offense was committed in its territory ... submit the case without undue delay to its competent authorities for the purpose of prosecution through proceedings in accordance with the laws of that state."⁵ This *aut dedere aut judicare* implementation of an obligation to treat terrorist offenses as crimes universally recognized and proscribed flows from the moral and legal commitment of States to each other and the demands of sovereignty itself.

Breaking down the macro problem of terrorism into identifiable manifestations, nation States have accordingly negotiated and ratified a web of multilateral antiterrorism conventions built on the cornerstone of sovereign enforcement of applicable norms. However, the persistence of transnational terrorism as a feature of the international community shows that the plethora of conventions focusing on domestic enforcement bolstered by multilateral cooperation is no panacea.⁶ The attacks of September 11, 2001 highlighted this striking systematic failure and prompted renewed interest in the possibility of an internationally accepted general definition of terrorism and an international forum to prosecute terrorist offenders.

The shock of September 11 regenerated debate over suitability and sufficiency of domestic adjudication for crimes of transnational terrorism. In particular, the perception that fundamental weaknesses plagued the normative structure sparked reassessment about the linkages between international terrorism and the prohibitions derived from international law. Given the inability of domestic forums to eradicate transnational terrorism, it was perhaps inevitable that the aftermath of September 11 would engender a groundswell of support for the creation of an international judicial forum to prosecute such terrorists. Even as they acknowledge that national courts are the backbone for the systematic prosecution of international terrorists, some scholars observe that an international forum would "symbolize global justice for global crimes."⁷ In addition, in the words of one prominent international lawyer, if "we're thinking in terms of a global war on terrorism in the long-term, it would be better to try [bin Laden] in an international forum where we could get the input,

---

This latter course is rendition.... [A] people or king is not absolutely bound to surrender a culprit, but ... either to surrender or to punish him.").

[5] International Convention for the Suppression of Terrorist Bombings, art. 8, ¶ 1, G.A. Res. 164, U.N. GAOR, 52d Sess., Supp. No. 49, at 389, U.N. Doc. A/52/49 (Dec. 15, 1997) [hereinafter *Terrorist Bombing Convention*].

[6] M. CHERIF BASSIOUNI, INTERNATIONAL TERRORISM: MULTILATERAL CONVENTIONS (1937–2001) (2001); M. Cherif Bassiouni, *Legal Control of International Terrorism: A Policy Oriented Assessment*, 43 HARV. INT'L L.J. 83, 90 (2001).

[7] Anne-Marie Slaughter, *Luncheon Address: Rogue Regimes and the Individualization of International Law*, 36 NEW ENG. L. REV. 815, 820 (2002) (comments based on a more detailed explication found in Anne-Marie Slaughter & William Burke-White, *An International Constitutional Moment*, 43 HARV. INT'L L.J. 1 [2002]).

but also the condemnation of judges from all the world's legal systems under both national and international law."[8]

The September 11 attacks raised the corollary question whether terrorist acts are properly prosecutable within the existing structure of international humanitarian law or whether change is needed. There has been significant debate over the typology of crimes against humanity and speculation over the advisability of adding a stand-alone offense of "terrorism" to the existing array of offenses specified within the crimes against humanity rubric.[9] One other possible approach would be to deem terrorism as a discrete crime against humanity under the category of "other inhumane acts." This essay examines whether terrorism ought to be incorporated within the existing understanding of crimes against humanity or should be added as a substantive offense in its own right within the context of a multilateral convention dedicated to the corpus of crimes against humanity. We conclude that a separate offense of "terrorism" as a subcomponent of crimes against humanity law would not materially advance the core purposes of the international criminal law regime.

II. THE CURRENT ANTITERRORISM CONVENTIONS APPROACH

International interest in addressing terrorist acts dates to the League of Nations era.[10] In 1926, the International Congress of Penal Law recommended that the Permanent

---

[8] *Burden of Proof: America's Legal War on Terrorism: Are There Rules for Hunting Terrorists? Could bin Laden be Brought to Trial?* (CNN television broadcast Oct. 6, 2001), cited in David J. Scheffer, *The Future of Atrocity Law*, SUFFOLK TRANSNAT'L L. REV. 389, 390 n. 3 (2002). This view perhaps represents a modern incarnation of the views articulated by the then-Secretary of State Thomas Jefferson in a letter dated April 18, 1793:

> Compacts ... between nation and nation, are obligatory on them by the same moral law which obliges individuals to observe their compacts ... It is true that nations are to be judges for themselves; since no one nation has a right to sit in judgment over another, but the tribunal of our conscience remains, and that also of the opinion of the world. These will review the sentence we pass in our own case, and as we respect these, we must see that in judging ourselves we have honestly done the part of impartial and rigorous judges.

THOMAS JEFFERSON, 8 WRITINGS OF THOMAS JEFFERSON 11 (1904).

[9] *See Rome Statute of the International Criminal Court*, United Nations Diplomatic Conference of Plenipotentiaries on the Establishment of an International Criminal Court, July 17, 1998, U.N. Doc. A/CONF.183/9 (1998) [hereinafter *Rome Statute*] (listing the following *acti rei* as crimes against humanity and proffering internationally accepted definitions of key terms within the specified offenses: Murder; Extermination; Enslavement; Deportation or forcible transfer of population; Imprisonment or other severe deprivation of physical liberty in violation of fundamental rules of international law; Torture; Rape, sexual slavery, enforced prostitution, forced pregnancy, enforced sterilization, or any other form of sexual violence of comparable gravity; Persecution against any identifiable group or collectivity on political, racial, national, ethnic, cultural, religious, gender as defined in paragraph 3, or other grounds that are universally recognized as impermissible under international law, in connection with any act referred to in this paragraph or any crime within the jurisdiction of the Court; Enforced disappearance of persons; The crime of apartheid; Other inhumane acts of a similar character intentionally causing great suffering, or serious injury to body or to mental or physical health).

[10] *Voeu of the International Congress of Penal Law Concerning an International Criminal Court* (1926), *reprinted in Historical Survey of the Question of International Criminal Jurisdiction, Memorandum Submitted by the Secretary-General* 74, U.N. Doc. A/CN.4/7Rev.1 (May 27, 1949)

Court of International Justice "be competent to judge individual liabilities" incurred as a result of crimes considered as international offenses "which constitute a threat to world peace."[11] This proposal initially died on the vine of international diplomacy. However, similar proposals were made in subsequent years. The assassination of King Alexander of Yugoslavia in Marseilles on October 9, 1934, for example, prompted the French government to propose an international convention for the suppression of terrorism in a letter to the Secretary-General of the League of Nations.[12] The core of the French proposal was a suggestion that an international criminal court would be the most feasible forum for addressing political crimes of an international character, and the Council of the League responded by establishing a Committee of Experts to prepare a preliminary draft of "an international convention to assure the repression of conspiracies or crimes committed with a political and terrorist purpose."[13] From November 1 to November 16, 1937, the International Conference for the Repression of Terrorism met in Geneva and adopted a Convention for the Creation of an International Criminal Court.[14] This effort to establish an international forum to respond to terrorism was implicitly rejected by the international community after only one State (Italy) ratified the multilateral treaty.

Although the proposed 1937 Convention never entered into force, it remains highly relevant to the current debate for two reasons. First, the jurisdiction of the international court proposed in the 1937 treaty derived solely from the consent of the affected States,[15] and the court was limited to applying the "least severe" domestic law of either the State in which the crimes were committed or the State of the offender's nationality.[16] In effect, the 1937 Convention created an internationalized process for applying the substantive law of different domestic systems, which is the antithesis of modern arguments that an international forum is essential for applying the international norms against terrorism. The approach of the 1937 Convention is essentially

---

(translating the original French text found in Premier congrès international de droit pénal, Actes du congrès 634).

[11] Id. This strain of thought eventually led to the development of a draft statute for a criminal chamber of the Permanent International Court of Justice. International Law Association, *Report of the Thirty-fourth Conference* 113–25 (1927).

[12] *Historical Survey of the Question of International Criminal Jurisdiction, Memorandum Submitted by the Secretary General* 16, U.N. Doc. A/CN.4/7Rev.1 (May 27, 1949).

[13] Id. *See also* 15 LEAGUE OF NATIONS O.J. 1760 (1934) (containing the text of the full resolution passed by the Council).

[14] Convention for the Prevention and Punishment of Terrorism, *opened for signature* Nov. 16, 1937, League of Nations Doc. C.546(I).M.383(I)1937.V, 19 LEAGUE OF NATIONS O.J. 23 (1938), *reprinted in* M. CHERIF BASSIOUNI, INTERNATIONAL TERRORISM: MULTILATERAL CONVENTIONS (1937–2001) 71 (2001) [hereinafter 1937 *Convention*].

[15] 1937 *Convention*, *supra* note 14, art. 21 (referring to the obligation of the domestic States to enact criminal legislation to punish the acts defined in the underlying multilateral treaty and empowering those same States to "commit the accused to trial" before the International Criminal Court). This provision differs from the jurisdictional provisions of the Rome Statute of the International Criminal Court, which allow the ICC to bypass nonconsenting states in establishing personal jurisdiction over their citizens. *See Rome Statute*, *supra* note 9, arts. 12–19.

[16] 1937 *Convention*, *supra* note 14, art. 21.

the precursor for the Lockerbie Bombing Court[17] and stands in sharp contrast to current efforts to portray transnational terrorism as an international problem that requires a generalized international definition and jurisdiction. Second, it is important to note that every one of the multilateral antiterrorism conventions adopted since the 1937 Convention have adhered to its pattern by defining specific terrorist acts as substantive violations of international law and specifically requiring sovereign States to enact domestic criminal legislation for the purpose of punishing those acts. This uniform historical pattern undercuts arguments that the very nature of transnational terrorism requires articulation of terrorism as a crime against humanity.

III. DEFINITIONAL UNCERTAINTY

The clarity with which international law categorizes and condemns discrete manifestations of terrorism actually masks the indeterminacy of the underlying definitional framework. "Terrorism" is a concept caught in a kaleidoscope of conflicting sociological, political, psychological, moral, and yes, legal perspectives. The claim that "what looks, smells and kills like terrorism is terrorism"[18] belies the reality that the international community has unsuccessfully sought to reach agreement on a comprehensive definition of the term for more than a century.[19] No comprehensive definition has achieved universal acceptance, whether approached from a moral,[20] psychological,[21] or historical[22] perspective. Despite the fact that non-State

---

[17] The Scottish Court in The Netherlands was an internationalized process applying Scottish law to prosecute the Libyan nationals responsible for the 1988 bombing of Pan Am Flight 103. *See* http://www.scotcourts.gov.uk/index1.asp?path=%2Fhtml%2Flockerbie%2Easp (Jan. 30, 2003). *See* Michael P. Scharf, *The Lockerbie Model of Transfer of Proceedings*, in II INTERNATIONAL CRIMINAL LAW: MULTILTERAL AND BILATERAL ENFORCEMENT MECHANISMS (M. Cherif Bassiouni ed., 3rd ed. 2008).

[18] General Assembly, *Debate on Measures to Eliminate International Terrorism*, U.N. GAOR, 56th Sess., 12th plen. mtg. at 18, U.N. Doc. A/56/PV.12 (Oct. 1, 2001) (Statement of Sir Jeremy Greenstock, Ambassador from the United Kingdom).

[19] Thomas M. Franck & Bert B. Lockwood, Jr., *Preliminary Thoughts Towards an International Convention on Terrorism*, 68 AM. J. INT'L L. 69 (1974).

[20] C. A. J. Coady, *The Morality of Terrorism*, 60 PHIL. 47, 52 (1985).

[21] Martha Crenshaw, *The Psychology of Terrorism: An Agenda for the 21st Century*, 21 POL. PSYCHOL. 405, 406 (2000).

[22] Gilbert Guillaume, *Terrorism and International Law*, 53 INT'L & COMP. L.Q. 537, 540 (2004). In the context of international law, it would appear to us that the adjective "terrorist" may be applied to any criminal activity involving the use of violence in circumstances likely to cause bodily harm or a threat to human life, in connection with an enterprise whose aim is to provoke terror. Three conditions thus have to be met: (a) the perpetration of certain acts of violence capable of causing death, or at the very least severe physical injury. Certain texts of domestic and European law go further than this, however, and consider that the destruction of property even without any danger for human life may also constitute a terrorist act; (b) an individual or collective enterprise that is not simply improvised – in other words, an organized operation or concerted plan reflected in coordinated efforts to achieve a specific goal (which, for example, excludes the case of the deranged killer who shoots at everyone in sight); (c) the pursuit of an objective: to create terror among certain predetermined persons, groups or, more commonly, the public at large (thus differentiating terrorism from the political assassination of a single personality, such as that of Julius Caesar or Brutus).

participants in a noninternational armed conflict are fully subject to prosecution for their warlike acts,[23] and will often be simultaneously subject to the jurisdiction of courts with substantive authority over terrorism, criminal law generally disfavors reliance on terms such as "terrorism" that are perceived to lack objectivity, precision, and emotive neutrality. Some have even argued that applying the label "terrorist" to a non-State actor in a noninternational armed conflict carries a pejorative taint that creates an undesirable disincentive to abide by the laws and customs of war.[24]

The paradox in a post–September 11 world is that the UN Security Council *requires* nations to "accept and carry out"[25] resolutions that oblige them to act against "terrorists" and "terrorism" but has not reached consensus on what those terms mean. Giving operative legal significance to vaguely defined terms could be seen as undermining the world's "normative and moral stance against terrorism."[26] As noted earlier, rather than relying on an overarching definitional framework couched as a crime against humanity with uncertain pedigree and feigned international acceptance, the international community developed a patchwork of norms and conventions that seek to prevent and punish specific manifestations of terrorist activities.[27]

IV. TERRORIST ACTS AS *JUS IN BELLO* VIOLATIONS

The *sine qua non* of any crime against humanity is that the underlying criminal acts constitute, in the aggregate, "a widespread or systematic attack directed against

---

[23] YORAM DINSTEIN, THE CONDUCT OF HOSTILITIES UNDER THE LAW OF INTERNATIONAL ARMED CONFLICT 31 (2d ed. 2004) (clarifying that *jus in bello* merely prescribes the offenses under which lawful combatants can be brought to trial. With regard to unlawful combatants, *jus in bello* "merely takes off the mantle of immunity from the defendant, who is therefore accessible to penal charges for any offense committed against the domestic legal system.").

[24] See M. Cherif Bassiouni, *The New Wars and the Crisis of Compliance with the Law of Armed Conflict by Non-State Actors*, 98 J. CRIM. L. & CRIMINOLOGY 711(2008).

[25] UN Charter, art. 25.

[26] UN High-level Panel on Threats, Challenges and Change, A *More Secure World: Our Shared Responsibility*, ¶ 159, U.N. Doc. A/59/565 (Dec. 2, 2004).

[27] Convention on Offenses and Certain Other Acts Committed on Board Aircraft, Sept. 14, 1963, 20 U.S.T. 2941, 704 U.N.T.S. 219 [hereinafter *Tokyo Hijacking Convention*]; Hague Convention for the Suppression of Unlawful Seizure of Aircraft, Dec. 16, 1970, 22 U.S.T. 1641, 860 U.N.T.S. 105 [hereinafter *Hague Hijacking Convention*]; Montreal Convention for the Suppression of Unlawful Acts Against the Safety of Civil Aviation, Sept. 23, 1971, 24 U.S.T. 565, 974 U.N.T.S. 177 [hereinafter *Montreal Hijacking Convention*]; Protocol for the Suppression of Unlawful Acts of Violence at Airports Serving International Civil Aviation, Feb. 24, 1988, 1589 U.N.T.S. 474, 27 I.L.M. 627; Convention on the High Seas, Apr. 29, 1958, 13 U.S.T. 2312, 450 U.N.T.S. 82; United Nations Convention on Law of the Sea, Dec. 10, 1982, U.N. Doc. A/Conf.62/122, 21 I.L.M. 1261; Convention on the Prevention and Punishment of Crimes Against Internationally Protected Persons, Including Diplomatic Agents, Dec. 14, 1973, 28 U.S.T. 1975, 1035 U.N.T.S. 167; Convention on the Safety of United Nations and Associated Personnel, G.A. Res. 49/59, U.N. Doc. A/Res/49/59 (Feb. 17, 1995); Convention for the Suppression of Unlawful Acts Against the Safety of Maritime Navigation, Mar. 10, 1988, 1678 U.N.T.S. 221; Protocol for the Suppression of Unlawful Acts Against the Safety of Fixed Platforms Located on the Continental Shelf, Mar. 10, 1988, 1678 U.N.T.S. 304; International Convention Against the Taking of Hostages, Dec. 17, 1979, T.I.A.S. 11,081, 1316 U.N.T.S. 205; *Terrorist Bombing Convention*, *supra* note 5.

a civilian population."[28] Although the "attack" for the purpose of charging a perpetrator may or may not have a purely military character, almost any conceivable terrorist acts that could rise to the level of a crime against humanity would be covered by the existing framework of *jus in bello* as a violation of the established laws and customs of war. At present, there does not appear to be a class of terrorist acts that warrant specification as an articulated crime against humanity to prevent acquittals of those perpetrators clever or lucky enough to exploit lacunae in current case law.

Undercutting the very essence of terrorist tactics and motivations, the participants in all conflicts are required by international humanitarian law to distinguish "at all times" between civilians and protected civilian objects and are permitted to "direct their operations only against military objectives."[29] This principle of distinction is celebrated as a cornerstone of the law of war.[30] Civilians may never be deliberately attacked unless and for such time as they directly participate in hostilities,[31] and by extension the war crime of first importance in both international[32] and noninternational[33] armed conflicts is that of "[i]ntentionally directing attacks against the civilian population as such or against individual civilians not taking direct part in the hostilities." Both Protocol I[34] and Protocol II[35] expressly prohibit "acts or threats of violence the primary purpose of which is to spread terror among the civilian population." The wave of terrorist acts that provided the context for the negotiation of the 1977 Additional Protocols was conducted by "the alphabet soup terrorists of the past, the IRA, ETA, PLO, RAF, and others [that] were political organizations with political goals."[36] Hence, it is wholly logical that the texts specifically address and condemn the use of terror as a tactic.

Terrorists therefore commit criminal acts outside the protected framework of international humanitarian law. They cannot hide behind a shield of combatant immunity in the same manner as lawful combatants; they are always subject to prosecution

---

[28] See Rome Statute, *supra* note 9, art. 7 ("For the purpose of this Statute, 'crime against humanity' means any of the following acts when committed as part of a widespread or systematic attack directed against any civilian population, with knowledge of the attack.").

[29] Protocol I Additional to the Geneva Conventions of 12 August 1949 (Relating to the Protection of Victims of International Armed Conflicts), Dec. 12, 1977, U.N. Doc. A/32/144, Annex I, art. 48, *reprinted in* 16 I.L.M. 1391 (1977) [hereinafter *Protocol I*].

[30] Jakob Kellenberger, *International Humanitarian Law at the Beginning of the 21st Century*, (Sept. 5, 2002), *available at* http://www.icrc.org/Web/Eng/siteeng0.nsf/iwpList74/EFC5A1C8D8 DD70B9C1256C36002EFC1E.

[31] *Protocol I*, *supra* note 29, art. 51(2)(3).

[32] *Rome Statute*, *supra* note 9, art. 8(2)(b)(1).

[33] *Id.* art. 8(2)(e)(1).

[34] *Protocol I*, *supra* note 29, art. 51(2).

[35] Protocol Additional to the Geneva Conventions of 12 August 1949 (Relating to the Protection of the Victims of Non-International Armed Conflicts), Annex II, art. 13(2), Dec. 12, 1977, 26 I.L.M. 561 (1978) [hereinafter *Protocol II*].

[36] RALPH PETERS, NEW GLORY: EXPANDING AMERICA'S GLOBAL SUPREMACY 155 (2005) (adding that "no matter how brutal their actions or unrealistic their goals, their common intent was to gain a people's independence or to force their ideology on society").

for their actions irrespective of their subjective motivations.[37] Domestic courts around the world have, without exception, rejected assertions of combatant immunity raised by defendants in terrorism related cases.[38] This was recently reaffirmed by a Canadian court in the case of Mohammed Momin Khawaja. Khawaja was involved in an al-Qaeda-inspired plot that spanned three continents to build and detonate ammonium nitrate-rich fertilizer bombs. The plot surfaced during an investigation by the British Security Services, and the day after his arrest in Ottawa, his co-conspirators were arrested in London.[39] Khawaja was convicted in Canada, and his seven co-conspirators were sentenced to life imprisonment by British authorities.

The parallel structure of multilateral conventions prohibiting specific manifestations of terrorism makes clear that the definitional framework is coextensive with conduct that would also violate the core prohibitions of the laws and customs of war. Though nowhere do they use the word "terrorism," the three International Civil Aviation Organization (ICAO) conventions[40] defining offenses against plane and passenger safety are widely acknowledged to represent the first true antiterrorism conventions. The Hague Convention of 1970 (Hijacking Convention) constitutes

---

[37] In a classic treatise, Professor Julius Stone described the line between lawful participants in conflict and unprivileged or "unprotected" combatants as follows:

> The distinction draws the line between personnel who, on capture, are entitled under international law to certain minimal treatment as prisoners of war, and those not entitled to such protection. 'Non-combatants' who engaged in hostilities are one of the classes deprived of such protection ... Such unprivileged belligerents, though not condemned by international law, are not protected by it, but are left to the discretion of the belligerents threatened by their activities.

JULIUS STONE, LEGAL CONTROLS ON INTERNATIONAL CONFLICT 549 (1954).

[38] Termed the "shoe bomber," Richard Reid pled guilty to attempted multiple murders for his attempt to blow up a *civilian* airliner *in* flight using a bomb built into the sole of his shoe. His attempt was foiled by alert fellow passengers. Announcing the sentence of life imprisonment, U.S. District Judge William Young rejected the assertion of combatant immunity as follows:

> Here in this court, where we deal with individuals as individuals, and care for individuals as individuals, as human beings we reach out for justice, you are not an enemy combatant. You are a terrorist. You are not a soldier in any war. You are a terrorist. To give you that reference, to call you a soldier gives you far too much stature. Whether it is the officers of government who do it or your attorney who does it, or that happens to be your view, you are a terrorist. And we do not negotiate with terrorists. We do not treat with terrorists. We do not sign documents with terrorists. We hunt them down one by one and bring them to justice. So war talk is way out of line in this court. You are a big fellow. But you are not that big. You're no warrior. I know warriors. You are a terrorist. A species of criminal guilty of multiple attempted murders.

http://www.cnn.com/2003/LAW/01/31/reid.transcript/; *see also* United States v. Reid, No. 1:02-cr-10013-WGY (D. Mass. Jan. 16, 2002).

[39] R. v. Khawaja, File No. 04-G30282 (Ont. Sup. Ct. Oct. 29, 2008) (Can.); *see also* CrimA 6659/06, 1757/07, 8228/07, 3621/08 A & B v. Israel [2008], *available at* http://www.elyon1.court.gov.il/files_eng/06/590/066/n04/06066590.n04.pdf (Supreme Court of Israel sitting as Court of Criminal Appeals); Munaf v. Geren, 128 S. Ct. 2207 (2008).

[40] Tokyo Hijacking Convention, *supra* note 27; Hague Hijacking Convention, *supra* note 27; Montreal Hijacking Convention, *supra* note 27.

the model subsequently used for the modern antiterrorism conventions, including the several regional conventions adopted between 1971 and 2002.[41]

Echoing the original language of the 1937 League of Nations Convention, the 1994 General Assembly Resolution on "Measures to Eliminate International Terrorism" does provide a general definition of terrorism that contrasts with the more modern multilateral conventions by proscribing:

> [c]riminal acts intended or calculated to provoke a state of terror in the general public, a group of persons or particular persons for political purposes are in any circumstance unjustifiable, whatever the considerations of a political, philosophical, ideological, racial, ethnic, religious or any other nature that may be invoked to justify them.[42]

The difference in the General Assembly context was the inclusion of State terrorism and the clear intent to disallow any exceptions. However, the modern conventions returned to the familiar foundations drawn from the laws and customs of war. The 1999 Terrorist Financing Convention, for example, defines terrorism as:

> [a]ny ... act intended to cause death or serious bodily injury to a civilian, or to any other person not taking an active part in the hostilities in a situation of armed conflict, when the purpose of such act, by its nature or context, is to intimidate a population, or to compel a Government or an international organization to do or to abstain from doing any act.[43]

Recent practice has reinforced the jurisprudential value of these prohibitions in that the deliberate use of terror as a military tactic cannot constitute a viable basis for legalized violence. In convicting one perpetrator, the International Criminal Tribunal for the former Yugoslavia (ICTY) opined that "the prohibition against terror is a specific prohibition within the general prohibition of attack on civilians," the latter of which constitutes "a peremptory norm of international law."[44] In other words, there can never be an attack that is expressly intended to provoke terror in the civilian

---

[41] Organization of American States, Convention to Prevent and Punish the Acts of Terrorism Taking the Form of Crimes against Persons and Related Extortion That Are of International Significance, Feb. 2, 1971, 27 U.S.T. 3949, 1986 U.N.T.S. 195 [hereinafter *OAS Convention*]; Council of Europe, European Convention on the Suppression of Terrorism, Jan. 27, 1977, 1137 U.N.T.S. 93, Europ. T.S. No. 90 [hereinafter *COE Convention*]; South Asian Association for Regional Cooperation, Regional Convention on Suppression of Terrorism, Nov. 4, 1987; League of Arab States, Arab Convention for the Suppression of Terrorism, Apr. 22, 1998, *available at* http://www.al-bab.com/arab/docs/league/terrorism98.htm; Organization of African Unity Convention on the Prevention and Combating of Terrorism, June 14, 1999, OAU Doc. AHG/Dec. 132 (XXXV) [hereinafter *OAU Convention*]; Convention of the Organisation of the Islamic Conference on Combating International Terrorism, July 1, 1999, *reprinted in* U.N.Doc. A/54/637, Annex (Oct. 11, 2008) [hereinafter *OIC Convention*]; Treaty on Cooperation among States Members of the Commonwealth of Independent States in Combating Terrorism, June 4, 1999; Inter-American Convention Against Terrorism, June 3, 2002, 42 I.L.M. 19.

[42] *Measures to Eliminate Terrorism*, G.A. Res. 49/60, ¶ I.3, U.N. Doc. A/RES/49/60 (Dec. 9, 1994).

[43] International Convention for the Suppression of the Financing of Terrorism art. 2(1)(b), G.A. Res. 54/109, U.N. Doc. A/RES/54/109 (Feb. 25, 2009) [hereinafter *Terrorist Financing Convention*].

[44] Prosecutor v. Galić, Case No. IT-98-29-T, Judgment & Opinion, ¶¶ 66, 94–100 (Dec. 5, 2003), *available at* http://www.icty.org/x/cases/galic/tjug/en/gal-tj031205e.pdf.

population or political structure that comports with the laws and customs of war. Indeed, the International Committee of the Red Cross (ICRC) Commentary notes that military operations that seek to inflict terror "are particularly reprehensible, occur frequently, and inflict particularly cruel suffering on the civilian population."[45] Likewise, in upholding the convictions in the *AFRC* case, the Appeals Chamber of the Special Court for Sierra Leone accepted that convictions for "acts of terrorism" could lie for the three appellants who engaged in a "common plan to carry out a campaign of terrorising and collectively punishing the civilian population of Sierra Leone ... in order to achieve the ultimate objective of gaining and exercising political power and control over the territory of Sierra Leone."[46] As this book was going to press, Bosnian Serb leader Radovan Karadžić was being tried at the ICTY, *inter alia*, on the charge of unlawfully inflicting terror upon civilians.[47]

In short, this established jurisdictional framework conveys an extensive and growing punitive capacity over terrorist acts. For example, the 2005 Council of Europe Convention on the Prevention of Terrorism required States Parties to adopt three new criminal offenses (along with penalties commensurate with their severity): "public provocation to commit a terrorist offense," recruitment for terrorism, and training for terrorism.[48] Any of those acts committed in the context of conflict aimed at facilitating deliberate attacks against civilians for the purpose of causing indiscriminate terror would already violate well-established international humanitarian law. Furthermore, using the recurring formula that typifies the multilateral regime, the modern conventions seeking to prevent and punish terrorist acts embody the broadest possible jurisdictional authority for domestic courts.[49] The proponents of a new international crime against humanity should bear the burden of establishing

---

[45] COMMENTARY ON THE ADDITIONAL PROTOCOLS OF 8 JUNE 1977 TO THE GENEVA CONVENTIONS OF 12 AUGUST 1949 ¶ 4785 n.19 (Claude Pilloud, Yves Sandoz, Christophe Swinarski & Bruno Zimmermann eds., 1987).

[46] Prosecutor v. Brima, Kamara and Kanu, Case No. SCSL-04-16-A, Judgment, ¶ 70, (Feb. 22, 2008) [hereinafter *AFRC Appeals Judgment*]; *see* Prosecutor v. Brima, Kamara and Kanu, Case No. SCSL-04-16-T, Judgment, ¶¶ 1633, 2113, 2117, 2121 (June 27, 2007), *available at* http://www.sc-sl.org/CASES/ArmedForcesRevolutionaryCouncilAFRCComplete/AFRCJudgment/tabid/173/Default.aspx.

[47] Prosecutor v. Karadžić, Case No. IT-95-5/18-PT, Amended Indictment, ¶¶ 44–52 (Apr. 28, 2000), *available at* http://icr.icty.org/LegalRef/CMSDocStore/Public/English/Indictment/NotIndexable/IT-95-5%2318/IND253R0000051360.TIF.

[48] Council of Europe, Convention on the Prevention of Terrorism, arts. 5–7, *opened for signature* May 16, 2005, E.T.S. No. 196.

[49] *Terrorist Financing Convention*, *supra* note 43, art. 7.
1. Each State Party shall take such measures as may be necessary to establish its jurisdiction over the offences set forth in article 2 when:
(a) The offence is committed in the territory of that State;
(b) The offence is committed on board a vessel flying the flag of that State or an aircraft registered under the laws of that State at the time the offence is committed;
(c) The offence is committed by a national of that State.
2. A State Party may also establish its jurisdiction over any such offence when:
(a) The offence was directed towards or resulted in the carrying out of an offence referred to in article 2, paragraph 1, subparagraph (a) or (b), in the territory of or against a national of that State;

its usefulness on the international landscape by illustrating existing gaps in coverage or condemnation that could be remedied. Moreover, an effort to augment existing *jus in bello* principles could actually result in more frequent acts of terrorism by introducing new uncertainty and imprecision into the jurisprudential dialogue.

V. TERRORISM AS A CRIME AGAINST HUMANITY

The key to whether the *jus in bello* framework discussed earlier applies to acts of terrorism is the "armed conflict threshold."[50] By their terms, the relevant international humanitarian law conventions do not apply to "situations of internal disturbances and tensions such as riots and isolated and sporadic acts of violence."[51] Expanding the corpus of crimes against humanity could provide a harmonized legal framework applicable in both times of armed conflict or peace.[52] Nevertheless, in situations falling outside of armed conflict, terrorist acts are proscribed by the comprehensive framework of multinational antiterrorism conventions that outlaw hostage taking, hijacking, aircraft and maritime sabotage, attacks at airports, attacks against diplomats and government

> (b) The offence was directed towards or resulted in the carrying out of an offence referred to in article 2, paragraph 1, subparagraph (a) or (b), against a State or government facility of that State abroad, including diplomatic or consular premises of that State;
> (c) The offence was directed towards or resulted in an offence referred to in article 2, paragraph 1, subparagraph (a) or (b), committed in an attempt to compel that State to do or abstain from doing any act;
> (d) The offence is committed by a stateless person who has his or her habitual residence in the territory of that State;
> (e) The offence is committed on board an aircraft which is operated by the Government of that State.
> 3. Upon ratifying, accepting, approving or acceding to this Convention, each State Party shall notify the Secretary-General of the United Nations of the jurisdiction it has established in accordance with paragraph 2. Should any change take place, the State Party concerned shall immediately notify the Secretary-General.
> 4. Each State Party shall likewise take such measures as may be necessary to establish its jurisdiction over the offences set forth in article 2 in cases where the alleged offender is present in its territory and it does not extradite that person to any of the States Parties that have established their jurisdiction in accordance with paragraphs 1 or 2.
> 5. When more than one State Party claims jurisdiction over the offences set forth in article 2, the relevant States Parties shall strive to coordinate their actions appropriately, in particular concerning the conditions for prosecution and the modalities for mutual legal assistance.
> 6. Without prejudice to the norms of general international law, this Convention does not exclude the exercise of any criminal jurisdiction established by a State Party in accordance with its domestic law.

Id.

[50] See Abella v. Argentina, Case 11.137, Inter-Am. C.H.R., Report No. 55/97, OEA/Ser.L/V/II.98, doc. 6 rev. (1998).
[51] *Rome Statute*, supra note 9, art. 8(2)(d). *See also* Waldemar Solf, *The Status of Combatants in Non-International Armed Conflicts Under Domestic Law and Transnational Practice*, 33 AM. U. L. REV. 53, 62–62 (1983) (quoting article 1(2) of Protocol II, *supra* note 35).
[52] Prosecutor v. Kunarac, Kovač & Vuković, Case No. IT-96-23 & IT-96-23/1-A, Judgment, ¶ 86 (June 12, 2002) [hereinafter *Kunarac et al. Judgment*].

officials, attacks against UN peacekeepers, use of bombs or biological, chemical, or nuclear materials, and providing financial support to terrorist organizations.[53]

Even though they cover a wide range of terrorist acts, there are some remaining gaps in the regime of the peacetime antiterrorism conventions. For example, assassinations of businessmen, engineers, journalists, and educators are not covered, whereas similar attacks against diplomats and public officials are prohibited. Attacks or acts of sabotage by means other than explosives against a passenger train or bus, an office building, or a water supply or power plant are not covered, whereas similar attacks against an airplane or an ocean liner would be included. Placing anthrax into an envelope would not be covered, nor would most forms of cyberterrorism. Additionally, acts of psychological terror that do not involve physical injury are not covered, even though placing fake bombs in a public place or sending fake anthrax through the mail can be every bit as traumatizing to a population as an actual attack, and can have significant and widespread financial consequences.

Should such acts be deemed crimes against humanity within the existing framework of international criminal law? Crimes against humanity are defined by the Rome Statute of the International Criminal Court as including murder or inhumane acts of a similar character intentionally causing great suffering or serious injury to body or to mental or physical health, when "committed as part of a widespread or systematic attack directed against any civilian population with knowledge of the attack."[54] The Rome Statute further defines "attack directed against any civilian population" as "a course of conduct involving the multiple commission of acts ... pursuant to or in furtherance of a State or organizational policy to commit such attack."[55] Recent decisions by the International Criminal Tribunals for the former Yugoslavia (ICTY) and Rwanda (ICTR) have reaffirmed that crimes against humanity can be disconnected from armed conflicts, and that the requirement of a State connection is not absolute, so long as an "organizational policy" can be established.[56]

The September 11 events provided a focal point for reexamination of the Rome Statute requirement that there be a nexus between the charged offense as a crime against humanity and a State or organizational plan or policy. Al-Qaeda and its supporters acted as private citizens in declaring war on the United States, its citizens, and its values and carried out their attacks with a scope and intensity that arguably rises to the level of armed conflict by any common-sense definition. In the official fatwa signed by bin Laden and four others on February 23, 1998, the leaders of al-Qaeda declared their objective, which is presumably the derivative goal of al-Qaeda:

> The ruling to kill the Americans and their allies – civilians and military – is an individual duty for every Muslim who can do it in any country in which it is possible

---

[53] Michael Scharf, *Defining Terrorism as the Peacetime Equivalent of War Crimes: Problems and Prospects*, 36 CASE W. RES. J. INT'L L. 359, 359–74 (2004).
[54] Rome Statute, *supra* note 9, art. 7(1).
[55] *Id.* art. 7(2)(a).
[56] William A. Schabas, *Theoretical and International Framework: Punishment of Non-State Actors in Non-International Armed Conflict*, 26 FORDHAM INT'L L.J. 907, 929–30 (2003).

to do it, in order to liberate the al-Aqsa Mosque and the holy mosque [Mecca] from their grip, and in order for their armies to move out of all the lands of Islam, defeated and unable to threaten any Muslim.... We – with God's help – call on every Muslim who believes in God and wishes to be rewarded to comply with God's order to kill the Americans and plunder their money wherever and whenever they find it. We also call on Muslim ulema, leaders, youths, and soldiers to launch the raid on Satan's U.S. troops and the devil's supporters allying with, and to displace those who are behind them so that they may learn a lesson.[57]

Some scholars noted that "it can safely be assumed that al-Qaeda – an avowedly political and comprehensively structured entity – has an 'organizational policy.'"[58] By extension, many commentators would posit that a wave of terrorist attacks committed by a non-State entity during peacetime, resulting in thousands of civilian deaths, could be prosecuted as the crime against humanity of murder. Thus, for example, commentators have opined that the September 11 attacks could be deemed a crime against humanity because: (1) they targeted civilians; (2) they resulted in the deaths of more than 3,000 people; (3) they were part of a string of attacks that included the earlier bombing of the World Trade Center in 1993, bombings in Saudi Arabia in 1995 and 1996, bombings of U.S. embassies in Africa in 1998, and the attack on the U.S.S. *Cole* in October 2000; and (4) they constituted a systematic attack against the two World Trade Center towers, the Pentagon, and an attempt against the White House.[59]

The delegates to the Rome Conference included the explicit requirement for a State or organizational plan or policy associated with a particular pattern of criminality as a response to the strong opposition to an unqualified disjunctive "widespread or systematic."[60] As a matter of historical and factual experience, crimes against humanity have been characterized by a State or organizational policy dimension.[61] This is the perspective that prompted the *Kunarac* Appeals Chamber to flatly conclude (in the context of ICTY practice) that "nothing in the Statute or in customary international law ... required proof of the existence of a plan or policy to commit these crimes."[62] The necessary exclusion of random or isolated individual acts from proper consideration as crimes against humanity implies the instigation or encouragement of some

---

[57] RAYMOND IBRAHIM, THE AL QAEDA READER 13 (2007).
[58] Mark A. Drumbl, *Judging the 11 September Terrorist Attack*, 24 HUM. RTS. Q. 323, 337 (2002).
[59] Mireille Delmas-Marty, *Global Crime Calls for Global Justice*, 10 EUR. J. CRIME, CRIM. L. & CRIM. JUST. 286 (2002) (suggesting the September 11 attacks meet the ICC definition of a crime against humanity); Mark A. Drumbl, *Victimhood in our Neighborhood: Terrorist Crime, Taliban Guilt, and the Asymmetries of the International Legal Order*, 81 N.C. L. REV. 1 (2002).
[60] ROBERT CRYER ET AL., AN INTRODUCTION TO INTERNATIONAL CRIMINAL LAW AND PROCEDURE 196 (2007).
[61] Guénaël Mettraux, *Crimes Against Humanity in the Jurisprudence of the International Criminal Tribunals for the Former Yugoslavia and for Rwanda*, HARV. INT'L L.J. 237, 281(2002) (opining that the existence of the plan or policy element appears to be merely a factor for assessing the nature of the attack directed against the civilian population, which is the completely uncontroversial and necessary component of any crimes against humanity prosecution).
[62] *Kunarac et al. Judgment, supra* note 52, ¶ 98.

external actor,[63] namely the "state or organization," in the words of the Rome Statute. On the other hand, one of the preeminent experts in the field advocates a restrictive interpretation of the phrase "organizational policy" that would include the policy guidance of a sovereign State but would exclude a non-State actor, even a transnational terrorist network like al-Qaeda. In M. Cherif Bassiouni's view, the only entities legally capable of committing crimes against humanity are the suborganizational elements of sovereign States such as the Gestapo, the KGB, or the Ministry of Interior.[64]

However, if Bassiouni is correct in his interpretation of the policy requirement, the phrase "state or organizational plan or policy" found in article 7(2)(a) would be internally redundant. There is no evidence in the drafting history of the Rome Statute to support the conflation of the two terms into one functional concept. On the other hand, the ICTY Appeals Chamber's rejection of an element of State or organizational policy is based on a "largely literal reading" of texts that do not purport to contain modern formulations, which is compounded by "a debatable interpretation of a relatively small number of texts."[65]

Assuming that non-State actors are in fact legally capable of committing crimes against humanity, the acts of any large-scale group such as the Mafia, organized narco-trafficking or terrorist organization, or even a gang capable of committing "widespread or systematic crimes" would be sufficiently covered by the specifically listed categories of crimes against humanity. In such a case, there is no need to list terrorism as a separate crime against humanity; rather, the specific act is already covered in the crimes against humanity of murder, persecution, or other identifiable crime. Other types of terrorism, such as widespread and systematic hijackings, hostage takings, acts of sabotage, or cyber attacks against the civilian population, resulting in pervasive fear and financial losses but few deaths, pose a more difficult question, namely: Should such terrorist acts be deemed to fall within the "other inhumane acts" category of crimes against humanity?

Any prosecution of a previously unidentified crime against humanity must comport with the principle of *nullum crimen sine lege*.[66] This principle protects the fundamental rights of the accused from infringement by capricious or arbitrary prosecution for acts that were not recognized as crimes when they were committed.[67] Even though crimes against humanity may be prosecuted "whether or not in violation of the domestic law of the court where perpetrated,"[68] the Rome Statute is clear that the perpetrator's acts must be committed "with knowledge of" the larger attack directed against the civilian population.[69] Moreover, mindful of the subjective and

---

[63] Margaret McAuliffe de Guzman, *The Road From Rome: The Developing Law of Crimes Against Humanity*, 22 HUM. RTS. Q. 335, 374 (2000).
[64] William A. Schabas, *State Policy As An Element of International Crimes*, 98 J. CRIM. L. & CRIMINOLOGY 953, 973 (2008).
[65] *Id.* at 981.
[66] ANTONIO CASSESE, INTERNATIONAL CRIMINAL LAW 145 (2003).
[67] *Id.*
[68] Agreement for the Prosecution and Punishment of Major War Criminals of the European Axis and Establishing the Charter of the International Military Tribunal, annex art. 6, Aug. 8, 1945, 59 Stat. 1544, 82 U.N.T.S. 270.
[69] *Rome Statute*, *supra* note 9, art. 7(1).

perhaps shifting meaning of crimes against humanity concepts, the Assembly of States Parties adopted Elements of Crimes that specify that:

> [the crimes] must be strictly construed, taking into account that crimes against humanity as defined in article 7 are among the most serious crimes of concern to the international community as a whole, warrant and entail individual criminal responsibility, and require conduct which is impermissible under generally applicable international law, as recognized by the principal legal systems of the world.[70]

To prosecute an individual for a previously unrecognized crime against humanity but still pay proper heed to the principle, one must study established customary international law to see if it speaks to the crime.[71] Thus, proceeding against a particular act that might be characterized as a crime against humanity under a preexisting jurisprudentially justified category is far more defensible than relying on a newly created crime of terrorism with an uncertain pedigree.

Related to the *nullum crimen sine lege* principle is the general prohibition of *ex post facto* law: the retroactive application of criminal penalties to acts that were not criminalized at the time they were committed.[72] Freedom from retroactive punishment has been established in various human rights treaties and has gained acceptance as a fundamental human right.[73] This does not, however, prevent courts from refining, elaborating on, or clarifying existing rules, nor does it prevent courts from relying on judicial precedent from other jurisdictions.[74] Both *nullum crimen sine lege* and *ex post facto* are judicial guarantees that are generally recognized as being indispensable under international law.[75]

The category of "other inhumane acts" enjoys a particularly strong assurance of compliance with *nullum crimen sine lege*, because it has been a recognized crime against humanity since its incorporation into the Nuremberg charter.[76] The crime of "other inhumane acts" originated in article 6(c) of the Nuremberg Charter and was also included in the Tokyo Charter as well as Allied Control Council Law No. 10 applicable in occupied Germany.[77] The crime of inhumane acts was "designed as a residual category, as it was felt undesirable for this category to be exhaustively enumerated. An exhaustive categorization would merely create opportunities for

---

[70] International Criminal Court, Elements of Crimes, *available at* http://www.icc-cpi.int/NR/rdonlyres/9CAEE830-38CF-41D6-AB0B-68E5F9082543/0/Element_of_Crimes_English.pdf (last visited Feb. 7, 2010).

[71] CASSESE, *supra* note 66, at 743.

[72] *Id.* at 742.

[73] *Id.*

[74] *Id.*

[75] KNUT DÖRMANN, ELEMENTS OF WAR CRIMES UNDER THE ROME STATUTE OF THE INTERNATIONAL CRIMINAL COURT 410 (2002).

[76] Charter of the International Military Tribunal, Aug. 8, 1945, 59 Stat. 1544, 82 U.N.T.S. 284, 288, *available at* http://www.yale.edu/lawweb/avalon/imt/proc/imtconst.htm.

[77] *See* Prosecutor v. Stakić, Case No. IT-97-24-A, Appeal Judgment, ¶ 315 (Mar. 22, 2006), *available at* http://www.un.org/icty/stakic/appeal/judgement/index.htm [hereinafter *Stakić Appeals Judgment*].

evasion of the letter of the prohibition."[78] Some courts have found that convictions of the same accused for both the crime of inhumane acts and the crime of torture are cumulative.[79]

As recognized in the judgments of previous war crimes tribunals, other inhumane acts have included economic discrimination, confiscation, pillage and plunder of Jewish property,[80] beatings and general inhumane treatment,[81] forcible transfer,[82] confinement in inhumane conditions,[83] and sexual violence in the form of forced public nudity.[84] In the Iraqi High Tribunal, Taha Yassin Ramadan was convicted of that crime for razing the fields and orchards of Dujail and destroying the fruit trees or the verdant agricultural area. The lifestyle and affluence of the families of Dujail died as the orchards were pulled from the ground. As international humanitarian law is applied more frequently, the Trial Chamber decision to convict Taha Yassin Ramadan for the crime of inhumane acts may become the very embodiment of that catch-all crime. After all, destroying the sustenance and prosperity of an entire village is the epitome of acts "intentionally causing great suffering, or serious injury to the body or to the mental or physical health."[85] Most recently, the Special Court for Sierra Leone's Appeals Chamber identified forced marriage as an "other inhumane act" and upheld the conviction of the perpetrator of this crime as a crime against humanity.[86]

VI. CONCLUSION: WEIGHING THE PROS AND CONS OF CHARACTERIZING TERRORISM AS A DISCRETE CRIME AGAINST HUMANITY

The authors can imagine some theoretical advantages to characterizing some incidents of terrorism as a new discrete crime against humanity. For example, this would create universal jurisdiction (and trigger a duty to prosecute or extradite) at the national level with respect to terrorist acts that are not presently covered by the laws of war or one of the dozen multilateral antiterrorism conventions in peacetime. It would also create uniformity of jurisdiction and prosecutorial obligation with regard to any States that have ratified the *Proposed Crimes Against Humanity Convention*

---

[78] Prosecutor v. Kupreškić et. al., Case No. IT-95-16-T, Judgment, ¶ 563 (Jan. 14, 2000) (cautioning however that there "is a concern that this category lacks precision and is too general to provide a safe yardstick for the work of the Tribunal and hence, that it is contrary to the principle of the 'specificity' of criminal law. It is thus imperative to establish what is included within this category").
[79] Prosecutor v. Milan Martić, Case No. IT-95-11-T, Judgment, ¶ 477 (June 12, 2007).
[80] Matthew Lippman, *Crimes Against Humanity*, 17 B.C. THIRD WORLD L.J. 171, 201 (1997).
[81] Prosecutor v. Tadić, Case No. IT-94-1-T, Judgment, ¶ 730 (May 7, 1997).
[82] *Stakić Appeals Judgment*, *supra* note 77, ¶ 317.
[83] Prosecutor v. Kvočka et al., Case No. IT-98-30/1-T, Trial Judgment, ¶¶ 206–09 (Nov. 2, 2001).
[84] Prosecutor v. Akayesu, Case No. ICTR-96-4-T, Judgment, ¶ 697 (Sept. 2, 1998).
[85] *See* Law of the Supreme Iraqi Criminal Tribunal (Law No. 10), Oct. 18, 2005, AL-WAQA'I AL-IRAQIYA [Official Gazette of the Republic of Iraq] No. 4006, art. 12(First)(J), *available at* www.law.case.edu/saddamtrial/documents/IST_statute_official_english.pdf.
[86] *AFRC Appeals Judgment*, *supra* note 46, ¶¶ 169–203.

but have not ratified the various antiterrorism conventions. Moreover, such crimes could be prosecuted by the International Criminal Court as well as by national courts, providing a third alternative when domestic prosecution and extradition to another State are legally or politically unfeasible.

There are, nevertheless, no compelling values served by deeming terrorism as a crime against humanity through the vehicle of a new Convention. Indeed, in the opinion of the authors, the creation of a wholly new specified offense under the rubric of crimes against humanity is inadvisable for several reasons. First, most widespread terrorist acts are already covered by the laws of war or would constitute the existing crime against humanity of murder, without having to address the thorny definitional question of what is terrorism. There are no lacunae that can be constructively addressed.

Second, the determination of whether an alleged act short of mass murder (such as systematic kidnappings by a terrorist group) qualifies as an "other inhumane act" type of crimes against humanity is best handled as a judicial determination made on a case-by-case basis, taking into account the nature of the alleged act, the context in which it took place, the personal circumstances of the victims, and the physical, mental, and moral effects of the perpetrator's conduct upon the victims.[87]

Finally, the effort to achieve international consensus on the inclusion of a specific crime against humanity of "terrorism" would introduce a whole new level of uncertainty and politicization into the existing legal structures and definitions. The effort could therefore undermine the fundamental human rights of the perpetrator and the efficacy of existing prohibitions and punitive forums.

---

[87] *Id.* ¶ 178.

12

Crimes Against Humanity and the International Criminal Court

Kai Ambos*

This chapter examines the question of the need for a specialized Convention for Crimes against Humanity from the perspective of the existing protection granted by the International Criminal Court (ICC) Statute. The ICC's role in the prevention and prosecution of crimes against humanity is predicated on its normative framework, especially article 7 of the ICC Statute. A critical analysis of this provision and its comparison with the definition in the *Proposed International Convention on the Prevention and Punishment of Crimes Against Humanity* (*Proposed Convention*) lies at the heart of this chapter. A second, related issue to be dealt with is the ICC's effective capacity to prevent and prosecute crimes against humanity. This issue touches on one of the fundamental cornerstones of the criminal law: its possible effect of deterrence.

I. INTRODUCTION: HISTORICAL BACKGROUND AND RATIONALE OF CAH

The concept of Crimes Against Humanity (CAH) in its modern usage can be traced as far back as the declaration of May 28, 1915 by the governments of France, Great Britain, and Russia, relating to the massacres of the Armenian population in Turkey. In this declaration, the atrocities committed were described as "crimes against humanity for which all members of the Turkish Government will be held responsible together with its agents implicated in the massacres."[1] The novelty in this case was that the crimes were committed by citizens of a State on their own fellow citizens and not those of another State. The Nuremberg Trials were similar in nature, for they dealt with crimes committed by Germans against fellow Germans.[2] However, a historical overview of the development of CAH shows that the Nuremberg Charter was

---

* I thank my (former) research assistants Ousman Njikam (The Hague) and Dr. Stefanie Bock (Göttingen) for their assistance and Timothy Campbell (Göttingen) for language revision. I also thank Leila Sadat for useful comments.

[1] Egon Schwelb, *Crimes Against Humanity*, 23 Brit. Y.B. Int'l L. 178, 181 (1946). *See also* John P. Cerone, *The Jurisprudential Contributions of the ICTR to the Legal Definition of Crimes Against Humanity*, 14 New Eng. J. Int'l & Comp. L. 191, 191–92 (2008).

[2] Roger S. Clark, *Crimes Against Humanity at Nuremberg, in* The Nuremberg Trial and International Law 193, 195–98 (George Ginsburgs & Vladimir Nikolaevich Kudriavtsev eds., 1990).

not a legislative act that created a new crime, but rather articulated a crime already embedded in the fabric of customary international law.[3] This is evidenced by at least three instruments: the Martens Clause of the 1899 and 1907 Hague Conventions,[4] referring to the "laws of humanity"; the already mentioned Joint Declaration of May 28, 1915, condemning "crimes against humanity and civilization"[5]; and the 1919 Report of the Commission on the Responsibility of the Authors of War, supporting individual criminal responsibility for "violations of the laws of humanity."[6] It is noteworthy that with respect to historic recognitions of "laws of humanity" and CAH, the reach of these principles was potentially quite broad, perhaps as far-reaching as human rights. They dealt with a wide range of conducts, performed by either State or non-State actors, and in times of war or peace.[7]

Yet, the definition of CAH has thus far been vague and, in many respects, contradictory. A more refined definition of CAH, reflecting the historical developments, was only achieved with the ICC Statute. Article 7 represents both a "codification" and a "progressive development" of international law.[8] It unites the distinct legal features that may be thought of as the "common law" of CAH.[9] Yet, to understand the *rationale* of CAH, one must dig deeper and go beyond the mere positivist analysis of Statutes and other norms. History teaches us that the State always had an important role in the organization and actual commission of CAH. This historical fact lends a strong argument to a concept of CAH as a State crime in the sense of Richard Vernon's definition: "a moral inversion, or travesty, of the state;"[10] "an abuse of state

---

[3] *Cf.* Darryl Robinson, *Defining Crimes Against Humanity at the Rome Conference*, 93 AM. J. INT'L L. 43, 44 (1999).

[4] The Preamble to the Convention with Respect to the Laws and Customs of War on Land, July 29, 1899, 32 Stat. 1803, and the Preamble to the Convention Respecting the Laws and Customs of War on Land, with annexed Regulations, Oct. 18, 1907, 36 Stat. 2277, T.S. No. 539, specify that in cases not included in the Hague Regulations, "the inhabitants and the belligerents remain under the protection and the rule of the principles of the law of nations, as they result from the usages established among civilized peoples, from the laws of humanity, and the dictates of the public conscience."

[5] Schwelb, *supra* note 1; *see also* UN WAR CRIMES COMM'N, HISTORY OF THE UNITED NATIONS WAR CRIMES COMMISSION AND THE DEVELOPMENT OF THE LAWS OF WAR 35 (1948).

[6] The 1919 Report Presented to the Preliminary Peace Conference by the Commission on the Responsibility of the Authors of War and on Enforcement of Penalties for Violations of the Laws and Customs of War, recommended the establishment of a high tribunal to try persons belonging to enemy countries who were guilty of "offences against the laws and customs of war or the laws of humanity," excerpted in M. CHERIF BASSIOUNI, CRIMES AGAINST HUMANITY IN INTERNATIONAL CRIMINAL LAW 553–65 (2d ed. 1999).

[7] *Cf.* JORDAN J. PAUST ET AL., INTERNATIONAL CRIMINAL LAW, CASES AND MATERIALS 703 (2007).

[8] *Cf.* UN Charter art. 13; *cf. also* Roger S. Clark, *Crimes Against Humanity and The Rome Statute of the International Criminal Court*, *in* INTERNATIONAL AND NATIONAL LAW IN RUSSIA AND EASTERN EUROPE 139–56 (Roger Clark et al. eds., 2001).

[9] David Luban, *A Theory of Crimes against Humanity*, 29 YALE J. INT'L L. 85, 93 et seq. (2004), summarizing these legal features as follows: "Crimes against humanity are international crimes committed by politically organized groups acting under color of policy, consisting of the most severe and abominable acts of violence and persecution, and inflicted on victims because of their membership in a population or group rather than their individual characteristics." *Id.* at 108.

[10] Richard Vernon, *What is Crime against Humanity?*, 10 J. POL. PHIL. 231, 233 (2002).

power involving a systematic inversion of the jurisdictional resources of the state;"[11] "a systematic inversion: powers that justify the state are, perversely, instrumentalized by it, territoriality is transformed from a refuge to a trap, and the modalities of punishment are brought to bear upon the guiltless."[12]

The problem with this definition is that it is limited to the classical relation between a State and its citizen residing in its territory, leaving out other extraterritorial State-citizen relations and relations of a State with foreign citizens.[13] In addition, the definition does not account for non-State actors, at least not explicitly. One may replace "State" with "non-State actor" to accommodate the concept to the now-recognized standing of the latter as a potential perpetrator of CAH. Still, this would not be enough because there is clearly a difference between a State's obligation under international law to guarantee the rule of law and protect its citizens and a similar (emerging) duty of a non-State actor over the territory under its control. All in all, it is therefore more convincing to develop a concept of CAH without so much focusing on the entity behind these crimes. This does not deny the eminent political connotation of CAH; indeed it stresses the "distinctive perversion of politics"[14] underlying CAH; it takes up David Luban's idea of CAH as "politics gone horribly wrong,"[15] as "politics gone cancerous,"[16] launching a double assault on individuality (the individual and political "quality of being human," "humanness") and groups ("the set of individuals," "sociability," "humankind"):[17]

> First the phrase 'crimes against humanity' suggest offenses that aggrieve not only the victims and their own communities, but all human beings, regardless of their community. Second, the phrase suggests that these offences cut deep, violating the core humanity that we all share and that distinguishes us from other natural beings.[18]
>
> [T]he humanness that crimes against humanity violates lies in our status as political animals.... crimes against humanity offend against that status in two ways: by perverting politics, and by assaulting the individuality and sociability of the victims in tandem.[19]
>
> [C]rimes against humanity ... represent an affront to our nature as political animals, our double character as unsociably social individuals who combine self-awareness and self-interest with a natural need for society of others.... Crimes against humanity assault our individuality by attacking us solely because of the groups to which we belong, and they assault our sociability by transforming political communities into death traps.[20]

---

[11] *Id.* at 242.
[12] *Id.* at 245.
[13] See the convincing critique of Luban, *supra* note 9, at 94 n. 28.
[14] *Id.*
[15] *Id.* at 108.
[16] *Id.* at 116.
[17] *Id.* at 86 et seq. Vernon, although critical of the element of humanness, shares the idea of an attack on humankind in the sense of entity and diversity, *id.* at 238 et seq.
[18] Luban, *supra* note 9, at 86 (footnote omitted).
[19] *Id.* at 120.
[20] *Id.* at 159–60.

CAH, so understood, provide for a penal protection against the transgression of the most basic laws protecting our individuality as political beings and our sociability as members of – again – political communities. The transgressor, that is, the criminal against humanity, becomes an enemy and legitimate target of all humankind,[21] a *hostis humani generis*, which, in principle, anyone ("the people") may bring to justice. Although this consequence gives rise to certain concerns,[22] the underlying concept of CAH is also convincing in that it explains the gist of CAH without invoking a mere positivist analysis, and in that it avoids overinclusiveness by criminalizing only violations of the most fundamental human rights. From a methodological perspective, such an approach is convincing because it makes clear that the quest for a correct and rational construction of the law ("right law") must take precedence over pure policy considerations.

Thus, there seems to be at least some common ground and understanding as to what amounts to a CAH and what the prosecutor has to prove. As such, article 7 serves as a good starting point for discussing a specialized convention on CAH.

II. STRUCTURE AND KEY ELEMENTS OF ARTICLE 7 OF THE ICC STATUTE

A. *A Twofold Structure: Context (Chapeau) and Individual Acts*

Article 7 of the ICC Statute has a similar structure to the respective provisions in the ICTY and ICTR Statutes (articles 5 and 3 respectively); they only differ as to the chapeau. Article 7 consists of a context element (chapeau, *Gesamttat*) and a list of inhumane acts that must be committed within the described context. In other words, the chapeau sets out the conditions under which the commission of the individual acts amounts to a crime against humanity.[23] The chapeau reads as follows: "For the

---

[21] *Id.* at 139, 160; for the same consequence see Vernon, *supra* note 10, at 234.

[22] The "civil lawyer" is first reminded of the polemical and controversial debate of a criminal law for enemies (*Feindstrafrecht, derecho penal del enemigo, diritto penal del nemico*) taking place in particular in continental Europe and Latin America and directed in particular at terrorist offenders. Such a special criminal law is to be rejected. For a more or less full account, see the two volumes Derecho penal del enemigo (Manuel Cancio & Carlos Gómez-Jara Diez eds., 2006); *see also* Diritto penal del nemico: Un dibattito internazionale (Massimo Donini & Michele Papa eds., 2007). For my view see Kai Ambos, *Feindstrafrecht*, 124 Schweizerische Zeitschrift für Strafrecht 1 (2006); in Spanish see Kai Ambos, *Derecho penal del enemigo, in* I Derecho penal del enimigo, *supra*, at 119; updated version in Kai Ambos, El derecho penal frente a amenazas extremas 81–145 (2007); in Italian see Kai Ambos, *Il diritto penale del nemico, in* Diritto penal del nemico, *supra*, at 29. Secondly, such a CAH concept may give rise, as Luban himself acknowledged, to a dangerous people's (vigilante) justice and jurisdiction, Luban, *supra* note 9, at 140, 160; he proposes to counter potential abuses by delegating the *jus puniendi* to national and international tribunals which satisfy the minimum standards of "natural justice," *i.e.*, guarantee a fair trial, *id.* at 142–43, 145, 160.

[23] *Cf.* Herman von Hebel & Darryl Robinson, *Crimes within the Jurisdiction of the Court, in* The International Criminal Court: The Making of the Rome Statute – Issues, Negotiations, Results 91 (Roy S. Lee ed., 1999).

purpose of this Statute, crimes against humanity means any of the following acts when committed as part of a widespread or systematic attack directed against any civilian population, with knowledge of the attack."

Four key requirements follow from this chapeau, namely:

- the disjunctive widespread or systematic test;
- the "civilian population" element as to the object of the attack;
- a special mental requirement;
- the existence of individual acts to be committed within the framework of the attack.

It follows further from this chapeau that a nexus to an armed conflict and a special discriminatory intent is no longer required.

B. The Context Element

The historical development and rationale of the context element have been discussed elsewhere.[24] Summing up this discussion, it may be recalled that the context element has continued to change throughout its history, but some kind of context by means of a *link to an authority or power*, be it a State, organization or group, has always been required; although the reference to "organizational policy" in article 7(2) makes clear that the provision also applies to non-State actors,[25] these actors must be in a position to act like a State, that is, they must possess a similar capacity of organization and force.[26] The context element was thus converted into the "international element"[27] in CAH, which renders certain criminal conduct a matter of international concern.[28] The *rationale* of this "internationalization" of certain crimes was their special gravity, often accompanied by the unwillingness or inability

---

[24] Kai Ambos & Steffen Wirth, *The Current Law of Crimes against Humanity. An Analysis of UNTAET Regulation 15/2000*, 13 CRIM. L.F. 1, 3 et seq. (2002); KAI AMBOS, INTERNATIONALES STRAFRECHT. STRAFANWENDUNGSRECHT, VÖLKERSTRAFRECHT UND EUROPÄISCHES STRAFRECHT § 7 marginal numbers (mn.) 174 et seq. (2d ed. 2008).

[25] *But see* M. CHERIF BASSIOUNI, THE LEGISLATIVE HISTORY OF THE ICC: INTRODUCTION, ANALYSIS AND INTEGRATED TEXT 151–52 (2005). Convincingly against Bassiouni's view, see William A. Schabas, *Crimes against Humanity: The State Plan or Policy Element*, in THE THEORY AND PRACTICE OF INTERNATIONAL CRIMINAL LAW 358 et seq. (Leila Sadat & Michael Scharf eds., 2008). In any case, Bassiouni himself recognizes an "extension to non-state actors by analogy" if they act pursuant to a policy. BASSIOUNI, *supra* note 6, at 245.

[26] *See* Ambos, *supra* note 24, § 7 mn. 188 with further references; in a similar vein, see BASSIOUNI, THE LEGISLATIVE HISTORY OF THE ICC, *supra* note 25, at 245 (non-State actors "partake of the characteristics of state actors in that they exercise some dominion or control over territory and people, and carry out 'policy' which has similar characteristics of those of 'state action or policy'"); *see also* Schabas, *supra* note 25, at 359 ("state-like bodies").

[27] Prosecutor v. Tadić, Case No. IT-94-1-A and IT-94-1-A *bis*, Judgment in Sentencing Appeal, Separate Opinion of Judge Shahabuddeen (Jan. 26, 2000); BASSIOUNI, *supra* note 6, at 243 (cf. the title of Chapter 6: "The International or Jurisdictional Element").

[28] Claus Kress, *Der Jugoslawien-Strafgerichtshof im Grenzbereich zwischen internationalem bewaffneten Konflikt und Bürgerkrieg*, in VÖLKERRECHTLICHE VERBRECHEN VOR DEM JUGOSLAWIEN TRIBUNAL, NATIONALEN GERICHTEN UND DEM INTERNATIONALEN STRAFGERICHTSHOF 15, 53–55

of national criminal justice systems to prosecute them. Indeed, as discussed earlier, CAH may be understood as a State crime in the sense of the "systematic inversion" of the powers justifying the State's existence.

1. The Widespread-Systematic Test

Article 7 turns the individual acts listed in the provision into CAH if they fulfill the widespread-systematic test. The very purpose of the test is to ensure that single, isolated, or random acts do not constitute CAH.[29] Whereas the term "widespread" implies, in a more quantitative sense, that an act be carried out on a large scale and involving a high number of victims,[30] "systematic" has a rather qualitative meaning, requiring that the act be carried out as a result of methodical planning.[31] The case law always opted for a disjunctive or alternative reading, that is, it held that the

---

(Horst Fischer & Sascha Rolf Lüder eds., 1999); Beth van Schaack, *The Definition of Crimes Against Humanity: Resolving the Incoherence*, 37 COLUM. J. TRANSNAT'L L. 787, 819 (1999); Matthew Lippman, *Crimes Against Humanity*, 17 B.C. THIRD WORLD L.J. 171, 173, 183 (1997) (quoting Robert H. Jackson, head of the United States delegation at the London Conference in 1945 where the Nuremberg Charter was negotiated); recently, see Cerone, *supra* note 1, at 195 ("nexus requirement"); in the same vein, see Stefan Kirsch, *Zweierlei Unrecht*, *in* FESTSCHRIFT FÜR RAINER HAMM 283, 285 et seq. (Regina Michalke et al. eds., 2008) considering the context element, however, as a mere jurisdictional element; in English, see Stefan Kirsch, *Two Kinds of Wrong: On the Context Element of Crimes against Humanity*, 22 LEIDEN J. INT'L L. 525 (2009) and for a more detailed discussion, see Stefan Kirsch, DER BEGEHUNGSZUSAMMENHANG DER VERBRECHEN GEGEN DIE MENSCHLICHKEIT 107 et seq. (2009).

[29] See also Prosecutor v. Milutinović et al., Case No. IT-05-87-T, Judgment, ¶ 150 (Feb. 26, 2009); Prosecutor v. Katanga & Ngudjolo, Doc. No. ICC-01/04-01/07-717, Decision on the Confirmation of Charges, ¶ 394 (Sept. 30, 2008); conc. Prosecutor v. Al Bashir, No. ICC-02/05-01/09-3, Decision on the Prosecution's Application for a Warrant of Arrest against Omar Hassan Ahmad Al Bashir, ¶ 81 (Mar. 4, 2009); thereto Robert Cryer, *The Definition of International Crimes in the Al Bashir Arrest Warrant*, 7 J. INT'L CRIM. L. 283 (2009); Prosecutor v. Bemba Gombo, Doc. No. ICC-01/05-01/08-424, Decision Pursuant to Article 61(7)(a) and (b) of the Rome Statute on the Charges of the Prosecutor Against Jean-Pierre Bemba Gombo, ¶ 83 (June 15, 2009). *See also* Rodney Dixon, revised by Christopher Hall, *Crimes Against Humanity*, *in* COMMENTARY ON THE ROME STATUTE OF THE INTERNATIONAL CRIMINAL COURT, OBSERVERS NOTES, ARTICLE BY ARTICLE Art. 7 mn. 4 (Otto Triffterer ed., 2d ed. 2008).

[30] The important definitional element is the number of victims, not the number of acts. *Katanga and Ngudjolo Confirmation of Charges, supra* note 29, ¶ 395. Thus, a single act may be sufficient if it is "of extraordinary magnitude." This is the (correct) view of the ICTY since the Rule 61 decision in the *Vucovar hospital* case. Prosecutor v. Mrkšić et al., Case No. IT-95-13-R61, Decision on Review of Indictment Pursuant to Rule 61 (Apr. 3, 1996). In a similar vein, see *Bemba Gombo Confirmation of Charges, supra* note 29, ¶ 83; for a discussion and further references, see Ambos & Wirth, *supra* note 24, at 20–21; Ambos, *supra* note 24, § 7 mn. 184 n.781; for a good recent discussion, see Chile Eboe-Osuji, *Crimes against Humanity: Directing Attacks against a Civilian Population*, 2 AFR. J. LEGAL STUD. 118, 120 (2008); *see also* Cerone, *supra* note 1, at 197. For another view ("repeated" acts), see the Iraqi High Tribunal in the Al-Dujail Judgment, see Kai Ambos & Said Pirmurat, *Das Todesurteil gegen Saddam Hussein*, 62 JURISTEN ZEITUNG 822, 824 (2007); Bernhard Kuschnik, *The Legal Findings of Crimes against Humanity in the Al-Dujail Judgments of the Iraqi High Tribunal: A Forerunner for the ICC?*, 7 CHINESE J. INT'L L. 459, 472 (2008), both with references.

[31] *See, e.g.*, Prosecutor v. Akayesu, Case No. ICTR-96-4-T, Judgment, ¶ 579 (Sept. 2, 1998) (defining "widespread" "as massive, frequent, large-scale action, carried out collectively with considerable

"attack" could either be widespread or systematic.[32] Yet, article 7 seems to obscure this apparently clear interpretation by defining the context element of paragraph 1 ("attack directed against any civilian population") in its paragraph 2 as "a course of conduct involving the multiple commission of acts ..., pursuant to or in furtherance of a State or organizational policy to commit such attack." This definition replaces "widespread" with "multiple commissions of acts" and "systematic" with "a State or organizational policy;" yet, more importantly, it no longer phrases these two elements in the alternative mode, but interconnects them insofar as the "multiple commission" must be based on a "policy." This means that the policy element is indispensable and its absence cannot be compensated, for example, by a particularly high number of acts and/or victims. In other words, sheer quantity does not convert a number of acts into CAH; otherwise, a serial killer would qualify as a criminal against humanity for the mere fact that he acted on a large scale. Instead, the decisive element is that of a policy: Only its existence turns multiple acts into CAH.[33] This is also confirmed by the concept of CAH as an eminently political crime defended earlier (*supra* Section I).

In fact, the policy element has developed out of the already mentioned requirement for a link to a State or a non-State authority and as such can already be found in the post–World War II case law and the ILC Draft Codes.[34] Although the case law of the ICTY and ICTR has denied several times that this element is required by customary international law,[35] its explicit inclusion in article 7(2) is

---

seriousness and directed against a multiplicity of victims;" and "systematic" "as thoroughly organized and following a regular pattern on the basis of a common policy involving substantial public or private resources"). For a detailed analysis of the case law, see Ambos & Wirth, *supra* note 24, at 18 et seq. The Iraqi High Tribunal also used the terms "large scale" and "methodical" for widespread and systematic, see Kuschnik, *supra* note 30, at 471 with references. *See also Katanga and Ngudjolo Confirmation of Charges*, *supra* note 29, ¶ 397 with references to the relevant case law of the ad hoc Tribunals; conc. *Al Bashir Arrest Warrant*, *supra* note 29, ¶ 81.

[32] For one of the leading and first decisions, see *Akayesu Trial Judgment*, *supra* note 31, ¶ 579; most recently *Bemba Gombo Confirmation of Charges*, *supra* note 29, ¶ 82. For further references, see Kai Ambos, *Selected Issues Regarding the "Core Crimes" in International Criminal Law*, in INTERNATIONAL CRIMINAL LAW: QUO VADIS? (Nouvelles Etudes Penales 19) 219, 243 (AIDP ed., 2004); Ambos, *supra* note 24, § 7 mn. 185.

[33] *See also* Darryl Robinson, *The Elements of Crimes Against Humanity*, in THE INTERNATIONAL CRIMINAL COURT: ELEMENTS OF CRIMES AND RULES OF PROCEDURE AND EVIDENCE 57, 63 (Roy S. Lee ed., 2001) ("[D]isjunctive test ... coupled with a ... conjunctive test (multiple and policy)."); *id.* at 64 ("[P]olicy element ... unites otherwise unrelated inhumane acts ....").

[34] For the respective references, see Ambos & Wirth, *supra* note 24, at 26.

[35] Prosecutor v. Kunarac et al., Case No. IT-96-23 & IT-96-23/1-A, Judgment, ¶ 98 (June 12, 2002); Prosecutor v. Vasiljević, Case No. IT-98-32-T, Judgment, ¶ 36 (Nov. 29, 2002); Prosecutor v. Limaj et al., Case No. IT-03-66-T, Judgment, ¶ 184 (Nov. 30, 2005); Prosecutor v. Krajisnik, Case No. IT-00-39-T, Judgment, ¶ 706 (Sept. 27, 2006); Prosecutor v. Muvunyi, Case No. ICTR-2000-55A-T, Judgment, ¶ 512 (Sept. 12, 2006) with further references in fn. 716. See on this case law the mostly critical literature GUÉNAËL METTRAUX, INTERNATIONAL CRIMES AND THE AD HOC TRIBUNALS 172 n.93 (2005); *see also* BASSIOUNI, *supra* note 6, at 243 et seq.; MACHTELD BOOT, GENOCIDE, CRIMES AGAINST HUMANITY, WAR CRIMES: NULLUM CRIMEN SINE LEGE AND THE SUBJECT MATTER JURISDICTION OF THE ICC, ¶ 458 et seq. (2002); Ambos & Wirth, *supra* note 24, at

sound. This element makes clear that some kind of link with a State or a de facto power and thus organization and planning, by means of a policy,[36] is necessary to categorize otherwise ordinary crimes as CAH. It thus offers an important guideline to delimitate ordinary crimes from CAH. Another question is what kind of policy is exactly required. The old debate between active conduct and mere inaction or toleration of atrocities, reflected in the contradictory wording of the Elements of Crimes and a corresponding footnote,[37] discussed elsewhere,[38] must be decided in favor of a broad interpretation of the policy concept.[39] Given its contested status in customary international law and the general meaning of "policy" inaction, toleration or acquiescence in the face of CAH must be considered sufficient. There is, however, a difference between a systematic and a widespread attack. Whereas in the former, a certain guidance of the individual perpetrators with regard to the prospective victims may be typical, a widespread attack that is not at the same time systematic will very often be accompanied by a policy only consisting of deliberate inaction, toleration, or acquiescence.

2. The Civilian Population as Object of the Attack

I have argued elsewhere that this element should be deleted from article 7 because it cannot be reconciled with an essentially humanitarian concept of CAH as defended in this work (*supra* Section I), namely to protect humanness and humankind and

---

28 et seq.; STEPHAN MESEKE, DER TATBESTAND DER VERBRECHEN GEGEN DIE MENSCHLICHKEIT NACH DEM RÖMISCHEN STATUT DES IStGH 139 (2004); GERHARD WERLE, VÖLKERSTRAFRECHT mn. 768 (2d ed. 2007); ROBERT CRYER ET AL., AN INTRODUCTION TO INTERNATIONAL CRIMINAL LAW AND PROCEDURE 196–97 (2007); Cerone, *supra* note 1, at 198; Schabas, *supra* note 26, at 349 et seq. (demonstrating convincingly that a State plan or policy was always required). The European Parliament recently issued a resolution to recognize all sexual offenses as CAH, independent of a systematic context. EUR. PARL. DOC. RC-B6–0022/2008 (2008), *available at* http://www.europarl.europa.eu/sides/getDoc.do?pubRef=-//EP//NONSGML+MOTION+P6-RC-2008–0022+0+DOC+PDF+V0//EN.

[36] See *Katanga & Ngudjolo Confirmation of Charges*, *supra* note 29, ¶ 396.

[37] The third paragraph of the Introduction to the Elements of Crimes concerning art. 7 reads: "It is understood that 'policy to commit such attack' requires that the State or organisation actively promote or encourage such an attack against a civilian population." Preparatory Comm'n of the Int'l Criminal Court, Draft Report of the Preparatory Commission for the International Criminal Court: Finalized Draft Text of the Elements of Crimes, 9, PCNICC/2000/INF/3/Add.2 (Sept. 9, 2002) [hereinafter Introduction to the Elements of Article 7]. However, footnote 6 attached to this sentence provides: "A policy which has a civilian population as the object of the attack would be implemented by State or organisational action. Such a policy may, in exceptional circumstances, be implemented by a deliberate failure to take action, which is consciously aimed at encouraging such attack. The existence of such a policy cannot be inferred solely from the absence of governmental or organisational action." *Id.* at 9 n.6 (emphasis added). On the difficult negotiations, see Robinson, *supra* note 33, at 75 et seq.

[38] *Cf.* Ambos & Wirth, *supra* note 24, at 28 et seq., 34; Ambos, *supra* note 32, at 244–45; Ambos, *supra* note 24, § 7 mn. 187.

[39] For apparently the same view, see Robinson, *supra* note 33, at 79 (referring to the Report of the Commission of Experts for the former Yugoslavia requiring "deliberate inaction to encourage the crimes").

thereby the fundamental human rights of *all* persons against widespread and systematic violations.[40] The ICTY recognized this problem previously in *Kupreškić et al.* when it stated:

> One fails to see why only civilians and not also combatants should be protected by these rules (in particular by the rule prohibiting persecution), given that these rules may be held to possess a broader humanitarian scope and purpose than those prohibiting war crimes.[41]

Nevertheless, the ICTY even held in some instances that the civilian population must be the "primary" rather than an incidental target of the attack, that is, it apparently further restricted CAH by overstating the civilian population ("directed at") element.[42] Yet, even a conservative reading of CAH does not require more than an intentional targeting of the civilian population.[43]

Be that as it may, the fact that the drafters of the ICC Statute maintained this requirement shows that they still do not recognize CAH as a crimes concept in its own right, but rather as an extension of war crimes into peace times only. Yet, apart from the inconsistency of such a conservative definition of CAH with its rationale, on a more technical level, a definition of "civilian" according to International Humanitarian Law (IHL) meets insurmountable difficulties if applied to peace time. Whereas the term can formally be defined with regard to an (international) armed conflict in a negative sense as referring to those persons who are *not* members of military organizations or groups as defined in article 4(a) of the Third Geneva Convention (article 50 of Additional Protocol I), in peace time, a recourse to this definition is not possible because IHL is not applicable during peace time. In fact, in peace time, all persons are civilians (i.e., non-combatants), and it is exactly during this time when CAH should fulfill the function of filling the gap left by armed-conflict crimes. The protection must therefore be extended to all persons, including soldiers.[44]

While the ad hoc tribunals in *Kupreškić et al.*, as shown earlier, have already recognized the dilemma generated by the civilian population requirement, they are, as the ICC, bound by the wording of their Statutes and thus cannot get around the problem. One may stress the term "population" arguing that the requirement focuses rather on the collective nature of the attack (against "a population") than on

---

[40] Ambos, *supra* note 32, at 245 et seq., 247; Ambos, *supra* note 24, § 7 mn. 189 et seq.; for a broad interpretation, see Ambos & Wirth, *supra* note 24, at 22 et seq.

[41] Prosecutor v. Kupreškić, Case No, IT-95-16-T, Judgment, ¶ 547 (Jan. 24, 2000).

[42] *Kunarac Appeals Judgment*, *supra* note 35, ¶ 91; Prosecutor v. Blaškić, Case No. IT-95-14-A, Judgment, ¶ 106 (July 29, 2004); Prosecutor v. Kordić & Čerkez, Case No. IT-95-14/2-A, Judgment, ¶ 96 (Dec. 17, 2004); Prosecutor v. M. Lukić & S. Lukić, Case No. IT-98-32/1-T, Judgment, ¶ 874 (July 20, 2009). This view has been adopted by the SCSL. Prosecutor v. Fofana & Kondewa, Case No. SCSL-04-14-T, Judgment, ¶ 114 (Aug. 2, 2007); Prosecutor v. Fofana & Kondewa, Case No. SCSL-04-14-A, Judgment, ¶ 299 (May 28, 2008).

[43] For a good discussion, see Eboe-Osuji, *supra* note 30, at 120 et seq.

[44] For the same result, see ANTONIO CASSESE, INTERNATIONAL CRIMINAL LAW 122–23 (2d ed. 2008); ROBERT KOLB, DROIT INTERNATIONAL PENAL 97 (Helbing Lichtenhahn 2008); RICCARDO

the (civilian or military) individuals affected,[45] and thus confirms that there must be a multiplicity of victims (going against a strictly alternative reading of the "widespread or systematic" requirement),[46] but this does not make the term "civilian" disappear. Similarly, one may opt for a broad interpretation of "civilian," but this interpretation must not, in light of the principle of legality (article 22 (2)), be stretched beyond the reasonable meaning of the term.[47] Thus, the only clear solution is a legislative one, that is, to delete the civilian population requirement entirely.

3. The Knowledge Requirement

The chapeau of article 7 requires explicitly that the accused be aware of the attack of which his individual act forms part. This implies a twofold test: On the one hand, the perpetrator must know of the existence of the attack; on the other hand, he must know that his individual act forms part of this attack.[48] The knowledge requirement constitutes an additional mental element to be distinguished from the general *mens rea* requirement of article 30.[49] This follows both from the fact that "knowledge" is explicitly mentioned in article 7 and from the Elements of Crimes, where knowledge is also required separately in the Elements for each of the enumerated individual acts of CAH. If one were to understand the knowledge requirement as part of the general mental element, paragraph 3 of article 30 would have to be interpreted in the sense of a risk-based approach (see below).[50] This is another good reason to interpret the knowledge requirement as an additional mental element. In structural terms, the knowledge requirement connects the individual acts with the overall attack by means of the perpetrator's mind. It thus ensures that single, isolated acts that are only carried out on the occasion of an overall attack, "using the opportunity," do not qualify as CAH and therefore cannot be prosecuted under article 7.

The case law holds that the accused must be aware that his act forms part of the collective attack.[51] There is, however, certain controversy as to the specific *contents*

BORSARI, DIRITTO PUNITIVO SOVRANAZIONALE COME SISTEMA 73 (CEDAM 2007); *see also* MESEKE, *supra* note 35, at 156.

[45] In a similar vein, see Luban, *supra* note 9, at 104, who however does not renounce the civilian requirement.

[46] Ambos & Wirth, *supra* note 24, at 21; against this view, see Luban, *supra* note 9, at 108 n.84, arguing for a broad interpretation of the population requirement in the sense of "any" population, *id.* at 105 et seq.

[47] For the ICTY's broad interpretation, see Prosecutor v. Galić, Case No. IT-98-29-A, Judgment, ¶ 144 (Nov. 30, 2006); *Milutinović et al. Trial Judgment, supra* note 29, ¶ 147, both with further references. *But see* ALEXANDER ZAHAR & GÖRAN SLUITER, INTERNATIONAL CRIMINAL LAW 205 et seq. (2007).

[48] Ambos, *supra* note 32, at 249. Against a mental requirement, see Kirsch, *supra* note 28, at 286.

[49] Ambos & Wirth, *supra* note 24, at 39–40.

[50] This is possible, Ambos, *supra* note 32, at 250; Ambos, *supra* note 24, § 7 mn. 197, but it will certainly generate controversy.

[51] Prosecutor v. Kordić and Čerkez, Case No. IT-95-14/ 2-T, Judgment, ¶187 (Feb. 26, 2001); Prosecutor v. Tadić, Case No. IT-94-1-A, Judgment, ¶ 248, 255 (July 15, 1999); *Kupreškić Trial*

of this knowledge and its *object of reference*.⁵² As to the latter, the risk-orientated or risk-based approach proposed by the *Blaškić* Trial Chamber is convincing. According to this approach, knowledge also includes the conduct "of a person taking a deliberate risk in the hope that the risk does not cause injury."⁵³ This was confirmed by the *Kunarac* Appeals Chamber upholding the Trial Chamber's view that the perpetrator must, at least, have known "the risk that his acts were part of the attack."⁵⁴ This approach extends knowledge from "full" or "positive" knowledge well into the field of recklessness, and thus clarifies the obscure concept of "constructive knowledge" introduced by other Chambers.⁵⁵ Thus, a perpetrator has knowledge of the attack if he is aware of the risk that his conduct is objectively part of such a broader attack. As to the knowledge of the contents of the attack, it is sufficient that the perpetrator is aware of the existence of the attack in general without possessing detailed knowledge of its particularities and circumstances.⁵⁶ In other words, the perpetrator must (only) know the facts related to the attack that increase the dangerousness of his conduct for the victims or render this conduct a contribution to the crimes of others.⁵⁷ This standard corresponds to the risk-based approach.

The risk-based approach also shows its superiority in cases where the perpetrator carries out one of the underlying acts at a moment when the *attack* is only *imminent* or just *begins*. In such a situation, positive knowledge of an overall attack cannot exist because the attack does not exist in the first place. The Elements of Crimes

---

Judgment, *supra* note 41, ¶ 556; Prosecutor v. Vasiljević, Case No. IT-98-32-A, Judgment, ¶ 30 (Feb. 25, 2004); *Limaj et al. Trial Judgment, supra* note 35, ¶ 190; *Krajišnik Trial Judgment, supra* note 35, ¶ 706; Prosecutor v. Bisengimana, Case No. ICTR-00-60-T, Judgment, ¶ 57 (Apr. 13, 2006); *Bemba Gombo Confirmation of Charges, supra* note 29, ¶ 87.

⁵² *See* Ambos & Wirth, *supra* note 24, at 37 et seq.

⁵³ Prosecutor v. Blaškić, Case No. IT-95-14-T, Judgment, ¶ 254 (Mar. 3, 2000), referring to Frédéric Desportes & Francis Le Gunehec, Le Nouveau Droit Pénal 445 (14th ed. 2007) ("[D]e la personne qui prend un risque de façon délibérée, tout en espérant que ce risque ne provoque aucun dommage.").

⁵⁴ *Kunarac Appeals Judgment, supra* note 35, ¶ 102 (quoting from the Trial Judgment, *infra* note 64, ¶ 434); conc. *Vasiljević Appeals Judgment, supra* note 51, ¶ 37; Prosecutor v. Martić, Case No. IT-95-11-T, Judgment, ¶ 49 (June 12, 2007); Prosecutor v. Mrkšić, Case No. IT-95-13/1-T, Judgment, ¶ 439 (Sept. 27, 2007); *see also M. Lukić and S. Lukić Trial Judgment, supra* note 42, ¶ 877.

⁵⁵ Prosecutor v. Tadić, Case No. IT-94-1-T, Judgment, ¶ 656–59 (May 7, 1997); *Tadić Appeals Judgment, supra* note 51, ¶ 248 (does not mention constructive knowledge); Prosecutor v. Kayishema & Ruzindana, Case No. ICTR-95-1-T, Judgment, ¶¶ 133–34 (May 21, 1999); Prosecutor v. Rutaganda, Case No. ICTR-96-3-T, Judgment, ¶ 71 (Dec. 6, 1999); *Kupreškić Trial Judgment, supra* note 41, ¶¶ 556–57; Prosecutor v. Musema, Case No. ICTR-96-13, Judgment, ¶ 206 (Jan. 27, 2000); Prosecutor v. Ruggiu, Case No. ICTR-97-32-I, Judgment, ¶ 20 (June 1, 2000); *Kordić Trial Judgment, supra* note 51, ¶ 185. For a critical discussion of this concept, see Ambos & Wirth, *supra* note 24, at 38–39; Ambos, *supra* note 32, at 250; Ambos, *supra* note 24, § 7 mn. 198.

⁵⁶ *See, e.g., Kunarac Appeals Judgment, supra* note 35, ¶ 102; Prosecutor v. Simba, Case No. ICTR-01-76-T, Judgment, ¶ 421 (Dec. 13, 2005); *Katanga and Ngudjolo Confirmation of Charges, supra* note 29, ¶ 401; *Arrest Warrant Al Bashir, supra* note 29, ¶ 87. See also Introduction to the Elements of Crime, *supra* note 37, ¶ 2 (Ambos & Wirth, *supra* note 37) on CAH: "should not be interpreted as requiring proof that the perpetrator had knowledge of all characteristics of the attack … ;" on the negotiations, see Robinson, *supra* note 33, at 72.

⁵⁷ Ambos & Wirth, *supra* note 24, at 41.

provide that in such a situation, it is sufficient that the perpetrator intends "to further such an attack"[58] or intends "the conduct to be part of a[n] attack." The drafters obviously intended that in such situations, the requirement for knowledge should be replaced by the perpetrator's desire to bring about the relevant facts. Yet, although it is true that future events (*in casu* the development of an incipient into a full-fledged attack) cannot be known but only hoped for or desired, one can be aware of the risk that a certain conduct will lead to a certain result.[59] In other words, a participant in an incipient attack cannot know for certain that the attack will develop into a full-fledged attack, but he can certainly be aware of a risk to that effect.[60]

4. The Individual Acts and the Context Element

The list of individual crimes forming part of a crime against humanity has gradually increased. Whereas the ICTY Statute included acts such as deportation, imprisonment, torture and rape, the International Law Commission went a step further and included discrimination based on racial, ethnic or religious grounds, forcible transfer, forced disappearance, enforced prostitution, and other forms of sexual violence.[61] Article 7 of the ICC Statute further extends the list, including sexual crimes such as forced pregnancy, enforced sterilization, or any other form of sexual violence of comparable gravity. A detailed analysis of these acts and their general mental element (article 30) has been done elsewhere.[62] Here it suffices to say that article 7 represents clear progress compared to the codifications so far, if only for the fact that it provides for more or less precise definitions in its paragraph 2.

As to the relationship between the individual acts and the context element, one has to start from the wording of article 7. Paragraph 1 provides that the enumerated criminal acts must be "committed *as part of* a widespread or systematic attack" (emphasis added). From this follows, first, the material or objective requirement that "the crimes must be committed in the context of widespread or systematic crimes ...."[63] Yet, the underlying acts need not constitute the attack itself;[64] they

---

[58] Elements of Crimes, *supra* note 37, Introduction to the Elements of article 7, ¶ 2; *see also* Robinson, *supra* note 33, at 73.

[59] WOLFGANG FRISCH, VORSATZ UND RISIKO 341 et seq. (1983): "Notwendig ist das Wissen um das der Handlung eigneude und (normative) ihre Tatbestandsmäßigkeit begründende Risiko ...". *Id.* at 341.

[60] For the same result, see Ambos & Wirth, *supra* note 24, at 40.

[61] *Draft Code of Crimes against Peace and Security of Mankind*, Report of the International Law Commission on Its Forty-Eighth Session, art. 18, U.N. GAOR, 51st Sess., Supp. No. 10, at 9, U.N. Doc. A/51/10 (1996).

[62] Ambos & Wirth, *supra* note 24, at 43 et seq., 46 et seq.; Ambos, *supra* note 32, at 251 et seq.; Ambos, *supra* note 24, § 7 mn. 199 et seq.

[63] *Tadić Appeals Judgment*, *supra* note 51, ¶ 248, 255; *Kordić Trial Judgment*, *supra* note 51, ¶ 187; *Kupreskic Trial Judgment*, *supra* note 41, ¶ 556; *Decision on the Confirmation of the Charges against Bemba Gombo*, *supra* note 29, ¶ 84; *see also* Dixon (revised by Hall), *supra* note 29, art. 7 mn. 10; Mettraux, *supra* note 35, at 161–62; Ambos & Wirth, *supra* note 24, at 35–36.

[64] *Prosecutor v. Kunarac*, Case No. IT-96-23-T and IT-96-23/1-T, Judgment, ¶ 417 (Feb. 22, 2001); *Kunarac Appeals Judgment*, *supra* note 35, ¶ 85; *Tadić Appeals Judgment*, *supra* note 51, ¶ 248;

must only "form part of such an attack"[65] or take place "in the context of" such an attack.[66] Relevant criteria for determining if the required nexus exists are the characteristics, the aims, the nature, or the consequences of the act.[67] Second, as a consequence of the (subjective) knowledge element just discussed, "the accused must have *known* that his acts, 'fitted into such a pattern.'"[68] If one follows the convincing risk-based approach, it is sufficient that the perpetrator is aware of the risk of acting in the context of an attack. Further, as the "attack" always entails a policy element, as already shown above, the perpetrator must also be aware, at least of the risk, of acting pursuant to such a policy but not knowing the details of this policy.[69]

A more precise definition of the link required between the individual acts and the context may be derived from the *rationale* of CAH. If it consists, as already argued earlier, of the protection against the particular dangers of the multiple or repeated commission of crimes, actively supported or at least tolerated by a (de facto) authority, this very policy of support or toleration – that is, the context of an overall attack – increases the destructive effect of the individual act and the risk or danger for the victim. Compare, for example, the case of an ordinary killing in the course of a robbery and a killing of a political opponent. In the former case, there is no official support or toleration for the killing. In the latter case, this very support or toleration increases the risk for the potential victim, shields the perpetrators from prosecution, and may transform the otherwise ordinary killing into a CAH. Thus, an adequate test to determine whether a certain act was part of the attack, and therefore amounts to a CAH, is to ask whether the act would have produced a less destructive and dangerous effect for the victim if it had not taken place within the framework of an attack and pursuant to a policy.[70]

5. Renunciation of Armed Conflict Nexus and Discriminatory Motive

Although article 7 maintains the element of a civilian population, and thus stops short of a (complete) emancipation from IHL, at least it renounces the requirement of a

---

Kayishema Trial Judgment, *supra* note 55, ¶ 135; Prosecutor v. Bagilishema, Case No. ICTR-95-1A-T, Judgment, ¶ 82. (June 7, 2001).
[65] Kunarac Trial Judgment, *supra* note 64, ¶ 417; *see also* Kayishema Trial Judgment, *supra* note 55, ¶ 135.
[66] Kunarac Trial Judgment, *supra* note 64, ¶ 419.
[67] Decision on the Confirmation of the Charges against Bemba Gombo, *supra* note 29, ¶ 86.
[68] Tadić Appeals Judgment, *supra* note 51, ¶¶ 248, 255; Kordić Trial Judgment, *supra* note 51, ¶ 187; Kupreskic Trial Judgment, *supra* note 41, ¶ 556. On this mental element, see also Cerone, *supra* note 1, at 200 (without, however, clearly distinguishing between the general mental element and the special knowledge requirement).
[69] *See also* Introduction to the Elements, *supra* note 37, ¶ 2, on CAH: "should not be interpreted as requiring proof that the perpetrator had knowledge of ... the precise details of the plan or policy of the State or organization." On the negotiations, see Robinson, *supra* note 33, at 73. *See also* Ambos & Wirth, *supra* note 24, at 42.
[70] *See* Ambos & Wirth, *supra* note 24, at 36; *see also* Pablo Parenti, *Los Crímenes Contra la Humanidad y el Genocidio en el Derecho Internacional*, *in* LOS CRÍMENES CONTRA LA HUMANIDAD Y EL GENOCIDIO EN EL DERECHO INTERNACIONAL: ORIGEN Y EVOLUCIÓN DE LAS FIGURAS, ELEMENTOS TÍPICOS, JURISPRUDENCIA INTERNACIONAL 59–60 (Pablo Parenti et al. eds., 2007). *See contra* Mettraux, *supra* note 35, at 251, 252.

nexus with an armed conflict. This requirement dates back to the Nuremberg precedent and gave CAH – apart from protecting the drafters from their own prosecution[71] – the legitimacy they could otherwise not have had at that time.[72] In current ICL, this requirement is, however, out of place, as correctly held by the *Tadić* Appeals Chamber, despite its inclusion in article 5 of the ICTY Statute in the early days of the ICTY.[73]

Article 7 of the ICC Statute, contrary to article 3 of the ICTR Statute, no longer requires a special discriminatory intent or motive, namely that the act must have been committed on national, political, ethnic, racial, or religious grounds. Apart from the confusion between intent and motive,[74] it is, since the *Tadić Appeals Judgment*, clear that such a discriminatory intent is only required for persecution as a CAH.[75] This is confirmed by the wording of article 7(1)(h) of the ICC Statute referring to certain (albeit in fact unlimited)[76] grounds as the basis for the conduct.[77]

III. THE ICC, ARTICLE 7 OF THE ICC STATUTE, AND A SPECIAL CONVENTION

A. *The Proposed Article 3 Compared to Article 7 of the ICC Statute*

Whereas article 2 in the original draft of the proposed CAH convention substantially deviated from the CAH definition of article 7 of the ICC Statute,[78] article

---

[71] See Schabas, *supra* note 26, at 349 (referring to Robert Jackson's statement at the London conference).
[72] For the history and rationale of this requirement, see Ambos & Wirth, *supra* note 24, at 3 et seq.
[73] Prosecutor v. Tadić, Case No. IT-94-1-AR72, Decision on the Defence Motion for Interlocutory Appeal on Jurisdiction, ¶ 140 (Oct. 2, 1995) [hereinafter *Tadić Jurisdiction Decision*]. "[T]here is no logical or legal basis for [a war nexus] and it has been abandoned in subsequent State practice with respect to crimes against humanity." *Id.* at ¶ 141. "[A] settled rule of customary international law that crimes against humanity do not require a connection to international armed conflict. Indeed … customary international law may not require a connection between crimes against humanity and any conflict at all …." *Id.*
[74] Intent and motive must be distinguished. The principle of culpability requires that the perpetrator acts with a certain state of mind, normally with intent; his possible motives (the reason for his action) are irrelevant in this respect. The distinction has, in the meantime, also been recognized by the Appeals Chamber of the ICTY and ICTR. *See Tadić Appeals Judgment*, *supra* note 51, ¶¶ 270, 272; Prosecutor v. Jelisić, Case No. IT-95-10-A, Judgment, ¶ 49 (July 5, 2001); Prosecutor v. Niyitegeka, Case No. ICTR-96-14-A, Judgment, ¶ 52 (July 9, 2004); Prosecutor v. Kvočka et al., Case No. IT-98-30/1-A, Judgment, ¶ 106 (Feb. 26, 2005); Prosecutor v. Limaj et al., Case No. IT-03-66-A, Judgment, ¶ 109 (Sept. 17, 2007); *see also* Mettraux, *supra* note 35, at 211; Zahar & Sluiter, *supra* note 47, at 180; José Manuel Gómez-Benítez, *El Exterminio de Grupos Políticos en el Derecho Penal Internacional etc.*, 4 Revista de Derecho y Proceso Penal 147, 151 (2000); Ambos & Wirth, *supra* note 24, at 45.
[75] *Tadić Appeals Judgment*, *supra* note 51, ¶ 284, 288 et seq. For a discussion, see Ambos & Wirth, *supra* note 24, at 44.
[76] This is not a closed list, because the grounds must only be "universally recognized as impermissible under international law." This broad formulation causes Luban, *supra* note 9, at 107, to argue that the discriminatory intent requirement has been brought "into parity with the population requirement" (which he also interprets broadly, *supra* note 46).
[77] *Cf.* Ambos, *supra* note 32, at 259.
[78] The original draft article 2, compared with the chapeau of article 7 of the ICC Statute, added the term "intentionally" between "committed" and "as part …" and finished the chapeau (after

3 of the September 2009 draft of the proposed convention essentially tracks the "official" definition.[79] Thus, on the one hand, my earlier criticism of the definition of CAH remains valid as it is directed against the wording of article 7 of the ICC Statute; on the other hand, however, it is striking that the drafters of the *Proposed Convention*, with their all-too-conservative approach, gave up certain clarifications they had achieved with the prior definition:

a) As to the *civilian population requirement* retained by the *Proposed Convention*, it is, because of the rationale of CAH as explained earlier (*supra* Section I), more convincing to delete this requirement. To retain it is particularly confusing in light of the purpose of the *Proposed Convention*, namely to complement the ICC regime. Why do the drafters want to retain a serious restriction of the traditional offense definition instead of using the opportunity to enlarge CAH by abolishing this controversial restriction?

b) It is to be welcomed that the drafters have now deleted their original reference to "a conflict of an international or non-international character...."[80] For with this reference the drafters ran the risk of reintroducing the *(armed) conflict requirement*. Admittedly, the respective part was open to at least two, albeit contradictory, interpretations. A conservative reading would be that the part "conflict of ..." refers to the State and non-State actors mentioned and thus reintroduces the traditional war requirement. A modern interpretation, in line with the renunciation of this requirement, would limit the conflict reference to non-State actors, that is, it would serve to accord these actors a certain weight. This interpretation was confirmed by paragraph 2(a) of the older draft article 2 where it was made clear that CAH may be committed "in times of war or peace." In any case, it is a wise decision and avoids confusion that now any reference to an (armed) conflict in paragraph (1) of article 3 has been deleted.

c) It is equally to be welcomed that the new article 3 deletes the terms "intentionally" or "knowingly" in the chapeau.[81] Apparently, the purpose of this reference was to define the *general mens rea requirement* of the underlying acts. Yet, it was superfluous, since the general mental element was provided for in article 3–1 last clause and in article 4–2 ("knowingly or intentionally") of the original draft (no longer contained in the September draft

---

"civilian population") with the following text: "or knowingly by agents of a state or state organization, or by members of a non-state actor group engaging in a conflict of an international or non-international character...".

[79] Editor's Note: The final text of the *Proposed International Convention on the Prevention and Punishment of Crimes Against Humanity*, in this volume, App. I, is virtually identical to the September Draft referred to by the author with respect to the text of article 3 (definition of the crime).

[80] See *supra* note 78.

[81] For the original draft article 2, see *supra* note 78.

or later iterations of the Convention!) – in an identical fashion to article 30 (1) of the ICC Statute. In addition, the use of the term "intentional" entailed another problem as to its concrete meaning. The drafters apparently understood it in a volitional sense. Even though this corresponds to the core meaning of this term, it must not be overlooked that, in traditional common law, intent or intention was always understood in both a volitional and cognitive sense.[82] Modern English law still includes in the definition of intention, apart from purpose, "foresight of certainty," that is, only the core meaning of intent or intention is reserved to desire, purpose, and so on.[83] Also, the U.S. Model Penal Code, which served as a reference for the ICC Statute in many regards, while distinguishing between "purpose" and "knowledge" (section 2.02 (a)), defines the former in a cognitive sense by referring to the perpetrator's "conscious object" with regard to conduct and result.[84] Last, but not least, article 30 of the ICC Statute itself recognizes a cognitive side of intent when it defines it in paragraph 2(b) as being aware (in relation to a consequence) "that it will occur in the ordinary course of events." All these issues are no longer relevant with a view to the new September draft, but it is surprising that the drafters *totally renounced a (general) definition of the mental element* required for CAH.

d) The September draft, relying on article 7 of the ICC Statute, also contains the *special knowledge requirement* with regard to the overall attack. It was not clear whether the omission of this requirement in the original draft of the proposed convention was deliberate or based on a misunderstanding of the meaning of this special mental element as opposed to the general mental element. In any case, the absence of this requirement would sever the link between the individual acts and the overall attack or policy; it is therefore correct, that the drafters reintroduced it.

---

[82] See GLANVILLE WILLIAMS, THE MENTAL ELEMENT IN CRIME 20 (1965) ("Intention is a state of mind consisting of knowledge of any requisite circumstances plus desire that any requisite result shall follow from one's conduct, or else of foresight that the result will certainly follow."). See also GEORGE P. FLETCHER, RETHINKING CRIMINAL LAW 440 (2000) (1978) (tracing this doctrinal tradition to the nineteenth-century utilitarian John Austin).

[83] ANDREW ASHWORTH, PRINCIPLES OF CRIMINAL LAW 170 et seq. (171) (6th ed. 2009); ANDREW P. SIMESTER & G. ROBERT SULLIVAN, CRIMINAL LAW: THEORY AND DOCTRINE 120 et seq. (3d ed. 2007). See also *R. v. Woollin*, where the House of Lords, with regard to a murder charge, defined intention referring to "virtual certainty" as to the consequence of the defendant's actions. R. v. Woollin [1999] 1 Crim. App. 8, 20–21 (H.L.) (U.K.) ("[T]he jury should be directed that they are not entitled to find the necessary intention unless they feel sure that death or serious bodily harm was a virtual certainty (barring some unforeseen intervention) as a result of the defendant's actions …"). See also Judicial Studies Board, *Specimen Directions*, § 12, *available at* www.jsboard.co.uk/criminal_law/cbb/index.htm (last visited September 10, 2009).

[84] The respective part of section 2.02(a) reads: "A person acts purposely with respect to a material element of an offense when … if the element involves the nature of his conduct or a result thereof, it is his conscious object to engage in conduct of that nature or to cause such a result …" (emphasis added). See also FLETCHER, *supra* note 82, at 440 et seq.

e) The *Proposed Convention* no longer contains the clarification that the acts can be committed by both *State and non-State actors*.[85] Whereas this clarification is not strictly necessary because paragraph 1 of the original draft already referred explicitly to non-State actors and the reference to an "organizational" policy must also be interpreted to that effect, it is certainly useful, especially in light of the continuing resistance of certain non-State actors to comply with ICL. Further, paragraph 2(a) of the original draft omitted the qualifier "multiple" before commission and thus reduced the *quantitative element* in CAH ("widespread") to even one act. This has correctly been changed because it entails an expansion of the offense definition that, albeit sound for policy reasons, is inconsistent with the "widespread" requirement of CAH. It is deplorable, however, that the September draft deleted the definition of *"organizational policy"* in paragraph 2(b) of the original draft, considering that it provided a very useful clarification of a highly controversial term.

In sum, although the *Proposed Convention's* adoption of the ICC definition is certainly to be welcomed as far as it deletes the unnecessary and confusing changes of the original draft, it misses the chance of improving and clarifying the definition of CAH with a view to its rationale as explained above (*supra* Section I). It is especially unfortunate that the drafters, apparently in an all-too-conservative and diplomatic mood, did not take issue with the civilian population requirement. Thus, as a result, the offense definition proposed, by essentially repeating article 7 of the ICC Statute, does not offer broader protection than the ICC's legal regime.

B. *The Limited Role of the ICC in the Prevention and Repression of CAH*

Apart from the mere normative limitation due to a narrow offense definition as just discussed, there are various other limitations that may speak in favor of a specialized CAH Convention. The first and most obvious one is that the ICC has a *jurisdiction* that is basically limited to the territory and nationals of its State Parties (article 12(2)), unless there is an ad hoc acceptance of jurisdiction under article 12(3) or a UN Security Council referral (article 13(b)). The *Proposed Convention*, like any other specialized convention on international crimes, offers the States the possibility to commit themselves to the fight against CAH without having to accept, at the same time, the jurisdiction of the ICC. On the other hand, its ratification could be the first step toward ratification of the ICC Statute.

Another limitation follows from the principle of *complementarity* and the ICC's subsidiarity toward national jurisdictions. It provides States with a strong tool to

---

[85] Article 2(2)(a) of the original draft defining "attack" as a "course of conduct ... whether by a State or non-State actor."

impede the ICC's exercise of jurisdiction, as long as they are willing and able to prosecute CAH themselves. The implicit pressure on national jurisdictions could be increased by a specialized Convention because it would create an additional normative obligation whose force would increase with time. Ultimately, such a Convention could serve as a trigger, similar to the Genocide Convention, for the intervention of the international community in the face of CAH.[86] In addition, the complementarity regime explicitly requires *"sufficient gravity"* for a case to be admissible before the ICC (article 17(4); *see also* article 53(1)(b) and (2)(b)). This special gravity threshold establishes an *additional* threshold, that is, it operates independently of the gravity of ICC crimes as such.[87] As a result, there may be CAH that do not pass the gravity test of article 17(4) but that would be covered by the *Proposed Convention*.

Last but not least, it is quite clear that the ICC does not have the *capacity* to prosecute all CAH, perhaps not even the sufficiently grave ones in the sense of article 17(4).[88] In fact, at the time of this writing the ICC has, in only four situations (the Democratic Republic of the Congo, Uganda, the Central African Republic, and Sudan) initiated formal investigations (article 53) dealing with CAH (see the list in the annex to this chapter). In many other situations, where the commission of CAH is of general knowledge and the ICC has jurisdiction, no formal investigations have been initiated. One of the most dramatic examples is perhaps the case of Colombia, where the Court's jurisdiction has existed since November 1, 2002 (article 126(2), date of ratification: August 5, 2002). Thus, it is clear that an effective prevention and prosecution of CAH is impossible without the active contribution and enforcement of national jurisdictions.

C. *Deterrence and ICL*

Clearly, the argument in favor of a new CAH Convention rests on the premise that the sheer existence of (international) criminal law norms has a deterrent effect. Indeed, the proponents of a specialized Convention display a great trust in the deterrence capacity of (international) criminal law norms. For them, the absence of a specialized convention leaves millions of victims "outside the protection of international criminal law" and "beyond the reach of international criminal law."[89] In light

---

[86] For the related discussion on the "responsibility to protect," see David Scheffer, in this volume.
[87] *Cf.* Prosecutor v. Lubanga, Doc. No. ICC-01/04-01/06-8, Decision concerning Pre-Trial Chamber I's Decision of 10 February 2006 and the Incorporation of Documents into the Record of the Case against Mr. Thomas Lubanga Dyilo, ¶ 41 (Feb. 24, 2006) ("[T]his gravity threshold is in addition to … the crimes included in articles 6 to 8 of the Statute …".). For a discussion and further references, see MOHAMMED EL ZEIDY, THE PRINCIPLE OF COMPLEMENTARY IN THE INTERNATIONAL CRIMINAL LAW 36 et seq. (2008) and Kai Ambos, *The Legal Framework of Transitional Justice: A Systematic Study with a Special Focus on the Role of the ICC, in* BUILDING A FUTURE ON PEACE AND JUSTICE 19, 73–74 (Kai Ambos et al. eds., 2009).
[88] On the limitations, see also Kai Ambos, *Prosecuting International Crimes at the National and International Level: Between Justice and Realpolitik, in* INTERNATIONAL PROSECUTION OF HUMAN RIGHTS CRIMES 55 (Wolfgang Kaleck et al. eds., 2006).
[89] Background paper of July 31, 2008, circulated before the Crimes Against Humanity Initiative's April Experts' Meeting, April 12–15, 2009, St. Louis, MO.

of such apodictic affirmations, some critical questions seem warranted: Will the mere drafting and adoption of yet another convention change the situation of the potential victims of CAH? Do these kinds of conventions and norms have any deterrent effect on the potential perpetrators at all? Do we have any reliable information as to the possible deterrent effect of the ICC?

The deterrent effects of criminal law have to be assessed in the overall context of the possible preventive effects of criminal law. Deterrence forms, in this context, part of the theories of negative general prevention and, as such, has three dimensions referring to the conditions of a given society to prevent crimes, to the individual circumstances of prevention with a view to the perpetrator and victims, and last but not least, to the prevention of recidivistic offenders.[90] Empirical research on deterrence has been the object of criminal law theory and, more recently, criminological research for centuries. Yet, the results of this research only have a limited value, because human behavior is influenced by various psychological and social factors that make it difficult, if not impossible, to consider law-abiding behavior as the consequence of the deterrent effect of criminal law. In fact, we know little about the deterrent effects of criminal law, and research results are contradictory.[91] The only thing we know with relative certainty is that the most important deterrence factor is the existence of a (more or less) functioning criminal justice system,[92] which entails the risk of detection and prosecution.[93] Whereas the gravity of a sanction (period and nature of punishment) is less, if at all, important,[94] the probability of punishment is of crucial importance.[95]

These general considerations also apply to ICL and its tribunals, but there are some additional factors to be taken into account. First of all, the existence of international criminal tribunals – as a direct enforcement mechanism of ICL – is still a quite recent phenomenon, and sustainable deterrence results may only be seen in the mid- or long term.[96] In any case, most authors believe, despite the absence of

---

[90] Arthur Kreuzer, *Prävention durch Repression*, in ANGEWANDTE KRIMINOLOGIE ZWISCHEN FREIHEIT UND SICHERHEIT 205, 205 (Heinz Schöch & Jörg-Marin Jehle eds., 2004).

[91] Dieter Dölling & Dieter Hermann, *Befragungsstudien zur negativen Generalprävention: Eine Bestandsaufnahme*, in KRIMINALITÄT, ÖKONOMIE UND EUROPÄISCHER SOZIALSTAAT 133, 162 (Hans-Jörg Albrecht & Horst Entorf eds., 2003); Kreuzer, *supra* note 90, at 207 et seq. In a meta-analysis of twenty-eight studies on deterrence Hermann Eisele, Die general- und spezialpräventive Wirkung strafrechtlicher Sanktionen. Methoden, Ergebnisse, Metaanalyse (Ph.D. dissertation, University of Heidelberg 1999) shows that nine of the studies confirm the deterrent effects, nine negate such effects, and ten present differentiated answers.

[92] FRANZ STRENG, STRAFRECHTLICHE SANKTION 31 (2d ed. 2002).

[93] ANDREW VON HIRSCH ET AL., CRIMINAL DETERRENCE AND SENTENCE SEVERITY 1 (1999); Kreuzer, *supra* note 90, at 216; *see also* Mark Drumbl, A Hard Look at the Soft Theory of International Criminal Law, in Sadat & Scharf, *supra* note 25, at 1, 14 ("likelihood of getting caught").

[94] VON HIRSCH ET AL., *supra* note 93, at 40–47; BERND-DIETER MEIER, KRIMINOLOGIE 262 (2003); Kreuzer, *supra* note 90, at 216–17.

[95] Jürgen Antony & Horst Entorf, *Zur Gültigkeit der Abschreckung im Sinne der ökonomischen Theorie der Kriminalität: Grundzüge einer Meta-Studie*, in KRIMINALITÄT, ÖKONOMIE UND EUROPÄISCHER SOZIALSTAAT 167, 170 (Hans-Jörg Albrecht & Horst Entorf eds., 2003).

[96] For criticism on short-term effects, see Herbert Jäger, *Hört das Kriminalitätskonzept vor der Makrokriminalität auf? – Offene Fragen und Denkansätze*, in VOM RECHT DER MACHT ZUR

hard empirical data,[97] in an (albeit limited) deterrent effect of ICL and international criminal tribunals on the condition that their decisions are promptly and consequently enforced and exemptions from prosecution and punishment – for example, in the course of national peace processes – are excluded.[98] This view is supported by

> MACHT DES RECHTS – INTERDISZIPLINÄRE BEITRÄGE ZUR ZUKUNFT INTERNATIONALER STRAFGERICHTSBARKEIT 45, 57 (Frank Neubacher & Anne Klein eds., 2006).
>
> [97] Julian G. Ku & Jide Nzelibe, *Do International Criminal Tribunals Deter or Exacerbate Humanitarian Atrocities?*, 84 WASH. U. L. REV. 777, 790 (2006); David Koller, *The Faith of the International Criminal Lawyer*, 40 N.Y.U. J. INT'L L. & POL. 1019, 1029 (2008); Payam Akhavan, *Beyond Impunity: Can International Criminal Justice Prevent Future Atrocities?*, 95 AM. J. INT'L L. 7, 9 (2001); Leila Sadat, *Exile, Amnesty and International Law*, 81 NOTRE DAME L. REV. 955, 998 (2006).
>
> [98] Pierre Hazan, *Measuring the Impact of Punishment and Forgiveness: A Framework for Evaluating Transitional Justice*, 88 ICRC INT'L REV. 19, 35 (2006), finds that "warring parties take the risk of prosecution into account" but the "deterrent effect soon diminishes without prompt indictments and arrests." William Whitney Burke-White, *Complementarity in Practice: The International Criminal Court as Part of a System of Multi-Level Global Governance in the Democratic Republic of Congo*, 18 LEIDEN J. INT'L L. 559, 58 (2005) (affirming that the ICC investigation provides some deterrent effect on rebel leaders in the DRC); *see also* Paul Seils & Marieke Wierda, Int'l Ctr. for Transitional Justice, The International Criminal Court and Conflict Mediation 19 (2005), www.ictj.org/en/news/pubs/index.html (last visited Sept. 10, 2009); Thomas Unger & Marieke Wierda, *Pursuing Justice in Ongoing Conflict: A Discussion of Current Practice*, in AMBOS ET AL., *supra* note 87, at 269 n.15 (explaining that the ICC has a deterrent effect by the likelihood "that there will be consequences" just as in national criminal law). According to Richard Goldstone, *Historical Evolution – From Nuremberg to the International Criminal Court*, 25 PENN ST. INT'L L. REV. 763, 767 68 (2007), the ICTY's supervision of military actions contributed to the fact that only a relatively small number of civilians were hit by NATO bombs during the Kosovo conflict. *See also* Jan Klabbers, *Just Revenge? The Deterrence Argument in International Criminal Law*, 12 FINNISH Y.B. INT'L L. 249 et seq. (2001); Daniel Ntanda Nsereko, *The Role of the International Criminal Tribunals in the Promotion of Peace and Justice: The Case of the ICC*, 19 CRIM. L.F. 373, 376–77, 392 (2008). According to Cryer et al., *supra* note 35, at 30, "deterrence is unlikely to be possible if potential offenders take the view that they may be able to obtain exemption from prosecution." Graham T. Blewitt, *The Importance of a Retributive Approach to Justice*, in THE LEGACY OF NUREMBERG: CIVILISING INFLUENCE OR INSTITUTIONALIZED VENGEANCE 39, 45 et seq. (David A. Blumenthal & Timothy McCormack eds., 2008) admits that "the mere existence of courts … will never bring a complete end to widespread atrocities" but still believes that courts do act as a deterrent and prevent the commission of crime. Sadat, *supra* note 97, at 998–99, sees some "deterrent value" in "sporadic enforcement of international humanitarian law" but also states "that the international criminal justice system has not yet reached the stage at which its deterrent value may be fairly assumed." Recently, Jens David Ohlin, *Peace, Security, and Prosecutorial Discretion*, in THE EMERGING PRACTICE OF THE ICC 185, 202 et seq. (Carsten Stahn & Göran Sluiter eds., 2008), sees deterrence as consequentialist justifications of international criminal law. On the other hand, Nick Grono & Adam O'Brien, *Justice in Conflict? The ICC and Peace Processes*, in COURTING CONFLICT? JUSTICE, PEACE AND THE ICC IN AFRICA 13, 17 (Nicholas Waddell & Phil Clark eds., 2008), emphasize the negative effects of the deterrent power, *i.e.*, that government officials "cling to power at all costs." Rama Mani, *Reparation as a Component of Transitional Justice: Pursuing 'Reparative Justice' in the Aftermath of Violent Conflict*, in OUT OF THE ASHES 53, 76 (Koen de Feyter et al. eds., 2005), argues that reparations have a larger deterrent effect than penal sanctions. For the argument that nonprosecution would undermine the effectiveness of deterrence, see also David A. Crocker, *Punishment, Reconciliation, and Democratic Deliberation*, 5 BUFF. CRIM. L. REV. 509, 536–37 (2002); Darryl Robinson, *Serving the Interests of Justice: Amnesties, Truth Commissions and the International Criminal Court*, 14 EUR. J. INT'L L. 481, 489 (2003); Rodrigo Uprimny & Maria Paula Saffon, *Justicia transicional y justicia restaurativa: tensiones y complementariedades*, in ENTRE EL PERDÓN

the prevailing case law of the ad hoc tribunals, which generally identifies deterrence as an important, if not the primary, purpose of sentencing in international criminal law.[99] Thus, clearly, the deterrent effect of an international criminal tribunal,

Y EL PAREDÓN. PREGUNTAS Y DILEMAS DE LA JUSTICIA TRANSICIONAL 211, 225–26 (Angelika Rettberg ed., 2005); Laura M. Olson, *Provoking the Dragon on the Patio: Matters of Transitional Justice: Penal Repression vs. Amnesties*, 88 ICRC INT'L REV. 275, 291 (2006); for a critique of this argument, see Jaime Malamud-Goti, *Transitional Government in the Breach: Why Punish State Criminals?*, *in* I TRANSITIONAL JUSTICE: GENERAL CONSIDERATIONS 189, 196 (Neil J. Kritz ed., 1995); Juan E. Méndez, *National Reconciliation, Transnational Justice and the International Criminal Court*, 15 ETHICS INT'L AFF. 25, 30–31 (2001). For Danilo Zolo, *Peace through Criminal Law?*, 2 J. INT'L CRIM. JUST. 727, 732 (2004), there is "little or no deterrent power;" for a similar critical view with regard to the ICTY, see Mary Penrose, *Lest We Fail: The Importance of Enforcement in International Criminal Law*, 15 AM. U. INT´L L. REV. 321, 325 (2000); Michael Smidt, *The International Criminal Court: An Effective Means of Deterrence?*, 167 MIL. L. REV. 156, 188 (2001); Oliver Tolmein, *Strafrecht als Instrument zur Schaffung von Frieden: Das Beispiel des ICTY*, *in* HUMANITÄRES VÖLKERRECHT 493, 507 (Jana Hasse et al. eds., 2001); CHRISTINA MÖLLER, VÖLKERSTRAFRECHT UND INTERNATIONALER STRAFGERICHTSHOF – KRIMINOLOGISCHE, STRAFTHEORETISCHE UND RECHTSPOLITISCHE ASPEKTE 501 (2003); Drumbl, *supra* note 93, at 14–15 (stressing the "unproven assumption of perpetrator rationality in the context of mass violence" and the selective enforcement of ICL); for a very positive evaluation of the ICTY and ICTR, see Akhavan, *supra* note 98, arguing that these tribunals "raised accountability," *id.* at 9, and had "relative success," *id.* at 31, so that even "diehard cynics" can no longer "deny the preventive effects of prosecuting murderous rulers," *id.* at 30.

[99] Prosecutor v. Delalić, Case No. IT-96-21-A, Judgment, ¶ 800 (Feb. 20, 2001); Prosecutor v. Kordić & Čerkez, Case No. IT-95-14/2-A, Judgment, ¶ 1076 (Dec. 17, 2004); Prosecutor v. Krajišnik, Case No. IT-00-39-A, Judgment, ¶ 775 (Mar. 17, 2009); Prosecutor v. Mrkšić & Šljivančanin, Case No. IT-95-13/1-A, Judgment, ¶ 415 (May 5, 2009); Prosecutor v. Delalić, Case No. IT-96-21-T, Judgment, ¶ 1234 (Nov. 16, 1998); Prosecutor v. Furundžija, Case No. IT-95-17/1-T, Judgment, ¶ 288 (Dec. 10, 1998); Prosecutor v. Tadić, Case No. IT-94-1-T*bis*-R117, Judgment, ¶ 9 (Nov. 11, 1999); Prosecutor v. Jelisić, Case No. IT-95-10-T, Judgment, ¶ 116 (Dec. 14, 1999); *Kupreškić Trial Judgment*, *supra* note 41, ¶ 848; *Blaškić Trial Judgment*, *supra* note 53, ¶ 761; *Kordić and Čerkez Trial Judgment*, *supra* note 51, ¶ 847; Prosecutor v. Todorović, Case No. IT-95-9/1-S, Judgment, ¶ 30 (July 31, 2001); *Vasiljević Trial Judgment*, *supra* note 35, ¶ 273; Prosecutor v. Naletilić & Martinović, Case No. IT-98-34-T, Judgment, ¶ 739 (Mar. 31, 2003); Prosecutor v. Simić, Case No. IT-95-9-T, Judgment, ¶ 1059 (Oct. 17, 2003); Prosecutor v. Nikolic, Case No. IT-02-60/1-S, Judgment, ¶ 88 et seq. (Dec. 2, 2003); Prosecutor v. Galić, Case No. IT-98-29-T, Judgment, ¶ 757 (Dec. 5, 2003); Prosecutor v. Brdjanin, Case No. IT-99-36-T, Trial Judgment, ¶¶ 1090-91 (Sept. 1, 2004); Prosecutor v. Strugar, Case No. IT-01-42-T, Judgment, ¶ 458 (Jan. 31, 2005); *Limaj et al. Trial Judgment*, *supra* note 35, ¶ 723; Prosecutor v. Hadžihasanović & Kubura, Case No. IT-01-47-T, Judgment, ¶ 2072 (Mar. 15, 2006); Prosecutor v. Zelenović, Case No. IT-96-23/2-S, Judgment, ¶ 33 (Apr. 4, 2007); *Martić Trial Judgment*, *supra* note 54, ¶ 484; *Mrkšić Trial Judgment*, *supra* note 54, ¶ 683; Prosecutor v. Haradinaj, Case No. IT-04-84-T, Judgment, ¶ 484 (Apr. 3, 2008); Prosecutor v. Boškoski & Tarčulovski, Case No. IT-04-82-T, Judgment, ¶ 587 (July 10, 2008); *Milutinović et al. Trial Judgment*, *supra* note 29, ¶ 1144; *M. Lukić and S. Lukić Trial Judgment*, *supra* note 42, ¶ 1049; *Rutaganda Trial Judgment*, *supra* note 55, ¶ 456; *Musema Trial Judgment*, *supra* note 55, ¶ 986; Prosecutor v. Kajelijeli, Case No. ICTR-98-44A-T, Judgment, ¶ 945 (Dec. 1, 2003); Prosecutor v. Ntakirutimana, Case No. ICTR-96-10 & ICTR-96-17-T, Judgment, ¶ 882 (Feb. 21, 2003); Prosecutor v. Niyitegeka, Case No. ICTR-96-14-T, Judgment, ¶ 484 (May, 16 2003); Prosecutor v. Kamuhanda, Case No. ICTR-95-54A-T, Judgment, ¶ 754 (Jan. 22, 2004); Prosecutor v. Ndindabahizi, Case No. ICTR-2001-71-I, Judgment, ¶ 498 (July 15, 2004); Prosecutor v. Rutaganira, Case No. ICTR-95-1-C, Judgment, ¶ 110 (Mar. 14, 2005); Prosecutor v. Karera, Case No. ICTR-01-74-T, Judgment, ¶ 571 (Dec. 7, 2007); Prosecutor v. Kalimanzira, Case No. ICTR-05-88-T, Judgment, ¶ 741 (June 22, 2009); Prosecutor v. Renzaho, Case No. ICTR-97-31-T, Judgment, ¶ 814 (July 14, 2009). *See also* Prosecutor v. Tadić, Case No.

especially a permanent one such as the ICC, ultimately depends on its capacity to enforce its judgments.[100] Although the relatively poor track record of the ad hoc tribunals – in more than 14 years, the ICTY has completed only 86 cases with 120 accused,[101] and the ICTR has delivered final judgments for no more than 36 accused so far[102] – seems to demonstrate a limited enforcement capacity and sheds some doubt on their overall deterrence effect,[103] it can hardly be denied that the very existence of international criminal tribunals, especially the ICC as a permanent and forward-looking one, sends the clear signal to the perpetrators of international core crimes that they are not beyond the reach of the law and may ultimately be held accountable for their acts.[104] In fact, the establishment of these tribunals has considerably increased the risk of punishment of the responsible,[105] especially of high-level perpetrators, because they normally act rationally and therefore take into account the possibility of punishment as an important factor in their decision making.[106]

As to the ICC in particular, U.S. economist Daniel Sutter, one of the followers of the economics of crime movement, has argued that it "is unlikely to have a very *dramatic* deterrent effect" and "to affect *greatly* a desperate regime's political calculus."[107] Yet, Sutter fails to explain what he means by a "dramatic" as opposed to a "normal" or "ordinary" effect. Neither does he explain when a certain cause has a "great" as opposed to "little" effect. At any rate, would it not be sufficient if the ICC would have *any* deterrent effect at all, if it would affect a regime's calculus *at all*? In fact, given the restrictions built into the ICC's legal regime and its obvious capacity problems, most international criminal lawyers would be more than happy if the

---

IT-94-1-A and IT-94-1-A *bis*, Judgment in Sentencing Appeals, ¶ 48 (Jan. 26, 2000); Prosecutor v. Aleksovski, Case No. IT-95-14/1-A, Judgment, ¶ 185 (Mar. 24, 2000); Prosecutor v. Blaškić, Case No. IT-95-14-A, Judgment, ¶ 678 (July 29, 2004); Prosecutor v. Plavšić, Case No. IT-00-39&40/1-S, Judgment, ¶ 22 (Feb. 27, 2003); *Kayishema & Ruzindana Trial Judgment, supra* note 55, sentence ¶ 2; *Simba Trial Judgment, supra* note 56, ¶ 429; *Muvunyi Trial Judgment, supra* note 35, ¶ 532; Prosecutor v. Seromba, Case No. ICTR-2001-66-I, Judgment, ¶ 376 (Dec. 13, 2006); Prosecutor v. Nchamihigo, Case No. ICTR-01-63-T, Judgment, ¶ 383 (Nov. 12, 2008); Prosecutor v. Bagosora, Case No. ICTR-98-41-T, Judgment, ¶ 2260 (Dec. 18, 2008); Prosecutor v. Bikindi, Case No. ICTR-01-72-T, Judgment, ¶ 443 (Dec. 2, 2008).

[100] For the same view, see some of the authors quoted in *supra* note 98.
[101] *See* http://www.icty.org/sections/TheCases/KeyFigures (last visited Sept. 10, 2009).
[102] *See* http://69.94.11.53/default.htm (last visited Sept. 10, 2009).
[103] Crit. in this sense, see Tolmein, *supra* note 98, at 507; Ku & Nzelibe, *supra* note 97, at 808; Koller, *supra* note 97, at 1027–28.
[104] *Kordić and Čerkez Appeals Judgment, supra* note 99, ¶ 1078; *Krajišnik Trial Judgment, supra* note 35, ¶ 1137; *Zelenović Trial Judgment, supra* note 99, ¶ 34.
[105] Frank Neubacher, Kriminologische Grundlagen einer internationalen Strafgerichtsbarkeit 424 (2005); Frank Neubacher, *Strafzwecke und Völkerstrafrecht*, 59 Neue Juristische Wochenschrift 966, 968 (2006). In a similar vein, see *Prosecutor v. Nikolić, supra* note 99, ¶ 88.
[106] Neubacher, *Strafzwecke, supra* note 105, at 968–69. *See also* Ron Sievert, *A New Perspective on the International Criminal Court: Why the Right Should Embrace the ICC and How America Can Use It*, 68 U. Pitt. L. Rev. 77, 99 (2006). In a similar vein, see *Delalić Trial Judgment, supra* note 99, ¶ 1234. For a critical view, see Jäger, *supra* note 96, at 57; Ku & Nzelibe, *supra* note 97, at 807.
[107] Daniel Sutter, *The Deterrent Effects of the International Criminal Court, in* International Conflict Resolution 9, 23 (Stefan Voigt et al. eds., Mohr Siebeck 2006) (emphasis added).

Court were able "to deter kleptocrats seeking to loot their country, yet still interested in spending their ill-gotten riches abroad ...."[108]

In any case, to get the whole picture, one should not view the ICC as an isolated tool to fight impunity but, as already argued above (*supra* Section II), as an integral part of the international criminal justice system. The ICC is, above all, a complement to national jurisdictions, especially to the jurisdiction of the territorial State. The ICC is a criminal court with very limited powers, dependent on the cooperation of States and worldwide accession to its Statute. Thus, its capacity for enforcement, and with it its deterrent effect, depends on the cooperation of the international community. More concretely, the ICC's enforcement capacity depends on the cooperation of the territorial State or, if this State is unwilling to cooperate, on a regime change through internal or external pressure.

Given the limited powers and functions of the ICC, its objectives and goals are also limited. Nobody familiar with international criminal justice and the ICC expects "dramatic" or "great" effects; limited effects and deterrence, if only of some of those most responsible, would indeed mean a considerable improvement compared to the *status quo ex ante* without an ICC. In any case, prosecution by the ICC, respecting internationally recognized standards for fair trials and the presumption of innocence, serves the idea of justice and truth about past crimes better than on-the-spot extrajudicial killings, let alone Iraq-style military invasions. Criminal law is, above all, about the confirmation of certain moral values, and if these values are internalized by the addressees of the norms (as a consequence of primary prevention),[109] deterrence may work indirectly.

Summing up these considerations, a specialized CAH Convention may have a positive impact on compliance and may deter future criminals. While CAH may not entirely disappear as a result of the Convention's adoption, it is realistic to expect that the signal such a Convention sends would not remain unheard among potential criminals against humanity.

ANNEX: CAH IN THE CURRENT FORMAL INVESTIGATIONS (ART. 53) OF THE ICC (AS OF OCTOBER 1, 2009)

I. Situation in the Democratic Republic of the Congo

Prosecutor v. Katanga and Ngudjolo, Doc. No. ICC-01/04-01/07-717, Decision on the Confirmation of Charges (Sept. 30, 2008)

- widespread or systematic attack, ¶¶ 389 et seq.
- murder, ¶¶ 240 et seq. (charge confirmed at pp. 209–10)
- sexual slavery, ¶¶ 428 et seq. (charge confirmed at p. 211)
- rape, ¶¶ 437 et seq. (charge confirmed at p. 212)
- other inhumane acts, ¶¶ 445 et seq. (charge declined at p. 212)

---

[108] *Id.*, at 23.
[109] Kreuzer, *supra* note 90, at 215.

II. Situation in Uganda

Warrant of Arrest for Joseph Kony issued on 8 July, 2005, as amended on 27 September, 2005, Doc. No. ICC-02/04-01/05-53 (Sept. 27, 2005)

- count 1 (p. 12), sexual enslavement
- count 2 (p. 12), rape
- count 6 (p. 13), enslavement
- count 10 (p. 14), murder
- count 11 (p. 14), enslavement
- count 16 (p. 15), murder
- count 20 (p. 16), murder
- count 21 (p. 16), enslavement
- count 22 (p. 17), inhumane acts
- count 27 (p. 18), murder
- count 28 (p. 18), enslavement
- count 29 (p. 18), inhumane acts

Warrant of Arrest for Vincent Otti, Doc. No. ICC-02/04-01/05-54 (July 8, 2005)

- count 1 (p. 12), sexual enslavement
- count 3 (p. 13), rape
- count 6 (p. 13), enslavement
- count 10 (p. 14), murder
- count 11 (pp. 14–15), enslavement
- count 16 (p. 16), murder
- count 20 (p. 17), murder
- count 21 (p. 17), enslavement
- count 22 (p. 17), inhumane acts
- count 27 (p. 18), murder
- count 28 (p. 19), enslavement
- count 29 (p. 19), inhumane acts

Warrant of Arrest for Okot Odhiambo, Doc. No. ICC-02/04-01/05-56 (July 8, 2005)

- count 11 (p. 10), enslavement
- count 16 (p. 11), murder

Warrant of Arrest for Dominic Ongwen, Doc. No. ICC-02/04-01/05-57 (July 8, 2005)

- count 27 (p. 9), murder
- count 28 (p. 9), enslavement
- count 29 (p. 9), inhumane acts

Warrant of Arrest for Raska Lukwiya, Doc. No. ICC-02/04-01/05-55 (July 8, 2005)[110]

- count 6 (p. 9), enslavement

III. Situation in Darfur, Sudan

Warrant of Arrest for Ahmad Harun, Doc. No. ICC-02/05-01/07-2 (Apr. 25, 2007)

- count 1 (p. 6), persecution
- count 2 (p. 6), murder
- count 4 (pp. 6–7), murder
- count 9 (pp. 7–8), forcible transfer
- count 10 (p. 8), persecution
- count 11 (p. 8), murder
- count 13 (p. 8), rape
- count 17 (p. 9), inhumane acts
- count 20 (p. 10), forcible transfer
- count 21 (p.10), persecution
- count 22 (p. 10), murder
- count 24 (p. 11), murder
- count 28 (p. 11), murder
- count 34 (p. 12), imprisonment or severe deprivation of liberty
- count 35 (p. 12), torture
- count 39 (p. 13), persecution
- count 40 (p. 13), murder
- count 42 (pp. 13–14), rape
- count 48 (pp. 14–15), inhumane acts
- count 51 (p. 15), forcible transfer

Warrant for Arrest for Ali Kushayb, Doc. No. ICC-02/05-01/07-3 (Apr. 27, 2007)

- count 1 (p. 6), persecution
- count 2 (p. 6), murder
- count 4 (p. 7), murder
- count 9 (p. 8), forcible transfer
- count 10 (p. 8), persecution
- count 11 (p. 8), murder
- count 13 (pp. 8–9), rape
- count 17 (p. 9), inhumane acts
- count 20 (p. 10), forcible transfer
- count 21 (p.10), persecution

---

[110] The proceedings were terminated because of the death of the suspect. Prosecutor v. Kony et al., Doc. No. ICC-02/04-01/05-248, *Decision to Terminate the Proceedings against Raska Lukwiya* (July 11, 2007).

- count 22 (p. 10), murder
- count 24 (p. 11), murder
- count 25 (p. 11), murder
- count 28 (pp. 11–12), murder
- count 29 (p. 12), murder
- count 34 (p. 13), imprisonment or severe deprivation of liberty
- count 35 (p. 13), torture
- count 39 (p. 14), persecution
- count 40 (p. 14), murder
- count 42 (p. 14), rape
- count 48 (pp. 15–16), inhumane acts
- count 51 (p. 16), forcible transfer

Warrant of Arrest for Omar Hassan Ahmad Al Bashir, Doc. No. ICC-02/05-01/09-1 (Mar. 4, 2009)

- count 3 (p. 7), murder
- count 4 (p. 7), extermination
- count 5 (p. 7), forcible transfer
- count 6 (p. 8), torture
- count 7 (p. 8), rape

IV. Situation in the Central African Republic

Prosecutor v. Bemba Gombo, Doc. No. ICC-01/05-01/08-424, Decision Pursuant to Article 61(7)(a) and (b) of the Rome Statute on the Charges of the Prosecutor Against Jean-Pierre Bemba Gombo (June 15, 2009)

- widespread or systematic attack, ¶¶ 73 et seq.
- murder, ¶¶ 128 et seq. (charge confirmed at p. 185)
- rape, ¶¶ 159 et seq. (charge confirmed at p. 185)
- torture, ¶¶ 189 et seq. (charge declined at p. 185)

13

Crimes Against Humanity and the Responsibility to Protect

David Scheffer*

I. INTRODUCTION

The drafting of a comprehensive International Convention on Crimes Against Humanity (Convention) raises the fundamental question of whether and how the emerging principle of *the responsibility to protect* (R2P) will be integrated with the legal obligations set forth in a finalized Convention. It is entirely possible to draft the Convention without any reference to R2P and without even any inference of the relationship between the defined crimes against humanity set forth in the Convention and the State responsibility measures that frame the application of R2P. Indeed, the anticipated approach to such a drafting exercise might be to set forth a State responsibility to criminalize well-defined crimes against humanity in domestic law for purposes solely of individual criminal responsibility, but to remain silent with respect to the responsibility of the State itself, including its government and military, to protect civilian populations from the commission of crimes against humanity by the State and its institutional organs.

In this chapter, I propose a more ambitious methodology. The reason R2P arises as a challenge for State action and, in more extreme circumstances, Security Council action, is because of the commission of genocide, crimes against humanity, ethnic cleansing, or war crimes (hereinafter together referred to as "atrocity crimes"[1]) of such gravity that a moral and arguably legal duty arises to end the criminal conduct. The procedure by which individuals, such as political, military, and even some religious, media, and business leaders, have been targeted for investigation and prosecution of atrocity crimes before international and hybrid criminal tribunals since 1993 creates a legal framework within which to examine how States and the

---

* David Scheffer is the Mayer Brown/Robert A. Helman Professor of Law and Director of the Center for International Human Rights at Northwestern University School of Law. He was the first U.S. Ambassador-at-Large for War Crimes Issues (1997–2001). Portions of this chapter are drawn from the author's prior writings: *Atrocity Crimes Framing the Responsibility to Protect*, in THE RESPONSIBILITY TO PROTECT: THE GLOBAL MORAL COMPACT FOR THE 21st CENTURY 77–98 (Richard Cooper & Juliette Voinov Kohler eds., 2009); *Atrocity Crimes Framing the Responsibility to Protect*, 40 CASE W. RES. J. INT'L L. 111–35 (2008).

[1] See David Scheffer, *The Merits of Unifying Terms: "Atrocity Crimes" and "Atrocity Law,"* 2 GENOCIDE STUD. & PREVENTION 81 (2007); David Scheffer, *Genocide and Atrocity Crimes*, 1 GENOCIDE STUD. & PREVENTION 229 (2006); David Scheffer, *The Future of Atrocity Law*, 25 SUFFOLK TRANSNAT'L L. REV. 389, 394–98 (2002).

international community can recognize situations demanding timely and effective responses – hence, the responsibility to protect. But the enormous strides that have been taken to establish individual criminal responsibility, including for perpetration of crimes against humanity, do not address the fundamental premise of R2P. Governments and international organizations such as the Security Council are the agents of R2P in response to actions that usually entail the purposeful acts of governments and their military forces, which in turn are led by individuals who unleash the institutional power but are themselves increasingly subject to the enforcement of international criminal law. If the Convention requires only that the State Party ensure, domestically and internationally, that the individual perpetrator of crimes against humanity is prosecuted and punished, then R2P will be of limited relevance to the Convention. One can point to prosecution of perpetrators of crimes against humanity as a means of protecting civilian populations and thus of meeting an R2P objective. This self-evident proposition may be worth noting, but it does not address the larger issue of how the Convention should directly invoke R2P, if at all.

In addition to its focus on individual criminal responsibility, the Convention could include State responsibility provisions that 1) prohibit and thus render illegal the commission of crimes against humanity by any State Party entity, and 2) require the States Parties to the Convention to act, as a matter of legal obligation, in accordance with R2P principles as set forth in the *2005 World Summit Outcome*.[2]

This chapter examines the meaning and scope of R2P, explores the crimes against humanity that would activate an R2P duty, and proposes language for the Convention to incorporate the prohibition on commission of crimes against humanity and the duty to advance R2P as obligations of States Parties to the Convention.

II. MEANING AND SCOPE OF THE RESPONSIBILITY TO PROTECT

The principle of the responsibility to protect, about which much has been conceived, examined, and written since 2001,[3] at its core stands for the responsibility of governments and of the international community to protect populations from genocide, war crimes, ethnic cleansing, and crimes against humanity – four categories of

---

[2] *2005 World Summit Outcome Resolution*, G.A. Res. A/RES/60/1, ¶¶ 138–39, U.N. Doc. A/RES/60/1 (Oct. 24, 2005).

[3] *See* THE INT'L COMM'N ON INTERVENTION AND STATE SOVEREIGNTY, THE RESPONSIBILITY TO PROTECT: REPORT OF THE INTERNATIONAL COMMISSION ON INTERVENTION AND STATE SOVEREIGNTY (2001), *available at* http://www.iciss.ca/pdf/Commission-Report.pdf; The Secretary-General, *Report of the Secretary-General's High-level Panel on Threats, Challenges, and Change*, delivered to the General Assembly, U.N. Doc. A/59/565 (Dec. 8, 2004); The Secretary-General, *In Larger Freedom: Towards Development, Security and Human Rights for All*, delivered to the General Assembly, U.N. Doc. A/59/2005 (Mar. 21, 2005); GARETH EVANS, THE RESPONSIBILITY TO PROTECT: ENDING MASS ATROCITY CRIMES ONCE AND FOR ALL (2008); ALEX J. BELLAMY, A RESPONSIBILITY TO PROTECT: THE GLOBAL EFFORT TO END MASS ATROCITIES (2009); RESPONSIBILITY TO PROTECT: THE GLOBAL MORAL COMPACT FOR THE 21st CENTURY (Richard H. Cooper & Juliette Voinov Kohler eds., 2009); The Secretary-General, *Implementing the Responsibility to Protect*, U.N. Doc. A/63/677 (Jan. 21, 2009).

crimes that I term *atrocity crimes* for purposes of accuracy when describing such crimes and for simplicity as a means of communicating with the global populace. Preceded by three major initiatives over a five-year period to describe and define it, R2P today rests essentially on the formulation set forth in the *2005 World Summit Outcome*.[4]

It is worthwhile at this juncture to set forth the full text of the two paragraphs of the *2005 World Summit Outcome*, which articulate R2P in terms of a principle that was adopted by the Member States of the United Nations in a nonbinding General Assembly resolution 60/1 in 2005, and which remains applicable today, albeit with differing degrees of support among nations. The text of paragraphs 138 and 139 follows:

> 138. Each individual State has the responsibility to protect its populations from genocide, war crimes, ethnic cleansing and crimes against humanity. This responsibility entails the prevention of such crimes, including their incitement, through appropriate and necessary means. We accept that responsibility and will act in accordance with it. The international community should, as appropriate, encourage and help States to exercise this responsibility and support the United Nations in establishing an early warning capability.
>
> 139. The international community, through the United Nations, also has the responsibility to use appropriate diplomatic, humanitarian and other peaceful means, in accordance with Chapters VI and VIII of the Charter, to help to protect populations from genocide, war crimes, ethnic cleansing and crimes against humanity. In this context, we are prepared to take collective action, in a timely and decisive manner, through the Security Council, in accordance with the Charter, including Chapter VII, on a case-by-case basis and in cooperation with relevant regional organizations as appropriate, should peaceful means be inadequate and national authorities are manifestly failing to protect their populations from genocide, war crimes, ethnic cleansing and crimes against humanity. We stress the need for the General Assembly to continue consideration of the responsibility to protect populations from genocide, war crimes, ethnic cleansing and crimes against humanity and its implications, bearing in mind the principles of the Charter and international law. We also intend to commit ourselves, as necessary and appropriate, to helping States build capacity to protect their populations from genocide, war crimes, ethnic cleansing and crimes against humanity and to assisting those which are under stress before crises and conflicts break out.[5]

The Security Council reaffirmed these provisions in resolution 1674 (2006) on the protection of civilians in armed conflict.[6] Thereafter, these increasingly prominent

---

[4] See David Scheffer, *Atrocity Crimes Framing the Responsibility to Protect*, 40 CASE W. RES. J. INT'L L. 111, 112–17 (2008).
[5] *2005 World Summit Outcome Resolution, supra* note 2, ¶¶ 138–39.
[6] S.C. Res. 1674, ¶ 4, U.N. Doc. S/RES/1674 (Apr. 28, 2006) ("[The Security Council] *reaffirms* the provisions of paragraphs 138 and 139 of the 2005 World Summit Outcome Document regarding the responsibility to protect populations from genocide, war crimes, ethnic cleansing and crimes against humanity.").

provisions were acknowledged in Security Council resolution 1706 (2006) regarding Darfur[7] and in the Report of the Secretary-General on the Protection of Civilians (October 2007).[8] The latter document cited the World Summit Outcome provisions on R2P as a "cardinal achievement." On January 12, 2009, the Report of the Secretary-General on "Implementing the responsibility to protect" was issued with a thorough examination of the mandate and its historical, legal, and political context, and a proposal for a three-pillar strategy stressing "the value of prevention and, when it fails, of early and flexible response tailored to the specific circumstances of each case."[9]

What does R2P, as described in the 2005 World Summit Outcome, precisely establish relating to crimes against humanity and a new Convention on crimes against humanity? Compared to earlier studies drafted by experts and by the UN Secretary-General, the 2005 World Summit Outcome was the result of intensive political negotiations at the United Nations that, for better or worse, provided for a realistic appraisal of the concept.[10] The result was a sharpened focus for R2P that articulated an extremely significant, albeit narrow, principle of international relations. The exercise also points to an arguably emerging, though neither codified nor necessarily enforceable, norm of international law.[11] Doubtless there will be efforts in the years ahead to broaden the prism of R2P in an effort to protect civilian populations from a wider range of threats beyond atrocity crimes, and probably for good reason.

The responsibility to protect remains a controversial principle among a large number of governments for varied reasons.[12] One example pertains to the related issue of protection of civilians in armed conflict, which has long been a significant agenda item before the Security Council. As reported by the Global Centre for the Responsibility to Protect:

> the sensitivities around the inclusion of R2P within the protection of civilians' agenda have increased in recent months. There are concerns that the [Protection of Civilians in Armed Conflict] agenda is being needlessly politicized by the introduction of R2P into the [Security] Council's work and resolutions on the protection of civilians, as those who seek to roll back the 2005 endorsement of R2P raise

---

[7] S.C. Res. 1706, pmbl., U.N. Doc. S/RES/1706 (Aug. 31, 2006).
[8] The Secretary-General, *Report of the Secretary-General on the Protection of Civilians in Armed Conflict*, ¶ 11, U.N. Doc. S/2007/643 (Oct. 28, 2007).
[9] The Secretary-General, *Implementing the Responsibility to Protect*, at 1–2, U.N. Doc. A/63/677 (Jan. 21, 2009).
[10] *See* Alex J. Bellamy, *Whither the Responsibility to Protect? Humanitarian Intervention and the 2005 World Summit*, 20 ETHICS & INT'L AFF. 143 (2006).
[11] *See* Carsten Stahn, *Responsibility to Protect: Political Rhetoric or Emerging Legal Norm?*, 101 AM. J. INT'L L. 99 (2007).
[12] *See* U.N. SCOR, 61st Sess., 5577th mtg., U.N. Doc. S/PV.5577 (Dec. 4, 2006), *available at* http://www.un.org/Depts/dhl/resguide/scact2006.htm (follow "S/PV.5577" hyperlink); U.N. SCOR, 61st Sess., 5474th mtg., U.N. Doc. S/PV.5474 (June 22, 2006), *available at* http://www.un.org/Depts/dhl/resguide/scact2006.htm (follow "S/PV.5474" hyperlink).

questions about the protection of civilians in the attempt to challenge hard-won consensus reached on both issues.[13]

The narrow prism – responding to the threat or reality of atrocity crimes against civilian populations – may prove to be precisely the foundation on which R2P must first demonstrate its strength of purpose and persuasiveness as a guiding principle of world affairs and perhaps ultimately as a binding norm of international law. Indeed, a broader mandate for R2P in the years ahead may burden it with so much political controversy and dissent among international lawyers that it would collapse as a declared commitment, even with respect to atrocity crimes, before it would have an opportunity to be fully tested.

The 2005 *World Summit Outcome* repeatedly identifies four categories of crimes – genocide, war crimes, ethnic cleansing, and crimes against humanity – as the only basis for prevention and collective action under R2P. The identification of these atrocity crimes as the sole premise for prevention or action under R2P derives much of its legitimacy from the jurisprudence of the international and hybrid criminal tribunals built during the 1990s, including the International Criminal Tribunals for the former Yugoslavia (ICTY) and Rwanda (ICTR), the Special Court for Sierra Leone (SCSL), and the International Criminal Court (ICC).[14] During that decade and into the twenty-first century, such crimes were prosecuted against individual perpetrators in the regions and nations falling within the jurisdiction of these courts. Even atrocity crimes committed during the Pol Pot tyranny of 1975 to 1979 are finally being prosecuted against surviving senior leaders of the Khmer Rouge and at least one other major perpetrator before the Extraordinary Chambers in the Courts of Cambodia.[15]

Atrocity crimes were codified as the subject matter jurisdiction of the ICC in considerable detail. That court will carry forth the ever-expanding mission of individual criminal responsibility for such crimes into the future. It thus has become increasingly implausible to extend the basis for judicial intervention to enforce individual criminal responsibility for atrocity crimes, and yet perpetuate a global system that tolerates, through inaction in prevention or response, the commission of such crimes against civilian populations. The International Commission on Intervention and State Sovereignty report, *The Responsibility to Protect*, revealed the disconnect in logic between the judicial activism of the 1990s and the continued impotence of the international community to respond effectively – be it politically, economically,

---

[13] GLOBAL CTR. FOR THE RESPONSIBILITY TO PROTECT, POLICY BRIEF: THE RELATIONSHIP BETWEEN THE RESPONSIBILITY TO PROTECT AND THE PROTECTION OF CIVILIANS IN ARMED CONFLICT 1 (2009), *available at* http://globalr2p.org/pdf/GCR2PPolicyBrief-ProtectCivConflict.pdf.

[14] *See generally* WILLIAM A. SCHABAS, THE UN INTERNATIONAL CRIMINAL TRIBUNALS: THE FORMER YUGOSLAVIA, RWANDA, AND SIERRA LEONE (2006); WILLIAM A. SCHABAS, AN INTRODUCTION TO THE INTERNATIONAL CRIMINAL COURT (3d ed. 2007).

[15] *See* David Scheffer, *The Extraordinary Chambers in the Courts of Cambodia*, *in* 3 INTERNATIONAL CRIMINAL LAW 219–55 (M. Cherif Bassiouni ed., 3d ed. 2008); for daily developments, see the Cambodia Tribunal Monitor, http://www.cambodiatribunal.org.

diplomatically, or militarily – to atrocity crimes against civilian populations.[16] The logical next step was to connect atrocity crimes to R2P, a step the U.N. General Assembly took in 2005 when it crafted the somewhat narrow basis in atrocity crimes for R2P.

III. THE SUBSTANTIALITY TEST

For the purpose of understanding what justifies implementation of R2P, the *2005 World Summit Outcome* restricts the analysis to the four sets of crimes described as genocide, war crimes, ethnic cleansing, and crimes against humanity. If one considers that in order for R2P to be triggered, the commission of any one of these atrocity crimes must occur on a societal level involving a large number of potential or actual victims, then one can discover the starting point for a proper understanding of the relationship between R2P and atrocity crimes and, more particularly, between R2P and crimes against humanity. In the context of that relationship, the possibility for some codified wording in the Convention that associates a State Party's obligation to implement R2P alongside criminal enforcement of crimes against humanity should become more apparent.

In my view, the responsibility to protect only arises when a "substantiality test" that has been largely developed by the international and hybrid criminal tribunals is met. This is a logical requirement for R2P, because the concept only deals with the mega-crimes that assault civilian populations wholesale, and seeks to compel governments (and hopefully the host government of the crime), as well as the international community, working through the United Nations and regional organizations, to act decisively and with timely effect to prevent or stop the commission of atrocity crimes. Examples of where R2P would have served high moral purpose in the 1990s, based on the substantiality test, are Bosnia and Herzegovina from 1992 through 1995, Rwanda in 1994, the Democratic Republic of the Congo in the late 1990s, Sierra Leone in the mid- to late 1990s, and in Darfur since 2003. Early notions of R2P actually appeared in the multinational interventions into Kosovo and East Timor in 1999.

R2P is as much a principle of prevention as it is of response. Yet, R2P cannot possibly be a viable concept if it is defined as a means of reacting to the most speculative suggestion of some relatively minor and isolated threat of atrocity crimes. The threat has to have some meaningful content. The speculation about it must be centered on the plausible possibility of a crime of some magnitude. Otherwise, R2P would become part of the daily musings of diplomats, analysts, academics, journalists, nongovernmental activists, and others about all manner of threats in the world. R2P would become meaningless if it were all things to all people. Therefore, even when considering R2P in its preventive capacity, the content of

---

[16] *See* THE RESPONSIBILITY TO PROTECT: REPORT OF THE INTERNATIONAL COMMISSION ON INTERVENTION AND STATE SOVEREIGNTY, *supra* note 3.

the threat to civilian populations remains important and must demonstrate some meaningful magnitude. Principles of substantiality that apply to ongoing atrocity crimes are also relevant to examining what is required to trigger R2P as a measure of prevention.

Crimes against humanity have long demanded substantiality as a prerequisite to criminal liability. If the substantiality test were to be diluted by, for example, not requiring a "widespread or systematic attack directed against any civilian population," then there would be little purpose in discussing a connection between crimes against humanity and R2P. The Convention should only intersect with R2P if the substantiality test is met. If it is contemplated that the Convention defines crimes against humanity with the option that particular acts can be criminalized even if they are minor in character and fall short of any meaningful level of magnitude, then the Convention would have to distinguish between those minimalist actions and other acts that in fact satisfy the substantiality test and hence are relevant to an R2P analysis.

The prosecutions for crimes against humanity before the Nuremberg Tribunal after World War II focused on actions that typically involved large numbers of victims and were orchestrated in a systematic or widespread manner by high-level political, military, judicial, or business leaders.[17] The ICTY, which in its Statute does not stipulate any literal substantiality test for crimes against humanity, has established in its jurisprudence that an "attack" under this category of crimes must be "directed against a civilian 'population' rather than against a limited and randomly selected number of individuals."[18] The ICTY has found that a crime against humanity "may be widespread or committed on a large scale by the 'cumulative effect of a series of inhumane acts or the singular effect of an inhumane act of extraordinary magnitude.'"[19]

The second prong of a crime against humanity – that it be "systematic" rather than, or in addition to being, "widespread" – has been explained by the ICTY in this manner:

> The systematic character refers to four elements which ... may be expressed as follows: [1] the existence of a political objective, a plan pursuant to which the attack is perpetrated or an ideology, in the broad sense of the word, that is, to destroy, persecute or weaken a community; [2] the perpetration of a criminal act on a very large scale against a group of civilians or the repeated and continuous commission of inhumane acts linked to one another; [3] the preparation and use of significant public or private resources, whether military or other; [4] the implication of

---

[17] See WHITNEY HARRIS, TYRANNY ON TRIAL: THE TRIAL OF THE MAJOR GERMAN WAR CRIMINALS AT THE END OF THE WORLD WAR II AT NUREMBERG, GERMANY 1945–1946, at 281–451 (1954).

[18] Prosecutor v. Kunarac, Kovač and Voković, Case No. IT-96-23/1-A, Judgment, ¶ 90 (June 12, 2002) [hereinafter Kunarac Appeals Judgment]. See Prosecutor v. Kunarac, Kovač and Voković, Case No. IT-96-23-T, Judgment, ¶ 421 (Feb. 22, 2001) [hereinafter Kunarac Trial Judgment].

[19] See Prosecutor v. Kordić and Čerkez, Case No. IT-95-14/2-T, Judgment, ¶ 179 (Feb. 26, 2001) [hereinafter Kordić Judgment].

high-level political and/or military authorities in the definition and establishment of the methodical plan.[20]

In one ICTY judgment, where the key requirement of crimes against humanity – that they be "widespread or systematic" – required the Tribunal to consider what factors were involved, the judges looked to "the number of victims" and "the employment of considerable financial, military or other resources and the scale or the repeated, unchanging and continuous nature of the violence committed against a particular civilian population."[21]

These requirements of high-level orchestration and magnitude for the commission of crimes against humanity also frame, both in a logical and pragmatic sense, the requirements of R2P. They strengthen the argument for the importance of the R2P principle because the substantiality requirement creates the self-evident and imperative need for an effective response, be it from the national government where the assault on the civilian population is occurring or, if that is implausible or unlikely, from the international community.

As noted earlier, if the crimes against humanity to be codified in a Convention reflect the substance of article 7 (Crimes Against Humanity) of the Rome Statute[22] but offer the option to deviate with respect to the substantiality test, then any such deviation would eliminate R2P as a relevant factor in responding to the commission of the particular crime against humanity. It would be implausible for R2P to be undertaken by a government or international organization or otherwise by the international community for a single murder, act of torture, or disappearance because none would qualify as a crime against humanity to which the substantiality test developed by the tribunals and determinative of R2P applies.

In the Elements of Crimes for the Rome Statute of the ICC, a clear marker was established for the magnitude of crime required to qualify as a crime against humanity. The introduction to the section on "Crimes Against Humanity" reads in part:

> "Attack directed against a civilian population" in these context elements is understood to mean a course of conduct involving the multiple commission of acts referred to in article 7, paragraph 1, of the Statute [the listing of crimes against humanity] against any civilian population, pursuant to or in furtherance of a State or organizational policy to commit such attack. The acts need not constitute a military attack. It is understood that "policy to commit such attack" requires that the State or organization actively promote or encourage such an attack against a civilian population.[23]

---

[20] Prosecutor v. Blaškić, Case No. IT-95-14-T, Judgment, ¶ 203 (Mar. 3, 2000) [hereinafter *Blaškić Judgment*] (footnotes omitted); *see also* Prosecutor v. Naletilić and Martinović, Case No. IT-98-34-T, Judgment, ¶ 232 (Mar. 31, 2003).

[21] *See* Prosecutor v. Jelisić, Case No. IT-95-10-T, Judgment, ¶ 53 (Dec. 14, 1999).

[22] *See Rome Statute of the International Criminal Court*, art. 7, United Nations Diplomatic Conference of Plenipotentiaries on the Establishment of an International Criminal Court, July 17, 1998, U.N. Doc. A/CONF.183/9 (1998) [hereinafter *Rome Statute*].

[23] *See* Preparatory Comm'n for the Int'l Criminal Court, *Finalized Draft Text of the Elements of Crimes*, 9, U.N. Doc. PCNICC/2000/1/Add.2 (Nov. 2, 2000) (emphasis added).

There is a further explanation:

> A policy which has a civilian population as the object of the attack would be implemented by State or organizational action. Such a policy may, in exceptional circumstances, be implemented by a deliberate failure to take action, which is consciously aimed at encouraging such attack. The existence of such a policy cannot be inferred solely from the absence of governmental or organizational action.[24]

Both of these explanatory requirements for crimes against humanity bear on the substantiality test and would be relevant for an invocation of R2P under or in connection with the Convention. The jurisprudence of the ICTY and ICTR offer additional guidance on the substantiality test that triggers crimes against humanity. When examining these criteria, however, it remains important not to automatically translate the substantiality required for a criminal prosecution of a crime against humanity with the justification for R2P, particularly military action under R2P. The former concerns accountability for a particular individual and his or her perpetration of a crime that meets the threshold requirements of a crime against humanity. A far larger set of factors come into play when determining, as a matter of policy, whether to initiate R2P measures against a foreign government or other organized force on foreign territory to protect a civilian population at risk of crimes against humanity. The tribunals and the Convention, if drafted to cover only individual criminal responsibility, focus on crimes already committed and establish important criteria for such crimes. But governments, international organizations, and the international community, when confronted with the threat or reality of crimes against humanity, will take additional considerations to mind when determining whether or not to take preventive or responsive action under R2P. Nonetheless, the tribunals' judgments offer some guidance for how to evaluate the commission, or likely commission, of crimes against humanity so as to determine the merits of an R2P action. The ICTY, for example, has ruled that,

> [i]t is sufficient to show that enough individuals were targeted in the course of the attack, or that they were targeted in such a way as to satisfy the Chamber that the attack was in fact directed against a civilian 'population', rather than against a limited and randomly selected number of individuals.[25]

The ICTY has further held that "a crime may be widespread or committed on a large scale by the 'cumulative effect of a series of inhumane acts or the singular effect of an inhumane act of extraordinary magnitude.'"[26] The "systematic" character of an attack on a civilian population requires the four elements set forth above and reiterated in the *Blaskic* Judgment.[27] Thus, in determining the justification for an

---

[24] *Id.* at 9 n.6 (emphasis added).
[25] *Kunarac Appeals Judgment*, *supra* note 18, ¶ 90; *see Kunarac Trial Judgment*, *supra* note 18, ¶ 424.
[26] *Kordić Judgment*, *supra* note 19, ¶ 179.
[27] *Blaškić Judgment*, *supra* note 20.

R2P action based on crimes against humanity, several factors addressing magnitude, continuous commission, planning, and leadership must be considered.

IV. SPECIFIC CRIMES AGAINST HUMANITY AND THE R2P CONTEXT

When one examines specific crimes against humanity, the calculus for R2P can become quite challenging. Not all crimes against humanity would qualify easily for an R2P response if taken in isolation of any other crime against humanity (including ethnic cleansing) or of war crimes or genocide. Indeed, when examining the modern list of crimes against humanity, one might roughly categorize a first basket of widespread or systematic murder, extermination, deportation or forcible transfer of population, persecution in the form of ethnic cleansing, and enforced disappearance of persons as the most realistic grounds for action under R2P. Other crimes against humanity, such as apartheid, sexual violence, torture, enslavement, imprisonment, or "other inhumane acts," may well rise to the level of inhumanity triggering the political will to take an R2P action. But this second basket of crimes against humanity can be deeply institutionalized within a society and may be divorced from international or noninternational armed conflicts generating global interest. Even if the elements of the particular crime against humanity can be established, it may be far more difficult to justify the kinds of governmental and institutional responses under R2P for this second basket of crimes against humanity than for the first basket described above. The best that might be accomplished in such "slow-motion" atrocities is using the R2P principle for diplomatic or economic pressures against the perpetrator government.

For example, the *enforced disappearance of persons* might involve a situation not unlike that which existed in Argentina and Chile in the 1970s, when an estimated 8,000 to 20,000 Argentine civilians and at least 3,000 Chilean civilians disappeared by action of State authorities.[28] Although individual criminal responsibility can be, and has been, associated with such events, the crime is one that may evolve slowly and steadily and may not attract international attention so as to warrant an R2P action. But if the enforced disappearance involves a very large number of civilians over a short period of time – such as occurred near Srebrenica in July 1995, and appeared possible in Kosovo during April and May 1999 – then the significance of the crime is much more apparent. It was soon confirmed that the disappeared at Srebrenica were about 8,000 murdered men and boys.[29] The disappeared in Kosovo

---

[28] *See* Amnesty Int'l, Argentina and Chile: The International Community's Responsibility Regarding Crimes Against Humanity: Trials in Spain for Crimes Against Humanity Under Military Regimes in Argentina and Chile 1–2, AI Index AMR 03/01/98, May 28, 1998, *available at* http://web.amnesty.org/library/Index/ENGAMR030011998?open&of=ENG-332; *see also* Edy Kaufman & Patricia Weis Fagen, *Extrajudicial Executions: An Insight into the Global Dimensions of a Human Rights Violation*, Hum. Rts. Q., Nov. 1981, at 81.

[29] Cent. and E. Eur. Law Initiative of the Am. Bar Ass'n & the Sci. and Human Rights Program of the Am. Ass'n for the Advancement of Sci., Political Killings in Kosova/

initially numbered about 100,000, but within a matter of weeks that number fell dramatically as the situation on the ground clarified that most of the individuals survived.[30] The higher number was a plausible estimate at the time given the unknown whereabouts of so many civilians during the armed conflict in Kosovo. Moreover, vast numbers of people who have potentially disappeared during a particular period of time should not only trigger justifiable concern for their fate but also an investigation to clarify the situation. R2P action, including military intervention, would stand a better chance of being seriously considered in response to such large-scale disappearances – particularly when they occur in the midst of an armed conflict that has already seized international attention, and even if those believed to have disappeared later emerge alive. At the time of crisis, the outcome remains unknown, and this uncertainty could influence greatly how decisions to respond are reached under the R2P principle. The victims of Srebrenica surely would have preferred that governments, NATO, and the United Nations, immediately implemented R2P despite the unknowns and uncertainties of those critical days in July 1995.

A second example is *sexual violence*, which is established as a crime against humanity in the Rome Statute constituting acts of "[r]ape, sexual slavery, enforced prostitution, forced pregnancy, enforced sterilization, or any other form of sexual violence of comparable gravity."[31] Where such sexual violence is occurring with requisite magnitude in the context of other crimes against humanity – such as deportation, murder, extermination, or ethnic cleansing (as a form of persecution) – it may prove easier to justify R2P action than if there were only an orchestrated campaign of sexual violence sweeping across a country. But as an isolated crime, sexual violence may have a very difficult time first qualifying as a crime against humanity and, even if that is accomplished, then triggering an international response under R2P beyond diplomatic gestures. Despite this high hurdle, sex and human trafficking under the definitional category of "enslavement" are gaining enough prominence in intergovernmental affairs to create a premise for R2P in largely nonmilitary contexts and, consequently, should have a positive impact on the kind of sexual violence that either is or can become a crime against humanity.

Apartheid is not only a "slow-motion" crime against humanity – it poses particular challenges for R2P. The international community's experience with apartheid in South Africa never seriously contemplated military intervention to eliminate the

---

Kosovo (1999) *available at* http://shr.aaas.org/kosovo/pk/p1_2.html (estimating that "approximately 10,500 [individuals were killed] and a 95 percent confidence interval with an approximate range between 7,500 and 13,750 individuals killed between March 20 and June 12, 1999"); *see generally Report of the Secretary-General pursuant to General Assembly resolution 53/85: The fall of Srebrenica*, G.A. Res. 549, ¶¶ 346–60, U.N. Doc. A/54/549 (Nov. 15, 1999) (discussing the killing of hundreds of unarmed men and boys).

[30] U.S. STATE DEP'T, FACT SHEET: ETHNIC CLEANSING IN KOSOVO (1999), *available at* http://www.state.gov/www/regions/eur/rpt_990422_ksvo_ethnic.html ("150,000 to 500,000 military-age men remain missing in Kosovo"); *see* Human Rights Watch, *Under Orders: War Crimes in Kosovo* (2001), *available at* http://www.hrw.org/reports/2001/kosovo/undword.htm.

[31] *Rome Statute*, *supra* note 22, art. 7 § 1(g).

State policy and practice of apartheid. Nonmilitary measures were used to pressure the South African government, including economic sanctions and extensive diplomatic efforts.[32] The same may be the case today and in the future if apartheid or apartheid-like practices emerge elsewhere on the globe. Although nonmilitary options would dominate most policy making when confronted with apartheid as a crime against humanity, military options in some situations might be plausible options for some governments. If, for example, Arab governments or Iran were to embrace the theory that Israeli occupation practices in the West Bank constitute apartheid,[33] one can imagine an R2P rationale being employed by such governments to justify Arab or Iranian military action to "liberate" the West Bank from apartheid as a crime against humanity. There would be intense controversy over whether the alleged apartheid, under those circumstances, would warrant a military R2P response, particularly in the absence of a UN Security Council authorizing resolution under Chapter VII of the UN Charter. But it is not inconceivable – as the ebb and flow of democracy, authoritarianism, and religious extremism continue to alter the contours of governance in nations – that apartheid can take hold with a vengeance and become a target of R2P.

Imprisonment or other severe deprivation of physical liberty in violation of fundamental rules of international law and *torture* exist as matters of common practice in many countries.[34] They would qualify as crimes against humanity if all of the fundamental requirements – substantiality, breadth of application, planning, leadership engagement – are met. The R2P response in such cases can fairly easily be crafted in diplomatic and perhaps economic ways, but it would be extraordinary (though not impossible) to contemplate military action under R2P to "rescue" large numbers of individuals tortured or arbitrarily imprisoned as a crime against humanity. Nonetheless, when either one of these crimes is paired with other significant crimes against humanity, it can form part of the mosaic for an assertive R2P response.

As a matter of law, the invocation of *ethnic cleansing* in the mandates of R2P is a nontechnical expression for what in fact is a subcategory of the crime against humanity of *persecution*. That being said, ethnic cleansing is a very powerful term, so much so that there is a growing basis for regarding it as a crime against humanity deserving of its own designation under the modern list of crimes against humanity. Ethnic cleansing is, by its very nature, an amalgamation of numerous crimes against humanity in any particular situation. In its simplest terms, ethnic cleansing is the discriminatory assault on an identifiable group within the civilian population for the

---

[32] See DAVID CORTRIGHT & GEORGE A. LOPEZ, THE SANCTIONS DECADE: ASSESSING UN STRATEGIES IN THE 1990s, at 4, 7, 118 (2000); *see also* Goler Teal Butcher, *The Unique Nature of Sanctions Against South Africa, and Resulting Enforcement Issues*, 19 N.Y.U. J. INT'L L. & POL. 821, 821 (1987).

[33] See JIMMY CARTER, PALESTINE: PEACE NOT APARTHEID 189, 215 (2006).

[34] See AMNESTY INT'L, AMNESTY INTERNATIONAL REPORT 2006: THE STATE OF THE WORLD'S HUMAN RIGHTS, AI Index POL 10/004/2006 (introduction by Irene Khan), *available at* http://asiapacific.amnesty.org/library/pdf/POL100042006ENGLISH/$File/POL1000406.pdf.

purpose of removing that group permanently from territory sought by the perpetrators of the assault. The means used to achieve the aims of the assault can range across the entire spectrum of crimes against humanity but has at its core the crime of persecution.

The crime of persecution, as it is defined in article 7(2)(g) of the Rome Statute of the ICC, "means the intentional and severe deprivation of fundamental rights contrary to international law by reason of the identity of the group or collectivity."[35] The ICTY Appeals Chamber has defined the crime of persecution as:

> [a]n act or omission that: (1) discriminates in fact and which denies or infringes upon a fundamental right laid down in international customary or treaty law (the *actus reas*); and (2) was carried out deliberately with the intention to discriminate on one of the listed grounds [of the ICTY Statute], specifically race, religion or politics (the *mens rea*).[36]

These attributes must be combined, of course, with the substantiality requirements of a crime against humanity, such as knowledge of a widespread or systematic attack against a civilian population. There are a large number of individual acts that, when taken in conjunction with other acts, may constitute the crime of persecution or may, when done individually, qualify as persecution if the magnitude of the act is large or widespread enough to qualify as a crime against humanity.

In the ICC Statute, the crime of persecution has a fairly narrow application but one that works satisfactorily for the "crime" of ethnic cleansing. Persecution is described as:

> [a crime] against any identifiable group or collectivity on political, racial, national, ethnic, cultural, religious, gender as defined in paragraph 3 ['the two sexes, male and female, within the context of society'], or other grounds that are universally recognized as impermissible under international law, *in connection with any act referred to in this paragraph or any crime within the jurisdiction of the Court.*[37]

The condition that the discriminatory attack takes place in connection with another crime against humanity, genocide, or a war crime firmly associates persecution with other atrocity crimes. In effect, the crime of persecution adds discriminatory intent to the underlying crime or, in the case of genocide, supplements the more narrowly defined genocidal intent to destroy in whole or in part a racial, religious, national, or ethnic group.

Within the framework of the crime against humanity called persecution, then, can be found the many actions that may characterize a campaign of *ethnic cleansing*. Since the mid-1980s, the phenomenon of ethnic cleansing has swept over the Kurdish region of Iraq and over Bosnia and Herzegovina, Croatia, Kosovo, Darfur, and other atrocity zones. A useful example of how to identify ethnic cleansing,

---

[35] *Rome Statute*, *supra* note 22, art. 7(2)(g).
[36] Prosecutor v. Stakić, Case No. IT-97-24-A, Judgment, ¶ 327 (Mar. 22, 2006).
[37] *Rome Statute*, *supra* note 22, art. 7 § 1(h) (emphasis added).

within the framework of the crime of persecution, can be seen in the ICTY Trial Chamber judgment of *Prosecutor v. Momcilo Krajišnik*. Krajišnik was President of the Bosnian Serb Assembly and was charged with crimes against humanity in connection with the ethnic cleansing campaign in Bosnia and Herzegovina from 1991 to 1992. While charging Krajišnik with and convicting him of the individual crimes against humanity of extermination (or murder in the alternative), deportation, and other inhumane acts (forced transfer) – all of which clearly contributed to the ethnic cleansing campaign – the ICTY also convicted him of the crime of persecution in a manner emblematic of the "crime" of ethnic cleansing.

The ICTY Trial Chamber I judges in *Krajišnik* first noted that:

> not every denial of a fundamental human right will be serious enough to constitute a crime against humanity. The underlying act committed on discriminatory grounds, considered in isolation or in conjunction with other acts, must be of the same gravity as other crimes listed under Article 5 of the [ICTY] Statute [namely, crimes against humanity].[38]

The judges found that, when taken together, various restrictive and discriminatory measures, not even listed explicitly as crimes against humanity in the ICTY Statute, nonetheless constituted the crime of persecution.[39] Then they examined acts that were charged in the indictment against Krajišnik with persecution as a crime against humanity. These acts included: killings, cruel or inhumane treatment, forced transfer or deportation, unlawful detention, establishment and perpetuation of inhumane living conditions, forced labor, human shields, appropriation or plunder of property, destruction of private property, and destruction of cultural monuments and sacred sites. In each of these acts, the Trial Chamber found a discriminatory intent, thus establishing the crime of persecution. Taken together, these discriminatory acts demonstrated ethnic cleansing. The Trial Chamber did not define a crime of ethnic cleansing as the end result of its lengthy exposition on the many discriminatory acts against Muslims and Croats that Krajišnik was found to have perpetrated, but it did thoroughly document ethnic cleansing and essentially defined it as the conjunction of numerous crimes of persecution.[40]

Discovering ethnic cleansing within the Statutes and jurisprudence of the international and hybrid criminal tribunals is important for the future of R2P as a principle on which governments, international organizations, and the international community can act with confidence in the legitimacy of their cause. Since ethnic cleansing became a popular term to describe what was occurring in Bosnia and Herzegovina, as well as parts of Croatia, in the early 1990s, its usage has only increased as similar patterns of discriminatory conduct have unfolded in other atrocity zones. Darfur

---

[38] Prosecutor v. Krajišnik, Case No. IT-00-39-T, Judgment, ¶ 735 (Sept. 27, 2006) (footnote omitted).
[39] *Id.*
[40] *Id.* ¶ 741.

would be the most obvious contemporary example of ethnic cleansing on a massive scale.[41]

Ethnic cleansing is a powerful justification for R2P. Since ethnic cleansing typically takes some amount of time to launch and press to its final conclusion, and since it can often meet armed resistance and delay in being fully achieved, there is some room for R2P to take hold. If the political will exists, governments, alliances, and international organizations can respond by whatever means prove most effective in reversing the tide of ethnic cleansing. Ethnic cleansing has achieved a legal framework – premised so far on persecution as a crime against humanity – on which to justify the entire range of R2P options for action, depending, of course, on the precise circumstances of the particular campaign of ethnic cleansing. If ethnic cleansing were to achieve the status as a separately codified crime against humanity, perhaps in the Convention itself or through amendment to article 7 of the ICC Statute, then the UN mandate for R2P will be recognized for its prescient understanding of the realities of many modern assaults on civilian populations. Even if such codification does not take place in the near future, there is strong reason to conclude that ethnic cleansing has a de facto identity as a crime against humanity that also yields the possibility of being paired with genocide or war crimes. Thus, ethnic cleansing could be viewed as an atrocity crime warranting implementation of R2P to prevent its commencement or to stop its continuation.

V. CODIFYING R2P IN THE PROPOSED CONVENTION

The Proposed International Convention on the Prevention and Punishment of the Crimes Against Humanity (Proposed Convention) will be focused primarily on confirming the criminality under international law of crimes against humanity and of obligating States Parties to cooperate in the international investigation and prosecution of such crimes, as well as to legislate amendments to their respective criminal codes so as to enable their domestic courts to fully prosecute atrocity crimes and extradite alleged perpetrators when necessary or desirable to face justice. But if R2P is to have any tangible relevance to the codification of individual criminal responsibility for crimes against humanity as envisaged by the *Proposed Convention*, then State responsibility of the States Parties for engaging in crimes against humanity and for implementing the responsibility to protect principle are inevitable issues that should be addressed. Otherwise, the *Proposed Convention* risks serving largely as a well-intentioned supplement to the work on individual criminal responsibility

---

[41] See Int'l Comm'n of Inquiry on Darfur, *Report of the Int'l Comm'n of Inquiry on Darfur to the Secretary General* 56, 115 (2005), *available at* www.un.org/News/dh/sudan/com_inq_darfur.pdf; *see also* INT'L CRISIS GROUP, DARFUR: THE FAILURE TO PROTECT (2005), *available at* http://www.crisisgroup.org/home/index.cfm?id=3314&l=1; *see also* LEE FEINSTEIN, DARFUR AND BEYOND: WHAT IS NEEDED TO PREVENT MASS ATROCITIES 3 (2007), *available at* http://www.cfr.org/content/publications/attachments/DarfurCSR22.pdf.

already underway in the international and hybrid criminal tribunals and in national criminal codes *without necessarily changing the dynamic of State performance*.

I recommend the incorporation of the following provision in the *Proposed Convention* to address the State responsibility requirements pertaining to crimes against humanity and the responsibility to protect. The two concepts are critical, in my view, because it would be awkward to require States Parties to act in accordance with R2P and yet not have a parallel prohibition on State-initiated policies and perpetration of crimes against humanity. The provision, which could be added to article 8 ("Obligations of the State Parties") of the *Proposed Convention*, should read as follows:

> Each State Party shall 1) not plan or execute any policy that involves the commission of any Crimes Against Humanity by any governmental, military, paramilitary, or any other entity of such State Party; 2) not cooperate with any State or organ or associated entity thereof or any non-State group or institution in the planning or execution of any Crimes Against Humanity; and 3) pursuant to paragraphs 138 and 139 of the *2005 World Summit Outcome* of the United Nations General Assembly (G.A. Res. A/RES/60/1, ¶¶ 138–39, U.N. Doc. A/RES/60/1 (Oct. 24, 2005)), implement the responsibility to protect principle, particularly as it relates to Crimes Against Humanity (including acts of persecution viewed as ethnic cleansing).

A different formulation for drafting, albeit with no change in meaning, would be two sentences, one of negative obligation and the other of positive obligation, as follows:

> Each State Party shall 1) not plan or execute any policy that involves the commission of any Crimes Against Humanity by any governmental, military, paramilitary, or any other entity of such State Party; and 2) not cooperate with any State or organ or associated entity thereof or any non-State group or institution in the planning or execution of any Crimes Against Humanity. Pursuant to paragraphs 138 and 139 of the *2005 World Summit Outcome* of the United Nations General Assembly (G.A. Res. A/RES/60/1, ¶¶ 138–39, U.N. Doc. A/RES/60/1 (Oct. 24, 2005)), each State Party shall implement the responsibility to protect principle, particularly as it relates to Crimes Against Humanity (including acts of persecution viewed as ethnic cleansing).

The first subpart of the presented State responsibility provision confirms what is likely a *jus cogens* principle of customary international law – the prohibition on State action to commit crimes against humanity – and yet firmly establishes it in treaty law. I do not underestimate that pressing for such a provision immensely complicates the primary objective of the *Proposed Convention* to ensure the criminalization and prosecution of crimes against humanity with respect to individual human perpetrators. But we all surely know that the famous Nuremberg judgment, "[c]rimes against international law are committed by men, not by abstract entities,"[42]

---

[42] Nazi Conspiracy and Aggression: Opinion and Judgment 223 (1947), *available at* http://www.loc.gov/rr/frd/Military_Law/pdf/NT_Nazi-opinion-judgment.pdf.

must stand side by side with the stark reality that governments and military organizations led by men and women plan and execute atrocity crimes, including crimes against humanity, and thus act illegally as institutions and with State responsibility. The *Proposed Convention* should recognize this reality, fill the gap, and thus constitute a comprehensive treatment of crimes against humanity.

The second subpart of the State responsibility provision adds the important duty that a State Party not cooperate with other entities to violate the prohibition on crimes against humanity. Finally, the obligation to advance R2P is set forth in the third subpart (or second full sentence in the second formulation) of the State responsibility provision. The particularity of crimes against humanity contained therein is simply meant to acknowledge the subject matter – crimes against humanity – of the *Proposed Convention* but not deny the relevance of R2P with respect to genocide or war crimes.

If such a State responsibility provision were to be incorporated in the *Proposed Convention*, then any noncompliance by a State Party with such provision could trigger application of article 26 ("Dispute Settlement Between States Parties") and perhaps ultimately bring such a matter to the International Court of Justice for adjudication. However, there might be additional value in providing for States Parties to seek assistance from the Security Council, as envisaged by the 2005 *World Summit Outcome*, to take action that confronts crimes against humanity under the responsibility-to-protect principle. This would be particularly helpful whether or not the interested State Party is a member of the Security Council at the time. The additional provision might supplement the third subpart of the State responsibility provision above and read:

> Each State Party acknowledges its right as a Member of the United Nations to take collective action and to seek consideration of and action by the Security Council with respect to any commission of crimes against humanity giving rise to the responsibility to protect populations from such crimes (including the crime of persecution known as ethnic cleansing) as well as genocide and war crimes.

VI. CONCLUSION

In this chapter, I have examined how a CAH Convention relates to and might be integrated with the responsibility-to-protect principle. This has required an understanding of the meaning and scope of R2P, which is a more limited principle in United Nations practice than was envisaged after several years of study and preparation of expert reports. One important feature of crimes against humanity drawn from the constitutional character and jurisprudence of the international and hybrid tribunals is the substantiality test, which requires sufficient gravity in the commission of the crimes in order to be defined as crimes against humanity for which individual criminal responsibility holds. But the limited character of R2P necessarily influences which crimes against humanity would be relevant to any likely application of R2P. A future Convention should recognize the critical role of State responsibility with respect to crimes against humanity and broaden the document's reach to the governments, military forces, and other State Party organs and entities that can act institutionally to commit crimes against humanity. Finally, a future Convention should require States Parties to accept the duty to advance the responsibility to protect principle as a matter of treaty law.

14

Re-enforcing Enforcement in a Specialized Convention on Crimes Against Humanity

Inter-State Cooperation, Mutual Legal Assistance, and the Aut Dedere Aut Judicare *Obligation*

Laura M. Olson*

The fight against impunity for serious crimes under international law, such as genocide, war crimes, and crimes against humanity, continues. A new effort in this fight focusing on crimes against humanity is the Crimes Against Humanity Initiative launched by Washington University Law's Whitney R. Harris World Law Institute to study the international law regarding crimes against humanity and to draft a multilateral treaty condemning and prohibiting such crimes.[1] The Crimes Against Humanity Initiative identified a need for a specialized convention on crimes against humanity,[2] because "most crimes against humanity remain outside the ambit of a universal treaty, unless they involve a situation within the jurisdiction of the International Criminal Court. Even in that case, no provision for State Responsibility exists, and no mechanisms for *interstate enforcement* are provided for."[3]

The key to effectively fighting impunity is robust enforcement mechanisms. Thus, a new specialized convention on crimes against humanity should aim to bridge gaps in enforcement[4] by providing "much-needed provisions on interstate cooperation in investigation and punishment of perpetrators of crimes against humanity, filling both a normative gap, and providing critically important enforcement mechanisms."[5] This should include "fostering the notion that states have an obligation to prosecute. Such an obligation, however, must be coupled with providing the realistic capacity

---

* This chapter was completed prior to the author's appointment as Supervisory Program Analyst to the U.S. Department of Homeland Security's Office for Civil Rights and Civil Liberties, and the views expressed herein do not represent the position or views of the U.S. Department of Homeland Security or the U.S. Government.
[1] Details on the Crimes Against Humanity Initiative undertaken by the Whitney R. Harris World Law Institute at Washington University School of Law are *available at* http://law.wustl.edu/crimesagainsthumanity/.
[2] Crimes Against Humanity Initiative, Final Report of the April Experts' Meeting, April 12–15, 2009, St. Louis, MO, ¶ 3 [hereinafter April Experts' Meeting Report] (on file with the Crimes Against Humanity Initiative at the Whitney R. Harris World Law Institute and the author).
[3] *Id.* ¶ 4 (emphasis added).
[4] *Id.* ¶ 34.
[5] *Id.* ¶ 5. Similar needs have been identified with respect to international terrorism. *See, e.g.,* M. Cherif Bassiouni, *Legal Control of International Terrorism: A Policy-Oriented Assessment*, 43 HARV. INT'L L.J. 83 (2002).

to prosecute which, for many states, will necessarily involve prosecutions requiring interstate cooperation in the form of mutual legal assistance."[6]

This chapter addresses enforcement measures with regard to crimes against humanity, focusing on forms of inter-State cooperation. In doing so, it generally describes various forms of, and challenges to, cooperation and then discusses some possible solutions to such challenges that should be incorporated in a new, specialized convention on crimes against humanity in order to reinforce enforcement. Particularly for the latter discussion, comparisons will be made to existing treaties – both those dealing specifically with forms of inter-State cooperation and those that serve a broader objective – as well as to the *Proposed International Convention on the Prevention and Punishment of Crimes Against Humanity* (*Proposed Convention*) developed by the Crimes Against Humanity Initiative.[7]

The chapter begins with a discussion of the obligation to extradite or prosecute (*aut dedere aut judicare*) not only because such an obligation is crucial to ending impunity but also because from that obligation flows the need for various forms of inter-State cooperation, if either prong – extradition or prosecution – is to be effective. Then, various forms of inter-State cooperation in penal matters will be reviewed, particularly extradition and mutual legal assistance.

I. *AUT DEDERE AUT JUDICARE*

To effectively end impunity with regard to crimes against humanity and facilitate inter-State cooperation, States must be required to prosecute alleged perpetrators of such crimes and/or to extradite them to a State willing and able to do so. This obligation is referred to as *aut dedere aut judicare*, meaning the duty to extradite or prosecute.

Aut dedere aut judicare is derived from the phrase originally expressed by Hugo Grotius in 1624: *aut dedere ... aut punire* (extradite or punish).[8] Grotius considered "that a general obligation to extradite or punish exists with respect to all offenses by which another state is particularly injured."[9] His view was that the injured State had a natural right to punish the perpetrator, thus a State holding the perpetrator must either extradite or punish the perpetrator because if it did not, it would be interfering with the injured State's right,[10] as well as the common interest that all States have in suppressing international crimes.[11]

---

[6] April Experts' Meeting Report, *supra* note 2, ¶ 34.
[7] *Proposed International Convention on the Prevention and Punishment of Crimes Against Humanity*, August 2010 [hereinafter *Proposed Convention*], in this volume, App. I.
[8] HUGO GROTIUS, II DE JURE BELLI AC PACIS, ch. XXI, §§ III, IV (1625), *in* CLASSICS OF INTERNATIONAL LAW 526–29 (James B. Scott ed., F. Kelsey trans., 1925). In 1973, M. Cherif Bassiouni "postulated the Grotian maxim as *aut punire* to *aut judicare*, since the purpose of contemporary criminal law is to *judicare* those who are believed to have committed a crime, and not to *punire* until after guilt has been established." M. Cherif Bassiouni, *The Duty to Prosecute and/or Extradite*: Aut Dedere Aut Judicare, *in* II INTERNATIONAL CRIMINAL LAW 35, 35 (M. Cherif Bassiouni ed., 3d ed. 2008) (footnotes omitted).
[9] M. CHERIF BASSIOUNI & EDWARD M. WISE, AUT DEDERE AUT JUDICARE: THE DUTY TO EXTRADITE OR PROSECUTE IN INTERNATIONAL LAW 5 (1995).
[10] Id.
[11] For a short elaboration of the historical perspective, see Bassiouni, *supra* note 8, at 36–41.

Today, only 102 (of 267) international criminal law treaties recognize the duty to prosecute and only 70 recognize the duty to extradite.[12] Whether there exists a customary international law obligation to prosecute or extradite with regard to *all* international crimes remains controversial, given inconsistent State practice.[13] A more accepted assertion, however, is that there exists such an obligation[14] for a *specific* type of international crime – *jus cogens* crimes, such as crimes against humanity.[15] The prohibition against these crimes is *erga omnes*, thus must be respected by all States.[16]

---

[12] *Id.* at 42 (footnote omitted); *see also* Michael J. Kelly, *Cheating Justice by Cheating Death: The Doctrinal Collision for Prosecuting Foreign Terrorists – Passage of* Aut Dedere Aut Judicare *into Customary Law and Refusal to Extradite Based on the Death Penalty*, 20 ARIZ. J. INT'L & COMP. L. 491, 497 (2003).

[13] Michael Plachta, *(Non-)Extradition of Nationals: A Neverending Story?*, 13 EMORY INT'L L. REV. 77, 125–26 (1999); BASSIOUNI & WISE, *supra* note 9, at 20–21; Bassiouni, *supra* note 8, at 45. *See also* Diane Orentlicher, *Immunities and Amnesties*, in this volume; Diane F. Orentlicher, *Settling Accounts: The Duty to Prosecute Human Rights Violations of a Prior Regime*, 100 YALE L.J. 2537 (1991); Naomi Roht-Arriaza, *State Responsibility to Investigate and Prosecute Grave Human Rights Violations in International Law*, 78 CALIF. L. REV. 449, 489–92 (1990). Some members of the International Law Commission do not view the principle of *aut dedere aut judicare* as either customary law or *jus cogens*. Int'l Law Comm'n, *Second Report on the Obligation to Extradite or Prosecute* (aut dedere aut judicare), ¶ 26, U.N. Doc. A/CN.4/585 (June 11, 2007) (prepared by Zdzislaw Galicki, Special Rapporteur). However, the International Law Commission has also indicated that:

> There is no consensus among the doctrine as it concerns this question, although a large and growing number of scholars joins the opinion supporting the concept of an international legal obligation *"aut dedere aut judicare"* as a general duty based not only on the provisions of particular international treaties, but also on generally binding customary norms, at least as it concerns certain categories of crimes.

Int'l Law Comm'n, *Preliminary Report on the Obligation to Extradite or Prosecute* (aut dedere aut judicare), ¶ 40, U.N. Doc. A/CN.4/571 (June 7, 2006) (prepared by Zdzislaw Galicki, Special Rapporteur). "[A]t least in terms of the list of 'crimes under international law' (i.e. genocide, crimes against humanity, crimes against United Nations and associated personnel and war crimes) ..., [the International Law Commission] considers them ... subject to the obligation of *aut dedere aut judicare*." *Id.* ¶ 26.

[14] "[I]t remains a legal obligation with respect to *jus cogens* crimes." Bassiouni, *supra* note 8, at 45; *see also* M. CHERIF BASSIOUNI, CRIMES AGAINST HUMANITY IN INTERNATIONAL CRIMINAL LAW 224 (2d revised ed. 1999). Mark S. Ellis, *Combating Impunity and Enforcing Accountability as a Way to Promote Peace and Stability – The Role of International War Crimes Tribunals*, 2 J. NAT'L SECURITY L. & POL'Y 111, 115 (2006).

[15] For a discussion of crimes against humanity as *jus cogens* crimes, see BASSIOUNI, *supra* note 14, at 210–17.

> But clearly a "state action or policy" aimed at committing "crimes against humanity" creates state responsibility for its violation of a *jus cogens* norm. In addition, since there is an international duty to prosecute or extradite such violators, a state that fails to do so would also breach its international legal duty and be in further violation of the principles of state responsibility. Thus, if conduct creates state responsibility because it constitutes the violation of a *jus cogens* norm, then it should follow that those individuals who carry out the "state action or policy" are also in breach of the same *jus cogens* norm.

Id. at 212 (footnote omitted).

[16] *See* M. Cherif Bassiouni, *International Crimes: Jus Cogens and Obligatio Erga Omnes*, LAW & CONTEMP. PROBS., Autumn 1996, at 63, 69; Lee M. Caplan, *State Immunity, Human Rights and Jus Cogens: A Critique of the Normative Hierarchy Theory*, 97 AM. J. INT'L L. 741, 741–42 (2003); Ellis, *supra* note 14, at 115.

It is generally agreed that the *jus cogens* crimes of war crimes, genocide, and crimes against humanity are subject to universal jurisdiction.[17] Whereas "[s]ome ... consider the exercise of universal jurisdiction permissive[, o]thers consider it mandatory when coupled with *aut dedere aut judicare* (effectively allowing universal jurisdiction to lift *aut dedere aut judicare* into customary law in connection with *jus cogens* crimes):"[18]

> [U]niversal jurisdiction adheres only to the most egregious offenses .... [B]ecause the international order has traditionally enforced international criminal law through domestic enforcement mechanisms, it has developed and applied the *aut dedere aut judicare* principle to these crimes .... [T]he duty to extradite or prosecute under customary international law applies as a *mandatory, affirmative obligation* for serious crimes such as war crimes, crimes against humanity, and genocide. This affirmative duty follows from the common interest that all states have in the suppression of these crimes.[19]

Given the debate on the customary nature of the obligation *aut dedere aut judicare*, practically speaking, a specialized convention on crimes against humanity must include the obligation to extradite and/or prosecute in order to meet the stated, primary objective of the treaty – ending impunity.[20] Whether inclusion of the principle *aut dedere aut judicare* in the new treaty is based on the view that it merely reflects an existing obligation under customary international law with regard to crimes against humanity,[21] or whether it establishes a conventional obligation binding States Parties, it remains crucial to leave no doubt with States as to their obligations concerning alleged perpetrators of crimes against humanity. Article 9 of the *Proposed Convention* reflects the principle of *aut dedere aut judicare*.[22]

---

[17] Universal jurisdiction is mentioned here only as it relates to the obligation of *aut dedere aut judicare*. For a discussion of universal jurisdiction, see Payam Akhavan, *The Universal Repression of Crimes Against Humanity before National Jurisdictions: The Need for a Treaty-Based Obligation to Prosecute*, in this volume (discussing the need for a treaty that creates obligations of universal repression). "The foundation for the application of the universality principal to war crimes, as well as 'crimes against humanity,' stems from the proceedings before the IMT and the subsequent prosecutions." BASSIOUNI, *supra* note 14, at 235 (footnote omitted).

[18] Kelly, *supra* note 12, at 501 (footnote omitted); *see* Akhavan, *supra* note 17.

[19] Lee A. Steven, Note, *Genocide and the Duty to Extradite or Prosecute: Why the United States Is in Breach of Its International Obligations*, 39 VA. J. INT'L L. 425, 441–43 (1999) (footnotes omitted).

[20] April Experts' Meeting Report, *supra* note 2, ¶ 3.

[21] "[I]t remains a legal obligation with respect to *jus cogens* crimes." Bassiouni, *supra* note 8, at 45.

[22] 1. Each State Party shall take necessary measures to establish its competence to exercise jurisdiction over crimes against humanity when the alleged offender is present in any territory under its jurisdiction, unless it extradites him or her to another State in accordance with its international obligations or surrenders him or her to the International Criminal Court, if it is a State Party to the Rome Statute, or to an international criminal tribunal whose jurisdiction it has recognized.

2. In the event that a State Party does not, for any reason not specified in the present Convention, prosecute a person suspected of committing crimes against humanity, it shall, pursuant to an appropriate request, either surrender such a person to another State willing to prosecute fairly and effectively, to the International Criminal Court, if it is a State Party to the Rome Statute, or to a competent international tribunal having jurisdiction over crimes against humanity.

Proposed Convention, *supra* note 7, art. 9; *see also id.* art. 8(9).

The most expansive form of this principle would be to require it based on universal jurisdiction.[23]

Whether *aut dedere aut judicare* imposes alternative or coexistent duties, as the principle has not been "expressed with sufficient specificity,"[24] remains unsettled. If the latter is true, then a State can choose whether to prosecute or extradite. If the options, however, are alternatives, then the duty to extradite is regarded as primary and the duty to prosecute arises when extradition cannot be granted.[25] Unless explicitly provided in a treaty provision, the present status of the principle *aut dedere aut judicare*

> does not warrant an assertion that *judicare* is "subordinated" to *dedere* to the effect that the requested state's first obligation is to deliver up the offender sought and that it is allowed to institute its own criminal proceedings only after it has showed that extradition is prohibited on legal grounds.[26]

The obligation to extradite and/or prosecute found in the *Proposed Convention*[27] requires States that do not prosecute alleged perpetrators to extradite them; this language indicates a coexistent duty between the two options. A new convention should not express a preference between *dedere* or *judicare*, because which is preferable depends on the specific situation.[28] Some factors to consider in making the determination include: where was the impact of the offense felt, which jurisdiction has the greater interest in prosecuting the offense, which jurisdiction has the most comprehensive case, the location of evidence, the nationality and residence of the accused, and the severity of the sentence the accused is likely to receive in each jurisdiction.[29]

Unlike other treaties containing the obligation to prosecute or extradite, the *Proposed Convention*[30] explicitly incorporates qualitative criteria with respect to

---

[23] See generally Akhavan, *supra* note 17. If the new treaty were to require mandatory rather than permissive jurisdiction, this could result in fewer States joining the treaty (particularly if no reservations are permitted), because not all States recognize universal jurisdiction. See generally M. Cherif Bassiouni, *Universal Jurisdiction for International Crimes: Historical Perspectives and Contemporary Practice*, 42 Va. J. Int'l L. 81 (2001).

[24] Bassiouni, *supra* note 14; *see also* Bassiouni, *supra* note 8, at 41–42; Plachta, *supra* note 13, at 128.

[25] Bassiouni, *supra* note 14, at 219–20; Plachta, *supra* note 13, at 128.

[26] Plachta, *supra* note 13, at 129 (footnote omitted); *see also* Bassiouni, *supra* note 14, at 220.

[27] *Proposed Convention*, *supra* note 7, art. 9(2).

[28] Plachta, *supra* note 13, at 133 ("Instead of having a fixed hierarchy of alternative obligations embodied in the principle *aut dedere aut judicare*, it is more desirable to base the decision of whether to prosecute in the requested country or surrender the person sought on mutual consultations between the appropriate authorities of the states involved. There may be cases in which it will be preferable for the accused to be tried in a foreign state, rather than his home country. The problem becomes even more delicate when an offense is committed in the territory of both the requesting and the requested states, each of which are therefore entitled to claim jurisdiction based on the principle of territoriality. A general and rigid rule of refusing to extradite nationals in such cases would reduce the effectiveness of extradition as a major tool to combat transnational crime.").

[29] Plachta, *supra* note 13, at 133–34, (*citing* Swystun v. United States [1988], 40 C.C.C.3d 222, 227–28 (Man. Q.B.) (Can.)).

[30] *Proposed Convention*, *supra* note 7, art. 9(2).

prosecutions undertaken by the State or international tribunal to which the person is surrendered. These criteria provide that the prosecution must be done "fairly and effectively."[31] If a new convention on crimes against humanity is to incorporate these qualitative terms, the drafters should consider also including them with regard to prosecution by the requested State as well as the extradition process.[32]

Explicit inclusion of such language may not be absolutely necessary given the general obligation to interpret a treaty in good faith.[33] However, to address the problem that arose in *Lockerbie*[34] requires not only giving meaning to these qualitative terms[35] but also resolving the question in international criminal law as to "whether the duty to extradite supersedes that of prosecution when the national law of the requested state prohibits extradition (*e.g.*, of its nationals), when that state cannot fairly and effectively prosecute."[36] Addressing these issues is necessary for effective enforcement, but it may not be practical to do so in detail in a new treaty without risking nonratification by those States unsatisfied with the solutions. The drafters of a new convention on crimes against humanity could consider some minimal language, such as that included in the recently adopted International Convention for the Protection of All Person from Enforced Disappearance:

> Any person against whom proceedings are brought in connection with an offence of enforced disappearance shall be guaranteed fair treatment at all stages of proceedings. Any person tried for an offence of enforced disappearance shall benefit from a fair trial before a competent, independent and impartial court established by law.[37]

A new, specialized treaty on crimes against humanity must incorporate the principle *aut dedere aut judicare*. However, it must not stop there. A new treaty must – to the extent possible – ensure that the obligation can function in practice:

> Practical problems in fulfilling the obligation under *judicare* do not necessarily result from a lack of goodwill on the part of the requested state. Rather, the impunity of the offender and the frustration of justice should be viewed, on the one hand, as a result of [, for example,] the requested state's inability to break with the

---

[31] Bassiouni, *supra* note 8, at 42; *see also* BASSIOUNI, *supra* note 14, at 220.
[32] Bassiouni, *supra* note 8, at 42; Plachta, *supra* note 13, at 130–32; *see Proposed Convention*, *supra* note 7, art. 2(2)(b).
[33] "A treaty shall be interpreted in good faith in accordance with the ordinary meaning to be given to the terms of the treaty in their context and in the light of its object and purpose." Vienna Convention on the Law of Treaties art. 13(1), *opened for signature* May 23, 1969, 1155 U.N.T.S. 331.
[34] The United States and the United Kingdom issued indictments against two Libyans for the explosion of Pan American Airways Flight 103 over Lockerbie, Scotland on December 21, 1988. Libya refused to extradite its nationals, arguing that it had a priority right to prosecute. The United States and the United Kingdom contended that no prosecution in Libya would be effective and claimed a priority right over Libya for extradition. Bassiouni, *supra* note 8, at 43; *see* Michael Scharf, *The Lockerbie Model of Transfer of Proceedings*, *in* II INTERNATIONAL CRIMINAL LAW, *supra* note 8, at 521.
[35] Bassiouni, *supra* note 8, at 42; Plachta, *supra* note 13, at 130–32.
[36] BASSIOUNI, *supra* note 14, at 220.
[37] International Convention for the Protection of All Persons from Enforced Disappearance art. 11(3), *opened for signature* Feb. 6, 2007, E/CN.4/2005/WG.22/WP.1/Rev.4 (2005) (not yet in force).

rule of non-extradition of nationals, and, on the other hand, its inability to overcome difficulties inherently involved in prosecuting and punishing offenders for crimes committed abroad.[38]

Without effective mechanisms in place for extradition and prosecution, neither the *aut dedere aut judicare* obligation, nor the objective of ending impunity can be fulfilled. The next section discusses some of these mechanisms – forms of inter-State cooperation.

II. FORMS OF INTER-STATE COOPERATION IN CRIMINAL MATTERS

Inter-State cooperation in criminal matters constitutes "the deliberate provision of support for criminal proceedings in a different *forum*."[39] Particularly for international crimes, such as crimes against humanity, inter-State cooperation is the linchpin for effective enforcement. The drafters of the *Proposed Convention* recognize this and provide for both vertical (with international tribunals) and horizontal (with States) cooperation in article 8.[40]

The *Proposed Convention* also requires its States Parties to take the necessary measures to give effect to the treaty's cooperation provisions.[41] This section discusses the following forms of inter-State cooperation: extradition, mutual legal assistance, transfer of criminal proceedings, enforcement of the effects of another State's penal judgments, and the transfer of the enforcement of sentences. In addressing these forms of cooperation, some of the practical challenges to successful cooperation – some arising out of issues of State sovereignty and others due to individual rights[42] – will be presented. In response to these challenges, some possible solutions (some appearing in existing treaties) are suggested that may be incorporated in a new, specialized treaty on crimes against humanity.

A. Extradition

In article 12 and Annex 2, the *Proposed Convention* addresses one of the two prongs of the principle of *aut dedere aut judicare*: extradition.[43] The proposed article attempts to address the difficulties that can impede the efficiency and effectiveness

---

[38] Plachta, *supra* note 13, at 135.
[39] COMMENTARY ON THE ROME STATUTE OF THE INTERNATIONAL CRIMINAL COURT 1504 (Otto Triffterer ed., 2d ed. 2008) [hereinafter ROME STATUTE COMMENTARY].
[40] *Proposed Convention, supra* note 7, art. 8(D)(17).
[41] (1) Each State Party shall enact necessary legislation and other measures as required by its Constitution or legal system to give effect to the provisions of the present Convention ....
   Id. art. 8(1); *see also id.* art. 8(D)(17)–(18).
[42] ROME STATUTE COMMENTARY, *supra* note 39, at 1504. *See generally* Steven W. Becker & Cave Janus, *Increased Cooperation Between Law Enforcement and Intelligence Agencies After September 11, 2001, in* II INTERNATIONAL CRIMINAL LAW, *supra* note 8, at 71.
[43] *Proposed Convention, supra* note 7, art. 12, Annex 2.

of extradition as a form of inter-State cooperation. This article of the *Proposed Convention* tracks much of the language of the International Convention for the Protection of All Persons from Enforced Disappearance.[44]

Without a specific bilateral extradition treaty pertaining to the specific extraditable offense, most States cannot extradite. To remove this obstacle, the *Proposed Convention* provides clearly that crimes against humanity are to be considered an extraditable offense in existing extradition treaties between the States Parties.[45] The *Proposed Convention* also requires that crimes against humanity be included as an extraditable offense in any future extradition treaty concluded.[46]

In addition to requiring a bilateral treaty, many States need national legislation to provide the legal basis for extradition. "National legislation varies as to its content and specificity. Most States require the existence of a treaty in addition to national legislation. Diversity in national judicial and administrative practices is also quite significant."[47] These variances can hinder consistent and effective extradition. To eliminate the need for a bilateral treaty or national legislation, the *Proposed Convention* itself establishes the legal basis for extradition for crimes against humanity.[48] This assists in addressing the problem that approximately half of the States do not have legislation containing provisions on extradition.[49] Even if national legislation exists, it may not include crimes against humanity; the *Proposed Convention* provision ensures that such crimes are covered. In an earlier draft of this work, I suggested that the *Proposed Convention* should include more details on how States are to cooperate in extradition using the language found in extradition treaties, as well as other criminal law treaties,[50] as a guide. The *Proposed Convention* does so in Annex 2.

Even though bilateral treaties and national legislation on extradition vary, two requirements have reached the level of customary law[51] and must be included. These two requirements are double criminality[52] and the principle of speciality.[53] Each will be discussed in turn.

First, double criminality requires that the "crime charged in the requesting state must also be found in the criminal laws of the requested state."[54] Application of this

---

[44] International Convention for the Protection of All Persons from Enforced Disappearance, *supra* note 37, art. 13.
[45] *Proposed Convention*, *supra* note 7, art. 12, Annex 2(A)(1).
[46] *Id.* art. 12, Annex 2(A)(2).
[47] M. Cherif Bassiouni, *The Modalities of International Cooperation in Penal Matters*, *in* II INTERNATIONAL CRIMINAL LAW, *supra* note 8, at 3, 5.
[48] *Proposed Convention*, *supra* note 7, art. 12, Annex 2(B)(3).
[49] Bassiouni, *supra* note 47, at 5.
[50] For example, UN Convention Against Transnational Organized Crime art. 16, *adopted* Nov. 15, 2000, 2225 U.N.T.S. 209; UN Convention Against Corruption art. 44, *adopted* Oct. 31, 2003, G.A. Res. 58/4, U.N. Doc. A/RES/58/4 (Oct. 31, 2003); UN Convention Against Illicit Traffic in Narcotic Drugs and Psychotropic Substances art. 6, *opened for signature* Dec. 20, 1988, U.N. Econ. & Soc. Council, U.N. Doc. E/CONF.82/15, Corr. 1 and Corr. 2.
[51] Bassiouni, *supra* note 47, at 5.
[52] Double criminality is also referred to as dual criminality. *Id.*
[53] Speciality is also referred to as specialty. *Id.*
[54] *Id.*

requirement varies in national practice: "some states require the crime be identical in the two legal systems, while others require only that the underlying facts give rise to a criminal charge in the requested state's legal system."[55] Given the differences in States' legal systems, particular acts often are not criminalized similarly by States. Thus, requiring that crimes be identical in both the requesting and requested States can effectively block extradition.

An earlier version of the *Proposed Convention* took the broader approach to fulfill the double criminality requirement: "that the underlying facts give rise to a criminal charge in the requested state's legal system,"[56] rather than requiring that the crime be identical in the two States. The May Interim Draft Convention included a specific provision explicitly adopting the broader approach: "The States Parties ... agree to cooperate ... irrespective of any definitional difference in their respective statutes, provided that the facts in question would be deemed sufficient under their respective statutes to investigate, prosecute, and punish a person for crimes against humanity."[57] The *Proposed Convention*, however, contains no such provision.[58] The broader approach is preferable because it not only responds to differences in legal systems, but is also particularly relevant to ensuring extradition for crimes against humanity. Many States do not have specific legislation criminalizing crimes against humanity as such, but they do have legislation criminalizing the underlying crime such as murder, torture, or rape.

Whereas double criminality has generally been considered to concern the substantive crime, the *Pinochet* case[59] raised another aspect of double criminality, which is "jurisdictional double criminality":

> Counsel for Pinochet argued that certain charges, notably those relating to torture and conspiracy to torture, were not extradition crimes because at the time of their commission there was no jurisdiction in the United Kingdom for such crimes *committed abroad*. Such jurisdiction was only established by section 134 of the Criminal Justice Act of 1988, which was passed to allow ratification of the 1984 Convention against Torture and Other Cruel, Inhuman or Degrading Treatment or Punishment, and which entered into force on September 29, 1988. The majority concluded that the double criminality requirement must be satisfied at the time of the commission of the offense, with the consequence that torture committed in Chile, or elsewhere outside Spain, before September 29, 1988, does not constitute an extradition crime in the United Kingdom.[60]

---

[55] *Id.* (footnote omitted).
[56] *Id.*
[57] Interim Draft International Convention on the Prevention and Punishment of Crimes Against Humanity, May 2009, art. 1(2) [hereinafter May Interim Draft Convention] (on file with the Crimes Against Humanity Initiative at the Whitney R. Harris World Law Institute).
[58] Such a reference is included with respect to *ne bis in idem. Proposed Convention, supra* note 7, art. 17.
[59] *See* Christine M. Chinkin, *International Decision, United Kingdom House of Lords, (Spanish request for extradition), Regina v. Bow Street Stipendiary Magistrate, ex parte Pinochet Ugarte (No. 3).* [1999] 2 WLR 827, 93 AM. J. INT'L L. 703 (1999); *see generally* THE PINOCHET CASE: ORIGINS, PROGRESS, AND IMPLICATIONS (Madeleine Davis ed. 2003).
[60] Chinkin, *supra* note 59, at 706 (footnotes omitted) (emphasis added).

As universal jurisdiction is generally permissive, not mandatory, a similar situation could arise with regard to crimes against humanity. It is suggested that the drafters of a specialized convention on crimes against humanity consider addressing this "Pinochet problem."

Second, the principle of speciality provides that a person who has been extradited from one country to another may only be prosecuted on the charges for which he or she has been extradited.[61] The principle of speciality ensures that the rights of the requested State as well as those of the concerned person are respected.[62]

This principle is provided in the *Proposed Convention*: "No person extradited for crimes against humanity shall be tried in the requesting State for any other crime than that for which extradition was granted unless the requested State or person so consents."[63] However, crimes against humanity are often jointly committed with war crimes and genocide. Given the special nature of such international crimes, particularly the *aut dedere aut judicare* obligation accompanying them, the drafters of the specialized convention should consider excluding or, at a minimum, including a waiver for international crimes. Particularly, in order to safeguard the extradited person's rights, the drafters should also consider including a provision ensuring that the person is not re-extradited to a third State.[64]

Whereas these issues can pose challenges to extradition, grounds for refusal remain great obstacles to extradition.[65] These exclusions include charges considered to be political offenses, imposition of certain penalties, such as the death penalty, occurrence of double jeopardy, application of statutes of limitations, or the person concerned being a national of the requested State.[66]

Political offenses usually constitute mandatory grounds for refusal of extradition. For acts to constitute crimes against humanity, they must occur on a widespread or

---

[61] Bassiouni, *supra* note 47, at 5.

[62] *See, e.g.*, United States v. Moss, 344 F. Supp. 2d 1142 (W.D. Tenn. 2004) (finding that the rule of specialty required the dismissal of the money laundering counts in the indictment, as the Costa Rican extradition resolution and the written assurance by the United States provided that defendant could not be prosecuted for money laundering). *See generally* Jacques Semmelman, *The Doctrine of Speciality in Criminal Cases*, N.Y. L.J. (Jan. 3, 2008).

[63] *Proposed Convention*, *supra* note 7, art. 12, Annex 2(E)(11).

[64] *See*, for example, the UN Model Treaty on Extradition: "A person extradited under the present Treaty shall not be proceeded against, sentenced, detained, re-extradited to a Third State ...." UN Model Treaty on Extradition art. 14(1), *adopted by* U.N. Doc. A/RES/45/116 (Dec. 14, 1990), *subsequently amended by* UN Doc. A/RES/52/88 (Dec. 12, 1997).

[65] Bassiouni, *supra* note 47, at 5.

> Perhaps most problematic for extradition cases involving acts of terrorism is the political offense exception. Many modern extradition treaties specifically exempt political offenses from extradition, since liberal and democratic governments developed a strong antipathy toward the idea of surrendering dissidents into the hands of a despotic government. There are, however, no recognized criteria as to what constitutes a "political" offense, nor is there a rule of international law prohibiting the extradition of political offenders. As a result, the decision whether to extradite rests on subjective criteria, as determined by the holding government.

> Christopher C. Joyner, *International Extradition and Global Terrorism: Bringing International Criminals to Justice*, 25 Loy. L.A. Int'l & Comp. L. Rev. 493, 501 (2003) (footnote omitted).

[66] Bassiouni, *supra* note 47, at 5.

systematic basis; therefore, crimes against humanity often are the result of a State policy. Hence, to avoid abuse of this exclusion with regard to crimes against humanity, crimes against humanity must be clearly and expressly excluded from constituting political offenses or having connection with a political offense. The *Proposed Convention* does this,[67] "[r]eflecting the need established over the years in extradition practice to narrow down the application of the political offence exception."[68]

The drafters had also suggested that claims of immunity and superior orders should be explicitly excluded from the exceptions to extradition in the *Proposed Convention*.[69] Exclusion of claims of immunity would assist in eliminating exceptions that have blocked extradition, hindering accountability. The extent of the scope of immunities to be explicitly excluded in the treaty warrants further discussion. As Diane Orentlicher notes, "[r]ecent developments in law and practice suggest that States are unlikely to agree to text that commits States Parties not to invoke immunities ratione personae in the context of inter-State criminal proceedings."[70]

The *Proposed Convention* provides that extradition shall not be "barred by claims of official capacity."[71] The removal in the final text of superior orders as nonapplicable refusal grounds eliminates confusion, because it was out of place in the May Interim Draft Convention: "[I]t is of a different nature than the other refusal grounds. The possibility of a successful claim on a defense is not relevant at this stage in the proceedings."[72]

The drafters could also consider expressly excluding amnesties and statutes of limitations as grounds for refusal. Whereas that would be in direct contradiction to the approach taken by the UN Model Treaty on Extradition, which provides as mandatory grounds for refusal of extradition immunity "for any reason, including lapse of time or amnesty,"[73] the UN Model Treaty on Extradition was drafted to cover all types of crimes. Here, the special nature of crimes against humanity cannot be forgotten, that is, immunities, amnesties, and statutes of limitations are not to be applied to *jus cogens* crimes.[74]

---

[67] See *Proposed Convention, supra* note 7, art. 12, Annex 2(D)(5).
[68] Demostenes Chryssikos, *Commentary on the United Nations Model Law on Extradition, in* II INTERNATIONAL CRIMINAL LAW, *supra* note 8, at 377, 379. *See generally* CHRISTOPHER L. BLAKSLEY, TERRORISM, DRUGS, INTERNATIONAL LAW, AND THE PROTECTION OF HUMAN LIBERTY 264–70 (1992) (providing an overview of the political offense exception).
[69] May Interim Draft Convention, *supra* note 57, art. 10(4) (bracketed text).
[70] *See* Orentlicher, *Immunities and Amnesties, supra* note 13, at 202, in this volume.
[71] *Proposed Convention, supra* note 7, art. 12, Annex 2(D)(5).
[72] Elies van Sliedregt, Remarks on Enforcement Issues at the Crimes Against Humanity Initiative Hague Intersessional Experts' Meeting, Leiden University, The Hague, Netherlands (June 11–12, 2009), at 4 (presenter's notes on file with author).
[73] UN Model Treaty on Extradition, *supra* note 64, art. 3(e).
[74] "Crimes against humanity as defined by this Convention shall not be subject to any statute of limitations." *Proposed Convention, supra* note 7, art. 7. *See generally* Roht-Arriaza, *supra* note 13; Orentlicher, *Immunities and Amnesties, supra* note 13; Orentlicher, *Settling Accounts: The Duty to Prosecute Human Rights Violations of a Prior Regime, supra* note 13. *But see* John Dugard, *Is the Truth and Reconciliation Process Compatible with International Law? An Unanswered Question*, 13 S. AFR. J. HUM. RTS. 258, 267 (1997); John Dugard, *Dealing with Crimes of the Past: Is Amnesty Still an Option?*, 12 LEIDEN J. INT'L L. 1001 (1999). *See, e.g.*, Convention on the Non-Applicability of

Furthermore, it is appropriate and consistent with other treaties[75] to include an antidiscrimination clause and an *ordre public* exception.[76]

The most significant and common impediment to extradition is the denial by States to extradite their own nationals.[77] In particular, this "extradition problem arose between common law and civil law countries when the latter refused to accept treaty provisions obligating them to surrender all requested offenders, including their own nationals."[78] The *Proposed Convention* does not directly tackle this issue. The drafters could consider including language to make clear that the obligation to extradite applies to "*all* persons"; however, this may be unacceptable for some States, particularly civil law countries, because many States' constitutions contain such an exclusion.[79] However, "[n]otwithstanding all of the convincing arguments against [refusal to extradite nationals], as well as the proposals to modify states' policies with respect to this form of international cooperation in criminal matters, there is nothing to indicate that it will soon be abandoned."[80] Thus, focus should perhaps better be placed on ensuring that, if extradition fails to occur, prosecution in the home State must take place, because even though "some states have provided for a jurisdictional basis to domestically prosecute their own nationals ..., the actual exercise of such jurisdiction is rare."[81]

Unlike a previous version of the *Proposed Convention*, which stipulated that assurances may be asked of the requesting State with regard to fair trial rights,[82] the final text posits that failure to provide fair trial rights may be grounds for denial of extradition.[83] Given the prohibition on the death penalty in many, particularly European, States,[84] I suggested in an earlier draft of this work that the drafters should provide that assurances may be sought with regard to nonimposition of or the carrying out of the death penalty. The *Proposed Convention* now does so.[85]

Statutory Limitations to War Crimes and Crimes Against Humanity arts. 1, 4, *opened for signature* Nov. 26, 1968, 754 U.N.T.S. 73; European Convention on the Non-Applicability of Statutory Limitation to Crimes Against Humanity and War Crimes art. 1, Jan. 25, 1974, E.T.S. 082.

[75] *See, e.g.,* UN Model Treaty on Extradition, *supra* note 64, art. 3(b); European Convention on Extradition, Dec. 13, 1957, E.T.S. No. 024, art. 3(2).
[76] van Sliedregt, *supra* note 72, at 4.
[77] Bassiouni, *supra* note 47, at 5. *See generally* John G. Kester, *Some Myths of United States Extradition Law*, 76 GEO. L.J. 1441 (1988) (providing a critical review of the extradition process).
[78] Plachta, *supra* note 13, at 95.
[79] Bassiouni, *supra* note 47, at 5.
[80] Plachta, *supra* note 13, at 77.
[81] Bassiouni, *supra* note 47, at 5. The UN Model Law provides two ways of addressing the matter of extradition of nationals of the requested State: either establish a mandatory or optional ground for refusal or have the law remain silent on this point, thus not expressly including such a ground for refusal. UN Office of Drugs and Crime, UN Model Law on Extradition § 11 (2004), *available at* http://www.unodc.org/pdf/model_law_extradition.pdf. *See* Chryssikos, *supra* note 68, at 379.
[82] May Interim Draft Convention, *supra* note 57, art. 10(6).
[83] *Proposed Convention, supra* note 7, art. 12, Annex 2(D)(8)–(9).
[84] *See generally* Kelly, *supra* note 12.
[85] *Proposed Convention, supra* note 7, art. 12, Annex 2(D)(10).

Finally, it must be recalled that extradition is always restricted by the principle of *non-refoulement*. The *Proposed Convention* models its *non-refoulement* provision[86] after that found in the International Convention for the Protection of All Persons from Enforced Disappearance.[87] In a previous version of the *Proposed Convention*, the drafters had failed – although this has been rectified in the final text – to include the novel addition found in the International Convention for the Protection of All Persons from Enforced Disappearance. This treaty not only requires States to consider human rights violations when determining whether a person may be returned, but also humanitarian law violations.[88] As the prohibitions, the violations of which constitute crimes against humanity, developed out of international humanitarian law,[89] inclusion of international humanitarian law in such a provision in a specialized convention on crimes against humanity is appropriate. Furthermore, in order to best ensure proper implementation of the principle of *non-refoulement*, it must be made clear that the principle prohibits transfer from one State authority to another State authority with no requirement to cross territorial boundaries.[90] Thus, it is suggested that the word "State" in article 18(1) of the *Proposed Convention* be replaced by "State authorities."[91]

A new, specialized treaty on crimes against humanity presents the opportunity to address barriers to enforcement. In this regard, it needs to alleviate to the extent possible the lengthy and cumbersome extradition practice.

---

[86] 1. No State Party shall expel, return (*"refouler"*) or extradite a person to another State where there are substantial grounds for believing that such a person would be in danger of being subjected to crimes against humanity.
2. For the purpose of determining whether there are such grounds, the competent authorities shall take into account all relevant considerations including, where applicable, the existence in the State concerned of a consistent pattern of gross, flagrant or mass violations of human rights or of serious violations of international humanitarian law.
Id. art. 18.

[87] 1. No State Party shall expel, return ("refouler"), surrender or extradite a person to another State where there are substantial grounds for believing that he or she would be in danger of being subjected to enforced disappearance.
2. For the purpose of determining whether there are such grounds, the competent authorities shall take into account all relevant considerations, including, where applicable, the existence in the State concerned of a consistent pattern of gross, flagrant or mass violations of human rights or of serious violations of international humanitarian law.
International Convention for the Protection of All Persons from Enforced Disappearance, *supra* note 37, art. 16.

[88] *Id.* art. 16(2).

[89] See Roger S. Clark, *History of Efforts to Codify Crimes Against Humanity: From the Charter of Nuremberg to the Statute of Rome*, in this volume; M. Cherif Bassiouni, *Revisiting the Architecture of Crimes Against Humanity: Almost a Century in the Making with Ambiguities Remaining*, in this volume.

[90] *See, e.g.*, Comm. Against Torture, *Consideration of Reports Submitted by States Parties Under Article 19 of the Convention: Conclusions and Recommendations of the Committee Against Torture – United States of America*, ¶ 20, U.N. Doc. CAT/C/USA/CO/2 (July 25, 2006) (stating its concern "that the State Party considers that the non-refoulement obligation ... does not extend to a person detained outside its territory").

[91] *Proposed Convention*, *supra* note 7, art. 18(1).

B. Mutual Legal Assistance

This section addresses the second prong of *aut dedere aut judicare*: prosecution. If a State is to prosecute effectively, it is likely to need judicial assistance, particularly if the crime was not committed on its territory. Judicial assistance between States – whether with regard, for example, to witness testimony, physical evidence, or the freezing of assets[92] – began traditionally through "letters rogatory" between the concerned States. However, this process is often long, with no obligation on the requested State to accept or, even if it does, with no guarantee that the requested evidence would be in a form usable by the requesting State.[93] To address some of these obstacles, States began in the 1960s to conclude bilateral and regional multilateral mutual legal assistance treaties.[94] However, the number of such treaties is low, as is the number of States having domestic legislation addressing judicial cooperation.[95] Thus, to be effective at combating impunity, a specialized convention on crimes against humanity must include measures to guarantee and expedite effective fulfillment of requests of one State's courts to those of another.[96]

As a starting point, given the relative paucity of mutual legal assistance treaties[97] *accompanied by* implementing legislation, a new convention on crimes against humanity should establish the basis for such required cooperation. The *Proposed Convention* does so. It stipulates that "[l]egal assistance between States Parties ... may be afforded on the basis of the present Convention and without the need for reliance on a bilateral treaty or national legislation."[98]

Mutual legal assistance treaties contain substantively similar requirements and exclusions as found in extradition treaties and national legislation, including double

---

[92] For further discussion on the freezing of assets, see, e.g., RESPONDING TO MONEY LAUNDERING: AN INTERNATIONAL PERSPECTIVE (Ernesto U. Savona ed., 1997); PAOLO BERNASCONI, NEW JUDICIAL INSTRUMENTS AGAINST INTERNATIONAL BUSINESS CRIMES (1995); Bassiouni, *supra* note 47, at 13–19.

[93] Bassiouni, *supra* note 47, at 8.

[94] *Id.* Regional instruments include, for example, the European Convention on Mutual Legal Assistance in Criminal Matters, Nov. 20, 1959, E.T.S. No. 030; Inter-American Convention on Mutual Legal Assistance in Criminal Matters, May 23, 1992, O.A.S.T.S. No. 75; Arab League Agreement for Judicial Cooperation (Riyadh Convention), Apr. 6, 1983, *available at* http://www.unhcr.org/refworld/docid/3ae6b38d8.html. *See generally* Bruce Zagaris, *Developments in International Judicial Assistance and Related Matters*, 18 DENV. J. INT'L L. & POL'Y 339 (1990); William M. Hannay, *The Legislative Approach to the Political Offense Exception*, *in* LEGAL RESPONSES TO INTERNATIONAL TERRORISM 115 (M. Cherif Bassiouni ed., 1988).

[95] Bassiouni, *supra* note 47, at 8.

[96] *See Proposed Convention*, *supra* note 7, art. 13, Annex 3.

[97] Multilateral mutual legal assistance treaties include the European Convention on Mutual Legal Assistance in Criminal Matters, *supra* note 95; First Additional Protocol to the European Convention on Mutual Legal Assistance in Criminal Matters, Oct. 15, 1975, E.T.S. No. 086; Second Additional Protocol to the European Convention on Mutual Legal Assistance in Criminal Matters, Nov. 8, 2001, E.T.S. No. 182; Inter-American Convention on Mutual Legal Assistance in Criminal Matters, *supra* note 95; Arab League Agreement on Extradition and Judicial Cooperation, *supra* note 95.

[98] *Proposed Convention*, *supra* note 7, art. 13, Annex 3(1).

criminality, speciality, and the political offense exception.[99] These can raise difficulties to ensuring effective legal assistance, hindering enforcement. Thus, solutions like those discussed earlier with regard to extradition[100] must be incorporated in provisions of a specialized crimes against humanity convention concerning mutual legal assistance. The *Proposed Convention* has done so to a limited extent: "Legal assistance may not be refused based upon claims of official capacity ..., or that the crime was of a political nature."[101] This specific limitation found in the *Proposed Convention* recognizes the circumstances that usually surround occurrences of crimes against humanity and thus better ensures accountability. This approach is preferable when compared to the general provision in the International Convention for the Protection of All Persons from Enforced Disappearance,[102] which gives no *specific* limitations on refusals to provide assistance, even though enforced disappearances occur in similar circumstances as crimes against humanity and, in fact, can amount to crimes against humanity.

The International Convention for the Protection of All Persons from Enforced Disappearance, adopted in 2006, provides very little guidance on mutual legal assistance.[103] This stands in contrast to contemporary international criminal law treaties such as the UN Convention Against Transnational Organized Crime,[104] the UN Convention Against Corruption,[105] and the UN Convention Against Illicit Traffic in Narcotic Drugs and Psychotropic Substances.[106] These treaties include extremely detailed articles on mutual legal assistance that incorporate, *inter alia*, the purposes for which assistance may be requested, the grounds for refusal, creation of a central authority to handle requests, and the procedures for making a request. Such detail helps ensure that States can successfully and effectively assist one another. These specific articles actually create a "mini" mutual legal assistance treaty within the larger treaty.

---

[99] Bassiouni, *supra* note 47, at 8–9.
[100] *See supra* Section II.A.
[101] *Proposed Convention*, *supra* note 7, art. 13, Annex 3(I)(15).
[102] 1. States Parties shall afford one another the greatest measure of mutual legal assistance in connection with criminal proceedings brought in respect of an offence of enforced disappearance, including the supply of all evidence at their disposal that is necessary for the proceedings.
   2. Such mutual legal assistance shall be subject to the conditions provided for by the domestic law of the requested State Party or by applicable treaties on mutual legal assistance, including, in particular, the conditions in relation to the grounds upon which the requested State Party may refuse to grant mutual legal assistance or may make it subject to conditions.
   International Convention for the Protection of All Persons from Enforced Disappearance, *supra* note 37, art. 14.
[103] *Id*.
[104] UN Convention Against Transnational Organized Crime, *supra* note 50, art. 18.
[105] UN Convention Against Corruption, *supra* note 50, art. 46.
[106] UN Convention Against Illicit Traffic in Narcotic Drugs and Psychotropic Substances, *supra* note 50, art. 7. The Rome Statute of the International Criminal Court, *opened for signature* July 17, 1988, 2187 U.N.T.S. 90, also contains detailed provisions on mutual legal assistance; however, the Rome Statute focuses on vertical State-International Criminal Court cooperation, rather than horizontal State-State cooperation.

These international criminal law treaties, however, also stipulate that the detailed provisions apply only if no other treaty, bilateral or multilateral, governs mutual legal assistance between the States Parties.[107] In this way, the "mini" mutual legal assistance treaty within the general international criminal law treaty does not override a treaty specifically on mutual legal assistance, which is most likely more detailed, and also does not risk interfering with previously adopted national implementing legislation. Yet, incorporation of a "mini" mutual legal assistance treaty permits these substantive criminal law treaties to fill the gap existing between those States Parties with no specific mutual legal assistance treaty.

Earlier versions of the *Proposed Convention* carved a middle path in addressing mutual legal assistance. The May Interim Draft Convention, for example, contained more detail than the International Convention for the Protection of All Persons from Enforced Disappearance but remained far from containing a "mini" mutual legal assistance treaty.[108] Because successful cooperation between States is key to enforcement, it is suggested that a new, specialized convention on crimes against humanity would be more effective with inclusion of provisions such as those in the treaties mentioned earlier or, for example, in the UN Model Treaty on Mutual Legal Assistance[109] or other multilateral mutual legal assistance treaties.[110] Because such provisions are not novel, States should not be overly reluctant to accept these additional provisions in another treaty, particularly with the stipulation that the new provisions do not affect existing obligations. In this way, the new treaty would not interfere with existing mutual legal assistance treaties but nevertheless would ensure the basis for effective cooperation where none already exists. The inclusion of Annex 3 is therefore a welcome addition, creating a "mini" mutual legal assistance treaty without overriding more detailed treaty obligations existing between States Parties.[111]

One of the more significant challenges with regard to inter-State cooperation has been with regard to evidence. The *Proposed Convention* takes a novel approach to the admissibility of foreign-obtained evidence with respect to the various forms

---

[107] UN Convention Against Transnational Organized Crime, *supra* note 50, art. 18(6); UN Convention Against Corruption, *supra* note 50, art. 46(6); UN Convention Against Illicit Traffic in Narcotic Drugs and Psychotropic Substances, *supra* note 50, art. 7(6). For a critique of mutual legal assistance treaties, see CarrieLyn Donigan Guymon, *International Legal Mechanisms for Combating Transnational Organized Crime: The Need for a Multilateral Convention*, 18 BERKELEY J. INT'L L. 53, 81–85 (2000); Paul Gully-Hart, *Loss of Time Through Formal and Procedural Requirements in International Co-operation*, in PRINCIPLES AND PROCEDURES FOR A NEW TRANSNATIONAL CRIMINAL LAW: DOCUMENTATION OF AN INTERNATIONAL WORKSHOP, FREIBURG, MAY 1991, at 248 (Albin Eser & Otto Logodny eds., 1992); Jimmy Gurulé, *The 1988 U.N. Convention Against Illicit Traffic in Narcotic Drugs and Psychotropic Substances – A Ten Year Perspective: Is International Cooperation Merely Illusory?*, 22 FORDHAM INT'L L.J. 74 (1998).
[108] May Interim Draft Convention, *supra* note 57, art. 11.
[109] UN Model Treaty on Mutual Legal Assistance, G.A. Res. 45/117, U.N. Doc. A/RES/45/117 (Dec. 14, 1990).
[110] *See* examples *supra* note 97.
[111] *Proposed Convention*, *supra* note 7, art. 13, Annex 3(C)(5).

of inter-State cooperation, including mutual legal assistance.[112] The *Proposed Convention* states:

> States Parties may, for purposes of the present Convention, recognize the validity of evidence obtained by another State Party even when the legal standards and procedure for obtaining such evidence do not conform to the same standards of a given State Party. Such non-conformity shall not be grounds for exclusion of evidence, provided that the evidence is deemed credible and that it is obtained in conformity with international standards of due process.[113]

This approach is in contrast to multilateral and bilateral treaties providing that the law of evidence to be applied is the law of the forum State. Recognizing the validity of evidence gathered by another State, even when the legal standards and procedures fail to conform with the requesting State's standards, may pose constitutional and other difficulties for State implementation. This approach would be particularly difficult for common law countries to implement.[114] In common law countries, the defense must be able to vigorously test the prosecution's evidence, because there exists "no independent fact-finder in charge of gathering evidence as in civil law systems and police may or may not operate with prosecutorial supervision."[115] The drafters may need to consider modification of this provision in order for it to be acceptable to States, because not even the European Union has adopted mutually admissible evidence.[116] Inclusion of a provision encouraging requested States to honor specific conditions on, for example, the gathering of evidence asked by the requesting State would assist in addressing the challenges of foreign-obtained evidence.

Finally, as with all forms of inter-State cooperation, mutual legal assistance raises concerns of individual rights. One issue is that mutual legal assistance treaties benefit governments, not individual defendants; individuals cannot make use of such treaties.[117] As Cherif Bassiouni has noted, "[g]overnments can make exclusive use of evidence they exchange between themselves and can, subject to their respective laws, deny access by the interested individuals to evidence that they have received from foreign governments, including exculpatory evidence when such individuals are accused of the commission of a crime."[118] Even though the

---

[112] "This paragraph shall apply to all aspects of the present Convention including, but not limited to: extradition, mutual legal assistance, transfer of criminal proceedings, enforcement of judicial orders, transfer and execution of foreign penal sentences, and recognition of foreign penal judgments." *Id.*, *supra* note 7, art. 11(2).
[113] *Id.*
[114] *See generally* Curt Markees, *The Difference in Concept Between Civil and Common Law Countries As To Judicial Assistance and Cooperation in Criminal Matters*, in II A TREATISE ON INTERNATIONAL CRIMINAL LAW 171, 173–76 (M. Cherif Bassiouni & Ved P. Nanda eds., 1973).
[115] van Sliedregt, *supra* note 72, at 4. *See generally* L. Song Richardson, *Due Process for the Global Crime Age: A Proposal*, 41 CORNELL INT'L L.J. 347 (2008).
[116] *See* van Sliedregt, *supra* note 72, at 3.
[117] *See generally* Bassiouni, *supra* note 47, at 9.
[118] *Id.*

Proposed Convention indicates more clearly than in previous drafts the understanding that only governmental or law enforcement authorities – not private individuals – may request assistance,[119] the *Proposed Convention* does seek to protect individual rights by ensuring that "[l]egal assistance shall be refused if the person who is the subject of the request is being tried for crimes against humanity or for another crime under the laws of the requested State which constitute one or more of the constituent acts listed in article 3(1), or if the person has already been tried for such crime or crimes and acquitted or convicted, and has fulfilled the penalty for said conviction."[120]

C. Transfer of Criminal Proceedings

To maximize the prospects for accountability for alleged perpetrators of crimes against humanity, it may be advantageous for a State to transfer criminal proceedings to another State. Such transfers are undertaken as "the transferee State has more significant contacts with the parties, and is therefore a *forum conveniens*,"[121] or, in contrast, when the transferring State is a *forum non conveniens*, or for public policy reasons to achieve the best interests of justice.[122] "Transfer of criminal proceedings is therefore a way of avoiding the prospects of impunity, facilitating the prosecution of multi-state complex crimes, resolving conflicts between states arising out of political considerations relating to a given case, and serving the interests of justice."[123]

No State is required to accept the transfer of proceedings unless a treaty and national legislation so mandate.[124] Although no bilateral treaties regulate this form of inter-State cooperation,[125] a regional instrument does exist – the 1972 European Convention on the Transfer of Criminal Proceedings in Criminal Matters.[126] This form of cooperation is also referenced in international criminal law treaties.[127]

The *Proposed Convention* avoids blockage of transfer due to lack of a treaty or national legislation by so stipulating.[128] It also provides various permissible reasons for transferring criminal proceedings in Annex 4.[129]

---

[119] *See* van Sliedregt, *supra* note 72, at 4. *See* Bassiouni, *supra* note 47, at 9.
[120] *Proposed Convention*, *supra* note 7, art. 13, Annex 3(I)(16).
[121] Bassiouni, *supra* note 47, at 12.
[122] *Id.*
[123] M. Cherif Bassiouni, *Introduction to Transfer of Criminal Proceedings*, in II INTERNATIONAL CRIMINAL LAW, *supra* note 8, at 515, 517.
[124] *Id.* at 515.
[125] Bassiouni, *supra* note 47, at 12.
[126] European Convention on the Transfer of Criminal Proceedings in Criminal Matters, May 15, 1972, E.T.S. No. 052, 865 U.N.T.S. 99.
[127] *See, e.g.*, UN Convention Against Transnational Organized Crime, *supra* note 50, art. 21; UN Convention Against Corruption, *supra* note 50, art. 47; UN Convention Against Illicit Traffic in Narcotic Drugs and Psychotropic Substances, *supra* note 50, art. 8.
[128] *Proposed Convention*, *supra* note 7, art. 14, Annex 4(1).
[129] *Id.* art. 14, Annex 4(2)-(3).

The question arises whether the drafters should include a provision explicitly stating that regional agreements on the transfer of criminal proceedings, such as the European Convention,[130] supersede obligations arising under a new convention on crimes against humanity.[131] The advantage to that approach is that such agreements provide much more detailed obligations, facilitating such transfers. This approach reflects that taken with regard to mutual legal assistance provisions found in treaties serving a broader goal.[132]

D. Enforcement of the Effects of States Parties' Penal Judgments

Historically States have not recognized (and most so continue) the penal judgments of other States, considering penal judgments to be an exercise of national sovereignty.[133] However, "based on the fictional distinction between recognizing the consequences of penal judgment and recognizing the penal judgment itself,"[134] States, based on foreign judgments, extradite persons, freeze and seize assets, and – as discussed below – execute foreign penal sentences.[135]

The *Proposed Convention* provides for recognition of foreign penal judgments in order to increase inter-State cooperation by "making the consequences of foreign penal judgments more widely applicable in other states' domestic legal proceedings."[136] The *Proposed Convention* does this by stipulating that recognition and enforcement are based on the Convention itself, requiring neither a bilateral treaty nor specific national legislation.[137] The *Proposed Convention* takes an approach similar to other criminal law treaties.[138] This is essential, as currently the only treaty specifically addressing this matter is the European Convention on the International Validity of Criminal Judgments.[139]

Of course such recognition need not and should not provide a blank check. Similar to provisions on extradition and mutual legal assistance, recognition should be contingent on, for example, respect for due process, satisfaction of double criminality, and consistency with the State's public policy.[140]

---

[130] European Convention on the Transfer of Criminal Proceedings in Criminal Matters, *supra* note 126.
[131] May Interim Draft Convention, *supra* note 57, art. 12 (commentary).
[132] See *supra* text accompanying note 107.
[133] Bassiouni, *supra* note 47, at 11.
[134] *Id.*
[135] *Id.*
[136] *Id.* at 12. *Proposed Convention, supra* note 7, art. 16, Annex 6.
[137] *Proposed Convention, supra* note 7, art. 16, Annex 6(1).
[138] See, *e.g.*, UN Convention Against Transnational Organized Crime, *supra* note 50, art. 16; UN Convention Against Corruption, *supra* note 50, art. 44; UN Convention Against Illicit Traffic in Narcotic Drugs and Psychotropic Substances, *supra* note 50, art. 6.
[139] European Convention on the International Validity of Criminal Judgments, May 28, 1970, E.T.S. No. 070, 973 U.N.T.S. 57. Bassiouni, *supra* note 47, at 11.
[140] Bassiouni, *supra* note 47, at 11. See exceptions provided for in the *Proposed Convention, supra* note 7, Annex 6(3) ("A State Party may, however, refuse to execute, enforce, give effect to, or rely on another State Party's penal judgments if the judgment in question was obtained by fraud or

E. Transfer of Convicted Persons for the Execution of Their Sentences

The objectives of transferring convicted persons for the execution of their sentences are twofold: rehabilitative and humanitarian. Returning sentenced persons to their home countries enhances their resocialization and brings them closer to their families.[141]

However, as discussed earlier, most States do not recognize, and thus do not enforce, the penal judgments of other States. Nevertheless, under the theory that execution of foreign sentences is merely the administrative execution of the consequences of a foreign penal judgment, not enforcement of the judgment itself,[142] States engage in such cooperation.

One of the main advantages of such cooperation is that if a State, otherwise hesitant or unwilling to extradite a person (particularly their own national) due to concerns about respect for his/her rights and/or treatment, may agree to do so contingent on the person being returned to the requested State to serve out his/her sentence if convicted.[143] In this way, humane treatment concerns can be addressed while also ensuring accountability.

Multilateral, regional, and bilateral treaties on this subject exist.[144] However, the *Proposed Convention* provides, in article 15 as supplemented by Annex 5, a basis for the transfer of a person convicted of crimes against humanity from one State Party to another, eliminating the need for any separate treaty or national legislation, thus facilitating the process.[145] This approach is more specific than other criminal law treaties that generally stipulate that States Parties may enter into such agreements.[146]

Transfers of convicted persons to another State for execution of their sentences occur relatively infrequently,[147] although this practice is gaining momentum lately.[148] The reticence may be in large part due to the predominant concern of transferring

---

duress or was issued on the basis of procedures that violate international standards of fairness, or are in conflict with domestic public policy.").

[141] Bassiouni, *supra* note 47, at 9. *See generally* M. Cherif Bassiouni, *United States Policies and Practices on the Execution of Foreign Sentences*, in II INTERNATIONAL CRIMINAL LAW, *supra* note 8, at 551.

[142] Bassiouni, *supra* note 47, at 10.

[143] Canada's Supreme Court ruled that extradition of Canadian citizens is permitted under the Charter of Rights and Freedom if, *inter alia*, the person convicted would be transferred back to Canada to serve his/her sentence. Plachta, *supra* note 13, at 138.

[144] *See* Mohamed Abdul-Aziz, *International Perspective on Transfer of Prisoners and Execution of Foreign Penal Judgments*, in II INTERNATIONAL CRIMINAL LAW, *supra* note 8, at 529, 537–44. For example, one of the main multilateral treaties is the European Convention on Transfer of Sentenced Persons, *opened for signature* Mar. 21, 1983, E.T.S. No. 112.

[145] *Proposed Convention*, *supra* note 7, art. 15, Annex 5(1).

[146] *See, e.g.*, UN Convention Against Transnational Organized Crime, *supra* note 50, art. 17; UN Convention Against Corruption, *supra* note 50, art. 45; UN Convention Against Illicit Traffic in Narcotic Drugs and Psychotropic Substances, *supra* note 50, art. 6(12).

[147] Bassiouni, *supra* note 47, at 11.

[148] Abdul-Aziz, *supra* note 144, at 529.

States that enforcing States will fail to carry out the sentence as ordered.[149] A concern of particular magnitude when dealing with crimes against humanity is that the enforcing State may assert application of its laws on commutation of sentences.[150] Given its objective to enhance enforcement, the *Proposed Convention* appropriately provides that: "Conditional release and other measures provided for in the transferred-to State shall be in accordance with its laws and applicable regulations. No pardon or other similar measure of clemency, however, shall be extended to the transferred person without the consent of the transferring State."[151]

Such a provision assuages some States' concerns, particularly when they transfer a convicted individual back to his/her *own* State for execution of his/her sentence. This provision contrasts with that in the UN Model Agreement on the Transfer of Foreign Prisoners,[152] permitting pardons and amnesties to be granted by both the sentencing and the administering State.[153] That this Model Agreement is general and concerns all crimes, explains such permissiveness; it does not specifically address the most serious of crimes, such as crimes against humanity.

III. CONCLUSION

Treaty provisions clearly establishing the mechanisms for inter-State enforcement remain essential for combating impunity with regard to crimes against humanity. The reality of treaty negotiations mandates practical and strategic proposals and may require having to accept less than ideal solutions. Nevertheless, if this new, specialized treaty on crimes against humanity is to meet the objectives set out by the Crimes Against Humanity Initiative, it must contain robust provisions on inter-State cooperation. Emphasis must be placed on re-enforcing enforcement provisions.

The previous versions of the *Proposed Convention* clearly recognized the importance of inter-State cooperation but required further development of these provisions in order to facilitate implementation. This indeed occurred as the drafters continued to elaborate on the text. Yet, when expediting and facilitating accountability through enforcement, safeguarding the rights of the accused must not be forgotten. In general, inter-State enforcement mechanisms center on respect for State sovereignty. Thus, although developing the various forms of inter-State cooperation remains crucial, protection of individual rights, not only State sovereignty, must be ensured.

---

[149] Bassiouni, *supra* note 47, at 11.
[150] *Id.*
[151] *Proposed Convention, supra* note 7, art. 15, Annex 5(3).
[152] Seventh United Nations Congress on the Prevention of Crime and the Treatment of Offenders, Milan, Aug. 26-Sept. 6, 1985, *Model Agreement on the Transfer of Foreign Prisoners and Recommendations for the Treatment of Foreign Prisoners, Note by the Secretariat*, provision 22, U.N. Doc. A/CONF.121/10 (Apr. 25, 1985) (endorsed by the General Assembly, G.A. Res. 40/32, U.N. Doc. A/RES/40/32 (Nov. 29, 1985)).
[153] Abdul-Aziz, *supra* note 144, at 535.

In conclusion, reference to an important proposal in the *Proposed Convention* must be made: the creation of a Voluntary Trust Fund.[154] Implementation of State obligations is central to success in the fight against impunity. Such a Fund, which provides States Parties with technical assistance and capacity building, can play a crucial role in ensuring that enforcement provisions adopted in the new treaty are effective in practice.

---

[154] *Proposed Convention, supra* note 7, art. 19(E)(14).

15

Why the World Needs an International Convention on Crimes Against Humanity

Gregory H. Stanton

Until the nineteenth century, the map of international law looked much like the world maps of the Middle Ages. Those who used such maps sailed into oceans filled with sea monsters, with whole continents missing, and others labeled *Terra Incognita*. Slavery was accepted. No woman could own property, much less vote. Torture was normal in criminal investigations, and felonies were punishable by death. Mankind lived "on a darkling plain swept with confused alarms of struggle and flight, where ignorant armies clash by night."[1]

The nineteenth century brought hope of human progress: the abolition of slavery in most of the world, the women's suffrage movement in Europe and America, and with the Red Cross, the beginning of humanitarian laws of war. But it also brought machine guns and colonial domination made more efficient by modern transportation and communication. The 1648 Treaty of Westphalia limited international law to relationships between States and still allowed States to conduct their "internal" or "domestic" affairs without hindrance.[2] States had licenses to hunt down their own citizens with impunity. With few exceptions, individuals were not the subjects of international law.

New monsters arose in the twentieth century. Nazi and Communist regimes murdered more people than all wars combined. Two World Wars threatened the very foundations of human civilization and opened the era of Total War, when distinctions between combatants and civilians dissolved. On August 6 and 9, 1945, nuclear attacks on Hiroshima and Nagasaki incinerated 200,000 civilian lives in just three days. The Cold War began an ice age in international relations kept cold by the threat of mutual nuclear annihilation. Colonial wars to hold onto empires and nationalist wars to break them up left a world filled with military dictators and warlords, where impunity reigned.

I. THE UNITED NATIONS AND THE HUMAN RIGHTS CONVENTIONS

Yet on top of the rubble of the twentieth century stood visionary leaders determined to impose world order under law. They created the United Nations, adopted the

---

[1] Matthew Arnold, *Dover Beach, in* NEW POEMS 112, 114 (1867), *available at* http://www.victorianweb.org/authors/arnold/writings/doverbeach.html.
[2] Treaty of Westphalia: Peace Treaty between the Holy Roman Emperor and the King of France and Their Respective Allies, Fr.-Holy Roman Empire, Oct. 24, 1648, 1 Consol. T.S. 198.

Genocide Convention, the Universal Declaration of Human Rights, and the human rights Covenants. They adopted conventions against war crimes, torture, slavery, apartheid, discrimination, and for the rights of women, children, and refugees.

The United Nations left the Westphalian paradigm in place because it is an organization of States, represented by governments, not an organization of nations or peoples. Many States are threatened by the claims of nations and peoples. It is little wonder that the United Nations is pro-State and anti-nation. As Leo Kuper, my mentor in genocide studies, observed in his classic book, *Genocide*, "the sovereign territorial state claims, as an integral part of its sovereignty, the right to commit genocide, or engage in genocidal massacres, against people under its rule, and the United Nations, for all practical purposes, defends this right."[3]

To enforce the human rights conventions, the States that constitute the United Nations were unwilling to create the international institutions to enforce them. They ignored one of the four crucial attributes of law.

The legal anthropologist Leo Pospíšil, who was my teacher at Yale Law School, wrote that for law to be law, it must have four attributes. He defined law as institutionalized social control:

1. made by decision of a legitimate authority,
2. intended to be applied universally to similar situations in the future,
3. that is obligatory, and
4. that is enforced by physical or cultural sanctions.[4]

Skeptics about the reality of international criminal law, such as John Bolton,[5] usually question whether there are any sanctions to enforce it. For many years, the only courts that could enforce the law of nations were national courts, and after 1922 (and then only for State versus State disputes), the Permanent Court of International Justice and its successor, the International Court of Justice in The Hague.

II. NUREMBERG AND TOKYO

The war crimes trials of the Young Turk triumvirate after World War I and the Nuremberg and Tokyo war crimes tribunals after World War II opened a new era in the enforcement of international criminal law. For the first time, international tribunals tried individuals for their crimes. And for the first time, in article 6(c) of the Nuremberg Charter, crimes that had before only been tried by individual States were called "crimes against humanity." They were "against humanity" because they are threats to the common dignity of the human race. They are universal crimes, made

---

[3] Leo Kuper, Genocide: Its Political Use in the Twentieth Century 161 (1981).
[4] Leo Pospíšil, Anthropology of Law: A Comparative Theory 95 (1974).
[5] Former U.S. Ambassador to the United Nations in the George W. Bush administration, former Assistant Secretary of State for International Organization Affairs in the George H.W. Bush administration.

universal not just by the laws of individual States but by the common conscience of mankind. They are *jus cogens*.

Legal positivists objected because they saw no place where such laws had been promulgated to warn those who might break them. They violated the principle of "legality." Constitutionalists like Senator Robert Taft objected because they were, he said, the application of *ex post facto* law.

The best answer was offered by Justice Jackson in his opening statement at the Nuremberg trials:

> It is true, of course, that we have no judicial precedent for the Charter. But International Law is more than a scholarly collection of abstract and immutable principles. It is an outgrowth of treaties and agreements between nations and of accepted customs.... International Law is not capable of development by the normal processes of legislation for there is no continuing international legislative authority. Innovations and revisions in International Law are brought about by the action of governments ....[6]

The Nuremberg Charter outlined the blueprint for the law of crimes against humanity, and the Nuremberg tribunal laid the foundations for the building of the international institutions to enforce that law. But Nuremberg left completion of the blueprints and construction of the rest of the cathedral for future generations.

III. THE GENOCIDE CONVENTION

The normative blueprints were drawn as the United Nations drafted international conventions. First and foremost, the International Convention on the Prevention and Punishment of the Crime of Genocide was adopted by the United Nations in 1948 and entered into force in 1951.[7] Its drafters considered genocide to be the ultimate crime against humanity because the intention of genocide is to eliminate an irreplaceable part of the human race – a national, ethnic, racial, or religious group.

Lemkin considered genocide to be the crime of crimes because it impoverishes every human being by eliminating part of the diversity that enriches the entire human race. Genocide is like extinction of a species. It reduces the creativity that results when cultures and peoples interact. It is no accident that the Enlightenment began in Northern Europe when people speaking different languages from many traditions could challenge the orthodoxies of the day. It is no accident that the greatest sources of the world's music have been where cultures meet – in Europe, America, Brazil, South Africa, the Congo.

---

[6] Statement of Justice Robert Jackson, Nov. 21, 1945, *in* 2 Trial of the Major War Criminals before the International Military Tribunal: Proceedings Volumes 147 (1947–1949), *available at* http://avalon.law.yale.edu/imt/11-21-45.asp.

[7] International Convention on the Prevention and Punishment of the Crime of Genocide, *adopted* Dec. 9, 1948, 78 U.N.T.S. 277.

Raphael Lemkin's original intent for the Convention is often lost in analysis of the *travaux* left by the drafters of the Convention. The Convention left out much that Lemkin originally proposed, including the many early warning signs of genocide included in his own definition of the crime, in which by "nation" he meant also an ethnicity, society, and polity:

> Generally speaking, genocide does not necessarily mean the immediate destruction of a nation, except when accomplished by mass killings of all members of a nation. It is intended rather to signify a coordinated plan of different actions aiming at the destruction of essential foundations of the life of national groups, with the aim of annihilating the groups themselves. The objectives of such a plan would be disintegration of the political and social institutions, of culture, language, national feelings, religion, and the economic existence of national groups, and the destruction of the personal security, liberty, health, dignity, and even the lives of the individuals belonging to such groups. Genocide is directed against the national group as an entity, and the actions involved are directed against individuals, not in their individual capacity, but as members of the national group.[8]

The international lawyers and diplomats who actually drafted the Genocide Convention fell short of Lemkin's definition and of Lemkin's dream. They narrowed the concept to omit cultural, political, and economic destruction of groups, and destruction of the personal security, liberty, health, and dignity of individuals belonging to those groups. So they eliminated the early stages of the genocidal process, significantly weakening the Convention as an instrument for prevention.

As I have outlined elsewhere, genocide develops in predictable, logical stages.[9] The eight stages of genocide are not linear, but each stage is logically necessary for subsequent stages. Every genocide that I have studied has included each of the stages, which are:

1. Classification – groups are defined as "us" versus "them."
2. Symbolization – the target group is named and identified by symbols, such as language and dress, sometimes even forced to wear symbols like the yellow star.
3. Dehumanization – the victim group is vilified as subhuman "rats," "cockroaches," "cancer" or "disease," or "filth," deserving eradication to purify the society.
4. Organization – hate groups form, train, and arm for killing.
5. Polarization – the hate groups drive moderates out of the political arena through assassination, imprisonment, and terror.

---

[8] Raphael Lemkin, Axis Rule in Occupied Europe: Laws of Occupation, Analysis of Government, Proposals for Redress 79 (1944).
[9] Gregory Stanton, *The Eight Stages of Genocide*, in The Genocide Studies Reader 127 (Samuel Totten & Paul Bartrop eds., 2009), available at http://www.genocidewatch.org/aboutgenocide/8stagesofgenocide.html.

6. Preparation – plans are made for a "final solution," militias are trained and mobilized, victims are driven into concentration camps or ghettos, trial massacres test the response of other states.
7. Extermination – mass killing begins and continues until it is stopped by force.
8. Denial – from the beginning, the perpetrators deny they are persecuting or killing the victims, and continue their denials for many years after the genocide.

Lemkin understood that the deprivations of fundamental human rights in the early stages of genocide – systematic discrimination and persecution – are early warning signs of the genocidal process. The relationship between the crime against humanity of persecution and the crime of genocide is direct, as the article 6(c) judgments at Nuremberg show. But this connection, so well understood by Lemkin, was omitted from the Genocide Convention.

The framers of the Genocide Convention were unable to establish new institutions to enforce it. Although they referred to an international court to try perpetrators, it was not established until the International Criminal Court came into being in 2002. They also established no international monitoring institution to prevent genocide.

The framers made article 1 of the convention so vague that States Parties merely "undertake to prevent and to punish" genocide, without defining their legal obligation to do so.[10] Although some claim that the decision of the International Court of Justice (ICJ) in *Bosnia and Herzegovina v. Serbia and Montenegro* declared a duty to prevent genocide, its decision restricted the duty to States with direct influence and means to prevent the genocide, as well as knowledge that the genocide would likely occur.[11]

The International Convention for the Prevention and Punishment of the Crime of Genocide was born without teeth to prevent genocide. Could the United States,

---

[10] Convention on the Prevention and Punishment of the Crime of Genocide art. 1, Dec. 9, 1948, 78 U.N.T.S. 277.

[11] Although the International Court of Justice, in *Bosnia and Herzegovina v. Serbia and Montenegro*, held that Serbia violated the duty to prevent genocide at Srebrenica, the duty to prevent remains so narrow that it only applies to those with direct influence over those who might commit genocide.

> In view of their undeniable influence and of the information, voicing serious concern, in their possession, the Yugoslav federal authorities should, in the view of the Court, have made the best efforts within their power to try and prevent the tragic events then taking shape, whose scale, though it could not have been foreseen with certainty, might at least have been surmised. The FRY leadership, and President Milošević above all, were fully aware of the climate of deep-seated hatred which reigned between the Bosnian Serbs and the Muslims in the Srebrenica region. Yet the Respondent has not shown that it took any initiative to prevent what happened, or any action on its part to avert the atrocities which were committed. It must therefore be concluded that the organs of the Respondent did nothing to prevent the Srebrenica massacres, claiming that they were powerless to do so, which hardly tallies with their known influence over the VRS. As indicated above, for a State to be held responsible for breaching its obligation of prevention, it does not need to be proven that the

or the United Kingdom, or France, for example, have been charged with failure to prevent the genocide in Rwanda, though each of them had the means, influence, and knowledge that the genocide was likely to occur? For that matter, could they have been brought to the ICJ for failure to prevent the genocidal massacre at Srebrenica, though there is now evidence that their intelligence services knew in advance the killings were coming?

It should be clear by now that the Genocide Convention has failed to stop genocide. Genocide Watch counts fifty-five genocides and politicides since World War II,[12] with a death toll of more than seventy million – more deaths than from all wars combined.

IV. THE AD HOC TRIBUNALS

On the punishment side, the picture is somewhat more hopeful. With the creation of the special international tribunals – the ICTY, the ICTR, the Special Court for Sierra Leone, and the tribunals for East Timor and Cambodia – the Genocide Convention has begun to cut some teeth. But they still bite only after a genocide is over.

The International Criminal Tribunal for the former Yugoslavia (ICTY) took Nuremberg's blueprint and updated it, but still left major structural flaws. Crimes against humanity still had to be connected to international conflict. No provisions in the UN Security Council resolution creating the ICTY called on UN member States to arrest the suspects. So the tribunal first had to determine whether there was an international conflict, and in its first years had almost no defendants arrested and detained for trial.

I drafted UN Resolution 955,[13] which created the International Criminal Tribunal for Rwanda (ICTR), and set forth its Statute. That Statute removed the nexus requirement to international conflict, and the tribunal's subject matter jurisdiction includes crimes committed by non-State actors in violation of Optional Protocol II and Common Article 3 of the Geneva Conventions. When State Department lawyers expressed misgivings because the United States is not a party to Optional Protocol II, I reminded them that the UN Security Council has the legitimate authority to adopt such a resolution whether or not the United States is a party to the Optional Protocol. Learning from the difficulty the ICTY was facing in arresting

> State concerned definitely had the power to prevent the genocide; it is sufficient that it had the means to do so and that it manifestly refrained from using them.
>
> Such is the case here. In view of the foregoing, the Court concludes that the Respondent violated its obligation to prevent the Srebrenica genocide in such a manner as to engage its international responsibility.
>
> Application of the Convention on the Prevention and Punishment of the Crime of Genocide (*Bosnia and Herzegovina v. Serbia and Montenegro*), Summary of the Judgment of 26 February 2007, ¶¶ 437–38 (Feb. 26, 2007), *available at* http://www.icj-cij.org/docket/files/91/13687.pdf.

[12] Genocide Watch, *Genocides, Politicides, and Other Mass Murder Since 1945, With Stages in 2008*, http://www.genocidewatch.org/aboutgenocide/genocidespoliticides.html.
[13] S.C. Res. 955, U.N. Doc. S/RES/955 (Nov. 8, 1994).

suspects, I also drafted UN Security Council Resolution 978,[14] urging UN member States to arrest and detain persons in their territory against whom there was sufficient evidence of participation in the Rwandan genocide, and to inform the ICTR of their arrest. The result was that most of the principal defendants were in custody within a year. Perhaps we have moved a step forward from the day when Justice Jackson said there is no continuing legislative authority to make international law.

The ICTR has built a much stronger jurisprudence of genocide than the ICTY, mainly because Rwanda so clearly suffered genocide. The ICTR's judgments have greatly strengthened the law of genocide. They have put the first sharp teeth into the Genocide Convention. The ICTR has resolved many issues, such as how to define a group (subjectively, from the point of view of the perpetrator),[15] whether mass rape is an act of genocide (it is),[16] and when hate speech is incitement to commit genocide.[17] Beginning with its path-breaking *Akayesu* judgment[18] and continuing through its far-reaching decision on incitement in the *Media* case (*Nahimana et al.*),[19] the ICTR has provided the legal basis for reclaiming much of what Lemkin lost to the Stalinists at the drafting of the Genocide Convention. The ICTR's judgments are not favored by scholars with a narrow view of the Genocide Convention,[20] but they are restoring Lemkin's original intent to the Convention.

---

[14] S.C. Res. 978, U.N. Doc. S/RES/978 (Feb. 27, 1995).

[15] *See* Prosecutor v. Kayishema & Ruzindana, Case No. ICTR 95-1-T, Judgment, ¶¶ 97–98 (May 21, 1999) [hereinafter *Kayishema and Ruzindana Trial Judgment*].

[16] Prosecutor v. Akayesu, Case No. ICTR-96-4-T, Judgment (Sept. 2, 1998), *available at* www.un.org/ictr/english/judgements/akayesu.html [hereinafter *Akayesu Trial Judgment*].

[17] *Akayesu Trial Judgment, supra* note 16, ¶ 516 ("The *mens rea* required for the crime of direct and public incitement to commit genocide lies in the intent to directly prompt or provoke another to commit genocide. It implies a desire on the part of the perpetrator to create by his actions a particular state of mind necessary to commit such a crime in the minds of the person(s) he is so engaging. That is to say that the person who is inciting to commit genocide must have himself the specific intent to commit genocide, namely, to destroy, in whole or in part, a national, ethnical, racial or religious group, as such.").

[18] *Akayesu Trial Judgment, supra* note 16.

[19] Prosecutor v. Nahimana et al., Case No. ICTR-99-52-T, Judgment & Sentence (Dec. 3, 2003). The *Nahimana* trial court's decision is especially important because it finally defines the distinction between hate speech and incitement to commit genocide. This issue had never before been resolved in international criminal law. Judge Pillay's brilliant opinion noted the importance of incitement in the planning and execution of genocide. Judge Pillay cited the careful planning and financing that Nahimana and his codefendants marshaled as heads of Radio Television Libre de Milles Collines, the infamous hate radio station that literally gave coordinates to killing squads. Ngeze's *Kangura*, the Hutu Power newspaper that helped create the culture of dehumanization and hatred crucial to the genocide, was found to be causally connected to whipping the Hutu militias into a killing frenzy. Barayagwiza's distribution of weapons and Ngeze's incitement by megaphone to the killers were also found to causally contribute to the genocide. Judge Pillay cut through the arguments on genocidal intent by citing the defendants' numerous public statements: "Let's exterminate them;" "Exterminate the cockroaches (Tutsis)." Judge Pillay noted that the *Streicher* case at Nuremberg did not require a direct effect to prove incitement, and noted that incitement to violent crime is not protected speech even in the most liberal countries, such as the United States.

[20] *See, e.g.*, Diane F. Orentlicher, *Criminalizing Hate Speech: A Comment on the ICTR's Judgment in* The Prosecutor v. Nahimana, et al., 13 Hum. Rights Br. 1 (2006).

Legally, the framers bound the definition of genocide in the strait-jacket of "specific or special intent" (*dolus specialis*) of German-Roman law, so that proving genocide becomes difficult after the fact and nearly impossible while genocide is being committed. Short of interception of written orders, the intent of the perpetrator is extremely hard to prove during the chaos and secrecy of war. As Melson and others have shown, most genocides occur *during* civil or international wars.[21] The fatal consequences of the special intent requirement have been evident in the refusal to name the killing in Rwanda and Darfur "genocide" until the killing is finished. While action was needed, lawyers argued interminably over whether the events constituted "genocide." Such "definitionalism" has rendered the Genocide Convention a playground for lawyers, but a killing field for victims.

Restrictive definitions of the special intent requirement by Judge Cassese and others on the ICTY (following Professor William Schabas's influential treatise[22]) prevented it from finding anyone guilty of genocide until the historic *Krstić* judgment of 2004.[23] Finally, in the *Krstić* trial judgment, the ICTY explicitly relied on the jurisprudence developed by the ICTR and found General Krstić guilty of genocide and conspiracy to commit genocide. In the trial court's outstanding legal analysis, it discussed the specific intent requirement in terms of the Genocide Convention's fundamental purpose evidenced in the Convention's *travaux*, and relied on the ICTR's *Akayesu*[24] and *Kayishema and Ruzendana*[25] judgments, where specific intent to commit genocide was held not to require a premeditated plan, not to require acts intended to destroy the whole group, and not to require direct participation by the defendants. But the stranglehold of the "special intent" doctrine was again applied by the *Krstić* Appeals Chamber, which effectively retried the case and overturned the Trial Chamber's findings of fact and the Trial Chamber's judgment, absolving Krstić of guilt for genocide but finding him guilty of aiding and abetting genocide. The Appeals Chamber explicitly referred to German law on "specific intent" in its ruling.[26]

V. THE INTERNATIONAL CRIMINAL COURT

Now we finally have an International Criminal Court. Luis Moreno-Ocampo has proven to be an aggressive prosecutor, and we can hope that the court will adopt the ICTR's jurisprudence of genocide, not the ICTY's. We already have one indicator: He has brought charges against three of the top leaders of the genocide and crimes against humanity in Darfur, including President Omar al-Bashir. He has

---

[21] ROBERT MELSON, REVOLUTION AND GENOCIDE (1992).
[22] WILLIAM SCHABAS, GENOCIDE IN INTERNATIONAL LAW (2000).
[23] Prosecutor v. Krstić, Case No. IT-98-33-A, Judgment (Apr. 19, 2004) [hereinafter *Krstić Appeal Judgment*].
[24] *Akayesu Trial Judgment*, supra note 16.
[25] *Kayishema and Ruzindana Trial Judgment*, supra note 15.
[26] *Krstić Appeal Judgment*, supra note 23, ¶ 141.

taken up the gauntlet thrown down by the UN Commission of Inquiry, which found that certain individuals may have committed genocide in Darfur, to be determined later by a court, but the Commission could not find genocidal intent by the government of Sudan.[27] The specific intent requirement imposed such high standards of proof that even after more than 100,000 violent deaths in Darfur and systematic bombing of Darfuri villages by the Sudanese Air Force, the International Commission of Inquiry on Darfur (the Cassese Commission) could not find specific intent by the Sudanese government to commit genocide in Darfur.[28] It should be apparent by now that the invocation of the specific intent requirement has emasculated the preventive muscle of the Genocide Convention.

The International Criminal Court (ICC) Prosecutor's initial failure to obtain an arrest warrant for genocide against al-Bashir from the ICC's Pre-Trial Chamber demonstrates the continuing limits of the Genocide Convention and the concomitant need for an International Convention on Crimes Against Humanity to deal with the precursors to genocide evident in murder, torture, mass rape, and other forms of persecution of a group.

The statute of the Extraordinary Chambers in the Courts of Cambodia (the Khmer Rouge Tribunal) also includes genocide, war crimes, and crimes against humanity in its jurisdiction, without the nexus requirement to conflict. I have personally been deeply involved in the twenty-eight-year campaign to establish the Khmer Rouge Tribunal, having founded the Cambodian Genocide Project in 1981 and written the first drafts of its internal rules of procedure. In that tribunal, the need for clear definition of crimes against humanity is especially important, because due to the restricted nature of the Genocide Convention, most of the crimes committed by the Khmer Rouge were against political and economic groups, and therefore do not fit the conventional definition of genocide.

Beside the Genocide Convention, several other international conventions have been especially important in defining crimes against humanity. The *Apartheid* convention[29] outlaws the most extreme forms of racial discrimination. However, it stops short of outlawing discrimination based on religion, nationality, and even ethnicity. The Convention Against Torture[30] comes closest to making a crime against humanity subject to universal jurisdiction, which must not be confused with extraterritorial reach for domestic law. Modern States have recently seemed reluctant to treat even piracy as a crime of universal jurisdiction, though it is often cited as the classic case of such a crime.

---

[27] Int'l Comm'n of Inquiry on Darfur, *Report of the International Commission of Inquiry on Darfur to the Secretary-General*, ¶ 520, U.N. Doc. S/2005/60 (Feb. 1, 2005). The Commission was chaired by Judge Cassese.

[28] Int'l Comm'n of Inquiry on Darfur, *Report to the Secretary-General* (Jan. 25, 2005), *available at* http://www.un.org/news/dh/sudan/com_inq_darfur.pdf.

[29] International Convention on the Suppression and Punishment of the Crime of Apartheid, Nov. 30, 1973, 1015 U.N.T.S. 243.

[30] Convention against Torture and Other Cruel, Inhuman or Degrading Treatment or Punishment, Dec. 10, 1984, 1465 U.N.T.S. 85.

The most important codification of Crimes Against Humanity is, of course, article 7 of the Rome Statute of the International Criminal Court[31] with its related Elements of Crimes.[32] The Rome Statute codifies crimes against humanity that are subject to its jurisdiction. But it has three major weaknesses.

1. The ICC Statute does not impose any direct obligation on States Parties to the ICC to outlaw these crimes under their own national law. Given the resource limitations of the ICC, the result is that although a few "big fish" may be prosecuted by the ICC if they are citizens of States Parties or commit their crimes in State-Parties to the ICC, the "small fry" may commit such crimes with impunity unless they are prosecuted by national courts. If the crimes have not been outlawed by national law, or national law is not enforced, they may literally get away with mass murder, mass rape, and the other crimes against humanity defined by the ICC Statute, because most will escape prosecution by the ICC.

The ICC will never be able to enforce the international law of crimes against humanity against most who violate it. It may try the worst offenders if they can be driven from power and brought before it. But the ICC was never meant to replace the national judicial systems of the world. It was meant to complement them. National courts will always be the primary place where international law is enforced. In doing so, they fulfill the function that Myres McDougal called "*le dédoublement fonctionel*," the double function of national courts to enforce both national and international law.

2. More than half of the people in the world are citizens of countries that are not States Parties to the ICC. They remain unprotected by the Rome Statute even with regard to the national leaders and warlords who might be prosecuted by the ICC. Unless the crimes against humanity defined by that Statute have been enacted into national law, they even remain unprotected by their own national law. The *Terra Incognita* and the open seas uncharted by international criminal law are still inhabited by monsters of the deep.

3. For crimes against humanity to become customary international criminal law, as the *Krstić* trial judgment held the crime of genocide has become,[33] they must be defined consistently in an international convention that is ratified by a large majority of the nation States of the world. An international convention would make that possible. Even States that do not wish to submit to the jurisdiction of the International Criminal Court could ratify such a convention, enact national laws against the crimes it defines, and by State practice render it *jus cogens*.

---

[31] *Rome Statute of the International Criminal Court*, art. 7, United Nations Diplomatic Conference of Plenipotentiaries on the Establishment of an International Criminal Court, July 17, 1998, U.N. Doc. A/CONF.183/9 (1998) [hereinafter *Rome Statute*].

[32] Preparatory Comm'n for the Int'l Criminal Court, *Finalized Draft Text of the Elements of Crimes*, 9, U.N. Doc. PCNICC/2000/1/Add.2 (Nov. 2, 2000).

[33] Prosecutor v. Krstić, Case No. IT-98-33-T, Judgment, ¶ 541 (Aug. 1, 2001).

VI. CRIMES AGAINST HUMANITY ARE RAMPANT TODAY

Crimes against humanity continue unabated around the world. Although the United Nations adopted the Torture Convention, torture remains widespread. Christopher J. Einolf's statistical analysis shows a decline in the use of torture after it was legally prohibited by European governments in the nineteenth century. But torture made a dramatic comeback in the twentieth century. Einholf argues that torture is most commonly used against people who are marginalized members of society, such as slaves, foreigners, prisoners of war, members of racial, ethnic, and religious outsider groups, and, in wartime, those suspected of treason. The twentieth century's increase in the number and severity of wars and the breakdown of the distinction between combatants and civilians have all caused torture to become more common.[34]

Rape remains a significant global problem. One out of three women worldwide has been raped or sexually assaulted.[35] A large number of victims are under the age of fifteen.[36] The rate of mass rape has reached such terrible proportions in Eastern Congo that World Vision reports that two-thirds of women in its relief camps have been raped,[37] and *The Journal of Humanitarian Relief* reports that same figure for villages all over the Eastern Congo.[38] One result of gang rape is fistula, which causes women to become sterile and incontinent, and to be shunned by their communities. Many victims of gang rape are children. If they survive the rapes, they often remain traumatized for life. The same hordes who committed the Rwandan genocide still roam the forests of Eastern Congo, raping and killing. They have been joined by the Congolese Army and dozens of militias. Lately, they have also been raping men.[39] The Senior Reproductive Health Adviser for the U.S. Agency for International Development and many other international aid workers have visited hospitals in the Congo where rape victims are treated. Women have described having rifles thrust up their vaginas, of being forced to watch while gangs raped their daughters and then slit their throats, of their babies bleeding to death after gang rapes. Rape is a global problem, not just a problem of poor countries. One in three women and thirteen percent of men in the United States will be sexually assaulted in their lifetimes.[40]

Forced deportation has left the world strewn with refugee and displaced persons camps. The UNHCR estimates that there are currently forty-two million people

---

[34] Christopher J. Einolf, *The Fall and Rise of Torture: A Comparative and Historical Analysis*, 25 Soc. Theory 101–21 (2007).
[35] George Mason Univ. Sexual Assault Servs., *Worldwide Sexual Assault Statistics 2005*, citing International Statistics, www.sexualassault.virginia.edu/statistics_international.htm.
[36] Stop Violence against Women, The Advocates for Human Rights, Prevalence of Sexual Assault, www.stopvaw.org/Prevalence_of_Sexual_Assault.html.
[37] World Vision, *Congo: Rape Disturbingly Common* (Nov. 2008), http://www.worldvision.org/news.nsf/news/congo-crisis-200811.
[38] Stefan Kirchner, *Hell on Earth – Systematic Rape in Eastern Congo*, J. Humanitarian Assistance, Aug. 6, 2007, *available at* http://jha.ac/2007/08/06/hell-on-earth-systematic-rape-in-eastern-congo/.
[39] Jeffrey Gettleman, *Symbol of Unhealed Congo: Male Rape Victims*, N.Y. Times, Aug. 5, 2009, at A1.
[40] The World Health Org., Sexual Violence Facts, www.who.int/violence_injury_prevention.

who have been uprooted from their homes.⁴¹ More than two million each have been displaced by the wars in Pakistan and Darfur, alone. In Darfur, the forcible transfer of the population from their villages, combined with attacks on them, has cost at least 300,000 lives, according to the UN Undersecretary for Humanitarian Affairs John Holmes, who said his estimate was a conservative figure.⁴²

The common element in most crimes against humanity is persecution. This is a return to Nuremberg, which tried genocide as a crime of persecution and murder. The Rome Statute of the ICC restores the criminality of persecution of groups excluded from protection by the Genocide Convention, including "any identifiable group or collectivity on political, racial, national, ethnic, cultural, religious, and gender … grounds."⁴³ It also defines "extermination" to include "the intentional infliction of conditions of life, inter alia the deprivation of access to food and medicine, calculated to bring about the destruction of part of the population."⁴⁴ Deliberate starvation of people or creation of artificial famines is thus finally and clearly made an international crime against humanity.

VII. WHY THE WORLD NEEDS AN INTERNATIONAL CONVENTION ON CRIMES AGAINST HUMANITY

If crimes against humanity continue to be so widespread, why should we expect an international convention on crimes against humanity to be any use in preventing and prosecuting them? Why would such a convention not meet the same fate as the Genocide Convention, almost never invoked for prevention, seldom enforced by prosecution? What practical use would such a convention be?

First, it would define the crimes universally. It would solidify the definitions, providing a strong counterforce against erosion and watering down of the definitions by advocates of "national security," "counterinsurgency," and the "war on terror," most recently seen in the contemptible redefinition of "torture" by Justice Department lawyers in the Bush administration. The progress of international criminal law has been through the development of emerging norms, formulated in treaties and conventions. These norms can then be enforced through the establishment of enforcement mechanisms.⁴⁵

Second, the convention would extend the reach of the rule of law on crimes against humanity beyond the ICC and international tribunals, and would implant uniform definitions of crimes against humanity into the laws of States around the

---

⁴¹ Tim Irwin, Office of the U.N. High Comm'r for Refugees, *UN Refugee Chief Cites Pressing Needs as Those Uprooted Tops 42 million*, June 16, 2009, http://www.unhcr.org/4a37c9076.html.

⁴² *Darfur deaths "could be 300,000,"* BBC NEWS, Apr. 23, 2008, http://news.bbc.co.uk/2/hi/africa/7361979.stm.

⁴³ *Rome Statute, supra* note 31, art. 7(1)(h).

⁴⁴ *Id.* art. 7 (2)(b).

⁴⁵ See M. Cherif Bassiouni, *Revisiting the Architecture of Crimes Against Humanity: Almost a Century in the Making with Ambiguities Remaining – The Need for a Specialized Convention*, in this volume.

world. Gradually, a global body of case law would develop, which would define crimes against humanity in many countries. Today, few countries have statutes outlawing crimes against humanity, though many of the crimes are covered by other parts of their criminal codes. To unify the law of crimes against humanity would have a similar effect to the unification of European law by the Napoleonic Code or of U.S. commercial law by the Uniform Commercial Code.

Third, an international convention would increase pressure on governments that commit crimes against humanity because they would be violating international law that will become *jus cogens*. The convention would develop into customary international law.

Fourth, an international convention, in conjunction with the ICC Statute, will provide a common body of law that will facilitate international technical assistance to train law enforcement officers to enforce it. Special academies could be established for such training, and it could become part of the police and legal training in police academies and law schools around the world.

Fifth, the convention will set forth provisions for interstate cooperation in enforcement, and by universalizing the law on crimes against humanity will facilitate extradition and international judicial assistance.

Sixth, the convention will provide a 'halfway house' for States that are not yet members of the ICC to enact the law on crimes against humanity into their domestic law.

VIII. THE COPERNICAN REVOLUTION IN INTERNATIONAL CRIMINAL LAW

A Copernican Revolution is underway in international criminal law. In the Westphalian universe, individual rights revolved around the State and were defined by States. States could literally get away with mass murder within their borders. In the world of the responsibility to protect, the responsibility of States revolves around universal human rights.

Today the Westphalian paradigm that permitted States to commit horrible crimes against their citizens has been stood on its head. The emerging norm of international law is "the responsibility to protect," building on the work of Dr. Frances Deng,[46] which redefines sovereignty as the duty of States to protect the rights of people in their territories and even beyond. It is the logical extension of the concept of popular sovereignty expressed in the American Declaration of Independence[47] and the French *Déclaration des droits de l'Homme et du citoyen*.[48]

---

[46] FRANCIS M. DENG ET AL., SOVEREIGNTY AS RESPONSIBILITY (1996).
[47] THE DECLARATION OF INDEPENDENCE (U.S. 1776), *available at* http://www.ushistory.org/Declaration/document/index.htm.
[48] Déclaration des droits de l'Homme et du citoyen (Fr. 1789), *available at* http://www.hrcr.org/docs/frenchdec.html.

Among the most visionary Copernicans who have led this revolution is Professor M. Cherif Bassiouni. Along with leaders like Bill Pace, Philippe Kirsch, and others, Professor Bassiouni has left us the lasting legacy of the International Criminal Court. In this project, we now meet to fulfill Professor Bassiouni's lifetime vision of an International Convention on Crimes Against Humanity. It will obligate all States Parties to pass laws against the crimes defined in it.

This project will contribute to completion of the blueprints. After further deliberations by the best minds in the world, the Convention can then be submitted to a process of adoption and ratification by governments of States.

When the first Gothic cathedrals were designed, skeptics said they could not be built – that their walls would crumble under their own weight. There was no reinforced concrete then and no steel beams had been invented to strengthen the structures. But medieval architects had studied the arches of the great mosques of Persia and Moorish Spain and knew the skeptics were wrong. Notre Dame de Chartres began to rise in 1194. And its walls did not fall. They reached to the heavens. Its windows allowed light to penetrate into the deepest recesses of the church, just as the Reformation and the Enlightenment soon did in the world of ideas. Hundreds of cathedrals were built all over Europe and the world. Their magnificence is still an inspiration to us today.

Law, like blueprints written on paper, must be built into the structures of human life. The nations of the world must enact the provisions of this International Convention into their national laws. Using national courts, the nave and the transept of the cathedral of international criminal law will be built, block by national block. And someday, after our lifetimes, great windows will light it, not with the color of human blood, but with the green of the grass, the blue of the sky, and the gold of the sun.

Washington University School of Law

Whitney R. Harris World Law Institute
Crimes Against Humanity Initiative

August 2010. Original: English

Proposed International Convention on the Prevention and Punishment of Crimes Against Humanity

Preamble

The States Parties to the present Convention,

Conscious that all people are united by common bonds and share certain common values,

Affirming their belief in the need to effectively protect human life and human dignity,

Reaffirming their commitment to the purposes and principles of the United Nations, outlined in its Charter, and to the universal human rights norms reflected in the Universal Declaration of Human Rights and other relevant international instruments,

Mindful of the millions of people, particularly women and children, who over the course of human history have been subjected to extermination, persecution, crimes of sexual violence, and other atrocities that have shocked the conscience of humanity,

Emphasizing their commitment to spare the world community and their respective societies the recurrence of atrocities, by preventing the commission of crimes against humanity, and prosecuting and punishing the perpetrators of such crimes,

Determined to put an end to impunity for the perpetrators of crimes against humanity by ensuring their fair and effective prosecution and punishment at the national and international levels,

Recognizing that fair and effective prosecution and punishment of the perpetrators of crimes against humanity necessitates good faith and effective international cooperation,

Recognizing that effective international cooperation is dependent upon the capacity of individual States Parties to fulfill their international obligations, and that ensuring the capacity of each State Party to fulfill its obligations to prevent and punish crimes against humanity is in the interest of all States Parties,

Recalling that it is the duty of every State to exercise its criminal jurisdiction over those responsible for international crimes, including crimes against humanity,

Recalling the contributions made by the statutes and jurisprudence of international, national, and other tribunals established pursuant to an international legal instrument, to the affirmation and development of the prevention and punishment of crimes against humanity,

Recalling that crimes against humanity constitute crimes under international law, which may give rise to the responsibility of States for internationally wrongful acts,

Recalling Article 7 and other relevant provisions of the Rome Statute of the International Criminal Court,

Declaring that in cases not covered by the present Convention or by other international agreements, the human person remains under the protection and authority of the principles of international law derived from established customs, from the laws of humanity, and from the dictates of the public conscience, and continues to enjoy the fundamental rights that are recognized by international law,

Have agreed as follows:

Explanatory Note

What follows are cross-references to other international instruments. For full commentary on the Convention and description of the choices made therein, see the Comprehensive History of the Proposed CAH Convention.

1. *The word "Punishment" tracks the Genocide Convention.*
2. *Preambular paragraphs 1, 4, 6 and 9 draw heavily from the Preamble to the Rome Statute of the International Criminal Court.*
3. *Preambular paragraph 3 draws upon the Preamble to the Enforced Disappearance Convention.*
4. *Preambular paragraphs 5, 6 and 7 include language specifically directed at both prevention and punishment.*
5. *Preambular paragraph 8 is intended to forcefully emphasize the importance of capacity building to ensuring the effective operation of the present Convention.*
6. *The reference in preambular paragraph 10 to "other tribunals established pursuant to an international legal instrument" includes mixed-model tribunals such as the Special Court for Sierra Leone.*
7. *Preambular paragraph 11 acknowledges that crimes against humanity may give rise to the responsibility of States for internationally wrongful acts. This does not mean that State responsibility necessarily attaches. See Article 1 and accompanying Explanatory Note.*
8. *Preambular paragraph 13 is inspired by the Martens Clause appearing in the Preamble to the Hague Convention of 1907 and by Article 10 of the Rome Statute.*

Contents

Article 1   *Nature of the Crime*
Article 2   *Object and Purposes of the Present Convention*
Article 3   *Definition of Crimes Against Humanity*
Article 4   *Individual Criminal Responsibility*
Article 5   *Responsibility of Commanders and Other Superiors*
Article 6   *Irrelevance of Official Capacity*
Article 7   *Non-applicability of Statute of Limitations*
Article 8   *Obligations of States Parties*
Article 9   *Aut Dedere Aut Judicare (Prosecute or Extradite)*
Article 10 *Jurisdiction*
Article 11 *Evidence*
Article 12 *Extradition*
Article 13 *Mutual Legal Assistance*
Article 14 *Transfer of Criminal Proceedings*
Article 15 *Transfer of Convicted Persons for the Execution of Their Sentences*
Article 16 *Enforcement of the Effects of States Parties' Penal Judgments*
Article 17 *Ne Bis in Idem*
Article 18 *Non-refoulement*
Article 19 *Institutional Mechanisms*
Article 20 *Federal States*
Article 21 *Signature, Ratification, Acceptance, Approval, or Accession*
Article 22 *Entry into Force*
Article 23 *Reservations*
Article 24 *Amendment*
Article 25 *Interpretation*
Article 26 *Dispute Settlement Between States Parties*
Article 27 *Authentic Texts*
Annex 1   *Use of Terms*
Annex 2   *Extradition*
    A. *Crimes Against Humanity as Extraditable Offenses*
    B. *Legal Basis for Extradition*
    C. *Modalities of Extradition*
    D. *Grounds for Refusal of Extradition*
    E. *Rule of Specialty*
    F. *Multiple Requests for Extradition*
Annex 3   *Mutual Legal Assistance*
    A. *Types of Mutual Legal Assistance*
    B. *Transmission of Information*
    C. *Obligations Under Other Applicable Treaties*
    D. *Transfer of Detained Persons*
    E. *Form of Requests for Mutual Legal Assistance*

    F. *Execution of Requests for Mutual Legal Assistance*
    G. *Witnesses*
    H. *Limited Use of Information*
    I. *Refusal of Requests for Mutual Legal Assistance*
Annex 4 *Transfer of Criminal Proceedings*
Annex 5 *Transfer of Convicted Persons for the Execution of Their Sentences*
Annex 6 *Enforcement of the Effects of States Parties' Penal Judgments*

Article 1
Nature of the Crime

Crimes against humanity, whether committed in time of armed conflict or in time of peace, constitute crimes under international law for which there is individual criminal responsibility. In addition, States may be held responsible for crimes against humanity pursuant to principles of State responsibility for internationally wrongful acts.

Explanatory Note

1. *States Parties to the present Convention who are also Parties to the Rome Statute are bound by their obligations under that Statute. The obligations arising under the present Convention are therefore compatible with the Rome Statute. In addition, the provisions of the present Convention regulate the bilateral relations between the States Parties to the Rome Statute. The present Convention also offers an opportunity for States that are not parties to the Rome Statute to regulate their bilateral relations with other States, whether Parties to the Rome Statute or not.*
2. *The prohibition against crimes against humanity exists under customary international law and this provision incorporates the customary international law development, which recognizes that crimes against humanity may be committed in time of armed conflict and in time of peace.*
3. *Article 1, like preambular paragraph 11, acknowledges that crimes against humanity may give rise to the responsibility of States for internationally wrongful acts should breaches of the present Convention be attributable to a State Party in accordance with the International Law Commission's Draft Articles on Responsibility of States for Internationally Wrongful Acts adopted in 2001.*
4. *Specific reference to State responsibility underscores the applicability of State responsibility principles to the present Convention.*

Article 2
Object and Purposes of the Present Convention

1. The States Parties to the present Convention undertake to prevent crimes against humanity and to investigate, prosecute, and punish those responsible for such crimes.
2. To these ends, each State Party agrees:
    (a) To cooperate, pursuant to the provisions of the present Convention, with other States Parties to prevent crimes against humanity;

(b) To investigate, prosecute and punish persons responsible for crimes against humanity fairly and effectively;
(c) To cooperate, pursuant to the provisions of the present Convention, with other States Parties, with the International Criminal Court if the State is a Party to the Rome Statute, and with other tribunals established pursuant to an international legal instrument having jurisdiction over crimes against humanity, in the fair and effective investigation, prosecution and punishment of persons responsible for crimes against humanity; and
(d) To assist other States Parties in fulfilling their obligations in accordance with Article 8 of the present Convention.

Explanatory Note

1. *This provision highlights the three core "pillars" of the present Convention: prevention, punishment, and effective capacity building to facilitate such prevention and punishment.*
2. *The reference in paragraph 2(c) to other international tribunals includes the ad hoc tribunals such as the International Criminal Tribunal for the former Yugoslavia and the International Criminal Tribunal for Rwanda, as well as mixed-model tribunals established pursuant to an international legal instrument, such as the Special Court for Sierra Leone, and the Extraordinary Chambers in the Courts of Cambodia. With regard to this provision's reference to a State Party cooperating with the International Criminal Court, it should be noted that States Parties to the Rome Statute may have such an obligation. States which are not Party to the Rome Statute have no such obligation absent a referral by the Security Council or voluntary acceptance of the Court's jurisdiction, but may cooperate with the International Criminal Court. This provision recognizes that such States may cooperate with the International Criminal Court, but does not impose an independent obligation to do so.*
3. *The reference in Article 2(d) to assisting "States Parties in fulfilling their obligations" includes the obligations in Article 8 to facilitate State capacity building.*

Article 3
Definition of Crimes Against Humanity

1. For the purpose of the present Convention, "crimes against humanity" means any of the following acts when committed as part of a widespread or systematic attack directed against any civilian population, with knowledge of the attack:
(a) Murder;
(b) Extermination;

(c) Enslavement;
(d) Deportation or forcible transfer of population;
(e) Imprisonment or other severe deprivation of physical liberty in violation of fundamental rules of international law;
(f) Torture;
(g) Rape, sexual slavery, enforced prostitution, forced pregnancy, enforced sterilization, or any other form of sexual violence of comparable gravity;
(h) Persecution against any identifiable group or collectivity on political, racial, national, ethnic, cultural, religious, gender as defined in paragraph 3, or other grounds that are universally recognized as impermissible under international law, in connection with any act referred to in this paragraph or in connection with acts of genocide or war crimes;
(i) Enforced disappearance of persons;
(j) The crime of apartheid;
(k) Other inhumane acts of a similar character intentionally causing great suffering, or serious injury to body or to mental or physical health.

2. For the purpose of paragraph 1:
   (a) "Attack directed against any civilian population" means a course of conduct involving the multiple commission of acts referred to in paragraph 1 against any civilian population, pursuant to or in furtherance of a State or organizational policy to commit such attack;
   (b) "Extermination" includes the intentional infliction of conditions of life, *inter alia* the deprivation of access to food and medicine, calculated to bring about the destruction of part of a population;
   (c) "Enslavement" means the exercise of any or all of the powers attaching to the right of ownership over a person and includes the exercise of such power in the course of trafficking in persons, in particular women and children;
   (d) "Deportation or forcible transfer of population" means forced displacement of the persons concerned by expulsion or other coercive acts from the area in which they are lawfully present, without grounds permitted under international law;
   (e) "Torture" means the intentional infliction of severe pain or suffering, whether physical or mental, upon a person in the custody or under the control of the accused; except that torture shall not include pain or suffering arising only from, inherent in or incidental to, lawful sanctions;
   (f) "Forced pregnancy" means the unlawful confinement of a woman forcibly made pregnant, with the intent of affecting the ethnic composition of any population or carrying out other grave violations of international law. This definition shall not in any way be interpreted as affecting national laws relating to pregnancy;

(g) "Persecution" means the intentional and severe deprivation of fundamental rights contrary to international law by reason of the identity of the group or collectivity;

(h) "The crime of apartheid" means inhumane acts of a character similar to those referred to in paragraph 1, committed in the context of an institutionalized regime of systematic oppression and domination by one racial group over any other racial group or groups and committed with the intention of maintaining that regime;

(i) "Enforced disappearance of persons" means the arrest, detention or abduction of persons by, or with the authorization, support or acquiescence of, a State or a political organization, followed by a refusal to acknowledge that deprivation of freedom or to give information on the fate or whereabouts of those persons, with the intention of removing them from the protection of the law for a prolonged period of time.

3. For the purposes of the present Convention, it is understood that the term "gender" refers to the two sexes, male and female, within the context of society. The term "gender" does not indicate any meaning different from the above.

Explanatory Note

1. The text of paragraphs 1 and 2 incorporates the definition contained in Article 7 of the Rome Statute, with two necessary modifications of language specific to the International Criminal Court in subparagraph 1(h), whereby the following language was used: "gender as defined in paragraph 3," and "or in connection with acts of genocide or war crimes."
2. No substantive changes to Article 7 of the Rome Statute have been made.
3. As used in paragraph 1(k) of the present Convention, "[o]ther inhumane acts of a similar character" could be interpreted, in keeping with Articles II(b) and II(c) of the Genocide Convention, as including acts which cause the same harmful results as the acts listed in subparagraphs (a) through (j).

Article 4
Individual Criminal Responsibility

1. A person who commits a crime against humanity shall be individually responsible and liable for punishment in accordance with the present Convention.
2. In accordance with the present Convention, a person shall be criminally responsible and liable for punishment for a crime against humanity if that person:
   (a) Commits such a crime, whether as an individual, jointly with another or through another person, regardless of whether that other person is criminally responsible;

(b) Orders, solicits or induces the commission of such a crime which in fact occurs or is attempted;
(c) For the purposes of facilitating the commission of such a crime, aids, abets or otherwise assists in its commission or its attempted commission, including providing the means for its commission;
(d) In any other way contributes to the commission or attempted commission of such a crime by a group of persons acting with a common purpose. Such contribution shall be intentional and shall either:
  (i) Be made with the aim of furthering the criminal activity or criminal purpose of the group, where such activity or purpose involves the commission of a crime against humanity; or
  (ii) Be made in the knowledge of the intention of the group to commit the crime;
(e) Directly and publicly incites others to commit crimes against humanity;
(f) Attempts to commit such a crime by taking action that commences its execution by means of a substantial step, but the crime does not occur because of circumstances independent of the person's intentions. However, a person who abandons the effort to commit the crime or otherwise prevents the completion of the crime shall not be liable for punishment under the present Convention for the attempt to commit that crime if that person completely and voluntarily gave up the criminal purpose.
3. No provision in the present Convention relating to individual criminal responsibility shall affect the responsibility of States under international law for internationally wrongful acts.

Explanatory Note

This provision draws upon Article 25 of the Rome Statute.

Article 5
Responsibility of Commanders and Other Superiors

In addition to other grounds of criminal responsibility under the present Convention for crimes within the jurisdiction of a court:

1. A military commander or person effectively acting as a military commander shall be criminally responsible for crimes within the jurisdiction of a court committed by forces under his or her effective command and control, or effective authority and control as the case may be, as a result of his or her failure to exercise control properly over such forces, whereas,
   (a) That military commander or person either knew or, owing to the circumstances at the time, should have known that the forces were committing or about to commit such crimes; and

(b) That military commander or person failed to take all necessary and reasonable measures within his or her power to prevent or repress their commission or to submit the matter to the competent authorities for investigation and prosecution.

2. With respect to superior and subordinate relationships not described in paragraph 1, a superior shall be criminally responsible for crimes within the jurisdiction of a court committed by subordinates under his or her effective authority and control, as a result of his or her failure to exercise control properly over such subordinates, where:
   (a) The superior either knew, or consciously disregarded information which clearly indicated, that the subordinates were committing or about to commit such crimes; and
   (b) The crimes concerned activities that were within the effective responsibility and control of the superior; and
   (c) The superior failed to take all necessary and reasonable measures within his or her power to prevent or repress their commission or to submit the matter to the competent authorities for investigation and prosecution.

Explanatory Note

This provision is from Article 28 of the Rome Statute.

Article 6
Irrelevance of Official Capacity

1. The present Convention shall apply equally to all persons without any distinction based on official capacity. In particular, official capacity as a Head of State or Government, a member of a Government or parliament, an elected representative or a government official shall in no case exempt a person from criminal responsibility under the present Convention, nor shall it, in and of itself, constitute a ground for reduction of sentence.
2. Immunities or special procedural rules which may attach to the official capacity of a person, whether under national or international law, shall not bar a court from exercising its jurisdiction over such a person.

Explanatory Note

1. This language draws heavily upon Article 27 of the Rome Statute. However, in paragraph 2 of this Article, "the Court" has been changed to "a court," meaning any duly constituted judicial institutions having jurisdiction.
2. Paragraph 2 draws upon the dissenting opinion of Judge Van den Wyngaert from the ICJ's judgment in the Case Concerning the Arrest

Warrant of 11 April 2000 (Democratic Republic of the Congo v. Belgium), Judgment of 14 February 2002, and supports a different and more expansive principle than Article 27(2) of the Rome Statute.

Article 7
Non-applicability of Statute of Limitations

Crimes against humanity as defined by the present Convention shall not be subject to any statute of limitations.

Explanatory Note

1. *This language draws upon Article 29 of the Rome Statute.*
2. *States Parties to the present Convention undertake to adopt, in accordance with their respective constitutional processes, any legislative or other measures necessary to ensure that statutory or other limitations shall not apply to the prosecution and punishment of crimes against humanity as defined in the present Convention and that, where they exist, such limitations shall be abolished.*

Article 8
Obligations of States Parties

1. Each State Party shall enact necessary legislation and other measures as required by its Constitution or legal system to give effect to the provisions of the present Convention and, in particular, to take effective legislative, administrative, judicial and other measures in accordance with the Charter of the United Nations to prevent and punish the commission of crimes against humanity in any territory under its jurisdiction or control.

A. Legislation and Penalties

2. Each State Party shall adopt such legislative and other measures as may be necessary to establish crimes against humanity as serious offenses under its criminal law, as well as its military law, and make such offenses punishable by appropriate penalties which take into account the grave nature of those offenses, the harm committed, and the individual circumstances of the offender. In addition, such a person may be barred from holding public rank or office, be it military or civilian, including elected office.
3. Each State Party shall adopt such legislative and other measures as may be necessary to ensure that a military commander or person effectively acting as a military commander shall be criminally responsible for crimes against humanity as set forth in Article 5, paragraph 1.

4. Each State Party shall adopt such legislative and other measures as may be necessary to ensure that, with respect to superior and subordinate relationships not described in paragraph 3, a superior shall be criminally responsible for crimes against humanity as set forth in Article 5, paragraph 2.
5. Each State Party shall adopt such legislative and other measures as may be necessary to ensure in its legal system that the victims of crimes against humanity have the right to equal and effective access to justice, and the right to adequate, effective and prompt reparation for harm suffered, including, where appropriate:
   (a) Restitution;
   (b) Compensation;
   (c) Rehabilitation;
   (d) Satisfaction, including restoration of reputation and dignity; and
   (e) Measures to ensure non-repetition.
   Each State Party shall ensure that, in the event of the death of a victim of crimes against humanity, his or her heirs shall be entitled to the same rights to equal and effective access to justice, and to adequate, effective and prompt reparation.
6. Each State Party shall adopt such legislative and other measures as may be necessary, consistent with its legal principles, to establish the liability of legal persons for participation in crimes against humanity. Subject to the legal principles of the State Party, the liability of legal persons may be criminal, civil or administrative. Such liability shall be without prejudice to the criminal liability of the natural persons who have committed the offense. Each State Party shall, in particular, develop administrative measures designed to provide reparation to victims, and to ensure that legal persons held liable in accordance with this article are subject to effective, proportionate and dissuasive criminal or non-criminal sanctions, including monetary sanctions.

B. Investigation and Prosecution

7. Upon receiving information that a person who has committed or who is alleged to have committed crimes against humanity may be present in its territory, the State Party concerned shall take such measures as may be necessary under its domestic law to investigate the facts contained in the information.
8. Upon being satisfied that the circumstances so warrant, the State Party in whose territory the person who has committed or who is alleged to have committed crimes against humanity is present shall take the necessary and appropriate measures under its domestic law so as to ensure that person's presence for the purpose of prosecution or extradition.
9. States Parties shall prosecute or extradite those charged with or suspected of committing crimes against humanity.
10. Each State Party shall ensure that any individual who alleges that he or she has been subjected to crimes against humanity in any part of the territory

under its jurisdiction has the right to complain to the competent legal authorities and to have his or her case promptly and impartially examined by the competent judicial authorities.
11. Each State Party shall take appropriate measures in accordance with its domestic legal system and within its means to provide effective protection from potential retaliation or intimidation for witnesses and experts who give testimony concerning crimes against humanity and, as appropriate, for their relatives and other persons close to them. Such measures may include, *inter alia*, without prejudice to the rights of the accused, including the right to due process:
    (a) Establishing procedures for the physical protection of such persons such as, to the extent necessary and feasible, relocating them and permitting, where appropriate, non-disclosure or limitations on the disclosure of information concerning the identity and whereabouts of such persons;
    (b) Providing evidentiary rules to permit witnesses and experts to give testimony in a manner that ensures the safety of such persons, such as permitting testimony to be given through the use of communications technology such as video or other adequate means.

C. Prevention

12. Each State Party shall endeavor to take measures in accordance with its domestic legal system to prevent crimes against humanity. Such measures include, but are not limited to, ensuring that any advocacy of national, racial, or religious hatred that constitutes incitement to discrimination, hostility, or violence shall be prohibited by law.
13. States Parties may call upon the competent organs of the United Nations to take such action in accordance with the Charter of the United Nations as they consider appropriate for the prevention and punishment of crimes against humanity.
14. States Parties may also call upon the competent organs of a regional organization to take such action in accordance with the Charter of the United Nations as they consider appropriate for the prevention and punishment of crimes against humanity.
15. States Parties shall develop educational and informational programs regarding the prohibition of crimes against humanity including the training of law enforcement officers, military personnel, or other relevant public officials in order to:
    (a) Prevent the involvement of such officials in crimes against humanity;
    (b) Emphasize the importance of prevention and investigations in relation to crimes against humanity;
16. Each State Party shall ensure that orders or instructions prescribing, authorizing, or encouraging crimes against humanity are prohibited. Each State Party shall guarantee that a person who refuses to obey such

an order will not be punished. Moreover, each State Party shall take the necessary measures to ensure that persons who have reason to believe that crimes against humanity have occurred or are planned to occur, and who report the matter to their superiors or to appropriate authorities or bodies vested with powers of review or remedy are not punished for such conduct.

D. Cooperation

17. States Parties shall cooperate with States or tribunals established pursuant to an international legal instrument having jurisdiction in the investigation, prosecution, and punishment of crimes against humanity.
18. States Parties shall afford one another the greatest measure of assistance and cooperation in the course of any investigation or prosecution of persons alleged to be responsible for crimes against humanity irrespective of whether there exist between said States Parties any treaties on extradition or mutual legal assistance.

E. Capacity Building

19. States Parties shall to the extent possible provide one another capacity building assistance on an individual basis or through the mechanisms outlined in Article 19.

Explanatory Note

1. *This provision draws upon similar language from other international criminal law conventions. Paragraph 1 of this provision provides that measures taken by States Parties to prevent and repress crimes against humanity must be in accordance with the Charter of the United Nations. It should also be understood, however, that the obligation to prevent crimes against humanity includes the obligation not to provide aid or assistance to facilitate the commission of crimes against humanity by another State. See ILC Draft Articles on Responsibility of States for Internationally Wrongful Acts, Article 16, commentary paragraph (9). See also the ICJ's judgment in the Application of the Convention on the Prevention and Punishment of the Crime of Genocide (Bosnia and Herzegovina v. Serbia and Montenegro), Judgment of 26 February 2007, paragraphs 425–38. This is consistent with Article 1 of the present Convention.*

2. *With regard to paragraph 2, it is understood that the obligations of States Parties apply to all institutions and organs of the State without exception including, inter alia, military courts and any other special proceedings. The language regarding penalties is drawn from Article 4(1) of the Torture Convention. The current provision acknowledges, however, that States Parties may have different*

obligations arising under regional human rights conventions, and earlier language requiring penalties to be no less severe than those applicable for the most serious crimes of a similar nature has been removed. With regard to barring individuals found responsible for crimes against humanity from holding public rank or office, the permissive "may" was included to avoid possible contradiction with the jurisprudence of the European Court of Human Rights. There is, however, language in Velásquez Rodríguez v. Honduras (Merits), Inter-Am. Ct. H.R., 29 July 1988, Ser. C, No. 4, to support the proposition that persons who abused power to commit crimes against humanity could be barred from holding public office.

3. *Paragraphs 3 and 4 require States Parties to enact legislation to ensure that military commanders and other superiors are criminally responsible for crimes against humanity committed by subordinates under their effective command and control, or effective authority and control as the case may be, as a result of the commander or superior's failure to exercise control over such subordinates.*

4. *Paragraph 5 draws upon the General Assembly's Resolution adopting Basic Principles and Guidelines on the Right to a Remedy and Reparation for Victims of Gross Violations of International Human Rights Law and Serious Violations of International Humanitarian Law, UN Doc. A/RES/60/147 (March 21, 2006).*

5. *In order to avoid impunity or de facto immunity for those persons who act collectively or within a legal structure, States Parties should enact legislation capable of reaching such entities. Paragraph 6 draws heavily upon Article 26 of the UN Convention Against Corruption to oblige States Parties to adopt appropriate legislation and develop administrative measures designed to provide reparation to victims.*

6. *Paragraph 7 is from Article 7(1) of the Terrorist Bombing Convention. It also covers persons who have committed crimes against humanity or alleged to have done so.*

7. *Paragraph 8 is from Article 7(2) of the Terrorist Bombing Convention.*

8. *Paragraph 9 recognizes the obligation of aut dedere aut judicare.*

9. *Paragraph 10 draws upon Article 13 of the Torture Convention but includes language clarifying that the State Party's obligation extends to "any part of the" territory under its jurisdiction.*

10. *Paragraph 11 draws upon Article 32 of the UN Convention Against Corruption.*

11. *The language of paragraph 12 is from Article 20 of the ICCPR.*

12. *Paragraph 13 is from Article VIII of the Genocide Convention. This is consistent with paragraph 1 of the present provision, which provides that any measures taken by States Parties to prevent and punish crimes against humanity must be in accordance with the Charter of the United Nations.*

13. The term competent used here means the appropriate body within the regional instrument and also those bodies acting within its constituent instrument.
14. Paragraphs 15 and 16 oblige States Parties to develop education and training sessions in order to give effect to the obligation to prevent crimes against humanity. These paragraphs draw heavily upon Article 23 of the Enforced Disappearance Convention.
15. The Summary of Recommendations of the Genocide Prevention Task Force Report sets forth specific policy measures for education and prevention, which cannot be incorporated into normative provisions of the present Convention. However, if the present Convention has a treaty body that recommends specific measures to States Parties, such a body may use these recommendations.
16. Recognizing that capacity building is one of the core functions of the present Convention, paragraph 19 provides that States Parties, to the extent possible, shall provide one another capacity building assistance. Providing capacity building technical assistance to States Parties is one of the mandated functions of the permanent Secretariat to be established pursuant to Article 19, paragraphs 10 and 11.
17. Although it defines the obligations of States Parties, this article makes no explicit reference to State responsibility. Both preambular paragraph 11 and Article 1 explicitly recognize that crimes against humanity are crimes under international law which may give rise to the responsibility of States for internationally wrongful acts.

Article 9
Aut Dedere Aut Judicare (Prosecute or Extradite)

1. Each State Party shall take necessary measures to establish its competence to exercise jurisdiction over crimes against humanity when the alleged offender is present in any territory under its jurisdiction, unless it extradites him or her to another State in accordance with its international obligations or surrenders him or her to the International Criminal Court, if it is a State Party to the Rome Statute, or to another international criminal tribunal whose jurisdiction it has recognized.
2. In the event that a State Party does not, for any reason not specified in the present Convention, prosecute a person suspected of committing crimes against humanity, it shall, pursuant to an appropriate request, either surrender such a person to another State willing to prosecute fairly and effectively, to the International Criminal Court, if it is a State Party to the Rome Statute, or to a competent international tribunal having jurisdiction over crimes against humanity.

Explanatory Note

1. Paragraph 1 draws upon Article 9(2) of the Enforced Disappearance Convention.
2. Paragraph 2 reflects the principle *aut dedere aut judicare*.
3. With regard to this provision's reference to a State Party surrendering an accused individual to the International Criminal Court, it should be noted that States Parties to the Rome Statute may have such an obligation. States which are not Party to the Rome Statute may have no such obligation, but may cooperate with the International Criminal Court. This provision recognizes that such States may cooperate with the International Criminal Court, but does not impose an independent obligation to do so.

Article 10
Jurisdiction

1. Persons alleged to be responsible for crimes against humanity shall be tried by a criminal court of the State Party, or by the International Criminal Court, or by an international tribunal having jurisdiction over crimes against humanity.
2. Each State Party shall take the necessary measures to establish its competence to exercise jurisdiction over persons alleged to be responsible for crimes against humanity:
    (a) When the offense is committed in any territory under its jurisdiction or onboard a ship or aircraft registered in that State or whenever a person is under the physical control of that State; or
    (b) When the person alleged to be responsible is one of its nationals; or
    (c) When the victim is one of its nationals and the State Party considers it appropriate.
3. Each State Party shall likewise take such measures as may be necessary to establish its competence to exercise jurisdiction over the offense of crimes against humanity when the alleged offender is present in any territory under its jurisdiction, unless it extradites or surrenders him or her to another State in accordance with its international obligations or surrenders him or her to an international criminal tribunal whose jurisdiction it has recognized.
4. The present Convention does not preclude the exercise of any other competent criminal jurisdiction compatible with international law and which is exercised in accordance with national law.
5. For purposes of cooperation, jurisdiction shall be deemed to exist whenever the person responsible for, or alleged to be responsible for, crimes against humanity is present in the State's territory or the State Party is in a position to exercise physical control over him or her.

Explanatory Note

1. It is understood that the reference in paragraph 1 to "an international tribunal having jurisdiction," is with respect to any State Party that shall have accepted the jurisdiction of such tribunal. This provision also recognizes the principle of complementarity embodied in the Rome Statute.
2. Paragraph 2 draws upon the language of Article 9(1) of the Enforced Disappearance Convention. This provision is intended to avoid litigation over the scope of territorial application.
3. Paragraph 3 draws upon Article 9(2) of the Enforced Disappearance Convention and Article 5(2) of the Torture Convention.
4. Paragraph 4 draws upon Article 9(3) of the Enforced Disappearance Convention.
5. Paragraph 5 is intended to ensure that there exists no jurisdictional gap in a State Party's capacity to exercise jurisdiction over a person who is responsible for, or is alleged to be responsible for, crimes against humanity, and would apply to persons transiting a State Party's territory even where the State Party is not in a position to exercise physical control over the person.

Article 11
Evidence

1. The rules of evidence required for prosecution shall be those in existence under the national laws of the State Party conducting the investigation, prosecution, or post-trial proceedings but shall in no way be less stringent than those that apply in cases of similar gravity under the law of said State Party.
2. States Parties may, for purposes of the present Convention, recognize the validity of evidence obtained by another State Party even when the legal standards and procedure for obtaining such evidence do not conform to the same standards of a given State Party. Such non-conformity shall not be grounds for exclusion of evidence, provided that the evidence is deemed credible and that it is obtained in conformity with international standards of due process. This paragraph shall apply to all aspects of the present Convention including, but not limited to: extradition, mutual legal assistance, transfer of criminal proceedings, enforcement of judicial orders, transfer and execution of foreign penal sentences, and recognition of foreign penal judgments.
3. In relation to the collection of evidence, States Parties shall endeavor to conform with international standards of due process.

Explanatory Note

1. Paragraph 1 recognizes that in multilateral and bilateral treaties the law of evidence that applies is the law of the forum State.
2. In connection with mutual legal assistance and as currently reflected in Article 13 and Annex 2, it is also possible for requesting States to ask that specific conditions be employed or procedures followed in the taking of evidence by the requested State. Paragraph 2 permits States to recognize the validity of evidence obtained by another State Party, even where the requested conditions or procedures are not followed, provided that the evidence is deemed credible and that it is obtained in conformity with international standards of due process, including the obligation under Article 15 of the Torture Convention, which would exclude any statement made as a result of torture.
3. Paragraph 3 obliges States to endeavor to conform to international standards of due process in the collection of evidence.

Article 12
Extradition

States Parties shall afford one another the greatest measure of assistance in connection with extradition requests made with respect to crimes against humanity in accordance with the provisions of Annex 2.

Explanatory Note

The obligation to extradite or prosecute persons responsible for, or alleged to be responsible for, crimes against humanity is found in Article 8, paragraph 9 and Article 9 of the present Convention. Applicable modalities are provided in Annex 2.

Article 13
Mutual Legal Assistance

States Parties shall afford one another the greatest measure of assistance in connection with investigations, prosecutions and judicial proceedings brought with respect to crimes against humanity in accordance with the provisions of Annex 3.

Explanatory Note

The modalities by which States Parties are obliged to afford one another mutual legal assistance are outlined in Annex 3, which is drawn from the mutual legal assistance provisions of Article 46 of the UN Convention Against Corruption.

Article 14
Transfer of Criminal Proceedings

States Parties having jurisdiction in a case involving crimes against humanity may engage in a transfer of criminal proceedings in accordance with Annex 4.

Explanatory Note

The modalities by which States Parties may engage in a transfer of criminal proceedings under the present Convention are contained in Annex 4, which is based on the European Transfer of Proceedings Convention and its Protocol.

Article 15
Transfer of Convicted Persons for the Execution of Their Sentences

States Parties may transfer to one another a person convicted of crimes against humanity in their respective legal systems for purposes of the execution of such convicted person's sentence in accordance with the provisions of Annex 5.

Explanatory Note

The modalities by which States Parties may transfer persons convicted of crimes against humanity for the execution of their sentences are outlined in Annex 5, which is based on the European Convention on the Transfer of Sentenced Persons as well as the Inter-American Criminal Sentences Convention.

Article 16
Enforcement of the Effects of States Parties' Penal Judgments

A State Party may recognize and enforce the effects of another State Party's penal judgments in accordance with the provisions of Annex 6.

Explanatory Note

This provision acknowledges that States may recognize and enforce the effects of another State Party's penal judgments. The modalities for such recognition and enforcement are found in Annex 6, which is based on the European Convention on the International Validity of Criminal Judgments.

Article 17
Ne Bis in Idem

A person effectively prosecuted for crimes against humanity and convicted or acquitted cannot be prosecuted by another State Party for the same crime based on the same or substantially same facts underlying the earlier prosecution.

Explanatory Note

1. *This provision recognizes the ne bis in idem principle, which is found in many international instruments, including Article 14(7) of the ICCPR, Article 20 of the Rome Statute, Article 10 of the ICTY Statute, and Article 9 of the ICTR Statute.*
2. *This provision recognizes that for the ne bis in idem principle to apply as a bar to a subsequent prosecution, the first prosecution must have been conducted "effectively." Pursuant to Annex 1(b), "effectively" means diligently, independently and impartially in a manner not designed to shield the person concerned from criminal responsibility for crimes against humanity and consistent with an intent to bring the person concerned to justice, bearing in mind respect for the principle of the presumption of innocence.*

Article 18
Non-refoulement

1. No State Party shall expel, return (*"refouler"*) or extradite a person to another State where there are substantial grounds for believing that such a person would be in danger of being subjected to crimes against humanity.
2. For the purpose of determining whether there are such grounds, the competent authorities shall take into account all relevant considerations including, where applicable, the existence in the State concerned of a consistent pattern of gross, flagrant or mass violations of human rights or of serious violations of international humanitarian law.

Explanatory Note

1. *This provision draws upon Article 16 of the Enforced Disappearance Convention, which is in turn drawn from Article 8 of the Enforced Disappearance Declaration. A similar obligation, specific to torture, is found in the Torture Convention.*

2. *Paragraph 1 also draws upon Article 3(1) of the Torture Convention.*
3. *The non-refoulement provision of the present Convention is limited to situations involving crimes against humanity because such crimes form the core subject matter of the present Convention. In this regard, the present Convention follows the approach of the Enforced Disappearance Convention and the Torture Convention.*

Article 19
Institutional Mechanisms

A. Conference of States Parties

1. A Conference of States Parties to the present Convention is hereby established to improve the capacity of and cooperation between States Parties to achieve the objectives set forth in the present Convention and to promote and review its implementation.
2. The Secretary-General of the United Nations shall convene the Conference of States Parties not later than one year following the entry into force of the present Convention. Thereafter, regular meetings of the Conference of States Parties shall be held every three years. With regard to the first convening of the Conference of States Parties by the Secretary-General of the United Nations, the Secretary-General shall provide the necessary secretariat services to the Conference of States Parties to the Convention. The secretariat provided by the Secretary-General of the United Nations shall:
    (a) Assist the Conference of States Parties in carrying out the activities set forth in this article and make arrangements and provide the necessary services for the sessions of the Conference of States Parties;
    (b) Upon request, assist States Parties in providing information to the Conference of States Parties as envisaged in paragraphs 5 and 6; and
    (c) Ensure the necessary coordination with the secretariats of relevant international and regional organizations.
3. Each State Party shall have one representative in the Conference who may be accompanied by alternates and advisers. The Conference of States Parties shall adopt rules of procedure and rules governing the functioning of the activities set forth in this article, including rules concerning the admission and participation of observers and the payment of expenses incurred in carrying out those activities.

B. Committee

4. For the purpose of achieving the objectives set forth in paragraph 1 of this article, the Conference of States Parties shall establish the "Committee Established Pursuant to the International Convention on the Prevention and Punishment of Crimes Against Humanity" (the Committee).

5. The Committee shall have ten members. The members of the Committee shall be experts in matters relevant to the present Convention who are designated by the States Parties and elected by the Conference of States Parties. The members of the Committee shall be elected for a term of four years. They shall be eligible for re-election once. However, the term of five of the members elected at the first election shall expire at the end of two years. Immediately after the first election, the names of these five members shall be chosen by lot in a manner designated by the Conference of States Parties.
6. The Committee shall establish its own rules of procedure and shall agree upon activities, procedures and methods of work to achieve the objectives set forth in paragraph 1, including:
   (a) Facilitating activities by and between States Parties under the present Convention;
   (b) Facilitating the exchange of information among States Parties on successful practices for preventing and punishing crimes against humanity;
   (c) Cooperating with relevant international and regional organizations and mechanisms and non-governmental organizations;
   (d) Making appropriate use of relevant information produced by other international and regional mechanisms for preventing and punishing crimes against humanity in order to avoid unnecessary duplication of work;
   (e) Making recommendations to improve the present Convention and its implementation;
   (f) Taking note of the technical assistance requirements of States Parties with regard to the implementation of the present Convention and recommending any action it may deem necessary in that respect;
   (g) Establishing financial rules and regulations for the functioning of the Committee and the Secretariat; and
   (h) Managing the Voluntary Trust Fund established by the States Parties pursuant to paragraph 14.
7. For the purpose of paragraph 6, the Committee shall acquire the necessary knowledge of the measures taken by States Parties in implementing the present Convention and the difficulties encountered by them in doing so through information provided by States Parties and through such supplemental review mechanisms as may be established by the Committee.
8. The Committee shall examine the most effective way of receiving and acting upon information, including, *inter alia*, information received from States Parties and from competent international organizations. Input received from relevant non-governmental organizations duly accredited in accordance with procedures to be decided upon by the Committee may also be considered. Each State Party shall provide the Committee with information on its programs, plans and practices to implement the present Convention, including:

(a) The adoption of national implementing legislation;
(b) The establishment of administrative mechanisms fulfilling the prevention requirements contained in the present Convention;
(c) Reports on data gathering regarding its obligations under the present Convention including, but not limited to, the number of allegations, investigations, prosecutions, convictions, extraditions and mutual legal assistance requests.

9. The information provided by the States Parties shall be considered by the Committee, which shall issue such comments, observations or recommendations as it may deem appropriate. The comments, observations or recommendations shall be communicated to the State Party concerned, which may respond to them on its own initiative or at the request of the Committee. The Committee may also request States Parties to provide additional information on the implementation of the present Convention.

10. The Committee shall establish a permanent Secretariat to facilitate its activities, procedures and methods of work to achieve the objectives set forth in paragraphs 1, 5, 6 and 7. The Committee may establish such other subsidiary bodies as may be necessary.

C. Secretariat

11. The Secretariat's functions shall be:
    (a) Providing technical assistance to States in the process of acceding to the present Convention;
    (b) Providing technical assistance, including appropriate capacity building assistance, to States Parties in fulfilling their obligations under the present Convention;
    (c) Disseminating information between States Parties;
    (d) Facilitating mutual legal assistance and other aspects of cooperation between States Parties, including facilitating cooperation in matters involving the appearance of witnesses and experts in judicial proceedings, and in effectively protecting such persons;
    (e) Receiving and compiling information from States Parties as required by the Committee; and
    (f) Ensuring the necessary coordination with the secretariats of relevant international and regional organizations.

12. The Secretariat shall be headquartered at _____.

D. Expenses

13. The expenses of the Conference of States Parties, the Committee, the Secretariat, and any other subsidiary bodies shall be provided from the following sources:

(a) Contributions of States Parties assessed in accordance with an agreed scale of assessment, based on the scale adopted by the United Nations for its regular budget and adjusted in accordance with the principles on which that scale is based;
(b) Funds contributed on a voluntary basis by governments, inter-governmental organizations, non-governmental organizations, private organizations, foundations, and individuals.

E. Voluntary Trust Fund

14. The States Parties shall establish a Voluntary Trust Fund managed by the Committee to provide States Parties with technical assistance and capacity building needed in support of efforts to carry out the obligations arising under the present Convention.

Explanatory Note

1. *This article draws heavily upon Articles 112, 116 and 117 of the Rome Statute, Articles 63 and 64 of the UN Convention Against Corruption, and Articles 26 and 29 of the Enforced Disappearance Convention.*
2. *Paragraph 2 of this provision will be subject to approval by the competent organs of the United Nations, including reimbursement by the States Parties to the United Nations for expenses incurred by the organization.*
3. *The experience of States Parties with this body and its functions will determine how it will evolve in the future and what role it will assume over and above the mandate mentioned in the Convention such as fact-finding for purposes of developing an early warning system.*
4. *With regard to paragraph 12, an appropriate Headquarters Agreement will need to be negotiated with the host country, subject to approval by the Conference of States Parties.*

Article 20
Federal States

The provisions of the present Convention shall apply to all parts of federal States without any limitations or exceptions.

Explanatory Note

This language is from Article 41 of the Enforced Disappearance Convention.

Article 21
Signature, Ratification, Acceptance, Approval, or Accession

1. The present Convention shall be open for signature by all States at _____ until _____.
2. The present Convention shall be subject to ratification, acceptance or approval by signatory States. Instruments of ratification, acceptance or approval shall be deposited with the Secretary-General of the United Nations.
3. The present Convention shall be open to accession by all States. Instruments of accession shall be deposited with the Secretary-General of the United Nations.

Explanatory Note

This article draws upon Article 125 of the Rome Statute.

Article 22
Entry into Force

1. The present Convention shall enter into force on the thirtieth (30th) day following the date of deposit of the twentieth (20th) instrument of ratification, acceptance, approval, or accession with the Secretary-General of the United Nations.
2. For each State ratifying, accepting, approving, or acceding to the present Convention after the deposit of the twentieth (20th) instrument of ratification, acceptance, approval, or accession, the Convention shall enter into force on the thirtieth (30th) day after the deposit by such State of its instrument of ratification, acceptance, approval, or accession.

Explanatory Note

Paragraphs 1 and 2 draw upon Article 126 of the Rome Statute.

Article 23
Reservations

No reservations may be made to the present Convention.

Explanatory Note

1. *This language is from Article 120 of the Rome Statute.*
2. *It is understood that national legislative systems vary and that these variances will apply to modalities of aut dedere aut judicare and*

that States may make declarations about their respective national legal systems and procedures. This applies particularly to Articles 9, 10, 11, 12, 13, 14, 15, and 16 of the present Convention.

Article 24
Amendment

1. Any State Party to the present Convention may propose amendments thereto. The text of any proposed amendment shall be submitted to the Secretary-General of the United Nations, who shall promptly circulate it to all States Parties.
2. No sooner than three months from the date of notification, the Conference of States Parties, at its next meeting, shall, by a majority of those present and voting, decide whether to take up the proposal. The Conference may deal with the proposal directly or convene a Review Conference if the issue involved so warrants.
3. The adoption of an amendment at a meeting of the Conference of States Parties or at a Review Conference on which consensus cannot be reached shall require a two-thirds majority of States Parties.
4. Amendments to the present Convention shall enter into force one year after instruments of ratification or acceptance have been deposited with the Secretary-General of the United Nations by two-thirds of the States Parties and shall be binding on those States Parties that have accepted them; other States Parties who have not accepted the amendments shall continue to be bound by the provisions of the present Convention and any earlier amendments that they have accepted.
5. The Secretary-General of the United Nations shall circulate to all States Parties any amendment adopted at a meeting of the Conference of States Parties or at a Review Conference.

Explanatory Note

This article draws heavily upon Article 121 of the Rome Statute.

Article 25
Interpretation

The terms of the present Convention shall also be interpreted in the light of internationally recognized human rights standards and norms.

Explanatory Note

It is self-evident that the customary international law of treaty interpretation applies (codified in the Vienna Convention on the Law of Treaties). This article is also intended to ensure that the terms of the present Convention are interpreted in accordance with the regional human rights obligations of States Parties under the European Convention on Human Rights, the American Convention on Human Rights, and the African Charter on Human and Peoples' Rights, as well as in accordance with specific obligations established by treaty bodies with respect to different human rights conventions.

Article 26
Dispute Settlement Between States Parties

Any dispute between two or more States Parties concerning the interpretation or application of the present Convention, including those relating to the responsibility of a State for alleged breaches thereof, that cannot be settled through negotiation shall, at the request of one of them, be submitted to arbitration. If within six months from the date of the request for arbitration the Parties are unable to agree on the organization of the arbitration, any one of those Parties may refer the dispute to the International Court of Justice for a final and binding decision by a request in conformity with the Statute of the Court.

Explanatory Note

This provision draws upon Article 30(1) of the Torture Convention, Article 42(1) of the Enforced Disappearance Convention, and Article IX of the Genocide Convention.

Article 27
Authentic Texts

The original of the present Convention, of which the Arabic, Chinese, English, French, Russian, and Spanish texts are equally authentic, shall be deposited with the Secretary-General of the United Nations, who shall send certified copies thereof to all States.

Explanatory Note

This language is from Article 128 of the Rome Statute.

Annex 1
Use of Terms

For the purposes of the present Convention:

(a) "Fair," "fairly" or "fairness" means in accordance with norms of due process recognized by international law, consistent with the minimum guarantees in criminal proceedings, as contained in the International Covenant on Civil and Political Rights;

(b) "Effective," "effectively" or "effectiveness" means diligently, independently and impartially in a manner not designed to shield the person concerned from criminal responsibility for crimes against humanity and consistent with an intent to bring the person concerned to justice, bearing in mind respect for the principle of the presumption of innocence;

(c) "Person" means a natural person or legal entity.

Explanatory Note

The definitions of "fair" and "effective" in paragraphs (a) and (b) are designed to ensure that States may not use sham investigations or legal proceedings to thwart their obligations to investigate, prosecute or extradite. The definition in paragraph (b) draws heavily upon the ne bis in idem principle articulated in Article 10 of the ICTY Statute and Article 20 of the Rome Statute.

Annex 2
Extradition

A. Crimes Against Humanity as Extraditable Offenses

1. Crimes against humanity shall be deemed to be included as an extraditable offense in any extradition treaty existing between States Parties before the entry into force of the present Convention.
2. States Parties undertake to include crimes against humanity as an extraditable offense in any extradition treaty subsequently to be concluded between them.

B. Legal Basis for Extradition

3. In the absence of relevant national legislation or other extradition relationship, States Parties shall consider the present Convention as the legal basis for extradition in order to fulfill their obligation to prosecute or extradite persons alleged to be responsible for crimes against humanity pursuant to Article 8, paragraph 9 and Article 9.

C. Modalities of Extradition

4. In the absence of relevant national legislation or other extradition relationship, States Parties may use all or some of the following modalities provided in this Annex.

D. Grounds for Refusal of Extradition

5. For the purposes of extradition between States Parties, crimes against humanity shall not be regarded as a political offense or as an offense connected with a political offense. Accordingly, a request for extradition for crimes against humanity may not be refused on this ground alone, nor shall extradition be barred by claims of official capacity subject to Article 6, paragraph 1.
6. It shall be grounds for denial of extradition that the person sought is being tried for crimes against humanity or for another crime under the laws of the requested State based on facts which constitute one or more of the constituent acts listed in Article 3, paragraph 1, or that the person sought has already been tried for such crime or crimes and acquitted or convicted, and has fulfilled the penalty for said conviction. It shall also be grounds for denial of extradition if the requested State Party ascertains that the person sought for extradition may be subjected to crimes against humanity in the requesting State as provided for in Article 18.
7. It shall be grounds for denial of extradition that the requested State has substantial grounds for believing that the request for extradition has been made for the purpose of prosecuting or punishing a person on account of that person's race, religion, nationality, ethnic origin, political opinions, sex

or status, or that the person's right to a fair and impartial trial may be prejudiced for any of those reasons.
8. It shall be grounds for denial of extradition that the judgment of the requesting State has been rendered *in absentia*, the convicted person has not had sufficient notice of the trial or the opportunity to arrange for his or her defense, and the person has not or will not have the opportunity to have the case retried in his or her presence.
9. It shall be grounds for denial of extradition that the person has not received or would not receive the minimum guarantees in criminal proceedings, as contained in Article 14 of the International Covenant on Civil and Political Rights.
10. Extradition may be refused if the offense of crimes against humanity carries a penalty not provided for in the requested State, unless the requesting State gives such assurance as the requested State considers sufficient that the penalty not provided for in the requested State will not be imposed or, if imposed, will not be carried out.

E. Rule of Specialty

11. No person extradited for crimes against humanity shall be tried in the requesting State for any other crime than that for which extradition was granted unless the requested State or person extradited so consents.

F. Multiple Requests for Extradition

12. In cases of multiple requests for extradition, the State Party in whose territory the person alleged to be responsible for crimes against humanity has been found may take into consideration the following factors in determining priority:
    (a) The territory where one or more of the constitutive acts considered part of the crime has taken place;
    (b) The nationality of the offender(s);
    (c) The nationality of the victim(s); and
    (d) The forum most likely to have the greater ability and effectiveness in carrying out the prosecution, and which provides greater fairness and impartiality.

Explanatory Note

1. *Paragraph 1 draws upon Article 13(2) of the Enforced Disappearance Convention.*
2. *Paragraph 2 draws upon Article 13(3) of the Enforced Disappearance Convention.*
3. *Paragraph 3 ensures that, in the absence of relevant national legislation or an existing bilateral or multilateral extradition relationship, the present Convention shall provide the legal basis upon which a*

State Party may fulfill its obligation to extradite or prosecute in accordance with Article 8, paragraph 9 and Article 9.

4. Paragraph 4 ensures that, in the absence of relevant national legislation or an existing bilateral or multilateral extradition relationship, the present Convention may define the modalities by which a State Party may fulfill its obligation to extradite or prosecute in accordance with Article 8, paragraph 9 and Article 9.

5. Paragraph 5 draws upon Article 13(1) of the Enforced Disappearance Convention with regard to political offenses. With regard to claims of official capacity, this paragraph is consistent with Article 6, paragraph 1 of the present Convention, which precludes any official capacity as an applicable defense.

6. With regard to paragraph 6, in order to uphold the substance of the principle ne bis in idem, it should not matter whether a State or a State Party has tried a person. In any event, the requested State will have to determine whether the prosecution was fair and effective.

7. Paragraph 7 draws upon Article 3(b) of the UN Model Treaty on Extradition.

8. Paragraph 8 draws upon Article 3(g) of the UN Model Treaty on Extradition.

9. Paragraph 9 is draws upon Article 3(f) of the UN Model Treaty on Extradition.

10. Paragraph 10 is similar to, but broader than, Article 4(d) of the UN Model Treaty on Extradition, and recognizes that States may have differing obligations with respect to regional human rights treaties.

11. Paragraphs 6 through 9 provide mandatory grounds for refusal of extradition, while paragraph 10 provides an optional ground for refusal. Potential additional optional grounds for refusal are provided in the UN Model Treaty on Extradition, Article 4.

Annex 3
Mutual Legal Assistance

1. Legal assistance between States Parties shall be afforded to the fullest extent possible under relevant laws, treaties, agreements, and arrangements of the requested State Party and may be afforded on the basis of the present Convention and without the need for reliance on a bilateral treaty or national legislation.

A. Types of Mutual Legal Assistance

2. Legal assistance to be afforded in accordance with this Annex may be requested for any of the following purposes:
   (a) Taking evidence or statements from persons;
   (b) Effecting service of judicial documents;
   (c) Executing searches and seizures, and freezing of assets;
   (d) Examining objects and sites;
   (e) Providing information, evidentiary items and expert evaluations;
   (f) Providing originals or certified copies of relevant documents and records, including government, bank, financial, corporate or business records;
   (g) Identifying or tracing proceeds of crime, property instrumentalities or other things for evidentiary purposes;
   (h) Facilitating the voluntary appearance of persons in the requesting State Party;
   (i) Any other type of assistance that is not contrary to the domestic law of the requested State Party.

B. Transmission of Information

3. Without prejudice to domestic law, the competent authorities of a State Party may, without prior request, transmit information relating to crimes against humanity to a competent authority in another State Party where they believe that such information could assist the authority in undertaking or successfully concluding inquiries and criminal proceedings or could result in a request formulated by the latter State Party pursuant to the present Convention.

4. The transmission of information pursuant to paragraph 3 of this Annex shall be without prejudice to inquiries and criminal proceedings in the State of the competent authorities providing the information. The competent authorities receiving the information shall comply with a request that said information remain confidential, even temporarily, or with restrictions on its use. However, this shall not prevent the receiving State Party from disclosing in its proceedings information that is exculpatory to an accused person. In such a case, the receiving State Party shall notify the transmitting State Party prior to the disclosure and, if so requested, consult with the transmitting State Party. If, in an exceptional case, advance notice is not

possible, the receiving State Party shall inform the transmitting State Party of the disclosure without delay.

C. Obligations Under Other Applicable Treaties

5. The provisions of this Annex shall not affect the obligations under any other treaty, bilateral or multilateral, that governs or will govern, in whole or in part, mutual legal assistance.

D. Transfer of Detained Persons

6. A person who is being detained or is serving a sentence in the territory of one State Party whose presence in another State Party is requested for purposes of identification, testimony or otherwise providing assistance in obtaining evidence for investigations, prosecutions or judicial proceedings in relation to crimes against humanity may be transferred if the following conditions are met:
   (a) The person freely gives his or her informed consent;
   (b) The competent authorities of both States Parties agree, subject to such conditions as those States Parties deem appropriate.

E. Form of Requests for Mutual Legal Assistance

7. Requests for legal assistance shall be made in writing or, where possible, by any means capable of producing a written record, in a language acceptable to the requested State Party, under conditions allowing that State Party to establish authenticity. The Secretary-General of the United Nations shall be notified of the language or languages acceptable to each State Party at the time it deposits its instrument of ratification, acceptance or approval of or accession to the present Convention. In urgent circumstances and where agreed by the States Parties, requests may be made orally but shall be confirmed in writing forthwith.

8. A request for legal assistance shall contain:
   (a) The identity of the authority making the request;
   (b) The subject matter and nature of the investigation, prosecution or judicial proceedings to which the request relates and the name and functions of the authority conducting the investigation, prosecution or judicial proceedings;
   (c) A summary of the relevant facts, except in relation to requests for the purpose of service of judicial documents;
   (d) A description of the assistance sought and details of any particular procedure that the requesting State Party wishes to be followed;
   (e) Where possible, the identity, location and nationality of any person concerned; and
   (f) The purpose for which the evidence, information or action is sought.

9. The requested State Party may request additional information when it appears necessary for the execution of the request in accordance with its domestic law or when it can facilitate such execution.

F. Execution of Requests for Mutual Legal Assistance

10. A request shall be executed in accordance with the domestic law of the requested State Party and, to the extent not contrary with the domestic law of the requested State Party and where possible, in accordance with the procedures specified in the request.

G. Witnesses

11. Wherever possible and consistent with fundamental principles of domestic law, when an individual is in the territory of a State Party and has to be heard as a witness or expert by the judicial authorities of another State Party, the first State Party may, at the request of the other, permit the hearing to take place by video conference if it is not possible or desirable for the individual in question to appear in person in the territory of the requesting State Party. States Parties may agree that the hearing shall be conducted by a judicial authority of the requesting State Party and attended by a judicial authority of the requested State Party.

H. Limited Use of Information

12. The requesting State Party shall not transmit or use information or evidence furnished by the requested State Party for investigations, prosecutions or judicial proceedings other than those stated in the request without the prior consent of the requested State Party. Nothing in this paragraph shall prevent the requesting State Party from disclosing in its proceedings information or evidence that is exculpatory to an accused person. In the latter case, the requesting State Party shall notify the requested State Party prior to the disclosure and, if so requested, consult with the requested State Party. If, in an exceptional case, advance notice is not possible, the requesting State Party shall inform the requested State Party of the disclosure without delay.

I. Refusal of Requests for Mutual Legal Assistance

13. States Parties shall not decline to render mutual legal assistance pursuant to this Annex on the ground of bank secrecy.
14. Legal assistance may be refused if the request is not made in conformity with the provisions of this Annex.
15. Legal assistance may not be refused based upon claims of official capacity subject to Article 6, paragraph 1, or that the crime was of a political nature.

16. Legal assistance shall be refused if the person who is the subject of the request is being tried for crimes against humanity or for another crime under the laws of the requested State based on facts which constitute one or more of the constituent acts listed in Article 3, paragraph 1, or if the person has already been tried for such crime or crimes and acquitted or convicted, and has fulfilled the penalty for said conviction. It shall also be grounds for refusal of mutual legal assistance if the requested State Party ascertains that the person who is the subject of the request may be subjected to crimes against humanity in the requesting State.

Explanatory Note

1. *Much of the text of this Annex draws upon the mutual legal assistance provisions of Article 46 of the UN Convention Against Corruption.*
2. *For additional modalities of effectuating mutual legal assistance, States Parties may look to model legislation such as the UN Model Treaty on Mutual Assistance in Criminal Matters or to the relevant conventions of regional bodies.*

Annex 4
Transfer of Criminal Proceedings

1. Whenever a State Party, having jurisdiction over a person charged with crimes against humanity, agrees with another State Party, also having jurisdiction pursuant to Article 10, to cede jurisdiction and to transfer the record of the proceedings undertaken to the requesting State Party, the transfer procedure shall be established by agreement between their respective competent authorities. Such a procedure shall be based on the present Convention and shall not require the existence of a bilateral treaty between the respective States Parties or national legislation.
2. A transfer may occur when it is in the best interest of justice, and when it enhances fair and effective prosecution.
3. A State Party may request another State Party to take over proceedings in any one or more of the following cases:
   (a) If the suspected person is ordinarily resident in the requested State;
   (b) If the suspected person is a national of the requested State or if that State is his or her State of origin;
   (c) If the suspected person is undergoing or is to undergo a sentence involving deprivation of liberty in the requested State;
   (d) If proceedings for the same or other offenses are being taken against the suspected person in the requested State;
   (e) If it considers that transfer of the proceedings is warranted in the interests of arriving at the truth and in particular that the most important items of evidence are located in the requested State;
   (f) If it considers that the enforcement in the requested State of a sentence, if one were passed, is likely to improve the prospects for the social rehabilitation of the person sentenced;
   (g) If it considers that the presence of the suspected person cannot be ensured at the hearing of proceedings in the requesting State and that his or her presence in person at the hearing of proceedings in the requested State can be ensured;
   (h) If it considers that it could not itself enforce a sentence if one were passed, even by having recourse to extradition, and that the requested State could do so.

Explanatory Note

1. *This provision draws upon the European Transfer of Proceedings Convention and includes in paragraph 3 the situations listed in Article 8 of that convention defining when States may make such transfer requests.*
2. *Grounds for refusal have not been included in light of the diversity of national legal systems.*

Annex 5
Transfer of Convicted Persons for the Execution of Their Sentences

1. States Parties may transfer to one another a person convicted of crimes against humanity in their respective legal systems for purposes of the execution of such convicted person's sentence on the basis of the present Convention and without the need for a bilateral treaty between the States Parties or national legislation.
2. The transfer shall require the consent of the transferring State Party, the transferred-to State Party, and the person to be transferred, who shall waive any rights to challenge his or her conviction in the transferring State, along with the agreement of the transferred-to State Party to execute the sentence as decided in the transferring State in accordance with its penal laws and applicable regulations.
3. Conditional release and other measures provided for in the transferred-to State shall be in accordance with its laws and applicable regulations. No pardon or other similar measure of clemency, however, shall be extended to the transferred person without the consent of the transferring State.

Explanatory Note

This provision draws upon the Convention on the Transfer of Sentenced Persons as well as the Inter-American Criminal Sentences Convention. States Parties may also wish to look to model legislation of relevant organizations, to regional directives, and to sub-regional agreements.

Annex 6
Enforcement of the Effects of States Parties' Penal Judgments

1. Recognition and enforcement of a State Party's penal judgment shall be based on the present Convention and shall not require a bilateral treaty between the respective States Parties, or national legislation, other than that which may be required under the Constitution or national law of each State Party to implement the present Convention.
2. Cooperation and assistance between States Parties, particularly with regards to giving effect to Annexes 3 through 6, and which, in accordance with the laws of a given State Party, are barred if predicated on a foreign penal judgment or which require a treaty or national legislation having for effect the recognition of a foreign penal judgment, shall instead rely on the present Convention with respect to the enforcement or reliance upon a foreign penal judgment.
3. A State Party may, however, refuse to execute, enforce, give effect to, or rely on another State Party's penal judgments if the judgment in question was obtained by fraud or duress, or was issued on the basis of procedures that violate international standards of due process, or are in conflict with domestic public policy.

Explanatory Note

This provision draws upon the European Convention on the International Validity of Criminal Judgments.

INTERNATIONAL CONVENTION ON THE PREVENTION AND PUNISHMENT OF CRIMES AGAINST HUMANITY

Table of Abbreviations and Instruments Cited in the Convention and Explanatory Notes

African Charter	African [Banjul] Charter on Human and People's Rights, 1982, 1520 U.N.T.S 217 (entry into force Oct. 21, 1986).
American Convention on Human Rights	American Convention on Human Rights, 1969, O.A.S.T.S. No. 36, 1144 UNTS 123 (entry into force July 18, 1978).
Apartheid Convention	International Convention on the Suppression and Punishment of the Crime of *Apartheid*, 1973, G.A. Res. 3068 (XXVIII) of Nov. 30, 1973, UN Doc. A/9030, 1015 U.N.T.S 243 (entry into force July 18, 1976).
CAH	Crime(s) Against Humanity.
Comprehensive History of the Proposed CAH Convention	Leila Nadya Sadat, *A Comprehensive History of the Proposed International Convention on the Prevention and Punishment of Crimes Against Humanity*, in FORGING A CONVENTION FOR CRIMES AGAINST HUMANITY (Cambridge Univ. Press, 2011). For the website of the Washington University School of Law Whitney R. Harris World Law Institute Crimes Against Humanity Initiative, see http://law.wustl.edu/crimesagainsthumanity/.
European Convention on the Transfer of Sentenced Persons	Convention on the Transfer of Sentenced Persons, 1983, Europ. T.S. No. 112, Strasbourg (Mar. 21, 1983) (entry into force July 1, 1985).
ECHR	European Convention for the Protection of Human Rights and Fundamental Freedoms, 1950, Europ. T.S. No. 5, 213 UNTS 222, Rome, (Sep. 4, 1950) (entry into force Sep. 3, 1953).
Enforced Disappearance Convention	International Convention on the Protection of All Persons from Enforced Disappearance, 2006, G.A. Res. 61/177, UN GAOR 61st Sess., Supp. No. 49, at 207, UN Doc. A/RES/61/177 (Dec. 20, 2006) (not yet in force).
Enforced Disappearance Declaration	Declaration on the Protection of All Persons from Enforced Disappearance, 1992, G.A. Res. 47/133, UN GAOR 47th Sess., Supp. No. 49, at 207, UN Doc. A/47/49 (1992).

European Convention on the International Validity of Criminal Judgments	European Convention on the International Validity of Criminal Judgments, 1970, Europ. T.S. No. 70, Criminal Judgments, The Hague, (May 28, 1970) (entry into force July 26, 1974).
European Evidence Warrant	Council Framework Decision on the European Evidence Warrant for the purpose of obtaining objects, documents and data for use in proceedings in criminal matters, 2008, O.J. (L 350) 72, Council Framework Decision 2008/978/JHA (entry into force Feb. 8, 2009).
European Mutual Assistance Convention	European Convention on Mutual Assistance in Criminal Matters, 1959, Europ. T.S. No. 30, Mutual Assistance in Criminal Matters, Strasbourg, (April 20, 1959) (entry into force 12 June 1962).
European Statutory Limitations Convention	European Convention on the Non-Applicability of Statutory Limitation to Crimes against Humanity and War Crimes, 1974, Europ. T.S. No. 82, Crimes against Humanity and War Crimes, Strasbourg (Jan. 25, 1974) (entry into force June 26, 2003).
European Transfer of Proceedings Convention	European Convention on the Transfer of Proceedings in Criminal Matters, 1972, Europ. T.S. No. 73, Criminal Proceedings, Strasbourg, (May 15, 1972) (entry into force Mar. 30, 1978).
Genocide Convention	Convention on the Prevention and Punishment of the Crime of Genocide, 1951, G.A. Res. 260 (III), UN Doc. No. A/180, 78 UNTS 277 (Dec. 9, 1948) (entry into force Jan. 12, 1951).
Genocide Prevention Task Force Report	Madeleine Albright & William Cohen, Preventing Genocide: A Blueprint for U.S. Policymakers (2008), *available at*: http://www.usip.org/genocide_taskforce/report.html.
Hijacking Convention	Convention for the Suppression of Unlawful Seizure of Aircraft, 1970, (The Hague, Dec. 18, 1970), T.I.A.S. No. 7192, 22 U.S.T. 1641, 860 UNTS 105 (entry into force Oct. 14, 1971).
ICCPR	International Covenant on Civil and Political Rights, 1976, G.A. Res. 2200 (XXI), Supp. No. 16, UN Doc. A/6316 (Dec. 16, 1966) (entry into force Mar. 23, 1976).
ICJ	International Court of Justice

ICTR Statute	Statute of the International Criminal Tribunal for the Prosecution of Persons Responsible for Genocide and Other Serious Violations of International Humanitarian Law Committed in the Territory of Rwanda and Rwandan Citizens Responsible for Genocide and Other Such Violations Committed in the Territory of Neighbouring States, between 1 January 1994 and 31 December 1994, 1994, S.C.Res. 955, UN Doc. S/RES/955 (Nov. 8, 1994), as amended by S.C.Res. 1431, UN Doc. S/RES/1431 (Aug. 14, 2002).
ICTY Statute	Statute of the International Criminal Tribunal for the Prosecution of Persons Responsible for Serious Violations of International Humanitarian Law Committed in the Territory of the Former Yugoslavia since 1991, UN Doc. S/25704 at 36, Annex (1993) & S/25704/Add.1 (1993), adopted by Security Council on May 25, 1993, UN Doc. S/RES/827 (1993).
ILC Draft Articles on the Responsibility of States for Internationally Wrongful Acts	Report of the International Law Commission on the work of its fifty-third session, 23 April – 1 June and 2 July – 10 August 2001, 2001, UN GAOR, 56th Sess., UN Doc. A/56/10 (2001).
Inter-American Criminal Sentences Convention	Inter-American Convention on Serving Criminal Sentences Abroad, 1993, O.A.S.T.S. No. 76 (June 9, 1993) (entry into force April 13, 1996).
Inter-American Extradition Convention	Inter-American Convention on Extradition, 1981, O.A.S.T.S. No. 60 (Feb. 25, 1981) (entry into force Mar. 28, 1992).
Inter-American Mutual Assistance Convention	Inter-American Convention on Mutual Assistance in Criminal Matters, 1992, O.A.S.T.S. No. 75 (May 23, 1992) (entry into force April 14, 1996).
Nuclear Terrorism Convention	International Convention for the Suppression of Acts of Nuclear Terrorism, 2005, G.A. Res. 59/290 (LIX), Annex, UN Doc. A/59/766 (April 13, 2005) (entry into force July 7, 2007).
Nürnberg Principles	Principles of International Law Recognized in the Charter of the Nürnberg Tribunal and in the Judgment of the Tribunal, 1950, Int'l Law Comm'n, delivered to the General Assembly, UN Doc. A/1316 (1950).

Rabat Declaration	Convention on Extradition and Mutual Legal Assistance in Counter-Terrorism, 2008, Annex to the letter dated 14 August 2008 from the Chargé d'affaires a.i. of the Permanent Mission of Morocco to the United Nations addressed to the Secretary-General. A/62/939 – S/2008/567 (08–47023) (not in force).
Rome Statute	Rome Statute of the International Criminal Court, 1998, 2187 UNTS 90 (entry into force July 1, 2002).
Statutory Limitations Convention	Convention on the Non-Applicability of Statutory Limitations to War Crimes and Crimes Against Humanity, 1970, G.A. Res. 2391 (XXIII) UN Doc. A/7218, 754 UNTS 73 (Nov. 26, 1968) (entry into force Nov. 11, 1970).
Terrorist Bombings Convention	International Convention for the Suppression of Terrorist Bombings, 1997, G.A. Res. 52/164, UN Doc. A/RES/52/164 (Jan. 12, 1998) (entry into force May 23, 2001).
Torture Convention	Convention against Torture and Other Cruel, Inhuman or Degrading Treatment or Punishment, 1987, G.A. Res. 39/46, Annex, UN GAOR, 39th Sess., UN Doc. A/39/51 (Dec. 10, 1984) (entry into force June 26, 1987).
UN Charter	Charter of the United Nations, 1945, 1 UNTS 16 (Oct. 24, 1945).
UN Model Assistance Treaty	United Nations Model Treaty on Mutual Assistance in Criminal Matters, 1990, G.A. Res. 45/117, UN Doc. A/RES/45/117 (Dec. 14, 1990).
UN Convention Against Corruption	United Nations Convention Against Corruption, 2003, G.A. Res. 58/4, UN Doc. A/58/422 (Oct. 31, 2003) (entry into force Dec. 14, 2005).
UN Convention Against Transnational Organized Crime	United Nations Convention Against Transnational Organized Crime, 2001, G.A. Res. 25/55, Annex I, UN GAOR, 55th Sess., Supp. No. 49, at 44, U.N. Doc. A/45/49 (Vol. I) (2001) (entry into force Sept. 29, 2003).
UN Model Extradition Treaty	United Nations Model Treaty on Extradition, 1990, G.A. Res. 45/116, Annex, UN Doc. A/RES/45/49 (Dec. 14, 1990).
World Summit Outcome Document	General Assembly Resolution 60/1: 2005 World Summit Outcome, 2005, G.A. Res. A/RES/60/1, UN Doc. A/RES/60/1 (Oct. 24, 2005).

Washington University School of Law

Whitney R. Harris World Law Institute
Initiative sur les crimes contre l'humanité

Août 2010. Original: anglais*

Proposition de Convention Internationale sur la Prévention et la Répression des crimes contre l'humanité

Préambule

Les États Parties à la présente Convention,

Conscients que tous les peuples sont unis par des liens étroits et qu'ils partagent certaines valeurs communes,

Affirmant leur conviction selon laquelle la vie humaine et la dignité humaine doivent être effectivement protégées,

Réaffirmant leur attachement aux buts et principes des Nations Unies, énoncés dans la Charte, et aux normes universelles des droits de l'homme reflétées dans la Déclaration universelle des droits de l'homme et les autres instruments internationaux pertinents,

Ayant à l'esprit les millions de personnes, en particulier des femmes et des enfants, qui, au cours de l'histoire de l'humanité, ont été soumis à l'extermination, à la persécution, à des violences sexuelles et à d'autres atrocités qui ont heurté profondément la conscience de l'humanité,

Soulignant leur engagement à épargner à la communauté internationale et à leurs peuples la répétition d'atrocités, en prévenant la commission de crimes contre l'humanité et en poursuivant et punissant les auteurs de tels crimes,

Déterminés à mettre un terme à l'impunité des auteurs de crimes contre l'humanité en s'assurant qu'ils soient équitablement et efficacement poursuivis et punis aux niveaux national et international,

Reconnaissant que les poursuites et la répression équitables et efficaces à l'encontre des auteurs de crimes contre l'humanité requièrent une coopération efficace et de bonne foi à l'échelle internationale,

Reconnaissant que l'efficacité de la coopération internationale repose sur la capacité des États Parties à remplir leurs obligations internationales, et qu'il est de l'intérêt

---

* The Crimes Against Humanity Initiative is grateful to Mélanie Deshaies, Lecturer in International Criminal Law and Laws of Armed Conflict at the University of Montreal and Former Associate Legal Officer at the ICTR/Y Appeals Chambers, for her invaluable work on the French translation of the Proposed Convention.

de tous les États Parties de s'assurer que chacun d'entre eux a la capacité de se conformer à ses obligations de prévenir et de réprimer les crimes contre l'humanité,

Rappelant qu'il est du devoir de chaque État de soumettre à sa juridiction pénale les responsables de crimes internationaux, y compris les crimes contre l'humanité,

Rappelant les contributions apportées par les autres statuts et la jurisprudence des tribunaux internationaux, nationaux et autres établis en vertu d'un instrument juridique international, dans l'affirmation et le développement de la prévention et de la répression des crimes contre l'humanité,

Rappelant que les crimes contre l'humanité constituent des crimes au regard du droit international qui peuvent engager la responsabilité des États pour fait internationalement illicite,

Rappelant l'article 7 et les autres dispositions pertinentes du Statut de Rome de la Cour pénale internationale,

Déclarant que, dans les cas non compris dans la présente Convention ou par d'autres accords internationaux, la personne humaine reste sous la sauvegarde et sous l'empire des principes du droit des gens, tels qu'ils résultent des usages établis, des lois de l'humanité et des exigences de la conscience publique, et qu'elle continue à jouir des droits fondamentaux qui sont reconnus par le droit international,

Sont convenus de ce qui suit:

Note explicative

Les notes qui suivent sont des renvois à d'autres instruments internationaux. Pour le commentaire complet relatif à la Convention et la description des choix reflétés dans celle-ci, consulter l'Historique général de la Proposition de Convention internationale sur la prévention et la répression des crimes contre l'humanité (« Comprehensive History of the Proposed CAH Convention »).

1. *Le terme « répression » est repris de la Convention sur le génocide.*
2. *Les paragraphes 1, 4, 6 et 9 du préambule s'appuient largement sur le préambule du Statut de Rome de la Cour pénale internationale.*
3. *Le paragraphe 3 du préambule s'appuie sur le préambule de la Convention sur les disparitions forcées.*
4. *Les paragraphes 5, 6 et 7 du préambule incluent des termes faisant directement référence à la fois à la prévention et à la répression.*
5. *Le paragraphe 8 du préambule vise à souligner avec force l'importance du renforcement des capacités pour assurer le fonctionnement efficace de la présente Convention.*
6. *La référence aux « autres tribunaux établis en vertu d'un instrument juridique international », qui apparaît au paragraphe 10 du préambule, inclut les tribunaux établis suivant le modèle de juridiction mixte tel que la Cour spéciale pour la Sierra Leone.*

7. *Le paragraphe 11 du préambule reconnaît que les crimes contre l'humanité peuvent engager la responsabilité des États pour fait internationalement illicite. Cela n'implique pas que la responsabilité des États soit nécessairement en cause. Voir l'article premier et sa note explicative.*
8. *Le paragraphe 13 du préambule s'inspire de la Clause de Martens qui apparaît dans le préambule de la Convention de La Haye de 1907, ainsi que de l'article 10 du Statut de Rome.*

TABLE DES MATIÈRES

Article 1   *Nature du crime*
Article 2   *Objet et buts de la présente Convention*
Article 3   *Définition de crimes contre l'humanité*
Article 4   *Responsabilité pénale individuelle*
Article 5   *Responsabilité des chefs militaires et autres supérieurs hiérarchiques*
Article 6   *Défaut de pertinence de la qualité officielle*
Article 7   *Imprescriptibilité*
Article 8   *Obligations des États Parties*
Article 9   *Aut dedere aut judicare (poursuivre ou extrader)*
Article 10   *Compétence*
Article 11   *Preuve*
Article 12   *Extradition*
Article 13   *Entraide judiciaire*
Article 14   *Transmission de procédures répressives*
Article 15   *Transfèrement de personnes condamnées aux fins de l'exécution de leur peine*
Article 16   *Exécution des jugements pénaux prononcés dans les États Parties*
Article 17   *Ne bis in idem*
Article 18   *Non-refoulement*
Article 19   *Mécanismes institutionnels*
Article 20   *États fédéraux*
Article 21   *Signature, ratification, acceptation, approbation ou adhésion*
Article 22   *Entrée en vigueur*
Article 23   *Réserves*
Article 24   *Amendement*
Article 25   *Interprétation*
Article 26   *Règlement des différends entre États Parties*
Article 27   *Textes authentiques*
Annexe 1   *Terminologie*
Annexe 2   *Extradition*
    A. *Crimes contre l'humanité en tant qu'infractions donnant lieu à l'extradition*
    B. *Base juridique pour l'extradition*
    C. *Modalités de l'extradition*
    D. *Motifs du refus d'une demande d'extradition*
    E. *Règle de la spécialité*
    F. *Demandes concurrentes d'extradition*
Annexe 3   *Entraide judiciaire*
    A. *Types d'entraide judiciaire*
    B. *Communication d'informations*
    C. *Obligations découlant d'autres traités applicables*

D. Transfèrement des personnes détenues
E. Forme des demandes d'entraide judiciaire
F. Exécution des demandes d'entraide judiciaire
G. Témoins
H. Utilisation restreinte des informations
I. Refus d'exécuter des demandes d'entraide judiciaire

Annexe 4   Transmission de procédures répressives
Annexe 5   Transfèrement de personnes condamnées aux fins de l'exécution de leur peine
Annexe 6   Exécution des jugements pénaux prononcés dans les États Parties

Article premier
Nature du crime

Les crimes contre l'humanité, qu'ils soient commis en temps de conflit armé ou en temps de paix, constituent des crimes du droit des gens pour lesquels la responsabilité pénale individuelle est engagée. De plus, les États peuvent être tenus responsables de crimes contre l'humanité en vertu des principes régissant la responsabilité des États pour fait internationalement illicite.

Note explicative

1. Les États Parties à la présente Convention qui sont également parties au Statut de Rome sont liés par les obligations qui découlent de ce Statut. Les obligations qui découlent de la présente Convention sont par conséquent compatibles avec le Statut de Rome. En outre, les dispositions de la présente Convention régissent les relations bilatérales entre les États Parties au Statut de Rome. La présente Convention offre aussi aux États qui ne sont pas parties au Statut de Rome l'opportunité de régir leurs relations bilatérales avec d'autres États, que ces derniers soient ou non parties au Statut de Rome.
2. L'interdiction des crimes contre l'humanité existe dans le droit international coutumier et cette disposition incorpore les développements de la coutume reconnaissant qu'un crime contre l'humanité peut être commis autant en temps de conflit armé qu'en temps de paix.
3. L'article premier, tout comme le paragraphe 11 du préambule, reconnaît que les crimes contre l'humanité peuvent engager la responsabilité des États pour fait internationalement illicite, à supposer que des violations de la présente Convention soient attribuables à un État Partie, conformément au Projet d'articles sur la Responsabilité de l'État pour fait internationalement illicite, adopté par la Commission du droit international en 2001.
4. La référence spécifique à la responsabilité de l'État fait ressortir l'applicabilité des principes régissant la responsabilité de l'État à la présente Convention.

Article 2
Objet et buts de la présente Convention

1. Les États Parties à la présente Convention s'engagent à prévenir les crimes contre l'humanité et à mener des enquêtes sur, à poursuivre et à punir les responsables de tels crimes.
2. À ces fins, chaque État Partie convient:

a) De coopérer, conformément aux dispositions de la présente Convention, avec les autres États Parties pour prévenir les crimes contre l'humanité;
b) De mener des enquêtes, ainsi que de poursuivre et de punir les personnes responsables de crimes contre l'humanité équitablement et efficacement;
c) De coopérer, conformément aux dispositions de la présente Convention, avec les autres États Parties, avec la Cour pénale internationale, si l'État est partie au Statut de Rome, et avec les autres tribunaux établis en application d'un instrument juridique international et ayant compétence à l'égard des crimes contre l'humanité, dans la conduite équitable et efficace d'enquêtes, de poursuites et l'imposition de sanctions aux personnes responsables de crimes contre l'humanité; et
d) D'aider les autres États Parties à s'acquitter de leurs obligations conformément à l'article 8 de la présente Convention.

Note explicative

1. *Cette disposition met en évidence les trois « piliers » centraux de la présente Convention, soit: la prévention, la répression et le renforcement efficace des capacités pour faciliter la prévention et la répression.*
2. *Au paragraphe 2 c), la référence aux autres tribunaux internationaux inclut les tribunaux ad hoc, tels que le Tribunal pénal international pour l'ex-Yougoslavie (TPIY) et le Tribunal pénal international pour le Rwanda (TPIR), de même que les tribunaux mixtes établis en application d'un instrument juridique international, comme la Cour spéciale pour la Sierra Leone, et les Chambres extraordinaires au sein des Tribunaux Cambodgiens. En ce qui concerne la référence dans cette disposition à un État Partie qui coopère avec la Cour pénale internationale, il apparaît utile de souligner que les États Parties au Statut de Rome peuvent avoir une telle obligation. Les États non parties au Statut de Rome ne sont pas tenus à une telle obligation, à moins d'un renvoi par le Conseil de sécurité ou de l'acceptation volontaire de la compétence de la Cour, mais ils disposent de la faculté de coopérer avec la Cour pénale internationale s'ils le souhaitent. Cette disposition reconnaît que ces États peuvent coopérer avec la Cour pénale internationale, mais elle n'impose pas une obligation indépendante à cet effet.*
3. *À l'article 2 d), la référence à l'assistance fournie aux États Parties pour les aider à « s'acquitter de leurs obligations » inclut les obligations énoncées à l'article 8 en matière de renforcement des capacités.*

Article 3
Définition de crimes contre l'humanité

1. Aux fins de la présente Convention, on entend par crime contre l'humanité l'un quelconque des actes ci-après lorsqu'il est commis dans le cadre d'une attaque généralisée ou systématique lancée contre toute population civile et en connaissance de cette attaque:
   a) Meurtre;
   b) Extermination;
   c) Réduction en esclavage;
   d) Déportation ou transfert forcé de population;
   e) Emprisonnement ou autre forme de privation grave de liberté physique en violation des dispositions fondamentales du droit international;
   f) Torture;
   g) Viol, esclavage sexuel, prostitution forcée, grossesse forcée, stérilisation forcée ou toute autre forme de violence sexuelle de gravité comparable;
   h) Persécution de tout groupe ou de toute collectivité identifiable pour des motifs d'ordre politique, racial, national, ethnique, culturel, religieux ou sexiste au sens du paragraphe 3, ou en fonction d'autres critères universellement reconnus comme inadmissibles en droit international, en corrélation avec tout acte visé dans le présent paragraphe ou en corrélation avec des actes de génocide ou des crimes de guerre;
   i) Disparitions forcées de personnes;
   j) Crime d'apartheid;
   k) Autres actes inhumains de caractère analogue causant intentionnellement de grandes souffrances ou des atteintes graves à l'intégrité physique ou à la santé physique ou mentale.
2. Aux fins du paragraphe 1:
   a) Par « attaque lancée contre une population civile », on entend le comportement qui consiste en la commission multiple d'actes visés au paragraphe 1 à l'encontre d'une population civile quelconque, en application ou dans la poursuite de la politique d'un État ou d'une organisation ayant pour but une telle attaque;
   b) Par « extermination », on entend notamment le fait d'imposer intentionnellement des conditions de vie, telles que la privation d'accès à la nourriture et aux médicaments, calculées pour entraîner la destruction d'une partie de la population;
   c) Par « réduction en esclavage », on entend le fait d'exercer sur une personne l'un quelconque ou l'ensemble des pouvoirs liés au droit de propriété, y compris dans le cadre de la traite des êtres humains, en particulier des femmes et des enfants;
   d) Par « déportation ou transfert forcé de population », on entend le fait de déplacer de force des personnes, en les expulsant ou par d'autres

moyens coercitifs, de la région où elles se trouvent légalement, sans motifs admis en droit international;

e) Par « torture », on entend le fait d'infliger intentionnellement une douleur ou des souffrances aiguës, physiques ou mentales, à une personne se trouvant sous sa garde ou sous son contrôle; l'acception de ce terme ne s'étend pas à la douleur ou aux souffrances résultant uniquement de sanctions légales, inhérentes à ces sanctions ou occasionnées par elles;

f) Par « grossesse forcée », on entend la détention illégale d'une femme mise enceinte de force, dans l'intention de modifier la composition ethnique d'une population ou de commettre d'autres violations graves du droit international. Cette définition ne peut en aucune manière s'interpréter comme ayant une incidence sur les lois nationales relatives à la grossesse;

g) Par « persécution », on entend le déni intentionnel et grave de droits fondamentaux en violation du droit international, pour des motifs liés à l'identité du groupe ou de la collectivité qui en fait l'objet;

h) Par « crime d'apartheid », on entend des actes inhumains analogues à ceux que vise le paragraphe 1, commis dans le cadre d'un régime institutionnalisé d'oppression systématique et de domination d'un groupe racial sur tout autre groupe racial ou tous autres groupes raciaux et dans l'intention de maintenir ce régime;

i) Par « disparitions forcées de personnes », on entend les cas où des personnes sont arrêtées, détenues ou enlevées par un État ou une organisation politique ou avec l'autorisation, l'appui ou l'assentiment de cet État ou de cette organisation, qui refuse ensuite d'admettre que ces personnes sont privées de liberté ou de révéler le sort qui leur est réservé ou l'endroit où elles se trouvent, dans l'intention de les soustraire à la protection de la loi pendant une période prolongée.

3. Aux fins de la présente Convention, le terme « sexe » s'entend de l'un et l'autre sexes, masculin et féminin, suivant le contexte de la société. Il n'implique aucun autre sens.

Note explicative

1. *Le texte des paragraphes 1 et 2 incorpore la définition prévue par l'article 7 du Statut de Rome, en apportant deux modifications à leur libellé rendues nécessaires par les termes se rapportant spécifiquement à la Cour pénale internationale au sous-paragraphe 1 h); ainsi, les expressions suivantes ont été utilisées: « sexe au sens du paragraphe 3 » et « en corrélation avec des actes de génocide ou des crimes de guerre ».*

2. Aucun changement substantiel n'a été apporté à l'article 7 du Statut de Rome.
3. Telle qu'utilisée dans le paragraphe 1 k) de la présente Convention, l'expression « [a]utres actes inhumains de caractère analogue » pourrait être interprétée, en lien avec les articles II b) et II c) de la Convention sur le génocide, comme incluant des actes qui causent les mêmes dommages que les actes énumérés dans les sous-paragraphes a) à j).

Article 4
Responsabilité pénale individuelle

1. Quiconque commet un crime contre l'humanité est individuellement responsable et peut être puni conformément à la présente Convention.
2. Conformément à la présente Convention, une personne est pénalement responsable et peut être punie pour un crime contre l'humanité si:
    a) Elle commet un tel crime, que ce soit individuellement, conjointement avec une autre personne ou par l'intermédiaire d'une autre personne, que cette autre personne soit ou non pénalement responsable;
    b) Elle ordonne, sollicite ou encourage la commission d'un tel crime, dès lors qu'il y a commission ou tentative de commission de ce crime;
    c) En vue de faciliter la commission d'un tel crime, elle apporte son aide, son concours ou toute autre forme d'assistance à la commission ou à la tentative de commission de ce crime, y compris en fournissant les moyens de cette commission;
    d) Elle contribue de toute autre manière à la commission ou à la tentative de commission d'un tel crime par un groupe de personnes agissant de concert. Cette contribution doit être intentionnelle et, selon le cas:
        i) Viser à faciliter l'activité criminelle ou le dessein criminel du groupe, si cette activité ou ce dessein comporte l'exécution d'un crime contre l'humanité; ou
        ii) Être faite en pleine connaissance de l'intention du groupe de commettre ce crime;
    e) Elle incite directement et publiquement autrui à commettre un crime contre l'humanité;
    f) Elle tente de commettre un tel crime par des actes qui, par leur caractère substantiel, constituent un commencement d'exécution mais sans que le crime soit accompli en raison de circonstances indépendantes de sa volonté. Toutefois, la personne qui abandonne l'effort tendant à commettre le crime ou en empêche de quelque autre façon l'achèvement ne peut être punie en vertu de la présente Convention pour sa tentative si elle a complètement et volontairement renoncé au dessein criminel.

3. Aucune disposition de la présente Convention relative à la responsabilité pénale des individus n'affecte la responsabilité des États en droit international pour fait internationalement illicite.

Note explicative

Cette disposition s'appuie sur l'article 25 du Statut de Rome.

Article 5
Responsabilité des chefs militaires et autres supérieurs hiérarchiques

Outre les autres motifs de responsabilité pénale au regard de la présente Convention pour des crimes relevant de la compétence d'un tribunal:

1. Un chef militaire ou une personne faisant effectivement fonction de chef militaire est pénalement responsable des crimes relevant de la compétence d'un tribunal commis par des forces placées sous son commandement et son contrôle effectifs, ou sous son autorité et son contrôles effectifs, selon le cas, lorsqu'il ou elle n'a pas exercé le contrôle qui convenait sur ces forces dans les cas où:
   a) Ce chef militaire ou cette personne savait, ou, en raison des circonstances, aurait dû savoir, que ces forces commettaient ou allaient commettre ces crimes; et
   b) Ce chef militaire ou cette personne n'a pas pris toutes les mesures nécessaires et raisonnables qui étaient en son pouvoir pour en empêcher ou en réprimer l'exécution ou pour en référer aux autorités compétentes aux fins d'enquête et de poursuites.
2. En ce qui concerne les relations entre supérieur hiérarchique et subordonnés non décrites au paragraphe 1, le supérieur hiérarchique est pénalement responsable des crimes relevant de la compétence d'un tribunal commis par des subordonnés placés sous son autorité et son contrôle effectifs, lorsqu'il ou elle n'a pas exercé le contrôle qui convenait sur ces subordonnés dans les cas où:
   a) Le supérieur hiérarchique savait que ces subordonnés commettaient ou allaient commettre ces crimes ou a délibérément négligé de tenir compte d'informations qui l'indiquaient clairement;
   b) Ces crimes étaient liés à des activités relevant de sa responsabilité et de son contrôle effectifs; et
   c) Le supérieur hiérarchique n'a pas pris toutes les mesures nécessaires et raisonnables qui étaient en son pouvoir pour en empêcher ou en réprimer l'exécution ou pour en référer aux autorités compétentes aux fins d'enquête et de poursuites.

Note explicative

Cette disposition vient de l'article 28 du Statut de Rome.

Article 6
Défaut de pertinence de la qualité officielle

1. La présente Convention s'applique à tous de manière égale, sans aucune distinction fondée sur la qualité officielle. En particulier, la qualité officielle de chef d'État ou de gouvernement, de membre d'un gouvernement ou d'un parlement, de représentant élu ou d'agent d'un État, n'exonère en aucun cas de la responsabilité pénale au regard de la présente Convention, pas plus qu'elle ne constitue en tant que telle un motif de réduction de la peine.
2. Les immunités ou règles de procédure spéciales qui peuvent s'attacher à la qualité officielle d'une personne, en vertu du droit interne ou du droit international, n'empêchent pas un tribunal d'exercer sa compétence à l'égard de cette personne.

Note explicative

1. *Cette disposition s'appuie largement sur l'article 27 du Statut de Rome. Toutefois, au paragraphe 2 de cette disposition, « la Cour » a été remplacée par « un tribunal », faisant référence à toute autorité judiciaire compétente dûment constituée.*
2. *Le paragraphe 2 s'inspire de l'opinion dissidente du Juge Van den Wyngaert dans la décision de la CIJ dans l'Affaire relative au mandat d'arrêt du 11 avril 2000 (République démocratique du Congo c. Belgique), Décision du 14 février 2002, et adhère à un principe différent et plus étendu que l'article 27 2) du Statut de Rome.*

Article 7
Imprescriptibilité

Les crimes contre l'humanité tels qu'ils sont définis par la présente Convention ne se prescrivent pas.

Note explicative

1. *Cette disposition s'appuie sur l'article 29 du Statut de Rome.*
2. *Les États Parties à la présente Convention s'engagent à prendre, conformément à leurs procédures constitutionnelles respectives, toutes les mesures législatives ou autres nécessaires pour assurer l'imprescriptibilité des crimes contre l'humanité tels qu'ils sont définis dans la présente*

Convention, tant en ce qui concerne les poursuites qu'en ce qui concerne la peine, et à assurer que là où des prescriptions existent en vertu de la loi ou autrement elles seront abolies.

Article 8
Obligations des États Parties

1. Chaque État Partie doit promulguer les mesures législatives et autres qui sont nécessaires, tel que l'exige sa constitution ou son système juridique, pour donner effet aux dispositions de la présente Convention et, en particulier, pour prendre des mesures efficaces de nature législative, administrative, judiciaire ou autre, en conformité avec la Charte des Nations Unies, pour prévenir et punir la commission de crimes contre l'humanité sur tout territoire soumis à sa compétence ou son contrôle.

A. Législation et peines

2. Chaque État Partie adopte les mesures législatives et autres qui sont nécessaires pour conférer le caractère d'infraction pénale grave, au regard de son droit pénal, ainsi que de son droit militaire, et rend ces infractions punissables par des peines appropriées qui tiennent compte de la nature grave de ces infractions, du dommage causé, et des circonstances individuelles propres au délinquant. En outre, une telle personne peut se voir interdire d'exercer une fonction ou une charge publique, qu'elle soit militaire ou civile, y compris une charge élective.

3. Chaque État Partie adopte les mesures législatives et autres qui sont nécessaires pour assurer qu'un chef militaire ou une personne faisant effectivement fonction de chef militaire sera responsable pénalement de crimes contre l'humanité comme le prévoit le paragraphe 1 de l'article 5.

4. Chaque État Partie adopte les mesures législatives et autres qui sont nécessaires pour assurer que, concernant les relations entre supérieur hiérarchique et subordonné non décrites au paragraphe 3, un supérieur sera responsable pénalement de crimes contre l'humanité comme le prévoit le paragraphe 2 de l'article 5.

5. Chaque État Partie adopte les mesures législatives et autres qui sont nécessaires pour assurer que, dans son système juridique, les victimes de crimes contre l'humanité ont un droit d'accès égalitaire et efficace à la justice, et un droit à une réparation adéquate, efficace et rapide du préjudice subi, comprenant, le cas échéant:
   a) La restitution;
   b) L'indemnisation;
   c) La réhabilitation;
   d) La satisfaction, y compris le rétablissement de la réputation et de la dignité de la victime; et
   e) Des mesures pour assurer la non-répétition.

Chaque État Partie assure que, dans le cas du décès d'une victime de crimes contre l'humanité, ses héritiers bénéficieront des mêmes droits à un accès égalitaire et efficace à la justice et à une réparation adéquate, efficace et rapide.

6. Chaque État Partie adopte les mesures législatives et autres qui sont nécessaires, conformément à ses principes juridiques, pour établir la responsabilité des personnes morales qui participent à des crimes contre l'humanité. Sous réserve des principes juridiques de l'État Partie, la responsabilité des personnes morales peut être pénale, civile ou administrative. Cette responsabilité est sans préjudice de la responsabilité pénale des personnes physiques qui ont commis les infractions. Chaque État Partie veille, en particulier, à développer des mesures administratives destinées à fournir une réparation aux victimes et assurer que les personnes morales tenues responsables conformément au présent article soient soumises à des sanctions efficaces, proportionnées et dissuasives, de nature ou non pénale, y compris des sanctions pécuniaires.

B. Enquêtes et poursuites

7. Lorsqu'il est informé que l'auteur ou l'auteur présumé de crimes contre l'humanité pourrait se trouver sur son territoire, l'État Partie concerné prend les mesures qui peuvent être nécessaires conformément à sa législation interne pour enquêter sur les faits portés à sa connaissance.
8. S'il estime que les circonstances le justifient, l'État Partie sur le territoire duquel se trouve l'auteur ou l'auteur présumé de crimes contre l'humanité prend les mesures nécessaires et appropriées en vertu de sa législation interne pour assurer la présence de cette personne aux fins de poursuite ou d'extradition.
9. Les États Parties doivent poursuivre ou extrader ceux qui sont accusés ou soupçonnés de commettre des crimes contre l'humanité.
10. Chaque État Partie assure à toute personne qui prétend avoir été soumise à des crimes contre l'humanité sur toute partie du territoire sous sa juridiction le droit de porter plainte devant les autorités légales compétentes et de faire examiner son cas promptement et impartialement par les autorités judiciaires compétentes.
11. Chaque État Partie prend, conformément à son système juridique interne et dans la limite de ses moyens, des mesures appropriées pour assurer une protection efficace contre des actes éventuels de représailles ou d'intimidation aux témoins et aux experts qui déposent concernant des crimes contre l'humanité et, s'il y a lieu, à leurs parents et à d'autres personnes qui leur sont proches. Ces mesures peuvent consister, notamment, sans préjudice des droits de l'accusé, y compris du droit à une procédure régulière:
    a) À établir, pour la protection physique de ces personnes, des procédures visant notamment, selon les besoins et dans la mesure du possible, à leur fournir un nouveau domicile et à permettre, s'il y a lieu,

que les renseignements concernant leur identité et le lieu où elles se trouvent ne soient pas divulgués ou que leur divulgation soit limitée;

b) À prévoir des règles de preuve qui permettent aux témoins et experts de déposer d'une manière qui garantisse leur sécurité, notamment à les autoriser à déposer en recourant à des techniques de communication telles que les liaisons vidéo ou d'autres moyens adéquats.

C. Prévention

12. Chaque État Partie doit s'efforcer de prendre des mesures conformément à son système juridique interne pour prévenir les crimes contre l'humanité. Ces mesures incluent, sans s'y limiter, la garantie que tout appel à la haine nationale, raciale ou religieuse qui constitue une incitation à la discrimination, à l'hostilité ou à la violence est interdit par la loi.

13. Les États Parties peuvent saisir les organes compétents de l'Organisation des Nations Unies afin que ceux-ci prennent, conformément à la Charte des Nations Unies, les mesures qu'ils jugent appropriées pour la prévention et la répression des crimes contre l'humanité.

14. Les États Parties peuvent également saisir les organes compétents d'une organisation régionale afin que ceux-ci prennent, conformément à la Charte des Nations Unies, les mesures qu'ils jugent appropriées pour la prévention et la répression des crimes contre l'humanité.

15. Les États Parties développent des programmes d'enseignement et d'information concernant la prohibition des crimes contre l'humanité, y compris la formation du personnel chargé de l'application des lois, du personnel militaire ou des autres agents de la fonction publique afin de:

    a) Prévenir l'implication de ces agents dans des crimes contre l'humanité;
    b) Souligner l'importance de la prévention et des enquêtes en matière des crimes contre l'humanité.

16. Chaque État Partie veille à ce que les ordres ou instructions prescrivant, autorisant ou encourageant les crimes contre l'humanité soient interdits. Chaque État Partie garantit qu'une personne qui refuse d'obéir à un tel ordre ne sera pas punie. De plus, chaque État Partie prend les mesures nécessaires pour assurer que les personnes qui ont des raisons de croire que des crimes contre l'humanité sont survenus ou sont planifiés pour survenir, et qui signalent le cas à leurs supérieurs hiérarchiques ou aux autorités ou instances investies de pouvoirs d'examen ou de redressement, ne seront pas punies en raison d'une telle conduite.

D. Coopération

17. Les États Parties coopèrent avec les États ou les tribunaux établis en vertu d'un instrument juridique international ayant compétence en matière d'enquête, de poursuite et de répression des crimes contre l'humanité.

18. Les États Parties s'accordent entre eux la plus grande assistance et coopération possible au cours d'une enquête ou d'une poursuite à l'encontre de personnes soupçonnées d'être responsables de crimes contre l'humanité sans égard au fait qu'il existe ou non des traités d'extradition ou d'entraide judiciaire entre lesdits États Parties.

E. Renforcement des capacités

19. Les États Parties se prêtent, dans la mesure du possible, mutuellement assistance en matière de renforcement des capacités sur une base individuelle ou par l'intermédiaire des mécanismes décrits à l'article 19.

Note explicative

1. Cette disposition s'inspire d'autres conventions internationales en matière de droit pénal. Le paragraphe 1 de la présente disposition prévoit que toutes mesures prises par les États Parties pour prévenir et réprimer les crimes contre l'humanité doivent être conformes à la Charte des Nations Unies. Toutefois, il est également entendu que l'obligation de prévenir les crimes contre l'humanité inclut l'obligation de ne pas prêter aide ou assistance aux fins de faciliter la commission de crimes contre l'humanité par un autre État. Voir le Projet d'articles sur la responsabilité de l'État pour fait internationalement illicite de la CDI, article 16, paragraphe 9) du commentaire. Voir également l'arrêt de la Cour internationale de justice (CIJ) dans l'affaire relative à l'application de la Convention pour la prévention et la répression du crime de génocide (Bosnie-Herzégovine c. Serbie et Monténégro), arrêt du 26 février 2007, paragraphes 425–38. Ceci est compatible avec l'article premier de la présente Convention.

2. En ce qui concerne le paragraphe 2, il est entendu que les obligations incombant aux États Parties s'appliquent à tous les institutions et organes d'un État sans exception, y compris les tribunaux militaires et toute autre forme de procédures spéciales. Les termes choisis pour décrire les peines sont tirés de l'article 4 1) de la Convention contre la torture. La version actuelle de la disposition reconnaît, toutefois, que les États Parties peuvent être tenus à des obligations différentes émanant de conventions régionales sur les droits de l'homme, et la formulation antérieure, qui requérait des peines non moins contraignantes que celles qui sont applicables pour les crimes les plus sérieux de même nature, a été supprimée. En ce qui concerne l'interdiction imposée à des personnes trouvées responsables de crimes contre l'humanité d'occuper des fonctions ou des charges publiques, le terme permissif « peut » a été utilisé afin d'éviter toute contradiction possible avec la jurisprudence de la Cour européenne des droits de l'homme. Néanmoins, certains termes de l'arrêt sur le fond dans l'affaire Velázquez Rodríguez c. Honduras,

Inter-Am. Ct. H.R., 29 juillet 1988, Sér. C, No. 4, permettent d'étayer la proposition selon laquelle les personnes qui ont abusé de leur autorité pour commettre des crimes contre l'humanité pourraient se voir interdire l'accès à des charges publiques.

3. Les paragraphes 3 et 4 exigent des États Parties qu'ils adoptent une législation pour assurer que les chefs militaires et autres supérieurs hiérarchiques soient tenus pénalement responsables pour les crimes contre l'humanité commis par des subordonnés placés sous leur commandement et contrôle effectifs, ou sous leur autorité et contrôle effectifs, selon le cas, lorsqu'ils ou elles n'ont pas exercé un tel contrôle sur ces subordonnés.

4. Le paragraphe 5 s'appuie sur la Résolution de l'Assemblée générale adoptant les Principes fondamentaux et directives concernant le droit à un recours et à réparation des victimes de violations flagrantes du droit international des droits de l'homme et de violations graves du droit international humanitaire, Doc. NU A/RES/60/147 (21 mars 2006).

5. Afin d'empêcher que les personnes qui agissent de concert ou au sein d'une structure juridique bénéficient de l'impunité ou de l'immunité de facto, les États Parties devraient promulguer des lois dont la portée s'étendent à ces entités. Le paragraphe 6 s'appuie largement sur l'article 26 de la Convention de l'ONU contre la corruption pour obliger les États Parties à adopter une législation appropriée et élaborer des mesures administratives conçues de manière à assurer une réparation aux victimes.

6. Le paragraphe 7 vient de l'article 7 1) de la Convention sur les attentats terroristes à l'explosif. Il couvre également les personnes qui ont commis ou sont soupçonnées d'avoir commis des crimes contre l'humanité.

7. Le paragraphe 8 vient de l'article 7 2) de la Convention sur les attentats terroristes à l'explosif.

8. Le paragraphe 9 reconnaît l'obligation *aut dedere aut judicare*.

9. Le paragraphe 10 s'inspire de l'article 13 de la Convention contre la torture mais comprend une formulation clarifiant que la portée de l'obligation d'un État Partie s'étend à « toute partie » du territoire soumis à sa compétence.

10. Le paragraphe 11 s'appuie sur l'article 32 de la Convention de l'ONU contre la corruption.

11. Le paragraphe 12 vient de l'article 20 du Pacte international relatif aux droits civils et politiques (PIDCP).

12. Le paragraphe 13 vient de l'article VIII de la Convention sur le génocide. Ceci est compatible avec le paragraphe 1 de la présente disposition, qui prévoit que toutes mesures prises par les États Parties pour prévenir et réprimer les crimes contre l'humanité doivent être conformes à la Charte des Nations Unies.

13. Le terme « compétent » utilisé ici signifie l'organe approprié au sein de l'instrument régional, de même que les organes qui agissent dans le cadre de cet instrument constitutif.
14. Les paragraphes 15 et 16 obligent les États Parties à développer des cours éducatifs et de formation afin de donner effet à l'obligation de prévenir les crimes contre l'humanité. Ces paragraphes s'appuient largement sur l'article 23 de la Convention sur les disparitions forcées.
15. Le résumé des recommandations du Rapport de la Commission d'étude sur la prévention du génocide (« Genocide Prevention Task Force ») énonce des mesures politiques précises pour l'éducation et la prévention, qu'il n'est pas possible d'intégrer dans les dispositions normatives de la présente Convention. Toutefois, si la présente Convention dispose d'un organe de traité qui recommande des mesures spécifiques aux États Parties, ledit organe pourrait alors utiliser ces recommandations.
16. Reconnaissant que le renforcement des capacités est l'une des fonctions centrales de la présente Convention, le paragraphe 19 prévoit que les États Parties, dans la mesure du possible, se prêtent assistance l'un à l'autre dans le renforcement des capacités. La fourniture d'une assistance technique en matière de renforcement des capacités est l'une des fonctions prévues aux termes du mandat du Secrétariat permanent, qui sera établi en vertu des paragraphes 10 et 11 de l'article 19.
17. Bien qu'il définisse les obligations des États Parties, cet article ne fait pas explicitement référence à la responsabilité étatique. Le paragraphe 11 du préambule, ainsi que l'article premier, reconnaissent tous les deux explicitement que les crimes contre l'humanité sont des crimes au regard du droit international qui peuvent donner lieu à la responsabilité des États pour fait internationalement illicite.

Article 9
Aut dedere aut judicare (poursuivre ou extrader)

1. Tout État Partie prend les mesures nécessaires pour établir sa compétence aux fins de connaître des crimes contre l'humanité quand l'auteur présumé de l'infraction se trouve sur tout territoire sous sa juridiction, sauf si ledit État l'extrade vers un autre État conformément à ses obligations internationales ou le remet à la Cour pénale internationale, s'il s'agit d'un État Partie au Statut de Rome, ou à un autre tribunal pénal international dont il a reconnu la compétence.
2. Dans les cas où un État Partie ne poursuit pas une personne soupçonnée d'avoir commis des crimes contre l'humanité pour toute raison qui n'est pas spécifiée dans la présente Convention, cet État doit, conformément

à une demande appropriée, soit remettre cette personne à un autre État qui est disposé à la poursuivre équitablement et efficacement, ou à la Cour pénale internationale, si cet État est partie au Statut de Rome, ou à un tribunal international qui a compétence à l'égard des crimes contre l'humanité.

Note explicative

1. *Le paragraphe 1 s'inspire de l'article 9 2) de la Convention sur les disparitions forcées.*
2. *Le paragraphe 2 reflète le principe aut dedere aut judicare.*
3. *Concernant la référence dans cette disposition à un État Partie qui remet une personne accusée à la Cour pénale internationale, il est utile de noter que les États Parties au Statut de Rome peuvent avoir une telle obligation. Les États qui ne sont pas parties au Statut de Rome peuvent ne pas être tenus à une telle obligation, mais ils disposent de la faculté de coopérer avec la Cour pénale internationale. Cette disposition reconnaît que ces États peuvent coopérer avec la Cour pénale internationale, mais elle n'impose pas une obligation indépendante à cet effet.*

Article 10
Compétence

1. Les personnes soupçonnées d'être responsables de crimes contre l'humanité seront jugées par un tribunal pénal de l'État Partie, ou par la Cour pénale internationale, ou par un tribunal international qui a compétence à l'égard des crimes contre l'humanité.
2. Chaque État Partie prend les mesures nécessaires pour établir sa compétence sur les personnes soupçonnées d'être responsables de crimes contre l'humanité:
    a) Quand l'infraction est commise sur tout territoire sous sa juridiction ou à bord d'un navire ou d'un aéronef immatriculé dans cet État ou chaque fois qu'une personne se trouve sous le contrôle physique de cet État; ou
    b) Quand la personne soupçonnée d'être responsable est l'un de ses ressortissants; ou
    c) Quand la victime est l'un de ses ressortissants et que l'État Partie le juge approprié.
3. Chaque État partie prend également les mesures nécessaires pour établir sa compétence aux fins de connaître des crimes contre l'humanité quand l'auteur présumé de l'infraction se trouve sur tout territoire sous sa juridiction, sauf si ledit État l'extrade, ou qu'il le remet à un autre État conformément à ses obligations internationales ou qu'il le remet à une juridiction pénale internationale dont il a reconnu la compétence.

4. La présente Convention n'écarte aucune compétence pénale supplémentaire compatible avec le droit international et exercée conformément aux lois nationales.
5. Pour les fins de la coopération, la compétence est présumée exister à chaque fois qu'une personne responsable ou soupçonnées d'être responsable de crimes contre l'humanité est présente sur le territoire de l'État ou que l'État Partie est en mesure d'exercer un contrôle physique sur cette personne.

Note explicative

1. *Il est entendu que la référence dans le paragraphe 1 à « un tribunal international qui a compétence » s'applique à tout État Partie qui a accepté la compétence d'un tel tribunal. Cette disposition reconnaît aussi le principe de complémentarité incorporé dans le Statut de Rome.*
2. *Le paragraphe 2 s'appuie sur l'article 9 1) de la Convention sur les disparitions forcées. Cette disposition vise à éviter les litiges sur la portée de l'application territoriale.*
3. *Le paragraphe 3 s'appuie sur l'article 9 2) de la Convention sur les disparitions forcées et l'article 5 2) de la Convention contre la torture.*
4. *Le paragraphe 4 s'appuie sur l'article 9 3) de la Convention sur les disparitions forcées.*
5. *Le paragraphe 5 a pour fin d'assurer qu'il n'y ait pas de vide juridictionnel affectant la capacité d'un État Partie à exercer sa compétence à l'égard d'une personne qui est responsable ou soupçonnée d'être responsable de crimes contre l'humanité; il pourrait, en outre, s'appliquer aux personnes qui transitent sur le territoire d'un État Partie, alors même que ledit État Partie n'est pas en mesure d'exercer un contrôle physique sur cette personne.*

Article 11
Preuve

1. Les règles de preuve requises pour exercer des poursuites sont les mêmes que celles qui sont prescrites par le droit interne de l'État Partie qui procède à l'enquête, aux poursuites ou aux procédures qui font suite à un procès; elles ne sont en aucun cas moins rigoureuses que les règles applicables aux affaires de gravité similaire en vertu du droit de cet État Partie.
2. Les États Parties peuvent, aux fins de la présente Convention, reconnaître la validité d'éléments de preuve obtenus par un autre État Partie même si les règles légales et de procédure régissant le rassemblement de tels éléments de

preuve ne sont pas conformes aux règles similaires d'un État Partie donné. De tels cas de non-conformité ne constituent pas des motifs d'exclusion d'un élément de preuve, pour autant que cet élément de preuve soit présumé crédible et qu'il ait été obtenu conformément aux normes internationales régissant le droit à une procédure équitable. Ce paragraphe s'applique à toutes les procédures décrites dans la présente Convention, y compris, mais sans s'y limiter: l'extradition, l'entraide judiciaire, la transmission de procédures répressives, l'exécution d'ordonnances judiciaires, la transmission et l'exécution de peines pénales étrangères et la reconnaissance de jugements pénaux étrangers.
3. En ce qui concerne le rassemblement d'éléments de preuve, les États Parties s'efforcent de se conformer aux normes internationales régissant le droit à une procédure équitable.

Note explicative

1. *Le paragraphe 1 reconnaît que dans les traités multilatéraux et bilatéraux, la loi applicable en matière de preuve est celle de l'État du for.*
2. *En ce qui concerne l'entraide judiciaire et tel que cela est actuellement reflété à l'article 13 et à l'Annexe 2, il est aussi possible, pour l'État requérant, de demander que la collecte des éléments de preuve se fasse suivant des conditions particulières ou que certaines procédures soient suivies par l'État visé par la demande. Le paragraphe 2 permet aux États de reconnaître la validité d'un élément de preuve obtenu par un autre État Partie, même lorsque les conditions ou les procédures demandées ne sont pas appliquées, pour autant que l'élément de preuve soit présumé crédible et qu'il ait été obtenu conformément aux normes internationales régissant le droit à une procédure équitable, incluant l'obligation, en vertu de l'article 15 de la Convention sur la torture, qui exclut toute déclaration faite sous la torture.*
3. *Le paragraphe 3 oblige les États à s'efforcer de se conformer aux normes internationales régissant le droit à une procédure équitable dans le rassemblement des éléments de preuve.*

Article 12
Extradition

Les États Parties s'accordent mutuellement l'entraide la plus large possible pour toute demande d'extradition relative à des crimes contre l'humanité conformément aux dispositions de l'Annexe 2.

Note explicative

L'obligation d'extrader ou de poursuivre les personnes responsables ou les personnes soupçonnées d'être responsables de crimes contre l'humanité est énoncée au paragraphe 9 de l'article 8 et à l'article 9 de la présente Convention. Les modalités applicables sont énoncées à l'Annexe 2.

Article 13
Entraide judiciaire

Les États Parties s'accordent mutuellement l'entraide judiciaire la plus large possible pour toute enquête, poursuite et procédure judiciaire relative à des crimes contre l'humanité conformément aux dispositions de l'Annexe 3.

Note explicative

Les modalités selon lesquelles les États Parties sont tenus de s'accorder une entraide judiciaire mutuelle sont énoncées à l'Annexe 3, laquelle s'appuie sur les dispositions de l'article 46 de la Convention de l'ONU contre la corruption.

Article 14
Transmission de procédures répressives

Les États Parties qui ont compétence pour connaître des affaires impliquant des crimes contre l'humanité peuvent procéder à une transmission de procédures répressives conformément à l'Annexe 4.

Note explicative

Les modalités selon lesquelles les États Parties peuvent procéder à une transmission de procédures répressives en vertu de la présente Convention sont décrites à l'Annexe 4, laquelle s'appuie sur la Convention européenne sur la transmission des procédures répressives et son Protocole.

Article 15
Transfèrement de personnes condamnées aux fins de l'exécution de leur peine

Les États Parties peuvent transférer du système judiciaire de l'un vers celui de l'autre une personne reconnue coupable de crimes contre l'humanité, aux fins de l'exécution de la peine imposée à cette personne, conformément aux dispositions de l'Annexe 5.

Note explicative

Les modalités selon lesquelles les États Parties peuvent transférer des personnes reconnues coupables pour crimes contre l'humanité aux fins d'exécution de leur peine sont décrites à l'Annexe 5, laquelle s'inspire de la Convention européenne sur le transfèrement des personnes condamnées ainsi que de la Convention interaméricaine sur l'exécution des décisions rendues par les juridictions pénales étrangères.

Article 16
Exécution des jugements pénaux prononcés dans les États Parties

Un État Partie peut reconnaître et exécuter les jugements pénaux d'un autre État Partie conformément aux dispositions de l'Annexe 6.

Note explicative

Cette disposition prend acte du fait que les États peuvent reconnaître et exécuter les jugements pénaux d'un autre État Partie. Les modalités de cette reconnaissance et de cette exécution se trouvent à l'Annexe 6, laquelle s'inspire de la Convention européenne sur la valeur internationale des jugements répressifs.

Article 17
Ne bis in idem

Une personne qui a été jugée efficacement pour crimes contre l'humanité et qui a été reconnue coupable ou acquittée ne peut pas être poursuivie par un autre État Partie pour le même crime si les faits constitutifs du crime sont similaires ou substantiellement similaires à ceux de la poursuite précédente.

Note explicative

1. *Cette disposition reconnaît l'application du principe « ne bis in idem » qui se retrouve dans plusieurs instruments internationaux, y compris à l'article 14 7) du PIDCP, à l'article 20 du Statut de Rome, à l'article 10 du Statut du TPIY et à l'article 9 du Statut du TPIR.*
2. *Cette disposition reconnaît que, pour que le principe « ne bis in idem » puisse constituer un obstacle à une poursuite subséquente, la première poursuite doit avoir été conduite « efficacement ». L'Annexe 1 b) prévoit que le terme « efficacement » signifie avec diligence, indépendance et impartialité et d'une manière qui ne vise pas à*

soustraire la personne concernée à sa responsabilité pénale pour crimes contre l'humanité et qui est compatible avec l'intention de traduire cette personne en justice, en gardant à l'esprit que le principe de la présomption d'innocence doit être respecté.

Article 18
Non-refoulement

1. Aucun État Partie n'expulsera, ne refoulera, ni n'extradera une personne vers un autre État où il y a des motifs sérieux de croire qu'elle risque d'être soumise à des crimes contre l'humanité.
2. Pour déterminer s'il y a de tels motifs, les autorités compétentes tiendront compte de toutes les considérations pertinentes, y compris, le cas échéant, de l'existence, dans l'État intéressé, d'un ensemble de violations systématiques graves, flagrantes ou massives des droits de l'homme, ou de violations sérieuses du droit international humanitaire.

Note explicative

1. *Cette disposition s'appuie sur l'article 16 de la Convention sur les disparitions forcées, laquelle est à son tour fondée sur l'article 8 de la Déclaration sur les disparitions forcées. Une obligation similaire se rapportant spécifiquement à la torture est incluse dans la Convention contre la torture.*
2. *Le paragraphe 1 s'appuie également sur l'article 3 1) de la Convention contre la torture.*
3. *La disposition relative au principe de non-refoulement est limitée aux situations impliquant des crimes contre l'humanité, car ces crimes constituent le sujet central de la présente Convention. À cet égard, la présente Convention suit la même approche que la Convention sur les disparitions forcées et la Convention sur la torture.*

Article 19
Mécanismes institutionnels

A. Conférence des États Parties

1. Une Conférence des États Parties à la présente Convention est instituée pour améliorer la capacité des États Parties à atteindre les objectifs énoncés dans la présente Convention et renforcer leur coopération à cet effet ainsi que pour promouvoir et examiner l'application de la présente Convention.

2. Le Secrétaire général de l'Organisation des Nations Unies convoquera la Conférence des États Parties au plus tard un an après l'entrée en vigueur de la présente Convention. Par la suite, la Conférence des États Parties tiendra des réunions ordinaires tous les trois ans. En ce qui concerne la convocation de la première réunion de la Conférence des États Partie par le Secrétaire général de l'Organisation des Nations Unies, ce dernier fournit les services de secrétariat nécessaires à la Conférence des États Parties à la Convention. Le secrétariat qui est fourni par le Secrétaire général de l'Organisation des Nations Unies:
    a) Aide la Conférence des États Parties à réaliser les activités énoncées dans le présent article, prend des dispositions et fournit les services nécessaires pour les sessions de la Conférence des États Parties;
    b) Aide les États Parties, sur leur demande, à fournir des informations à la Conférence des États Parties comme le prévoient les paragraphes 5 et 6; et
    c) Assure la coordination nécessaire avec le secrétariat des organisations régionales et internationales compétentes.
3. Chaque État Partie dispose d'un représentant à la Conférence qui peut être secondé par des suppléants et des conseillers. La Conférence des États Parties adopte un règlement intérieur et des règles régissant le fonctionnement des activités énoncées dans le présent article, y compris des règles concernant l'admission et la participation d'observateurs et le financement des dépenses encourues au titre de ces activités.

B. Comité

4. Aux fins d'atteindre les objectifs énoncés au paragraphe 1 du présent article, la Conférence des États Parties institue un « Comité établi conformément à la Convention internationale sur la prévention et la répression des crimes contre l'humanité » (le Comité).
5. Le Comité se compose de dix membres. Les membres du Comité sont des experts dans des domaines pertinents à la présente Convention qui sont désignés par les États Parties et élus par la Conférence des États Parties. Les membres du Comité sont élus pour quatre ans. Ils sont rééligibles une fois. Toutefois, le mandat de cinq des membres élus lors de la première élection prend fin au bout de deux ans. Immédiatement après la première élection, les noms de ces cinq personnes sont tirés au sort de la manière désignée par la Conférence des États Parties.
6. Le Comité établit son propre règlement intérieur et arrête des activités, des procédures et des méthodes de travail en vue d'atteindre les objectifs énoncés au paragraphe 1, notamment:
    a) Il facilite les activités menées par et entre les États Parties en vertu de la présente Convention;

b) Il facilite l'échange d'informations entre États Parties sur les pratiques efficaces pour prévenir et réprimer les crimes contre l'humanité;
c) Il coopère avec les organisations et mécanismes régionaux et internationaux ainsi qu'avec les organisations non gouvernementales compétents;
d) Il utilise de manière appropriée les informations pertinentes produites par d'autres mécanismes internationaux et régionaux visant à prévenir et à réprimer les crimes contre l'humanité afin d'éviter une répétition inutile d'activités;
e) Il formule des recommandations en vue d'améliorer la présente Convention et son application;
f) Il prend note des besoins d'assistance technique des États Parties en ce qui concerne l'application de la présente Convention et recommande les mesures qu'il peut juger nécessaires à cet égard;
g) Il établit les règles et règlements de gestion financières régissant le fonctionnement du Comité et du Secrétariat; et
h) Il administre le Fonds de contributions volontaires établi par les États Parties conformément au paragraphe 14.

7. Aux fins du paragraphe 6, le Comité s'enquiert des mesures prises et des difficultés rencontrées par les États Parties pour appliquer la présente Convention en utilisant les informations que ceux-ci lui communiquent et par le biais des mécanismes complémentaires d'examen qu'il pourra établir.

8. Le Comité examine le moyen le plus efficace de recevoir des informations et d'y réagir, y compris, notamment, les informations reçues d'États Parties et d'organisations internationales compétentes. Les contributions reçues d'organisations non gouvernementales dûment accréditées conformément aux procédures arrêtées par le Comité peuvent être également prises en compte. Chaque État Partie communique au Comité des informations sur ses programmes, plans et pratiques visant à mettre en œuvre la présente Convention, incluant:
   a) L'adoption de législation nationale d'application;
   b) L'établissement de mécanismes administratifs conçus pour satisfaire les exigences inhérentes à la prévention prévues par la présente Convention;
   c) Des rapports compilant les données relatives à ses obligations en vertu de la présente Convention, comprenant, mais sans s'y limiter, le nombre d'allégations, d'enquêtes, de poursuites, de condamnations, d'extraditions et de demandes mutuelles d'entraide judiciaire.

9. Les informations fournies par les États Parties sont examinées par le Comité, qui émet les commentaires, observations ou recommandations qu'il juge appropriés. Les commentaires, observations ou recommandations sont communiqués à l'État Partie concerné, lequel peut y répondre de sa propre initiative ou à la demande du Comité. Le Comité peut aussi demander aux

États Parties de fournir des informations additionnelles sur l'application de la présente Convention.

10. Le Comité établit un Secrétariat permanent pour faciliter ses activités, procédures et méthodes de travail en vue d'atteindre les objectifs énoncés aux paragraphes 1, 5, 6 et 7. Le Comité peut établir tout autre organe subsidiaire qu'il juge nécessaire.

C. Secrétariat

11. Le Secrétariat a pour fonctions de:
    a) Fournir une assistance technique aux États dans le processus d'adhésion à la présente Convention;
    b) Fournir une assistance technique, incluant l'assistance appropriée au renforcement des capacités, aux États Parties dans l'accomplissement de leurs obligations en vertu de la présente Convention;
    c) Diffuser des informations entre les États Parties;
    d) Faciliter l'entraide judiciaire mutuelle et d'autres aspects de la coopération entre les États Parties, y compris l'aide à la coopération en matières de comparution de témoins et d'experts dans les procédures judiciaires, ainsi qu'à la protection efficace de ces personnes;
    e) Recevoir et compiler les informations obtenues des États Parties à la demande du Comité; et
    f) Assurer la coordination nécessaire avec les secrétariats des organisations internationales et régionales compétentes.

12. Le Secrétariat a son siège à: _____.

D. Dépenses

13. Les dépenses de la Conférence des États Parties, du Comité, du Secrétariat et de tout autre organe subsidiaire sont financées par les sources suivantes:
    a) Les contributions des États Parties sont calculées selon un barème convenu de quotes-parts, fondé sur le barème adopté par l'Organisation des Nations Unies pour son budget ordinaire, et adapté conformément aux principes sur lesquels ce barème est fondé;
    b) Les fonds provenant de contributions volontaires de gouvernements, d'organisations intergouvernementales, d'organisations non gouvernementales, d'organismes privés, de fondations et de particuliers.

E. Fonds de contributions volontaires

14. Les États Parties établissent un Fonds de contributions volontaires relevant du Comité pour fournir aux États Parties une assistance technique et un soutien en matière de renforcement des capacités nécessaires à la poursuite de leurs efforts dans l'exécution de leurs obligations découlant de la présente Convention.

Note explicative

1. Cet article s'inspire largement des articles 112, 116 et 117 du Statut de Rome, des articles 63 et 64 de la Convention de l'ONU contre la corruption et des articles 26 et 29 de la Convention sur les disparitions forcées.
2. Le paragraphe 2 de cette disposition sera sujet à approbation par les organes compétents de l'Organisation des Nations Unies, incluant le remboursement par les États Parties aux Nations Unies des dépenses encourues par l'organisation.
3. L'expérience des États Parties auprès de cet organe et dans ses fonctions déterminera comment celui-ci évoluera dans le futur et quel rôle il assumera en plus du mandat indiqué dans la Convention tel que, par exemple, l'établissement de faits aux fins du développement d'un système d'alerte précoce.
4. En ce qui concerne le paragraphe 12, un accord de siège approprié devra être négocié avec le pays hôte, sous réserve de l'approbation par la Conférence des États Parties.

Article 20
États fédéraux

Les dispositions de la présente Convention s'appliquent, sans limitation ni exception aucune, à toutes les unités constitutives des États fédéraux.

Note explicative

Cette disposition vient de l'article 41 de la Convention sur les disparitions forcées.

Article 21
Signature, ratification, acceptation, approbation ou adhésion

1. La présente Convention est ouverte à la signature de tous les États le _____ jusqu'au _____.
2. La présente Convention est soumise à ratification, acceptation ou approbation par les États signataires. Les instruments de ratification, d'acceptation ou d'approbation seront déposés auprès du Secrétaire général de l'Organisation des Nations Unies.
3. La présente Convention est ouverte à l'adhésion de tous les États. Les instruments d'adhésion seront déposés auprès du Secrétaire général de l'Organisation des Nations Unies.

Note explicative

Cet article s'appuie sur l'article 125 du Statut de Rome.

Article 22
Entrée en vigueur

1. La présente Convention entrera en vigueur le trentième (30ᵉ) jour après la date de dépôt du vingtième (20ᵉ) instrument de ratification, d'acceptation, d'approbation ou d'adhésion auprès du Secrétaire général de l'Organisation des Nations Unies.
2. À l'égard de chaque État qui ratifie, accepte ou approuve le présent Statut ou y adhère après le dépôt du vingtième (20ᵉ) instrument de ratification, d'acceptation, d'approbation ou d'adhésion, la présente Convention entre en vigueur le trentième (30ᵉ) jour après le dépôt par cet État de son instrument de ratification, d'acceptation, d'approbation ou d'adhésion.

Note explicative

Les paragraphes 1 et 2 s'appuient sur l'article 126 du Statut de Rome.

Article 23
Réserves

La présente Convention n'admet aucune réserve.

Note explicative

1. *Ce libellé vient de l'article 120 du Statut de Rome.*
2. *Il est entendu que les régimes législatifs nationaux varient et que ces variations s'appliqueront aux modalités d'application du principe aut dedere aut judicare et que les États peuvent faire des déclarations au sujet de leurs systèmes juridiques et procédures nationaux respectifs. Ceci s'applique particulièrement aux articles 9, 10, 11, 12, 13, 14, 15 et 16 de la présente Convention.*

Article 24
Amendement

1. Tout État Partie à la présente Convention peut proposer des amendements à celle-ci. Le texte de toute proposition d'amendement est soumis au

Secrétaire général de l'Organisation des Nations Unies, qui le communique sans retard à tous les États Parties.
2. Trois mois au plus tôt après la date de cette communication, la Conférence des États Parties, à la réunion suivante, décide, à la majorité de ses membres présents et votants, de se saisir ou non de la proposition. La Conférence peut traiter cette proposition elle-même ou convoquer une conférence de révision si la question soulevée le justifie.
3. L'adoption d'un amendement lors d'une réunion de la Conférence des États Parties ou d'une conférence de révision requiert, s'il n'est pas possible de parvenir à un consensus, la majorité des deux tiers des États Parties.
4. Les amendements à la présente Convention entrent en vigueur à l'égard des États Parties qui les ont acceptés un an après que les deux tiers d'entre eux ont déposé leurs instruments de ratification ou d'acceptation auprès du Secrétaire général de l'Organisation des Nations Unies; les autres États Parties qui n'ont pas accepté les amendements continuent d'être liés par les dispositions de la présente Convention et par tout amendement antérieur qu'ils ont accepté.
5. Le Secrétaire général de l'Organisation des Nations Unies communique à tous les États Parties les amendements adoptés lors d'une réunion de la Conférence des États Parties ou d'une conférence de révision.

Note explicative

Cet article est largement inspiré de l'article 121 du Statut de Rome.

Article 25
Interprétation

Les dispositions de la présente Convention seront aussi interprétées à la lumière des règles et normes internationalement reconnues relatives aux droits de l'homme.

Note explicative

Il est évident que le droit coutumier international concernant l'interprétation des traités s'applique (codifié dans la Convention de Vienne sur le droit des traités). Cet article vise aussi à assurer que les termes de la présente Convention sont interprétés d'une manière compatible avec les obligations régionales relatives aux droits de l'homme incombant aux États Parties en vertu de la Convention européenne des droits de l'homme, de la Convention américaine des droits de l'homme, de la Charte africaine des droits de l'homme et des peuples, ainsi que conformément aux obligations spécifiques établies par des organes de traités en regard de diverses conventions relatives aux droits de l'homme.

Article 26
Règlement des différends entre États Parties

Tout différend entre deux ou plus des États Parties concernant l'interprétation ou l'application de la présente Convention, y compris ceux qui se rapportent à la responsabilité d'un État suite à la violation soupçonnée de celle-ci, qui ne peut pas être réglé par voie de négociation, est soumis à l'arbitrage à la demande de l'un d'entre eux. Si, dans les six mois qui suivent la date de la demande d'arbitrage, les parties ne parviennent pas à se mettre d'accord sur l'organisation de l'arbitrage, l'une quelconque d'entre elles peut soumettre le différend à la Cour internationale de Justice en déposant une requête conformément au Statut de la Cour afin que celle-ci rende une décision définitive et obligatoire.

Note explicative

Cette disposition s'inspire de l'article 30 1) de la Convention contre la torture, de l'article 42 1) de la Convention sur les disparitions forcées et de l'article IX de la Convention sur le génocide.

Article 27
Textes authentiques

L'original de la présente Convention, dont les textes anglais, arabe, chinois, espagnol, français et russe font également foi, sera déposé auprès du Secrétaire général de l'Organisation des Nations Unies, qui en fera tenir copie certifiée conforme à tous les États.

Note explicative

Ce libellé vient de l'article 128 du Statut de Rome.

Annexe 1
Terminologie

Aux fins de la présente Convention:

a) Les termes « équitable », « équitablement » ou « équité » signifient dans le respect des garanties d'un procès équitable reconnues par le droit international, compatibles avec les garanties minimales applicables aux procédures pénales, telles qu'énoncées dans le Pacte international relatif aux droits civils et politiques;

b) Les termes « efficace », « efficacement » ou « efficacité » signifient avec diligence, indépendance et impartialité d'une manière ne visant pas à soustraire la personne concernée à sa responsabilité pénale pour crimes contre l'humanité et compatible avec l'intention de traduire la personne concernée en justice, sans oublier le principe de la présomption d'innocence;

c) Le terme « personne » s'entend d'une personne physique ou d'une personne morale.

Note explicative

Les définitions des termes « équitable » et « efficace » aux paragraphes a) et b) visent à assurer que les États n'auront pas recours à des simulacres d'enquêtes ou de procédures légales afin de contourner leurs obligations d'enquêter, de poursuivre ou d'extrader. La définition énoncée au paragraphe b) s'appuie largement sur le principe « ne bis in idem » formulé à l'article 10 du Statut du TPIY et à l'article 20 du Statut de Rome.

Annexe 2
Extradition

A. Crimes contre l'humanité en tant qu'infractions donnant lieu à extradition

1. Les crimes contre l'humanité sont de plein droit compris au nombre des infractions donnant lieu à extradition dans tout traité d'extradition conclu entre des États Parties avant l'entrée en vigueur de la présente Convention.
2. Les États Parties s'engagent à inclure les crimes contre l'humanité au nombre des infractions qui justifient l'extradition dans tout traité d'extradition à conclure par la suite entre eux.

B. Base juridique pour l'extradition

3. En l'absence de législation nationale pertinente ou d'autre forme de relation en matière d'extradition, les États Parties considèrent la présente Convention comme base juridique de l'extradition aux fins de se conformer à leurs obligations de poursuivre ou d'extrader les personnes soupçonnées d'être les auteurs de crimes contre l'humanité en vertu du paragraphe 9 de l'article 8 et de l'article 9.

C. Modalités de l'extradition

4. En l'absence de législation nationale pertinente ou d'autre forme de relation en matière d'extradition, les États Parties peuvent recourir à tout ou partie des modalités suivantes décrites dans cette Annexe.

D. Motifs de refus d'une demande d'extradition

5. Pour les besoins de l'extradition entre États parties, les crimes contre l'humanité ne sont pas considérés comme une infraction politique ou une infraction connexe à une infraction politique. En conséquence, une demande d'extradition fondée sur des crimes contre l'humanité ne peut être refusée pour ce seul motif, et l'extradition ne peut non plus être empêchée en invoquant la qualité officielle sous réserve du paragraphe 1 de l'article 6.
6. Le fait qu'une personne recherchée soit jugée pour crimes contre l'humanité ou pour un autre crime prévu par les lois internes de l'État requis, lorsque ce crime est fondé sur des faits qui sont constitutifs de l'un ou plusieurs des actes énumérés au paragraphe 1 de l'article 3, ou le fait que la personne recherchée a déjà été jugée pour un tel crime ou de tels crimes et a été acquittée ou condamnée, et a servi la peine pour cette condamnation, constituent des motifs de refus d'extradition. Le fait que l'État Partie requis détermine que la personne recherchée pour extradition pourrait faire l'objet de crimes contre l'humanité dans l'État

requérant, constitue également un motif de refus d'extradition tel que le prévoit l'article 18.

7. Le fait que l'État requis ait des motifs sérieux de croire que la demande d'extradition a été présentée en vue de poursuivre ou de punir une personne en raison de sa race, de sa religion, de sa nationalité, de son origine ethnique, de ses opinions politiques, de son sexe ou de son statut, ou qu'il pourrait être porté atteinte au droit de cette personne à un procès équitable et impartial pour l'une de ces raisons, constituent des motifs de refus d'extradition.

8. Le fait que le jugement de l'État requérant a été rendu en l'absence de l'intéressé, que celui-ci n'a pas été prévenu suffisamment tôt de son procès ou n'a pas eu la possibilité de prendre des dispositions pour assurer sa défense, et n'a pas pu ou ne pourra pas faire juger à nouveau l'affaire en sa présence, constituent des motifs de refus d'extradition.

9. Le fait que la personne n'a pas bénéficié ou ne bénéficierait pas des garanties minimales prévues, au cours des procédures pénales, par l'article 14 du Pacte international relatif aux droits civils et politiques, constituent des motifs de refus d'extradition.

10. L'extradition peut être refusée si l'infraction de crimes contre l'humanité est passible d'une peine qui n'est pas prévue dans l'État requis, à moins que l'État requérant fournisse des assurances jugées suffisantes par l'État requis, à l'effet que la peine non prévue dans cet État ne sera pas prononcée ou, si elle l'est, ne sera pas appliquée.

E. Règle de la spécialité

11. Nulle personne extradée pour crimes contre l'humanité ne sera jugée dans l'État requérant pour tout crime autre que celui pour lequel l'extradition a été accordée, sauf si l'État requis ou la personne extradée y consent.

F. Demandes concurrentes d'extradition

12. Dans les cas où plusieurs demandes d'extradition sont présentées, l'État Partie sur le territoire duquel la personne soupçonnée d'être responsable de crimes contre l'humanité a été trouvée peut prendre les facteurs suivants en considération en déterminant la priorité de ces demandes:
    a) Le territoire sur lequel l'un ou plusieurs des actes constitutifs du crime s'est produit;
    b) La nationalité du ou des délinquant(s);
    c) La nationalité de la ou des victime(s); et
    d) Le forum le plus susceptible de faire preuve d'une plus grande capacité et efficacité à mener la poursuite et qui assurera la plus grande équité et impartialité.

Note explicative

1. *Le paragraphe 1 s'appuie sur l'article 13 2) de la Convention sur les disparitions forcées.*
2. *Le paragraphe 2 s'appuie sur l'article 13 3) de la Convention sur les disparitions forcées.*
3. *Le paragraphe 3 assure qu'en l'absence de législation nationale pertinente ou d'une relation bilatérale ou multilatérale existante en matière d'extradition, la présente Convention fournit la base juridique sur le fondement de laquelle un État Partie peut remplir son obligation d'extrader ou de poursuivre conformément au paragraphe 9 de l'article 8 et l'article 9.*
4. *Le paragraphe 4 assure qu'en l'absence de législation nationale pertinente ou d'une relation bilatérale ou multilatérale existante en matière d'extradition, la présente Convention peut définir les modalités suivant lesquelles un État Partie peut remplir son obligation d'extrader ou de poursuivre conformément au paragraphe 9 de l'article 8 et l'article 9.*
5. *Le paragraphe 5 s'appuie sur l'article 13 1) de la Convention sur les disparitions forcées en ce qui a trait aux infractions politiques. Concernant les prétentions à la qualité officielle, ce paragraphe est conforme au paragraphe 1 de l'article 6 de la présente Convention qui exclut que la capacité officielle puisse être invoquée comme moyen de défense applicable.*
6. *À l'égard du paragraphe 6, et afin de pouvoir assurer le respect du principe « ne bis in idem », le fait qu'un État ou un État Partie ait ou n'ait pas fait traduire une personne en justice ne porte pas à conséquence. Quoiqu'il en soit, l'État requis aura à déterminer si la poursuite était équitable et efficace.*
7. *Le paragraphe 7 s'appuie sur l'article 3 b) du Traité type d'extradition de l'ONU.*
8. *Le paragraphe 8 s'appuie sur l'article 3 g) du Traité type d'extradition de l'ONU.*
9. *Le paragraphe 9 s'appuie sur l'article 3 f) du Traité type d'extradition de l'ONU.*
10. *Le paragraphe 10 est similaire à l'article 4 d) du Traité type d'extradition de l'ONU, mais sa portée est plus large et il reconnaît que les obligations des États au regard des traités régionaux relatifs aux droits de l'homme peuvent différer.*
11. *Les paragraphes 6 à 9 prévoient des motifs obligatoires de refus de l'extradition, tandis que le paragraphe 10 prévoit un motif facultatif de refus. D'autres motifs possibles de refus sont prévus à l'article 4 du Traité type d'extradition de l'ONU.*

Annexe 3
Entraide judiciaire

1. L'entraide judiciaire entre les États Parties est accordée dans la plus grande mesure possible, autant que les lois, traités, accords et arrangements pertinents de l'État Partie requis le permettent, et peut être accordée sur le fondement de la présente Convention, sans qu'il ne soit nécessaire de recourir à un traité bilatéral ou une loi nationale.

A. Types d'entraide judiciaire

2. L'entraide judiciaire qui est accordée en application de la présente Annexe peut être demandée aux fins suivantes:
   a) Recueillir des témoignages ou des dépositions;
   b) Signifier des actes judiciaires;
   c) Effectuer des perquisitions et des saisies, ainsi que le gel des avoirs;
   d) Examiner des objets et visiter des lieux;
   e) Fournir des informations, des pièces à conviction et des estimations d'experts;
   f) Fournir des originaux ou des copies certifiées conformes de documents et dossiers pertinents, y compris des documents administratifs, bancaires, financiers ou commerciaux et des documents de société;
   g) Identifier ou localiser des produits du crime, des biens, des instruments ou d'autres choses afin de recueillir des éléments de preuve;
   h) Faciliter la comparution volontaire de personnes dans l'État Partie requérant;
   i) Fournir tout autre type d'assistance compatible avec le droit interne de l'État Partie requis.

B. Communication d'informations

3. Sans préjudice du droit interne, les autorités compétentes d'un État Partie peuvent, sans demande préalable, communiquer des informations concernant des crimes contre l'humanité à une autorité compétente d'un autre État Partie, si elles pensent que ces informations pourraient aider celle-ci à entreprendre ou à mener à bien des enquêtes et des poursuites pénales, ou amener ce dernier État Partie à formuler une demande en vertu de la présente Convention.

4. La communication d'informations conformément au paragraphe 3 de la présente Annexe se fait sans préjudice des enquêtes et poursuites pénales dans l'État dont les autorités compétentes fournissent les informations. Les autorités compétentes qui reçoivent ces informations accèdent à toute demande tendant à ce que lesdites informations restent confidentielles, même temporairement, ou à ce que leur utilisation soit assortie de restrictions. Toutefois, cela n'empêche pas l'État Partie qui reçoit les informations de révéler, lors de la procédure judiciaire, des informations à la décharge

d'un prévenu. Dans ce dernier cas, l'État Partie qui reçoit les informations avise l'État Partie qui les communique avant la révélation et, s'il lui en est fait la demande, consulte ce dernier. Si, dans un cas exceptionnel, une notification préalable n'est pas possible, l'État Partie qui reçoit les informations informe sans retard de la révélation l'État Partie qui les communique.

C. Obligations découlant d'autres traités applicables

5. Les dispositions de la présente Annexe n'affectent en rien les obligations découlant de tout autre traité bilatéral ou multilatéral régissant ou devant régir, entièrement ou partiellement, l'entraide judiciaire.

D. Transfèrement des personnes détenues

6. Toute personne détenue ou purgeant une peine sur le territoire d'un État Partie, dont la présence est requise dans un autre État Partie à des fins d'identification ou de témoignage ou pour qu'elle apporte de toute autre manière son concours à l'obtention de preuves dans le cadre d'enquêtes, de poursuites ou de procédures judiciaires relatives à des crimes contre l'humanité, peut faire l'objet d'un transfèrement si les conditions ci-après sont réunies:
    a) Ladite personne donne librement et en toute connaissance de cause son consentement;
    b) Les autorités compétentes des deux États Parties concernés y consentent, sous réserve des conditions que ces États Parties peuvent juger appropriées.

E. Forme des demandes d'entraide judiciaire

7. Les demandes d'entraide judiciaire sont adressées par écrit ou, si possible, par tout autre moyen pouvant produire un document écrit, dans une langue acceptable pour l'État Partie requis, dans des conditions permettant audit État Partie d'en établir l'authenticité. La ou les langues acceptables pour chaque État Partie sont notifiées au Secrétaire général de l'Organisation des Nations Unies au moment où ledit État Partie dépose son instrument de ratification, d'acceptation ou d'approbation ou d'adhésion à la présente Convention. En cas d'urgence et si les États Parties en conviennent, les demandes peuvent être faites oralement mais doivent être confirmées sans délai par écrit.
8. Une demande d'entraide judiciaire doit contenir les renseignements suivants:
    a) La désignation de l'autorité dont émane la demande;
    b) L'objet et la nature de l'enquête, des poursuites ou de la procédure judiciaire auxquelles se rapporte la demande, ainsi que le nom et les fonctions de l'autorité qui en est chargée;
    c) Un résumé des faits pertinents, sauf pour les demandes adressées aux fins de la signification d'actes judiciaires;
    d) Une description de l'assistance requise et le détail de toute procédure particulière que l'État Partie requérant souhaite voir appliquée;

e) Si possible, l'identité, l'adresse et la nationalité de toute personne visée; et
  f) Le but dans lequel le témoignage, les informations ou les mesures sont demandés.
9. L'État Partie requis peut demander un complément d'information lorsque cela apparaît nécessaire pour exécuter la demande conformément à son droit interne ou lorsque cela peut en faciliter l'exécution.

F. Exécution des demandes d'entraide judiciaire

10. Toute demande est exécutée conformément au droit interne de l'État Partie requis et, dans la mesure où cela ne contrevient pas au droit interne de l'État Partie requis et lorsque cela est possible, conformément aux procédures spécifiées dans la demande.

G. Témoins

11. Lorsque cela est possible et conforme aux principes fondamentaux du droit interne, si une personne qui se trouve sur le territoire d'un État Partie doit être entendue comme témoin ou comme expert par les autorités judiciaires d'un autre État Partie, le premier État Partie peut, à la demande de l'autre, autoriser son audition par vidéoconférence s'il n'est pas possible ou souhaitable qu'elle comparaisse en personne sur le territoire de l'État Partie requérant. Les États Parties peuvent convenir que l'audition sera conduite par une autorité judiciaire de l'État Partie requérant et qu'une autorité judiciaire de l'État Partie requis y assistera.

H. Utilisation restreinte des informations

12. L'État Partie requérant ne communique ni n'utilise les informations ou les éléments de preuve fournis par l'État Partie requis pour des enquêtes, poursuites ou procédures judiciaires autres que celles visées dans la demande sans le consentement préalable de l'État Partie requis. Rien dans le présent paragraphe n'empêche l'État Partie requérant de révéler, lors de la procédure, des informations ou des éléments de preuve à décharge d'un prévenu. Dans ce cas, l'État Partie requérant avise l'État Partie requis avant la révélation et, s'il lui en est fait la demande, consulte ce dernier. Si, dans un cas exceptionnel, une notification préalable n'est pas possible, l'État Partie requérant informe sans retard l'État Partie requis de la révélation.

I. Refus d'exécuter des demandes d'entraide judiciaire

13. Les États Parties n'invoquent en aucun cas le secret bancaire pour refuser l'entraide judiciaire prévue à la présente Annexe.
14. L'entraide judiciaire peut être refusée si la demande n'est pas faite conformément aux dispositions de la présente Annexe.

15. L'entraide judiciaire ne peut être refusée sur la base de prétentions à la qualité officielle sous réserve du paragraphe 1 de l'article 6, ou au motif que le crime était de nature politique.
16. L'entraide judiciaire est refusée si la personne concernée par la demande est jugée pour crimes contre l'humanité ou pour un autre crime prévu par les lois internes de l'État requis, lorsque ce crime est fondé sur des faits qui sont constitutifs de l'un ou plusieurs des actes énumérés au paragraphe 1 de l'article 3, ou si la personne a déjà été jugée pour un tel crime ou de tels crimes et a été acquittée ou condamnée, et a servi la peine pour cette condamnation. Constituent aussi des motifs de refuser l'entraide judiciaire le fait que l'État Partie requis détermine que la personne concernée par la demande pourrait faire l'objet de crimes contre l'humanité dans l'État requérant.

Note explicative

1. *Une grande partie du texte de cette Annexe s'inspire des dispositions concernant l'entraide judiciaire de l'article 46 de la Convention de l'ONU contre la corruption.*
2. *Pour des modalités additionnelles d'exécution de l'entraide judiciaire, les États Parties peuvent s'inspirer de lois types, comme le Traité type d'entraide judiciaire de l'ONU en matière pénale ou les conventions pertinentes d'organes régionaux.*

Annexe 4
Transmission de procédures répressives

1. Chaque fois qu'un État Partie, ayant compétence à l'égard d'une personne accusée de crimes contre l'humanité, s'entend, avec un autre État Partie ayant également compétence en vertu de l'article 10, pour céder sa compétence et transmettre le dossier des poursuites engagées à l'État Partie requérant, la procédure applicable à cette transmission est établie suivant un accord entre les autorités compétentes respectives. Cette procédure se base sur la présente Convention et ne requiert pas l'existence d'un traité bilatéral entre les États Parties concernés ou d'une loi nationale.
2. Une transmission peut survenir lorsque cela est dans le meilleur intérêt de la justice, et lorsque cela accroît l'équité et l'efficacité de la poursuite.
3. Un État Partie peut demander à un autre État Partie d'exercer la poursuite à sa place dans l'un ou plusieurs des cas suivants:
   a) si le prévenu a sa résidence habituelle dans l'État requis;
   b) si le prévenu est un ressortissant de l'État requis ou si cet État est son État d'origine;
   c) si le prévenu subit ou doit subir dans l'État requis une sanction privative de liberté;
   d) si le prévenu fait l'objet dans l'État requis d'une poursuite pour la même infraction ou pour d'autres infractions;
   e) s'il estime que la transmission est justifiée par l'intérêt de la découverte de la vérité et notamment que les éléments de preuve les plus importants se trouvent dans l'État requis;
   f) s'il estime que l'exécution dans l'État requis d'une éventuelle condamnation est susceptible d'améliorer les possibilités de reclassement social du condamné;
   g) s'il estime que la présence du prévenu ne peut pas être assurée à l'audience dans l'État requérant alors que sa présence physique peut être assurée à l'audience dans l'État requis;
   h) s'il estime qu'il n'est pas en mesure d'exécuter lui même une éventuelle condamnation, même en ayant recours à l'extradition, et que l'État requis est en mesure de le faire.

Note explicative

1. *Cette disposition s'inspire de la Convention européenne sur la transmission des procédures répressives et intègre, à son paragraphe 3, les situations énumérées à l'article 8 de cette convention définissant à quel moment les États peuvent soumettre de telles demandes de transmission.*
2. *Cette disposition ne prévoit pas de motifs de refus en raison de la diversité des systèmes juridiques nationaux.*

Annexe 5
Transfèrement de personnes condamnées aux fins de l'exécution de leur peine

1. Les États Parties peuvent procéder entre eux au transfèrement d'une personne condamnée pour crimes contre l'humanité dans leurs systèmes juridiques respectifs aux fins d'exécution de la peine imposée à cette personne, sur la base de la présente Convention et sans qu'un traité bilatéral entre ces États Parties ou une législation nationale ne soit requis.
2. Le transfèrement requiert, à la fois, le consentement de l'État Partie de condamnation, de l'État Partie d'exécution et de la personne qui doit être transférée, laquelle doit renoncer à tous ses droits de contestation à l'égard de sa condamnation dans l'État de condamnation, ainsi que l'accord de l'État Partie d'exécution à l'effet que la sentence sera exécutée telle que décidée dans l'État de condamnation, conformément aux lois pénales et règlements applicables de cet État.
3. La libération conditionnelle et les autres mesures exécutées dans l'État d'exécution s'appliquent conformément aux lois et règlements applicables de cet État. Toutefois, aucun pardon ou mesure comparable de clémence n'est appliqué à la personne transférée sans le consentement de l'État de condamnation.

Note explicative

Cette disposition s'inspire de la Convention sur le transfèrement des personnes condamnées ainsi que sur la Convention interaméricaine sur l'exécution des décisions rendues par les juridictions pénales étrangères. Les États Parties pourraient aussi souhaiter consulter des exemples de législations types d'organisations compétentes, des directives régionales et des accords sous-régionaux.

Annexe 6
Exécution des jugements pénaux prononcés dans les États Parties

1. La reconnaissance et l'exécution d'un jugement pénal prononcé dans un État Partie sont fondées sur la présente Convention et il n'est pas requis de traité bilatéral entre les États Parties concernés, ni de législation nationale, sauf dans la mesure où la constitution ou le droit interne de chaque État Partie l'exige aux fins de la mise en œuvre de la présente Convention.
2. La coopération et l'assistance entre les États Parties, particulièrement en regard de l'application des annexes 3 à 6, qui, suivant les lois d'un État Partie donné, ne peuvent procéder sur le fondement d'un jugement pénal étranger ou requièrent qu'un traité ou une loi nationale reconnaisse un jugement pénal étranger, dépendent plutôt de la présente Convention pour l'exécution de ou le fait de se fonder sur un jugement pénal étranger.
3. Un État Partie peut toutefois refuser d'exécuter, de faire respecter, de donner effet à ou de s'appuyer sur les jugements pénaux d'un autre État Partie si le jugement en question a été obtenu par la fraude ou la contrainte, ou a été rendu en application de procédures qui contreviennent aux normes internationales de procès équitable, ou qui sont contraires aux politiques publiques internes.

Note explicative

Cette disposition s'inspire de la Convention européenne sur la valeur internationale des jugements répressifs.

CONVENTION INTERNATIONALE POUR LA PRÉVENTION ET LA RÉPRESSION DES CRIMES CONTRE L'HUMANITÉ

Table des abréviations et instruments cités dans la Convention et dans les notes explicatives

Charte africaine	Charte africaine des droits de l'homme et des peuples [signée à Banjul], 1982, 1520 RTNU 217 (entrée en vigueur le 21 oct. 1986).
Convention américaine relative aux droits de l'homme	Convention américaine relative aux droits de l'homme, 1969, RTOÉA No. 36, 1144 RTNU 123 (entrée en vigueur le 18 juillet 1978).
Convention contre l'apartheid	Convention internationale sur l'élimination et la répression du crime d'apartheid, 1973, Rés. A.-G. 3068 (XXVIII) du 30 nov. 1973, Doc. NU A/9030, 1015 RTNU (entrée en vigueur le 18 juillet 1976).
CCH	Crime(s) contre l'humanité.
Historique général de la Proposition de Convention internationale sur la prévention et la répression des crimes contre l'humanité	Leila Nadya Sadat, *A Comprehensive History of the Proposed International Convention on the Prevention and Punishment of Crimes Against Humanity*, in Forging a Convention for Crimes Against Humanity (Cambridge Univ. Press, 2011). Pour le site internet de la « Washington University School of Law Whitney R. Harris World Law Institute Crimes Against Humanity Initiative », voir http://law.wustl.edu/crimesagainsthumanity/
Convention européenne sur le transfèrement de personnes condamnées	Convention sur le transfèrement des personnes condamnées, 1983, RTE No. 112, Strasbourg (21 mar. 1983) (entrée en vigueur le 1er juillet 1985).
CEDH	Convention européenne de sauvegarde des droits de l'homme et des libertés fondamentales, 1950, RTE No. 5, 213 RTNU 222, Rome (4 sept. 1950) (entrée en vigueur le 3 sept. 1953).
Convention sur les disparitions forcées	Convention internationale pour la protection de toutes les personnes contre les disparitions forcées, 2006, Rés. A.-G. 61/177 (20 déc. 2006) (non encore en vigueur).
Déclaration sur les disparitions forcées	Déclaration internationale pour la protection de toutes les personnes contre les disparitions forcées, 1992, Rés. A.-G. 47/133 (1992).
Convention européenne sur la valeur internationale des jugements répressifs	Convention européenne sur la valeur internationale des jugements répressifs, 1970, RTE No. 70, Criminal Judgments, La Haye, (28 mai 1970) (entrée en vigueur le 26 juillet 1974).

Mandat européen d'obtention de preuves	Décision-cadre du Conseil relative au mandat européen d'obtention de preuves tendant à recueillir des objets, des documents et des données en vue de leur utilisation dans le cadre de procédures pénales, 2008, O.J. (L 350) 72, Décision-cadre du Conseil 2008/978/JHA (entrée en vigueur le 8 févr. 2009).
Convention européenne d'entraide judiciaire en matière pénale	Convention européenne d'entraide judiciaire en matière pénale, 1959, RTE No. 30, Mutual Assistance in Criminal Matters, Strasbourg (20 avril 1959) (entrée en vigueur le 12 juin 1962).
Convention européenne sur l'imprescriptibilité	Convention européenne sur l'imprescriptibilité des crimes contre l'humanité et des crimes de guerre, 1974, RTE No. 82, Crimes contre l'humanité et crimes de guerre, Strasbourg (25 jan. 1974) (entrée en vigueur le 26 juin 2003).
Convention européenne sur la transmission des procédures répressives	Convention européenne sur la transmission des procédures répressives, 1972, RTE No. 73, Criminal Proceedings, Strasbourg (15 mai 1972) (entrée en vigueur le 30 mars 1978).
Convention sur le génocide	Convention pour la prévention et la répression du crime de génocide, 1951, Rés. A.-G. 260 (III), Doc. N-U A/180, 78 RTNU 277 (9 déc. 1948) (entrée en vigueur le 12 jan. 1951).
Report of the Genocide Prevention Task Force	Madeleine Albright & William Cohen, Preventing Genocide: A Blueprint for U.S. Policymakers (2008), disponible à: http://www.usip.org/genocide_taskforce/report.html
Convention pour la répression de la capture illicite d'aéronefs	Convention pour la répression de la capture illicite d'aéronefs, 1970, (La Haye, 18 déc. 1970), T.I.A.S. No. 7192, 22 U.S.T. 1641, 860 RTNU 105 (entrée en vigueur le 14 oct. 1971).
CIJ	Cour internationale de Justice
PIDCP	Pacte international relatif aux droits civils et politiques, 1976, Rés. A.-G. 2200 (XXI), Supp. No. 16, Doc. NU A/6316 (16 déc. 1966) (entrée en vigueur le 23 mars 1976).
Projet d'articles sur la Responsabilité de l'État pour fait internationalement illicite de la Commission du droit international	Rapport de la Commission du droit international sur les travaux de la 55e session, 23 avril – 1er juin et 2 juillet – 10 août 2001, 2001, UN GAOR, 55e Sess., Doc. NU A/56/10 (2001).

Statut du TPIR	Statut du Tribunal international chargé de juger les personnes présumées responsables d'actes de génocide ou d'autres violations graves du droit international humanitaire commis sur le territoire du Rwanda et les citoyens rwandais présumés responsables de tels actes ou violations commis sur le territoire d'États voisins entre le 1er janvier et le 31 décembre 1994, 1994, Doc. NU S/RES/955 (1994).
Statut du TPIY	Statut du Tribunal pénal international chargé de poursuivre les personnes présumées responsables de violations graves du droit international humanitaire commises sur le territoire de l'ex-Yougoslavie depuis 1991, Doc. NU S/25704 à 36, Annexe (1993) & S/25704/Add.1 (1993), adopté par le Conseil de Sécurité le 25 mai 1993, Doc. NU S/RES/827 (1993).
Convention interaméricaine sur l'exécution des décisions rendues par les juridictions pénales étrangères	Convention interaméricaine sur l'exécution des décisions rendues par les juridictions pénales étrangères, 1993, RTOÉA No. 76 (9 juin 1993) (entrée en vigueur le 13 avril 1996).
Convention interaméricaine sur l'extradition	Convention interaméricaine sur l'extradition, 1981, RTOÉA No. 60 (25 févr. 1981) (entrée en vigueur le 28 mars 1992).
Convention interaméricaine sur l'entraide juridique	Convention interaméricaine sur l'entraide juridique en matière pénale, 1992, RTOÉA No. 75 (23 mai 1992) (entrée en vigueur le 14 avril 1996).
Convention pour la répression des actes de terrorisme nucléaire	Convention internationale pour la répression des actes de terrorisme nucléaire, 2005, Rés. A.-G. 59/290 (LIX), Annexe, Doc. NU A/59/766 (13 avril 2005) (entrée en vigueur le 7 juillet 2007).
Principes de Nuremberg	Principes du droit international consacrés par le Statut du tribunal de Nuremberg et dans le jugement de ce tribunal, 1950, Comm'n du droit international, soumis à l'Assemblée générale, Doc. NU A/1316 (1950).
Déclaration de Rabat	Convention sur l'extradition et l'entraide judiciaire en matière de lutte contre le terrorisme, 2008, Annexe à la lettre datée du 14 août 2008 du chargé d'affaires a.i. de la Mission permanente du Maroc auprès des Nations Unies adressée au Secrétaire général. A/62/939 – S/2008/567 (08–47023) (non en vigueur).

Statut de Rome	Statut de Rome de la Cour pénale internationale, 1998, 2187 RTNU 90 (entré en vigueur le 1er juillet 2002).
Convention sur l'imprescriptibilité	Convention sur l'imprescriptibilité des crimes de guerre et des crimes contre l'humanité, 1970, Rés. A.-G. 2391 (XXIII), Doc. NU A/7218, 754 RTNU 73 (26 nov. 1968) (entrée en vigueur le 11 nov. 1970).
Convention pour la répression des attentats terroristes à l'explosif	Convention internationale pour la répression des attentats terroristes à l'explosif, 1997, Rés. A.-G. 52/164, Doc. NU A/RES/52/164 (12 janv. 1998) (entrée en vigueur le 23 mai 2001).
Convention contre la torture	Convention contre la torture et autres peines ou traitements cruels, inhumains ou dégradants, 1987, Rés. A.-G. 39/46, Annexe, (10 déc. 1984) (entrée en vigueur 26 juin 1987).
Charte de l'ONU	Charte des Nations Unies, 1945, 1 RTNU 16 (24 oct. 1945).
Traité type d'entraide judiciaire de l'ONU	Traité type d'entraide judiciaire en matière pénale, 1990, Rés. A.-G. 45/117, Doc. NU A/RES/45/117 (14 déc. 1990).
Convention de l'ONU contre la corruption	Convention des Nations Unies contre la corruption, 2003, Rés. A.-G. 58/4, Doc. NU A/58/422 (31 oct. 2003) (entrée en vigueur le 14 décembre 2005).
Convention de l'ONU contre la criminalité transnationale organisée	Convention des Nations Unies contre la criminalité transnationale organisée, 2001, Rés. A.-G. 25/55, Annexe I, (Vol. I) (2001) (entrée en vigueur le 29 septembre 2003).
Traité type d'extradition de l'ONU	Traité type d'extradition, 1990, Rés. A.-G. 45/116, Doc. NU A/RES/45/49 (14 déc. 1990).
Document final du Sommet mondial	Résolution adoptée par l'Assemblée générale 60/1. Document final du Sommet mondial de 2005, 2005, Rés. A.-G. A/RES/60/1, Doc. NU A/RES/60/1 (24 oct. 2005).

Washington University School of Law

Whitney R. Harris World Law Institute
Crimes Against Humanity Initiative

A Comprehensive History of the *Proposed International Convention on the Prevention and Punishment of Crimes Against Humanity*

By
Leila Nadya Sadat

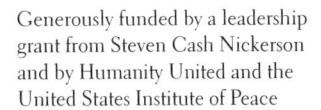

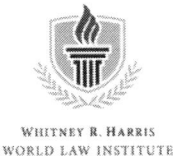

Generously funded by a leadership grant from Steven Cash Nickerson and by Humanity United and the United States Institute of Peace

CONTENTS

I. INTRODUCTION AND BACKGROUND 455
    Why a Specialized Convention on Crimes Against Humanity? 457
    Phases I and II of the Initiative 458
    Phase III of the Initiative 458

II. APRIL EXPERTS' MEETING IN ST. LOUIS, MISSOURI 460
    A. Plenary Sessions and Keynote Address 460
    B. Major Themes Elucidated During the Discussions 461
        1. The Continuing Problem of Atrocity Crimes 461
        2. The Obstacle of Semantic Indifference 462
        3. Capacity Building as an Important Dimension of the Issue 462
        4. Relationship of a Crimes Against Humanity Convention
           to the International Criminal Court 462
           a. Importance of the International Criminal Court 462
           b. The Normative Relationship Between Article 7 of the
              Rome Statute and the *Proposed Convention* 463
           c. The Possibility of a Protocol 464
        5. General Theoretical and Normative Concerns 464
        6. The Question of Universal Jurisdiction 465
        7. The Problem of Selectivity in International Criminal Justice 465
        8. Codification of Crimes Against Humanity and Its
           Relationship to Customary International Law 466
           a. Contributions of the Case Law of the ad hoc Tribunals
              to the Definition of the Crime 466
           b. Gender Crimes 467
        9. State Responsibility, the Critical Importance of
           Prevention and the Responsibility to Protect 467
        10. The Question of Amnesties and Immunities 468
        11. Crimes Against Humanity and Terrorism 468
        12. Interstate Cooperation and Mutual Assistance in
           Penal Matters 469
        13. Modes of Participation 469

III. THE HAGUE INTERSESSIONAL EXPERTS' MEETING 470
    A. Plenary Sessions and Keynote Address 470
    B. Major Themes Elucidated During the Discussions 473
        1. The Importance of Prevention 473
        2. Enforcement 473
           a. The Need to Bring States Within the Jurisdiction of the
              International Court of Justice 473

  b. Filling the Current Gaps in Domestic Legislation..................474
  c. The Possibility of Regional Courts..474
  d. Impact of the Disappearance of the ad hoc Tribunals.............474
  e. The Importance of Effective Mutual Legal Assistance 475
  f. The Need for Compliance Inducement Mechanisms
   such as a Treaty Monitoring Body..475
 3. Public Relations and the Need for Civil Society Involvement.....476
 4. The Responsibility to Protect 476
 5. The Possibility of an Additional Protocol to the Rome Statute 477
 6. The Definitional Question..477
IV. The Technical Advisory Session in St. Louis and Circulation
 of the November Draft Convention for Comment.......................478
V. The Washington, D.C. Meeting, March 11–12, 2010.....................479
 A. Opening Plenary Session and Keynote Address................................480
 B. Major Themes Elucidated During the Discussions 482
  1. Crimes Against Humanity and Gender Justice..............................482
  2. Peace and Justice Dilemmas 483
   a. The Difficulties Facing Humanitarian Workers 484
   b. Sudan and the African Situation More Generally...................484
   c. The Role of Prosecutors 484
   d. Amnesties and Truth Commissions 485
  3. Facilitating Effective Interstate Cooperation in the
   Prevention and Punishment of Crimes Against Humanity 485
   a. Cooperation with International Tribunals...............................485
   b. Cooperation Provisions of the Draft Convention 486
   c. The Normative Contribution of the Draft Convention
    Revisited..488
   d. The Relationship Between Enforcement and Prevention........489
  4. Crimes Against Humanity and U.S. Policy 489
   a. U.S. Role in International Humanitarian Law 490
   b. Existing U.S. Legislation on Atrocity Crimes and Its
    Shortcomings..491
   c. Possible U.S. Role in a Crimes Against
    Humanity Convention 492
   d. A Crimes Against Humanity Convention and Amnesties 493
   e. Alternatives to Ratification 493
   f. The UN Security Council and Crimes Against Humanity 494
  5. Crimes Against Humanity and State Responsibility to Protect 494
   a. The Responsibility to Protect Principle 494
   b. State Responsibility 496
   c. Lessons from the Inter-American Court of Human Rights 497
  6. Universal Jurisdiction, Complementarity and
   Capacity Building..498

       a. Complementarity at the ICC 498
       b. The Work of NGOs in Facilitating Complementarity 499
       c. Reparations for Victims 499
    C. Closing Plenary Session, Issuance of Resolutions
       and the Signing of the Washington Declaration 500
VI. MAY TECHNICAL ADVISORY SESSION 500
VII. CONCLUSION 501

Annex #1: St. Louis Experts' Meeting, List of Participants 549
Annex #2: St. Louis Experts' Meeting, Agenda 553
Annex #3: The Hague Intersessional Experts' Meeting, List of
    Participants 557
Annex #4: The Hague Intersessional Experts' Meeting, Agenda 561
Annex #5: Technical Advisory Session in St. Louis, List of
    Participants 563
Annex #6: List of Experts Submitting Comments on the
    November 2009 Draft Convention 565
Annex #7: Washington Conference, List of Participants 567
Annex #8: Washington Conference, Agenda 573
Annex #9: Technical Advisory Session in Chicago, List of
    Participants 577

Washington University School of Law

Whitney R. Harris World Law Institute
Crimes Against Humanity Initiative

A Comprehensive History of the *Proposed International Convention on the Prevention and Punishment of Crimes Against Humanity*

By

Leila Nadya Sadat*

I. INTRODUCTION AND BACKGROUND

1. In Spring 2008, under the direction of Professor Leila Nadya Sadat, the Whitney R. Harris World Law Institute of Washington University School of Law embarked upon a project to study the need for a comprehensive convention on crimes against humanity, analyze the necessary elements of such a convention and draft a proposed treaty. Since that time, this Crimes Against Humanity Initiative has proceeded in four phases, over a period of three years, as follows:
    - **Phase I**. Preparation of the project and methodological development, including the formation of the Initiative's Steering Committee;
    - **Phase II**. Private study of the project through the commission of working papers by leading experts, the convening of expert meetings and collaborative discussion of draft treaty language at expert meetings held in St. Louis and The Hague;
    - **Phase III**. Public discussion of the project through written consultation with additional experts and at an international conference convened in Washington, D.C. from March 11–12, 2010; and
    - **Phase IV**. Widening consultations with diplomats, academics and members of civil society, and organizing and participating in regional

---

* Henry H. Oberschelp Professor of Law and Director, Whitney R. Harris World Law Institute. This project could not have been undertaken without the generous financial support of Steven Cash Nickerson, the United States Institute of Peace, and Humanity United. I am indebted to Amitis Khojasteh, Yordanka Nedyalkova and B. Don Taylor III for their assistance in preparing this report.

conferences as part of a global awareness campaign focusing on the prevention and punishment of crimes against humanity.
2. In addition to other public outreach efforts, the expert papers, the *Proposed Convention* resulting from the work completed in Phases I-III and this *Comprehensive History* have been published in this volume.
3. As the initial scholarly work was undertaken, a preliminary draft text of the convention, prepared by Professor M. Cherif Bassiouni, was circulated to participants of the Initiative's first meeting (the April Experts' Meeting) to begin the drafting process (*see* paras. 16–46 *infra*). As the Initiative progressed, nearly 250 experts were consulted, many of whom submitted detailed comments (orally or in writing) on the various drafts of the *Proposed Convention* circulated, or attended meetings convened by the Initiative either in the United States or elsewhere. Between formal meetings, technical advisory sessions were held during which every comment received – whether in writing or communicated verbally – was discussed as the text was refined. The *Proposed Convention* went through seven major revisions (and innumerable minor ones) and was approved by the members of the Steering Committee in August 2010 as it now appears in Appendices I (in English) and II (in French) in this volume.[1]
4. The *Proposed Convention* builds upon and complements the ICC Statute by retaining the Rome Statute definition of crimes against humanity but adds robust interstate cooperation, extradition and mutual legal assistance provisions in Annexes 2–6. Universal jurisdiction was retained (but is not mandatory), and the Rome Statute served as the model for several additional provisions, including Articles 4–7 (Responsibility, Official Capacity, Non-Applicability of Statute of Limitations) and with respect to final clauses. Other provisions draw upon other international criminal law and human rights instruments, such as the recently negotiated Convention for the Protection of All Persons from Enforced Disappearance, the Terrorist Bombing Convention, the Convention Against Torture, the United Nations Conventions on Corruption and Organized Crime, the European Transfer of Proceedings Convention and the Inter-American Criminal Sentences Convention.
5. Although the Initiative benefited from the existence of current treaties, the creative work of the drafting process was to meld these and our own ideas into a single, coherent international convention that establishes the principle of State responsibility as well as individual criminal responsibility for the commission of crimes against humanity. The *Proposed*

---

[1] As used in this Comprehensive History, "draft convention" and "proposed convention" refer to interim versions of the *Proposed International Convention on the Prevention and Punishment of Crimes Against Humanity*; "Proposed Convention" refers to the text approved by the Steering Committee in August 2010, which appears in this volume as Appendix I (in English) and Appendix II (in French).

Convention innovates in many respects by attempting to bring prevention into the instrument in a much more explicit way than predecessor instruments, by including the possibility of responsibility for the criminal acts of legal persons, by excluding defenses of immunities and statutory limitations, by prohibiting reservations, and by establishing a unique institutional mechanism for supervision of the convention. Echoing its 1907 forbearer, it also contains its own Martens Clause in paragraph 13 of the Preamble. The twenty-seven Articles and six Annexes of the *Proposed Convention* represent a tremendous effort on the part of many individuals.

Why a Specialized Convention on Crimes Against Humanity?

6. Since the indictment and judgment of the International Military Tribunal at Nuremberg, there has been no specialized convention on crimes against humanity. The objective of the Crimes Against Humanity Initiative is to fill this gap.
7. The Convention for the Prevention and Punishment of the Crime of Genocide was the first international treaty of general application to codify the repression of atrocity crimes. As such, it was a seminal development. Nevertheless, it left large gaps both in terms of the groups that it protected and the scope of its obligations. As a result, only a fraction of the millions of victims over the past six decades has benefited from the provisions of the Genocide Convention. Although other treaties, such as the Apartheid Convention and the new Convention on Enforced Disappearance, condemn particular manifestations of crimes against humanity, most crimes against humanity remain outside the ambit of a universal treaty unless they involve a situation within the jurisdiction of the International Criminal Court. These include extermination, imprisonment, persecution and widespread sexual violence including rape, sexual slavery, enforced prostitution and forced pregnancy.
8. Like the Geneva Conventions of 1949 and the Genocide Convention, a crimes against humanity treaty will complement and reinforce the mission of the International Criminal Court by building upon the negotiations that led to the inclusion of crimes against humanity in the Rome Statute in 1998. At the same time, the Rome Statute provides a starting place, not a final destination, when it comes to the problem of mass atrocities. While the Rome Statute provides for the investigation and prosecution of individual offenders, not all States are parties, and the Court can only prosecute a very limited number of offenders given its size and statutory mandate. A comprehensive crimes against humanity convention could provide much-needed provisions on interstate cooperation in the

investigation and punishment of perpetrators of crimes against humanity, filling a normative gap and providing critically important enforcement mechanisms.

9. The Initiative's goal of ending impunity for those who commit crimes against humanity is also linked to the further development of the Responsibility to Protect doctrine. Under international law, States must not commit certain of the most serious international crimes and may have a duty to prosecute those responsible for their commission. The emerging Responsibility to Protect principle may also require States to affirmatively intervene to protect vulnerable populations from nascent or continuing international crimes under certain circumstances. A necessary condition precedent to the invocation of the Responsibility to Protect is a clear definition of the event which triggers that responsibility. A comprehensive crimes against humanity convention could reinforce the normative obligation not to commit crimes against humanity, as well as emphasize the duty of States to prevent the commission of atrocity crimes.

Phases I and II of the Initiative

10. Phases I and II of the Crimes Against Humanity Initiative were concluded in September 2009, following two experts' meetings held in St. Louis, Missouri and in The Hague in April and June, respectively, of 2009. The discussion at these meetings highlighted the need for the convention to be an effective tool of prevention and interstate cooperation and to provide for universal jurisdiction and State responsibility. It was agreed that the convention should complement the Rome Statute for the International Criminal Court, contain compliance inducement mechanisms, and include provisions emphasizing capacity building. An initial outline of the draft convention was prepared and circulated in October 2008 by Professor M. Cherif Bassiouni and in April 2009 a proposed draft text was circulated by Professor Bassiouni prior to the April Experts' Meeting in St. Louis. This text was revised following the extensive discussions in St. Louis, and a new draft, the May draft convention, was circulated to participants in the Experts' Meeting convened from June 11–12, 2009 in The Hague. A summary of the major themes and discussions in April and June are found in paragraphs 16 to 46 and 47 to 78 below.

Phase III of the Initiative

11. Following the meeting in The Hague on June 11–12, 2009, a new draft of the convention (the July draft) was circulated to a small Technical Advisory

Session of Experts, who met in St. Louis, Missouri, from August 21–23, 2009. The St. Louis August 2009 Technical Advisory Session recommended various changes to the draft convention's language, and a new version of the draft was circulated to the Steering Committee in September 2009. This text was revised further, and a new draft elaborated in November 2009 (the November draft convention).

12. Beginning in November 2009, more than 100 experts – some of whom had been present at earlier meetings, but most of whom had not been at either the April, June, or August meetings of the Initiative – were provided the November draft convention (in English) and invited to comment thereon. To provide relevant background on the progress of the Initiative, as well as the substantive discussions on previous iterations of the draft convention, these experts were also provided with an earlier version of this *Comprehensive History* that summarized Phases I and II (*Final Report on Phases I and II*).

13. A professional French translation of the November draft convention was circulated to French-speaking experts beginning in December 2009. Because the *Final Report on Phases I and II* was not translated, these experts were provided English-language versions of the report.

14. Through February 28, 2010, more than forty experts provided comments on either the English or French drafts of the *Proposed Convention*. Some comments were received orally in discussions with members of the Steering Committee or Harris Institute staff.[2] Many experts provided extremely detailed and helpful written comments. These included technical suggestions regarding terminology and consistency of word choice, and discussions of substantive issues. All comments received were circulated to and considered by the Steering Committee.

15. From March 11–12, 2010, a two-day international conference was held at the Brookings Institution in Washington, D.C. to discuss many of the major themes that had surfaced during earlier discussions of the project. A summary of the major themes and discussions at the March conference are found in paragraphs 85 to 165 below. At the conclusion of the meeting a Declaration was adopted by the Steering Committee calling upon States to adopt a comprehensive crimes against humanity convention. A copy of this document (*The Washington Declaration*) was circulated to participants at the meeting, and, as of this writing, has been signed by more than seventy-five distinguished experts and supporters of international criminal justice who participated in the work of the Initiative.[3]

---

[2] A list of experts offering written comments is found in Annex 6.
[3] *The Washington Declaration* appears in this volume and on the Harris Institute's website at http://law.wustl.edu/crimesagainsthumanity.

II. APRIL EXPERTS' MEETING IN ST. LOUIS, MISSOURI

A. Plenary Sessions and Keynote Address

16. On April 13–15, 2009, forty-six experts gathered at Washington University School of Law for the first public meeting of the Crimes Against Humanity Initiative.[4] The program was opened by Whitney R. Harris, the last surviving podium prosecutor of the Nuremberg trials, who reminded the group of the historical importance of the Nuremberg trials and the link between the commission of crimes against humanity and the destruction of civilization itself. Whitney received a standing ovation as his legacy was recognized and those present were reminded of the work that remained to be done. Following Whitney Harris' remarks, Professor Leila Nadya Sadat, Chair of the Initiative's Steering Committee, opened the meeting and urged the participants to think creatively and imaginatively about the issues to be discussed. Professor Sadat then thanked the members of the Initiative's Steering Committee and Harris Institute and law school staff before turning to the meeting's substantive program.

17. The agenda featured fourteen commissioned papers,[5] each of which addressed a particular aspect of the law and practice relating to crimes against humanity. The first set of papers by Gregory Stanton and Roger Clark addressed the social and historical context within which crimes against humanity take place and early legal efforts to define and ultimately punish the crime. An additional paper by David Crane addressed the "peace and justice" issue often raised regarding attempts to prosecute perpetrators, particularly high-ranking political and military leaders, for crimes against humanity during peace negotiations.

18. The second set of papers took up legal issues regarding the definition of crimes against humanity and its application to particular contexts, focusing on the work of the ad hoc tribunals since 1993 (Göran Sluiter), the "policy element" and the scope of the crime (Guénaël Mettraux), gender crimes (Valerie Oosterveld), ethnic cleansing (John Hagan), immunities and amnesties (Diane Orentlicher), and modes of participation (Elies van Sliedregt).

19. The third set of papers concerned the question of new conceptual paradigms, crimes against humanity and terrorism (Michael Scharf and Michael Newton) and a reconsideration of the "Nuremberg architecture" (M. Cherif Bassiouni).

20. The final set of issues involved enforcement, which became one of the most important foci of the St. Louis meeting. Three papers – on crimes against humanity and the International Criminal Court (Kai Ambos), crimes against

---

[4] A list of expert participants is found in Annex 1. The agenda is found in Annex 2.
[5] See Annex 2.

humanity and the Responsibility to Protect (David Scheffer), and crimes against humanity and national jurisdictions (Payam Akhavan) – formed the basis of the discussion of international criminal law enforcement in various fora and reconnected the end of the conference with the beginning by emphasizing the existing lacuna in the enforcement of international criminal law.

21. On Monday evening, the group was addressed by John Clint Williamson, United States Ambassador-at-Large for War Crimes Issues. Ambassador Williamson spoke in support of the Initiative and highlighted the important work his office was doing to support international justice. He also commented briefly upon his efforts to achieve a limited *rapprochement* between the United States and the International Criminal Court. On Tuesday evening, the group visited Holmes Lounge in historic Ridgley Hall at Washington University, where the twelfth conference of the Inter-Parliamentary Union was held in 1904. It was there, on September 13, 1904, that the Inter-Parliamentary Union issued its appeal for peace and adopted a resolution calling for a second Hague Peace Conference, paving the way for the convening of the 1907 Hague Peace Conference.

22. On both days, a preliminary draft convention, prepared by Professor M. Cherif Bassiouni with comments from various participants (April draft convention), was presented and debated. A revised draft based upon those discussions was then presented to the June Intersessional Meeting of the Crimes Against Humanity Initiative in The Hague (May draft convention).

B. Major Themes Elucidated During the Discussions

1. The Continuing Problem of Atrocity Crimes

23. A compelling case was made that the commission of atrocity crimes, and particularly crimes against humanity, is a continuing and difficult international problem. In one study noted by Professor Bassiouni, of the 310 conflicts from 1948 to 2008, estimated casualties ranged from 92 to 101 million victims, most of whom were civilians. In more than 90 percent of those cases, impunity was the rule.[6] While some participants voiced skepticism that "more law is good," arguing that atrocity trials do not necessarily deliver justice, others felt that punishment of individuals responsible for the commission of atrocity crimes (retributive justice) was a legitimate goal in and of itself. Most participants recognized that neither criminal trials nor alternative forms of justice, such as truth commissions, reparations, lustration, or indigenous models were sufficient in and of themselves to address

---

[6] See THE PURSUIT OF INTERNATIONAL CRIMINAL JUSTICE: A WORLD STUDY ON CONFLICTS, VICTIMIZATION, AND POST-CONFLICT JUSTICE (M. Cherif Bassiouni, ed. 2010).

the commission of mass atrocities. Rather, it was acknowledged that each of these mechanisms was useful and often several were needed during and following a given conflict to maximize peace and restore justice.

2. The Obstacle of Semantic Indifference

24. Several experts underscored the difficulties of rallying international attention and support for preventing and punishing crimes against humanity. Many noted that unless a crime was described as "genocide," its commission somehow seemed less of a problem and required no international response. Many participants were frustrated by this semantic indifference to the commission of crimes against humanity, which has resulted in the victimization of millions of human beings. It was also noted that in the case of the position of the United Nations Special Advisor on the Prevention of Genocide, recommendations had been made to expand the title to "Prevention of Genocide and Mass Atrocities;" however, ultimately, the decision was taken not to include the words "Mass Atrocities." This was perhaps due to fears that, as one participant put it, States are conscious that crimes against humanity cut "close to the bone." One participant suggested shortening the definition of the crime, to make it more easily understandable to the general public, in the way that the Genocide Convention uses a short definition.

3. Capacity Building as an Important Dimension of the Issue

25. Several participants noted that one critical issue for societies addressing the problem of mass atrocities and post-conflict justice was the need for additional capacity building of local institutions. Many participants offered useful suggestions as to how a crimes against humanity convention might address this problem, and noted that the anti-trafficking convention seemed particularly helpful in the case of Vietnam, and the ILO convention on the worst forms of child labor seemed to stimulate State responses in many cases. Other experts suggested perhaps the establishment of a secretariat or a treaty body associated with the convention that could assist with State capacity building. Another alternative was the creation of a voluntary fund for States like those found in many environmental treaties where reallocation of resources from wealthy to poorer nations has become important.

4. Relationship of a Crimes Against Humanity Convention to the International Criminal Court

a. Importance of the International Criminal Court

26. Much of the conference time was devoted to thinking about the relationship between the International Criminal Court and a new treaty condemning

crimes against humanity. Virtually unanimous support was expressed for the idea that the treaty should in no way hamper, but should instead support the ICC and build upon the ICC Statute. Many experts referred to the long and arduous process of negotiating the Rome Statute, the fragile compromises achieved, and the current difficulties of the Court, particularly in regard to political support from African States, as reasons to rely heavily upon the ICC Statute for definitional purposes and to ensure that a new treaty with provisions on interstate enforcement and State responsibility would complement the ICC regime.

b. The Normative Relationship Between Article 7 of the Rome Statute and the Proposed Convention

27. A fundamental question for the meeting was what to do with the definition in Article 7 of the Rome Statute. Several participants wrote superb papers proposing changes in the Article 7 definition. These proposals included dropping the "civilian population" requirement; deleting the "policy" element; expanding the list of gender crimes; including ethnic cleansing as a separate head of crime; and writing a new, shorter definition, harkening back to Article 6(c) of the Nuremberg Charter. Others noted that in spite of thoughtful arguments contending that the Rome Statute was not a codification of custom, but treaty law applicable only before the International Criminal Court, 108 States had already ratified the Rome Statute and were adopting domestic legislation tracking its provisions in order to fulfill their "complementarity" obligations.[7] Therefore, as a practical matter, changing the Rome Statute definition seemed impossible for those States and even implicated the law of treaties. Nonetheless, many experts continued to struggle with this question, as they believed that including the Rome Statute definition could be problematic in a multilateral interstate convention and were concerned that an international convention building upon it would not permit customary international law to evolve in a progressive manner. After much discussion, two possibilities emerged from the discussions that met with general approval.

28. First, the suggestion was made that the proposed convention essentially leave the definition open. A variation of this is found in Article 5 of the new Convention on Enforced Disappearance, which provides:

> The widespread or systematic practice of enforced disappearance constitutes a crime against humanity as defined in applicable international law and shall attract the consequences provided for under such applicable international law.

---

[7] As of this writing, 114 States are Parties to the Rome Statute.

29. A similar proposal was included as option 2 in Article 2 of the May draft convention. This solution preserves flexibility – States Parties to the Rome Statute could incorporate the Rome Statute definition or, as some States have already done, modify it slightly. Concerns about the legality principle caused some discomfort with this proposal for some participants, who suggested instead incorporating Article 7 of the Rome Statute verbatim, but with some modifications given the definition's inclusion in a separate treaty. This is option 1 in Article 2 of the May draft convention.

c. The Possibility of a Protocol

30. One idea that emerged during the two days of meetings was the possibility of a protocol to the Rome Statute as an alternative to a separate multilateral convention. It was suggested that this could put the convention on a shorter track and would signify support for the Rome Statute. Other crimes within the Rome Statute might also be included in such a protocol, which would then require adoption by the ICC Assembly of States Parties. It was noted, however, that adoption by the Assembly of States Parties (which would require a supermajority vote) might bog the convention down in a long process and might not offer the shorter track envisaged. Moreover, although it would be possible for ICC non-States Parties to ratify such a protocol, ICC non-States Parties might not be able to participate fully in the initial discussions of the Protocol if the venue were the ICC Assembly of States Parties, as opposed to a United Nations conference open to all. Finally, such a Protocol could include no provisions on State Responsibility or prevention.

5. General Theoretical and Normative Concerns

31. Many experts focused on the theory underlying crimes against humanity prosecutions, particularly as related to their definition and enforcement. As one participant remarked, perhaps the question was not whether the problem to be solved can be addressed in practice but whether it worked in theory. To put it another way, this expert observed that the question of what should be in a crimes against humanity convention depends upon which social interests one is trying to protect. Typically, crimes against humanity turn the normal state of affairs "on its head" because the State has turned against its own citizens. In that sense, crimes against humanity has a "State policy" requirement because it is about State power. Other theories, however, ground crimes against humanity either in international humanitarian law, as an additional protection for civilians during war time, or in human rights law, which provides the broadest and most universal grounds for the protection of human dignity.

6. The Question of Universal Jurisdiction

32. Many participants noted that crimes against humanity were traditionally considered "universal jurisdiction" crimes. Indeed, one paper suggested that a central feature of a crimes against humanity convention would be the inclusion of provisions on universal jurisdiction that would substantially strengthen the interstate enforcement regime applicable to the crimes. The biggest gap in international enforcement of crimes against humanity is that while complementarity focuses on national court jurisdiction, it only requires national courts to act in conjunction with a request from the International Criminal Court. If the Court's jurisdiction is not somehow engaged, there is no duty to try or extradite in the absence of legislation so providing. At the same time, substantial debate ensued as to the desirability of putting mandatory universal jurisdiction provisions in a treaty, as some States would be wary of ratifying a treaty instrument with provisions on universal jurisdiction, and the April draft convention included a clause suggesting that universal jurisdiction would be exercised only in limited circumstances. After substantial discussion, it was decided to put jurisdictional clauses in the crimes against humanity convention that tracked those already present in existing treaties, such as the Torture Convention, the Convention for the Suppression of Terrorist Bombings and the new Convention on Enforced Disappearance.

33. There was also considerable discussion of the failures of universal jurisdiction to materialize as a significant threat to "traveling tyrants," in part due to financial concerns. The example of Senegal was advanced, noting that it had argued it was unable to prosecute Hissène Habré due to the financial burden that such a trial would impose. The difficulty of convincing African States to ratify a new convention if there would be a duty (rather than an option) to exercise universal jurisdiction was also evoked.

7. The Problem of Selectivity in International Criminal Justice

34. The challenge posed by the objections of many African States to the issuance of the International Criminal Court's arrest warrant against Sudanese President al-Bashir was noted by several participants, who observed that it had been viewed in some quarters as an attack upon African dignity. The same issue was evoked with respect to the exercise of universal jurisdiction by "northern courts," which may promote criminal justice, but may not be considered legitimate if they are perceived as selectively targeting only these crimes committed in the southern hemisphere. Others responded that crimes against humanity are not committed lawfully by any sovereign, and that all victims, whether African, Asian, European, or Latin American, are entitled to

justice, both when they are victimized by their own States directly and when their States are unwilling or unable to protect them from being victimized by other actors. At the same time, it was acknowledged by the group that selectivity is a cause for concern and that consideration must be given as to how a crimes against humanity convention might address the issue.

8. Codification of Crimes Against Humanity and Its Relationship to Customary International Law

a. Contributions of the Case Law of the ad hoc Tribunals to the Definition of the Crime

35. This topic was the subject of a paper and a recurring theme throughout the discussions. The paper focused upon the ongoing difficulties in defining crimes against humanity and noted that even though the ICC Statute is an important codification, the legal team of the UN Secretary-General built upon, but modified, the ICC definition in developing the Statute for the Special Court of Sierra Leone. Thus, the paper concluded, there still appear to be uncertainties surrounding the crime and its definition. The paper also noted that in the summer of 1998, when the Rome Statute was adopted, only the *Tadić* jurisdictional decision (October 1995) and judgment (May 1997) had been handed down, meaning that case law from the International Criminal Tribunal for the former Yugoslavia (ICTY) and the International Criminal Tribunal for Rwanda (ICTR) could not have had much influence on the ICC codification, although there was considerably more jurisprudence by the time the Elements of Crimes were adopted in 2002. As for the post-Rome experience, a vigorous discussion ensued as to whether the contributions of the ad hoc tribunals had developed the law on crimes against humanity in a positive manner. Questions as to methodology, particularly in the "discovery" of customary international law, were raised, with the larger question remaining as to the overall relationship between the law of the ICC and customary international law.

36. Many participants noted the tension between the universality of the ICC Statute – in aspirational terms because the Statute has not yet achieved universal acceptance, and in practical terms because of the possibility of Security Council referrals regarding situations in non-States Parties – and the idea that customary international law regarding crimes against humanity could continue to evolve outside the Statute, including in other international courts and tribunals. At the same time, it was noted that Article 10 of the ICC Statute itself anticipates such a situation, and that "fragmentation" was perhaps not an undesirable structural consequence of the international legal order in all its diversity. The debates on these ideas resulted in the alternative formulations of Article 2 of the May draft convention.

b. Gender Crimes

37. The paper on gender crimes argued that in order to be relevant to the nature of current and future armed conflicts, a treaty codifying crimes against humanity should reflect a range of gender-based prohibited acts. The paper also critiqued the definition of gender in the Rome Statute and suggested that perhaps the term, if included in a crimes against humanity convention, should not be defined. Both the paper author and the discussant argued for further specification of gender violence in a crimes against humanity convention, noting that using umbrella terms like "other inhumane acts" did not adequately capture the specific nature and horror of gender crimes. Others noted the difficulty of modifying the Rome Statute definition to provide for additional gender based crimes, for the reasons noted above (*see* paras. 27–29, *supra*).

9. State Responsibility, the Critical Importance of Prevention and the Responsibility to Protect

38. Although no paper was commissioned specifically on the issue of State responsibility, the issue arose throughout the two and one-half days of meetings. Participants were in widespread agreement that the principal goal of a crimes against humanity convention should be to end impunity for those who commit crimes against humanity, especially where those individuals use the apparatus of the State as an instrument of victimization. As one participant noted, the principal evil of a crime against humanity is the insidious way in which the territory of a State is transformed from a place of refuge into a trap. Recalling recent international criminal prosecutions of former heads of State, as well as former governmental and military leaders, participants agreed that the goal of ending impunity seems best served by focusing on the individual criminal responsibility of those actors instrumental to the commission of crimes against humanity.

39. Noting that criminal prosecutions are primarily reactive, several participants highlighted the problem of prevention and suggested useful additions to the draft convention along those lines. Obviously, it is hoped, but not empirically demonstrable, that the prosecution of atrocity crimes will deter future atrocity crimes; indeed, it was observed that given the paucity of enforcement of the norms against genocide, war crimes and crimes against humanity, impunity remained the rule rather than the exception. At the same time, the paper on the Responsibility to Protect suggested language that would go further than requiring States to criminalize and prosecute individuals for committing crimes against humanity and would prohibit, and thus render illegal, the commission of crimes against humanity by any State Party, and require States Parties to the convention to act in accordance with the Responsibility to

Protect principles set forth in the 2005 World Summit Outcome document. While some participants were supportive of including such provisions in a crimes against humanity convention, others hesitated, questioning whether the principles enunciated are clear enough or opining that inclusion of such principles could hinder the adoption of a convention.

10. The Question of Amnesties and Immunities

40. Echoing the conclusions of the commissioned paper on the subject of amnesties and immunities, several participants argued that a crimes against humanity convention should include a specific prohibition on immunities but should not include a blanket prohibition of amnesties. For immunities, the question for the participants was not whether to include such a prohibition, but what form the prohibition should take. Much of the discussion centered on the state of the law following the *Arrest Warrant* case, with some suggesting that an immunity prohibition in a crimes against humanity convention should seek to progressively define the scope of immunity *ratione personae*. It was also suggested that a specific immunity prohibition should include a sentence excluding crimes against humanity from being characterized as official or public acts, which could serve to clarify what one participant described as the 'ambiguous' language of the *Arrest Warrant* case regarding private acts vis-à-vis immunity *ratione materiae*. Finally, it was suggested that any prohibition of immunities should not be limited to criminal prosecutions but extend to civil and administrative actions as well.

41. It was observed that recent attempts to codify a provision that would limit or prohibit the possibility of amnesty in the Rome Statute and the Convention on Enforced Disappearance had not borne fruit. It was noted that drafting an 'appropriate' amnesty provision might be particularly difficult in that a blanket prohibition could sweep too broadly, yet crafting appropriate exceptions could be problematic. The issue is already addressed to the extent that the *Proposed Convention* imposes a duty on States to prosecute those who commit crimes against humanity. In addition, the expert paper submitted by Professor Orentlicher noted that it could actually be counterproductive to include a prohibition on amnesties, as such could imply that no prohibition currently exists as a matter of customary international law in the absence of a treaty provision.

11. Crimes Against Humanity and Terrorism

42. Following some discussion, there seemed to be widespread agreement among the participants that it was unnecessary and potentially problematic to include

terrorism as a crime against humanity. Although some advantages could be envisioned, such as providing for universal jurisdiction over terrorist acts not currently covered by any of the existing terrorism conventions, it was felt that any attempt to include terrorism as a crime against humanity would suffer from the same definitional problem that has plagued States in this area—namely, the difficulty of States reaching a consensus on a general definition of terrorism. Moreover, the vast majority of those specific *acts* for which consensus could be achieved are already prohibited in one of the many existing terrorism conventions. Some of them are also already subsumed within the definition of crimes against humanity, such as mass murder under certain circumstances. Finally, it was observed that the Rome Statute does not include terrorism as a crime against humanity, and that the inclusion of terrorism in a crimes against humanity convention would therefore raise the concern repeatedly voiced that the convention should seek to complement the operation of the ICC rather than complicate its operations in any way.

12. Interstate Cooperation and Mutual Assistance in Penal Matters

43. It was widely agreed among the participants that bridging the enforcement "gap" should be one of the primary functions of a crimes against humanity convention. This must include fostering the notion that States have an obligation to prosecute rather than merely a discretionary ability to prosecute. Such an obligation, however, must be coupled with providing the realistic capacity to prosecute which, for many States, will necessarily involve prosecutions requiring interstate cooperation in the form of mutual legal assistance.

13. Modes of Participation

44. Much of the discussion of how a crimes against humanity convention should address modes of participation and individual criminal responsibility centered on two distinct issues: superior responsibility and joint criminal enterprise. There was widespread agreement that a distinct provision on superior responsibility should be included in the convention, and that this should incorporate the developments in the jurisprudence on this issue at the ad hoc international criminal tribunals. Most participants felt that the existing provision in the Rome Statute was the best option. Although it was pointed out that there are still some open questions regarding modes of participation and individual criminal responsibility arising from existing jurisprudence, and that certain aspects of the jurisprudence have been controversial, it was generally considered that most of these are not questions to be directly addressed in the text of a convention.

45. It was widely acknowledged that although some form of extended liability is necessary to address the "system criminality" inherent in crimes against humanity, the development of joint criminal enterprise at the ad hoc international criminal tribunals has been problematic. The doctrine should not be stretched to the point that it becomes a threat to equitable application of the law. One suggestion made was that participants should consider whether conspiracy should be included as a mode of participation. Although there was no consensus reached on this question, it was pointed out that the concept of conspiracy has become more palatable to civil law countries with the spread of anti-terrorism legislation.

46. Finally, at the conclusion of the St. Louis meeting, the Steering Committee determined to commission an additional paper on interstate enforcement, given the central importance of that issue. Laura Olson was commissioned to produce that paper during Summer 2009.

III. THE HAGUE INTERSESSIONAL EXPERTS' MEETING

A. *Plenary Sessions and Keynote Address*

47. On June 11–12, 2009, fifty-eight experts gathered at Leiden University's Campus Den Haag for the second public meeting of the Crimes Against Humanity Initiative.[8] The program was opened by the Honorable J.J. van Aartsen, Mayor of the City of The Hague, who welcomed the participants to the international city of peace and justice. Mayor van Aartsen stated that it was a great honor for the City of The Hague to host the meeting, noting in closing that "where lawlessness and absence of rights prevail, people cannot live in peace. Where injustice goes unpunished, old conflicts keep flaring up again."

48. The group was then addressed briefly by Judge Hans-Peter Kaul, Second Vice President of the International Criminal Court. Judge Kaul also welcomed the participants and expressed his own personal enthusiasm and support for the Crimes Against Humanity Initiative.

49. Steering Committee member Justice Richard Goldstone delivered an opening address in which he bridged the work of the April and June meetings, and drew upon the South African experience with apartheid and the current indictment of Sudanese President Omar al-Bashir by the International Criminal Court to illustrate the central role of enforcement to the success of any treaty addressing international crimes. He reminded the participants that the multilateral convention condemning apartheid was never enforced and that South African diplomats were welcomed in capitals across the

---

[8] A list of expert participants is found in Annex 3. The Agenda is found in Annex 4.

world during the apartheid era. This, he believed, may have prolonged the existence of South Africa's apartheid policies by as much as a decade. However, the situation in South Africa is now different. In that context, he noted that South Africa had announced it would arrest Sudanese President al-Bashir if he entered South Africa.

50. Justice Goldstone revisited several of the issues that had been discussed in St. Louis, including the relationship between the convention's definition of crimes against humanity and Article 7 of the Rome Statute, the need for more specific obligations of States, and the importance of workable enforcement mechanisms, including a treaty monitoring body. Justice Goldstone also reminded the participants of the need to remain ever-conscious of the victims of crimes against humanity, who are too often overlooked, and noted that to this end the convention should address State responsibility and might include non-State actors to facilitate the award of reparations to victims. Finally, he noted that the answer to those who might question the need for a crimes against humanity convention was twofold: first, such a treaty would confer jurisdiction in the International Court of Justice over crimes against humanity committed by States, thus avoiding the result in the case of *Bosnia and Herzegovina v. Serbia and Montenegro*; second, the treaty would oblige States to implement domestic legislation directed at crimes against humanity.

51. During the morning plenary session introducing the report of the St. Louis meeting, Steering Committee member M. Cherif Bassiouni drew upon his experience with the evolution of the Torture Convention from an academic idea to a political reality and described the need for a well-thought-out strategy possessing the greatest potential for the Initiative to lead to the adoption of an international instrument. He described the comparative benefits and disadvantages of the two options currently being considered, a comprehensive convention, and, as suggested in St. Louis, an additional protocol to the Rome Statute. Professor Bassiouni emphasized that the convention must seek to fill the enforcement gap that exists with regard to crimes against humanity, noting that effective extradition and mutual legal assistance provisions will be crucial to facilitating the bilateral cooperation necessary for the convention to be an effective tool in deterring crimes against humanity. He reminded the participants that the best is often the enemy of the good and urged all of them to focus on the end goal and be prepared, if necessary, to compromise on provisions of personal interest. He characterized the Initiative as an academic offering to the international community, one that seeks to accomplish a great objective.

52. Steering Committee member William Schabas also addressed the morning plenary session, warning the participants that a crimes against humanity convention must be drafted so as to achieve a delicate balance between codification and aspiration. He referenced the European Court of Human

Rights' decision in the *Soering* case as an example of treaty drafting which foreclosed progressive development by judicial interpretation. He also noted that the experience of the ad hoc international criminal tribunals demonstrates the benefit of permitting judges to progressively interpret the contours of customary international law. With regard to the interim draft treaty's definition of crimes against humanity, Professor Schabas noted that it had become clear during the St. Louis meeting that nothing about the draft treaty should have the potential for undermining the Rome Statute. He outlined the comparative benefits and disadvantages of having either a verbatim copy of the definition from Article 7 of the Rome Statute in the crimes against humanity convention, or no definition at all.

53. Three panel discussions were conducted during the remainder of the day. The first, chaired by Steering Committee member Juan Mendez, addressed the need for a crimes against humanity convention as a natural completion of the work begun with the Rome Statute, discussing the timing, feasibility, and scope of a convention. The second panel, chaired by Steering Committee member Ambassador Hans Corell, addressed enforcement issues, including extradition, mutual legal assistance, immunities and State responsibility. The third panel, chaired by Steering Committee Chair Leila Sadat, discussed ways in which the convention would complement the work of the International Criminal Court.

54. On Thursday evening, the group was addressed by Gareth Evans, former Foreign Minister of Australia and then President and CEO of the International Crisis Group. He recalled his travels through Asia as a young man and the friendships he developed with students from all over the region, including young Cambodians, all of whom later died in the mass atrocities committed by Pol Pot's regime. Evans noted that the knowledge and memory of what must have happened to those young men and women haunts him to this day. It was this memory, he said, that made him intensely committed to the Initiative and the ultimate adoption of a convention to fill the gap "which has all too obviously become apparent in the array of legal instruments available to deal with atrocity crimes, notwithstanding the emergence of the International Criminal Court." Finally, Evans said that he had every confidence that the Initiative "will bear real fruit."[9]

55. On Friday, a technical advisory session was held to discuss the May draft convention. Many technical and substantive suggestions were received as the participants discussed and debated the draft treaty language. It was noted that over the summer, Harris Institute staff under the direction of Professor Bassiouni and Professor Sadat would work to research and implement the suggestions made at the technical session. It was also decided that a drafting

---

[9] The text of Mr. Evans's remarks is found in this volume.

meeting would be convened in St. Louis in August, during which a limited number of participants from the two experts' meetings would work to refine the draft text.

B. Major Themes Elucidated During the Discussions

1. The Importance of Prevention

56. Many participants acknowledged that it will be vitally important for the convention to be an instrument for the fair and effective prosecution and punishment of those who commit crimes against humanity, but also felt that prevention should be the primary focus of the convention. Parallels were drawn to the Genocide Convention, with some participants noting that it is particularly weak vis-à-vis prevention and often used as a fig leaf behind which States hide to avoid their obligations. This experience should inform the Initiative. One participant spoke of the NATO bombing campaign in Kosovo as an example of the preventive potential of the convention. He noted that NATO commanders went to extraordinary lengths to avoid civilian casualties, due in no small part to their knowledge of the existence of the ICTY and its mandate.

57. It was then suggested that prevention must focus on education and capacity building among States. In this regard, several participants also noted the importance of "operationalizing" the emerging norm of the Responsibility to Protect and thought that the convention would benefit from explicitly recognizing the norm as a State obligation.

2. Enforcement

a. The Need to Bring States within the Jurisdiction of the International Court of Justice

58. Echoing the discussion at the April Experts' Meeting in St. Louis, many participants and panelists spoke to the need for the convention to specifically address the question of State responsibility. Many participants voiced strong support for the inclusion in the treaty of a dispute settlement mechanism vesting jurisdiction for inter-State disputes in the International Court of Justice (ICJ). As became painfully apparent with the ICJ's decision in the *Bosnia and Herzegovina v. Serbia and Montenegro* case, there is currently no mechanism for holding States responsible when they commit or are complicit in crimes against humanity. As such, there is currently no mechanism by which either aggrieved States or the victims of such crimes may seek reparations, leaving the vast majority of victims with no remedy. Moreover, at least one member of the International Court of Justice

continues to believe that the Genocide Convention does not provide a basis for the invocation of State responsibility, making it necessary to explicitly address this issue in the draft convention.

59. It was suggested that in addition to States, thought should be given to including non-State actors, including corporations, within the provisions of the treaty. If feasible, this would ensure that organizations which commit or are complicit in crimes against humanity may be held accountable for reparations to aggrieved States and victims.

b. Filling the Current Gaps in Domestic Legislation

60. It was generally agreed among participants that there is currently a vacuum in domestic legislation regarding international crimes in general, including crimes against humanity, and that one of the primary goals of effective enforcement under the convention should be to fill this gap. For example, it was noted that only two of the thirty African States Parties to the Rome Statute have implemented domestic legislation, and only five of thirty-one Commonwealth States have done so. This is also a problem among States not parties to the Rome Statute. Indeed, one participant pointed out that crimes against humanity are completely missing from U.S. law. Universal domestication of the obligations under the convention will be important to ensuring that there is no safe haven for those who commit crimes against humanity.

61. The suggestion was also made that alternatives to traditional domestic prosecutions should be considered. Specifically, with regard to the domestication of the convention's obligations to extradite or prosecute, the question was raised whether it would be sufficient for States to prosecute offenders domestically for "ordinary" crimes (*i.e.*, multiple counts of murder), as opposed to murder as a crime against humanity. It was also suggested that States might employ a strategy of deportation of suspected offenders rather than prosecution.

c. The Possibility of Regional Courts

62. One participant noted that the experience of both international criminal tribunals and domestic courts demonstrates that prosecuting crimes against humanity is logistically and technically difficult, and that States will need to have specialized units dedicated to atrocity crimes. Given these difficulties, and the lack of capacity apparent in many domestic criminal justice systems, it was suggested that thought should be given to the creation of regional courts that might more effectively prosecute offenders.

d. Impact of the Disappearance of the ad hoc Tribunals

63. Relevant to the discussion about the need for capacity building, several participants noted that with the impending closure of the various ad hoc

international criminal tribunals, there will be a significant number of professionals with expertise in the adjudication of crimes against humanity. Thought should be given to how this wealth of experience might be put to use in furtherance of the convention and its goals.

e. The Importance of Effective Mutual Legal Assistance

64. There was widespread agreement among the participants that effective mutual legal assistance among States is a necessary pre-requisite if the convention is to have any hope of fulfilling its potential. It was noted that concrete and enforceable mutual legal assistance obligations would "tighten the net," making it easier for States to prosecute those individuals responsible for crimes against humanity.
65. It was suggested that the convention would benefit by looking to the detailed mutual legal assistance provisions in other conventions, including specifically the UN Convention Against Corruption and the UN Convention Against Transnational Crime. It was also noted that the convention could include provisions on witness protection, modeled upon the UN Convention Against Corruption, and a provision on international subpoenas. A provision on subpoenas could benefit the prosecution of these crimes, which often cross State borders, and would constitute a much-needed progressive development in the field of mutual legal assistance.
66. Given the fundamental importance of mutual legal assistance in combating international crime, it was also suggested that perhaps there should be a convention aimed specifically at mutual legal assistance for international crimes. This suggestion met with widespread approval, in particular by some at the meeting representing NGOs, who noted that they have been supportive of such a convention for many years.

f. The Need for Compliance Inducement Mechanisms such as a Treaty Monitoring Body

67. Many of the participants said that the convention would benefit greatly by the inclusion of a treaty monitoring body. Such a body should have the capacity to receive and review compliance reports submitted by States and should be prepared to publicize any State Party's failure to abide by its obligations under the convention. Such a mechanism was thought by some to be an effective tool, with the capacity to raise the alarm when any situation threatened to deteriorate to the point where crimes against humanity might be committed.
68. Other participants felt that a treaty monitoring body should exist more in the form of a technical secretariat without any specific duty to "name and shame" non-compliant States. This body would exist to facilitate training

and capacity building where it is needed. The participants were in widespread agreement that many States lack the resources and/or the political will to prevent, investigate, or punish crimes against humanity. A treaty monitoring body equipped to provide support and training directly to such States would therefore benefit both the prevention and punishment dimensions of the convention. It was felt that training for domestic law enforcement would be particularly useful. One participant familiar with the domestic investigation of crimes against humanity in West Africa noted that he had been extremely impressed with the professionalism of the investigations. Others noted that the training of local law enforcement provided the best option for ensuring successful investigation and domestic prosecution.

3. Public Relations and the Need for Civil Society Involvement

69. The participants agreed that it would be crucial for the success of the Initiative to have the support of civil society. It will be important for the general population of the world to see the need for a convention, and for the plight of those affected by crimes against humanity to be made more relevant and highly visible. To this end, the Initiative will need high profile people and organizations to publicize and promote the need for a convention. Some participants noted that crimes against humanity suffer from a "perception" problem, in that crimes against humanity are viewed as less egregious violations than genocide. Accordingly, one of the great benefits of a convention would be its potential for addressing and correcting this perception. This was also discussed at the St. Louis Experts' Meeting, where the problem of semantic indifference was evoked (*see* para. 24, *supra*).

70. With regard to the importance of public opinion, it was noted that NGOs played an important role at the Rome Conference and were instrumental in marshalling public opinion in favor of ICC ratification in many States. Organizations such as the Coalition for the International Criminal Court, Amnesty International and Africa Legal Aid – all represented at the meeting – could play an important public relations role in promoting awareness of the convention among both States and the general public, as well as helping to galvanize public and political support for the convention. It was suggested that a special meeting for NGOs be convened, and that the Initiative involve them more deeply in formulating a political strategy.

4. The Responsibility to Protect

71. As in St. Louis, the participants held mixed views on whether, or to what degree, the convention should incorporate the developing norm recognizing the Responsibility to Protect. While some felt that the General

Assembly's resolution on the norm provides a sufficient basis for including it as an affirmative State obligation, others were less confident.

72. Some who supported "operationalizing" the Responsibility to Protect doctrine in the convention noted that the apparent intention of the current Secretary General to aggressively promote the norm provided an opportunity. Some suggested that including the norm as an affirmative State obligation represented a significant comparative added value of a comprehensive convention over an additional protocol to the Rome Statute. Finally, it was suggested that the principle of Responsibility to Protect could be recognized and affirmed in the Preamble.

5. The Possibility of an Additional Protocol to the Rome Statute

73. Many participants addressed the question posed by the morning speakers with regard to an optional protocol to the Rome Statute, voicing various degrees of support and concern. Some were concerned that many States which have ratified the Rome Statute have failed to domesticate its provisions. This caused some to question the need for any additional law, noting that attention should be paid to enforcing existing law.
74. Other participants pointed out that tying the Initiative to the Rome Statute in the form of an additional protocol raises particular problems for States that are not parties to the ICC. Thus, an additional protocol is bound to face political difficulties that a comprehensive convention would not raise. While it is certainly not the only State in such a position, the United States was mentioned as a specific example of one non-party State which would face particular political difficulties.
75. Ultimately, there was agreement with the Steering Committee's decision to proceed with the preparation of a convention and, at a later time, an additional protocol. It was noted that the additional protocol could be modeled upon the provisions of the convention.

6. The Definitional Question

76. As in the St. Louis meeting, there was a clear consensus among the experts in The Hague that the convention must complement the Rome Statute and do no harm to the ICC. On the question whether the convention should track Article 7 of the Rome Statute or have no definition of crimes against humanity, most participants felt that the lack of a definition would present problems for States in being able to domestically prosecute crimes against humanity. This could be a particular problem for States which are not parties to the Rome Statute, as they will have to decide how to define the crime domestically to give effect to the principle of legality. It was also

suggested that members of the public reading the convention should be able to understand directly from the convention what is prohibited, as is now the case with the Genocide Convention.

77. Ultimately, there was little support for the option of not including any definition in the convention. Although it was acknowledged that copying Article 7 raises technical issues, such as potential amendments to Article 7, it was generally agreed that these issues did not pose insurmountable difficulties. Some participants also noted that copying Article 7 will not foreclose States from progressively developing their own domestic statutes on crimes against humanity. Canada was raised as an example of one domestic jurisdiction which has implemented broader prohibitions on crimes against humanity than it was required to do by the Rome Statute.

78. Some participants advocated expanding the list of crimes in Article 7 to include issues of immediate concern to developing States, especially in the global "South." These would include economic and environmental crimes. The same question had also come up in the April Experts' Meeting in St. Louis. However thoughtful these and other suggestions were, the consensus remained that Article 7 should not be modified by the convention.

IV. THE TECHNICAL ADVISORY SESSION IN ST. LOUIS AND CIRCULATION OF THE NOVEMBER DRAFT CONVENTION FOR COMMENT

79. Following the Hague Intersessional Experts' Meeting in June, the draft treaty was revised in accordance with the input received during the June meeting. This work produced an amended treaty draft (July draft convention), which was circulated to the Steering Committee for review and comment.

80. On August 21–23, 2009, seven experts gathered at Washington University School of Law for a technical advisory session on the July draft convention.[10] During two full days of meetings, the participants reviewed and discussed each article of the text. At the successful conclusion of the meetings, the participants were able to reach a consensus on refinement of the July draft convention, which was then sent to the Steering Committee for comment in September (the September draft convention).

81. Following Steering Committee input and revision, the draft text was again refined, and an interim November draft convention was produced and circulated to more than 100 experts for comment. The convention was also

---

[10] A list of expert participants is found in Annex 5.

translated into French and sent to Francophone experts who commented on the French text.

82. Each of the experts who provided written comments on both the English and French draft conventions expressed broad support for the goals of the Initiative. Several experts whose schedules did not permit detailed review and comment nevertheless expressed their admiration for the work of the Initiative and their hopes for its success. A few experts expressed doubts as to whether States would take up the draft convention at this time but nonetheless applauded the Initiative's goals and progress. One expert noted that although skeptical at first, he was persuaded of the need for a convention following his review of the most recent draft. Echoing the problem of semantic indifference discussed during previous meetings (*see* paras. 24 and 69, *supra*), this expert noted that a convention focused on crimes against humanity might prod States which currently seem to be excessively focused on the label of "genocide" as a precondition to concern and action.

83. The only hesitations expressed went to the timing of the Initiative. While broad agreement was expressed as to its normative goals, it was underscored by some that the project should support rather than detract from the important work of the International Criminal Court. Additionally, some experts expressed their hope that the project would engage in "progressive" development of the law. That is, the concern was raised that it was likely that States might use the opportunity for a new convention to retreat from the application of the doctrine of universal jurisdiction or immunities, for example, and the Initiative was urged to elaborate a convention that would take a strong "anti-impunity" stand, given that States would likely water down the provisions later on during further study and negotiations.

84. It was impossible for the Steering Committee to adopt all comments received, particularly as many experts disagreed with each other. Each comment, however, was carefully considered during the final revisions of the draft text, and particularly where a clear consensus emerged, the text was modified accordingly.[11]

V. THE WASHINGTON, D.C. MEETING, MARCH 11–12, 2010

85. From March 11–12, 2010, nearly 100 experts gathered at the Brookings Institution, in Washington, D.C., for the final "capstone" conference of the Initiative's first three phases.[12] Like the April Experts' Meeting in St. Louis, the program opened with a presentation from Whitney R. Harris

---

[11] The list of experts providing written comments is found in Annex 6.
[12] A list of expert participants is found in Annex 7. The agenda is found in Annex 8. The discussion at the Washington meeting focused on the November 2009 draft of the *Proposed Convention*; therefore, all references to draft provisions in this section refer to the November draft convention.

who reminded the group of the historical importance of the Nuremberg trials and the link between the commission of crimes against humanity and the destruction of civilization itself. Whitney urged the group to finish the Nuremberg legacy by adopting a convention to prevent and punish crimes against humanity. These were Whitney Harris's final public remarks, for he passed away on April 22, 2010.[13]

86. The agenda featured an opening and a closing plenary session, six panels addressing issues that had surfaced during the Initiative's work, and keynote addresses by Stephen J. Rapp, U.S. Ambassador-at-Large for War Crimes Issues and Christian Wenaweser, Permanent Representative of Lichtenstein to the United Nations and President of the Assembly of States Parties to the Rome Statute of the International Criminal Court. The program was opened by Strobe Talbott, President of the Brookings Institution, who welcomed the participants and underscored the important role of Brookings Institution projects and scholars in shaping and informing U.S. foreign policy. Mark Wrighton, Chancellor of Washington University in St. Louis, then presented the University's "Global Philanthropy Award" to Steven Cash Nickerson for his leadership gifts to the Whitney R. Harris World Law Institute in support of the Crimes Against Humanity Initiative.

A. *Opening Plenary Session and Keynote Address*

87. Mary Werntz, Head of Regional Delegation for the United States and Canada for the International Committee of the Red Cross, delivered the opening address of the Conference. She spoke of the important work of the ICRC in the enforcement, application and development of international humanitarian law. She underscored the central importance of the four Geneva Conventions, the two Additional Protocols of 1977 and other instruments setting forth standards for the conduct of war. In response to questions, she noted that the ICRC believes that the current instruments are effective, and that efforts to reopen them in light of current criticisms might lead to a lowering of standards. During the question and answer period, she suggested that the ICRC was very much in favor of continuing to develop the law, and that the Crimes Against Humanity Initiative was very much consistent with the ICRC's thinking on these issues. Her advice was that, in terms of the political viability of the Initiative, it would be best to take a long-term view of State support and ratification.

88. During the opening plenary session, Professor Sadat presented the work of the Initiative to date, and outlined the reasons for the Initiative's work.

---

[13] Whitney Harris' remarks were communicated by videotape, and can be found on the Harris Institute website at http://law.wustl.edu/news/pages.aspx?id=7913.

Subsequently, Professor Bassiouni took the floor and underscored the need for the convention. He pointed to the obstacle of *realpolitik* that accompanies the Initiative, which may require State actors to open themselves to responsibility that the convention can bring about. He again noted the conclusions of a recent study (*see* para. 23, *supra*) that between 1948 and 2008 an estimated 92 to 101 million people, mostly civilians, died in 310 conflicts, with only about 866 persons having been prosecuted out of an estimated one million perpetrators. He observed that victims had received practically nothing.

89. Professor Bassiouni also evoked the high cost of international criminal justice and noted that the international community is presently facing dozens of failed States which will create a tremendous need for justice that may overwhelm the system. Hence, the need for more enforcement mechanisms. He observed that the Rome Statute system established a vertical relationship between the ICC and States Parties, but that no horizontal system exists between States, and that, for complementarity to engage, mechanisms of interstate cooperation based on the principle of extradite or prosecute must be established. The normative gap needed to be filled, and universal application expanded to cover not only States Parties to the ICC but non-States Parties as well.

90. As to the definition of crimes against humanity in the convention, the decision had been taken by the Steering Committee to use Article 7 of the Rome Statute verbatim to enhance acceptance of the convention and support for its adoption. In this way, the convention will directly expand the ICC's reach, scope and breadth. This meant that some weaknesses in Article 7 needed to be accepted.

91. Professor Bassiouni noted that non-State actors, in particular, posed challenges to current international law which contains no incentives for their compliance. In Professor Bassiouni's view, Article 7(2) of the Rome Statute was meant to refer to State policy, not to non-State actors, which creates a gap as well as a question of tactics: Maybe one option, he noted, would be to "pretend" that Article 7(2) does apply to non-State actors and hope that the ICC sees it that way.

92. Professor Bassiouni observed that the draft convention rested upon four pillars: the normative foundation composed of human rights law, international criminal law and international humanitarian law; prevention; the expansion of the principle of *aut dedere aut judicare*; and, finally, sanctions. The text, he noted, is well drafted and solid, resting on existing international criminal law treaties and principles, but with imaginative linkages.

93. In terms of political strategy, Professor Bassiouni noted that the draft convention began with a group of qualified experts, then expanded to consultations, resulting in many refinements to the text. The political process, he noted, would be challenging, but suggested that the audience could be

encouraged by the process that accompanied the elaboration and adoption of the Torture Convention. Professor Bassiouni explained how the Torture Convention also emerged from a combination of expert groups and governments and suggested that a six- to eight-year timeline would not be unreasonable; yet it would require a great deal of work and in the end, the text might be quite different than what we started with.

B. Major Themes Elucidated During the Discussions

1. Crimes Against Humanity and Gender Justice

94. This panel, chaired by The Honorable Christine Van den Wyngaert, was the first of six sessions convened by the Initiative for the two-day conference. The speakers were Elizabeth Abi-Mershed, Assistant Executive Secretary of the Inter-American Commission on Human Rights; David M. Crane, former Chief Prosecutor for the Special Court for Sierra Leone; Patricia Viseur Sellers, former legal advisor for Gender-Related Crimes at the International Criminal Tribunal for the former Yugoslavia; and Judge Inez Monica Weinberg de Roca, President of the United Nations Appeals Tribunal.

95. Judge Van den Wyngaert began by noting that because gender crimes became an explicit subcategory of offenses within the definition of crimes against humanity in Article 7 for the first time, gender justice was a novelty in the ICC Statute. This was a great achievement. Yet, there had been criticism of the definition of gender in Article 7(3) of the ICC Statute, in particular during the presentations on this issue at the April Experts' meeting in St. Louis. Nonetheless, for reasons already articulated (*see* paras. 27 and 37 *supra*) the Steering Committee chose to leave intact the fragile framework of the ICC definition of gender, even though the French translation of the ICC Statute translates "gender" as "sexe."

96. The panelists were asked to address three questions: (1) Whether we need a subcategory of gender crimes as crimes against humanity; (2) What to do about the potentially stigmatizing nature of gender crimes whose victims may not wish to come forward or be labeled as victims, for example, of "enforced prostitution"; and (3) Whether the phenomenon of gender crimes is a symptom of creeping penalization in international criminal law.

97. The panelists extensively discussed these issues in their own presentations and answered questions from the experts in the audience. The point was made that the Inter-American Commission has been able to advance the normative work of identifying and remedying gender-related human rights violations because the legal instruments in the Inter-American system permit individual petitions and the case law of the Inter-American Court of

Human Rights have emphasized the positive obligations of State and non-State actors. The work of the Special Court for Sierra Leone and the ICTY and ICTR has also contributed to an understanding of the gendered nature of atrocity crimes in certain contexts. Specifying what these violations entail in treaty instruments is important, particularly in the international criminal law context, for otherwise reliance on the category of "other inhumane acts" can give rise to problems of legality.

98. It was also noted that if specific normative content was missing, the question becomes "is prosecution of gender crimes permissive or required?" If it is permissive, then it becomes personnel-dependent and requires that someone like Patricia Viseur Sellers be present to raise the issue. The presence of women personnel is important, in any event, because of the stigmatization problem referred to by Judge Van den Wyngaert in her opening remarks. On the question whether victims should be able to raise new crimes before the ICC, for example, the panelists noted that in many cases even though those claims might be valid, raising them could fetter the Prosecutor's discretion and potentially impair the rights of the defense.

2. Peace and Justice Dilemmas

99. This panel was chaired by Justice Richard J. Goldstone. Other speakers included Richard Dicker, Director, International Justice Program of Human Rights Watch; Elizabeth Ferris, Senior Fellow at the Brookings Institution; Jerry Fowler, former President of The Save Darfur Coalition; and Max du Plessis, Professor at the University of KwaZulu-Natal in South Africa.

100. The discussions centered upon the balance between peace and justice. One panelist noted that justice was different from the political process because it is an end in itself and is essential to honoring victims and strengthening the rule of law. Negotiators need to strengthen their management of peace and justice, which is difficult to do as there is no universal blueprint. At the same time, one can draw lessons from experiences where these objectives have been managed well, in particular during the Dayton negotiations in 1995 and the Goma Peace negotiations in eastern Congo in 2008. It was suggested that diplomats, mediators, and others tend to have an overly negative reaction when justice enters the picture during a period of peace negotiations or when the deployment of peacekeepers is an issue. This causes pushback against justice initiatives, but is not warranted by the experience of the international community.

101. There was much discussion on the role of the Security Council in bringing about peace. It was observed by one expert that the Permanent Members of the Council had undermined the Council's authority and the work of the

International Criminal Court. It was also noted that Articles 13 and 16 of the ICC Statute functioned as a compromise but could also create a situation that was politicized or hypocritical.

a. The Difficulties Facing Humanitarian Workers

102. For humanitarians working in conflict situations, it was observed that the factual context is quite different than before. The number of actors has increased and diversified, with more than 250,000 humanitarian actors around the world. Although most humanitarians on the ground hope for justice, during a peace process, they may sometimes find themselves helping the perpetrators. It was suggested that humanitarian organizations should not be pressed to open their files to investigators.

b. Sudan and the African Situation More Generally

103. It was noted that the ICC Prosecutor's issuance of an arrest warrant for Sudanese President Omar al-Bashir had been criticized as disruptive of the peace process in Sudan. Yet, there was no ongoing peace process in Sudan at the time for the warrant to disrupt but instead it was *after* the ICC warrant request that a new peace process was initiated in Doha that led to some progress. The ICC moved forward with its process in a deliberate manner; however, one expert observed that the Security Council and governments did not pursue the peace process with the same sustained seriousness of purpose. Because of this disconnect, the reconciliation of justice and peace has not been achieved.

104. Others noted that the concern in Africa about the activities of the ICC emanates from an African perspective that sees the ICC as a threat to State sovereignty. The al-Bashir arrest warrant creates issues because Sudan is not a party to the ICC, and the Security Council's referral is seen as a cynical exercise of power involving a double standard. This is a serious concern. At the same time, it was noted that the African Union must be reminded that the Security Council's role in ICC prosecutions was foreseen and agreed to by the thirty African States Parties to the ICC.[14]

c. The Role of Prosecutors

105. It was argued that international prosecutors should ground themselves in non-partial adherence to the law and be free from corruption because of the highly political atmosphere in which they work. They must be independent, but not indifferent to the political landscape, which may affect the exercise of their discretion, such as the timing of an indictment or an arrest warrant. The audience was reminded that this is true of domestic prosecutors, as well.

---

[14] This issue was also raised at the April Experts' Meeting. *See* para. 34 *supra*.

d. Amnesties and Truth Commissions

106. The questions of amnesties and a truth and reconciliation commission for Sudan were raised during the discussion. It was observed that blanket amnesties would probably not be accepted, but that there might be some possibility for amnesties under the Rome Statute. It was also stressed that amnesties would not be effective outside of the country where granted, and that the ICC would ultimately have to address the question under its Statute.

107. The panel also discussed whether the proposed crimes against humanity convention should contain a provision on amnesties, an issue that had been raised at earlier meetings and by experts during the consultation process (*see* paras. 40–41 *supra*). It was observed that efforts had been made during the ICC Preparatory Committee discussions to offer an amnesty provision, but that had not been productive. Similarly, there was a proposed amnesty provision (prohibiting amnesties) in the Convention on Enforced Disappearance, but it did not receive consensus.

3. Facilitating Effective Interstate Cooperation in the Prevention and Punishment of Crimes Against Humanity

108. This panel, chaired by Ambassador Hans Corell, focused on effective interstate cooperation, a core issue in the proposed crimes against humanity convention. Panelists included Serge Brammertz, Chief Prosecutor, the International Criminal Tribunal for the former Yugoslavia; Professor Robert Cryer, Birmingham Law School; Professor Yoram Dinstein, Tel Aviv University; Laura Olson, The Constitution Project; and Professor Darryl Robinson, Queen's University.

a. Cooperation with International Tribunals

109. It was noted that there is virtually universal agreement that international cooperation is central to the work of international tribunals and international justice. Cooperation was central to the ICTY's early days and remains a key concern. Access to archives and documentation in countries where investigations are conducted is essential; so is access to witnesses in national and international prosecutions. At the ICTY, cooperation of third parties has been an issue, especially with respect to the acquisition and use of classified material in investigations and in tribunal proceedings.

110. It was also observed that cooperation between international and national institutions goes both ways. The ICTY, for instance, has been receiving and responding to requests for assistance coming from States in the region; at the moment, incoming requests are greater than outgoing requests. Cooperation also means not only fulfilling all technical requests for information, but also helping the Tribunal to succeed. In the case of the ICTY,

while the governments of Serbia and Croatia have provided technical assistance to the Tribunal, there is poor political support for its work in those countries and actions taken by the Tribunal are often criticized. In Serbia at the moment, 65 percent of the population opposes the arrest of General Mladic, which indicates that the Tribunal has failed to explain the importance of its work. This is an important problem for the international community.

111. A second factor influencing cooperation is the pressure which the international community places on individual States. The success of the ICTY is at least partly attributable to the decision of the United States to condition financial aid to Serbia upon the arrest of remaining fugitives as well as the commitment of the European Union to link accession prospects to the level of cooperation the former Yugoslav States provide to the Tribunal. The only chance that the ICTY has to fulfill its mandate is to ensure that incentives to require cooperation from the countries in the region remain in place.

112. Finally, the importance of capacity building was underscored. The ICTY Prosecutor noted a number of internal mechanisms at the ICTY that exist to facilitate cooperation, including a dedicated tracking unit, ICTY police who work with local police, a functioning assistance unit for public inquiries, and a special section to work with war crimes prosecutors from the region. One of the ICTY's top priorities at the moment is to organize the transfer of cases from the Tribunal to local institutions, because the ICTY's success will depend on how this transfer takes place.

113. Other experts also underscored the need for capacity building. It was noted that the ICC, although a permanent court, has the same problem as the tribunals – namely, it will need a completion strategy for each situation, as it cannot stay in situation countries forever. A major difference between the ICC and the ad hoc tribunals is that the latter built partners on the ground during their lifetime.

b. Cooperation Provisions of the Draft Convention

114. It was observed that the draft convention aimed at improving the horizontal enforcement of international criminal law, rather than its vertical application by the ICC, the ICTY, or other international tribunals. Robust enforcement is the key to fighting impunity, and stronger enforcement mechanisms than those currently available are needed. The greatest gaps exist at the horizontal level of interstate prosecutions and mutual legal assistance. For instance, where there is no extradition treaty between individual States, most States cannot extradite. The *Proposed Convention* establishes the legal basis for extradition for crimes against humanity and removes the political offense exception as a ground for refusal to extradite. This is important because crimes against humanity are often the result of State policy.

The draft text also addresses issues of mutual legal assistance, enforcement of another State's penal judgments and transfer of persons for execution of sentences.

115. One expert noted that often common and civil law countries have different standards of proof for extradition, which raises problems in interstate cooperation. Common law countries want to see evidence before extradition. Civil law countries merely require a description of the facts prior to extradition. Thus, it might be helpful to require States Parties to recognize that in ratifying the convention, they are setting aside national preferences on evidentiary standards.

116. Article 7 of the draft text[15] requires States to investigate if they received information that crimes against humanity have been or are being committed. Article 6(9) provides further that a State must prosecute those responsible for crimes against humanity.[16] States might worry about this, especially about the prospect of vexatious prosecutions. However, vexatious prosecutions are usually a concern in private suits, and although the above cited articles impose strong obligations on States, that should not be an insurmountable problem.

117. The draft of the *Proposed Convention* innovates as regards evidence. Article 9(2) permits a receiving State to recognize evidence from the sending State, even when this evidence, although credible and obtained fairly and effectively, does not conform to the rules of evidence in the receiving State.[17] The panel expressed support for this provision, but queried whether States would find it acceptable. It was recognized that after all the goal of the *Proposed Convention* is to the start the process of discussion and negotiation, not to end it. Thus, the above provision gives States something to discuss and take out if they need to compromise on other provisions.

118. The draft also provides that no statute of limitations shall apply to crimes against humanity,[18] which is a common impediment to extradition of offenders. At the same time, the convention includes provisions[19] for denial of extradition when substantial grounds exist to believe that a person might be sought for extradition for discriminatory reasons, that his or her trial rights may be denied, or that the possible penalty for the offense is not provided for in the law of the requested State.

119. The draft text is silent on the issue of the death penalty. However, it should be recalled that extradition must adhere to the principle of *non-refoulement*. The draft requires States to consider not only gross violations of human rights but also humanitarian law violations. If a State is to prosecute

---

[15] Now Article 9 of the *Proposed Convention*.
[16] Now Article 8(9) of the *Proposed Convention*.
[17] Now Article 11(2) of the *Proposed Convention*.
[18] Now Article 7 of the *Proposed Convention*.
[19] Now Annex 2(D) of the *Proposed Convention*.

effectively, it requires judicial assistance (*i.e.*, witness protection, freezing of assets), so a specialized convention requires special provisions regarding the movement of persons from one country to another. A new convention should establish the basis for such required cooperation.

120. The draft text also provides that legal assistance between States Parties can be predicated upon the convention itself, without the need for an additional mutual legal assistance treaty.[20] At the same time, the legal assistance provisions of the convention are meant to apply only if no other treaty governs the relevant obligations of States. To maximize prospects for accountability, the *Proposed Convention* allows a State to transfer detainees or criminal proceedings to another country.[21] It also gives States Parties the option to give effect to the penal judgments of other States.[22] The provisions governing the transfer of convicted persons are essential – the possibility that a defendant could be transferred back to serve his sentence in the requested country may facilitate extradition and counter impunity.[23] To ensure that no convicted individual receives pardon or commutation of sentence by his or her home State, the convention does not permit grants of clemency without the assent of the transferring State.[24]

121. Additionally, it was noted that Annex 2 on extradition does not explicitly address the issue of dual criminality. It was suggested that excluding the dual criminality requirement could be useful. It was also observed that even if it is theoretically possible to extradite without legislation, it can be difficult to convince a judge to apply the treaty in the absence of legislation.

c. The Normative Contribution of the Draft Convention Revisited

122. The point was made that some may doubt the utility of treaties such as the *Proposed Convention*. Treaties, however, help guide and construct our thinking and create normative constraints that shape human behavior. At the same time, on the issue of the normative contribution of the convention, objections were raised to a commentary note in the draft of the convention, suggesting that the policy element in Article 7 of the Rome Statute applies only to State actors. It was contended that this interpretation is problematic because it risks ruling out crimes against humanity committed by non-State actors and creates other issues under dual criminality. One participant, who had been a coordinator of Articles 7 and 7(2)(a) of the Rome Statute, noted that he did not feel that Article 7 contains such a limitation. Moreover, he argued that such an interpretation would contravene the law that, following the *Tadić* case, State and non-State

---

[20] See Article 13 and Annex 3 of the *Proposed Convention*.
[21] See Article 14 and Annex 4 of the *Proposed Convention*.
[22] See Article 16 and Annex 6 of the *Proposed Convention*.
[23] See Article 15 and Annex 5 of the *Proposed Convention*.
[24] See Annex 5(3) of the *Proposed Convention*.

actors are covered by the definition of crimes against humanity. A suggestion was made to delete the limiting language in the commentary, which was later accepted by the Steering Committee.

d. The Relationship between Enforcement and Prevention

123. An interesting point was raised regarding the pace of international justice. It was suggested that proceedings are slow and expensive – for example, by the time the ICTY wraps up its work (projected date 2013), it will have taken almost two decades and cost $2 billion to complete its work. By comparison, the Nuremberg Tribunal took 11 months. One expert suggested that a fact-finding procedure, created by the UN Security Council, like the equivalent of the international fact-finding committee established by Additional Protocol I, could be useful. Such a procedure could be activated between speculation about atrocities to come and future punishment therefore, before the acts become widespread and systematic. No mechanisms would be required, other than fact-finding, to discover what is happening. This would make a record and help to pressure States and the international community before a situation spirals completely out of control.
124. If there is to be a fact-finding commission, the question is who appoints it and who stands behind it. If the Security Council lends its imprimatur to a fact-finding commission, it will be possible for it to adopt binding and influential decisions.
125. It was suggested that the high cost of the international criminal justice system might be a result of its relative infancy. It is a long-term investment requiring large amounts of initial capital. In time, hopefully the International Criminal Court and internationalized courts will demonstrate their utility and competence and prove a less costly alternative to war.

4. Crimes Against Humanity and U.S. Policy

126. This panel was chaired by Andrew Solomon, Deputy Director for the Brookings Institution. The other panelists included John Clint Williamson, former U.S. Ambassador-at-Large for War Crimes Issues; Joseph Zogby, Staff Director of the U.S. Senate Subcommittee on Human Rights and the Law; Michael P. Scharf, Director of the Frederick K. Cox International Law Center, Case Western Reserve University School of Law; Elizabeth Andersen, Executive Director of the American Society of International Law; and Larry Johnson, former UN Assistant-Secretary-General for Legal Affairs.
127. At the outset, it was emphasized that while the present commitment of the United States to international criminal law and justice is often questioned, historically the United States has contributed a great deal to the development of international criminal law (*i.e.*, the Nuremberg trials, the ICTY and

the ICTR) and to its enforcement (*i.e.*, the prosecution of Charles Taylor at the SCSL). It was further noted that there has been a dramatic evolution of U.S. foreign policy towards the ICC under the Obama Administration. The attendance of Stephen Rapp, the U.S. Ambassador-at-Large for War Crimes Issues, at the Assembly of States Parties of the International Criminal Court was a positive step forward. Yet, despite the Obama administration's willingness to participate in and support the work of international bodies, it was observed that it is unlikely that the United States will become an ICC State Party any time soon.

a. U.S. Role in International Humanitarian Law

128. One expert made the point that the U.S. role in the establishment and administration of the International Criminal Tribunal for the former Yugoslavia was largely one of support and contribution. It was observed that the United States often took more progressive positions on matters of international humanitarian law than the UN Secretariat, the body in charge of drafting the ICTY Statute and related resolutions. For instance, when the Secretariat excluded the Additional Protocols to the Geneva Conventions and Common Article 3 from the ICTY Statute, then U.S. Ambassador to the United Nations, Madeleine Albright, made it clear that the United States did not agree. Furthermore, the United States generously contributed FBI and Department of Justice resources to the work of the ICTY. It also shared sensitive information with ICTY prosecutors (under Rule 70 of the ICTY Statute), which was used to obtain non-classified evidence for trial. Recently, the United States has remained a main supporter of the ICTY amidst pressure by other governments for the Tribunal to close down soon.

129. The same panelist also asserted that the United States led the effort to establish the International Criminal Tribunal for Rwanda and had taken, along with New Zealand, the initiative in drafting the Statute and empowering the Tribunal. Common Article 3 and the Geneva Protocols were explicitly included in the ICTR Statute. Furthermore, the United States was a major leader in establishing and securing General Assembly approval for the Special Court for Sierra Leone. The U.S. government has also consistently funded the Khmer Rouge Tribunal, even under former President George W. Bush.

130. It was also noted that although the United States is a major donor of development assistance for capacity-building and strengthening the rule of law in national jurisdictions, this assistance has two drawbacks. First, it is too little – tens of millions of dollars, instead of hundreds of millions – especially compared to European contributions. Second, this assistance has not properly aimed at fostering complementarity between the ICC and national

jurisdictions (possibly because of wishful thinking that the ICC would fail).

b. Existing U.S. Legislation on Atrocity Crimes and its Shortcomings

131. The panel observed that it was only in 2007 that the Unites States Senate created a standing Subcommittee on Human Rights and the Law. The subcommittee held the first hearing on the issue of genocide law in U.S. history. The hearing highlighted a gap in U.S. law (the Proxmire Act which implemented the Genocide Convention domestically) – namely, that the Act did not cover non-U.S. nationals who committed genocide abroad. In response, Senators Durbin and Coburn introduced the Genocide Accountability Act, which was adopted unanimously by both Houses of Congress and signed into law by President George W. Bush in 2007.

132. Similarly, the Subcommittee on Human Rights and the Law held a hearing on the issue of child soldiers. At the time, U.S. law did not provide for the prosecution or even deportation of persons responsible for the recruitment of child soldiers who resided in the United States. In 2008 the Child Soldiers Accountability Act was passed by Congress and signed into law by President George W. Bush.

133. The Human Rights Subcommittee has also received evidence which underscores shortcomings in domestic prosecutions of human rights violations. For example, Dr. Juan Roma-Goza gave testimony about his efforts, which went largely unheeded, to compel the U.S. government to prosecute his former torturers who were living in the United States. Similarly, an alleged perpetrator of the Srebrenica massacre known to reside in the state of Massachusetts was tried for visa fraud even though accused of crimes against humanity. It is believed that more than 1,000 individuals responsible for war crimes and crimes against humanity have found safe haven within the United States. Senators Durbin and Coburn have introduced a new Crimes Against Humanity bill to enable the prosecution of such individuals. The eventual adoption of this legislation promises to be an uphill battle, as would be the ratification of any future crimes against humanity convention. On a more positive note, Senator Durbin was instrumental in the passage of the Human Rights Enforcement Act, which creates a section within the U.S. Department of Justice with the mandate to prosecute human rights violators. The bill passed both Houses and was signed into law by President Obama in early 2010.

134. One panelist commented on the limitations of existing U.S. legislation on the issue of atrocity crimes. The Genocide Accountability Act (*see* para. 131 *supra*) is limited to the scope and requirements of the Genocide Convention, and neither contains an obligation to prosecute or extradite individuals

responsible for genocide taking place outside U.S. borders. Similarly, the War Crimes Act (18 U.S.C. § 2441) does not provide for universal jurisdiction and permits amnesty deals with non-citizens responsible for war crimes against other non-citizens before coming to the United States. Even the proposed crimes against humanity legislation by Senators Durbin and Coburn does not go far enough in requiring mandatory prosecutions and closing the door on amnesties for perpetrators of crimes against humanity.

135. Against this backdrop, it was observed that there were four ways in which a crimes against humanity convention could affect U.S. policy: (1) it could help end amnesty deals; (2) it could close gaps in existing domestic legislation; (3) it could facilitate cooperation with the ICC and other prosecution efforts around the world; and (4) it could add a new tool in the arsenal of atrocity prosecutions – indictments. To illustrate this last point, one panelist invoked the Pan Am 103 bombing prosecutions. Instead of using force against Libya after the bombing, the United States, relying on existing counter-terrorism conventions, went to the United Nations with indictments and secured Libya's agreement to a trial at a specially convened court in The Netherlands. There is no similar convention on crimes against humanity at the moment. A new crimes against humanity convention could provide the necessary basis for the issuance of indictments against perpetrators of crimes against humanity, outside the ICC framework.

c. Possible U.S. Role in a Crimes Against Humanity Convention

136. Currently, the U.S. government has no position on a crimes against humanity treaty. In fact, at the moment, except for a small group of government international criminal law experts, the U.S. government is largely unaware of the work of the Initiative and the call for the conclusion and adoption of a new international treaty to prevent and punish the commission of crimes against humanity. Even when the work of the Initiative becomes better known, U.S. officials from different departments and agencies, such as the Defense and Justice Departments, will have to study the *Proposed Convention* and weigh in on its consequences. U.S. policy is rarely imposed from above by top political appointees and is instead the product of the "least common denominator" of the interests of different government representatives.

137. In view of the above, U.S. participation in a new crimes against humanity convention is not just a question of securing Senate ratification. Instead, it will require concerted lobbying efforts of different agencies and offices within the Executive Branch as well. It was suggested that such efforts be directed first and foremost at the Democracy, Human Rights and Labor Bureau in the Department of State; the Office of the Legal Advisor and the War Crimes Office at the Department of State; a newly created section within the U.S. Department of Justice to prosecute serious human rights violations; and the JAG Offices in the Department of Defense.

138. In the process, it is also important for the Crimes Against Humanity Initiative to think about how to avoid getting caught up in a potential U.S. backlash against the ICC. The challenge is to make the *Proposed Convention* part of a continued U.S. engagement with issues of international justice, no matter what happens to U.S. policy towards the ICC in particular. To that end, the Initiative should endeavor to educate U.S. government stakeholders about what the *Proposed Convention* does or does not do, especially as regards its implications for potential liability of U.S. soldiers.

d. A Crimes Against Humanity Convention and Amnesties

139. It was repeatedly emphasized that a crimes against humanity convention should take a hard stance on amnesties for alleged perpetrators. Rights violators cannot be trusted, and amnesties erode the rule of law and add to cynicism. Furthermore, amnesties prevent the development of a historical record. Examples were given of ignominious amnesty offers: there is strong evidence that U.S. envoy Richard Holbrooke offered Radovan Karadzic immunity from prosecution in peace talks in the mid-1990s; in 2003 Charles Taylor, the former President of Liberia, was given a deal to seek exile in Nigeria and avoid international prosecution for his role in the Sierra Leone conflict; prior to the invasion of Iraq, Bahrain offered Saddam Hussein asylum should he want to leave the country, despite his long record of crimes against humanity; and even today many States are calling on the UN Security Council to quash the ICC indictment of President al-Bashir of Sudan.

e. Alternatives to Ratification

140. One possible route for the eventual *Proposed Convention* to become binding international law immediately, without lengthy negotiations and the need for country ratifications, was suggested – namely through its adoption, in whole or in part, by the UN Security Council in a Chapter VII resolution. This is what happened in the aftermath of September 11 when the Security Council drew upon an existing proposed treaty on terrorist financing in issuing a number of Chapter VII resolutions (*i.e.*, UN S.C. Res. 1368, 1373, and 1377). One panelist speculated that another Darfur could be the catalyst for adopting the *Proposed Convention* in a future Chapter VII resolution, much as the September 11 attacks were for the proposed terrorist financing treaty.

141. Another panelist commented on the alternatives to U.S. ratification of a crimes against humanity convention. She noted that while ratification is a long, difficult and uncertain process, other steps could be taken in the short to medium term, such as clarifying domestic law, filling in existing gaps, adopting best practices, and providing a common framework.

f. The UN Security Council and Crimes Against Humanity

142. The history of the establishment of the Special Tribunal for Lebanon offers an interesting glimpse into the positions of UN Security Council members on crimes against humanity. The Lebanon Tribunal is tasked to investigate and prosecute those responsible for the assassination of former Lebanese Prime Minister Rafiq al-Hariri. The Tribunal applies Lebanese law and has no jurisdiction to try any other crime under international humanitarian law. When the UN Secretariat attempted to include crimes against humanity in the Statute of the Tribunal, the Permanent Members of the Security Council objected. Some objections dealt with the threshold number of victims for crimes against humanity to exist (*i.e.*, is 60 victims enough?); other objections concerned the credibility of the Security Council if it recognized crimes against humanity as triable offenses in al-Hariri's assassination but not in the case of the 2006 Israel-Hezbollah war.

5. Crimes Against Humanity and State Responsibility to Protect

143. This panel was chaired by Professor William A. Schabas, Director of the Irish Centre for Human Rights, National University of Ireland, Galway. The other panelists included Professor Payam Akhavan, McGill University; Professor Edward C. Luck, International Peace Institute; The Honorable Daniel David Ntanda Nsereko, Judge at the International Criminal Court; Professor Dinah L. Shelton, George Washington University Law School; and Professor David J. Scheffer, Northwestern University Law School and former U.S. Ambassador-at-Large for War Crimes Issues.

144. Professor Schabas opened the discussion by observing that the panel topic of State Responsibility to Protect breaks down into two issues: State responsibility and responsibility to protect/prevent. He highlighted two relevant provisions in the draft convetion. Article 2(2)(a) on the object and purposes of the convention imposes obligations on States to "prevent" crimes against humanity, and Article 6(1) requires States Parties to implement the convention by adopting legislation in accordance with the convention.[25] Professor Schabas also suggested that the scope of obligations imposed by any future treaty on atrocity crimes will be interpreted in light of the ICJ decision in the *Bosnia and Herzegovina v. Serbia and Montenegro* case, which addressed issues of prevention under the Genocide Convention.

a. The Responsibility to Protect Principle

145. It was suggested that of the four crimes which the principle of the Responsibility to Protect (R2P) addresses, crimes against humanity have

---

[25] Now Article 8(1) of the *Proposed Convention*.

particular importance. Generally, genocide becomes known after the fact, war crimes involve individual acts, and ethnic cleansing does not have the same legal status as the other atrocity crimes. Thus, crimes against humanity are vital for the implementation of R2P in practice.

146. One panelist compared the draft text of the proposed convention and the 2005 World Summit Outcome on the Responsibility to Protect adopted by the UN General Assembly. There is significant overlap between the two documents – for instance, between Articles 2 and 6(12)[26] of the convention and paragraphs 138 and 139 of the World Summit Outcome. Yet, there are important distinctions. Paragraph 139 of the World Summit Outcome commits UN Member States to protect vulnerable populations both inside and outside their borders in accordance with Chapter VII of the UN Charter. In contrast, the draft crimes against humanity convention does not contain an explicit obligation for States to protect civilian populations, and it does not give civilians a right to protection as the Outcome provisions do. (One panelist took issue with this interpretation of paragraph 139, contending that it contains no obligation to respond, and that the United States would not have signed onto it if it did.) Furthermore, the draft language of the convention contains the words "prevent and suppress." While "protection" signifies proactive action, "suppression" usually refers to action after the fact. These are important differences that future policy makers and lawyers will have to parse out and make sense of.

147. One panelist expressed the view that the Security Council should not be front and center in R2P initiatives. He argued that States should not condition the discharge of their obligation to protect on Security Council authorization. Regional and sub-regional action can be more effective in responding to emerging conflicts. In addition, peace-keeping missions can be authorized by the UN General Assembly without the consent of the Security Council. Another panelist cautioned that R2P should be carefully distinguished from humanitarian intervention.

148. One panelist applauded the proposed convention as a real improvement over the Genocide Convention on the issue of prevention. The Genocide Convention emphasized punishment after the fact. The proposed convention, by contrast, has progressive provisions on prevention. It promotes multilateralism over unilateralism by encouraging States Parties to call upon the UN to take action, if needed. Unlike the Rome Statute, the convention does not contain language forbidding interference with internal political affairs and territorial integrity. The convention also requires States to develop educational and informational programs.[27] Such programs should aim to eradicate social ills and prevent the dissemination of hatred, which usually underlie and facilitate the commission of crimes against humanity. It was further suggested that besides education, the convention should also

---

[26] Now Article 8(13) of the *Proposed Convention*.
[27] See Article 8(15) of the *Proposed Convention*.

discuss and encourage constitutional reforms on self-determination, political and economic equality for all groups, and the principle of humanity.

b. State Responsibility

149. The panel urged the Steering Committee to include a strong State responsibility principle in the proposed convention. While a watered-down version of the principle exists in Articles 1 and 6(12)-(13)[28] of the convention, one expert felt that was not sufficient. Unless the obligation of State responsibility is made more explicit, it would be impossible to bring an action at the ICJ for the failure of a government to stop crimes against humanity under this convention. At the same time, it was recognized that selling a strong State responsibility provision to future States Parties of the convention could be difficult.

150. One panelist suggested that the obligation to protect should not only be stronger than what the convention envisages but also more expansive to include collective responsibility to intervene and prevent crimes. The questions of where, when, and how to intervene are difficult, but not impossible, to answer. The ICJ decision in *Bosnia and Herzegovina v. Serbia and Montenegro* established that the responsibility of States to prevent genocide extends to territories over which they have not only jurisdiction and effective control, but also influence. (Another panelist wondered what France's responsibility to intervene in Rwanda would have been under the rationale of this decision.) In addition, while imminence is required, States should not wait until the eleventh hour to intervene. Instead, the international community should create early warning systems to detect signs of mass incitement and radicalization. Atrocity crimes are not natural disasters, but manmade catastrophes, which makes them foreseeable and preventable. Finally, there is a misunderstanding about what counts as prevention. In the case of the Rwandan genocide, for instance, events might have unfolded differently had RTLM radio been shut down, instead of waiting for the Security Council to act.[29]

151. One panelist also argued for a broader view of how governments commit crimes. He rejected the narrow focus of the ICJ and the ICTY on specific intent, especially in genocide prosecutions. He urged that the draft convention should clarify that specific intent to commit crimes against humanity is not required to prove liability under its provisions. Another panelist explained that under Articles 138–139 of the World Summit Outcome document, an intent to commit crimes is not required for an R2P intervention. An intervention could be justified even in the absence of intent, if a State (especially a failed State) cannot exercise effective control over its territory and populations.

---

[28] See Articles 8(1) & 8(13)-(15) of the *Proposed Convention*.
[29] Ambassador Stephen Rapp made a similar point during his address at the Conference.

152. It was also suggested that the principle of the Responsibility to Protect should run to non-State actors and armed groups. Quite often States are not in control of their own territories. In such situations, the responsibility to protect the civilian population and prevent the commission of mass atrocities should bind non-State actors as well.
153. The question of what specific obligations should inform State responsibility under R2P and the proposed convention elicited thoughtful discussion. It was suggested that criminal sanctions for incitement and hate speech are a concern particular to genocide prevention, but could become problematic in the context of crimes against humanity. First, such penalties bump into freedom of expression issues; and second, it is unclear how to prosecute incitement when hate speech does not lead to violence in its aftermath. It was further pointed out that States refused to include incitement to commit crimes against humanity in the Rome Statute. At the same time, criminal sanctions for incitement and hate speech may be important tools to prevent the commission of atrocities.
154. One commentator identified specific duties which could inform State responsibility obligations – refraining from participation in the planning of crimes against humanity, engaging in and cooperating with ongoing investigations, and committing to R2P in binding treaty form. Another expert wondered how the latter obligation squared with domestic constitutional bans on military intervention in countries like Japan. The argument was advanced that the two may be compatible since there is a clear distinction between military intervention and prevention, especially if prevention takes the form of economic or political measures.
155. The panel also addressed the interesting question whether State responsibility should attach to diplomatic decisions that have impact on atrocity crimes. For instance, can Security Council Member States be held responsible for how they vote in the Security Council? One panelist related that the United States was attacked for its votes in 1993 and 1994 in connection with the situations in the former Yugoslavia and Rwanda. Another panelist added that in 1993 Bosnia and Herzegovina considered bringing the United Kingdom before the ICJ on the theory that its actions in the Security Council violated the Genocide Convention and the Convention on the Elimination of All Forms of Racial Discrimination. The same panelist argued that the ICJ has recognized an obligation on behalf of States to exercise pressure in conflict situations. Another panelist took the position that international law has not yet settled this issue.

c. Lessons from the Inter-American Court of Human Rights

156. One panelist reviewed the record of the Inter-American Court of Human Rights (IACtHR) on the issue of a State's responsibility to protect and prevent. The IACtHR has recognized a legal duty to prevent and investigate

human rights violations, but it has not distinguished between investigating past crimes and preventing future violations. The Court has also detailed specific measures to be taken to protect human rights. It has held that truth commissions are not a substitute for judicial processes and that amnesties cannot be used to limit responsibility. It has also ordered educational measures and training programs for individuals most at risk of violating human rights. Finally, in the *Miguel Castro* case, the Court referred to a duty of international cooperation and extradition.

6. Universal Jurisdiction, Complementarity and Capacity Building

157. This panel was chaired by Juan E. Méndez, Visiting Professor, Washington College of Law, American University. The other panelists included Gilbert Bitti, International Criminal Court; Francesca Varda, Coalition for the International Criminal Court; and Mohamed El-Zeidy, International Criminal Court.
158. At the outset, Professor Méndez reminded the audience of the importance of the three issues that the panel was designed to discuss. He noted that universal jurisdiction is a necessary weapon in the fight to end impunity, and the Initiative's Steering Committee carefully considered the concept in drafting the proposed convention. Complementarity, too, is key to the prevention of crimes against humanity, while capacity building has turned into one of the three main pillars of the proposed convention, alongside prevention and punishment.

a. Complementarity at the ICC

159. It was observed that as the cornerstone of the Rome Statute, the principle of complementarity protects State sovereignty. The International Criminal Court has addressed issues of complementarity mainly in cases involving its *proprio motu* and State referral jurisdiction. Some of the most important findings of the ICC on this issue, which could have implications for crimes against humanity prosecutions, include the following: (1) That national proceedings should encompass both the person and the conduct in question to foreclose ICC involvement; (2) That States should incorporate and national courts should apply the modes of liability recognized in the ICC Statute; (3) That although the meanings of "unwilling" and "unable" remain unclear, the Court has held, in the *Katanga* case (September 2009), that if a State has been inactive in investigating or prosecuting a particular accused, then the Court need not reach the question of unwillingness and inability in asserting jurisdiction.
160. One panelist distinguished between classical complementarity, which concerns the basis for the exercise of jurisdiction by the International Criminal Court, and positive complementarity, which deals with capacity building

and mutual assistance between national and international tribunals. He pointed out that while the origins of positive complementarity are sometimes traced to Nuremberg, that Tribunal was created not to enhance the capacity of domestic courts, but to establish jurisdiction over Nazi crimes committed against a stateless population. Similarly, the notion of positive complementarity is improperly attributed to the ICC. Instead, it originated with the ICTY, where the Office of the Prosecutor began sending so-called "category two" cases back to domestic courts while at the same time offering these courts assistance. He noted that the ICC probably will not engage in the kind of positive complementarity/capacity building witnessed at the ICTY and the ICTR – while it will encourage domestic prosecutions, it will not get involved in technical or financial support. However, he suggested that the ICC should consider cooperating with States by sharing databases of non-confidential information, involving local lawyers in OTP activities, assisting countries in meeting their international law obligations and strengthening their witness protection capabilities.

b. The Work of NGOs in Facilitating Complementarity

161. The panelists drew attention to the work of the Coalition for the International Criminal Court (CICC) at the national level. The CICC has helped identify local experts to advocate for the Rome Statute on the ground. In addition, the CICC has worked closely with national judiciaries to encourage and facilitate capacity building. The CICC has also provided support for and monitored the process of implementation of the ICC Statute by individual States. The implementation process has been slow and accompanied by many challenges, but has had the positive impact of modernizing State criminal codes and expanding State jurisdiction over international crimes. Jordan and Morocco were singled out for their specific advances towards implementation; Latin America and Africa were also noted as making good progress. It was also stated that 25 States have criminalized crimes against humanity as of early 2010. The example of the *Fujimori* case was advanced to illustrate how crimes against humanity jurisprudence at the international level is influencing national courts. In *Fujimori*, the Supreme Court of Peru relied upon precedent from the Inter-American Court of Human Rights to find that the national amnesty law was no longer applicable.

c. Reparations for Victims

162. The issue of victim compensation arose during the Question and Answer session. An expert from the audience observed that Article 6 of the November draft of the convention[30] leaves matters of reparations almost entirely to the

---

[30] Now Article 8 of the *Proposed Convention*.

discretion of individual States. He argued that instead, the international community should agree on an international mechanism for reparations. One panelist suggested that a trust fund for victims could be helpful.

C. Closing Plenary Session, Issuance of Resolutions and the Signing of the Washington Declaration

163. At the outset of the final plenary session, the Steering Committee requested the participants to observe a moment of silence in honor of the victims of crimes against humanity.
164. Professor Sadat then read aloud three resolutions in which the Steering Committee: (1) Expressed gratitude to Steven Cash Nickerson for his financial generosity and ongoing support, which enabled the Initiative to bring together the many minds who contributed to the development of the proposed convention; (2) Recognized Whitney R. Harris for his tireless dedication to the cause of international criminal justice and for his enthusiastic support of the work of the Initiative; and (3) Thanked the individuals and organizations who had taken part in the Initiative by reviewing and commenting on both the form and substance of the proposed convention. The Resolution noted that these contributions, stemming from many different legal systems, were invaluable in refining and finalizing the convention.
165. Finally, the Steering Committee concluded the meeting by adopting the *Washington Declaration* included in this Volume. The *Declaration* recognizes the plight of the millions of victims of crimes against humanity and calls upon States to adopt a comprehensive crimes against humanity convention incorporating certain fundamental principles.[31] A copy of the *Declaration* was circulated to participants at the meeting, and, as of this writing, has been signed by more than seventy-five distinguished experts and supporters of international criminal justice.

VI. MAY TECHNICAL ADVISORY SESSION

166. Following the conclusion of the Washington Conference, the draft convention was refined once more at another technical advisory session held in Chicago, Illinois, at DePaul University School of Law, from May 10–11, 2010.[32] The session considered the input received from experts in Fall and Winter of 2009–2010 and the comments from the Washington Conference. Portions of the text were redrafted and refined. The resulting draft was then sent to the Steering Committee for deliberation. After lengthy discussions,

---

[31] *The Washington Declaration* appears in this Volume and on the Harris Institute's website at http://law.wustl.edu/crimesagainsthumanity.
[32] A list of participants is found in Annex 9.

additional changes were incorporated and the text finalized. The result is the *Proposed International Convention on the Prevention and Punishment of Crimes Against Humanity*, found in Appendix I of this Volume, which was adopted by the Steering Committee in August 2010 (in English), and subsequently translated into French (Appendix II).

VII. CONCLUSION

167. During Phase IV of the Initiative's work, the *Proposed Convention* will be circulated to governments, United Nations decision makers, academics and NGOs to promote the work of the Initiative and create support for the adoption of a comprehensive international instrument on crimes against humanity. It is intended that States, NGOs and prominent personalities, including former Heads of State, will take part in this effort. The Initiative plans to convene and participate in regional meetings in, *inter alia*, Africa, the Americas, Asia, Europe and the Middle East to further these objectives.
168. It is hoped that by the end of Phase IV of the Initiative, the international community will have acquired the strong conviction that the adoption of a comprehensive international instrument on crimes against humanity is both urgently required and eminently feasible.

Washington University School of Law

Whitney R. Harris World Law Institute
Iniciativa sobre Crímenes de Lesa Humanidad

Agosto 2010. Original: Inglés[1]

Propuesta de Convención Internacional para la Prevención y la Sanción de los Crímenes de Lesa Humanidad

Preámbulo

Los Estados Partes en la presente Convención,

Conscientes de que todos los pueblos están unidos por estrechos lazos y comparten ciertos valores comunes,

Afirmando su creencia en la necesidad de proteger de forma efectiva la vida y la dignidad humana,

Reafirmando su compromiso con los propósitos y principios de las Naciones Unidas, enunciados en su Carta, y con las normas universales de derechos humanos reflejadas en la Declaración Universal de los Derechos Humanos y otros instrumentos internacionales pertinentes,

Teniendo presente que a lo largo de la historia de la humanidad millones de personas, particularmente mujeres y niños, han sido sometidos a exterminio, persecución, delitos de violencia sexual y otras atrocidades que han conmovido la conciencia de la humanidad,

Destacando su compromiso de evitar a la comunidad mundial y a sus respectivas sociedades la repetición de atrocidades, mediante la prevención de la comisión de crímenes de lesa humanidad y el enjuiciamiento y la sanción de los autores de dichos crímenes,

Decididos a poner fin a la impunidad de los autores de los crímenes de lesa humanidad garantizando su enjuiciamiento y sanción justo y efectivo a nivel nacional e internacional,

Reconociendo que un justo y efectivo enjuiciamiento y sanción de los autores de crímenes de lesa humanidad requiere buena fe y una eficaz cooperación internacional,

---

[1] La Iniciativa sobre Crímenes de Lesa Humanidad expresa su agradecimiento a Salvador Cuenca, que supervisó la traducción al español de la Propuesta de Convención como parte de un proyecto del Instituto Iberoamericano de La Haya para la paz, los derechos humanos y la justicia internacional (IIH).

Reconociendo que una cooperación internacional eficaz depende de la capacidad de los distintos Estados Partes para cumplir sus obligaciones internacionales, y que garantizar la capacidad de cada Estado Parte para cumplir sus obligaciones de prevenir y sancionar los crímenes de lesa humanidad redunda en interés de todos ellos,

Recordando que es deber de todo Estado ejercer su jurisdicción penal contra los responsables de crímenes internacionales, incluyendo los crímenes de lesa humanidad,

Recordando las contribuciones hechas por los estatutos y la jurisprudencia de los tribunales internacionales, nacionales y demás tribunales establecidos conforme a un instrumento jurídico internacional, a la afirmación y el desarrollo de la prevención y la sanción de los crímenes de lesa humanidad,

Recordando que los crímenes de lesa humanidad constituyen crímenes de derecho internacional que pueden dar lugar a responsabilidad de los Estados por hechos internacionalmente ilícitos,

Recordando el artículo 7 y otras disposiciones pertinentes del Estatuto de Roma de la Corte Penal Internacional,

Declarando que, en los casos no previstos en la presente Convención o en otros acuerdos internacionales, la persona humana queda bajo la protección y la autoridad de los principios del derecho internacional que se derivan de las costumbres establecidas, de las leyes de la humanidad y de las exigencias de la conciencia pública, y sigue gozando de los derechos fundamentales que son reconocidos por el derecho internacional,

Han convenido en lo siguiente:

Nota Explicativa

Lo que sigue son referencias cruzadas a otros instrumentos internacionales. Para un comentario exhaustivo de la Convención y la descripción de las opciones adoptadas en ella, véase la Historia Completa de la Propuesta de Convención Internacional para la Prevención y la Sanción de los Crímenes de Lesa Humanidad *(«Comprehensive History of the Proposed CAH Convention»).*

1. *La palabra "Sanción" se entiende en el mismo sentido que en la Convención sobre el Genocidio.*
2. *Los párrafos 1, 4, 6 y 9 del Preámbulo se basan en gran medida en el Preámbulo del Estatuto de Roma de la Corte Penal Internacional.*
3. *El párrafo 3 del Preámbulo se basa en el Preámbulo de la Convención contra las Desapariciones Forzadas.*
4. *Los párrafos 5, 6 y 7 del Preámbulo incluyen expresiones específicamente dirigidas tanto a la prevención como a la sanción.*
5. *El párrafo 8 del Preámbulo pretende destacar fuertemente la importancia del desarrollo de capacidades para garantizar el funcionamiento eficaz de la presente Convención.*

6. *La referencia del párrafo 10 del Preámbulo a "demás tribunales establecidos conforme a un instrumento jurídico internacional" incluye modelos mixtos de tribunales como el Tribunal Especial para Sierra Leona.*
7. *El párrafo 11 del Preámbulo reconoce que los crímenes de lesa humanidad pueden dar lugar a responsabilidad de los Estados por hechos internacionalmente ilícitos. Ello no quiere decir que conlleven necesariamente responsabilidad del Estado. Véase el artículo 1 y la nota explicativa que lo acompaña.*
8. *El párrafo 13 del Preámbulo se inspira en la Cláusula Martens que aparece en el Preámbulo de la Convención de La Haya de 1907 y en el artículo 10 del Estatuto de Roma.*

Índice

Artículo 1	Naturaleza del crimen
Artículo 2	Objeto y fines de la presente Convención
Artículo 3	Definición de Crímenes de Lesa Humanidad
Artículo 4	Responsabilidad penal individual
Artículo 5	Responsabilidad de los jefes y otros superiores
Artículo 6	Improcedencia del cargo oficial
Artículo 7	Imprescriptibilidad
Artículo 8	Obligaciones de los Estados Partes
Artículo 9	Aut dedere aut judicare (juzgar o extraditar)
Artículo 10	Competencia
Artículo 11	Pruebas
Artículo 12	Extradición
Artículo 13	Asistencia judicial recíproca
Artículo 14	Transmisión de procedimientos penales
Artículo 15	Traslado de personas condenadas para el cumplimiento de sus condenas
Artículo 16	Ejecución de las sentencias penales de los Estados Partes
Artículo 17	Ne bis in idem
Artículo 18	No devolución
Artículo 19	Mecanismos institucionales
Artículo 20	Estados federales
Artículo 21	Firma, ratificación, aceptación, aprobación, o adhesión
Artículo 22	Entrada en vigor
Artículo 23	Reservas
Artículo 24	Enmienda
Artículo 25	Interpretación
Artículo 26	Solución de controversias entre Estados Partes
Artículo 27	Textos auténticos
Anexo 1	Términos empleados
Anexo 2	Extradición
	A. Crímenes de Lesa Humanidad como delitos que dan lugar a extradición
	B. Base jurídica para la extradición
	C. Modalidades de extradición
	D. Motivos para denegar la extradición
	E. Principio de especialidad
	F. Múltiples solicitudes de extradición
Anexo 3	Asistencia judicial recíproca
	A. Tipos de asistencia judicial recíproca
	B. Transmisión de información
	C. Obligaciones dimanantes de otros tratados aplicables
	D. Traslado de personas detenidas

     E. *Forma de las solicitudes de asistencia judicial recíproca*
     F. *Cumplimiento de las solicitudes de asistencia judicial recíproca*
     G. *Testigos*
     H. *Utilización limitada de la información*
     I. *Denegación de las solicitudes de asistencia judicial recíproca*
Anexo 4 *Transmisión de procedimientos penales*
Anexo 5 *Traslado de personas condenadas para la ejecución de sus condenas*
Anexo 6 *Ejecución de las sentencias penales de los Estados Partes*

Artículo 1
Naturaleza del Crimen

Los crímenes de lesa humanidad, ya sean cometidos tanto en tiempo de conflicto armado como en tiempo de paz, constituyen crímenes de derecho internacional para los que existe responsabilidad penal individual. Además, los Estados pueden ser considerados responsables de crímenes de lesa humanidad conforme a los principios de responsabilidad del Estado por hechos internacionalmente ilícitos.

Nota explicativa

1. *Los Estados Partes en la presente Convención que también son Parte del Estatuto de Roma están vinculados por sus obligaciones de conformidad con dicho Estatuto. Las obligaciones que se derivan de la presente Convención son, por tanto, compatibles con el Estatuto de Roma. Además, las disposiciones de la presente Convención regulan las relaciones bilaterales entre los Estados Partes del Estatuto de Roma. La presente Convención también ofrece una oportunidad para que los Estados que no son partes en el Estatuto de Roma regulen sus relaciones bilaterales con otros Estados, ya sean Partes del Estatuto de Roma o no.*
2. *La prohibición de los crímenes de lesa humanidad existe con arreglo al derecho internacional consuetudinario, y esta disposición incorpora el desarrollo de dicho derecho internacional consuetudinario, que reconoce que los crímenes de lesa humanidad pueden ser cometidos tanto en tiempo de conflicto armado como en tiempo de paz.*
3. *El artículo 1, al igual que el párrafo 11 del preámbulo, reconoce que los crímenes de lesa humanidad pueden dar lugar a responsabilidad de los Estados por hechos internacionalmente ilícitos en el supuesto de que las violaciones de la presente Convención sean atribuibles a un Estado Parte de conformidad con el Proyecto de Artículos sobre la Responsabilidad del Estado por Hechos Internacionalmente Ilícitos adoptado en 2001 por la Comisión de Derecho Internacional.*
4. *La referencia específica a la responsabilidad del Estado pone de relieve la aplicabilidad de los principios de la responsabilidad del Estado en la presente Convención.*

Artículo 2
Objeto y fines de la presente Convención

1. Los Estados Partes en la presente Convención se comprometen a prevenir los crímenes de lesa humanidad y a investigar, juzgar y sancionar a los responsables de dichos crímenes.

2. Con estos fines, cada Estado Parte conviene en:
   (a) Cooperar con los demás Estados Partes, conforme a las disposiciones de la presente Convención, para prevenir los crímenes de lesa humanidad;
   (b) Investigar, juzgar y sancionar de manera justa y efectiva a los responsables de crímenes de lesa humanidad;
   (c) Cooperar, conforme a las disposiciones de la presente Convención, con los demás Estados Partes, con la Corte Penal Internacional si el Estado es Parte del Estatuto de Roma y con otros tribunales establecidos conforme a un instrumento jurídico internacional que tengan competencia sobre crímenes de lesa humanidad, en la investigación, enjuiciamiento y sanción justo y efectivo de las personas responsables de crímenes de lesa humanidad; y
   (d) Ayudar a los demás Estados Partes en el cumplimiento de sus obligaciones de conformidad con el artículo 8 de la presente Convención.

Nota explicativa

1. *Esta disposición pone de relieve los tres "pilares" centrales de la presente Convención: la prevención, la sanción y el desarrollo eficaz de capacidades para facilitar dicha prevención y sanción.*
2. *La referencia del párrafo 2(c) a otros tribunales internacionales incluye los tribunales ad hoc, como el Tribunal Penal Internacional para la Antigua Yugoslavia (TPIY) y el Tribunal Penal Internacional para Ruanda (TPIR), así como los modelos mixtos de tribunales establecidos conforme a un instrumento jurídico internacional, como el Tribunal Especial para Sierra Leona y las Salas Extraordinarias en los Tribunales de Camboya. Respecto a la referencia que hace esta disposición a que un Estado Parte coopere con la Corte Penal Internacional, cabe señalar que los Estados Partes del Estatuto de Roma pueden tener tal obligación. Los Estados que no son Parte en dicho Estatuto no tienen tal obligación en ausencia de una remisión por parte del Consejo de Seguridad o de la aceptación voluntaria de la competencia de la Corte, pero tienen la posibilidad de cooperar con la Corte Penal Internacional. Esta disposición reconoce que tales Estados pueden cooperar con la Corte Penal Internacional, pero no impone una obligación independiente de hacerlo.*
3. *La referencia del artículo 2(d) a ayudar a los "Estados Partes en el cumplimiento de sus obligaciones" incluye las obligaciones del artículo 8 de facilitar el desarrollo de capacidades del Estado.*

Artículo 3
Definición de Crímenes de Lesa Humanidad

1. A los efectos de la presente Convención, se entenderá por "crímenes de lesa humanidad" cualquiera de los actos siguientes cuando se cometa como parte de un ataque generalizado o sistemático contra una población civil y con conocimiento de dicho ataque:
   (a) Asesinato;
   (b) Exterminio;
   (c) Esclavitud;
   (d) Deportación o traslado forzoso de población;
   (e) Encarcelación u otra privación grave de la libertad física en violación de normas fundamentales de derecho internacional;
   (f) Tortura;
   (g) Violación, esclavitud sexual, prostitución forzada, embarazo forzado, esterilización forzada o cualquier otra forma de violencia sexual de gravedad comparable;
   (h) Persecución de un grupo o colectividad con identidad propia fundada en motivos políticos, raciales, nacionales, étnicos, culturales, religiosos, de género definido en el párrafo 3, u otros motivos universalmente reconocidos como inaceptables con arreglo al derecho internacional, en conexión con cualquier acto mencionado en el presente párrafo o con actos de genocidio o crímenes de guerra;
   (i) Desaparición forzada de personas;
   (j) El crimen de apartheid;
   (k) Otros actos inhumanos de carácter similar que causen intencionalmente grandes sufrimientos o atenten gravemente contra la integridad física o la salud mental o física.
2. A los efectos del párrafo 1:
   (a) Por "ataque contra una población civil" se entenderá una línea de conducta que implique la comisión múltiple de actos mencionados en el párrafo 1 contra una población civil, de conformidad con la política de un Estado o de una organización de cometer ese ataque o para promover esa política;
   (b) El "exterminio" comprenderá la imposición intencional de condiciones de vida, entre otras, la privación del acceso a alimentos o medicinas, encaminadas a causar la destrucción de parte de una población;
   (c) Por "esclavitud" se entenderá el ejercicio de los atributos del derecho de propiedad sobre una persona, o de algunos de ellos, incluido el ejercicio de esos atributos en el tráfico de personas, en particular mujeres y niños;

(d) Por "deportación o traslado forzoso de población" se entenderá el desplazamiento forzoso de las personas afectadas, por expulsión u otros actos coactivos, de la zona en que estén legítimamente presentes, sin motivos autorizados por el derecho internacional;

(e) Por "tortura" se entenderá causar intencionalmente dolor o sufrimientos graves, ya sean físicos o mentales, a una persona que el acusado tenga bajo su custodia o control; sin embargo, no se entenderá por tortura el dolor o los sufrimientos que se deriven únicamente de sanciones lícitas o que sean consecuencia normal o fortuita de ellas;

(f) Por "embarazo forzado" se entenderá el confinamiento ilícito de una mujer a la que se ha dejado embarazada por la fuerza, con la intención de modificar la composición étnica de una población o de cometer otras violaciones graves del derecho internacional. En modo alguno se entenderá que esta definición afecta a las normas de derecho interno relativas al embarazo;

(g) Por "persecución" se entenderá la privación intencional y grave de derechos fundamentales en contravención del derecho internacional en razón de la identidad del grupo o de la colectividad;

(h) Por "el crimen de apartheid" se entenderán los actos inhumanos de carácter similar a los mencionados en el párrafo 1 cometidos en el contexto de un régimen institucionalizado de opresión y dominación sistemáticas de un grupo racial sobre uno o más grupos raciales y con la intención de mantener ese régimen;

(i) Por "desaparición forzada de personas" se entenderá la aprehensión, la detención o el secuestro de personas por un Estado o una organización política, o con su autorización, apoyo o aquiescencia, seguido de la negativa a admitir tal privación de libertad o dar información sobre la suerte o el paradero de esas personas, con la intención de dejarlas fuera del amparo de la ley por un período prolongado.

3. A los efectos de la presente Convención, se entenderá que el término "género" se refiere a los dos sexos, masculino y femenino, en el contexto de la sociedad. El término "género" no tendrá más acepción que la que antecede.

Nota explicativa

1. *El texto de los párrafos 1 y 2 incorpora la definición contenida en el artículo 7 del Estatuto de Roma, con dos modificaciones necesarias respecto a los términos específicos de la Corte Penal Internacional en el apartado 1(h), mediante las cuales se utilizan las siguientes expresiones: "de género definido en el párrafo 3" y "en conexión [...] con actos de genocidio o crímenes de guerra".*

2. No se han hecho modificaciones sustanciales al artículo 7 del Estatuto de Roma.
3. Tal y como se utiliza en el párrafo 1(k) de la presente Convención, se podría interpretar que, de acuerdo con los artículos II(b) y II(c) de la Convención sobre el Genocidio, "[o]tros actos inhumanos de carácter similar" incluye actos que causan los mismos resultados perjudiciales que los enumerados en los apartados (a) a (j).

Artículo 4
Responsabilidad penal individual

1. Quien cometa un crimen de lesa humanidad será responsable individualmente y podrá ser penado de conformidad con la presente Convención.
2. De conformidad con la presente Convención, será penalmente responsable y podrá ser penado por la comisión de un crimen de lesa humanidad quien:
   (a) Cometa ese crimen por sí solo, con otro o por conducto de otro, sea éste o no penalmente responsable;
   (b) Ordene, proponga o induzca la comisión de ese crimen, ya sea consumado o en grado de tentativa;
   (c) Con el propósito de facilitar la comisión de ese crimen, sea cómplice o encubridor o colabore de algún modo en la comisión o la tentativa de comisión del crimen, incluso suministrando los medios para su comisión;
   (d) Contribuya de algún otro modo en la comisión o tentativa de comisión del crimen por un grupo de personas que tengan una finalidad común. La contribución deberá ser intencional y se hará:
      (i) Con el propósito de llevar a cabo la actividad o propósito delictivo del grupo, cuando una u otro entrañe la comisión de un crimen de lesa humanidad; o
      (ii) A sabiendas de que el grupo tiene la intención de cometer el crimen;
   (e) Haga una instigación directa y pública a que se cometan crímenes de lesa humanidad;
   (f) Intente cometer ese crimen mediante actos que supongan un paso importante para su ejecución, aunque el crimen no se consume debido a circunstancias ajenas a su voluntad. Sin embargo, quien desista de la comisión del crimen o impida de otra forma que se consume no podrá ser penado de conformidad con la presente Convención por la tentativa si renunciare íntegra y voluntariamente al propósito delictivo.
3. Nada de lo dispuesto en la presente Convención respecto de la responsabilidad penal de las personas naturales afectará a la responsabilidad del Estado conforme al derecho internacional por hechos internacionalmente ilícitos.

Nota Explicativa

Esta disposición se basa en el artículo 25 del Estatuto de Roma.

Artículo 5
Responsabilidad de los jefes y otros superiores

Además de otras causales de responsabilidad penal de conformidad con la presente Convención por crímenes de la competencia de un tribunal:

1. El jefe militar o el que actúe efectivamente como jefe militar será penalmente responsable por los crímenes de la competencia de un tribunal que hubieren sido cometidos por fuerzas bajo su mando y control efectivo, o su autoridad y control efectivo, según sea el caso, en razón de no haber ejercido un control apropiado sobre esas fuerzas cuando:
   (a) Hubiere sabido o, en razón de las circunstancias del momento, hubiere debido saber que las fuerzas estaban cometiendo esos crímenes o se proponían cometerlos; y
   (b) No hubiere adoptado todas las medidas necesarias y razonables a su alcance para prevenir o reprimir su comisión o para poner el asunto en conocimiento de las autoridades competentes a los efectos de su investigación y enjuiciamiento.
2. En lo que respecta a las relaciones entre superior y subordinado distintas de las señaladas en el apartado 1, el superior será penalmente responsable por los crímenes de la competencia de un tribunal que hubieren sido cometidos por subordinados bajo su autoridad y control efectivo, en razón de no haber ejercido un control apropiado sobre esos subordinados, cuando:
   (a) Hubiere tenido conocimiento o deliberadamente hubiere hecho caso omiso de información que indicase claramente que los subordinados estaban cometiendo esos crímenes o se proponían cometerlos; y
   (b) Los crímenes guardaren relación con actividades bajo su responsabilidad y control efectivo; y
   (c) No hubiere adoptado todas las medidas necesarias y razonables a su alcance para prevenir o reprimir su comisión o para poner el asunto en conocimiento de las autoridades competentes a los efectos de su investigación y enjuiciamiento.

Nota explicativa

Esta disposición procede del artículo 28 del Estatuto de Roma.

Artículo 6
Improcedencia del cargo oficial

1. La presente Convención será aplicable por igual a todos sin distinción alguna basada en el cargo oficial. En particular, el cargo oficial de una persona, sea Jefe de Estado o de Gobierno, miembro de un gobierno o parlamento, representante elegido o funcionario de gobierno, en ningún caso le eximirá de responsabilidad penal ni constituirá per se motivo para reducir la pena.
2. Las inmunidades y las normas de procedimiento especiales que conlleve el cargo oficial de una persona, con arreglo al derecho interno o al derecho internacional, no obstarán para que un tribunal ejerza su competencia sobre ella.

Nota explicativa

1. *Esta disposición se basa en gran medida en el artículo 27 del Estatuto de Roma. No obstante, en el párrafo 2 del presente artículo, "la Corte" se ha cambiado por "un tribunal", entendiéndose como cualquier institución judicial debidamente constituida que tenga competencia.*
2. *El párrafo 2 se basa en la opinión disidente de la Magistrada Van den Wyngaert en la sentencia de la CIJ en el caso relativo a la orden de detención de 11 de abril de 2000 (República Democrática del Congo contra Bélgica), Sentencia de 14 de febrero de 2002, y mantiene un principio diferente y más amplio que el artículo 27(2) del Estatuto de Roma.*

Artículo 7
Imprescriptibilidad

Los crímenes de lesa humanidad definidos en la presente Convención no prescribirán.

Nota explicativa

1. *Esta disposición se basa en el artículo 29 del Estatuto de Roma.*
2. *Los Estados Partes en la presente Convención se comprometen a adoptar, de conformidad con sus respectivos procedimientos constitucionales, las medidas legislativas o de otra índole que sean necesarias para asegurar que la prescripción de la acción penal y de la pena, establecida por ley o de otro modo, no se aplique a los crímenes de lesa humanidad definidos en la presente Convención y que, en caso de que exista, sea abolida.*

Artículo 8
Obligaciones de los Estados Partes

1. Cada Estado Parte promulgará la legislación necesaria y cualquier otra medida exigida por su Constitución o su ordenamiento jurídico para hacer efectivas las disposiciones de la presente Convención y, en particular, adoptará medidas legislativas, administrativas, judiciales y de otra índole eficaces, de conformidad con la Carta de las Naciones Unidas, para prevenir y sancionar la comisión de crímenes de lesa humanidad en cualquier territorio bajo su jurisdicción o control.

A. Legislación y Penas

2. Cada Estado Parte adoptará las medidas legislativas y de otra índole necesarias para tipificar los crímenes de lesa humanidad como delitos graves en su legislación penal y militar, y castigará dichos delitos con penas adecuadas que tengan en cuenta su gravedad, el daño cometido y las circunstancias personales del delincuente. Además, a dicha persona se le podrá inhabilitar para el ejercicio de cargo público, ya sea militar o civil, incluidos los cargos electivos.

3. Cada Estado Parte adoptará las medidas legislativas y de otra índole necesarias para asegurar que el jefe militar o el que actúe efectivamente como jefe militar sea penalmente responsable de crímenes de lesa humanidad, tal como enuncia el párrafo 1 del artículo 5.

4. Cada Estado Parte adoptará las medidas legislativas y de otra índole necesarias para asegurar que, en lo que respecta a las relaciones entre superior y subordinado distintas de las señaladas en el párrafo 3, el superior sea penalmente responsable de crímenes de lesa humanidad, tal como enuncia el párrafo 2 del artículo 5.

5. Cada Estado Parte adoptará las medidas legislativas y de otra índole necesarias para garantizar en su ordenamiento jurídico a las víctimas de crímenes de lesa humanidad el derecho a un acceso igual y efectivo a la justicia y el derecho a una reparación adecuada, efectiva y rápida del daño sufrido, incluyendo, cuando corresponda:
    (a) Restitución;
    (b) Indemnización;
    (c) Rehabilitación;
    (d) Satisfacción, incluyendo el restablecimiento de la reputación y la dignidad; y
    (e) Medidas para garantizar la no repetición.

    Cada Estado Parte velará por que, en caso de muerte de una víctima de crímenes de lesa humanidad, sus herederos tengan los mismos derechos a un acceso igual y efectivo a la justicia y a una reparación adecuada, efectiva y rápida.

6. Cada Estado Parte adoptará, en consonancia con sus principios jurídicos, las medidas legislativas y de otra índole que sean necesarias a fin de establecer la responsabilidad de personas jurídicas por su participación en crímenes de lesa humanidad. Con sujeción a los principios jurídicos del Estado Parte, la responsabilidad de las personas jurídicas podrá ser de índole penal, civil o administrativa. Dicha responsabilidad existirá sin perjuicio de la responsabilidad penal que incumba a las personas naturales que hayan cometido el delito. Cada Estado Parte, en particular, desarrollará medidas administrativas destinadas a conceder reparación a las víctimas y velará por que se impongan sanciones penales o no penales eficaces, proporcionadas y disuasivas, incluidas sanciones monetarias, a las personas jurídicas consideradas responsables con arreglo al presente artículo.

B. Investigación y Enjuiciamiento

7. El Estado Parte que reciba información que indique que en su territorio puede encontrarse el culpable o presunto culpable de crímenes de lesa humanidad tomará inmediatamente las medidas que sean necesarias de conformidad con su legislación nacional para investigar los hechos comprendidos en esa información.
8. El Estado Parte en cuyo territorio se encuentre el culpable o presunto culpable de crímenes de lesa humanidad, si estima que las circunstancias lo justifican, tomará las medidas necesarias que correspondan conforme a su legislación nacional a fin de asegurar la presencia de esa persona a efectos de enjuiciamiento o extradición.
9. Los Estados Partes enjuiciarán o extraditarán a los acusados o sospechosos de haber cometido crímenes de lesa humanidad.
10. Cada Estado Parte velará por que toda persona que alegue haber sido objeto de crímenes de lesa humanidad en cualquier parte del territorio bajo su jurisdicción tenga derecho a presentar una queja ante las autoridades legales competentes y a que su caso sea pronta e imparcialmente examinado por las autoridades judiciales competentes.
11. Cada Estado Parte adoptará medidas apropiadas, de conformidad con su ordenamiento jurídico interno y dentro de sus posibilidades, para proteger de manera eficaz contra eventuales actos de represalia o intimidación a los testigos y peritos que presten testimonio sobre crímenes de lesa humanidad, así como, cuando proceda, a sus familiares y demás personas cercanas. Sin perjuicio de los derechos del acusado, incluido el derecho a un proceso con las debidas garantías, dichas medidas podrán consistir, entre otras, en:
    (a) Establecer procedimientos para la protección física de esas personas, incluida, en la medida de lo necesario y posible, su reubicación, y permitir, cuando proceda, la prohibición total o parcial de revelar información sobre su identidad y paradero;

(b) Establecer normas probatorias que permitan que los testigos y peritos presten testimonio sin poner en peligro la seguridad de esas personas, por ejemplo, aceptando el testimonio mediante tecnologías de comunicación como la videoconferencia u otros medios adecuados.

C. Prevención

12. Cada Estado Parte procurará adoptar medidas de conformidad con su ordenamiento jurídico interno para prevenir crímenes de lesa humanidad. Dichas medidas incluyen, pero no se limitan a, garantizar que toda apología del odio nacional, racial o religioso que constituya incitación a la discriminación, la hostilidad o la violencia esté prohibida por la ley.
13. Los Estados Partes pueden recurrir a los órganos competentes de las Naciones Unidas a fin de que estos tomen, de conformidad con la Carta de las Naciones Unidas, las medidas que juzguen apropiadas para la prevención y la sanción de los crímenes de lesa humanidad.
14. Los Estados Partes pueden asimismo recurrir a los órganos competentes de una organización regional a fin de que estos tomen, de conformidad con la Carta de las Naciones Unidas, las medidas que juzguen apropiadas para la prevención y la sanción de los crímenes de lesa humanidad.
15. Los Estados Partes desarrollarán programas educativos e informativos sobre la prohibición de crímenes de lesa humanidad que incluyan la formación de los agentes encargados de la aplicación de la ley, personal militar u otros funcionarios públicos pertinentes a fin de:
    (a) Prevenir la participación de esos agentes en crímenes de lesa humanidad;
    (b) Resaltar la importancia de la prevención y de las investigaciones en materia de crímenes de lesa humanidad;
16. Cada Estado Parte prohibirá las órdenes o instrucciones que dispongan, autoricen o alienten crímenes de lesa humanidad. Cada Estado Parte garantizará que la persona que rehúse obedecer una orden de esta naturaleza no sea sancionada. Además, cada Estado Parte tomará las medidas necesarias para asegurar que las personas que tengan razones para creer que se han producido o están a punto de producirse crímenes de lesa humanidad y que informen a sus superiores o a las autoridades u órganos de control o de revisión competentes no sean sancionados por dicha conducta.

D. Cooperación

17. Los Estados Partes cooperarán en la investigación, el enjuiciamiento y la sanción de los crímenes de lesa humanidad con Estados o tribunales establecidos conforme a un instrumento jurídico internacional que tengan competencia.
18. Los Estados Partes se prestarán mutuamente la mayor asistencia y cooperación posible en el curso de cualquier investigación o enjuiciamiento de

presuntos responsables de crímenes de lesa humanidad, con independencia de si existen tratados de extradición o de asistencia judicial recíproca entre dichos Estados Partes.

E. Desarrollo de Capacidades

19. Los Estados Partes, en la medida de lo posible, se prestarán asistencia mutua en el desarrollo de capacidades a título individual o a través de los mecanismos enunciados en el artículo 19.

Nota Explicativa

1. *Esta disposición se basa en disposiciones similares de otras convenciones de derecho penal internacional. El párrafo 1 de esta disposición establece que las medidas adoptadas por los Estados Partes para prevenir y reprimir los crímenes de lesa humanidad deben ser conformes a la Carta de las Naciones Unidas. También se debe entender, no obstante, que la obligación de prevenir los crímenes de lesa humanidad incluye la obligación de no prestar ayuda o asistencia para facilitar la comisión de crímenes de lesa humanidad por otro Estado. Véase el párrafo (9) del comentario al artículo 16 del Proyecto de Artículos sobre la Responsabilidad del Estado por Hechos Internacionalmente Ilícitos de la Comisión de Derecho Internacional. Véase también la sentencia de la CIJ sobre la Aplicación de la Convención para la Prevención y la Sanción del Delito de Genocidio (Bosnia y Herzegovina contra Serbia y Montenegro), Sentencia de 26 de febrero de 2007, párrafos 425–38. Ello es compatible con el artículo 1 de la presente Convención.*

2. *Respecto al párrafo 2, se entiende que las obligaciones de los Estados Partes se aplican a todas las instituciones y órganos del Estado sin excepción, incluidos, entre otros, los tribunales militares y cualquier otro procedimiento especial. Las expresiones relativas a penas proceden del artículo 4(1) de la Convención contra la Tortura. La disposición actual reconoce, no obstante, que los Estados Partes pueden tener diferentes obligaciones derivadas de convenciones regionales de derechos humanos, y ha sido eliminado el texto anterior, que exigía que las penas no fueran menos severas que las aplicables por los crímenes más graves de la misma naturaleza. Con respecto a la prohibición de que las personas que resulten responsables de crímenes de lesa humanidad ejerzan cargo público, el término permisivo "podrá" se ha incluido para evitar posibles contradicciones con la jurisprudencia del Tribunal Europeo de Derechos Humanos. No obstante, parte del contenido de la sentencia sobre el caso Velásquez Rodríguez contra Honduras (Fondo), Corte Interamericana de Derechos Humanos, 29 de julio de 1988, Serie C, No. 4, apoya la proposición de que a las personas que abusaron de su poder para cometer crímenes de lesa humanidad se les pudiera inhabilitar para el ejercicio de cargos públicos.*

3. Los párrafos 3 y 4 exigen que los Estados Partes promulguen legislación para asegurar que los jefes militares y otros superiores sean penalmente responsables por los crímenes de lesa humanidad cometidos por subordinados bajo su mando y control efectivo, o su autoridad y control efectivo, según el caso, en razón de no haber ejercido control sobre esos subordinados.
4. El párrafo 5 se basa en la Resolución de la Asamblea General que aprueba los Principios y directrices básicos sobre el derecho de las víctimas de violaciones manifiestas de las normas internacionales de derechos humanos y de violaciones graves del derecho internacional humanitario a interponer recursos y obtener reparaciones, Doc. ONU A/RES/60/147 (21 de marzo de 2006).
5. A fin de evitar la impunidad o la inmunidad de facto de aquellas personas que actúan colectivamente o dentro de una estructura jurídica, los Estados Partes deberían promulgar legislación capaz de extenderse a dichas entidades. El párrafo 6 se basa en gran medida en el artículo 26 de la Convención de las Naciones Unidas contra la Corrupción para obligar a los Estados Partes a adoptar una legislación apropiada y a desarrollar medidas administrativas destinadas a conceder reparación a las víctimas.
6. El párrafo 7 procede del artículo 7(1) de la Convención sobre los atentados terroristas cometidos con bombas. También abarca a las personas que han cometido crímenes de lesa humanidad o que presuntamente lo hayan hecho.
7. El párrafo 8 procede del artículo 7(2) de la Convención sobre los atentados terroristas cometidos con bombas.
8. El párrafo 9 reconoce la obligación de «aut dedere aut judicare».
9. El párrafo 10 se basa en el artículo 13 de la Convención contra la Tortura, pero incluye una expresión que aclara que la obligación del Estado Parte se extiende a "cualquier parte del" territorio bajo su jurisdicción.
10. El párrafo 11 se basa en el artículo 32 de la Convención de las Naciones Unidas contra la Corrupción.
11. El texto del párrafo 12 procede del artículo 20 del PIDCP.
12. El párrafo 13 procede del artículo VIII de la Convención sobre el Genocidio. Esto es compatible con el párrafo 1 de la presente disposición, que establece que las medidas adoptadas por los Estados Partes para prevenir y sancionar los crímenes de lesa humanidad deben ser conformes a la Carta de las Naciones Unidas.
13. El término "competente" usado aquí significa el órgano apropiado dentro del instrumento regional y también aquellos órganos que actúen en el marco de su instrumento constitutivo.
14. Los párrafos 15 y 16 obligan a los Estados Partes a desarrollar cursos de educación y formación con el fin de hacer efectiva la obligación de prevenir los crímenes de lesa humanidad. Estos párrafos se basan en gran medida en el artículo 23 de la Convención contra las Desapariciones Forzadas.
15. El Resumen de las recomendaciones del Informe del Grupo de Trabajo para la Prevención del Genocidio («Genocide Prevention Task Force Report»)

enuncia medidas políticas específicas para la educación y la prevención que no se pueden incorporar a las disposiciones normativas de la presente Convención. Sin embargo, si la presente Convención tuviera un órgano del tratado que recomendara medidas específicas a los Estados Partes, dicho órgano podría utilizar tales recomendaciones.
16. Reconociendo que el desarrollo de capacidades es una de las funciones básicas de la presente Convención, el párrafo 19 establece que los Estados Partes, en la medida de lo posible, se prestarán asistencia mutua para el desarrollo de capacidades. La prestación de asistencia técnica a los Estados Partes para el desarrollo de capacidades es una de las funciones encomendadas a la Secretaría permanente que será establecida conforme a los párrafos 10 y 11 del artículo 19.
17. A pesar de que define las obligaciones de los Estados Partes, este artículo no hace referencia explícita a la responsabilidad del Estado. Tanto el párrafo 11 del preámbulo como el artículo 1 reconocen explícitamente que los crímenes de lesa humanidad son crímenes de derecho internacional que pueden dar lugar a responsabilidad de los Estados por hechos internacionalmente ilícitos.

Artículo 9
Aut dedere aut judicare (juzgar o extraditar)

1. Cada Estado Parte tomará las medidas necesarias para establecer su competencia sobre los crímenes de lesa humanidad en los casos en que el presunto autor se halle en cualquier territorio bajo su jurisdicción, salvo que dicho Estado lo extradite a otro Estado conforme a sus obligaciones internacionales, o lo entregue a la Corte Penal Internacional, si es un Estado Parte del Estatuto de Roma, o a otro tribunal penal internacional cuya competencia haya reconocido.
2. En el caso de que un Estado Parte, por cualquier motivo no especificado en la presente Convención, no enjuicie a una persona sospechosa de haber cometido crímenes de lesa humanidad, deberá, de conformidad con una solicitud apropiada, entregar a tal persona a otro Estado dispuesto a enjuiciarlo de manera justa y efectiva, o a la Corte Penal Internacional, si es un Estado Parte del Estatuto de Roma, o a un tribunal internacional competente que tenga jurisdicción sobre los crímenes de lesa humanidad.

Nota Explicativa

1. El párrafo 1 se basa en el artículo 9(2) de la Convención contra las Desapariciones Forzadas.
2. El párrafo 2 refleja el principio «aut dedere aut judicare».
3. Respecto a la referencia que hace esta disposición a que un Estado Parte entregue un acusado a la Corte Penal Internacional, cabe señalar que los

Estados Partes del Estatuto de Roma pueden tener tal obligación. Los Estados que no son Parte de dicho Estatuto pueden no tenerla, pero tienen la posibilidad de cooperar con la Corte Penal Internacional. Esta disposición reconoce que tales Estados pueden cooperar con la Corte Penal Internacional, pero no impone una obligación independiente de hacerlo.

Artículo 10
Competencia

1. Las personas presuntamente responsables de crímenes de lesa humanidad serán juzgadas o bien por un tribunal penal del Estado Parte, o bien por la Corte Penal Internacional, o bien por un tribunal internacional que tenga competencia sobre crímenes de lesa humanidad.
2. Cada Estado Parte tomará las medidas necesarias para establecer su competencia sobre personas presuntamente responsables de crímenes de lesa humanidad, en los siguientes casos:
    (a) Cuando los delitos se cometan en cualquier territorio bajo su jurisdicción o a bordo de una aeronave o un buque matriculados en ese Estado o siempre que una persona esté bajo el control material de dicho Estado; o
    (b) Cuando el presunto responsable sea nacional de ese Estado; o
    (c) Cuando la víctima sea nacional de ese Estado y este lo considere apropiado.
3. Cada Estado Parte tomará asimismo las medidas necesarias para establecer su competencia sobre los crímenes de lesa humanidad en los casos en que el presunto autor se halle en cualquier territorio bajo su jurisdicción, salvo que dicho Estado lo extradite o entregue a otro Estado conforme a sus obligaciones internacionales o lo entregue a un tribunal penal internacional cuya competencia haya reconocido.
4. La presente Convención no impide la actuación de ninguna otra jurisdicción penal competente compatible con el derecho internacional y que actúe de conformidad con las leyes nacionales.
5. A efectos de cooperación, se considerará que existe competencia siempre que el responsable, o presunto responsable, de crímenes de lesa humanidad se halle en el territorio del Estado o siempre que el Estado Parte esté en condiciones de ejercer control material sobre él.

Nota explicativa

1. *Se entiende que la referencia del párrafo 1 a "un tribunal internacional que tenga competencia" es aplicable a cualquier Estado Parte que haya aceptado la competencia de dicho tribunal. Esta disposición también reconoce el principio de complementariedad incorporado en el Estatuto de Roma.*

2. El párrafo 2 se basa en el texto del artículo 9(1) de la Convención contra las Desapariciones Forzadas. Esta disposición tiene por objeto evitar conflictos sobre el ámbito de aplicación territorial.
3. El párrafo 3 se basa en el artículo 9(2) de la Convención contra las Desapariciones Forzadas y el artículo 5(2) de la Convención contra la Tortura.
4. El párrafo 4 se basa en el artículo 9(3) de la Convención contra las Desapariciones Forzadas.
5. El párrafo 5 tiene por objeto asegurar que no exista un vacío competencial en la capacidad de un Estado Parte para ejercer su competencia sobre una persona que es responsable, o presuntamente responsable, de crímenes de lesa humanidad, y se aplicaría a personas en tránsito por el territorio de un Estado Parte incluso allá donde el Estado Parte no esté en condiciones de ejercer un control material sobre la persona.

Artículo 11
Pruebas

1. Las reglas probatorias necesarias para el enjuiciamiento serán aquellas existentes con arreglo a las leyes nacionales del Estado Parte que lleve a cabo la investigación, el enjuiciamiento o los procedimientos posteriores al juicio, pero no serán en modo alguno menos estrictas que aquellas que se apliquen en casos de similar gravedad con arreglo a la ley de dicho Estado Parte.
2. Los Estados Partes podrán, a efectos de la presente Convención, reconocer la validez de las pruebas obtenidas por otro Estado Parte incluso cuando las normas jurídicas y el procedimiento para la obtención de dichas pruebas no se ajusten a las mismas reglas de un Estado Parte determinado. Tal falta de conformidad no será motivo de exclusión de las pruebas, siempre que estas se consideren creíbles y hayan sido obtenidas de acuerdo con las normas internacionales relativas a las debidas garantías procesales. Este párrafo se aplicará a todos los aspectos de la presente Convención, lo que incluye, pero no se limita, a los siguientes: extradición, asistencia judicial recíproca, transmisión de procedimientos penales, ejecución de mandamientos judiciales, transmisión y cumplimiento de condenas penales extranjeras y reconocimiento de sentencias penales extranjeras.
3. En relación con la obtención de pruebas, los Estados Partes tratarán de ajustarse a las normas internacionales relativas a las debidas garantías procesales.

Nota Explicativa

1. El párrafo 1 reconoce que en tratados multilaterales o bilaterales la ley aplicable en materia de prueba es la ley del Estado del foro.

2. *En relación con la asistencia judicial recíproca, y tal como actualmente se refleja en el artículo 13 y el anexo 2, también es posible que los Estados requirentes pidan que sean empleadas condiciones específicas o que se sigan ciertos procedimientos en la obtención de pruebas por parte del Estado requerido. El párrafo 2 permite que los Estados reconozcan la validez de las pruebas obtenidas por otro Estado Parte, incluso en los casos en los que no se aplicaron las condiciones o los procedimientos solicitados, siempre que las pruebas se consideren creíbles y que hayan sido obtenidas de acuerdo con las normas internacionales relativas a las debidas garantías procesales, incluida la obligación que impone el artículo 15 de la Convención contra la Tortura, que excluiría cualquier declaración realizada como resultado de la tortura.*
3. *El párrafo 3 obliga a los Estados a intentar ajustarse a las normas internacionales relativas a las debidas garantías procesales en lo que se refiere a la obtención de pruebas.*

Artículo 12
Extradición

Los Estados Partes se prestarán mutuamente la mayor asistencia posible en relación con las solicitudes de extradición hechas respecto a crímenes de lesa humanidad de conformidad con las disposiciones del anexo 2.

Nota explicativa

La obligación de extraditar o juzgar a los responsables o presuntos responsables de crímenes de lesa humanidad se encuentra en el párrafo 9 del artículo 8 y en el artículo 9 de la presente Convención. Las modalidades aplicables se establecen en el anexo 2.

Artículo 13
Asistencia judicial recíproca

Los Estados Partes se prestarán la mayor asistencia posible en relación con investigaciones, procesos y actuaciones judiciales que se inicien con respecto a crímenes de lesa humanidad de conformidad con las disposiciones del anexo 3.

Nota explicativa

Las modalidades mediante las que los Estados Partes están obligados a prestarse asistencia judicial recíproca están enunciadas en el anexo 3, que procede de las disposiciones sobre asistencia judicial recíproca del artículo 46 de la Convención de las Naciones Unidas contra la Corrupción.

Artículo 14
Transmisión de procedimientos penales

Los Estados Partes que tengan competencia sobre un asunto que implique crímenes de lesa humanidad podrán realizar una transmisión de procedimientos penales de conformidad con el anexo 4.

Nota explicativa

Las modalidades mediante las que los Estados Partes podrán realizar una transmisión de procedimientos penales de conformidad con la presente Convención están contenidas en el anexo 4, que se basa en el Convenio Europeo sobre la Transmisión de Procedimientos en materia penal y su Protocolo.

Artículo 15
Traslado de personas condenadas para el cumplimiento de sus condenas

Los Estados Partes podrán trasladar de uno a otro a una persona condenada por crímenes de lesa humanidad en sus respectivas jurisdicciones a efectos del cumplimiento de la condena de dicha persona de acuerdo con las disposiciones del anexo 5.

Nota explicativa

Las modalidades mediante las que los Estados Partes podrán trasladar personas condenadas por crímenes de lesa humanidad para el cumplimiento de sus condenas se enuncian en el anexo 5, que se basa en el Convenio Europeo sobre Traslado de Personas Condenadas así como en la Convención Interamericana para el cumplimiento de condenas penales en el extranjero.

Artículo 16
Ejecución de las sentencias penales de los Estados Partes

Un Estado Parte podrá reconocer y ejecutar las sentencias penales de otro Estado Parte de conformidad con las disposiciones del anexo 6.

Nota explicativa

Esta disposición reconoce que los Estados podrán reconocer y ejecutar las sentencias penales de otro Estado Parte. Las modalidades de tal reconocimiento y ejecución se encuentran en el anexo 6, que se basa en el Convenio Europeo sobre la Validez Internacional de las Sentencias Penales.

Artículo 17
Ne bis in idem

Una persona efectivamente juzgada por crímenes de lesa humanidad y condenada o absuelta no puede ser enjuiciada por otro Estado Parte por el mismo crimen basándose en los mismos, o sustancialmente los mismos, hechos que fundamentan el anterior enjuiciamiento.

Nota explicativa

1. *Esta disposición reconoce el principio «ne bis in idem», que se encuentra en muchos instrumentos internacionales, incluido el artículo 14(7) del PIDCP, el Artículo 20 del Estatuto de Roma, el artículo 10 del Estatuto del TPIY y el artículo 9 del Estatuto del TPIR.*
2. *Esta disposición reconoce que, para que el principio «ne bis in idem» actúe como un impedimento para un enjuiciamiento posterior, el primer enjuiciamiento debe haber sido sustanciado "efectivamente". Conforme al anexo 1(b), "efectivamente" quiere decir de forma diligente, independiente e imparcial, de manera que no tenga por objeto sustraer a la persona de que se trate de su responsabilidad penal por crímenes de lesa humanidad y sea compatible con la intención de someter a la persona a la acción de la justicia, teniendo presente el respeto por el principio de presunción de inocencia.*

Artículo 18
No devolución

1. Ningún Estado Parte procederá a la expulsión, devolución o extradición de una persona a otro Estado cuando haya motivos fundados para creer que estaría en peligro de ser sometida a crímenes de lesa humanidad.
2. A los efectos de determinar si existen esas razones, las autoridades competentes tendrán en cuenta todas las consideraciones pertinentes, inclusive, cuando proceda, la existencia, en el Estado de que se trate, de un cuadro de violaciones sistemáticas graves, flagrantes o masivas de los derechos humanos o violaciones graves del derecho internacional humanitario.

Nota explicativa

1. *Esta disposición se basa en el artículo 16 de la Convención contra las Desapariciones Forzadas, que a su vez procede del artículo 8 de la Declaración contra las Desapariciones Forzadas. En la Convención contra la Tortura se encuentra una obligación similar, que es específica para la tortura.*
2. *El párrafo 1 también se basa en el artículo 3(1) de la Convención contra la Tortura.*

3. La disposición relativa al principio de no devolución («*non-refoulement*») de la presente Convención se limita a situaciones que impliquen crímenes de lesa humanidad, ya que tales crímenes constituyen el objeto central de la presente Convención. A este respecto, la presente Convención sigue el enfoque de la Convención contra las Desapariciones Forzadas y la Convención contra la Tortura.

Artículo 19
Mecanismos institucionales

A. Conferencia de Estados Partes

1. Por la presente Convención se establece una Conferencia de Estados Partes a fin de mejorar la capacidad de los Estados Partes y la cooperación entre ellos para alcanzar los objetivos enunciados en la presente Convención y para promover y examinar su aplicación.
2. El Secretario General de las Naciones Unidas convocará la Conferencia de Estados Partes a más tardar un año después de la entrada en vigor de la presente Convención. Posteriormente se celebrarán reuniones periódicas de la Conferencia de Estados Partes cada tres años. Respecto a la primera convocatoria de la Conferencia de Estados Partes por parte del Secretario General de las Naciones Unidas, el Secretario General prestará a la Conferencia de Estados Partes en la presente Convención los servicios de secretaría necesarios. La secretaría proporcionada por el Secretario General de las Naciones Unidas:
   (a) Prestará asistencia a la Conferencia de Estados Partes en la realización de las actividades enunciadas en el presente artículo y organizará los períodos de sesiones de la Conferencia de Estados Partes y les proporcionará los servicios necesarios;
   (b) Prestará asistencia a los Estados Partes que la soliciten en el suministro de información a la Conferencia de Estados Partes según lo previsto en los párrafos 5 y 6; y
   (c) Velará por la coordinación necesaria con las secretarías de otras organizaciones internacionales y regionales pertinentes.
3. Cada Estado Parte tendrá un representante en la Conferencia, que podrá hacerse acompañar de suplentes y asesores. La Conferencia de Estados Partes aprobará el reglamento y las normas que rijan la ejecución de las actividades enunciadas en el presente artículo, incluidas las normas relativas a la admisión y participación de observadores y el pago de los gastos que ocasione la realización de esas actividades.

B. Comité

4. Con el fin de alcanzar los objetivos enunciados en el párrafo 1 del presente artículo, la Conferencia de Estados Partes establecerá el "Comité establecido conforme a la Convención Internacional para la Prevención y la Sanción de los Crímenes de Lesa Humanidad" (el Comité).
5. El Comité tendrá diez miembros. Los miembros del Comité, que serán expertos en materias pertinentes en la presente Convención, serán designados por los Estados Partes y elegidos por la Conferencia de Estados Partes. Los miembros del Comité serán elegidos por cuatro años. Podrán ser reelegidos una vez. No obstante, el mandato de cinco de los miembros elegidos en la primera elección expirará a los dos años. Inmediatamente después de la primera elección, los nombres de esos cinco miembros serán seleccionados por sorteo de la forma indicada por la Conferencia de Estados Partes.
6. El Comité establecerá su reglamento interno y concertará actividades, procedimientos y métodos de trabajo con miras a lograr los objetivos enunciados en el párrafo 1, y en particular:
    (a) Facilitará las actividades realizadas por y entre los Estados Partes con arreglo a la presente Convención;
    (b) Facilitará el intercambio de información entre los Estados Partes sobre prácticas eficaces para prevenir y sancionar crímenes de lesa humanidad;
    (c) Cooperará con organizaciones y mecanismos internacionales y regionales, y organizaciones no gubernamentales pertinentes;
    (d) Aprovechará adecuadamente la información pertinente elaborada por otros mecanismos internacionales y regionales encargados de prevenir y castigar crímenes de lesa humanidad a fin de evitar una duplicación innecesaria de actividades;
    (e) Formulará recomendaciones para mejorar la presente Convención y su aplicación;
    (f) Tomará nota de las necesidades de asistencia técnica de los Estados Partes con respecto a la aplicación de la presente Convención y recomendará las medidas que considere necesarias al respecto;
    (g) Establecerá normas y reglamentos financieros para el funcionamiento del Comité y la Secretaría; y
    (h) Administrará el Fondo Fiduciario de Contribuciones Voluntarias establecido por los Estados Partes de conformidad con el párrafo 14.
7. A los efectos del párrafo 6, el Comité obtendrá el necesario conocimiento de las medidas adoptadas y de las dificultades encontradas por los Estados Partes en la aplicación de la presente Convención por conducto de la información que ellos le faciliten y de los demás mecanismos de examen que establezca el Comité.

8. El Comité tratará de determinar la manera más eficaz de recibir y procesar la información, incluida la que reciba de los Estados Partes y de organizaciones internacionales competentes. También se podrán considerar las aportaciones recibidas de organizaciones no gubernamentales pertinentes debidamente acreditadas conforme a los procedimientos acordados por el Comité. Cada Estado Parte proporcionará al Comité información sobre sus programas, planes y prácticas adoptados para aplicar la presente Convención, incluyendo:
   (a) La adopción de legislación nacional de aplicación;
   (b) El establecimiento de mecanismos administrativos que satisfagan las necesidades de prevención contenidas en la presente Convención;
   (c) Informes sobre la recopilación de datos respecto a sus obligaciones en virtud de la presente Convención, lo que incluye, pero no se limita al número de denuncias, investigaciones, enjuiciamientos, condenas, extradiciones y solicitudes de asistencia judicial recíproca.
9. La información proporcionada por los Estados Partes será examinada por el Comité, el cual podrá hacer los comentarios, observaciones o recomendaciones que considere apropiados. El Estado Parte interesado será informado de dichos comentarios, observaciones o recomendaciones, a los que podrá responder, por iniciativa propia o a solicitud del Comité. El Comité podrá también pedir a los Estados Partes informaciones complementarias sobre la aplicación de la presente Convención.
10. El Comité establecerá una Secretaría permanente para facilitar sus actividades, procedimientos y métodos de trabajo con miras a lograr los objetivos enunciados en los párrafos 1, 5, 6 y 7. El Comité podrá establecer los demás órganos subsidiarios que fueran necesarios.

C. Secretaría

11. Las funciones de la Secretaría serán:
    (a) Prestar asistencia técnica a los Estados en el proceso de adhesión a la presente Convención;
    (b) Prestar asistencia técnica a los Estados Partes en el cumplimiento de sus obligaciones de conformidad con la presente Convención, incluyendo una apropiada asistencia en el desarrollo de capacidades;
    (c) Difundir la información entre los Estados Partes;
    (d) Facilitar la asistencia judicial recíproca y otros aspectos de la cooperación entre los Estados Partes, incluyendo la cooperación en asuntos que impliquen la comparecencia de testigos y peritos en procedimientos judiciales, y proteger de forma efectiva a tales personas;
    (e) Recibir y recopilar la información de los Estados Partes según lo requiera el Comité; y
    (f) Velar por la coordinación necesaria con las secretarías de otras organizaciones internacionales y regionales pertinentes.

12. La Secretaría tendrá su sede en _____.

D. Gastos

13. Los gastos de la Conferencia de Estados Partes, el Comité, la Secretaría y cualquier otro órgano subsidiario se sufragarán de los recursos siguientes:
    (a) Cuotas de los Estados Partes prorrateadas de conformidad con una escala de cuotas convenida basada en la escala adoptada por las Naciones Unidas para su presupuesto ordinario y ajustada de conformidad con los principios en que se basa dicha escala;
    (b) Fondos aportados de forma voluntaria por gobiernos, organizaciones intergubernamentales, organizaciones no gubernamentales, organizaciones privadas, fundaciones y particulares.

E. Fondo Fiduciario de Contribuciones Voluntarias

14. Los Estados Partes establecerán un Fondo Fiduciario de Contribuciones Voluntarias administrado por el Comité con el fin de prestar a los Estados Partes la asistencia técnica y el desarrollo de capacidades necesarios para apoyar los esfuerzos por cumplir con las obligaciones que se deriven de la presente Convención.

Nota explicativa

1. *Este artículo se basa en gran medida en los artículos 112, 116 y 117 del Estatuto de Roma, los artículos 63 y 64 de la Convención de las Naciones Unidas contra la Corrupción y los artículos 26 y 29 de la Convención contra las Desapariciones Forzadas.*
2. *El párrafo 2 de esta disposición estará sujeto a aprobación por parte de los órganos competentes de las Naciones Unidas, incluido el reembolso por los Estados Partes a las Naciones Unidas de los gastos que ocasione la organización.*
3. *La experiencia de los Estados Partes con este órgano y sus funciones determinará cómo evolucionará en el futuro y qué papel asumirá más allá del mandato establecido en la Convención, tal como, por ejemplo, el de la determinación de los hechos a efectos del desarrollo de un sistema de alerta temprana.*
4. *Respecto al párrafo 12, habrá que negociar un Acuerdo de Sede adecuado con el país anfitrión, sujeto a aprobación por la Conferencia de Estados Partes.*

Artículo 20
Estados federales

Las disposiciones de la presente Convención serán aplicables a todas las partes constitutivas de los Estados federales, sin limitación ni excepción alguna.

Nota explicativa

Esta disposición procede del artículo 41 de la Convención contra las Desapariciones Forzadas.

Artículo 21
Firma, ratificación, aceptación, aprobación o adhesión

1. La presente Convención estará abierta a la firma de todos los Estados en _____ hasta _____.
2. La presente Convención estará sujeta a la ratificación, aceptación o aprobación de los Estados signatarios. Los instrumentos de ratificación, aceptación o aprobación serán depositados en poder del Secretario General de las Naciones Unidas.
3. La presente Convención estará abierta a la adhesión de cualquier Estado. Los instrumentos de adhesión serán depositados en poder del Secretario General de las Naciones Unidas.

Nota explicativa

Este artículo se basa en el artículo 125 del Estatuto de Roma.

Artículo 22
Entrada en vigor

1. La presente Convención entrará en vigor el trigésimo (30°) día a partir de la fecha en que se deposite en poder del Secretario General de las Naciones Unidas el vigésimo (20°) instrumento de ratificación, aceptación, aprobación o adhesión.
2. Respecto de cada Estado que ratifique, acepte o apruebe la presente Convención o se adhiera a ella después de que sea depositado el vigésimo (20°) instrumento de ratificación, aceptación, aprobación o adhesión, la Convención entrará en vigor el trigésimo (30°) día a partir de la fecha en que haya depositado su instrumento de ratificación, aceptación, aprobación o adhesión.

Nota explicativa

Los párrafos 1 y 2 se basan en el artículo 126 del Estatuto de Roma.

Artículo 23
Reservas

No se admitirán reservas a la presente Convención.

Nota Explicativa

1. Este texto procede del artículo 120 del Estatuto de Roma.
2. Se entiende que los sistemas legislativos nacionales varían, que estas variaciones se aplicarán a las modalidades de «aut dedere aut judicare» y que los Estados podrán hacer declaraciones sobre sus respectivos ordenamientos jurídicos y procedimientos nacionales. Ello se aplica particularmente a los artículos 9, 10, 11, 12, 13, 14, 15 y 16 de la presente Convención.

Artículo 24
Enmienda

1. Cualquier Estado Parte en la presente Convención podrá proponer enmiendas a ella. El texto de toda enmienda propuesta será presentado al Secretario General de las Naciones Unidas, que lo distribuirá sin dilación a los Estados Partes.
2. Transcurridos no menos de tres meses desde la fecha de la notificación, la Conferencia de Estados Partes decidirá en su siguiente reunión, por mayoría de los presentes y votantes, si ha de examinar la propuesta, lo cual podrá hacer directamente o previa convocación de una Conferencia de Revisión si la cuestión lo justifica.
3. La aprobación de una enmienda en una reunión de la Conferencia de Estados Partes o en una Conferencia de Revisión en la que no sea posible llegar a un consenso requerirá una mayoría de dos tercios de los Estados Partes.
4. Las enmiendas a la presente Convención entrarán en vigor un año después de que dos tercios de los Estados Partes hayan depositado en poder del Secretario General de las Naciones Unidas sus instrumentos de ratificación o de aceptación y serán obligatorias para aquellos Estados Partes que las hayan aceptado; los demás Estados Partes que no hayan aceptado las enmiendas seguirán obligados por las disposiciones de la presente Convención y las enmiendas anteriores que hayan aceptado.
5. El Secretario General de las Naciones Unidas distribuirá a los Estados Partes las enmiendas aprobadas en una reunión de la Conferencia de Estados Partes o en una Conferencia de Revisión.

Nota explicativa

Este artículo se basa en gran medida en el artículo 121 del Estatuto de Roma.

Artículo 25
Interpretación

Los términos de la presente Convención también se interpretarán a la luz de los principios y las normas de derechos humanos internacionalmente reconocidos.

Nota explicativa

Es evidente que el derecho internacional consuetudinario sobre la interpretación de los tratados (codificado en la Convención de Viena sobre el Derecho de los Tratados) es aplicable. Este artículo también tiene por objeto asegurar que los términos de la presente Convención sean interpretados de conformidad con las obligaciones regionales de derechos humanos de los Estados Partes en virtud del Convenio Europeo de Derechos Humanos, la Convención Americana sobre Derechos Humanos y la Carta Africana sobre los Derechos Humanos y de los Pueblos, así como de conformidad con las obligaciones específicas que con respecto a las diferentes convenciones de derechos humanos establezcan los organismos de dichos tratados.

Artículo 26
Solución de controversias entre Estados Partes

Toda controversia que surja entre dos o más Estados Partes con respecto a la interpretación o aplicación de la presente Convención, incluso las relativas a la responsabilidad de un Estado por supuestas violaciones de la misma, que no pueda solucionarse mediante negociación, se someterá a arbitraje a petición de uno de los Estados afectados. Si en el plazo de seis meses contados a partir de la fecha de presentación de la solicitud de arbitraje, las Partes no consiguen ponerse de acuerdo sobre la organización del mismo, cualquiera de las Partes podrá someter la controversia a la Corte Internacional de Justicia, mediante una solicitud presentada de conformidad con el Estatuto de la Corte, a fin de que pronuncie una decisión definitiva y obligatoria.

Nota explicativa

Esta disposición se basa en el artículo 30(1) de la Convención contra la Tortura, el artículo 42(1) de la Convención contra las Desapariciones Forzadas y el artículo IX de la Convención sobre el Genocidio.

Artículo 27
Textos auténticos

El original de la presente Convención, cuyos textos en árabe, chino, español, francés, inglés y ruso son igualmente auténticos, será depositado en poder del Secretario General de las Naciones Unidas, que enviará copia certificada a todos los Estados.

Nota explicativa

Este texto procede del artículo 128 del Estatuto de Roma.

Anexo 1
Términos empleados

A los efectos de la presente Convención:
  (a) "Justo", "justamente" o "justicia" significan de conformidad con las normas relativas a las debidas garantías procesales reconocidas por el derecho internacional, compatibles con las garantías mínimas de los procedimientos penales, tal como se contienen en el Pacto Internacional de Derechos Civiles y Políticos;
  (b) "Efectivo", "efectivamente" o "efectividad" significan de forma diligente, independiente e imparcial, de manera que no tenga por objeto sustraer a la persona de que se trate de su responsabilidad penal por crímenes de lesa humanidad y sea compatible con la intención de someter a la persona a la acción de la justicia, teniendo presente el respeto por el principio de presunción de inocencia.
  (c) "Persona" designa a una persona natural o una entidad jurídica.

Nota explicativa

Las definiciones de "justo" y de "efectivo" de los apartados (a) y (b) tienen por objeto asegurar que los Estados no puedan utilizar investigaciones simuladas o procedimientos legales para eludir sus obligaciones de investigar, enjuiciar o extraditar. La definición del párrafo (b) se basa en gran medida en el principio «ne bis in idem» formulado en el artículo 10 del Estatuto del TPIY y el artículo 20 del Estatuto de Roma.

Anexo 2
Extradición

A. Crímenes de lesa humanidad como delitos que dan lugar a extradición

1. Los crímenes de lesa humanidad estarán comprendidos de pleno derecho entre los delitos que den lugar a extradición en todo tratado de extradición celebrado entre Estados Partes antes de la entrada en vigor de la presente Convención.
2. Los Estados Partes se comprometen a incluir los crímenes de lesa humanidad entre los delitos susceptibles de extradición en todo tratado de extradición que celebren entre sí con posterioridad.

B. Base jurídica para la extradición

3. En ausencia de legislación nacional pertinente u otra relación en materia de extradición, los Estados Partes considerarán la presente Convención como la base jurídica para la extradición a fin de cumplir su obligación de juzgar o extraditar a las personas presuntamente responsables de crímenes de lesa humanidad conforme al párrafo 9 del artículo 8 y al artículo 9.

C. Modalidades de extradición

4. En ausencia de legislación nacional pertinente u otra relación en materia de extradición, los Estados Partes podrán utilizar todas o algunas de las siguientes modalidades establecidas en el presente anexo.

D. Motivos para denegar la extradición

5. A efectos de extradición entre Estados Partes, los crímenes de lesa humanidad no serán considerados delitos políticos o delitos conexos a un delito político. En consecuencia, una solicitud de extradición por crímenes de lesa humanidad no podrá ser denegada por este único motivo ni se impedirá la extradición mediante alegación de cargo oficial con sujeción a lo dispuesto en el párrafo 1 del artículo 6.
6. Serán motivos para denegar la extradición que la persona reclamada esté siendo juzgada por crímenes de lesa humanidad o por otro crimen conforme a la legislación del Estado requerido basándose en hechos que constituyan uno o más de los actos enumerados en el párrafo 1 del artículo 3, o que la persona reclamada ya haya sido juzgada por tal crimen o crímenes y haya sido absuelta, o haya resultado condenada y haya cumplido la pena impuesta por dicha condena. También será motivo para denegar la extradición si el Estado Parte requerido comprueba que la persona reclamada para la extradición puede ser objeto de crímenes de lesa humanidad en el Estado requirente, tal como prevé el artículo 18.

7. Serán motivos para denegar la extradición que el Estado requerido tenga razones fundadas para creer que la solicitud de extradición se ha formulado con miras a procesar o sancionar a una persona a causa de su raza, religión, nacionalidad, origen étnico, opiniones políticas, sexo o condición, o que el derecho de esa persona a un juicio justo e imparcial pueda resultar perjudicado por alguna de esas razones.
8. Serán motivos para denegar la extradición que la sentencia del Estado requirente haya sido dictada en rebeldía, que no se avisara con suficiente antelación a la persona condenada de que iba a comparecer en juicio o no se le diera la oportunidad de organizar su defensa, y que la persona no tenga ni tendrá la posibilidad de participar en la revisión de la causa.
9. Serán motivos para denegar la extradición que la persona no haya tenido ni vaya a tener un proceso penal con las garantías mínimas que se establecen en el artículo 14 del Pacto Internacional de Derechos Civiles y Políticos.
10. Podrá denegarse la extradición si el crimen de lesa humanidad está castigado con una pena no prevista en el Estado requerido, a menos que el Estado requirente garantice suficientemente, a juicio del Estado requerido, que no se impondrá la pena no prevista en el Estado requerido y que, si se impone, no será ejecutada.

E. Principio de especialidad

11. Ninguna persona extraditada por crímenes de lesa humanidad será juzgada en el Estado requirente por un crimen distinto de aquel para el que se concedió la extradición a menos que el Estado requerido o la persona extraditada lo consientan.

F. Múltiples solicitudes de extradición

12. En los casos de múltiples solicitudes de extradición, el Estado Parte en cuyo territorio haya sido encontrada la persona presuntamente responsable de crímenes de lesa humanidad podrá tomar en consideración los siguientes factores para determinar la prioridad de dichas solicitudes:
    (a) El territorio en el que hayan tenido lugar uno o más de los actos constitutivos que se consideran parte del crimen;
    (b) La nacionalidad del delincuente o delincuentes;
    (c) La nacionalidad de la víctima o víctimas; y
    (d) La jurisdicción que, con más probabilidad, tenga una mayor capacidad y efectividad para llevar a cabo el enjuiciamiento, y que ofrezca un mayor grado de justicia e imparcialidad.

Nota explicativa

1. *El párrafo 1 se basa en el artículo 13(2) de la Convención contra las Desapariciones Forzadas.*

2. *El párrafo 2 se basa en el artículo 13(3) de la Convención contra las Desapariciones Forzadas.*
3. *El párrafo 3 asegura que, en ausencia de legislación nacional pertinente o de una relación bilateral o multilateral existente en materia de extradición, la presente Convención proporcionará la base jurídica sobre la cual un Estado Parte podrá cumplir su obligación de extraditar o juzgar de conformidad con el párrafo 9 del artículo 8 y el artículo 9.*
4. *El párrafo 4 asegura que, en ausencia de legislación nacional pertinente o de una relación bilateral o multilateral existente en materia de extradición, la presente Convención podrá definir las modalidades mediante las que un Estado Parte podrá cumplir su obligación de extraditar o juzgar de conformidad con el párrafo 9 del artículo 8 y el artículo 9.*
5. *El párrafo 5 se basa en el artículo 13(1) de la Convención contra las Desapariciones Forzadas respecto a los delitos políticos. Con respecto a alegaciones de cargo oficial, este párrafo es compatible con el párrafo 1 del artículo 6 de la presente Convención, que impide que se alegue cualquier cargo oficial como defensa aplicable.*
6. *Respecto al párrafo 6, a fin de respetar el contenido esencial del principio «ne bis in idem», no debería importar si un Estado o un Estado Parte ha juzgado a una persona. En cualquier caso, el Estado requerido tendrá que determinar si el enjuiciamiento fue justo y efectivo.*
7. *El párrafo 7 se basa en el artículo 3(b) del Tratado Modelo de Extradición de las Naciones Unidas.*
8. *El párrafo 8 se basa en el artículo 3(g) del Tratado Modelo de Extradición de las Naciones Unidas.*
9. *El párrafo 9 se basa en el artículo 3(f) del Tratado Modelo de Extradición de las Naciones Unidas.*
10. *El párrafo 10 es similar al artículo 4(d) del Tratado Modelo de Extradición de las Naciones Unidas, pero más amplio, y reconoce que los Estados pueden tener obligaciones diferentes en lo que respecta a los tratados regionales de derechos humanos.*
11. *Los párrafos 6 a 9 proporcionan motivos para denegar obligatoriamente la extradición, mientras que el párrafo 10 proporciona un motivo para denegarla facultativamente. Otros motivos posibles para denegar facultativamente la extradición se prevén en el artículo 4 del Tratado Modelo de Extradición de las Naciones Unidas.*

Anexo 3
Asistencia judicial recíproca

1. La asistencia judicial entre los Estados Partes se prestará en la mayor medida posible conforme a las leyes, tratados, acuerdos y arreglos pertinentes del Estado Parte requerido y podrá prestarse sobre la base de la presente Convención y sin la necesidad de depender de un tratado bilateral o de legislación nacional.

A. Tipos de asistencia judicial recíproca

2. La asistencia judicial que se preste de conformidad con el presente anexo podrá solicitarse para cualquiera de los fines siguientes:
   (a) Recibir testimonios o tomar declaración a personas;
   (b) Presentar documentos judiciales;
   (c) Efectuar inspecciones e incautaciones y embargos preventivos de activos;
   (d) Examinar objetos y lugares;
   (e) Proporcionar información, elementos de prueba y evaluaciones de peritos;
   (f) Entregar originales o copias certificadas de los documentos y expedientes pertinentes, incluida la documentación pública, bancaria y financiera, así como la documentación social o comercial de sociedades mercantiles;
   (g) Identificar o localizar el producto del crimen, los bienes, los instrumentos u otros elementos con fines probatorios;
   (h) Facilitar la comparecencia voluntaria de personas en el Estado Parte requirente;
   (i) Prestar cualquier otro tipo de asistencia autorizada por el derecho interno del Estado Parte requerido.

B. Transmisión de información

3. Sin menoscabo del derecho interno, las autoridades competentes de un Estado Parte podrán, sin que se les solicite previamente, transmitir información relativa a crímenes de lesa humanidad a una autoridad competente de otro Estado Parte si creen que esa información podría ayudar a la autoridad a emprender o concluir con éxito indagaciones y procesos penales o podría dar lugar a una solicitud formulada por este último Estado Parte con arreglo a la presente Convención.

4. La transmisión de información con arreglo al párrafo 3 del presente anexo se hará sin perjuicio de las indagaciones y procesos penales que tengan lugar en el Estado de las autoridades competentes que facilitan la información. Las autoridades competentes que reciben la información deberán acceder a toda solicitud de que se respete su carácter confidencial, incluso

temporalmente, o de que se impongan restricciones a su utilización. Sin embargo, ello no obstará para que el Estado Parte receptor revele, en sus actuaciones, información que sea exculpatoria de una persona acusada. En tal caso, el Estado Parte receptor notificará al Estado Parte transmisor antes de revelar dicha información y, si así se le solicita, consultará al Estado Parte transmisor. Si, en un caso excepcional, no es posible notificar con antelación, el Estado Parte receptor informará sin demora al Estado Parte transmisor de dicha revelación.

C. Obligaciones dimanantes de otros tratados aplicables

5. Lo dispuesto en el presente anexo no afectará a las obligaciones dimanantes de otros tratados bilaterales o multilaterales vigentes o futuros que rijan, total o parcialmente, la asistencia judicial recíproca.

D. Traslado de personas detenidas

6. La persona que se encuentre detenida o cumpliendo una condena en el territorio de un Estado Parte y cuya presencia se solicite en otro Estado Parte para fines de identificación, para prestar testimonio o para que ayude de alguna otra forma a obtener pruebas necesarias para investigaciones, procesos o actuaciones judiciales respecto de crímenes de lesa humanidad podrá ser trasladada si se cumplen las condiciones siguientes:
   (a) La persona, debidamente informada, da su libre consentimiento;
   (b) Las autoridades competentes de ambos Estados Partes están de acuerdo, con sujeción a las condiciones que estos consideren apropiadas.

E. Forma de las solicitudes de asistencia judicial recíproca

7. Las solicitudes de asistencia judicial se presentarán por escrito o, cuando sea posible, por cualquier medio capaz de registrar un texto escrito, en un idioma aceptable para el Estado Parte requerido, en condiciones que permitan a dicho Estado Parte determinar su autenticidad. Cada Estado Parte notificará al Secretario General de las Naciones Unidas, en el momento de depositar su instrumento de ratificación, aceptación o aprobación de la presente Convención o de adhesión a ella, el idioma o idiomas que le son aceptables. En situaciones de urgencia, y cuando los Estados Partes convengan en ello, las solicitudes podrán hacerse oralmente, debiendo ser confirmadas sin demora por escrito.
8. Toda solicitud de asistencia judicial contendrá lo siguiente:
   (a) La identidad de la autoridad que hace la solicitud;
   (b) El objeto y la índole de las investigaciones, los procesos o las actuaciones judiciales a que se refiere la solicitud y el nombre y las funciones de la autoridad encargada de efectuar dichas investigaciones, procesos o actuaciones judiciales;
   (c) Un resumen de los hechos pertinentes, salvo cuando se trate de solicitudes de presentación de documentos judiciales;

(d) Una descripción de la asistencia solicitada y pormenores sobre cualquier procedimiento particular que el Estado Parte requirente desee que se aplique;
(e) De ser posible, la identidad, ubicación y nacionalidad de toda persona interesada; y
(f) La finalidad para la que se solicita la prueba, información o actuación.

9. El Estado Parte requerido podrá pedir información adicional cuando sea necesaria para dar cumplimiento a la solicitud de conformidad con su derecho interno o para facilitar dicho cumplimiento.

F. Cumplimiento de las solicitudes de asistencia judicial recíproca

10. Se dará cumplimiento a toda solicitud con arreglo al derecho interno del Estado Parte requerido y, en la medida en que ello no lo contravenga y sea factible, de conformidad con los procedimientos especificados en la solicitud.

G. Testigos

11. Siempre que sea posible y compatible con los principios fundamentales del derecho interno, cuando una persona se encuentre en el territorio de un Estado Parte y tenga que prestar declaración como testigo o perito ante autoridades judiciales de otro Estado Parte, el primer Estado Parte, a solicitud del otro, podrá permitir que la audiencia se celebre por videoconferencia si no es posible o conveniente que la persona en cuestión comparezca personalmente en el territorio del Estado Parte requirente. Los Estados Partes podrán convenir en que la audiencia esté a cargo de una autoridad judicial del Estado Parte requirente y en que asista a ella una autoridad judicial del Estado Parte requerido.

H. Utilización limitada de la información

12. El Estado Parte requirente no transmitirá ni utilizará, sin previo consentimiento del Estado Parte requerido, la información o las pruebas proporcionadas por el Estado Parte requerido para investigaciones, procesos o actuaciones judiciales distintos de los indicados en la solicitud. Nada de lo dispuesto en el presente párrafo impedirá que el Estado Parte requirente revele, en sus actuaciones, información o pruebas que sean exculpatorias de una persona acusada. En este último caso, el Estado Parte requirente notificará al Estado Parte requerido antes de revelar la información o las pruebas y, si así se le solicita, consultará al Estado Parte requerido. Si, en un caso excepcional, no es posible notificar con antelación, el Estado Parte requirente informará sin demora al Estado Parte requerido de dicha revelación.

I. Denegación de las solicitudes de asistencia judicial recíproca

13. Los Estados Partes no invocarán el secreto bancario para denegar la asistencia judicial recíproca con arreglo al presente anexo.
14. La asistencia judicial podrá ser denegada cuando la solicitud no se haga de conformidad con lo dispuesto en el presente anexo.
15. La asistencia judicial no podrá ser denegada con base en la alegación de cargo oficial con sujeción a lo dispuesto en el párrafo 1 del artículo 6, ni en el carácter político del crimen.
16. La asistencia judicial será denegada cuando la persona objeto de la solicitud esté siendo juzgada por crímenes de lesa humanidad o por otro crimen conforme a la legislación del Estado requerido basándose en hechos que constituyan uno o más de los actos enumerados en el párrafo 1 del artículo 3, o cuando la persona ya haya sido juzgada por tal crimen o crímenes y haya sido absuelta, o haya resultado condenada y haya cumplido la pena impuesta por dicha condena. También será motivo para denegar la asistencia judicial recíproca si el Estado Parte requerido comprueba que la persona objeto de la solicitud puede ser víctima de crímenes de lesa humanidad en el Estado requirente.

Nota explicativa

1. *Gran parte del texto de este anexo se basa en las disposiciones sobre la asistencia judicial recíproca del artículo 46 de la Convención de las Naciones Unidas contra la Corrupción.*
2. *Para modalidades adicionales de efectuar la asistencia judicial recíproca, los Estados Partes pueden mirar modelos de legislación, como el Tratado Modelo de Asistencia Recíproca en asuntos penales de las Naciones Unidas, o las convenciones pertinentes de los organismos regionales.*

Anexo 4
Transmisión de procedimientos penales

1. Siempre que un Estado Parte que tenga competencia sobre una persona acusada de crímenes de lesa humanidad esté de acuerdo con otro Estado Parte, que también tenga competencia conforme al artículo 10, en ceder su competencia y transmitir el expediente de los procedimientos iniciados en el Estado requirente, el procedimiento de transmisión se establecerá mediante acuerdo entre sus respectivas autoridades competentes. Dicho procedimiento se basará en la presente Convención y no exigirá la existencia de un tratado bilateral entre los Estados Partes respectivos o legislación nacional.
2. Podrá producirse una transmisión cuando redunde en el mejor interés de la justicia y cuando mejore el enjuiciamiento justo y efectivo.
3. Un Estado Parte podrá pedir a otro Estado Parte que asuma un procedimiento en uno o varios de los casos siguientes:
   (a) Si el sospechoso tiene su residencia habitual en el Estado requerido;
   (b) Si el sospechoso es nacional del Estado requerido o si este último Estado es su Estado de origen;
   (c) Si el sospechoso está cumpliendo o va a cumplir en el Estado requerido una condena que implique privación de libertad;
   (d) Si contra el sospechoso se está instruyendo en el Estado requerido un procedimiento por el mismo crimen u otros crímenes;
   (e) Si considera que la transmisión del procedimiento está justificada para facilitar el descubrimiento de la verdad y en particular si los elementos de prueba más importantes se hallan en el Estado requerido;
   (f) Si considera que es probable que la ejecución de una posible condena en el Estado requerido mejora las posibilidades de readaptación social del condenado;
   (g) Si considera que no puede garantizarse la comparecencia del sospechoso en la audiencia que habría de celebrarse en el Estado requirente mientras dicha comparecencia pueda garantizarse en el Estado requerido;
   (h) Si considera que no está en condiciones de ejecutar por sí mismo una posible condena, incluso recurriendo a la extradición, siempre que el Estado requerido esté en condiciones de hacerlo.

Nota explicativa

1. *Esta disposición se basa en el Convenio Europeo sobre la Transmisión de Procedimientos en materia penal e incluye en el párrafo 3 las situaciones enumeradas en el artículo 8 de dicho Convenio, que define los casos en los que los Estados podrán hacer las peticiones de transmisión.*
2. *Los motivos de denegación no han sido incluidos dada la diversidad de ordenamientos jurídicos nacionales.*

Anexo 5
Traslado de personas condenadas para el cumplimiento de sus condenas

1. Los Estados Partes podrán trasladar de uno a otro a una persona condenada por crímenes de lesa humanidad en sus respectivas jurisdicciones a efectos del cumplimiento de la condena de dicha persona sobre la base de la presente Convención y sin la necesidad de un tratado bilateral entre los Estados Partes o de legislación nacional.
2. El traslado requerirá el consentimiento del Estado Parte de condena, del Estado Parte de cumplimiento y de la persona que sea trasladada, la cual renunciará a cualquier derecho a impugnar su condena en el Estado de condena, junto con el acuerdo del Estado Parte de cumplimiento para ejecutar la condena tal como se decidió en el Estado de condena, de conformidad con sus leyes penales y reglamentos aplicables.
3. La libertad condicional y demás medidas previstas en el Estado de cumplimiento serán conforme a sus leyes y reglamentos aplicables. No obstante, no se extenderá a la persona trasladada ningún indulto u otra medida de clemencia similar sin el consentimiento del Estado de condena.

Nota explicativa

Esta disposición se basa en el Convenio Europeo sobre Traslado de Personas Condenadas así como en la Convención Interamericana para el cumplimiento de condenas penales en el extranjero. Los Estados Partes podrán también querer mirar modelos de legislación de organizaciones pertinentes, directivas regionales y acuerdos subregionales.

Anexo 6
Ejecución de las sentencias penales de los Estados Partes

1. El reconocimiento y la ejecución de una sentencia penal de un Estado Parte se basarán en la presente Convención y no requerirán un tratado bilateral entre los Estados Partes respectivos ni legislación nacional distinta de la que pueda ser exigida con arreglo a la Constitución o las leyes nacionales de cada Estado Parte a fin de aplicar la presente Convención.
2. En cambio, la cooperación y la asistencia entre los Estados Partes, particularmente en lo que respecta a hacer efectivos los anexos 3 a 6, y que, de conformidad con las leyes de un Estado Parte determinado, estén prohibidas si se fundamentan en una sentencia penal extranjera o que exijan un tratado o legislación nacional que tenga por efecto el reconocimiento de una sentencia penal extranjera, dependerán de la presente Convención en lo que respecta a la ejecución o el reconocimiento de una sentencia penal extranjera.
3. Un Estado Parte podrá, no obstante, negarse a cumplir, ejecutar, hacer efectiva o reconocer las sentencias penales de otro Estado Parte si la sentencia en cuestión se obtuvo mediante fraude o coacción, o se dictó en base a procedimientos que violan las normas internacionales relativas a las debidas garantías procesales, o están en conflicto con el orden público interno.

Nota explicativa

Esta disposición se basa en el Convenio Europeo sobre la Validez Internacional de las Sentencias Penales.

CONVENCIÓN INTERNACIONAL PARA LA PREVENCIÓN Y LA SANCIÓN DE LOS CRÍMENES DE LESA HUMANIDAD

Tabla de abreviaturas e instrumentos citados en la Convención y las notas explicativas

Carta Africana	Carta Africana sobre los Derechos Humanos y de los Pueblos [Carta de Banjul], 1982, 1520 UNTS 217 (entrada en vigor: 21 de octubre de 1986).
Carta de las Naciones Unidas	Carta de las Naciones Unidas, 1945, 1 UNTS 16 (24 de octubre de 1945).
CEDH	Convenio Europeo para la Protección de los Derechos Humanos y de las Libertades Fundamentales, 1950, E.T.S. No. 5, 213 UNTS 222, Roma (4 de septiembre de 1950) (entrada en vigor: 3 de septiembre de 1953).
CIJ	Corte Internacional de Justicia
CLH	Crimen(es) de Lesa Humanidad.
Convención Americana sobre Derechos Humanos	Convención Americana sobre Derechos Humanos, 1969, Serie sobre Tratados, O.E.A., No. 36, 1144 UNTS 123 (entrada en vigor: 18 de julio de 1978).
Convención contra el Apartheid	Convención Internacional sobre la Represión y el Castigo del Crimen de *Apartheid*, 1973, Res. A.G. 3068 (XXVIII), de 30 de noviembre de 1973, Doc. ONU A/9030, 1015 UNTS 243 (entrada en vigor: 18 de julio de 1976).
Convención contra la Tortura	Convención contra la Tortura y Otros Tratos o Penas Crueles, Inhumanos o Degradantes, 1984, Res. A.G. 39/46, anexo, ONU, Asamblea General, Documentos Oficiales, 39° período de sesiones, Doc. ONU A/39/51 (10 de diciembre de 1984) (entrada en vigor: 26 de junio de 1987).
Convención contra las Desapariciones Forzadas	Convención Internacional para la Protección de todas las personas contra las desapariciones forzadas, 2006, Res. A.G. 61/177, ONU, Asamblea General, Documentos Oficiales, 61er período de sesiones, Doc. ONU A/RES/61/177 (20 de diciembre de 2006) (aún no ha entrado en vigor).
Convención de las Naciones Unidas contra la Corrupción	Convención de las Naciones Unidas contra la Corrupción, 2003, Res. A.G. 58/4, Doc. ONU A/58/422 (31 de octubre de 2003) (entrada en vigor: 14 de diciembre de 2005).

Convención de las Naciones Unidas contra la Delincuencia Organizada Transnacional	Convención de las Naciones Unidas contra la Delincuencia Organizada Transnacional, 2001, Res. A.G. 25/55, anexo I, ONU, Asamblea General, Documentos Oficiales, 55° período de sesiones, Suplemento No. 49, p. 44, Doc. ONU A/55/49 (Vol. I) (2001) (entrada en vigor: 29 de septiembre de 2003).
Convención Interamericana para el cumplimiento de condenas penales en el extranjero	Convención Interamericana para el cumplimiento de condenas penales en el extranjero, 1993, Serie sobre Tratados, O.E.A., No. 76 (9 de junio de 1993) (entrada en vigor: 13 de abril de 1996).
Convención Interamericana sobre Asistencia Mutua en Materia Penal	Convención Interamericana sobre Asistencia Mutua en Materia Penal, 1992, Serie sobre Tratados, O.E.A., No. 75 (23 de mayo de 1992) (entrada en vigor: 14 de abril de 1996).
Convención Interamericana sobre Extradición	Convención Interamericana sobre Extradición, 1981, Serie sobre Tratados, O.E.A., No. 60 (25 de febrero de 1981) (entrada en vigor: 28 de marzo de 1992).
Convención sobre el Genocidio	Convención para la Prevención y la Sanción del delito de Genocidio, 1951, Res. A.G. 260 (III), Doc. ONU No. A/180, 78 UNTS 277 (9 de diciembre de 1948) (entrada en vigor: 12 de enero de 1951).
Convención sobre la Imprescriptibilidad	Convención sobre la Imprescriptibilidad de los Crímenes de Guerra y de los Crímenes de Lesa Humanidad, 1970, Res. A.G. 2391 (XXIII), Doc. ONU A/7218, 754 UNTS 73 (26 de noviembre de 1968) (entrada en vigor: 11 de noviembre de 1970).
Convenio Europeo sobre Asistencia Recíproca en materia penal	Convenio Europeo sobre Asistencia Recíproca en materia penal, 1959, E.T.S. No. 30, Mutual Assistance in Criminal Matters, Estrasburgo (20 de abril de 1959) (entrada en vigor: 12 de junio de 1962).
Convenio Europeo sobre la Imprescriptibilidad	Convenio Europeo sobre la Imprescriptibilidad de los Crímenes de Lesa Humanidad y de los Crímenes de Guerra, 1974, E.T.S. No. 82, Crimes against humanity and War Crimes, Estrasburgo (25 de enero de 1974) (entrada en vigor: 26 de junio de 2003).
Convenio Europeo sobre la Transmisión de Procedimientos en materia penal	Convenio Europeo sobre la Transmisión de Procedimientos en material penal, 1972, E.T.S. No. 73, Criminal Proceedings, Estrasburgo (15 de mayo de 1972) (entrada en vigor: 30 de marzo de 1978).

Convenio Europeo sobre la Validez Internacional de las Sentencias Penales	Convenio Europeo sobre la Validez Internacional de las Sentencias Penales, 1970, E.T.S. No. 70, Criminal Judgments, La Haya (28 de mayo de 1970) (entrada en vigor: 26 de julio de 1974).
Convenio Europeo sobre Traslado de Personas Condenadas	Convenio sobre Traslado de Personas Condenadas, 1983, E.T.S. No. 112, Estrasburgo (21 de marzo de 1983) (entrada en vigor: 1 de julio de 1985).
Convenio para la represión de los actos de terrorismo nuclear	Convenio Internacional para la represión de los actos de terrorismo nuclear, 2005, Res. A.G. 59/290 (LIX), anexo, Doc. ONU A/59/766 (13 de abril de 2005) (entrada en vigor: 7 de julio de 2007).
Convenio para la represión de los atentados terroristas cometidos con bombas	Convenio Internacional para la represión de los atentados terroristas cometidos con bombas, 1997, Res. A.G. 52/164, Doc. ONU A/RES/52/164 (12 de enero de 1998) (entrada en vigor: 23 de mayo de 2001).
Convenio para la represión del apoderamiento ilícito de aeronaves	Convenio para la represión del apoderamiento ilícito de aeronaves, 1970, (La Haya, 18 de diciembre de 1970), T.I.A.S. No. 7192, 22 U.S.T. 1641, 860 UNTS 105 (entrada en vigor: 14 de octubre de 1971).
Declaración contra las Desapariciones Forzadas	Declaración sobre la Protección de todas las personas contra las desapariciones forzadas, 1992, Res. A.G. 47/133, ONU, Asamblea General, Documentos Oficiales, 47° período de sesiones, Suplemento No. 49, p. 207, Doc. ONU A/47/49 (1992).
Declaración de Rabat	Convenio de asistencia judicial y de extradición en casos de terrorismo, 2008, anexo de la carta de fecha 14 de agosto de 2008 dirigida al Secretario General por el Encargado de Negocios interino de la Misión Permanente de Marruecos ante las Naciones Unidas A/62/939 – S/2008/567 (08–47026) (no ha entrado en vigor).
Documento Final de la Cumbre Mundial	Resolución aprobada por la Asamblea General 60/1. Documento Final de la Cumbre Mundial 2005, 2005, Res. A.G. A/RES/60/1, Doc. ONU A/RES/60/1 (24 de octubre de 2005).
Estatuto de Roma	Estatuto de Roma de la Corte Penal Internacional, 1998, 2187 UNTS 90 (entrada en vigor: 1 de julio de 2002).

Estatuto del TPIR	Estatuto del Tribunal Penal Internacional para el enjuiciamiento de las personas responsables de Genocidio y de otras graves violaciones del Derecho Internacional Humanitario cometidas en el territorio de Ruanda y de los ciudadanos ruandeses responsables de Genocidio y de otras graves violaciones cometidas en el territorio de los Estados fronterizos, entre el 1 de enero de 1994 y el 31 de diciembre de 1994, 1994, Res. C.S. 955, Doc. ONU S/RES/955 (8 de noviembre de 1994), modificado por Res. C.S. 1431, Doc. ONU S/RES/1431 (14 de agosto de 2002).
Estatuto del TPIY	Estatuto del Tribunal Penal Internacional para el enjuiciamiento de las personas responsables de graves violaciones del Derecho Internacional Humanitario cometidas en el territorio de la antigua Yugoslavia desde 1991, Doc. ONU S/25704, p. 36, anexo (1993) & S/25704/Add.1 (1993), adoptada por el Consejo de Seguridad el 25 de mayo de 1993, Doc. ONU S/RES/827 (1993).
Exhorto europeo de obtención de pruebas	Decisión Marco del Consejo relativa al exhorto europeo de obtención de pruebas para recabar objetos, documentos y datos destinados a procedimientos en materia penal, 2008, DO (L 350) 72, Decisión Marco del Consejo, 2008/978/JAI (entrada en vigor: 8 de febrero de 2009).
Historia Completa de la Propuesta de Convención Internacional para la Prevención y la Sanción de los Crímenes de Lesa Humanidad	Leila Nadya Sadat, *A Comprehensive History of the Proposed International Convention on the Prevention and Punishment of Crimes Against Humanity*, in Forging a Convention for Crimes Against Humanity (Cambridge Univ. Press, 2011). Para la página web de la «Washington University School of Law Whitney R. Harris World Law Institute Crimes Against Humanity Initiative», véase http://law.wustl.edu/crimesagainsthumanity/.
Informe del Grupo de Trabajo para la Prevención del Genocidio	Madeleine Albright & William Cohen, Preventing Genocide: A Blueprint for U.S. Policymakers (2008), *disponible en:* http://www.usip.org/genocide_taskforce/report.html.
PIDCP	Pacto Internacional de Derechos Civiles y Políticos, 1976, Res. A.G. 2200 (XXI), Suplemento No. 16, Doc. ONU A/6316 (16 de diciembre de 1966) (entrada en vigor: 23 de marzo de 1976).

Principios de Nuremberg	**Principios de Derecho Internacional reconocidos por el Estatuto y por las sentencias del Tribunal de Nuremberg,** 1950, ONU, Asamblea General, Documentos Oficiales, 5º período de sesiones, Suplemento No. 12, Doc. ONU A/1316 (1950).
Proyecto de artículos sobre la responsabilidad del Estado por hechos internacionalmente ilícitos de la CDI	**Informe de la Comisión de Derecho Internacional en su 53º período de sesiones (23 de abril a 1º de junio y 2 de julio a 10 de agosto de 2001),** 2001, ONU, Asamblea General, Documentos Oficiales, 56º período de sesiones, Doc. ONU A/56/10 (2001).
Tratado Modelo de Asistencia Recíproca en asuntos penales de las Naciones Unidas	**Tratado Modelo de Asistencia Recíproca en asuntos penales,** 1990, Res. A.G. 45/117, Doc. ONU A/RES/45/117 (14 de diciembre de 1990).
Tratado Modelo de Extradición de las Naciones Unidas	**Tratado Modelo de Extradición,** 1990, Res. A.G. 45/116, anexo, Doc. ONU A/RES/45/116 (14 de diciembre de 1990).

Washington University School of Law

Whitney R. Harris World Law Institute
Crimes Against Humanity Initiative

St. Louis Experts' Meeting
April 13–15, 2009
ANNEX #1: LIST OF PARTICIPANTS

STEERING COMMITTEE MEMBERS

Chair: Professor Leila Nadya Sadat, Washington University in St. Louis School of Law; Director of the Whitney R. Harris World Law Institute

Professor M. Cherif Bassiouni, DePaul University College of Law; President Emeritus of the International Human Rights Law Institute

Ambassador Hans Corell, former Under-Secretary-General for Legal Affairs and the Legal Counsel of the United Nations

Justice Richard Goldstone, Fordham University School of Law; former Chief Prosecutor of the International Criminal Tribunals for the former Yugoslavia and for Rwanda

Mr. Juan Méndez, President, International Center for Transitional Justice

Professor William Schabas, Director, the Irish Centre for Human Rights, National University of Ireland, Galway

Judge Christine Van den Wyngaert, International Criminal Tribunal for the former Yugoslavia; International Criminal Court

EXPERT PARTICIPANTS

Professor David Akerson, Sturm College of Law, University of Denver

Professor Payam Akhavan, McGill University Faculty of Law

Professor Diane Marie Amann, University of California Davis School of Law

Professor Dr. Kai Ambos, Georg-August-Universität, Göttingen, Germany

Ms. Elizabeth Andersen, Executive Director, American Society of International Law

Ms. Evelyn Ankumah, Executive Director, Africa Legal Aid

Dr. Kelly Dawn Askin, Open Society Justice Initiative

Professor Elizabeth Borgwardt, Washington University in St. Louis

Dr. Frank Chalk, Concordia University

Professor Roger S. Clark, Rutgers University School of Law-Camden

Professor David Crane, Syracuse University College of Law

Ms. Margaret deGuzman, the Irish Centre for Human Rights, National University of Ireland, Galway

Professor Mark Drumbl, Washington & Lee University School of Law

Mr. Mark Ellis, International Bar Association

Dr. John Hagan, Northwestern University

Professor Hurst Hannum, Tufts University, The Fletcher School

Mr. Whitney R. Harris, former prosecutor for the International Military Tribunal at Nuremberg

Ambassador Feisal Amin Rasoul al-Istrabadi, Indiana University School of Law

Mr. Larry Johnson, former UN Assistant-Secretary-General for Legal Affairs

Professor David Luban, Georgetown University Law Center

Professor Larry May, Washington University in St. Louis

Mr. Guénaël Mettraux, former Associate Legal Officer and former defense counsel, International Criminal Tribunal for the former Yugoslavia

Professor Michael A. Newton, Vanderbilt University Law School

Ms. Laura M. Olson, American Society of International Law

Professor Valerie Oosterveld, University of Western Ontario Faculty of Law

Professor Diane Orentlicher, American University Washington College of Law

Professor Mark Osiel, T.M.C. Asser Institute, University of Amsterdam

Professor Naomi Roht-Arriaza, University of California, Hastings College of the Law

Dr. Leonard Rubenstein, Physicians for Human Rights

Professor Michael P. Scharf, Case Western Reserve University School of Law

Professor David Scheffer, Northwestern University School of Law

Ambassador Thomas A. Schweich, Washington University in St. Louis School of Law

Professor Elies van Sliedregt, Vrije Universiteit Amsterdam

Professor Göran Sluiter, University of Amsterdam

Dr. Gregory H. Stanton, Genocide Watch

Professor Jane Stromseth, Georgetown University Law Center

Mr. B. Don Taylor III, International Criminal Tribunal for the former Yugoslavia

Professor Melissa Waters, Washington University in St. Louis School of Law

Ambassador John Clint Williamson, U.S. Ambassador-at-Large for War Crimes Issues

WASHINGTON UNIVERSITY AND HARRIS INSTITUTE PERSONNEL

Chancellor Mark S. Wrighton, Washington University in St. Louis

Dean Kent Syverud, Dean and Ethan A.H. Shepley University Professor, Washington University School of Law

Ms. Amitis Khojasteh, Cash Nickerson Fellow, Whitney R. Harris World Law Institute

Ms. Linda McClain, Assistant Director, Whitney R. Harris World Law Institute

Mr. Michael Peil, Associate Dean for International Programs, Washington University School of Law

RAPPORTEURS

Ms. Kate Allen, Harvard Law School

Mr. Joseph Vincent Barrett, Harvard Law School

Ms. McCall Carter, Washington University in St. Louis School of Law

Ms. Miriam Gouvea Cohen, Harvard Law School

Ms. Margaret Wichmann, Washington University in St. Louis School of Law

Washington University School of Law

Whitney R. Harris World Law Institute
Crimes Against Humanity Initiative

St. Louis Experts' Meeting
April 13–15, 2009
ANNEX #2: AGENDA

MONDAY, APRIL 13, 2009

8:30 a.m. **Welcome and Opening Remarks**
- **Leila Nadya Sadat**, Washington University School of Law; Director, Harris World Law Institute
- **Whitney R. Harris**, Nuremberg Prosecutor

SECTION I: LEGAL, SOCIAL AND HISTORICAL CONTEXT

9:00–9:45 **History of Efforts to Codify Crimes Against Humanity**
- **Roger S. Clark**, Rutgers University School of Law, Camden (Author)
- **Frank Chalk**, Concordia University (Discussant)

9:45–10:30 **Why A Crimes Against Humanity Convention?**
- **Gregory H. Stanton**, Genocide Watch (Author)
- **Mark Drumbl**, Washington & Lee University School of Law (Discussant)

10:45–11:30 **Peace and Justice**
- **David Crane**, Syracuse University College of Law (Author)
- **Richard Goldstone**, Harvard Law School (Discussant)

SECTION II: LEGAL ISSUES

11:30–12:15 The Jurisprudence of the Ad Hoc Tribunals Since 1993 and Their Contribution to the Legal Definition of Crimes Against Humanity
- **Göran Sluiter**, University of Amsterdam (Author)
- **William Schabas**, National University of Ireland, Galway (Discussant)

12:15	Conclusion of Morning Session
	• **Kent Syverud**, Washington University School of Law; Dean and Ethan A.H. Shepley University Professor
1:45–2:30	Continuing Definitional Issues Regarding Crimes Against Humanity, Including the Policy Element and the Scope of the Crime
	• **Guénaël Mettraux**, formerly International Criminal Tribunal for the former Yugoslavia (Author)
	• **Mark Osiel**, T.M.C. Asser Institute, University of Amsterdam (Discussant)
2:30–3:15	Gender Crimes
	• **Valerie Oosterveld**, University of Western Ontario Faculty of Law (Author)
	• **Kelly Dawn Askin**, Open Society Justice Initiative (Discussant)
3:15–4:00	Ethnic Cleansing
	• **John Hagan**, Northwestern University (Author)
	• **Larry Johnson**, former UN Assistant-Secretary-General for Legal Affairs (Discussant)
4:15–5:30	Plenary Session – Introduction of Draft Convention
6:30	Evening Gala
	• **Remarks – Chancellor Mark S. Wrighton**, Washington University in St. Louis
	• **Keynote Address – John Clint Williamson**, U.S. Ambassador-at-Large for War Crimes Issues

TUESDAY, APRIL 14, 2009

SECTION II: LEGAL ISSUES (CONTINUED)

8:30–9:15	Immunities and Amnesties
	• **Diane Orentlicher**, American University, Washington College of Law (Author)
	• **Naomi Roht-Arriaza**, University of California, Hastings College of the Law (Discussant)
9:15–10:00	Modes of Participation

SECTION III: NEW CONCEPTUAL PARADIGMS

10:15–11:00	Crimes Against Humanity and Terrorism
	• **Michael P. Scharf**, Case Western Reserve University School of Law (Author)
	• **Michael A. Newton**, Vanderbilt University Law School (Author)
	• **Melissa Waters**, Washington University School of Law (Discussant)

11:00–11:45	Revisiting the Architecture of Nuremberg? Crimes Against Humanity and International Criminal Law • **M. Cherif Bassiouni**, DePaul University College of Law (Author) • **David Luban**, Georgetown University Law Center (Discussant)

SECTION IV: ENFORCEMENT ISSUES

1:15–2:00	Crimes Against Humanity and the International Criminal Court • **Kai Ambos**, Georg-August-Universität, Göttingen (Author) • **Betsy Andersen**, American Society of International Law (Discussant)
2:00–2:45	Crimes Against Humanity and the Responsibility to Protect • **David Scheffer**, Northwestern University School of Law (Author) • **Diane Marie Amann**, University of California Davis School of Law (Discussant)
2:45–3:30	Crimes Against Humanity and National Jurisdictions • **Payam Akhavan**, McGill University Faculty of Law (Author) • **Evelyn Ankumah**, Africa Legal Aid (Discussant)
3:45–5:45	Plenary Session – Resumed Discussion of Draft Convention

WEDNESDAY, APRIL 15, 2009

8:30–10:00	Executive Session (Steering Committee Members only)
10:00–12:00	Technical Advisory Session – Resumed Discussion of Draft Convention

Washington University School of Law

Whitney R. Harris World Law Institute
Crimes Against Humanity Initiative

The Hague Intersessional Experts' Meeting
June 11–12, 2009
ANNEX #3: LIST OF PARTICIPANTS

STEERING COMMITTEE MEMBERS

Chair: Professor Leila Nadya Sadat, Washington University in St. Louis School of Law; Director of the Whitney R. Harris World Law Institute

Professor M. Cherif Bassiouni, DePaul University College of Law; President Emeritus of the International Human Rights Law Institute

Ambassador Hans Corell, former Under-Secretary-General for Legal Affairs and the Legal Counsel of the United Nations

Justice Richard Goldstone, Fordham University School of Law; former Chief Prosecutor of the International Criminal Tribunals for the former Yugoslavia and for Rwanda

Mr. Juan Méndez, Scholar-in-Residence, the Ford Foundation

Professor William Schabas, Director, the Irish Centre for Human Rights, National University of Ireland, Galway

Judge Christine Van den Wyngaert, International Criminal Tribunal for the former Yugoslavia; International Criminal Court

EXPERT PARTICIPANTS

Judge Carmel A. Agius, International Criminal Tribunal for the former Yugoslavia

Judge Joyce Aluoch, International Criminal Court

Ms. Evelyn Ankumah, Executive Director, Africa Legal Aid

Ms. Silvana Arbia, Registrar of the International Criminal Court

Ms. Elizabeth Stubbins Bates, David Davies of Llandinam Research Fellow, London School of Economics and Political Science

Mr. Morten Bergsmo, Senior Researcher, International Peace Research Institute, Oslo, Norway

Professor Wim Blockmans, Rector, Netherlands Institute for Advanced Study in the Humanities and Social Sciences

Mr. Rob Bokhoven, Ministry of Justice, The Netherlands

Ms. Helen Brady, Special Tribunal for Lebanon, former Senior Appeals Counsel in the Office of the Prosecutor at the International Criminal Tribunal for the former Yugoslavia

Ms. Cynthia Chamberlain, Legal Officer, International Criminal Court

Sara Criscitelli, Prosecutions Coordinator, Office of the Prosecutor, International Criminal Court

Professor Robert Cryer, Birmingham Law School

Judge Pedro R. David, International Criminal Tribunal for the former Yugoslavia

Judge Fatoumata Diarra, First Vice-President of the International Criminal Court

Dr. David Donat-Cattin, Director, International Law and Human Rights Programme, Parliamentarians for Global Action

Mr. Gareth Evans, President and Chief Executive Officer, International Crisis Group

Ms. Claire Fourçans, Office of Public Counsel for the Defense, International Criminal Court

Dr. Fabricio Guariglia, Senior Appeals Counsel, Office of the Prosecutor, International Criminal Court

Mr. Christopher Hall, Amnesty International

Dr. Larissa van den Herik, Leiden University Faculty of Law

Mr. Omer Ismail, Advisor, ENOUGH! Project

Professor Mark W. Janis, University of Oxford and University of Connecticut School of Law

Dr. Chantal Joubert, The Netherlands Ministry of Justice

Judge Hans-Peter Kaul, Second Vice-President, International Criminal Court

Mr. Steven Kay, defense counsel before the International Criminal Tribunal for the former Yugoslavia

Mr. Xavier-Jean Keïta, Principal Counsel of the Office of Public Counsel for the Defence, International Criminal Court

Ms. Cecilia Kleffuer, Coalition for the International Criminal Court

Professor Dr. Geert-Jan Alexander Knoops, University of Utrecht

Judge Akua Kuenyehia, former First Vice-President, International Criminal Court

Judge O-Gon Kwon, Vice-President, International Criminal Tribunal for the former Yugoslavia

Ms. Catherine Marchi-Uhel, Head of Chambers, International Criminal Tribunal for the former Yugoslavia

Judge Theodor Meron, International Criminal Tribunal for the former Yugoslavia

Dr. Guénaël Mettraux, former Associate Legal Officer and former defense counsel, International Criminal Tribunal for the former Yugoslavia

Mr. George Mugwanya, Senior Appeals Counsel, International Criminal Tribunal for Rwanda

Mr. Steven Cash Nickerson, Executive Vice President, CFO and General Counsel, PDS Technical Services

Judge Daniel David Ntanda Nsereko, International Criminal Court

Ms. Laura M. Olson, President, Blackletter Consulting, LLC

Dr. Eugene O'Sullivan, Member of the Rules Committee and former defense counsel, International Criminal Tribunal for the former Yugoslavia

Mr. William Pace, Convener, Coalition for the International Criminal Court

Mr. Robert Petit, Co-Prosecutor for the Extraordinary Chambers in the Courts of Cambodia

Thomas Wayde Pittman, Senior Legal Officer, International Criminal Tribunal for the former Yugoslavia

Judge Kimberly Prost, International Criminal Tribunal for the former Yugoslavia

Mr. Stephen Rapp, Chief Prosecutor of the Special Court for Sierra Leone

Professor Elies van Sliedregt, Vrije Universiteit Amsterdam

Dr. Göran Sluiter, University of Amsterdam

Dr. Carsten Stahn, Programme Director, Grotius Centre for International Legal Studies, Leiden University-Campus Den Haag

Professor Albert Swart, University of Amsterdam

Mr. Krister Thelin, Member of the United Nations Human Rights Committee

Ms. Lorena Toyos-Flores, Legal Intern, International Criminal Court

Mr. Michaïl Wladimiroff, Wladimiroff & Waling

WASHINGTON UNIVERSITY AND HARRIS INSTITUTE PERSONNEL

Ms. Amitis (Amy) Khojasteh, Cash Nickerson Fellow, Whitney R. Harris World Law Institute

Ms. Linda McClain, Assistant Director of the Whitney R. Harris World Law Institute

Mr. Michael Peil, Associate Dean for International Programs, Washington University School of Law

Mr. B. Don Taylor III, Executive Director of the Whitney R. Harris World Law Institute and Cash Nickerson Fellow

RAPPORTEURS

Ms. Brianne McGonigle, University of Utrecht

Ms. Rumiana Yotova, Leiden University

Washington University School of Law

Whitney R. Harris World Law Institute
Crimes Against Humanity Initiative

The Hague Intersessional Experts' Meeting
June 11–12, 2009
ANNEX #4: AGENDA

THURSDAY, JUNE 11, 2009

8:30–8:45   **Welcome and Opening Remarks**
- **Leila Nadya Sadat**, Washington University School of Law; Director, Harris World Law Institute
- **Carsten Stahn**, Grotius Centre for International Legal Studies, Leiden University-Campus Den Haag

8:45–9:00   **Welcome Address**
- **Mr. J.J. van Aartsen**, Mayor of the City of The Hague

9:15–10:00   **Opening Address: Crimes Against Humanity and International Criminal Law**
- **Justice Richard Goldstone**, Fordham University School of Law; former Chief Prosecutor of the International Criminal Tribunals for the former Yugoslavia and for Rwanda

10:15–11:15   **Plenary Session: Report from April Experts' Meeting**
- **M. Cherif Bassiouni**, DePaul University College of Law; President Emeritus of the International Human Rights Law Institute
- **William Schabas**, Director, the Irish Centre for Human Rights, National University of Ireland, Galway
- Overview of Project; Presentation of April Report, **Leila Nadya Sadat**, Washington University School of Law

11:15–12:45   **Panel 1: Completing the Work of Rome: The Need for a Crimes Against Humanity Convention**
- Chair: **Juan Méndez**, Scholar-in-Residence, the Ford Foundation
- **M. Cherif Bassiouni**, DePaul University College of Law

- **Mark Janis**, University of Oxford and University of Connecticut School of Law
- **Leila Nadya Sadat**, Washington University School of Law
- **Richard Goldstone**, Fordham University School of Law

14:15–15:45   **Panel 2: Enforcement Issues**
- **Chair: Hans Corell**, former Under-Secretary-General for Legal Affairs and the Legal Counsel of the United Nations
- **Sara Criscitelli**, Prosecutions Coordinator, Office of the Prosecutor, International Criminal Court
- **Morten Bergsmo**, Senior Researcher, International Peace Research Institute, Oslo, Norway
- **Robert Cryer**, University of Birmingham
- **Elies van Sliedregt**, Vrije Universiteit Amsterdam

16:00–17:30   **Panel 3: Crimes Against Humanity and the International Criminal Court**
- **Chair: Judge Christine Van den Wyngaert**, International Criminal Tribunal for the former Yugoslavia; International Criminal Court
- **Thomas Wayde Pittman**, Senior Legal Officer, International Criminal Tribunal for the former Yugoslavia
- **Carsten Stahn**, Grotius Centre for International Legal Studies
- **Judge Kimberly Prost**, International Criminal Tribunal for the former Yugoslavia
- **Fabricio Guariglia**, Senior Appeals Counsel, Office of the Prosecutor, International Criminal Court
- **Evelyn Ankumah**, Executive Director, Africa Legal Aid

19:00   **Dinner at Pulchri Studio**
- **Keynote Address: Gareth Evans**, President & CEO of the International Crisis Group

FRIDAY, JUNE 12, 2009

8:30–10:00   **Steering Committee Meeting**
10:00–12:00   **Technical Advisory Session: Discussion of Draft Convention**
- **Chair: Leila Nadya Sadat**, Washington University in St. Louis School of Law
- **Presentation: M. Cherif Bassiouni**, DePaul University College of Law

14:00–16:30   **Technical Advisory Session (Resumed)**

Washington University School of Law

Whitney R. Harris World Law Institute
Crimes Against Humanity Initiative

Technical Advisory Session in St. Louis
August 21–23, 2009
ANNEX #5: LIST OF PARTICIPANTS

STEERING COMMITTEE MEMBERS

Chair: Professor Leila Nadya Sadat, Washington University in St. Louis School of Law; Director of the Whitney R. Harris World Law Institute

Professor M. Cherif Bassiouni, DePaul University College of Law; President Emeritus of the International Human Rights Law Institute.

EXPERT PARTICIPANTS

Mr. Morten Bergsmo, Senior Researcher, International Peace Research Institute, Oslo, Norway

Professor Robert Cryer, Birmingham Law School

Mr. Larry Johnson, former UN Assistant-Secretary-General for Legal Affairs

Dr. Guénaël Mettraux, former Associate Legal Officer and former defense counsel, International Criminal Tribunal for the former Yugoslavia

Dr. Göran Sluiter, University of Amsterdam, Faculty of Law

WASHINGTON UNIVERSITY AND HARRIS INSTITUTE PERSONNEL

Ms. Linda McClain, Assistant Director of the Whitney R. Harris World Law Institute

Mr. Michael Peil, Associate Dean for International Programs, Washington University School of Law

Mr. B. Don Taylor III, Executive Director of the Whitney R. Harris World Law Institute and Cash Nickerson Fellow

RAPPORTEURS

Ms. McCall Carter, Washington University in St. Louis School of Law

Ms. Margaret Wichmann, Washington University in St. Louis School of Law

Washington University School of Law

Whitney R. Harris World Law Institute
Crimes Against Humanity Initiative

ANNEX #6: LIST OF EXPERTS SUBMITTING COMMENTS ON THE NOVEMBER 2009 DRAFT CONVENTION

Mr. Hirad Abtahi, International Criminal Court

Senator Robert Badinter, Hauts-de-Seine Department, French Senate

Mr. Antoine Bernard, International Federation of Human Rights, International Secretariat Division

Judge Gilbert Bitti, International Criminal Court

Professor Gideon Boas, Monash University Law

Professor Neil Boister, University of Canterbury

Professor John Cerone, New England School of Law

Professor Hilary Charlesworth, Australian National University

Mr. Hicham Cherkaoui, Coalition Marocaine pour la Cour Pénale Internationale

Professor Christine Chinkin, The London School of Economics & Political Science

Dr. Philippe Currat, Dr en droit, Avocat au Barreau de Genève

Judge Liu Daqun, International Criminal Tribunal for the former Yugoslavia

Judge Sylvia Fernandez de Gurmendi, International Criminal Court

Professor Yoram Dinstein, Tel Aviv University

Mr. Nick Donovan, Aegis Trust

Professor John Dugard, Centre for Human Rights, University of Pretoria

Mr. Norman Farrell, International Criminal Tribunal for the former Yugoslavia

Mr. Benjamin Ferencz, former Nuremberg Prosecutor

Dr. Susan Harris-Rimmer, Australian National University

Dr. Chantal Joubert, The Netherlands Ministry of Justice

Professor Michael Kelly, Creighton University School of Law

Professor Dorean Koenig, The Thomas M. Cooley Law School

Professor Claus Kress, University of Cologne

Professor Suzannah Linton, The University of Hong Kong

Ms. Renifa Madenga, International Criminal Tribunal for Rwanda

Judge Sanji Mmasenono Monageng, International Criminal Court

Mr. Daryl Mundis, Special Tribunal for Lebanon

Professor Jordan Paust, University of Houston Law Center

Ms. Jelena Pejic, International Committee of the Red Cross

Mr. Robert Petit, Justice Canada, Crimes Against Humanity/War Crimes

Mr. Hugo Relva, Amnesty International

Professor Darryl Robinson, Queen's University

Mr. Eli Rosenbaum, U.S. Department of Justice, Criminal Division

Professor Marco Sassòli, Université de Genève

Professor Susana SáCouto, American University, Washington College of Law

Professor Wolfgang Schomburg, Durham Law School

Professor Albert Swart, University of Amsterdam

Judge Stefan Trechsel, International Criminal Tribunal for the former Yugoslavia

Judge Helmut Tuerk, Vice President, International Tribunal for the Law of the Sea

Professor H. G. van der Wilt, University of Amsterdam

Professor Beth Van Schaack, Santa Clara University School of Law

Ms. Patricia Viseur Sellers, International Criminal Law/Humanitarian Law Consultant

Judge Patricia Wald, U.S. Court Appeals, D.C. Circuit, and International Criminal Tribunal for the former Yugoslavia

Professor Andrew Williams, University of Warwick

Washington University School of Law

Whitney R. Harris World Law Institute
Crimes Against Humanity Initiative

Washington Conference
March 11–12, 2010
ANNEX #7: LIST OF PARTICIPANTS

STEERING COMMITTEE MEMBERS

Chair: Professor Leila Nadya Sadat, Washington University in St. Louis School of Law; Director of the Whitney R. Harris World Law Institute

Professor M. Cherif Bassiouni, DePaul University College of Law; President Emeritus of the International Human Rights Law Institute

Ambassador Hans Corell, former UN Under-Secretary-General for Legal Affairs

Justice Richard Goldstone, Georgetown University Law Center; former Chief Prosecutor of the International Criminal Tribunals for the former Yugoslavia and for Rwanda

Mr. Juan Méndez, Visiting Professor, Washington College of Law, American University, Washington D.C.

Professor William Schabas, Director, the Irish Centre for Human Rights, National University of Ireland, Galway

Judge Christine Van den Wyngaert, International Criminal Court

EXPERT PARTICIPANTS

Ms. Elizabeth Abi-Mershed, Assistant Executive Secretary, Inter-American Commission on Human Rights

Mr. Mike Abramowitz, United States Holocaust Memorial Museum

Mr. Anees Ahmed, Extraordinary Chambers in the Courts of Cambodia

Professor Payam Akhavan, McGill University

Ms. Elizabeth Andersen, Executive Director, American Society of International Law

Ms. Evelyn Ankumah, Executive Director, Africa Legal Aid

Mr. James Apple, President, International Judicial Academy

Ms. Cecile Aptel, International Justice Expert

Judge Micki I. Aronson, Administrative Appeals Judge, U.S. Social Security Administration

Professor John Barrett, St. John's University School of Law

Ms. Fatou Bensouda, Deputy Prosecutor, International Criminal Court

Mr. John Berger, Cambridge University Press

Mr. Gilbert Bitti, International Criminal Court

Dr. Michael Bohlander, Durham University Law School

Ms. Andrea Bosshard, First Secretary, Legal and Political Section, Embassy of Switzerland

Mr. Serge Brammertz, Prosecutor, International Criminal Tribunal for the former Yugoslavia

Mr. William Burke-White, U.S. Department of State

Mr. Scott Carlson, U.S. Department of State

Professor David Crane, former Chief Prosecutor, Special Court for Sierra Leone, Syracuse University College of Law

Professor Robert Cryer, Birmingham Law School

Judge Pedro David, International Criminal Tribunal for the former Yugoslavia

Ms. Mélanie Deshaies, University of Montreal

Mr. Richard Dicker, Human Rights Watch

Professor Yoram Dinstein, Tel Aviv University

Mr. Nick Donovan, Aegis Trust

Professor Max du Plessis, University of KwaZulu-Natal; Institute for Security Studies

Mr. Mohamed El Zeidy, International Criminal Court

Mr. Jerry Fowler, Save Darfur Coalition

Ms. Julia Fromholz, Human Rights First

Ms. Heloisa Griggs, Counsel, U.S. Senate Committee on the Judiciary, Subcommittee on Human Rights and the Law

Mr. Morton Halperin, Senior Advisor, Open Society Institute

Mr. Aung Htoo, General Secretary, Burma Lawyers Council

Mr. Larry Johnson, former UN Assistant-Secretary-General for Legal Affairs

Mr. Joseph Kamara, Acting Prosecutor, Special Court for Sierra Leone

Professor Michael Kelly, Creighton University School of Law

Mr. Michael Kleinman, Humanity United

Mr. Neil Kritz, United States Institute of Peace

Mr. Magnus Lennartsson, The Dag Hammarskjöld Foundation

Mr. Edward Luck, International Peace Institute

Mr. Henk Marquart Sholtz, Secretary-General, International Association of Prosecutors

Dr. Guénaël Mettraux, Defence Counsel, International Criminal Tribunal for the former Yugoslavia

Professor Sean Murphy, George Washington University Law School

Ms. Catherine Newcombe, U.S. Department of Justice

Mr. Steven Cash Nickerson, Executive Vice President, CFO and General Counsel, PDS Technical Services

Judge Daniel David Ntanda Nsereko, International Criminal Court

Professor Hèctor Alonso-Olàsolo, Utrecht University

Ms. Laura Olson, Senior Counsel, The Constitution Project

Mr. William Pace, Coalition for the International Criminal Court

Mr. Gregory Peterson, The Robert H. Jackson Center

Ambassador Constancio Pinto, Ambassador of the Democratic Republic of Timor-Leste to the United States

Judge Árpád Prandler, International Criminal Tribunal for the former Yugoslavia

Ambassador Stephen Rapp, U.S. Ambassador-at-Large for War Crimes Issues

Mr. Steve Riskin, United States Institute of Peace

Professor Darryl Robinson, Queen's University

Mr. Eli Rosenbaum, U.S. Department of Justice

Professor Michael Scharf, Case Western Reserve University School of Law

Professor David Scheffer, Northwestern University

Professor Dinah Shelton, George Washington University Law School

Professor Jane Stromseth, Georgetown University Law Center

Mr. Frederick Swinnen, International Criminal Tribunal for the former Yugoslavia

Mr. Colin Thomas-Jensen, The ENOUGH! Project

Mr. Igor Timofeyev, Paul, Hastings, Janofsky & Walker LLP

Judge Bakhtiyar Tuzmukhamedov, International Criminal Tribunal for Rwanda

Mr. Rob van Bokhoven, The Netherlands Ministry of Justice

Professor Elies van Sliedregt, Vrije Universiteit Amsterdam

Ms. Francesca Varda, Coalition for the International Criminal Court

Ms. Patricia Viseur Sellers, former Legal Advisor for Gender-Related Crimes, International Criminal Tribunal for the former Yugoslavia

Mr. John Washburn, Convener, American Non-Governmental Organizations Coalition for the International Criminal Court

Judge Inéz Mónica Weinberg de Roca, President, UN Appeals Tribunal

Ambassador Christian Wenaweser, Permanent Representative of Liechtenstein to the UN; President, Assembly of States Parties to the Rome Statute of the International Criminal Court

Ms. Mary Werntz, International Committee of the Red Cross

Ambassador John Clint Williamson, former U.S. Ambassador-at-Large for War Crimes Issues

Mr. Lawrence Woocher, United States Institute for Peace

HRH Prince Zeid Ra'ad Zeid Al-Hussein, Ambassador of the Hashemite Kingdom of Jordan to the United States

Mr. Mohamed El Zeidy, International Criminal Court

Ambassador Urs Ziswiler, Ambassador of Switzerland to the United States

Mr. Joseph Zogby, Chief Counsel to U.S. Senator Richard Durbin

WASHINGTON UNIVERSITY AND HARRIS INSTITUTE PERSONNEL

Chancellor Mark Wrighton, Washington University in St. Louis

Dean Kent Syverud, Washington University School of Law

Mr. B. Don Taylor III, Executive Director of the Whitney R. Harris World Law Institute and Cash Nickerson Fellow

Ms. Erika Detjen, Cash Nickerson Fellow, Whitney R. Harris World Law Institute

Mr. Jason Meyer, Cash Nickerson Fellow, Whitney R. Harris World Law Institute

Ms. Margaret Wichmann, Cash Nickerson Fellow, Whitney R. Harris World Law Institute

BROOKINGS INSTITUTION PERSONNEL

Mr. Strobe Talbott, President

Mr. Martin Indyk, Vice President for Foreign Policy

Ms. Erin Bourgois, Project Administrator

Ms. Elizabeth Ferris, Senior Fellow

Ms. Jacqueline Geis, Associate Director of Development, Foreign Policy

Ms. Natalie Lempert, Intern

Mr. Theodore Piccone, Senior Fellow

Mr. Andrew Solomon, Deputy Director

Ms. Chareen Stark, Senior Research Assistant

Ms. Erin Williams, Rapporteur

RAPPORTEURS

Ms. Rebecca Abou-Chedid, Georgetown University

Mr. Tajesh Adhihetty, Georgetown University

Mr. Justin Fraterman, Georgetown University

Mr. Yeghishe Kirakosyan, Georgetown University

Mr. Tom Odell, Georgetown University

Ms. Sarah Rivard, Georgetown University

Mr. Paul Schmitt, Georgetown University

Mr. Marc Sorel, Georgetown University

Washington University School of Law

Whitney R. Harris World Law Institute
Crimes Against Humanity Initiative

Washington Conference
March 11–12, 2010
ANNEX #8: AGENDA

THURSDAY, MARCH 11, 2010

9:00–9:30   Welcome and Opening Remarks
- Strobe Talbott, President, The Brookings Institution
- Mark S. Wrighton, Chancellor, Washington University in Saint Louis
- Presentation of the Global Philanthropy Award to Steven Cash Nickerson

9:30–10:00   Opening Address
- Introduction: William A. Schabas, Director, the Irish Centre for Human Rights, National University of Ireland, Galway
- Speaker: Mary Werntz, Head of Delegation, Regional Delegation for the United States and Canada, International Committee of the Red Cross

10:00–11:00   Plenary Session
- Introduction to the Crimes Against Humanity Initiative and Presentation of the Draft Convention
- Leila Nadya Sadat, Washington University School of Law, Henry H. Oberschelp Professor of Law; Director, Harris World Law Institute
- Remarks of Whitney R. Harris
- M. Cherif Bassiouni, DePaul University College of Law; President Emeritus of the International Human Rights Law Institute

11:15–12:45   Panel 1: Crimes Against Humanity and Gender Justice
- Chair: Judge Christine Van den Wyngaert, International Criminal Court

- **Elizabeth Abi-Mershed**, Inter-American Commission on Human Rights
- **Evelyn A. Ankumah**, Africa Legal Aid
- **David M. Crane**, Syracuse University; former Chief Prosecutor, Special Court for Sierra Leone
- **Patricia Viseur Sellers**, former Legal Advisor for Gender-Related Crimes, International Criminal Tribunal for the former Yugoslavia
- **Judge Inéz Mónica Weinberg de Roca**, UN Appeal Tribunal

12:45–2:00   **Lunch: Carnegie Endowment for International Peace**
- **Introduction: Leila Nadya Sadat**, Washington University School of Law, Henry H. Oberschelp Professor of Law; Director, Harris World Law Institute
- **Speaker: Ambassador Stephen J. Rapp**, U.S. Ambassador-at-Large for War Crimes Issues

2:00–3:30   **Panel 2: Peace and Justice Dilemmas**
- **Chair: Justice Richard J. Goldstone**, Georgetown University Law Center; former Chief Prosecutor of the International Criminal Tribunals for the former Yugoslavia and for Rwanda
- **Richard Dicker**, Human Rights Watch
- **Elizabeth Ferris**, The Brookings Institution
- **Jerry Fowler**, The Save Darfur Coalition
- **Max du Plessis**, University of KwaZulu-Natal

3:45–5:15   **Panel 3: Filling the Gaps: Facilitating Effective Interstate Cooperation in the Prevention and Punishment of Crimes Against Humanity**
- **Chair: Hans Corell**, former Under-Secretary-General for Legal Affairs and the Legal Counsel of the United Nations
- **Serge Brammertz**, Chief Prosecutor, International Criminal Tribunal for the former Yugoslavia
- **Yoram Dinstein**, Tel Aviv University
- **Robert Cryer**, Birmingham Law School
- **Laura Olson**, The Constitution Project
- **Darryl Robinson**, Queen's University

7:00   **Dinner** The Dupont Hotel
- **Introduction: Kent D. Syverud**, Washington University School of Law, Dean and Ethan A.H. Shepley University Professor
- Award Ceremony honoring the Crimes Against Humanity Initiative Steering Committee
- Presentation of the Whitney R. Harris World Law Institute World Peace Through Law Award to M. Cherif Bassiouni

FRIDAY, MARCH 12, 2010

10:00–11:30 **Panel 4: Crimes Against Humanity and U.S. Policy**
- **Chair: Andrew Solomon**, The Brookings Institution
- **Elizabeth Andersen**, American Society of International Law
- **Larry D. Johnson**, Columbia Law School, former UN Assistant-Secretary-General for Legal Affairs
- **Michael P. Scharf**, Case Western Reserve University School of Law
- **John Clint Williamson**, former U.S. Ambassador-at-Large for War Crimes Issues
- **Joseph R. Zogby**, Chief Counsel to U.S. Senator Richard Durbin

11:30–12:45 **Lunch** Carnegie Endowment for International Peace
- **Introduction: Justice Richard J. Goldstone**, Georgetown University Law Center; former Chief Prosecutor of the International Criminal Tribunals for the former Yugoslavia and for Rwanda
- **Speaker: Ambassador Christian Wenaweser**, Permanent Representative of Liechtenstein to the UN; President, Assembly of States Parties to the Rome Statute of the International Criminal Court

12:45–2:15 **Panel 5: Crimes Against Humanity and State Responsibility to Prevent**
- **Chair: William A. Schabas**, Director, the Irish Centre for Human Rights, National University of Ireland, Galway
- **Payam Akhavan**, McGill University
- **Edward C. Luck**, International Peace Institute
- **Judge Daniel David Ntanda Nsereko**, International Criminal Court
- **Dinah L. Shelton**, George Washington University Law School
- **David J. Scheffer**, Northwestern University; former U.S. Ambassador-at-Large for War Crimes Issues

2:30–4:00 **Panel 6: Universal Jurisdiction, Complementarity and State Capacity Building**
- **Chair: Juan E. Méndez**, Visiting Professor, Washington College of Law, American University
- **Gilbert Bitti**, International Criminal Court
- **Francesca Varda**, Coalition for the International Criminal Court
- **Mohamed El Zeidy**, International Criminal Court

4:00–5:30   **Plenary Session: Closing Ceremony and Presentation of the Conference Outcome Document**
- **Chair: Leila Nadya Sadat**, Washington University School of Law Henry H. Oberschelp Professor of Law; Director, Harris World Law Institute
- **M. Cherif Bassiouni**, DePaul University College of Law; President Emeritus of the International Human Rights Law Institute
- **Hans Corell**, former Under-Secretary-General for Legal Affairs and the Legal Counsel of the United Nations
- **Justice Richard J. Goldstone**, Georgetown University Law Center; former Chief Prosecutor of the International Criminal Tribunals for the former Yugoslavia and for Rwanda
- **Juan E. Méndez**, Visiting Professor, Washington College of Law, American University, Washington D.C.
- **William A. Schabas**, Director, the Irish Centre for Human Rights, National University of Ireland, Galway
- **Judge Christine Van den Wyngaert**, International Criminal Court

Washington University School of Law

Whitney R. Harris World Law Institute
Crimes Against Humanity Initiative

Technical Advisory Session in Chicago
May 10–11, 2010
ANNEX #9: LIST OF PARTICIPANTS

PARTICIPANTS

Professor M. Cherif Bassiouni, DePaul University College of Law; President Emeritus of the International Human Rights Law Institute

Mr. Larry Johnson, former UN Assistant-Secretary-General for Legal Affairs

Professor Leila Nadya Sadat, Washington University in St. Louis School of Law; Director of the Whitney R. Harris World Law Institute

Mr. Neill Townsend, Staff Attorney, Circuit Court of Cook County – Office of the Chief Judge, Cash Nickerson Fellow

WASHINGTON UNIVERSITY LAW

WHITNEY R. HARRIS WORLD LAW INSTITUTE

CRIMES AGAINST HUMANITY INITIATIVE

DECLARATION ON THE NEED FOR A COMPREHENSIVE CONVENTION ON CRIMES AGAINST HUMANITY

Whereas over the course of human history, millions of people, particularly women and children, have been subjected to murder, extermination, enslavement, deportation, persecutions and other atrocities that have shocked the conscience of humanity,

Whereas it was established in 1946 by the International Military Tribunal at Nuremberg that these "crimes against humanity" are crimes under international law for which the perpetrators could be prosecuted and punished,

Whereas in 1998, 120 States participating in the United Nations Diplomatic Conference of Plenipotentiaries on the Establishment of an International Criminal Court agreed upon a definition of crimes against humanity during the negotiations of the Rome Statute of the International Criminal Court,

Whereas it is the duty of every State to exercise its criminal jurisdiction over those responsible for international crimes, including crimes against humanity,

Whereas the Rome Statute of the International Criminal Court condemns crimes against humanity, and requires States to put an end to impunity by ensuring their prosecution and punishment at the national and international levels, but does not provide for universally effective inter-state cooperation,

Whereas since the Second World War, the world has seen hundreds of conflicts, in which tens of millions of victims have died, and only a limited number of perpetrators have been prosecuted,

Whereas there currently exists no international treaty providing for effective inter-state cooperation in the prosecution and punishment of crimes against humanity,

Whereas crimes against humanity constitute crimes under international law which give rise to the responsibility of States for internationally wrongful acts,

Whereas crimes against humanity continue to undermine the peace and security of the world, being the source of untold suffering and a threat to human civilization,

Whereas the Crimes Against Humanity Initiative has developed a draft *International Convention on the Prevention and Punishment of Crimes Against Humanity* (the "Draft Convention"), to which more than 200 experts from around the world have contributed,

Whereas the Draft Convention was further discussed at a Conference organized by the Initiative in Washington, D.C. on March 11-12, 2010,

Whereas the Steering Committee of the Initiative will, on its own responsibility, finalize the Draft Convention in the near future,

Now therefore we, the undersigned, adopt the following Declaration:

1. States should make adoption of a comprehensive convention on crimes against humanity a priority, so as to prevent the occurrence of crimes against humanity and to enhance the fair and effective prosecution and punishment of the perpetrators of such crimes.

2. The convention should adopt as its definition of crimes against humanity the provisions of article 7 of the Rome Statute of the International Criminal Court, in order to facilitate the integration of the convention's provisions into a comprehensive system of international criminal justice, while at the same time acknowledging that there may be cases not covered by the convention or by other international agreements, in which case the human person nevertheless remains under the protection and authority of the principles of international law.

3. The convention should embody provisions on immunities, official capacity, superior orders and statutory limitations that are consistent with existing international law.

4. The convention should include provisions explicitly providing for the responsibility of States for international wrongful acts for the commission of crimes against humanity and for the failure to prevent crimes against humanity, and provide a mechanism for the resolution in the event of a dispute that may arise between two or more States Parties concerning the interpretation or application of the convention, including a compromissory clause vesting jurisdiction in the International Court of Justice.

5. The convention should provide for a monitoring mechanism, or some other vehicle, so as to enhance the preventive elements of the convention, as well as to help ensure the capacity of States Parties to fulfill their obligations to prevent and punish crimes against humanity.

6. The convention should incorporate the principle *aut dedere aut judicare* and provide for universal jurisdiction over crimes against humanity, in accordance with international law.

7. The convention should incorporate provisions protecting the rights of the accused and suspects in inter-state proceedings, including the right to a fair trial, *ne bis in idem*, and conforming to internationally recognized standards of fairness and effectiveness in the collection of evidence.

8. The convention should explicitly focus on prevention, including the development of educational and informational programs, training of law enforcement officers and military personnel, development of State capacity, the adoption of legislation, and the promotion of effective inter-state cooperation and mutual legal assistance.

Done at Washington, D.C.

March 12, 2010

For the Steering Committee of the Initiative

M. Cherif Bassiouni

Hans Corell

Richard J. Goldstone

Juan E. Méndez

Leila Nadya Sadat

William A. Schabas

Christine Van den Wyngaert

The following persons who have participated in the process have declared that they support the Declaration:

Professor Payam Akhavan, McGill University, Centre for Human Rights and Legal Pluralism

Judge Carmel Agius, International Criminal Tribunal for the former Yugoslavia

Mr. Anees Ahmed, Extraordinary Chambers in the Courts of Cambodia; United Nations Assistance to Khmer Rouge Trials (UNAKRT)

Professor David Akerson, University of Denver, Sturm College of Law

Professor Payam Akhavan, McGill University

Professor Dr. Kai Ambos, Georg-August-Universität, Göttingen

Ms. Silvana Arbia, Registrar, International Criminal Court

Dr. Kelly Dawn Askin, Open Society Justice Initiative

Senator Robert Badinter, French Senate

Mr. Gilbert Bitti, International Criminal Court

Dr. Steven Blockmans, Deputy Head of the Research Department, T.M.C. Asser Instituut

Professor Wim Blockmans, Netherlands Institute for Advanced Study in the Humanities and Social Sciences

Dr. Gideon Boas, Monash University

Professor Neil Boister, University of Canterbury

Professor Frank Chalk, Concordia University; Director, Montreal Institute for Genocide and Human Rights Studies

Mr. Hicham Cherkaoui, Coordinator of Moroccan Coalition to the International Criminal Court

Professor Roger Clark, Rutgers University School of Law - Camden

Professor David Crane, Syracuse University College of Law

Professor Robert Cryer, University of Birmingham, Birmingham Law School

Dr. Philippe Currat, Avocat au Barreau de Genève

Judge Silvia Fernández de Gurmendi, International Criminal Court

Professor Margaret deGuzman, Temple University, Beasley School of Law

Professor Mélanie Deshaies, Université de Montréal

Mr. Nick Donovan, Aegis Trust

Professor Mark Drumbl, Washington & Lee University School of Law

Professor John Dugard, Centre for Human Rights, University of Pretoria

Professor Max du Plessis, University of KwaZulu-Natal, Durban

Mr. Mark Ellis, International Bar Association

Dr. Mohamed El Zeidy, International Criminal Court

The Honorable Gareth Evans, Professor, University of Melbourne

Mr. Benjamin B. Ferencz, United States Military Tribunals, Nuremberg

Mr. Donald M. Ferencz, Director, The Planethood Foundation

Mr. Whitney R. Harris, Former Prosecutor, International Military Tribunal at Nuremberg

Professor Mark Janis, University of Connecticut School of Law

Professor Larry Johnson, Columbia Law School

Professor Michael Kelly, Creighton University School of Law; President, AIDP, U.S. National Chapter

Dr. Young Sok Kim, Ewha Womans University College of Law

Professor Geert-Jan Knoops, University of Utrecht

Professor Dorean Marguerite Koenig, Thomas Cooley Law School; AIDP

Professor Claus Kress, University of Cologne

Judge O-Gon Kwon, Vice-President, International Criminal Tribunal for the former Yugoslavia

Professor Suzannah Linton, University of Hong Kong

Ms. Renifa Madenga, Office of the Prosecutor, International Criminal Tribunal for Rwanda

Mr. Henk Marquart-Scholtz, Secretary-General, International Association of Prosecutors

Professor Larry May, Vanderbilt University

Dr. Guénaël Mettraux, International Criminal Law Bureau

Dr. George Mugwanya, Senior Appeals Counsel, International Criminal Tribunal for Rwanda

Mr. Daryl Mundis, Chief of Prosecutions, Special Tribunal for Lebanon

Professor Michael Newton, Vanderbilt University Law School

Judge Daniel Nsereko, International Criminal Court

Mr. Robert Petit, Extraordinary Chambers in the Courts of Cambodia

Mr. Thomas Wayde Pittman, International Criminal Tribunal for the former Yugoslavia

Judge Árpád Prandler, International Criminal Tribunal for the former Yugoslavia

Professor Darryl Robinson, Queen's University

Professor Leonard Rubenstein, Center for Public Health & Human Rights, Johns Hopkins Bloomberg School of Public Health

Susana SáCouto, Director of War Crimes Research Office, American University Washington College of Law

Professor Michael Scharf, Case Western University

Ambassador David Scheffer, Professor and Director of the Center for International Human Rights, Northwestern University

Professor Wolfgang Schomburg, Durham University / Durham Law School; Former Judge (ICTY/ICTR)

Ms. Sandra Schulberg, Producer, "Nuremberg: It's Lesson for Today"

Professor Göran Sluiter, University of Amsterdam

Professor Gregory H. Stanton, George Mason University

Professor Jane Stromseth, Georgetown University Law Center

Judge Stefan Trechsel, International Criminal Tribunal for the former Yugoslavia

Professor H. G. van der Wilt, University of Amsterdam

Professor Beth Van Schaack, Santa Clara University Law

Professor Elies van Sliedregt, Vrije Universiteit, Amsterdam

Ms. Patricia Viseur-Sellers, International Criminal Law/Humanitarian Law Consultant

Judge Inés M. Weinberg de Roca, United Nations Appeals Tribunal

Mr. Peter H. Wilkitzki, General Director Criminal Law Federal Ministry of Justice, Berlin (retired); Lecturer, University of Cologne; Vice President, International Association of Penal Law (AIDP); President, German Group of AIDP

Mr. Mikhail Wladimiroff, Partner, Wladimiroff Advocaten

Supporters Updated: 29 September 2010

KIGALI DECLARATION
OF FIFTH COLLOQUIUM OF PROSECUTORS
OF INTERNATIONAL CRIMINAL TRIBUNALS

WE THE PROSECUTORS respectively of the International Criminal Court (ICC), the International Criminal Tribunal for the Former Yugoslavia (ICTY), the International Criminal Tribunal for Rwanda (ICTR), the Special Court for Sierra Leone (SCSL), the Extraordinary Chambers in the Courts of Cambodia (ECCC) and the Special Tribunal for Lebanon (STL) following constructive discussions on the occasion of the 5th Colloquium of International Prosecutors convened in Kigali, Rwanda from the 11th to the 13th of November 2009;

REITERATE

> that combating impunity through the international criminal justice process and other means is necessary for the maintenance of national and international peace, the rule of law, respect for human rights and the creation of the necessary environment for the maintenance of stable societies;

NOTE

> (i) the contribution of the international tribunals in combating impunity through the accountability of perpetrators responsible for serious violations of international humanitarian and criminal law and (ii) the need for the best practices established by these tribunals to be harnessed for the future;

STRESS

> the role of the United Nations in the establishment and maintenance of international tribunals to combat impunity;

AFFIRM

the importance of the development of effective residual mechanisms to ensure that the achievements of the international tribunals are sustained and that the conclusion of the tribunals' mandates does not permit the emergence of an impunity gap;

ACKNOWLEDGE

the significant cooperation of states that have enabled the international tribunals to discharge their respective mandates of combating impunity;

RECOGNIZE

the important role that national as well as regional legal systems and arrangements and civil society can and do play in combating impunity;

WELCOME

the consideration by the United Nations of the important question of the exercise of Universal Jurisdiction by States;

CONDEMN

all violence against non-combatants in situations of conflict, particularly violence against women and children, and call upon all conflicting parties to respect their legal obligations to such persons to prevent such violence and to punish its perpetrators;

URGE

the United Nations to maintain its significant role in the development and maintenance of measures to combat impunity;

CALL UPON ALL STATES

(i) to ensure that their legal systems and other regional legal arrangements to which they are party have the jurisdiction and the capacity to effectively prosecute international crimes or to extradite suspects of such crimes;

(ii) to provide full cooperation to all the international criminal tribunals and to execute all requests and orders for assistance from the tribunals including the arrest of all fugitives indicted by them;

(iii) to seriously consider the adoption of a Convention on the Suppression and Punishment of Crimes against Humanity;

(iv) that have not yet done so to become party to the Rome Statute of the International Criminal Court (ICC) and cooperate fully with the court in the execution of its mandate.

ADOPTED IN KIGALI, RWANDA
This 13th Day of November 2009

Luis Moreno-Ocampo
Prosecutor, ICC

Serge Brammertz
Prosecutor, ICTY

Joseph F. Kamara
Ag. Prosecutor, SCSL

ANEES AHMED
for William Smith
Ag. International Co- Prosecutor, ECCC

Daniel Bellemare
Prosecutor, STL

Hassan Bubacar Jallow
Prosecutor, ICTR

The Fourth Chautauqua Declaration
August 31, 2010

In the spirit of humanity and peace the assembled current and former international prosecutors and their representatives here at the Chautauqua Institution...

Recognizing the continuing need for justice and the rule of law as the foundation to international security, and cognizant of the legacy of all those who preceded us at Nuremberg and elsewhere:

Recognize the tenth anniversary of the Robert H. Jackson Center and its important mandate to preserve, promote, and advance the legacy of Justice Robert Jackson through education, exhibits, and events, which emphasize the current relevance of Jackson's ideas on individual freedom and justice;

Honor the life of our colleague and friend Whitney R. Harris, a prosecutor of the International Military Tribunal at Nuremberg who passed away this year; commend his drive and force in ensuring that the spirit of Nuremberg continued; and note the awarding posthumously to Whitney Harris the first annual Joshua Heintz Humanitarian Award for distinguished service to mankind;

Applaud the efforts of the states parties to the Rome Statute, and other delegations in Kampala this year in their willingness to openly take stock in the progress of international criminal law in general and the concrete recommendations to ensure justice for victims of international crimes; and for reaching consensus on a definition of the crime of aggression and for their determination to press for appropriate mechanisms for its enforcement and prosecution;

Noting that after thirty years of impunity the first judgment has been rendered in respect of the crimes of the Khmer Rouge in Cambodia;

Reflecting upon the fifteenth anniversary of the genocide at Srebrenica and the continuing need for the accountability of those responsible;

Expressing concern at the continuing plight of civilians caught up in armed conflict and particularly for those crimes committed against women and children;

Now do call upon the international community to:

Keep the spirit of the Nuremberg Principles alive by:

Ensuring the enforcement of the laws of armed conflict and in particular those relating to the protection of civilians;

Calling upon parties in armed conflict to respect international law applicable to the rights and protection of women and girls;

Ensuring that gender crimes are investigated and prosecuted appropriately;

States refraining from the use or threat of armed force and settling their disputes by peaceful means and in accordance with the United Nations Charter and international law;

Supporting and adequately funding the tribunals and courts in their work to maintain the rule of law at both the international and domestic level;

Implementing their obligations under international law in the sharing of information, investigating, prosecuting or transferring to an appropriate judicial body those who violate international criminal law to ensure accountability of all persons, including sitting heads of state;

Considering the adoption of a Convention on the Suppression and Punishment of Crimes against Humanity;

Signed in Mutual Witness:

Fatou Bensouda
International Criminal Court

David M. Crane
Special Court for Sierra Leone

Serge Brammertz
International Criminal Tribunal
for the former Yugoslavia

Benjamin Ferencz
International Military Tribunal,
Nuremberg

H. W. William Caming
International Military Tribunal,
Nuremberg

Richard Goldstone
International Criminal Tribunals for
Rwanda & the former Yugoslavia

Andrew Cayley
Extraordinary Chambers in the
Courts of Cambodia

Brenda Hollis
Special Court for Sierra Leone

Bongani Majola
International Criminal Tribunal
for Rwanda

Robert Petit
Extraordinary Chambers in the
Courts of Cambodia

Index

Abu Ghraib 156
AFRC case
  See Prosecutor v. Brima, Kamara, and Kanu
African Charter on Human Rights and Peoples'
    Rights 34
  amnesties 219
African Commission on Human and Peoples'
    Rights 219
aggression, crime of 16 fn 38, 49, 50, 52, 114
  and conspiracy 161
  lack of definition 52
  and the "policy" requirement 143
  See also Nuremberg Charter, crimes against
    peace
In re Ahlbrecht (No.2) 162
Aidid, Mohammed 61
al-Bashir, Omar 59, 188, 191, 206, 303, 352, 353,
    465, 470, 471, 484, 493
  See also Sudan
Albright, Madeleine 490
al-Hariri, Rafiq 494
al-Qaeda 269, 273–274, 275
In re Altstötter and others (Justice case) 162, 163,
    244
American Convention on Human Rights 34
  and amnesties 219
Amin, Idi 61
amnesties 202, 217–222, 333, 468, 485, 491–492,
    493
  and customary international law 217, 468
  in the Enforced Disappearance Convention
    220, 221 fn 86, 468, 485
  examples of amnesty deals or offers 62, 493
  Fujimori case 499
  jurisprudence of the Inter-American Court on
    Human Rights 498, 499
  and post-conflict justice 60, 62
  in the Rome Statute 485
  and treaty law 218–220
  in Treaty of Lausanne 49
  UN Model Agreement on the Transfer of
    Foreign Prisoners 343
  and U.S. legislation 492

Annan, Kofi 64
apartheid 16, 21, 25, 30 fn 4, 32, 38, 53 fn 37,
    108, 122–123, 153–154 fn 20, 314,
    470–471
  and crimes against humanity 21, 25, 29, 108,
    123, 314, 315–316, 353
  and the Draft Code of Offenses/Crimes
    15 fn 34, 25
  as a form of "attack" 122–123
  relationship to prosecution 30, 32
  and Responsibility to Protect 315–316
  in the Rome Statute 21, 25, 30 fn 4,
    53 fn 37
  See also International Convention on the
    Suppression and Punishment of the
    Crime of Apartheid
Arab League Agreement for Judicial Cooperation
    (Riyadh Convention) 336 fns 94, 97
Argentina
  Abella v. Argentina 272 fn 50
  and amnesties 62
  criminal law provisions 245
  enforced disappearance in 314
Armenia
  See genocide, Armenian
Arrest Warrant case (Congo v. Belgium)
  See International Court of Justice, Arrest
    Warrant case
Ashdown, Paddy 186–187
atrocity crimes xxiv–xxv, 2–7, 9, 177–201, 321,
    462, 496
  "atrocity law" 177, 183, 187, 189, 192, 201
  "criminology of mass atrocity" 177, 183, 184,
    187, 189, 192, 201
  categories of 306–307
  and early warning systems 5, 307, 496
  impunity for 461–462
  prevention of 458, 467, 496, 497
  and Responsibility to Protect 305–322
  U.S. legislation on 491
Australia 2, 173
  Polyukhovich v. The Commonwealth of
    Australia 163, 170

595

aut dedere aut judicare (duty to prosecute or extradite) 29, 38, 58, 262–263, 277, 324–329, 332, 336, 474, 481
  and complementarity 465, 481
  and customary international law 37–38, 325, 326
  origins of 324
  relationship to universal jurisdiction 34–35
  See also universal jurisdiction
Azerbaijan 96 fn 105

Bahrain 96 fn 105, 493
Balkans 2, 75, 177
  "burning tradition" in 177, 178, 186
  Balkan Wars 178
  and ethnic cleansing 178, 179, 248
  See also Bosnia; Croatia; Yugoslavia, former
Ball, Patrick 184–186, 187
Bassiouni, M. Cherif xviii, xxiv, 36, 38, 166, 339, 358, 461, 471, 481–482
  and the drafting of the *Proposed Convention* xxvii, 456, 458, 461, 472
  and the UN Commission of Experts on former Yugoslavia 56, 177, 179–181
Beijing Declaration and Platform for Action (Fourth World Conference on Women) 82 fn 19, 90
Belgium 69, 214
  criminal law provisions 231
  and immunities in genocide prosecutions 211 fn 39, 212
  proceedings against Senegal 34
  See also International Court of Justice, *Arrest Warrant* case
Bell-Fialkoff, Sudrew 181
Bergsmo, Morten 180
bin Laden, Osama 263–264, 273
Blair, Tony 71, 186
Bolton, John 346
Borkum Island case 247
Bosnia and Herzegovina 4, 192, 310
  Dayton negotiations 483
  domestic prosecutions of atrocity crimes 28, 148 fn 10, 174–175
  ethnic cleansing 180, 181, 317, 318
  forced pregnancy 91
  Prijedor report 180–181
  proceedings against the United Kingdom 497
  Prosecutor v. Rašević and Todović (Trial Judgment) 175 fn 115
  Prosecutor v. Todorović and Radić (Appeals Judgment) 148 fn 10
  rape in 91
  See also International Court of Justice, *Bosnia v. Serbia*; Srebrenica

Brownlie, Ian 36
Burkina Faso 67 fn 47, 68, 69
Burma (Myanmar) 4
Bush, George W. 356, 490, 491

Cambodia 1, 4
  and amnesties 62
  and forced displacement 2
  and forced marriage 98 fn 118
  genocide xxiii, 2–3, 309, 472
  See also Extraordinary Chambers in the Courts of Cambodia; Pol Pot
Canada 2, 68
  conditions on extradition 342 fn 143
  criminal law provisions 166, 170 fn 87
  domestic legislation on crimes against humanity 22–23 fn 69, 30, 41, 170, 259, 478
  domestic prosecutions of crimes against humanity 36, 41, 51, 166
  domestic prosecutions of terrorism 269
  R v. Désiré Munyaneza 41
  R.v. Finta 166
capacity building xxv, 5, 307, 323, 344, 458, 462, 469, 473, 474, 475–476, 486, 490, 498–499
Cassese, Judge Antonio 352, 353
Central African Republic 296, 304
Chad 34, 189, 196
Chamberlain, Sir Austen 6
Chile
  and amnesties 62
  and enforced disappearance 314
  See also Pinochet, Augusto; *Pinochet* case
China 46, 48, 69
Churchill, Sir Winston 60
Coalition for the International Criminal Court (CICC) 476, 499
Coburn, Tom 491–492
Colombia 296
Commission on the Responsibilities of the Authors of War and Enforcement of Penalties 45, 48, 50, 51
Committee on the Codification of International Law
  See International Law Commission
Common Article 3
  See Geneva Conventions
Compare, Blasé 67 fn 47, 69
Congo, Democratic Republic of 5, 10 fn 9, 310
  forced marriage 81
  Goma peace negotiations 483
  ICC prosecutions 296, 301
  rape 355
  See also International Court of Justice, *Arrest Warrant* case

conspiracy 143, 149, 161, 165, 223, 226, 249, 253–254, 470
  to commit genocide 15 fn 33, 226, 352
  Nuremberg jurisprudence on 161, 165, 223
  Pinkerton v. United States 252
Conte, Lansana 61
Control Council Law No. 10 xxiv fn 19, 12–13, 51, 54, 84, 162, 163–164, 165, 205
Convention Against Torture (Torture Convention) xxii, xxvii, 261, 262, 346, 353, 355, 456
  and amnesties 33, 217, 218–219
  aut dedere aut judicare provisions 29, 34–35, 37, 262, 353
  forms of criminal responsibility provisions 226
  official immunities provisions 210–211
  See also Pinochet case; torture
Convention on the Non-Applicability of Statutory Limitations to War Crimes and Crimes Against Humanity (Statutory Limitations Convention) 30, 36, 38
  and customary international law 32
  extradition provisions 28–29, 38
  and the "policy" requirement 168 fn 72, 171
  universal jurisdiction provisions 32, 38
Convention on the Prevention and Punishment of the Crime of Genocide (Genocide Convention) xvii, 3, 194, 261, 296, 346, 347–350, 356, 363, 457, 462, 478, 497
  and amnesties provisions 219
  and *Bosnia v. Serbia* xvii–xviii, 15, 494, 496
  and crimes against humanity 14–15, 30, 32
  definition of genocide 14, 53, 348
  and discriminatory intent 3, 53, 183, 317, 352
  and ethnic cleansing 182–184
  and forms of criminal responsibility provisions 226, 227
  "g" word 3
  and individual criminal responsibility 15
  and jurisdiction 14, 28
  limited application of xxii, xxiii, 3, 16, 147, 153, 183, 192, 348, 353, 457
  and nexus to armed conflict 14
  official immunities provisions 211, 211 fn 39, 212
  and the "policy" requirement 168 fn 72, 171
  and prevention 15, 348, 349, 473, 495
  and the Proxmire Act 491
  and State responsibility 15, 474
  universal jurisdiction provisions 30, 31–33
  See also genocide
Convention Respecting the Laws and Customs of War on Land (Fourth Hague Convention) xxix, 9
  Hague Peace Conference (1907) xxix–xxx, 461
  Martens Clause xxi, 9, 10, 44–45, 47–48, 280
Corell, Hans xviii, xxviii, 472, 485

crimes against peace
  See aggression; Nuremberg Charter, crimes against peace
crimes against humanity 3, 4, 305, 306, 309, 310, 314
  and amnesties 217–222, 485
  and apartheid 21, 25, 29, 108, 123, 314, 315–316, 353
  and the "attack" requirement 20, 21, 120–126, 143, 153–154, 160, 162
  chapeau elements in definition 19–21, 24, 26–27, 102–141, 147, 174, 176 fn 119, 282–283, 288, 292 fn 78, 293
  and the "civilian population" requirement 56, 117–120, 143, 153–154, 162, 163, 286–288, 293, 295, 311–314, 317, 463
  and customary international law 29, 30, 36–37, 106, 107 fn 25, 108, 110–113, 115, 121, 123–124, 129, 130–132, 134, 135, 139, 140–141, 280, 466
  definition in Control Council Law No. 10 12–13, 162, 165, 276
  definition in the Draft Code of Crimes/ Offenses 15–18, 51
  definition in ECCC Statute 105, 108 fn 27, 175
  definition in the ICC Elements of Crimes 25–27, 288
  definition in the ICTR Statute 19, 51, 53, 282
  definition in the ICTY Statute 19, 51, 53, 282
  definition in the Nuremberg Charter 8–12, 157–161, 276, 463
  definition in the Nuremberg Principles 13–14, 50, 161
  definition in the Rome Statute 19–25, 53, 55, 57, 107–108, 109, 114, 117, 119, 121, 122, 130–131, 134, 135, 137, 139, 141, 174 fn 110, 280, 282–295, 463
  definition in the SCSL Statute 166, 169
  definition in the Secretary General's report ("parallel definition") 106–107, 114, 120, 129, 130, 139
  definition in the Tokyo Tribunal Charter 12 fn 19, 106, 108, 161, 276
  domestic legislation on 30, 331, 474, 477–478, 499
  domestic prosecutions of 30, 474
  and deportation xxii fn 10, 9, 11, 13, 16–18, 41, 108, 158, 160 fn 43, 161 fn 44, 290, 314, 315, 318, 355–356
  and economic and environmental crimes 478
  and enforced disappearance 21, 24 fn 77, 108, 312, 314–315, 337
  and ethnic cleansing 182, 316–319
  and extermination 159, 318, 457

crimes against humanity (*cont.*)
  and gender-based crimes 13, 21, 78–101, 277, 315, 457, 463, 467, 482–483
  and genocide 3, 14–15, 32, 102
  and human rights law 33–34, 464
  and imprisonment 13, 18, 19 fn 47, 98, 108, 290, 314, 316, 457
  and individual criminal responsibility xxi, 280, 467
  and *mens rea* requirements 26–27, 53, 129–137, 167 fn 71, 288–290, 293–294
  and nexus to armed conflict 12–13, 14, 16, 17, 19, 29, 33, 51, 55, 114–116, 134–139, 283, 291–292, 350
  and official immunities 203–217, 468
  origins of xxi–xxii, 8–18, 44–46, 157 fn 27
  and "other inhumane acts" 18, 276–277, 278, 318, 467
  and persecution 9, 12, 14, 23, 81, 94, 316–319, 356, 457
  and the "policy" requirement 17–18, 21, 54–56, 108, 122, 123, 126–129, 135–137, 142–176, 283–284, 295, 333, 463
  and prosecution in specialized regional courts 474
  and Responsibility to Protect 4, 5, 7, 305–322, 458, 467–468, 473, 477, 494–495
  and semantic indifference 3, 462, 476, 479
  and the speciality principle 332
  and the substantiality test 311, 321
  and system criminality 223, 224, 470
  and the territoriality principle 28–42
  and terrorism 154 fn 24, 262–278, 468–469
  and torture 13, 17, 18, 19 fn 47, 21 fn 64, 29, 100, 290, 314, 316, 331, 353, 355
  and universal jurisdiction 28–42, 465
  and the "widespread and systematic" requirement 20, 33, 56, 120–122, 126–129, 143, 153–154, 158, 162, 167–175, 267–268, 284–286, 290, 311–314, 317, 332–333
crimes against humanity convention 2, 3, 5, 305
  and amnesties 468
  and capacity building 462
  and deterrence 301
  and a fact-finding commission 489
  and forms of criminal responsibility 226–227
  and gender-based crimes 81, 82–83, 100–101, 467
  and the Genocide Convention 15
  and individual criminal responsibility 5, 306, 319–320, 321, 467
  and national courts 2, 28, 40–41
  need for xvii–xviii, 2, 28, 29, 30, 40–41, 57–58, 323, 353, 354, 356–357, 358, 457–458, 465, 469, 471, 474
  and non-state actors 295, 474, 481, 488–489
  and official immunities 468
  and the "policy" requirement 176
  and prevention 58, 473
  and Responsibility to Protect 5, 7, 305, 306, 319–323, 473, 476–477
  and State Responsibility 5, 306, 319, 322, 467, 473
  and terrorism 264, 277–278, 468–469
  and a treaty monitoring body 475–476
Crimes Against Humanity Initiative xxv–xxx, 323, 324, 455, 458–459, 471
  April Experts' Meeting (St. Louis) 460–470
  June Experts' Meeting (The Hague) 470–478
  Phase III 455, 458–459, 461
  Phase IV xxx, 501
  Phases I and II 455, 458
  Steering Committee viii, xviii, xxviii, 481–482
  timing of 479
  Washington Conference 479–500
  See also Proposed International Convention on the Prevention and Punishment of Crimes Against Humanity
criminal responsibility, forms of 149, 164, 223–261
  aiding and abetting 236–241
  commission 228–234
  common purpose doctrine 231, 232
  conspiracy 223, 254, 470
  incitement 223, 254
  indirect perpetration 241–246
  instigation 234–236
  joint criminal enterprise (JCE) 149, 152, 155 fn 25, 223, 225, 231, 232, 246, 469, 470
  superior responsibility 223, 225, 254–261, 469
Croatia xxv fn 29, 180, 181, 317, 318, 486
Cryer, Robert 37
customary international law 6, 10, 18, 22–23, 40, 55, 58, 320, 354, 357, 463
  and amnesties 217, 468
  and *aut dedere aut judicare* 37–38, 325, 326
  and crimes against humanity 29, 30, 36–37, 106, 107 fn 25, 108, 110–113, 115, 121, 123–124, 129, 130–132, 134, 135, 139, 140–141, 280, 466
  and extradition 330
  and forms of criminal responsibility 228, 233, 238, 240, 241, 244, 247, 250, 257, 260
  and the Nuremberg Charter 157
  and official immunities 207–208, 209, 213, 215, 216
  and the "policy" requirement 142 fn 1, 145, 148, 149, 158, 167, 168–169, 173, 174, 175, 285
  and the principle of legality 276
  and the Rome Statute 22, 173, 463
  and universal jurisdiction 29–30, 36–40

Darfur 3, 5, 31 fn 9, 177, 178, 179, 184, 310, 352, 353, 356
  ethnic cleansing/genocide 187–201, 317, 318–319
  rape 190, 195–196
  Security Council Resolution on 308
Declaration des Droits de l'Homme et du Citoyen 357
Declaration Renouncing the Use, in Time of War, of Explosive Projectiles Under 400 Grammes Weight (St. Petersburg Declaration of 1868) 9 fn 7
deportation xxii fn 10, 9, 11, 13, 16–18, 41, 108, 158, 160 fn 43, 161 fn 44, 290, 314, 315, 318, 355–356
  and Rome Statute 9 fn 4
  as a terrorizing tactic 182
  See also crimes against humanity, deportation; forcible transfer
Deng, Frances 357
Diamond, Jared 194, 200
Documents of the Persecution of the Dutch Jewry 178
Doenitz, Admiral Karl 204 fn 11
Draft Code of Offenses/Crimes Against the Peace and Security of Mankind 15–18, 52, 58, 171–173
  See also International Law Commission
Durbin, Richard J. 491–492

East Timor
  multinational intervention in 310
  Special Panel for Serious Criminal Offenses (SPSC)/UNTAET Regulation 82 fn 20, 84, 87, 89, 90, 92, 93, 95, 105, 108 fn 27, 350
Einolf, Christopher J. 355
Einsatzgruppen case 162
enforced disappearance xxii fn 10, 21, 24 fn 77, 35, 290, 312, 337
  and amnesties 219, 220–221
  definition of 463
  and Responsibility to Protect 314–315
  and the Rome Statute 21, 24, 108
  See also crimes against humanity, enforced disappearance; International Convention for the Protection of All Persons from Enforced Disappearance
enforced prostitution
  See crimes against humanity; gender-based crimes
enforced sterilization
  See crimes against humanity; gender-based crimes
erga omnes crimes 325
Essen Lynching case 247
ethnic cleansing 3, 60, 244, 247–248, 305, 306, 309, 310, 314, 495
  categories of 182
  and crimes against humanity 182, 316–319
  in Darfur 187–201
  definition of 181–184, 201, 316–317, 318
  as euphemism 177, 178–179
  and genocide 182–183, 201
  as an independent crime 319
  as metaphor 177–201
  prevention of 178
  in Prijedor 180, 181–182, 247
  and Responsibility to Protect 316–319
  as a subcategory of persecution 315, 316–319
European Convention on Extradition 334 fn 75
European Convention on the International Validity of Criminal Judgments 341
European Convention on Mutual Legal Assistance in Criminal Matters 336 fns 94, 97
European Convention on the Non-Applicability of Statutory Limitations to Crimes Against Humanity and War Crimes 333–334 fn 74
European Convention on the Prevention of Terrorism 271
European Convention for the Protection of Human Rights and Fundamental Freedoms 33, 219
European Convention on the Transfer of Criminal Proceedings in Criminal Matters 340, 341, 456
European Convention on the Transfer of Sentenced Persons 342 fn 144
European Court of Human Rights 219
  Musayeva et al. v. Russia 220 fn 81
  Soering v. United Kingdom 472
Evans, Gareth 472, 473
evidence
  admissibility of foreign-obtained evidence 336, 338–339, 487
  before extradition 487
  gender-based evidence 97, 100
  of genocide/ethnic cleansing 183–184
  of "policy" 144–145
  of "specific intent" 183, 185
  utility of criminological evidence 183, 201
ex post facto law 50, 276, 347
  See also principle of legality
extradition 10 fn 8, 38, 324, 329–335, 471, 486–487
  and the death penalty exception 332, 334, 487
  and the double criminality requirement 330–332, 336, 488
  and duty to extradite 28, 32, 38, 325
  and duty to prosecute 325
  grounds for refusal to extradite 332–335, 487
  and *non-refoulement* 335, 487
  and the political offense exception 332, 337, 486
  and the speciality principle 330, 332, 337

Extraordinary Chambers in the Courts of Cambodia (ECCC) xxiii, xxiv, 40, 84, 309, 350, 353, 490
  definition of crimes against humanity 105, 108 fn 27, 175
  and gender-based crimes 84, 98 fn 118
  immunities provisions 206
  and the "policy" requirement 175
  See also Cambodia

Flick case 162
forced abortion/miscarriage
  See crimes against humanity; gender-based crimes
forced displacement xxii fn 10, 2, 177 fn 3, 179, 181, 182, 185, 188, 191
forced marriage
  See crimes against humanity; gender-based crimes
forced pregnancy
  See crimes against humanity; gender-based crimes
forcible transfer 17, 18, 154, 172, 290, 314
  in Darfur 356
  and "other inhumane acts" 277, 318
  in Pakistan 356
  See also deportation
France 12 fn 20, 69, 265, 350, 496
  Barbie case 118
  criminal law provisions 170, 229, 231, 241, 250, 252–253
  Declaration des Droits de l'Homme et du Citoyen 357
  domestic legislation on crimes against humanity xxii, 170
  domestic prosecutions of crimes against humanity 51, 118, 164–165
  Donald Rumsfeld case 209 fn 29
  French Resistance 164
  Ghadafi case 212 fn 45
  Joint Declaration (May 1915) 9, 45, 279
  Papon case 135, 164–165
  Touvier case 164
  Vichy regime 164

gender-based crimes against humanity 78–101, 467
  definition of gender 78–83
  enforced prostitution 22, 78, 83, 87, 89–90, 92, 93, 100, 290, 315, 457, 482
  enforced sterilization 78, 83, 92–93, 98, 99, 100, 101, 315
  forced abortion/miscarriage 92, 94, 98–99, 100, 101
  forced marriage 21 fn 64, 78, 81, 94, 97–98, 100, 101, 277
  forced pregnancy 22, 78, 83, 90–92, 99, 100, 101, 290, 315, 457

  gender-based persecution 78, 81, 83 fn 24, 94–97, 101
  in the inter-American system 482
  and "other inhumane acts" 467, 483
  rape xxv, 13, 20, 22, 61, 78, 79 fn 4, 83–86, 91, 92, 93, 95, 98, 100, 101, 108, 290, 315, 331, 353, 355, 457
  and the Rome Statute 81, 82, 94–96, 467, 482
  sexual slavery 22, 78, 79 fn 4, 83, 87–88, 89, 90, 92, 97, 98, 100, 101, 315, 457
  sexual violence crimes xxii fn 10, 22, 78, 79, 83–94, 95, 97, 98, 99, 100, 108, 189, 277, 290, 314, 315, 457
  See also crimes against humanity; Responsibility to Protect
Geneva Conventions (1949) and Additional Protocols I and II (1977) xvii, 9 fn 6, 29, 35, 89 fn 61, 261, 268, 287, 346, 457, 480, 490
  and amnesties 218–219
  Common Article 3 9 fn 6, 53, 152 fn 18, 350
  definition of "attack" in 123
  definition of "civilian" in 287
  fact-finding commission provisions 489
  grave breaches 35, 53, 212, 262
  official immunities provisions 212
  and superior responsibility 255
  universal jurisdiction provisions 29, 35–36
  See also international humanitarian law
genocide 3, 7, 9 fn 6, 177, 305, 306, 309, 310, 314, 321, 462, 494
  aiding and abetting genocide 352
  Armenian 9, 45, 61, 279
  conspiracy to commit genocide 226, 352
  in Darfur 187–201
  definition of 14, 53, 147
  and the Draft Code of Offenses/Crimes 15–16
  eight stages of 348–349
  and ethnic cleansing 182–184, 201, 319
  and the ICC Elements of Crimes 14–15 fn 31, 26
  and the ICTY Statute 19
  importance of spoken language 192–195
  incitement to commit genocide 351
  origins of word 14 fn 28
  precursors of 177–178, 184, 186, 187–201
  in Prijedor 56, 180
  relationship to persecution 30, 31–32, 317, 349, 356
  and state action 14 fn 31
  See also Convention on the Prevention and Punishment of the Crime of Genocide
Georgia 4
Germany 10–11, 23, 24–25 fn 79, 49, 60, 99 fn 126, 159, 161 fn 44, 163–164, 205, 215 fn 65, 276
  criminal law provisions 229, 231, 233, 241–242, 245, 250, 258, 260, 352

domestic prosecution for war crimes 51
"final solution" 177, 178–179
Ghadafi, Muammar 63, 67, 69, 212 fn 45
Ghana 76
Goldstone, Richard xxv, xxvii, 61, 470–471
Graven, Jean 149, 165
Great Britain
  See United Kingdom
Greve, Sophie 180
Grotius, Hugo 324
Guinea 61, 67

Habré, Hissène 34, 465
Harris, Whitney xvii, xxix–xxx, 460, 479–480, 500
Harun, Ahmad 179, 187 fn 68, 188
  See also International Criminal Court, Harun indictment
Harvard Research Project xxx
hate speech 351, 497
  and incitement to commit genocide 351, 497
Herak, Borislav 187
Hirohito, Emperor Michinomiya 205 fn 14
Hiroshima and Nagasaki 345
Hitler, Aldolf 24, 61, 204 fn 11
Holbrooke, Richard 493
Holmes, John 356
Holocaust 1, 129, 178
  See also Nuremberg Charter; Nuremberg Tribunal
Hunt, Judge David 151
Hussein, Saddam 61, 493
  See also Iraq
hybrid criminal tribunals
  See international criminal tribunals

immunities 151, 202, 203–217, 479
  functional immunity 203 fn 3
  personal immunity 203 fn 3
  Pinochet case 209–211
  ratione materiae immunity 203, 204–211
  ratione personae immunity 203, 209 fn 29, 211–217
  substantive immunity 204
imprisonment 181, 348
  and crimes against humanity 13, 18, 19 fn 47, 98, 108, 290, 314, 316, 457
  and Responsibility to Protect 316
India 6, 46
individual criminal responsibility 5, 155, 160, 224, 280, 305, 306, 319, 321, 469
  and a crimes against humanity convention 5, 306, 313, 319–320, 321, 456, 467
  and enforced disappearance 314
  and the Genocide Convention 15
  and the ICC 309
  relationship to State responsibility 5, 305, 467

In re (see name of party)
Inter-American Commission of Human Rights 219, 482–483
  Abella v. Argentina 272 fn 50
Inter-American Convention on Mutual Legal Assistance in Criminal Matters 336 fns 94, 97
Inter-American Convention on Serving Criminal Sentences Abroad 456
Inter-American Court of Human Rights (IACtHR) 219, 482–483, 497–498, 499
  amnesties jurisprudence 219, 499
  crimes against humanity jurisprudence 219 fn 79
  Miguel Castro case 498
  Velásquez-Rodríguez v. Honduras 34
international (ad hoc) criminal tribunals xxvi, 64, 103, 104, 108–109, 111–114, 129, 130, 138–141, 145, 153, 162, 170–175, 215 fn 65, 224, 226, 300, 305, 309, 318, 350–352, 466, 469–470, 472, 474–475, 485–486
  and the "civilian population" requirement 287–288
  consequences of closure 474–475
  and crimes against humanity prosecutions xxv, 103
  and customary international law 173
  and forms of criminal responsibility 155 fn 25, 225, 227, 228, 230, 232, 234, 237, 241, 242, 252, 469–470
  and gender-based crimes 78
  in the Holy Roman Empire 46
  and individual criminal responsibility 155, 319–320
  jurisdiction over atrocity crimes 102–103
  and official immunities 203, 205, 207, 217
  and the "policy" requirement 166–170, 173–175
  sentencing practices 298–299
  and the substantiality test 310–314, 321
  See also East Timor, Special Panel for Serious Criminal Offenses; Extraordinary Chambers in the Courts of Cambodia; International Criminal Tribunal for Rwanda; International Criminal Tribunal for the former Yugoslavia; Special Court for Sierra Leone
international armed conflict 9 fn 7, 10, 29, 35–36, 53, 268, 287
International Civil Aviation Organization Conventions (ICAO Conventions) 269
International Commission of Inquiry on Darfur (Cassese commission) 192, 353
International Commission on Intervention and State Sovereignty 309

International Committee of the Red Cross (ICRC) 345
  role in development of international humanitarian law 480
  on use of terror tactics 271
International Conference on Military Trials 134 fn 3, 159
International Conference for the Repression of Terrorism 265
International Congress of Penal Law 264
International Convention Against the Taking of Hostages 267 fn 27
International Convention on the Elimination of All Forms of Racial Discrimination 497
International Convention for the Protection of All Persons from Enforced Disappearance (Enforced Disappearance Convention) xxvii, 24 fn 77, 330, 456, 457, 463
  amnesties 220, 468, 485
  fair trial provisions 328
  mutual legal assistance provisions 337–338
  non-refoulement provision 335
  universal jurisdiction provisions 465
International Convention for the Suppression of the Financing of Terrorism (Terrorist Financing Convention) 270, 493
International Convention on the Suppression and Punishment of the Crime of Apartheid (Apartheid Convention) xxii, 25 fn 80, 30, 123, 346, 353, 457
  and the "policy" requirement 168 fn 72, 171
  relationship to the Genocide Convention 25 fn 85
  relationship to the Rome Statute 25 fn 85
  universal jurisdiction provisions 29, 32–33
  See also apartheid
International Convention for the Suppression of Terrorist Bombings (Terrorist Bombing Convention) 34, 232 fn 30, 252, 263, 456, 465, 471, 482
International Court of Justice (ICJ) 15, 321, 346, 350, 473–474, 496, 497
  Belgium v. Senegal 34
  Bosnia and Herzegovina v. Serbia and Montenegro (*Bosnia v. Serbia*) xvii–xviii, xxv, 15, 349–350, 471, 473, 494, 496
  Croatia v. Serbia xxv fn 29
  Democratic Republic of the Congo v. Belgium (*Arrest Warrant* case) 32, 34, 35, 37, 209 fn 29, 213–214, 215–216, 217 fn 69, 468
  Djibouti v. France 204 fn 9, 214 fn 54
  jurisdiction over crimes against humanity 457, 471, 473
  on the obligation to intervene 497
  and universal jurisdiction 34, 35, 37

International Covenant on Civil and Political Rights (ICCPR) 346
  duty to prosecute human rights violations 33, 34
  jurisdiction provisions 29
  locus delicti 29
  principle of legality 110
International Criminal Court (ICC) 2, 27, 36, 40, 51, 64, 66, 79, 309, 349, 352–354, 462–463, 486
  Assembly of States Parties 25–26, 57, 276, 464, 490
  and "complementarity" xviii, 28, 58, 225, 295–296, 354, 465, 498–499
  and the Elements of Crimes 14–15 fn 31, 25–27, 85, 87–88, 90–94, 276, 286, 288, 289–290, 312–313, 354, 466
  Harun indictment 179
  Iraq investigation 150
  limited capacity to prevent and prosecute crimes against humanity 295–296, 301
  outreach and legacy program 66
  relationship with the United States 461
  Security Council authority to confer jurisdiction 28, 31 fn 9, 215 fn 65, 222 fn 80, 295, 466, 483–484, 493
  See also Rome Statute
International Criminal Court Statute (ICC Statute)
  See Rome Statute
international criminal justice 461
  cost of 64, 481, 489
  deterrence effect of 62, 279, 296–301, 467
  enforcement of 297, 300, 346, 470
  and the selectivity problem 465–466
International Criminal Tribunal for Rwanda (ICTR) xxiv, 19, 28, 40, 51, 55, 79, 102–141, 148 fn 10, 158 fn 36, 166, 300, 309, 313, 350, 466, 483, 490
  definition of crimes against humanity 19, 51, 53, 102–141, 282
  on forms of criminal responsibility 232, 234, 235, 237, 240, 241, 243, 247, 255, 257, 260, 261
  and gender-based crimes 78–79, 83–85, 94, 95, 99–100
  genocide jurisprudence 102, 351, 352
  and nexus to armed conflict 51, 102 fn 3, 107, 273
  official immunities provisions 205
  and the "policy" requirement 126, 135, 166–169, 273
International Criminal Tribunal for the former Yugoslavia (ICTY) xxiv, 19, 28, 35, 40, 51, 55, 62, 102–141, 148 fn 10, 166, 172, 175 fn 113, 176 fn 119, 180, 230, 300, 309, 350–352, 466, 473, 483, 485–486, 489, 490, 496

on aggression 114
definition of crimes against humanity 19, 33, 51, 53, 102–141, 282, 290
definition in Secretary General's Report ("parallel definition") 106–107, 114, 120, 129, 130, 139
on ethnic cleansing 182
on forms of criminal responsibility 230, 232, 234, 235, 237, 239, 240, 241, 242–243, 245, 247, 248, 250, 251, 253–254, 255, 256, 257–258, 260, 261
and gender-based crimes 78–79, 83–85, 88, 94, 95, 99–100
genocide jurisprudence 31, 102, 351, 352
Milošević trial 184–187
on nexus to an armed conflict 20, 51, 107, 108, 110 fn 37, 111, 114–116, 122–124, 134–135, 273, 350
official immunities provisions 205, 208, 217 fn 71
on persecution 33, 95, 317, 318
and the "policy" requirement 54–55, 123, 126–129, 136–137, 166–169, 173, 273, 274, 275
and "positive complementarity" 499
and the substantiality test 311–314
on universal jurisdiction 36–37
on use of terror tactics 270–271
international humanitarian law 19, 29, 179, 181, 182, 291, 335, 345, 464, 480
and the armed conflict requirement 272
and combatant immunity 268–269
definition of "civilian" 287
and the principle of distinction 268
and terrorism 264, 268, 270
See also Geneva Conventions and Additional Protocols
International Labor Organization (ILO) 462
International Labor Organization on the Worst Forms of Child Labor 462
International Law Commission (ILC) 20 fn 57, 25, 38, 51, 55
on the *aut dedere aut aut judicare* principle 29 fn 1, 38
and the Draft Code of Offenses/Crimes Against the Peace and Security of Mankind 15–18, 25, 52, 171–173, 290
and forms of criminal responsibility 234, 235
and the Nuremberg Principles xxii, 11 fn 14, 13–14
and official immunities provisions 204, 207, 216–217
Third Report on the Obligation to Extradite or Prosecute 29 fn 1
International Military Tribunal for the Far East (Tokyo Tribunal) and Charter xxi, xxiv fn 19, 12 fn 19, 51, 54, 60, 160 fn 42, 346

definition of crimes against humanity xxiv fn 19, 12 fn 19, 106, 108, 161, 276
official immunities provisions 205
and "other inhumane acts" 276
and the "policy" requirement 161
See also crimes against humanity, definition in Tokyo Tribunal Charter
Inter-parliamentary union
St. Louis meeting xxix–xxx
inter-state cooperation 2, 38, 56–57, 262, 469, 471, 488–489
and effective enforcement of international legal norms 323, 329, 335, 343
focus of 324, 329–343
horizontal cooperation 329, 337 fn 106, 481, 486
vertical cooperation 28, 329, 337 fn 106, 481, 486
Iran 316
Iraq 75, 183, 277, 284 fn 30
coalition invasion of 4, 301
ethnic cleansing in 317
ICC investigation of 150
See also Hussein, Saddam
Israel 69, 212, 269 fn 39
and the 2006 Hezbollah war 494
Attorney General of Israel v. Eichmann 208 fn 27
domestic prosecutions of crimes against humanity 51, 208 fn 27
Nazi and Nazi Collaborators (Punishment) Law 170 fn 87
and the West Bank occupation 316
Italy 265
Ivory Coast 37, 73 fn 59
and amnesties 62

Jackson, Justice Robert xvii, 10, 60, 61, 159, 161, 347, 357
See also Nuremberg Tribunal
Japan 48, 88, 106, 205 fn 14, 497
Jefferson, Thomas 264 fn 8
Joint criminal enterprise (JCE)
See criminal responsibility, forms of
Joint Declaration of France, Great Britain, and Russia (May 1915) 9, 45, 279
Jordan 499
Judah, Tim 178
jus cogens 36–37, 38, 55, 320, 325, 326, 333, 347, 354, 357
Justice case
See *In re Altstötter and others*

Kabbah, Tejan 64, 67 fn 47, 71
Kambanda, Jean 205 fn 16
Karadžić, Radovan 271, 493
See also *Prosecutor v. Karadžić*
Katyn Forest massacre 54

Kenya 5
Khawaja, Mohammed Momin 269
Khmer Rouge
   See Cambodia; Extraordinary Chambers in the Courts of Cambodia
King Leopold 10 fn 9
Kirsch, Philippe 358
Kissinger, Henry 41–42
Kosovo 4, 184–187, 310
   battle of 180
   and enforced disappearance 314–315
   ethnic cleansing in 317
   Operation Horseshoe 180, 186
   war crimes chamber 28
Kosovo Liberation Army (KLA) 184–185
Krajišnik, Momčilo 318
   See also Prosecutor v. Krajišnik
Krstić, Radislav 183, 352
   See also Prosecutor v. Krstić
Kuper, Leo 346
Kurds
   ethnic cleansing 317
Kushayb, Ali 188
Kuwait 96 fn 105

Lansing, Robert 10 fn 8
Lauterpacht, Sir Hersch 8 fn 3, 17 fn 41
laws of war
   See international humanitarian law
League of Nations 56, 264, 265
Lebanon 69, 257 fn 156
   Kahan Commission 257 fn 156
      See also Special Tribunal for Lebanon
Lemkin, Raphael 14 fn 28, 28, 347–349, 351
"letters rogatory" 336
Liberia 59, 63, 67, 69, 70, 73–76
Libya 63, 64, 67
   See also Lockerbie case
Lincoln, Abraham 10 fn 8
Lockerbie case 265–266, 328, 492
London Conference of 1945 8–12, 50, 143 fn 3, 159 fn 38, 292 fn 71
Louis XVI 10 fn 9
Luban, David 280 fn 9, 281, 292 fn 76
Luck, Edward 6

Martens Clause
   See Convention Respecting the Laws and Customs of War on Land
Martens, Fyodor 44 fn 3
mass atrocity crimes
   See atrocity crimes
May Interim Draft Convention
   superior orders exception 333
   mutual legal assistance provision 338
   double criminality requirement 331

May, Judge Richard 186
McDougal, Myres 354
Medical case 92
Melson, Robert 352
Méndez, Juan xviii, xxviii, 472, 498
military intervention/action 2, 5, 313, 315–316
Milošević, Slobodan 180 fn 23, 208, 349 fn 11
   ICTY trial 184–187, 205–206 fn 16
Ministries case 162
Mladić, Radko 486
Morocco 499
Moscow Declaration (1943) 50
Mukherjee, Pranab 6
mutual legal assistance 336–340, 469, 471, 475
   and admissible evidence 338–339
   and effective prosecution 336
   international subpoena provisions 475
   limitations on refusal to assist 336–337
   and protection of defendants' rights 336–337
   specialized convention on 475

national courts
   and crimes against humanity definitions 153, 170–171
   and the ICC 30–31, 295–296
   and the law of immunities 215–216 fn 65
   role in prosecuting international crimes 28, 40–42, 224–226, 227, 354, 358
   terrorist prosecutions 263
   and universal jurisdiction 28–42, 225, 465
NATO 184–185, 187, 315, 473
Naumann, Klaus 187
The Netherlands 9, 69
   Dutch criminal law provisions 231, 239, 241–242, 246, 250, 253, 258, 260
   Public Prosecutor v. Menten 164
   See also Lockerbie case
New Zealand 490
   domestic legislation on crimes against humanity 22–23 fn 69
Nigeria 61, 70, 75, 76, 493
"night and fog" decree 24
non-international armed conflict 9 fn 6, 53, 267, 268
non-refoulement
   See extradition
Nuremberg Charter (Charter of the International Military Tribunal at Nuremberg) 8, 13, 19, 21–22, 24, 54, 103, 106
   article 6 8, 10–11, 105, 164, 165
   crimes against humanity xxi, 8–12, 15, 20, 50, 114, 117, 120, 124, 129, 134, 137, 157, 276, 346–347, 463
   crimes against peace 8, 12 fn 16, 13, 15, 50, 161, 165
   official immunities provisions 204, 207

and persecution 23, 54, 158, 356
and the "policy" requirement 149 fn 11, 157–161
and the "semi-colon Protocol" 8 fn 2, 11–12, 105
and war crimes 8, 13, 15, 50, 161, 165
Nuremberg Principles (Principles of International Law Recognized in the Charter of the Nuremberg Tribunal and in the Judgment of the Tribunal) xxi, 13–14, 161
official immunities provisions 207–208, 211 fn 40, 214, 215
See also International Law Commission
Nuremberg Tribunal (International Military Tribunal) 11, 20, 23, 24, 60, 147, 223, 279, 311, 346, 347, 489, 499
Judgment 12 fn 18, 159–161, 165, 205, 207, 320–321, 349, 457
See also Nuremberg Charter; Nuremberg Principles

Obama, Barack 491
Ocampo, Luis Moreno 352
Ottoman Empire
See genocide, Armenian; Turkey

Pace, William 358
Pakistan 356
Pascal, Blaise 45
"peace or justice" debate 60–77, 221–222, 483–485
Permanent Court of International Justice 264–265, 346
See also International Court of Justice
persecution 9, 12, 14, 81, 94–96, 356
on cultural grounds 16
and ethnic cleansing 315, 316–319
and gender 21–22, 78–100
and Nuremberg Charter 23, 54, 158, 356
on political, racial, and religious grounds 158, 348
relationship to apartheid 30, 32
relationship to genocide 30, 31–32, 317, 349, 356
and Responsibility to Protect 316–319
and the Rome Statute 23, 81, 94–96, 317
on "social grounds" 17
Peru
Miguel Castro case 498
Fujimori case 499
Petrovic, Drazen
categories of ethnic cleansing 182–184, 201
Pillay, Judge Navanethem 351 fn 19
Pinochet, Augusto 209–211
See also *Pinochet* case; United Kingdom
Pinochet case 35, 41
double criminality 331–332
and the law of immunities 209–211
and prohibitions on torture 35, 209–211, 331

piracy 10 fn 8, 37, 353
Pohl case 256–257
the "policy" requirement 142–176
and an accurate historical record 145, 146
and customary international law 142 fn 1, 145, 148, 149, 158, 167, 168–169, 173, 174, 175, 285
definition and scope of 142–143, 147–148, 149–150
and ethnic cleansing 181
evidentiary consequences of 143, 144–145, 147, 150, 151–152, 154–176
and gravity of the offense 146–147
in ICTY/ICTR case law 166–170
and impunity 152–153, 164–165 fn 64
in national legislation 170
and official immunities 151, 156
relationship to conspiracy 143, 149
relationship to incitement/instigation 149
relationship to joint criminal enterprise 149, 152
and State responsibility 145
and the "widespread and systematic attack" requirement 153–154, 158, 162, 167–175
in World War II case law 157–166
Portugal 32, 38
Pospisil, Leo 346
Pot, Pol 61
See also Cambodia
Preparatory Committee for the Establishment of an International Criminal Court 20, 26
principle of legality (*nullum crimen sine lege*) 22 fn 69, 48, 50, 106 fn 19, 110–113, 120–121, 134, 140, 227, 229, 247 fn 109, 288, 347, 478, 483
Proposed Convention for the Prevention and Punishment of Terrorism (1937 Convention) 265, 270
Proposed International Convention on the Prevention and Punishment of Crimes Against Humanity (*Proposed Convention*) xxi, xxvii, 202, 224, 226, 319–320, 456–457, 501
alternatives to ratification 493
amnesties provisions 202, 218, 220–222, 333, 457, 468
aut dedere aut judicare provisions 326, 327–329
and convention monitoring body xxviii, 457
definition of crimes against humanity 279, 292–295, 463, 471, 472, 477–478, 481
dispute settlement provisions 321
and educational programs 495
enforcement of the effects of states parties' judgments provisions 341, 487, 488
evidentiary provisions 338–339
extradition provisions xxvii, 330–335, 456, 486–487, 488

Proposed International Convention (cont.)
and forms of criminal responsibility provisions 228, 230, 234, 235–236, 238, 241, 245–246, 250, 252, 253–254, 260–261
and gender-based crimes provisions 81–83
and inter-State cooperation xxvii, 323–344, 456
and Martens Clause xxviii, 457
mutual legal assistance provisions xxvii, 336–340, 456, 487
ne bis in idem provisions 331 fn 58
non-refoulement provisions 335
official immunities provisions xxvii, xxviii, 202, 208–212, 215, 216–217, 333
optional protocol alternative to xviii, 57, 464, 471, 477
pillars of 481
and prevention xviii, xxviii, 58, 458, 473, 495
reservations provisions 457
and Responsibility to Protect 319–321, 458, 467–468, 473
and the Rome Statute xviii, xxvii, 82, 234, 235, 241, 245–246, 254, 260–261, 292–296, 456, 457, 458, 462–472, 477, 495
and State responsibility xxviii, 320–323, 456, 496–497
statutes of limitation provisions xxvii, xxviii, 333, 457, 487
transfer of convicted persons provisions 342–343, 487
transfer of criminal proceedings provisions 340–341, 488
universal jurisdiction provisions xxvii, 327 fn 23, 456
Voluntary Trust Fund for Victims provisions 344, 500
Prosecutor v. Akayesu (Trial Judgment) xxii, 84, 93–94, 100, 104, 109, 122–123, 125, 126, 129, 132, 135, 138, 148 fn 10, 153–154 fn 20, 167 fn 71, 192, 236 fn 51, 240, 277 fn 54, 284–285 fns 31–32, 351, 352
Prosecutor v. Bagilishema 132–133, 140
Prosecutor v. Blaškić (Appeals Judgment) 33, 118 fn 69, 120, 129 fn 108, 175 fn 113
Prosecutor v. Blaškić (Trial Judgment) 121, 124, 127, 129, 135–136, 167 fn 70, 235, 256 fn 154, 257, 289, 312 fn 20, 313
Prosecutor v. Brđanin (Appeals Judgment) 242–244
Prosecutor v. Brđanin (Trial Judgment) 95 fn 102, 248, 249
Prosecutor v. Brima et al. (AFRC case) (Appeals Judgment) 97 fn 117, 98 fn 120, 100 fn 133, 271, 277 fn 86
Prosecutor v. Brima et al. (AFRC case) (Trial Judgment) 79 fn 4, 85 fn 36, 97, 103 fn 5, 169
Prosecutor v. Delalić (Čelebići case) (Appeals Judgement) 255, 256 fn 153, 257

Prosecutor v. Delalić (Čelebići case) (Trial Judgement) 84 fn 31, 102 fn 1, 240, 255, 256 fn 153, 257, 300 fn 106
Prosecutor v. Fofana & Kondewa (Trial Judgment) 103 fn 5, 169, 297 fn 42
Prosecutor v. Furundžija 37, 79 fn 4, 84, 102 fn 1, 171 fn 93, 173 fn 108, 174, 208 fn 27, 237, 240, 251 fn 133
Prosecutor v. Gacumbitsi 85 fn 35, 104, 133 fn 126
Prosecutor v. Hadžihasanović and Kubura (Appeals Decision on Joint Challenge to Jurisdiction) 256
Prosecutor v. Jelisić (Trial Judgment) 55, 192, 312 fn 21
Prosecutor v. Karadžić (Decision on Pre-Trial Motion on Issue of Immunities) 217–218 fn 71
Prosecutor v. Katanga and Ngudjolo 31, 79 fn 4, 88, 245, 284–285 fns 30–31, 286 fn 36, 290–291 fns 64–65, 301–302, 351 fn 15, 498
Prosecutor v. Kayishema and Ruzindana (Trial Judgment) 102 fn 3, 126 fn 102, 132, 135, 138, 153–154 fn 20, 167 fn 71, 176 fn 118, 352
Prosecutor v. Kordić and Čerkez (Trial Judgment) 127, 167 fn 70, 168, 311 fn 19, 313 fn 26
Prosecutor v. Krajišnik (Trial Judgment) 318
Prosecutor v. Krnojelac (Trial Judgment) 232 fn 34, 236, 250
Prosecutor v. Krstić (Appeals Judgment) 352
Prosecutor v. Krstić (Trial Judgement) 183, 352, 354
See also Krstić, Radislav
Prosecutor v. Kunarac et al. (Appeals Judgment) 54–55, 85 fn 34, 86, 100, 118–120, 126 fn 102, 127–129, 136–137, 138 fn 137, 139, 168, 169 fn 80, 274, 289, 297 fn 42, 311 fn 18, 313 fn 25
Prosecutor v. Kunarac et al. (Trial Judgment) 79 fn 4, 84–85, 86, 88, 100, 116, 118, 124–125, 127, 139, 148 fn 10, 167, 168, 171 fn 93, 174 fn 109, 290–291 fns 64–66, 311 fn 18, 313 fn 25
Prosecutor v. Kupreškić (Trial Judgment) 32 fn 10, 36 fn 30, 118 fn 63, 167 fn 70, 168, 176 fn 118, 277 fn 78, 287
Prosecutor v. Kvočka (Appeals Judgment) 249–250, 292 fn 74
Prosecutor v. Kvočka (Trial Judgment) 85 fn 35, 94 fn 93, 249–250, 277 fn 83
Prosecutor v. Lubanga 98–99, 233, 296 fn 87
Prosecutor v. Martić (Trial Judgment) 119–120, 277 fn 79, 289 fn 54

Prosecutor v. Milutinovic et al. 113–114, 116, 119, 121 fn 82, 124, 125, 135 fn 131, 249 fn 123, 284 fn 29, 288 fn 47
Prosecutor v. Musema 84 fn 31, 102 fn 3, 126 fn 102, 132, 138, 289 fn 55
Prosecutor v. Nahimana et al. (Media case) 95, 351
Prosecutor v. Nikolić (Rule 61 Decision) 104 fn 7, 154 fn 21, 167 fn 70
Prosecutor v. Niyitegeka 84 fn 31, 100, 292 fn 74
Prosecutor v. Sesay et al. (Trial Judgment) 70 fn 53, 87 fn 49, 88, 103 fn 5, 169
Prosecutor v. Stakić (Appeals Judgment) 243 fn 89, 276 fn 77, 277 fn 82, 317 fn 36
Prosecutor v. Stakić (Trial Judgment) 182, 233
Prosecutor v. Tadić (Appeals Judgment) 35, 104, 110 fn 36, 112–113, 114–115, 121, 124 fn 88, 131, 132, 133, 134, 139, 228, 232, 245, 247–248, 250, 251, 252, 253, 288 fn 51, 290 fns 63–64, 292, 466, 488
Prosecutor v. Tadić (Jurisdictional Appeals Decision) 20 fn 60, 104, 109, 114, 152 fn 18, 292
Prosecutor v. Tadić (Trial Judgment) 100, 104, 109, 112, 115, 116, 117–119, 120–121, 122, 123–124, 126, 130, 132, 134, 138, 154 fn 22, 158 fn 32, 167 fn 70, 176 fn 118, 236, 237, 240 fn 73, 245, 277 fn 81, 289 fn 55, 466, 488
Prosecutor v. Vasiljević (Trial Judgment) 116 fn 54, 153 fn 20, 169, 285 fn 35, 289 fn 54
protection of civilians 6, 306, 464, 465, 495, 497
  and Responsibility to Protect 2, 305, 308
  and Secretary General's Report on 308
  and Security Council resolution on 307

R2P
  See Responsibility to Protect
Ramadan, Taha Yassin 277
rape 355, 457
  as an act of genocide 351
  in Bosnia xxv, 91
  in the Congo 355
  in Darfur 190, 195–196
  in Rwanda 355
  in Sierra Leone 63, 74
  and war crimes 22
  See also gender-based crimes
Reid, Richard ("shoe bomber") 269 fn 38
reparations 63, 156, 461, 473, 474, 499–500
Responsibility to Protect (R2P) 2–7, 305–322, 357, 467–468, 473, 476–477, 494–497
  and apartheid 315–316
  conceptual limits of the doctrine 4
  and customary international law 6

elements 2
and enforced disappearance 314–315
and ethnic cleansing 316–319
examples of application 4–5, 310
and humanitarian intervention 495
and imprisonment 316
institutional challenges to the doctrine 5
and military intervention/action 2, 5, 313, 315–316, 497
and non-State actors 497
and persecution 316–319
political challenges to the doctrine 5–6, 308, 309
relationship to crimes against humanity 4, 5, 7, 305–322, 458, 467–468, 473, 477, 494–495
responsibility of States 2, 5, 305, 312, 458
responsibility of the international community 2, 305–307, 312
and the "right to intervene" 4
Secretary General's Report on implementation of 6, 308
and sexual violence 315
and the substantiality test 310–314
and torture 316
Revolutionary United Front (RUF) 63, 65 fn 44, 68, 70, 73 fn 59
Robespierre, Maximilien 10 fn 9
Rodrigues, Calero 173
Rome Statute 18, 25, 26, 28, 36, 40, 108–109, 126, 141, 158, 176, 224, 466, 474, 477, 478
  amnesties provisions 468, 485
  crimes against humanity provisions xxiv–xxv, 19–25, 30, 33, 53, 57, 107–108, 109, 114, 117, 119, 121, 122, 130–131, 134, 135, 137, 139, 141, 173–174, 273, 312, 354
  and customary international law xxiv, 22, 173, 463
  deportation provisions 9 fn 4
  enforcement provisions 354
  and ethnic cleansing 317
  on forms of criminal responsibility 225, 228, 229, 230, 232–233, 234–235, 237, 238, 241, 246, 250, 252, 254, 255–261, 469, 497
  and freedom of expression 497
  and gender-based crimes 22, 78, 81–84, 87, 89, 90–97, 101, 315, 467, 482
  and hate speech 497
  immunities provisions 206, 214, 215, 216
  jurisdiction provisions 28, 31, 206, 265 fn 15, 295, 309
  lack of inter-State cooperation provisions xxiv
  mens rea requirements 26–27, 288, 290, 294
  mutual legal assistance provisions 337 fn 106
  and nexus to armed conflict 55, 108

Rome Statute *(cont.)*
  persecution provisions 17, 23, 30 fn 4, 81, 94–95, 317, 356
  and the "policy" requirement 108, 150, 168 fn 72, 171, 173–174, 273, 274, 481, 488–489
  and the *Proposed Convention* xviii, xxvii, 82, 234, 235, 241, 245–246, 254, 260–261, 456, 457–458, 462–464, 472, 477, 495
  universal jurisdiction provisions 28, 30–31
  and the "willing and able" requirement 31, 153, 296, 498
  and war crimes 150–151
  See also International Criminal Court
RuSHA case *(The United States of America vs. Ulrich Greifelt, et al.)* 244
Russia
  invasion of Georgia 4
  Joint Declaration (May 1915) 9, 45, 279
  Martens, Fyodor 44 fn 3
  Musayeva et al. v. Russia 220 fn 81
  See also Soviet Union
Rwanda xxii, xxiv, 1, 4, 75, 152, 310, 350, 352, 496
  gaccaca courts 28
  genocide 41, 192, 194–195, 496
  rape 355
  See also International Criminal Tribunal for Rwanda

Sadat, Leila vii, xiii, xviii, 455, 460, 472, 480, 500
Sankoh, Foday 63
Schabas, William xviii, xxvii, 55, 207 fn 21, 259, 352, 471–472, 494
Scheffer, David 177, 183, 184, 186, 187, 201
Senegal 34, 465
September 11 2001 263, 264, 267, 273, 274, 493
sexual slavery
  See gender-based crimes, sexual slavery
sexual violence
  See gender-based crimes, sexual violence; Responsibility to Protect, sexual violence
Sierra Leone 310, 493
  conflict in 63–76
  crimes against humanity in 64
  forced marriage in 81
  rape in 63, 74
  See also Special Court for Sierra Leone
slavery (enslavement) xxii fn 10, 346
  and crimes against humanity 10, 11–13, 16–19, 105, 121, 122, 157, 158, 161, 314, 315
  racial 193
  slave labor 9
  slave trade 10
  See also gender-based crimes, sexual slavery
Somalia 5
South Africa
  and amnesties 62
  apartheid 25 fn 84, 32, 38, 315–316, 470–471
  See also apartheid; International Convention on the Suppression and Punishment of the Crime of Apartheid
Soviet Union 12 fn 20, 50
  See also Nuremberg Tribunal; Russia
Spain 358
  Pinochet case 41, 209, 210 fn 32, 331
  domestic prosecutions of atrocity crimes 212 fn 44
Special Court for Sierra Leone (SCSL) 40, 63–76, 79, 104, 108, 139, 166, 169, 309, 466, 483, 490
  academic consortium 65
  definition of crimes against humanity 108, 114, 117, 119, 122, 130, 138, 166, 169, 466
  and gender-based crimes 78–79, 83–85, 87–90, 92 fn 81, 93, 94, 97–98, 99–100, 271
  immunities provisions 206, 207–208, 215 fn 65
  jurisdiction over atrocity crimes 102–103
  mandate 65, 75
  nexus to armed conflict requirement 114, 137
  notice pleading in indictments 66–67
  Operation Justice 59, 67–74, 76, 77
  Outreach and Legacy program 65–66, 75
  "policy" element 169
  on use of terror tactics 271
  witness management 66
  See also Sierra Leone
Special Tribunal for Lebanon 11 fn 13, 494
  official immunities provisions 205 fn 15, 215–216 fn 65
  See also Lebanon
Srebrenica 1, 183, 491
  and enforced disappearance 314–315
  genocide xviii, xxv, 349 fn 11, 350
  See also Bosnia and Herzegovina; International Court of Justice, *Bosnia v. Serbia*
Sri Lanka 5, 6
  operations against the Tamil Tigers 6
Stalin, Josef 24, 60
State Responsibility 5, 305, 323, 325 fn 15, 458, 464, 467–468, 496–497
  and crimes against humanity convention 319–322, 463, 471, 473, 496–497
  as a duty to implement domestic crimes against humanity legislation 5, 305, 319
  and the Genocide Convention 15, 474
  and the Martens Clause xxi
  political challenges to 5
  and the *Proposed Convention* xxviii, 456
  and Responsibility to Protect 5, 305, 467–468
  specific provisions on 306, 320, 497
Streicher, Julius 160, 351 fn 19

Sudan 31 fn 9, 59, 179, 187–201, 206, 296, 303–304, 353, 484, 485
    See also al-Bashir, Omar; Darfur
superior responsibility
    See criminal responsibility, focus of
Sutter, David 300–301

Taft, Robert 347
Taylor, Charles 59, 61, 63, 65, 67–70, 72–76, 208, 215 fn 65, 490, 493
terrorism 6, 262–278
    anti-terrorism conventions 263, 264–266, 270 fn 41, 272–273, 277, 492
    aut dedere aut judicare 262–263
    definition of 266–267, 270, 469
    domestic prosecutions 263
    international prosecutions 263
    relationship to crimes against humanity 154 fn 24, 262–278, 468–469
    relationship to war crimes 267–272
    and the Rome Statute 469
    use of terror tactics 270–271
Timor Leste
    See East Timor
Tokyo Tribunal
    See International Military Tribunal for the Far East
torture 37, 55, 78, 98, 346, 353, 355, 356
    and crimes against humanity 13, 17, 18, 19 fn 47, 21 fn 64, 29, 100, 290, 314, 316, 331, 353, 355
    and "other inhumane acts" 277
    Pinochet case 35, 209–211, 331
    and Responsibility to Protect 316
    sexual 79 fn 4, 100
    See also Convention Against Torture
Treaty of Lausanne (1923) 9 fn 5, 49
Treaty of Sèvres (1920) 9 fn 5, 49
Treaty of Versailles (1919) 45, 49
Treaty of Westphalia (1648) 345
truth commissions 63, 75, 461, 485, 498
Turkey 9, 45, 49, 51
    post-World War I trials of Turkish officials 9 fn 5, 45, 49, 346
    Young Turk Triumvirate 346
    See also genocide, Armenian

Uganda 296, 302–303
United Kingdom 12 fn 20, 72, 75, 350, 497
    domestic jurisprudence on immunities 213–214
    DPP for Northern Ireland v. Maxwell 239, 251 fn 132
    implementation of Genocide Convention 226, 227
    International Criminal Court Act of 258, 2001

Joint Declaration (May 1915) 9, 45, 279
Pinochet case 41, 209–211
United Nations 4, 15, 75, 76, 83, 307, 308, 310, 315, 321, 345–346, 347, 492
United Nations Charter 10
    Article 2(7) 4
    Article 13 22 fn 68, 280 fn 8
    Article 25, 267
    Article 51 20 fn 61
    Chapter VI 307
    Chapter VII 28, 31 fn 9, 307, 316, 495
United Nations Commission of Experts to Investigate Violations of International Humanitarian Law in the former Yugoslavia 56, 177, 179–180
United Nations Commission on Human Rights 20 fn 57
United Nations Convention Against Corruption 337, 456, 475
United Nations Convention Against Illicit Traffic in Narcotic Drugs 337
United Nations Convention Against Transnational Organized Crime 337, 456
United Nations General Assembly 4, 6, 22 fn 68
    Affirmation of the Principles of International Law Recognized by the Charter of the Nuremberg Tribunal xxi–xxii, 13, 15, 161, 207
    on the definition of gender 81, 96
    and the Draft Code of Offenses/Crimes Against the Peace and Security of Mankind 15, 52
    and the establishment of the ICC xxii–xxiii fn 11
    on ethnic cleansing in Bosnia 181–182
    power to authorize peace-keeping missions 495
    resolution on aggression 52
    resolutions on the punishment of perpetrators of war crimes and crimes against humanity 38–40
    on terrorism 262, 266, 270
    World Summit Outcome 307, 310, 477, 495
United Nations High Commissioner for Refugees 355–356
United Nations Human Rights Committee 33–34, 219
    Bautista de Arellana v. Colombia 33
United Nations Model Agreement on the Transfer of Foreign Prisoners 343
United Nations Model Treaty on Extradition 333
United Nations Model Treaty on Mutual Legal Assistance 338
United Nations Office of the Special Advisor on Gender Issues (OSAGI) 79, 80
United Nations Secretary General 64, 170
    Report on the ICTR 166, 171 fn 92
    Report on the ICTY 106–107, 114, 120, 129, 130, 139, 166

United Nations Secretary General (cont.)
  Report on implementing the Responsibility to Protect 308
  Report on the protection of civilians in armed conflict 308
United Nations Security Council 5, 52, 65, 308, 316, 350, 483, 489, 493, 496, 497
  and the definition of gender 81, 96
  power to confer jurisdiction on the ICC 28, 31 fn 9, 215 fn 65, 222 fn 80, 295, 466, 483–484, 493
  Resolution on Darfur 308
  Resolution on the establishment of ICTR 19, 107, 166, 205, 215 fn 65, 350–351
  Resolution on the establishment of ICTY 19, 107, 110, 115, 166, 205, 215 fn 65, 350
  Resolution on the establishment of the Special Court for Lebanon 11 fn 13, 494
  Resolution on the protection of civilians 307
  Resolution on Sierra Leone 64, 206 fn 17
  and Responsibility to Protect 5, 305, 306, 321, 495
  on Rwanda 496
  on terrorism 267, 493
  See also United Nations Charter; United Nations Commission of Experts to Investigate Violations of International Humanitarian Law in the former Yugoslavia
United Nations Special Advisor on the Prevention of Genocide 462
United Nations Special Rapporteur on Violence Against Women 80
United Nations War Crimes Commission 158, 162
United States 12 fn 20, 48, 50, 349, 489–493, 497
  Alien Tort Claims Act 238 fn 57
  Bauman v. DaimlerChrysler Corp. 238 fn 57
  Child Soldiers Accountability Act 491
  the Declaration of Independence 357
  and domestic legislation on crimes against humanity 474, 491–492
  and the ICC 461, 490, 493
  Model Penal Code 26 fn 88, 294
  and the Nuremberg Tribunal 163
  Pinkerton v. United States 252
  and the "political question" doctrine 156
  Presbyterian Church of Sudan v. Talisman Energy 238
  Senate Subcommittee on Human Rights and the Law 491
  State Department survey on Darfur 187, 189–192
  and support of the ICTR 490
  and support of the ICTY 486, 490
  United States v. Medina 257 fn 156
  and the World Summit Outcome 495

Universal Declaration of Human Rights 346
universal jurisdiction 217, 277, 353, 465, 469, 479, 491–492, 498
  and atrocity crimes 326
  aut dedere aut judicare 18, 327, 465
  and crimes against humanity 28–42, 465
  and customary international law 29–30, 36–40
  and genocide 14
  and the ICC 28
  mandatory 28–42, 327 fn 23, 332, 456, 465
  and national courts 28–42, 225, 465
  permissive 28–42, 327 fn 23, 332, 456
  and piracy 353
  See also Proposed International Convention on the Prevention and Punishment of Crimes Against Humanity, universal jurisdiction provisions

Van den Wyngaert, Judge Christine xviii, xxviii, 482, 483
Vernon, Richard 280–281
Vienna Convention on Diplomatic Relations 213 fn 48
Vienna Convention on the Law of Treaties 112–113, 328
Vienna Declaration and Programme of Action 81–82, 90
Vietnam 357 fn 156, 462
von Schirach, Baldur 160

Walker, Ambassador William 187
war
  See international armed conflict
war crimes xvii, xxiv–xxv, 8, 9, 16–17 fn 38, 24–25 fn 79, 32, 36, 50, 102–103, 148, 150, 153, 161, 165, 227, 491–492, 494–495
  and amnesties 62
  and crimes against humanity 3, 9 fn 6, 13–14, 16, 24 fn 79, 50, 55, 114, 115, 117, 287, 332
  domestic prosecutions for 41, 152 fn 17
  and ethnic cleansing 319
  and gender-based crimes 22, 79 fn 4, 86, 89 fn 61, 90, 91
  General Assembly resolutions on the punishment of war criminals 38–40
  and "grave breaches" 29
  and ICC Elements of Crimes 26, 27 fn 94
  and the ICTY Statute 19
  men rea requirements 137
  and nexus to armed conflict 102, 133, 138, 150, 152, 353
  and official immunities 208 fn 27, 215–216 fn 65, 217–218 fn 71
  and persecution 317

and the "policy" requirement 158
relationship to terrorism 267–272
and Responsibility to Protect 305–310, 314, 321
and universal jurisdiction 29, 326
    See also Geneva Conventions and Additional Protocols
Washington Declaration on the Need for a Comprehensive Convention on Crimes Against Humanity (Washington Declaration) 459, 477, 500
West Bank 316
Wilson, Woodrow
    Fourteen Points 56
Women's International War Crimes Tribunal for the Trial of Japan's Military Sexual Slavery 88

World Summit Outcome (2005) 4, 5, 306, 307, 308, 309, 310, 321, 468, 495, 496

Yugoslavia, former xxiv, 62, 178, 179
    assassination of King Alexander 265
    Dayton negotiations 483
    EU accession 486
    UN Commission on former Yugoslavia 56, 177, 179–181
    See also Balkans; Bosnia; Croatia; International Criminal Tribunal for the former Yugoslavia

Zedong, Mao 179
Zimbabwe 219

Made in the USA
Middletown, DE
12 June 2020